6/02

‖‖‖‖‖‖‖‖‖‖‖‖‖‖‖‖
3000 800053 19208
St. Louis Community College

Meramec Library
St. Louis Community College
11333 Big Bend Blvd.
Kirkwood, MO 63122-5799
314-984-7797

WITHDRAWN

D1208545

Spain in the Southwest

St. Louis Community College
at Meramec
Library

Spain in the Southwest

A NARRATIVE HISTORY
of Colonial New Mexico, Arizona, Texas, and California

John L. Kessell

UNIVERSITY OF OKLAHOMA PRESS • NORMAN

ALSO BY JOHN L. KESSELL

Mission of Sorrows: Jesuit Guevavi and the Pimas, 1691–1767
(Tucson, 1970)

Friars, Soldiers, and Reformers: Hispanic Arizona and the Sonora Mission Frontier, 1767–1856 (Tucson, 1976)

Kiva, Cross, and Crown: The Pecos Indians and New Mexico, 1540–1840 (Washington, D.C., 1979; Albuquerque, 1987)

The Missions of New Mexico, Since 1776 (Albuquerque, 1980)

(with Rick Hendricks, et al.) *The Journals of don Diego de Vargas, New Mexico, 1691–1704* 6 vols. (Albuquerque, 1989–2002)

Publication of this book is made possible through the generosity of the Southwestern Mission Research Center and Edith Kinney Gaylord.

Frontispiece and title page: Franciscan friar and Pecos Indians, New Mexico, mid-seventeenth century, by Roy Andersen. *Courtesy of the artist and Pecos National Historical Park.*

Kessell, John L.
    Spain in the Southwest : a narrative history of colonial New Mexico, Arizona, Texas, and California / John L. Kessell.
        p.   cm.
    Includes bibliographical references and index.
    ISBN 0–8061–3407–0
    1. Southwest, New—History—To 1848. 2. Southwest, New—Discovery and exploration—Spanish. 3. New Mexico—History—To 1848. 4. Arizona—History—To 1912. 5. Texas—History—To 1846. 6. California—History—To 1846. 7. Indians of North America—First contact with Europeans—Southwest, New. 8. Spaniards—Southwest, New—History. I. Title.
F799 .K38   2002
979'.02—dc 21   2001048070

The paper in this book meets the guidelines for permanence and durability of the Committee on Production Guidelines for Book Longevity of the Council on Library Resources. ♾

Copyright © 2002 by the University of Oklahoma Press, Norman, Publishing Division of the University. All rights reserved. Manufactured in the U.S.A.

1   2   3   4   5   6   7   8   9   10

CONTENTS

ILLUSTRATIONS

FIGURES

Maps

PREFACE

In the beginning, invading Spaniards did possess impressive advantages—imperial state and militant church, long-range sailing capability, firearms, horses, immunity to smallpox and measles, and more—but they, too, had to urinate.

Try as they might, not even white men could hide so familiar an urgency. Smelly and bearded, these emigrants and their multihued servants also had to eat, sleep, and cover their bodies. They laughed, bled, and craved sexual release; they fought to protect their mates and young and enslaved their enemies. And no observant Native American failed to notice.

In the hemispheric collision begun in 1492, Europeans and the medley of humanity crowding their camps had more in common culturally, and less racially, than Indians did. Still, both sides were of the same species—so many diverse groups, but all of the same species. Because we in today's multicultural United States seek with such earnestness to discover strength and progress in our contemporary diversity —while either pridefully proclaiming we are the Other or deep down still fearing the Other—we tend to project ethnic differences back into the past at the expense of human commonalities.

Initially, even though Europeans and Native Americans were from worlds far apart geographically, in basic, acultural, human terms, I think they understood each other very well.[1] Their ready, mutual comprehension of military, ritual, and sexual power helps explain their alliances and misalliances: Spaniards with Indians, Indians with Spaniards, Spaniards with other Europeans, Indians with other Indians.

Nahuatl-speaking chroniclers in the Valley of Mexico treated invading Spaniards as yet another political entity to reckon with. Keresan-speaking Pueblo Indians in New Mexico supplied maize to the army of Francisco Vázquez de Coronado as the intruders brutalized Tiwa-speaking Pueblo Indians. Nomadic Chichimecas imitated Spaniards, joining together in mounted confederations and assaulting Spanish towns. Lipan Apaches in Texas and Jicarillas in New Mexico invited Christian missionaries among them to enlist Spanish allies against Comanches, who in turn acquired guns by allying with Frenchmen.

Even though both sides possessed the capacity to understand one another, often they professed not to. Christian superiority always got in the way. How satisfying to Spanish egos that these barbaric, godless others appeared to stand in awe of them, taking the strangers for gods or sons of the sun. But what better way to explain the unexpected—blessing or curse, albino buffalo, lightning bolt, or the mystical Spanish nun María Jesús de Agreda? It came down from the sky.

In the realm of the spiritual, all peoples believed in supernatural phenomena, nonhuman beings descending or ascending, emerging from an underworld or being lifted up into the heavens. Trouble was, Spanish Roman Catholics had little tolerance for any but their own supernaturals. And when Native Americans temporarily halted the colonial march—as in New Mexico in 1680—they reserved special ire for the symbols of Christianity, mutilating Catholic priests and defecating in chalices. They well understood the price of imposed religion.

Spaniards, observing factionalism among Native peoples, rarely asked more than, are they for us or against us, our king, and our holy Catholic faith? Despite their preoccupations with such matters, Europeans could scarcely conceive that Indians had reasons of their own—personal or kinship affairs; expansion of territorial, occupational, or trade boundaries; rivalries of sacred or profane leaders—reasons enough to embrace or resist these steel-age intruders, that is, to use them in one way or another.

When Europeans were captured or thrown involuntarily among Indians and stripped of overt cultural and technological advantages, they survived in a variety of ways that said more about their individual personalities than their Christian ethnicity. To stay alive, they grasped at similarities.

Alvar Núñez Cabeza de Vaca came to recognize in thousands of strange faces fellow human beings, playful, cruel, loyal, and nasty, just as were his own kind. But Cabeza de Vaca's revelation did not prevail; neither did the pope's assertion of Indian humanness, nor the thousands of Spaniards who devoted their lives to defending the Natives' human rights.

More typical was the patronizing attitude of warrior knights like Gaspar Pérez de Villagrá, versifying chronicler of the New Mexico conquest. Emboldened by steel, black powder, and lead, Pérez de Villagrá could attribute noble, even classical behavior to the Native people of Acoma, if only to set them up literarily as worthy opponents for Spanish arms to vanquish physically and spiritually.

Rustic Diego Romero, however, twice convicted by the Inquisition of antisocial behavior in the 1660s, longed to become a white Indian and exercise his honorific title as chief captain of Plains Apaches. By contrast, Jean l'Archeveque, surviving among Caddos in the 1680s, permitted himself to be painfully tattooed to conceal his loathing for them.

The Indians of Pecos Pueblo understood selectively. Only by scrupulous attention to the outward signs of Roman Catholicism were they able in 1760 to parody so convincingly Bishop Pedro Tamarón's solemn visitation. They had no trouble either when it came to matters of exchange. In the bishop's words:

> In trade and temporal business where profit is involved, the Indians and Spaniards of New Mexico understand one another completely. In such matters they are knowing and avaricious. This does not extend to the spiritual realm, with regard to which they display great tepidity and indifference.[2]

Indians, too, could be arrogant and brutal, and Spaniards caring. If we select the facts to fit preconceived stereotypes, we can make the story come out rather the way we want, which is the nature of propaganda, not history. We can smear or glorify any group by stringing together mostly atrocities or mostly acts of high humanity. If, however, the peoples of the colonial Southwest were more alike than diverse, sharing similar inconstant natures, then we need have no favorites.

Even after the initial shock of the American encounter, new-found islands, continents, and oceans kept crowding and refining the Padrón Real at the Casa de Contratación in Sevilla. And, as Spaniards sought to reconcile fable, Christian scripture, and geography, the climate of wonder persisted. It made men giddy.

Three great swells of Spanish exploration and discovery rolled north from Mexico across the coasts and high deserts of the western borderlands. The first, set in motion by Columbus, lasted from the medieval (yet visibly Mesoamerican) quest of Francisco Vázquez de Coronado to the failed business ventures of Juan de Oñate and Sebastián Vizcaíno, from about 1540 to 1610. During the second, in the 1680s and 1690s, questing gave way to imperial defense, as Indian nations fought back and Frenchmen challenged Spain's exclusivity west of the Mississippi. By the third, from the 1770s through the 1790s, Spanish explorers who shared the enlightened world of Thomas Jefferson reasserted Spain's quixotic claims, erecting on the land cairns and crosses before Russians, Englishmen, or Anglo-Americans did.

Not that these three swells rose on a calm sea. Always there was movement— hunters, prospectors, slavers, traders, white Indians: they were ever out there—even when the authorities, in the interest of consolidation, decreed otherwise. Exploration progressed, sometimes steadily, sometimes fitfully, as Spaniards compiled practical geographical observations, pushed beyond the mirage, and dared even to settle there.

The rich mines of Zacatecas, discovered in the late 1540s, gave undying prospect of what could be. Mining strikes, of themselves, drew billows of humanity as mirage after mirage was proved up. Yet beyond an imaginary, wavy line drawn across northern New Spain through Sonora, Nueva Vizcaya, Coahuila, and Nuevo León well below the present Mexico-U.S. border, the strikes played out. North of that line, despite ever-present hope of new bonanzas, government incentives replaced mineral wealth. The first settlers, *los primeros pobladores*—recruited and subsidized by church and state—fought to build shelters, wrest subsistence and, occasionally, profit from the land, and raise families. Most stayed, and generations begot generation. The yield from mines, however, figured hardly at all in the colonial Southwest.

My intention was to call this book "Beyond the Mirage: Spain in the Southwest," but, alas, in the interest of marketing, I agreed to drop the nonessential, romantic prefix. Even *Spain in the Southwest*, while conveying some idea of what and where to a reader from the contemporary United States, rests on an ahistoric construct. The western borderlands—roughly New Mexico, Arizona, Texas, and California, plus adjoining parts of the north Mexican states—never possessed a regional identity during the Spanish colonial period. All lay well north of Mexico City, viceregal capital of New Spain, and represented the farthest reaches of Spanish expansion, like the extended fingers of an upraised hand. They are listed in the subtitle in the order of their initial Spanish occupation.[3]

Although Florida figures in the story early and Louisiana late, both are peripheral. Most of the action takes place west of an imaginary diagonal across North America from Nacogdoches in east Texas to Nootka Sound on Vancouver Island. New Mexico, with its earlier beginning in 1598 and ten times the countable population of Arizona, Texas, or California at the end in 1821, occupies the heartland. While Native and Euroamerican migrants ebb and flow and intermingle across the entire "Southwest," in the following pages, the sharper focus is on people culturally Hispanic.

Three trunk routes funneled men-at-arms, missionaries, and settler families northward from New Spain. A central corridor, the earliest, led up through Nueva Galicia and Nueva Vizcaya to New Mexico, first colonized in 1598, and west to the Hopi mesas of today's north-central Arizona (1629). Another ascended on the east through Nuevo León and Coahuila on into east Texas (1689), and the third, bearing northwest up the Pacific slope, divided in Sinaloa. Sonora developed higher on the mainland and from it dependent Pimería Alta, which soon extended into present-day southern Arizona (1701). (The name *Arizona* in the colonial period applied only to a small, ranchers' and prospectors' settlement just south of today's Arizona-Sonora border.) West across the Gulf of California, Sinaloa and Sonora gave birth to the Californias, first Antigua or Baja California (1697) and later, Nueva or Alta California (1769).

Settled at different times for different purposes, each colony maintained lines of communication, immigration, and supply with points to the south, but not with each other. A late-eighteenth-century project to bind these disparate territories administratively and extend webs of intercourse between them—the General Command of the Provincias Internas—foundered in the vastness of the scene. Hence, what passes today for "Mexican" food in Santa Fe, Tucson, San Antonio, and Monterey is so notably distinct. So, too, are certain Hispanic surnames listed in the four cities' telephone directories. And because Spain's claims always vastly exceeded the reality of Spanish occupation, the Southwest reached out in daring exploratory probes to the South Platte River of Nebraska, the Great Basin of Utah, and the ice floes of Alaska.

It all began with Columbus. Rather than sign on abruptly in Chapter 1 with

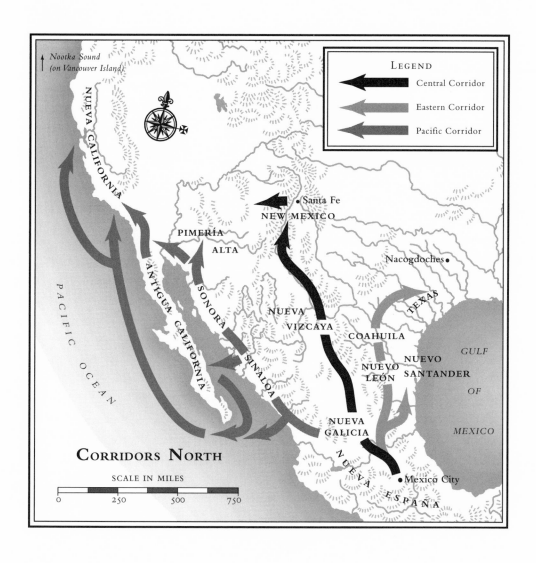

Nootka Sound
(on Vancouver Island)

NUEVA CALIFORNIA

LEGEND

Central Corridor

Eastern Corridor

Pacific Corridor

PACIFIC OCEAN

PIMERÍA ALTA

ANTIGUA CALIFORNIA

SONORA

SINALOA

NUEVA VIZCAYA

• Santa Fe

NEW MEXICO

Nacogdoches •

TEXAS

COAHUILA

NUEVO LEÓN

NUEVO SANTANDER

GULF

OF

MEXICO

NUEVA GALICIA

NUEVA ESPAÑA

• Mexico City

CORRIDORS NORTH

SCALE IN MILES

0   250   500   750

Spaniard in a boat. After Códice Florentino, central New Spain, sixteenth century. Redrawn by Jerry L. Livingston. *From Kessell,* Kiva, Cross, and Crown.

the outfit of Francisco Vázquez de Coronado in 1540 or with developer Juan de Oñate in 1598, we should enter the Caribbean by sail. From there, Spanish influence spread south, west, and north. The striking continuity of exploration, encounter, exploitation, alliance, warfare, extermination, conversion, and accommodation justifies starting at the beginning.

For three centuries, the northern frontier was a dynamic periphery of the Spanish empire. Even in 1821, when independent Mexico emerged out of New Spain, all the governors in the far north were still Spaniards born in the mother country. Three took the oath of allegiance. One quit. Each had warned higher authorities that the United States coveted New Mexico, Arizona, Texas, and California. And none would have been surprised by the redefinition of their provinces—in a scant twenty-five years—as the American Southwest.

This retelling is based on the secondary and published primary sources cited in notes and bibliography. To their many authors and editors, I extend grateful thanks. If putting the pieces together my way heightens interest in the region's Spanish colonial past, I shall be delighted.

For unfailing encouragement, I am indebted to master teacher Vi Matthews, who listened to me read aloud what I had written chapter by chapter and, subsequently, consented to marry me. Before sending the manuscript to press, I engaged Sarah Whalen, professional editor and longtime friend, to question obscurity and smooth the bumps. The book is better for her efforts. At the University of Oklahoma Press, Editor-in-Chief Charles E. Rankin, with the encouragement of Director John Drayton, captained the able team of Managing Editor Alice Stanton and Assistant Editor Julie Shilling. My thanks to those artists and curators who helped me acquire or gave their permission for the use of illustrations. Cartographer Deborah Reade of Santa Fe prepared the fine series of maps, and the Southwestern Mission Research Center of Tucson covered their cost, then added a generous subvention. To all, for making *Spain in the Southwest* the book readers now hold in their hands, I am enormously grateful.

Spain in the Southwest

1   Sons of the Sun

Among all these peoples, it was held for very certain that we came from the sky, because about all the things that they do not understand or have information regarding their origins, they say that such phenomena come from the sky.

—Alvar Núñez Cabeza de Vaca, 1542

By the same Indian, he [the cacique] answered him saying that with respect to what he [the governor] said about being the son of the sun, let him dry up the great river [the Mississippi] and he would believe him.

—Cacique Quigaltam's response to Hernando de Soto, 1542

Shorn of every outward sign of his Spanish superiority, unkempt castaway Alvar Núñez Cabeza de Vaca begged to survive. His dreams of fame and domination had collapsed. As he quested for food, water, and shelter, enough to stay alive, scales fell from the former conquistador's eyes. These Native peoples who abused, befriended, or stood in awe of him were not so different from himself. They shared the same emotions: fear, grief, joy. They, too, could be caring and tender, prank-ish, or falsehearted and hateful.

Cabeza de Vaca saw analogies between Native societies and his own on every side. He performed tasks for them that he would never have done as a nobleman at home. These people, like Europeans, wanted others to do the work. They had allies and enemies among neighboring nations, carried on seasonal activities, com-merce, diplomacy, and warfare.

It interested don Alvar that some of the Natives conveyed their belief that he and his companions had come down from the sky. To most Spaniards, their arse-nals and egos intact, the image was clear. These barbarous peoples, momentarily enlightened by God, were acknowledging the heavenly or divine mission of

Christians to convert and uplift them. To Cabeza de Vaca, however, the Natives' expression signaled no such submission. He knew them better. Things beyond their ken simply fell from the sky.

All the confident, early-sixteenth-century enterprises of Florida began badly and ended worse. Waves from the eruptive Spanish conquest of the Greater Antilles, they washed up on the peninsula every few years for a generation.

According to the record, robust, red-bearded don Juan Ponce de León, a venturesome knight who never underwent an ordeal like Cabeza de Vaca's, came first. Honoring the season, Ponce de León bestowed on what he mistook for a big island the Spanish adjective for the feast of Easter, *la Pascua Florida*. By Christian reckoning, it was the Saturday after Easter, April 2, 1513. Next day, he landed.[1]

No individual better personified the nature and continuity of Spanish expansion at the end of fifteenth century and beginning of the sixteenth than Juan Ponce de León. Illegitimate son of a powerful Andalusian noble, he was born, nevertheless, in the north, in the province of Valladolid, heartland of spare, intolerant Old Castile, in 1474. Apprenticed as page to a great lord while still in his teens, don Juan plunged into the exhilarating final stage of the *Reconquista,* the Catholic reconquest of Spain from the Moors.

Directing their artillery, soldiery, and propaganda against the Muslims' last Iberian kingdom in the mountains of Granada, Their Catholic Majesties Isabel and Fernando prevailed as never before. They caught their people up in a popular war that intensified Spaniards' militant Christianity and honed their fighting skills.

Instead of the Reconquista of reality, which had been on again, off again since the eighth century as Christians, Jews, and Muslims not only tolerated each other but also caroused, Spaniards of the 1480s embraced with fervor the myth of an unbroken, triumphal Christian crusade. It electrified their spirits. Then came 1492.

Never in Spain was there such a year. Early in January, Granada surrendered. In March, by royal decree, practicing Jews were given four months to convert to Christianity or leave the country; 150,000 would go. In April, after considerable third-party brokering, Columbus—Cristóbal Colón, Genoese navigator and mystic—signed contracts with Isabel and Fernando enabling him to pursue his "enterprise of the Indies." Also that year, a Spaniard, Rodrigo Borgia, was elected pope, and Antonio de Nebrija compiled a grammar of Castilian, proclaiming it a language of empire.

On August 3, Columbus sailed westward with three small ships and crews toward the riches of the Orient. At 2:00 A.M. on October 12, after a harrowing but speedy voyage, lookout Rodrigo de Triana sighted an island in the Caribbean.[2] From the Alhambra of Granada to San Salvador, hardly a break had occurred. No mere coincidence to Spaniards, the miracle of 1492 was divine providence.

On his second voyage, in 1493, with seventeen ships and more than twelve hundred males, including young Juan Ponce de León, Columbus inadvertently exported the Reconquista to the Western Hemisphere. The Genoese had his own commercial and spiritual agenda. When he faltered, however, his royal patrons imposed their own familiar program: acquisition of more riches and territory for Castile and the conversion to Roman Catholicism of subjected peoples.

Crews and passengers aboard Columbus's fleet in 1493 marveled at the dream-like string of green mountaintops rising out of placid waters. Shore parties cautiously examining deserted Carib huts shuddered at what seemed to be unmistakable signs of cannibalism.

After an unintended fight with six reckless Caribs in a canoe, Columbus gave a naked young woman as a slave to his friend Michele de Cuneo, who had captured her. When Cuneo tried to force himself upon her in his cabin, she clawed him and then shrieked while he beat her with a rope. "Finally," he recalled, "we came to an agreement in such manner that I can tell you that she seemed to have been brought up in a school of harlots."[3]

Coasting a big, mountainous island that Columbus named San Juan Bautista, today's Puerto Rico, the company put into a bay where sweet-water streams allowed them to refill the ships' water casks. The Natives of a large village all disappeared into the jungle. These were Tainos, edgy because painted Carib war parties had been preying upon them. If Juan Ponce de León fancied this island at first sight, he did not say; fifteen years later, however, he would conquer it. By then, some Tainos would welcome the Spaniards.

The word Europeans heard as *Taino* meant "good" or "noble" and distinguished these people from the "bad" Caribs. Far the most populous cultural group in the Caribbean, the sedentary, Arawak-speaking Tainos of the Greater Antilles, hundreds of thousands—some said millions—in 1493, lived in chiefdoms of large villages. Their thatched-roof and pole houses clustered around plazas or ball courts. They cultivated mainly manioc, or cassava, and also maize, beans, and peanuts. Skillful hunting and gathering on sea and land provided abundant protein.

Of the Tainos' elaborate ceremonial life, Spaniards seemed most amused or appalled by their veneration of *zemis,* small cotton, wood, or stone images representing spirits. Their easily recognizable hereditary chiefs, or *caciques,* to whom Columbus and his people gave names, wielded centralized authority over definable regions, traded surpluses, and dealt in war and peace with neighboring chiefdoms.[4]

Horror ran through the expeditionary force when the ships reached Española. Of La Navidad, the seaside camp where Columbus had left thirty-nine men on his first voyage, there remained only charred ruins and mutilated bodies with their eyes plucked out. These rapacious Spaniards' demands for gold and women, and their

Columbus meets the Tainos as King Fernando gives his blessing in this allegorical woodcut from Giuliano Dati's edition of the discoverer's 1493 letter. *Courtesy of the Rare Books Division, The New York Public Library, Astor, Lennox, and Tilden Foundations.*

quarreling among themselves, had cost them their lives. The Tainos of Cacique Caonabó had retaliated. With heavy heart, Columbus directed the fleet eastward along the coast against wind and current in search of a more propitious site for Spain's first New World city.[5]

Not far from present-day Puerto Plata on the north coast of the Dominican Republic, the admiral, viceroy, and captain general contented himself on January 2, 1494, with a "well-situated rock" that looked out on a handsome, open bay and a river. To the rear, a pass led through the mountains to the interior. There, surely, fortunes were to be had by setting Native Tainos to placer mine streams for gold.

It proved not so easy. Many of the men staggered off the ships sick. More fell ill almost at once, of an unhealthy climate, said the expedition's physician, but more specifically of intestinal parasites, venereal diseases, and other infectious maladies. Yet the resolute Columbus pressed on, laying out La Isabela, his trading post colony, named in honor of the queen. Across the bay, his people built a beehive-shaped kiln for making bricks, tiles, and pottery.

The ideal that construction in the Spanish Indies be orderly, lasting, and defensible was the crown's intent. Suddenly, the discovery had presented to the Renaissance mind a tabula rasa for neatly designed, grid-plan communities and societies free of medieval clutter. La Isabela, however, unique among European New World communities, perpetuated familiar medievalism. None of its principal buildings shared the same orientation: Columbus's 18-by-48-foot house, built of cut coral stone, packed earth plastered with lime, and red Mediterranean-style roof tiles and doubling as an arsenal; the first European church in the Western Hemisphere, a simple rectangle with adjoining bell tower; and a 113-foot-long storehouse, its heavy tile roof held up by eighteen interior stone pillars. Obviously, Columbus meant La Isabela to last.[6]

A majority of Spaniards who came to stay in 1493–94 were from the south of Spain, and their material baggage, such as the Andalusian scratch plow, later became standard in the New World. The enormous variety of artifacts in concurrent use in different regions of the Iberian Peninsula, in fact, underwent notable simplification as conquest culture crossed the Atlantic. Once an effective form of plow or cart or fishing gear had reached the Indies, there was simply no good reason to introduce other kinds not clearly superior.

The invaders, whether plant and animal husbandmen, traders, priests and professional men, or warriors, were mainly town and city dwellers. Their houses in Spain were intended mostly for extended family units, regardless of building materials, and as a rule were never as big or elaborate as their temples and council chambers.

The domesticated animals they brought, especially spirited Andalusian barb horses and snarling greyhound and mastiff attack dogs, astonished the Tainos. Cows, pigs, goats, and chickens also came ashore and multiplied. When allowed access, Natives took readily to this tamed and assorted meat supply, as they did to material items like candles or scissors that proved more efficient than their own. But they soon learned that the new technology came at the price of their freedom, even their lives. These strangers had plainly come to conquer.[7]

"When our small village was constructed," wrote Columbus's friend Cuneo, "the inhabitants of the island from one to two leagues around came to see us in a brotherly manner, saying that we were men of God that came from the sky."[8] Right away, the islanders learned that what most interested the men from the sky was gold from the earth.

Late in January 1494, Taino guides led two parties of Spaniards inland and they returned to La Isabela with grains and nuggets worth an estimated thirty thousand ducats. Columbus rejoiced. Forthwith, he dispatched this treasure to the crown, along with twenty-six West Indian slaves. Several hundred of the first European immigrants, disillusioned by toil and sickness, leapt at the chance to return to Spain in the dozen ships the admiral sent. Thus began an ebb and flow to and from the Indies, which depended on the news, good or bad.[9]

Among the two hundred unsalaried, volunteer *hidalgos* and *caballeros,* those nobles and gentlemen who paid their own way in 1493, more than a few bitterly resented the Genoese foreigner Columbus. He treated them no better than common laborers, employees of his trading or factory system, a demeaning affront to the conquest-and-spoils mentality of the Reconquista.

Dealing swiftly with the first of their revolts against his authority, Columbus ordered the expedition's chief accountant confined and several alleged conspirators hanged. Of all this, Juan Ponce de León evidently stayed clear.[10]

While fainter immigrants died or sought to return home, others adapted. They ate hard *yuca* bread made from the cassava's fleshy roots, fathered mestizo babies, and exploited the island's human and ecological resources. From stockades set up in the interior, they fought Taino resisters, branding and enslaving those taken as prisoners of war. And they sided with or against Columbus.

Gold finds southwest of La Isabela led to pit mining and the settlement of Santo Domingo on the south coast. When the amounts of gold bartered by the Indians dwindled, Columbus imposed a system of tribute. Finally, rumors of alleged misrule and a shipment to Spain of more than five hundred Indian slaves, which incensed the queen, resulted in the admiral's recall in 1500. But by that year, La Isabela, victim of dissension among colonists, disease, hurricane, and fire, had succumbed. The survivors had moved elsewhere.[11]

Spanish horseman and dog. After Lienzo de Tlaxcala, central New Spain, sixteenth century. Redrawn by Jerry L. Livingston. *From Kessell,* Kiva, Cross, and Crown.

Charming to his own kind and confident, don Juan Ponce de León got on well with people. He ingratiated himself soon enough with King Fernando's choice to replace Columbus as governor of Española, the incorruptible don Nicolás de Ovando, knight of the military order of Alcántara.

Ovando arrived in 1502 with twenty-nine ships and twenty-five hundred people, including officials of the first royal treasury office in the Indies and thirteen Franciscan friars. The ferocious July hurricane that sank or scattered the return fleet also leveled Santo Domingo, which was soon rebuilt on the west bank of the Ozama. From there, don Nicolás ruled.

First, he had to put down the uprising of Tainos under Cacique Cotubanamá in the food-producing eastern province of Higüey. In this vicious war, as usual pitting Taino allies of the Spaniards against other Tainos, Ponce de León campaigned as a captain. After the fighting, don Juan founded the new town of Salvaleón de Higüey where he directed construction of a hurricane-resistant stone house for himself. Although Ovando appointed him lieutenant governor of the area, Ponce de León did not get rich overnight, but he began building a base there. His Taino tributaries grew cassava, so he invested in a ship and supplied food to Santo

Domingo. He also wooed Leonor, a young Spanish woman of humble background employed at a nearby inn, married her, and began fathering a legitimate family.[12]

A planter and neighbor of Ponce de León's, hardly distinguishable from other ordinary Spaniards who had crowded Ovando's fleet, would achieve even greater fame, partly at don Juan's expense. Bartolomé de las Casas of Sevilla, whose father and uncle preceded him on Columbus's second voyage, at first resented the cry being raised by Dominican friars. How, these churchmen implored, could Christians in clear conscience enslave the Native peoples of the islands with such wanton brutality?

The question eventually penetrated Las Casas's consciousness. In time, he himself entered the Dominican order and was ordained a priest. Not, however, until he witnessed the cruel conquest of Cuba did he speak out. From then on, as the most zealous protector of Native Americans and critic of Spanish atrocities, fray Bartolomé de las Casas repeatedly stung the conscience of the crown. According to him, Juan Ponce de León, because of his barbaric mistreatment of Indians, deserved to burn in hell. But not everyone agreed.[13]

The rugged island of San Juan Bautista lay only eighty miles due east of Ponce de León's headquarters at Salvaleón on the Yuma River in extreme eastern Española. Don Juan may have traded with caciques on San Juan and even attempted a settlement in 1506. He knew there was gold on the island.

Negotiating a contract with Governor Ovando in the summer of 1508, and supplying the venture from Salvaleón, Ponce de León crossed over aboard his brigantine with some fifty followers, including a free black man, Juan Garrido. He picked up Cacique Agueybana as an emissary on the south coast, then sailed around to the north where he expected to find gold. He did, but not at first in impressive quantities. Still, don Juan went back to Española the following year to strike a more profitable bargain with Ovando and to bring over his family.

Again, he looked toward permanence. At his initial small settlement, which Ovando had ordered him to name Caparra, Ponce de León had another stone residence and arsenal erected. His closely controlled, allegedly nonviolent occupation of Puerto Rico might have succeeded but for politics.

In Spain, two deaths had complicated matters: Queen Isabel's in 1504 and Columbus's in 1506. The first occasioned a grave dynastic crisis and the second a vigorous renewal of Columbus's claims by his son and rightful heir, Diego. King Fernando, always the astute prince, had come through well, yet he saw no way around confirming Diego Colón's right to govern Española. That placed Ponce de León, Fernando's appointee as governor of Puerto Rico, in the middle.

Later, when members of the king's council upheld Diego's further claim to jurisdiction over Puerto Rico, Ponce de León, by 1512 a wealthy and renowned conquistador, turned over the governorship. At Fernando's request, however, he did not retire. Through agents at court, don Juan volunteered for further conquests. By seeking the royal patrimony of the king, rather than the competing feudal patrimony of the Colón family, Ponce de León further aligned himself with Fernando.

Tension between the crown and a potentially independent-minded New World aristocracy ran deep with Their Catholic Majesties, who had successfully put down such pretenders at home. Yet, to encourage the expansion of their empire by private enterprise, they and their successors kept offering rich men mighty concessions.

Ponce de León's patent from the crown to seek the fabled land or island of Bímini, issued to him exclusively over a similar bid by Columbus's younger brother Bartolomé, fit this mold.[14] By its terms, don Juan would be *adelantado,* a title and office transposed from the Castilian Reconquista, which gave the conquering entrepreneur broad authority over the territory and peoples he pacified, settled, and defended. If he succeeded, the crown moved quickly to supplant his political authority, appointing beholden governors and captains general, while allowing the rare fortunate adelantado his duly specified honorific and economic privileges.[15]

Don Juan's patent made no mention of waters that made old men young, although questing for such an elixir—or for the Seven Cities of Antilia or the Holy Grail—unquestionably had a hold on contemporary men's minds. Neither is there convincing evidence that a specific obsession with a fountain of perpetual youth drove the thirty-nine-year-old adelantado.

Ponce de León set sail from Puerto Rico early in March 1513. Aboard one of his three ships, the caravel *Santiago,* went plucky and experienced chief pilot Antón de Alaminos, from the Andalusian port of Palos, as well as two Spanish women, Beatriz and Juana Jiménez.

The course set by Alaminos carried them northwestward to San Salvador, where they put in to scrape the weeds off one of the ship's bottoms. Another couple of weeks saw them skirting the east side of the Lucayos, or Bahamas, previously discovered and frequented by Spaniards hunting Native slaves.

Finally, on April 3, the Sunday after Easter, Ponce de León stepped out of a bobbing longboat to take ritual possession in the king's name of an uncharted shore. "Believing that land to be an island," wrote an early chronicler,

> they named it *La Florida,* because it appeared very delightful, having many fresh groves, and it was all level, and also because they discover'd it at the season, which the Spaniards call *Pascua Florida.*

The party seems to have landed near Ponce de Leon Inlet, just south of today's Daytona Beach. Eyewitness at the surrender of Granada in 1492 and the founding of La Isabela in 1494, cool-handed, enterprising Juan Ponce de León in just two decades had brought Spaniards of record to North America.

Juan Ponce de León.
From Antonio de Herrera,
Historia general de los
hechos de los castellanos
(1601–1615).

As the little fleet coasted southward, don Juan noted that they were bucking a mighty current. Knowledge of the Gulf Stream, running against them at a steady five to six knots, would prove more valuable to Spain than the land they had found. The route of treasure fleets through the Straits of Florida, charted with the help of Antón de Alaminos, would provide an enduring reason for Spaniards to garrison inhospitable and unprofitable La Florida.

Standing out from the perilous Florida keys, to which someone aboard gave the name *Los Mártires,* the Martyrs, "because the high rocks at a distance look like men that are suffering," the ships slid northward into the Gulf of Mexico. In the second week of June, sailors clashed with inhabitants on an unnamed island, seemingly somewhere in the vicinity of Cape Sable or Cape Romano on present-day maps. When eighty war canoes of Calusa bowmen with shields, marshaled by a cacique called Calos or Carlos, came at them, don Juan thought it best to weigh anchor and report the discovery.[16]

During his absence from Caparra on Puerto Rico, where he had left his family, Caribs had struck overland, causing a number of casualties and burning twenty-nine of the thatch houses, the church, and the residence of don Alonso Manso, first Roman Catholic bishop to venture out to the Spanish Indies. One regrettable fatality, the result of a well-aimed Carib poisoned arrow, was Ponce de León's ferocious, red-coated war dog "Becerrillo," who must have been as big as a small calf.[17]

Don Juan did not return to La Florida for eight years. When he did, it was to repeat a routine he knew well. As at Salvaleón de Higüey and Caparra, he would select a site, found a settlement, and build a solid, stone residence.

Since his voyage of discovery, Ponce de León had been prodigally received at court in Spain, waged frustrating sea and land campaigns with island Caribs, suffered the death of doña Leonor, and arranged good marriages for his three daughters. His son Luis chose to become a Dominican friar.

At last, in 1521, don Juan had two ships crammed with the people, animals, and provisions to plant his new colony. "I also intend," he assured a new king, Emperor Carlos V, "to explore the coast of said island further, to see whether it is an island, or whether it connects with the land [of New Spain]."[18]

In that intention he failed. Having landed, probably near where he had been eight years earlier, perhaps because Cacique Carlos was rumored to have gold, Ponce de León ordered solid structures built. The nonfarming, arrow-shooting Calusas were no more welcoming than before. According to one version, don Juan, while restraining his colonists from returning evil for evil against the Indians, took an arrow himself deep in the thigh. Carried back aboard ship, he survived his festering wound only a short time, breathing his last at Puerto Príncipe on the north coast of Cuba in July 1521.

He was forty-seven. Although his Florida venture expired with him, Juan Ponce de León—conveying crossbows and pigs, Christian intolerance, and European diseases—had shown the way.[19]

Although less thrilling than questing and discovery, the mundane need for more workers also propelled Spaniards toward the mainland in three directions: south along the Spanish main, west to Yucatán and Mesoamerica, and north into the vastness of the Gulf of Mexico.

Mine owners, planters, and stock raisers on the Caribbean islands lamented how quickly the Natives were dying off. Certainly the warfare of conquest, over-work with pick and bar in the mines, malnutrition from unbalanced diets, and the shattering of cultural and family matrices all took their tolls. But the worst killers, especially under such conditions, came unintentionally on the breath and in the spittle and human waste of the invaders: European and African pathogens. At least as early as 1505, Spanish entrepreneurs had imported African blacks, or *bozales,* who added their continent's unfamiliar disease strains.

The smallpox epidemic of 1518–19, erupting at Santo Domingo and crossing swiftly to Puerto Rico and beyond, devastated the already diminished and exhausted Native population of the islands. Racked by insufferable fever and running pus-tules, Tainos of all ages dropped by the thousands. Within thirty years of La Isabela's founding, Spanish occupation of the islands had resulted in the virtual extinction of the Native Arawak peoples.[20]

Hints of their former lifeways and, of course, their biological contribution to the growing mestizo population endured. These mingled with the cultures and genes of involuntary African migrants brought in to replace dead Indians.

Thus traditional Caribbean societies vanished in a generation, to be replaced by a new and syncretic Euro-Afro-American one. Especially in the everyday realms of women, food preparation and child bearing, did the mixing proceed, while Spanish males, or those who aspired to be taken as such, clung to European mate-rial culture.[21]

Native slave raiding and discovery commingled. Ponce de León's tireless former pilot, Antón de Alaminos, between 1517 and 1519 personally set courses on three harrowing voyages of mixed motives while inspiring a fourth. Taken together, these sailings proved, even before don Juan's death, that La Florida and New Spain were indeed joined by an enormous arc of salt marsh, jungle, barrier island, and sand.

Alaminos led a dangerous but charmed life. In 1517, along the coast of Yucatán, he was among Francisco Hernández de Córdoba's crews, the first Europeans to gape at Mayan temples and then run for their lives. Half died in or as a result of combat. To fill their empty water casks, Alaminos proposed to the survivors a quick sail across from Yucatán to Florida to a bay he recognized from his voyage with Ponce de León. The Calusas captured one Spaniard and wounded half a dozen others, including Alaminos, when an arrow grazed his throat. Again aboard ship the following year, he steadfastly piloted Juan de Grijalva's follow-up to Yucatán and the compelling Mexican shore.

In 1519, ambitious, well-spoken, thirty-five-year-old Hernán Cortés pressed Alaminos into service on the one hundred-ton *Santa María de Concepción,* which carried to Spain the magnificent Aztec, or Nahua, treasure—a helmet filled with gold dust, objects of worked gold and silver, fine cotton cloth, brightly painted pictograph codices, and luminescent woven plumes—all meant to turn the young emperor's head in Cortés's favor.

After an unauthorized stop on the Cuban coast, the seasoned pilot pointed her bow for the fast-moving waters of the Florida Straits. After that, for three hundred years most of the inestimable treasure of the New World, along with the trans-shipped Oriental luxury goods of the Manila trade, would follow in the wake of Antón de Alaminos.

The concurrent Gulf Coast voyage he inspired, under little-known Alonso Alvarez de Pineda, closed the gap. Alaminos had made no secret of his calculations that a great unclaimed land mass must lie between Florida and central Mexico, per-haps concealing that hoped-for strait across North America. Francisco de Garay had listened carefully. Another tenacious veteran of Columbus's second voyage, Garay had found gold, raised pigs, and involved himself in the full suite of Caribbean endeavors. He then repaired to Spain, only to reappear as governor of Jamaica.

While sailing for Garay in 1519, Alvarez de Pineda was first to note the enor-mous discharge of the Mississippi River. He discovered more rivers but no strait. Surprised by the busy operations of Cortés at Veracruz, don Alonso found himself rebuffed and obliged to double back to the Río Pánuco.[22]

Draining a large area of Mexico's Sierra Madre Oriental and the tropical coast, the Río Pánuco flows into the sea at the present-day port of Tampico. In 1519, this territory belonged to the Huastec people, whose interlocking world consisted of autonomous hereditary chieftainships based on maize agriculture and strong enough to have resisted Aztec efforts to incorporate them.

Alvarez de Pineda sailed up the Pánuco and spent forty days careening his ships. The populous Huastec towns of thatched houses and semicircular temple mounds favorably impressed him. Moreover, the apparent scarcity of gold among these Natives suggested an alternative resource to exploit: slaves for export.

On the basis of Alvarez de Pineda's report, to which was appended a notable sketch of the whole Gulf of Mexico in recognizable outline, Francisco de Garay secured an adelantado contract to conquer and settle the land of Amichel, lying between La Florida and New Spain. That angered Hernán Cortés, who had not scrupled in 1519 to cast off the authority of Gov. Diego de Velásquez of Cuba and commence his own conquest of Mexico. Having succeeded brilliantly, Cortés would tolerate no interlopers on the mainland. In the case of Garay, he need not have worried. Fate prevailed.

The hardy Huastecs rose in 1520, killing Garay's agent, Alvarez de Pineda, and dozens of his men and flaying their carcasses. Survivors who escaped south, then returned overland two years later during Cortés's harsh conquest of the Huastecs, identified in horror the well-preserved, glovelike skins of comrades with their hair and beards still in place. Cortés, to mark this as his territory and foil a subsequent effort by Garay, founded a chartered municipality, the *villa* of Pánuco.

When colonizer Garay, who turned out to be a visionary bungler, finally got his hundreds of people under way in sweltering midsummer 1523, they first sailed farther north to the wrong river, the so-called Río de las Palmas, today's Soto la Marina. Dispirited and outmaneuvered, Garay went to consult Cortés in Mexico City and died shortly after a Christmas meal at the conqueror's table.

Again the Huastecs revolted, slaying several hundred abusive and scattered Spaniards and laying siege to the villa of Pánuco. Cortés's relief column arrived just in time, and Pánuco endured. As the northernmost outpost of Spanish civilization on the Gulf Coast, Pánuco would become the destination of the desperate human flotsam and jetsam cast on the waters from the next two quixotic plunges into the swamps of Florida.[23]

A signal victory of Christians over Muslims more than three centuries earlier, in 1212, had endowed him with a surname that otherwise would have been a joke: Cabeza de Vaca, or Cow's Head. Marking a strategic mountain trail with the skull of a cow, an ancestor on his mother's side had shown the way to Las Navas de Tolosa and been ennobled as reward. Ever since, the name had endured as a proud relic of the Reconquista. He preferred it even to that of his paternal grandfather, who had conquered the Guanches of the Canary Islands.

Born around 1490 in Jerez de Frontera, the Andalusian wine-making town, he himself, Alvar Núñez Cabeza de Vaca, had fought in Italy in battles between Christians. He had loyally served the Duke of Medina Sidonia in defending the right of Carlos, grandson of Fernando and Isabel, to rule Spain.

He need not have come to the New World. Cabeza de Vaca's place among the elite of Sevilla was secure when he accepted the position of treasurer and marshal, or second-in-command, of a touted expedition to settle the lands lying between the Río de las Palmas and the cape of La Florida. It would be led by Caribbean swash-buckler Pánfilo de Narváez, who had negotiated an adelantado contract. Six hundred people, mostly men, boarded five creaking ships moored at Sevilla's riverfront. Had Cabeza de Vaca known in 1527 the odds of his survival—eventually about one in seventy-five—he might have reconsidered.

Notorious for his haughty disregard of human life in the conquest of Cuba—which in retrospect appalled eyewitness Bartolomé de las Casas—the fair-skinned, red-bearded, hoarse and booming Narváez had also led an abortive maneuver by Governor Velásquez in 1520 to arrest Cortés. As a result, he had lost his right eye, gouged out by an opposing Spanish pikeman. Among Narváez's ranks on that occa-

Sebastian Munster's *Tabula Novarum Insularum*, 1538, showing Pánuco and Florida, but Yucatán erroneously as an island.

sion had been an ailing African porter who carried smallpox from islands to mainland, contributing greatly to the Aztecs' collapse.[24]

Sad for him, Narváez's luck had not changed. A quarter of his Florida colonists who had sailed from Sevilla in 1527 jumped ship at Santo Domingo. He had trouble acquiring supplies. A hurricane blew away two of his ships. Finally, in the spring of 1528, the remnant of his colony-to-be stood off the west coast of Florida, seemingly in the vicinity of Tampa Bay.

Cabeza de Vaca took issue with his leader's plan. To disembark on an inhospitable, unknown shore with roughly 260 footmen and 40 horsemen and march overland, while the ships coasted north seeking a better anchorage, seemed sheer folly to him. Yet, astride his horse with sword in hand, there was no stopping don Pánfilo.

Cabeza de Vaca, as a matter of honor, followed. What he remembered of his experiences, when he was able to record them more than eight years later, has gripped readers ever since: personal memoir as fantastic as any romance of chivalry; first North American captivity and travel narrative; spiritual journey of failed-conqueror-turned-holy man.[25]

How could he forget deadly clashes with Timucua and Apalachee Indians, month after month of sloughs and bogs and quicksand or tangled pines blown down by the wind, the sickening realization that the ships would never find them, miserable fevers and despair? Finally, with ingenuity born of desperation, the survivors began construction of five makeshift boats.

Late in September 1528, southwest of today's Tallahassee, the undone conquerors set out pushing and pulling these low-riding craft through shallow coastal marshes. Each boat was to bear fifty men and survival rations. They meant to keep the shore in sight and coast the arc west and south to Pánuco. None made it.

Cast up five weeks later onto a bleak island beach, evidently in the vicinity of present-day Galveston Island, the derelicts from Cabeza de Vaca's boat were given fish and roots by local Natives. They tried to relaunch their vessel but lost it and all their belongings in the surf. Now their plight seemed hopeless.

The Indians, probably Karankawas, came back and sat down with the dreary, half-dead, naked Europeans and, Cabeza de Vaca recounted, "with the great grief and pity they felt on seeing us in such a desperate plight, all of them began to weep loudly, and so sincerely that they could be heard a long way off."[26] Such commiseration made the Spaniards feel even worse. Taken to Indian lodges, warmed, and fed, they feared they were about to be sacrificed and eaten. For some of the castaways, who gradually starved even while cannibalizing the bodies of those who died before them, sacrifice would have been kinder. Most did not last through the first winter. Only one of the other boats, driven ashore nearby, had been accounted for; the other three and all aboard had vanished.

To stay alive, Cabeza de Vaca joined the local Gulf Coast peoples in their seasonal migrations, eating what they ate, sleeping where they slept, serving them, finally becoming a valued negotiator and trader between hostile groups. He learned words and phrases in a variety of languages. In his role as healer, evidently encouraged by his hosts, he combined the sign of the cross, Christian prayers, and breathing on his patients. If he understood the Natives correctly, there were several others of his expedition also still alive. Years passed.[27]

In 1534, during prickly pear harvest, Cabeza de Vaca came together by plan with the only other known survivors: Capt. Alonso del Castillo Maldonado of Salamanca; Andrés Dorantes de Carranza, an infantry officer from Extremadura; and Dorantes's slave, Estebanico, a black man from Azamor on the west coast of Morocco. Together, the four fled to the Coahuiltecan people Cabeza de Vaca called Avavares and passed the winter with them, then during 1535 crossed the continent: three white men and a black man, sons of the sun.

Originally, their goal had been Pánuco. Their route, however, always over native trails with Native guides, took them inland to the southwest, across the lower

Rio Grande, down into Nuevo León, back northwest diagonally through Coahuila and into Chihuahua. At times, thousands of Natives trooped along with this quartet of wondrous strange beings. Estebanico, spirited and theatrical, enjoyed the attention no end.

Recrossing the Rio Grande, which they cannot have known was the same river, near today's Ojinaga, they and their Indian escorts followed its course north and west to a point some seventy-five miles downriver from El Paso. From there, they again struck southwest, traversing northern Chihuahua and the Sierra Madre Occidental to the upper Río Yaqui, which they reached about Christmastime 1535. Here, at long last, they saw signs and heard terrified Native reports of other white men.[28]

Their emotions were a jumble. They had doubted they would ever see their own kind again. But these, obviously, were slavers, armed horsemen who struck terror into the hearts of the Natives who, Cabeza de Vaca remembered,

> brought us blankets that they had hidden for fear of the Christians and gave them to us and even told us how on many occasions the Christians had entered the land and destroyed and burned the villages and carried off half the men and all the women and children.

Some days later, when Cabeza de Vaca and Estebanico caught up with four mounted Spaniards, the latter were dumbfounded. Capt. Diego de Alcaraz, their leader, wanted to enslave the six hundred Natives who accompanied the castaways. How, the Indians pondered, could Alcaraz be of the same flesh as the four enchanted travelers? They simply would not believe it. Instead, wrote Cabeza de Vaca,

> they talked with one another saying that the Christians were lying, for we came from where the sun rises and they from where it sets; and that we cured the sick and they killed the healthy; and that we had come naked and barefoot and they well dressed and on horses and with lances; and that we did not covet anything, rather we returned everything that they gave us and were left with nothing, and the only aim of the others was to steal everything they found.[29]

Another irony escaped them all. Had the castaways made it to their original destination at Pánuco during November of 1528, they would have met the same smooth-talking slave operator as they were soon to meet on the opposite coast in 1536: Nuño Beltrán de Guzmán—an especially heinous character to his detractors.

Son of the illustrious Guzmán clan of Guadalajara northeast of Madrid, don Nuño, born around 1485, had arranged passage to the Indies in 1526. Clearly, his royal appointment as governor of Pánuco was part of the king's plan to rein in Hernán Cortés. Lacking any profitable alternative, Guzmán had licensed the taking of Huastec slaves—*esclavos de rescate,* men, women, and children allegedly already in bondage among the Natives, and *esclavos de guerra,* prisoners captured in allegedly just wars—branding them on the right side of the face, and shipping thousands to the Caribbean islands in exchange for livestock.[30]

In June 1536, hundreds of miles south of where they had been rudely reunited with Christians, Cabeza de Vaca and the others were graciously received by Guzmán at Compostela. Of don Nuño's career since late 1528, his guests knew nothing. Named president of the governing *audiencia,* or high tribunal, in Mexico City, he had clashed with the first bishop of New Spain, the indomitable Franciscan, fray Juan de Zumárraga. Guzmán's worst crime, in the bishop's eyes, was unbridled Indian slaving. The slaver, however, was too quick. Appropriating monies from the government treasury, Guzmán by late 1529 had begun a savage conquest of the Pacific slope northwest of Mexico City.

Don Nuño had convinced himself that other great cities lay to the north. From Pánuco, he had planned northern *entradas.* Tejo, an Indian servant from the valley of Oxitipa, had related how he journeyed as a boy with his father, a trader of multicolored tropical plumage, to some very large towns, or *pueblos.* Thus, it would seem that by 1527 or 1528, Spaniards had their first vague hearsay evidence of Pueblo Indian communities on the upper Rio Grande. What they chose to make of it, however, predetermined their sore disappointment.

How many of these very large pueblos were there, don Nuño had demanded, seven? Yes, seven, Tejo nodded. (Could these be, after all, the splendidly rich, lost Seven Cities of Antilia?) What did his father receive in exchange? Guzmán pressed Tejo, displaying samples of gold and silver. Yes, for sure, quantities of those metals, both of which abounded in that land. The streets, Tejo somehow conveyed, were in fact lined with silversmiths' shops. Further queries convinced the Spaniard that these cities lay a biblical forty days north across a wilderness. When he interviewed Cabeza de Vaca in 1536, Nuño de Guzmán inquired eagerly about them.

Don Nuño's grand design was to join sprawling Nueva Galicia to Pánuco, creating a sea-to-sea domain he would call, to spite Cortés, Mayor España, Greater Spain. But in 1533 he had lost the governorship of Pánuco, and his arch rival had returned from Spain enormously rich and licensed for further discoveries on the Pacific coast. Two years after Cortés's sailors found sterile Baja California, don Hernán himself, in 1535, had led hundreds of Spaniards and blacks to an ill-starred, short-lived colony at the Bahía de Santa Cruz, near today's La Paz.

Still, Guzmán seemed confident enough as he interrogated the only Spaniards to have actually seen the northern vastness from sea to sea. Don Nuño did not know at the time that he was about to be humbled, then jailed. The crown, quickening its reconquest of New Spain from the conquerors, was sending out an administrator to impose royal order on the chaotic colony.[31]

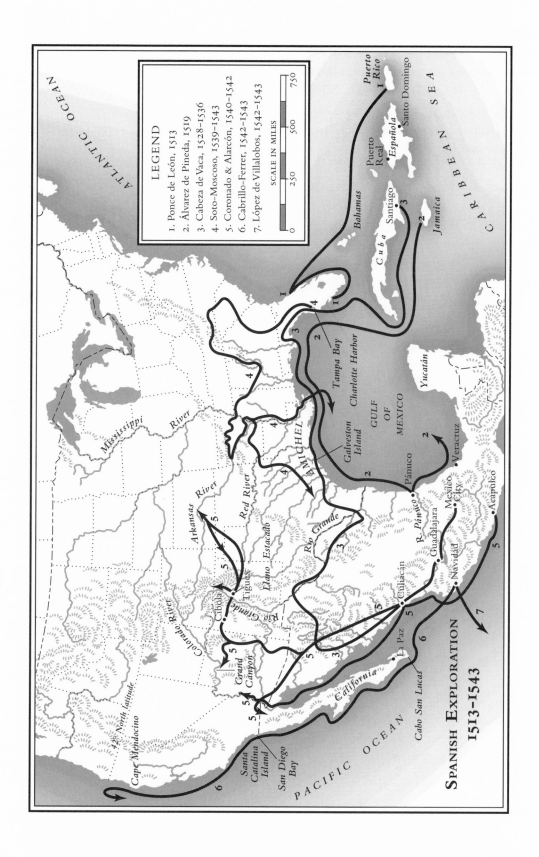

LEGEND

1. Ponce de León, 1513
2. Álvarez de Pineda, 1519
3. Cabeza de Vaca, 1528–1536
4. Soto-Moscoso, 1539–1543
5. Coronado & Alarcón, 1540–1542
6. Cabrillo-Ferrer, 1542–1543
7. López de Villalobos, 1542–1543

SCALE IN MILES

0   250   500   750

SPANISH EXPLORATION
1513–1543

ATLANTIC OCEAN

CARIBBEAN SEA

Puerto Rico
Santo Domingo
Puerto Real
Española
Santiago
Cuba
Jamaica
Bahamas

Tampa Bay
Charlotte Harbor
Yucatán
GULF OF MEXICO
Galveston Island
Pánuco
Veracruz
R. Pánuco
Mexico City
Guadalajara
Navidad
Acapulco
Culiacán

AMICHEL

Mississippi River
Arkansas River
Red River
Llano Estacado
Rio Grande
Colorado River
Río Grande
Tiguex
Cibola
Grand Canyon

California
La Paz
Cabo San Lucas

PACIFIC OCEAN

Cape Mendocino
42° North latitude
Santa Catalina Island
San Diego Bay

In 1535, the first viceroy of New Spain entered Mexico City with a huge retinue. Unless they came as personal representatives of the monarch, few Spanish *grandes,* the great lords who called the king cousin, ventured to the Indies. Don Antonio de Mendoza, a son of the captain general chosen to rule captured Granada, had distinguished himself in the royal service as warrior knight and diplomat. He had married Catalina de Vargas, lady-in-waiting to Queen Isabel. An especially judicious administrator, Mendoza moved at once to control competing cliques and increase revenues to the royal treasury.[32]

The following year, as Cabeza de Vaca and his companions neared Mexico City, crowds lined the roads to see these four survivors whom God had so miraculously delivered and the strange Indians who accompanied them. They entered the teeming capital on July 24, 1536, eve of the feast of Santiago, St. James, patron saint of all Spain. To their unaccustomed eyes, the festive throngs, bullfights, and receptions hosted by Viceroy Mendoza and don Hernán Cortés must have seemed like endless dreams.

During subsequent interviews, the castaways evidently did not greatly exaggerate what they had seen in the north. Cabeza de Vaca did tell of five ceremonial emerald arrow points he had been given and subsequently lost. In response to his questions about their origin, the Indians had told him

> that they were brought from some very high mountains that are toward the north, and that they bought them in exchange for plumes and parrot feathers; and they said that there were towns there with many people and very large houses.[33]

A small copper bell, likely traded up from Mesoamerica but thought to have originated in the north, heightened the illusion that the people of these northern towns must be metalworkers.

Politely, Cabeza de Vaca refused the viceroy's invitation to head an expedition of discovery, as did Castillo Maldonado. Dorantes later agreed, then backed out. Mendoza also offered him five hundred pesos for Estebanico, but Dorantes refused to sell. Instead, he allowed the viceroy to borrow the slave.

By the fall of 1537, Cabeza de Vaca had returned to Spain. Incredibly, he bid for Narváez's vacant grant to La Florida. Was it still a matter of honor? He had survived among Native Americans for years, but obviously chose not to remain one himself. He still wanted to conquer, but by exercising kindness. He and the other survivors had spent more than a month after their deliverance attempting to reassure and peacefully resettle the Indians of Sonora and Sinaloa so viciously disrupted by Guzmán's slavers. To make them faithful Christians and loyal vassals, Cabeza de Vaca informed the king, they "must be led by good treatment . . . this is a very sure way, and no other will suffice."[34] There were reformers at court who agreed with him, but few in the Indies.

Because the king had already awarded the contract for La Florida to another bidder, Cabeza de Vaca accepted the governorship of the Río de la Plata in South America. On the southern continent, his fantastic adventures continued. Finally, in 1544, enemies who despised his Indian sympathies staged a coup and shipped Cabeza de Vaca back to Spain a prisoner. By that time, La Florida had swallowed up another adelantado.

Sympathy for Indians was never a problem for Hernando de Soto, hero of the conquest of Peru. His was one of the great success stories. Born about 1500, probably at Jerez de los Caballeros in Extremadura, handsome and noble if not rich, don Hernando had borrowed money and sailed with the big expedition of 1514 to Panama.

Rising in the irregular ranks of conquerors, he led punitive expeditions against Indians, took slaves, invested, and joined impetuously and sadistically in subduing Nicaragua and Peru. With uninhibited élan, a flock of retainers, and a fortune estimated as high as 180,000 pesos, don Hernando returned to Spain in 1537. Conveying himself in style to court at Valladolid, he married doña Isabel de Bobadilla, a woman of high nobility and useful influence, and secured a governorship in the Indies. Wisely and courteously, Cabeza de Vaca refused to join him.[35]

News of Soto's adelantado contract "to conquer, pacify, and populate the lands that there are from the Province of the Río de las Palmas to Florida," executed at Valladolid on April 20, 1537, reached Mexico City soon enough, and the fleet carrying Soto himself and some seven hundred people made port at Santiago de Cuba in June 1538. Don Hernando also came as governor of Cuba, which would serve as his supply base. Since no one knew just where Tejo's and Cabeza de Vaca's rumored rich northern cities lay, the prospect that Soto's expedition might get there first moved Viceroy Mendoza to action.[36]

Securing royal permission, the viceroy planned a reconnaissance north of Nueva Galicia. Estebanico would serve as guide. As leader, Mendoza requested fray Marcos de Niza, who came highly recommended by his fellow Franciscan, Bishop Zumárraga. The well-traveled fray Marcos, from his order's province of Aquitaine in southwestern France, had been for nearly a decade a keen and critical observer of events in Central America and Peru.

The viceroy also assembled a number of the surviving Indians who had accompanied Cabeza de Vaca from the north. Having purchased them, he was sending them home as a gesture of goodwill.

Hernando de Soto. After a late-eighteenth-century engraving. *Courtesy of the Library of Congress.*

    In September 1538, fray Marcos and Estebanico left the viceregal capital
for Nueva Galicia. Overtaken en route, they traveled on with the numerous company of that troubled province's new governor, Mendoza's young protégé, don
Francisco Vázquez de Coronado y Luján. The governor was making haste to
Culiacán, northernmost town in the kingdom, which was reported under siege by
neighboring Indians.
    Fray Marcos carried instructions from Mendoza admonishing the Spaniards of

Culiacán to treat peaceful Indians well. The friar also was to tell the Natives, in the king's name, that they would no longer be enslaved or removed from their lands. That assurance seemed to undermine the local rebellion, and Ayapín, suspected leader, fled into the mountains. When he was captured, Coronado put him on trial as an example, ordered his execution, and had his body quartered.[37]

It was early March 1539 before fray Marcos, Estebanico, and a large party of Indians set out on foot northward from Culiacán. Natives along the way accorded them fine receptions. Beyond where the people had never seen a white man, they marveled at fray Marcos draped in his gray habit. "They tried to touch my garments, and called me Sayota, which in their language means 'man from heaven.'"

Two weeks before Easter, at a settlement he called Vacapa, the Franciscan decided to stay and collect information on his surroundings. He sent Estebanico ahead.

Gaudily decked out and playing on his reputation as a wonder worker, the black man strode on, accompanied by many Indians and a couple of greyhounds. If he heard anything remarkable, his orders were to wait for fray Marcos. What happened from here on is poorly recorded.

Estebanico sent back a cross as tall as a man, the agreed-upon sign for a phenomenal discovery. Learning that thirty days beyond him lay the first of seven, very large cities in a land called Cíbola, the slave did not wait but pressed on.

Following weeks behind, fray Marcos observed more and more turquoise and buffalo hides traded from Cíbola. Indeed, an Indian word for buffalo would become in Spanish cíbolo. The cities he sought were apparently distribution centers for buffalo products to the south and west, but what else besides skins and turquoise? Natives, by gesture and exclamation, fed the Franciscan's hopes. As instructed, he took symbolic possession of the lands through which he passed, erecting crosses. Then came news that stunned him, two reports of what had befallen Estebanico.

Nearing Cíbola, the black shaman had sent ahead a symbol of his authority. It had served him long and well with Cabeza de Vaca, a ceremonial gourd that, in fray Marcos's words, "had some strings of jingle bells, and two feathers, one white and the other red." Upon receipt, a headman of one of the six then-occupied Zuni Pueblo Indian towns reacted violently. Throwing the gourd to the ground, he shouted defiantly, according to two wounded survivors, "'I know these people, for these jingle bells are not the shape of ours. Tell them to turn back at once, or not one of their men will be spared.'" The bold Estebanico brushed aside the threat and came on, "with all his people, who must have numbered more than three hundred men, besides many women, and reached the city of Cíbola at sunset."

The visitors were not allowed to enter but were lodged in a house outside and given no food or water. "The next morning," so the story went, "when the sun had risen the height of a lance, Esteban went out of the house and some of the

Estebanico, by José Cisneros. *From the Collection of David J. and Carol Bryant Weber, by permission.*

chiefs followed him, whereupon many people came out of the city." When the black man and his escort tried to flee, the Zunis stopped them.

> We heard much shouting in the city, and we saw many men and women on the terraces, watching, but we never saw Esteban again. We believe that they shot him with arrows and also the others who were with him, as no one except ourselves escaped.[38]

Later Spanish accounts told a different story. The Zunis killed Estebanico because he demanded turquoise and women. They also considered him a liar. How was it that he represented powerful people he claimed were white when he himself was black? "A spy or guide of some nations that wanted to come and conquer them," he had to die.

In 1540, hundreds of miles west of Cíbola on the lower Colorado River, don Hernando Alarcón heard of Estebanico's death. Dispatched by order of Viceroy Mendoza from Acapulco in support of the later Coronado expedition, Alarcón had anchored his ships at the river's mouth and proceeded upstream in two launches, presenting himself to the Yuman-speaking Natives as a son of the sun. Conversing with an old man through an interpreter, don Hernando reported to Mendoza:

> I asked him about Cíbola and whether he knew if the people there had ever seen people like us. He answered no, except a negro who wore on his feet and arms some things that tinkled. Your Lordship must remember how this negro who went with Fray Marcos wore bells, and feathers on his ankles and arms, and carried plates of various colors. He arrived there a little more than one year ago. I asked him why they killed him. He replied that the chieftain of Cíbola asked the negro if he had any brothers, and he answered that he had an infinite number, that they had numerous arms, and that they were not very far from there. Upon hearing this, many chieftains assembled and decided to kill him so that he would not reveal their location to his brothers. For this reason they killed him and tore him into many pieces, which were distributed among the chieftains so that they should know that he was dead. He had a dog like mine, which the chieftain had killed a long time afterward.[39]

How ironic that a black man, carrying a symbol from one Native group that was offensive to another, should foreshadow Spanish conquest. Not two generations had passed since Columbus's first encounters in the Caribbean. For years, the Pueblo peoples deep in North America had heard from Native traders about white-skinned, bearded, glinting invaders to the south. Now, before the maize ripened again, they would meet them face to face.

2   Contact Face to Face

They [the Zuni elders] declare that it was foretold them more than fifty years ago that a people such as we are would come, and from the direction we have come, and that the whole country would be conquered.

—FRANCISCO VÁZQUEZ DE CORONADO TO ANTONIO DE MENDOZA, FROM THE PROVINCE OF CÍBOLA AND CITY OF GRANADA, AUGUST 3, 1540

Contact did not just happen. Driven by gnawing hunger on the one side and defense of their summer-solstice ceremonial, their homes, and their families on the other, Spaniards and Zunis came together violently in July 1540 and well understood each other's motives. Even at the cultural level, men on both sides must have sensed the spirit if not the letter of what was happening. Their advance parties had already clashed. The somber act of reading the *Requerimiento,* demanded by Spanish law before a conquistador could legally commence hostilities and take slaves, hardly boded well.

This surreal, nine-hundred-word manifesto drawn up by legalists at the Spanish court about 1512 was at once an invitation to submit peaceably and a declaration of war. Commenting on its usefulness, fray Bartolomé de las Casas admitted that he did not know whether to laugh or cry.

Close by their pueblo of Hawikuh, a crowd of Zuni men watched as several of the invaders, differently clad, moved forward. One, holding out in front of him what looked like a thin animal skin with markings on it, began to shout out loud. An Indian who had come with the outsiders and may have known the regional Piman trade language tried to interpret.

Many Native nations had already, of their own free will, become Christians. The Zunis must also.

A Zuni man, by Edward S. Curtis, 1903. *Courtesy of the Museum of New Mexico, no. 143712.*

> But if you do not do this or if you maliciously delay in doing it, I cer-
> tify to you that with the help of God we shall forcefully enter into your
> country and shall make war against you in all ways and manners that we can,
> and shall subject you to the yoke and obedience of the Church and of their
> highnesses.[1]

The resulting death and destruction would be their fault. The choice was up to them.

Zunis within earshot could not have grasped the divine or legalistic justification of European conquest, but they could read the Spaniards' eyes. These bizarre
beings stood armed and menacing. No line of sacred corn meal sprinkled on Mother
Earth would stop them.

Earlier, Native defenders had rallied fighting men from the other Zuni pueblos, prepared for war, and evacuated their women and children. "All those in the
city were warriors who remained to defend it," a Spanish soldier recalled. "Many
came out a crossbow shot, making great threats."

Not often did Spaniards misunderstand Indians who dared mock or oppose them.

> The general approached them in person, accompanied by two friars and the
> maestre de campo, to request them to surrender, as is customary in new
> lands. Their answer was the large number of arrows which they shot.

Nor did the Zunis, noting Coronado's gilded and plumed suit of armor, fail to
distinguish the Spaniards' leader. They nearly killed him. But for the good quality
of his helmet, dented by large rocks, and the quick action of *Maestre de campo* García
López de Cárdenas, who threw himself across his fallen general, they might have.

Ravenous, the attackers battled their way into the pueblo. There, admitted the
same soldier,

> we found something we prized more than gold or silver, namely, much
> maize, beans, and chickens larger than those of New Spain, and salt better
> and whiter than I have ever seen in my whole life.[2]

Salt would never do. Viceroy Mendoza and Coronado had invested tens of thousands of pesos in this enterprise. Many of the three hundred and more Spanish
horsemen, harquebusiers, and crossbowmen, mostly young, would-be conquerors
recently arrived in New Spain, had borrowed heavily to outfit themselves. Cousins,
friends, and strangers awaited big returns on their shares. All had seen how high
Cortés and his veterans lived. Tierra Nueva, this new land they were exploring for
Spain, must yield more than salt.

For the next twenty-two months, sustained by that hope, Coronado's medieval
cavalcade quested across canyon, basin and range, and endless plain for anything
that would make their investments pay.

Sensing futility early on, they blamed fray Marcos de Niza. After the murder of Estebanico the year before, fray Marcos had allegedly pressed on for a glimpse of Cíbola. He claimed to have seen one of the cities from afar. "This pueblo has a fine appearance," he had reported to Viceroy Mendoza in 1539,

> the best I have seen in these regions. The houses are as they had been described to me by the Indians, all of stone, with terraces and flat roofs, as it seemed to me from a hill where I stood to view it. The city is larger than the city of Mexico.

And this, the anxious friar understood, was the smallest of the seven. Rather than risk Estebanico's fate, he had hastily erected a cross and taken possession, naming that land the new kingdom of San Francisco. It was, he swore, "the greatest and best of all that have been discovered."[3]

The trusted Franciscan's eyewitness account had set entrepreneurial Mexico City on a roar. At last, the Seven Cities had been sighted. Moving adroitly, Mendoza headed off the rival interests of Hernán Cortés. To demonstrate his commitment, the viceroy had ridden with his entourage five hundred miles from Mexico City to Compostela, the capital and southernmost town in Nueva Galicia. There, he personally reviewed the expedition.

Besides the more than two hundred Spanish horsemen and sixty footmen, whose numbers grew en route, along with some women and children dependents, this New World army also counted a thousand or more imposing Mexican Indian allies, also on foot, and hundreds of unnamed supporting hands: cooks, herders, muleteers, and sundry retainers, many of them blacks. Fray Marcos and five other Franciscans with their Indian helpers and servants made up the priestly contingent.[4]

More than twenty years after the fact, in his chronicle of the entire disappointing venture, participant Pedro de Castañeda accused fray Marcos of lying. The Franciscan had only heard rumors of Cíbola in 1539, not seen it. Instead, wrote Castañeda, the friar, upon word of Estebanico's death, had turned around and fled south with his habit up to his waist.

A question remains. Why, if he lied, would he have gone back to the scene? Was his faith in rumors of northern cities so great? Was he so bold or so curious as to rely solely on hearsay and risk disillusion by volunteering to guide Coronado in 1540?

Elected father provincial, or superior, of the Franciscans in New Spain, fray Marcos had a perfect administrative excuse not to go. But he did go, only to deeply regret his decision. "When they got within sight of the first pueblo, which was Cíbola," continued Castañeda, "the curses that some hurled at fray Marcos were such that God forbid they may befall him." Coronado was not much kinder. "I can assure you," the general wrote defensively to Mendoza, "that he has not told

A Franciscan friar. After Diego Valadés,
Rhetórica Christiana, 1579. Redrawn by
Jerry L. Livingston. *From Kessell,* Kiva,
Cross, and Crown.

the truth in a single thing that he said, but everything is the opposite of what he
related, except the name of the cities and the large stone houses."[5]

Only the vanguard, a hundred or so Spaniards with Mexican Indian allies, had
attacked the Zuni pueblo. The main body of the army, departing Culiacán after
Coronado, did not arrive until November. Although, to wide-eyed Native observers
who saw them pass, European arms and armor stood out, more numerous even
among Spaniards were central and western Mexican *macanas,* obsidian-edged,
wooden swords; obsidian-pointed lances; slings; and padded cotton armor. Even the
points of the crossbow darts, manufactured in iron-poor New Spain, were wrought
of native copper.

Spanish chroniclers of the Coronado campaign characteristically all but ignored
the hundreds of fearsome Tlaxcalan, Aztec, and Tarascan warriors marching with
them as allies. Yet such a cohort must have awed the peoples of Tierra Nueva as
much as the metal Spaniards themselves. Zunis and their Pueblo neighbors, despite
the unconscious influence of centuries of tradition filtering up from Mesoamerica,
cannot have imagined the sight of these sturdy fighters displaying their Native
weapons and colorful feathered insignias, capes, and shields. In the assault on
Hawikuh, with Spanish horses and soldiers spent and Coronado unconscious, the
presence of Mexican Indian allies explains why the battle lasted less than an hour.[6]

The fragmented but interlocking Pueblo world invaded by the Spaniards and their Mexican auxiliaries in the summer of 1540 may have contained a hundred largely autonomous communes and accommodated sixty thousand people or twice that many. Archaeologists have estimated Native populations on the eve of contact by counting the number of concurrently used hearths, grinding stones, rooms, ceremonial chambers, or crop production areas, and figuring average family size, but these measures are far from precise. Some scholars suggest, without convincing evidence, that one or more of the lethal pandemics that swept central New Spain might have preceded Coronado and significantly reduced Pueblo population in the 1520s and 1530s.[7]

In 1540, Zunis evidently occupied six, not seven, close-built pueblos of multilevel, stone-and-earth houseblocks whose names Europeans came to render as Matsaki, Hawikuh, Kiakima, Halona, Kechipawa, and Kwakina. No outside entrances opened onto ground-floor rooms; inhabitants entered from above through hatches. Movable ladders permitted access to upper stories, each set back leaving a terrace or corridor. Coronado, displaying his European superiority, wondered if these barbaric people, who in the heat of July wore so little clothing, could possibly have built such structures by themselves. As he admitted to Mendoza,

> although they are not decorated with turquoises, nor made of lime or good bricks, nevertheless they are very good houses, three and four and five stories high, where there are very good homes and good rooms with corridors, and some quite good rooms underground and paved, which are built for winter, and which are something like estufas [warm, close rooms, stovelike].

Here, Coronado missed entirely the sacred significance of Pueblo kivas, or ceremonial chambers.

"So far as I can find out," he continued, "these Indians worship the water, because they say that it makes the maize grow and sustains their life."[8] Pedro de Castañeda commented that, unlike the Natives of New Spain, the Zunis had no rulers, but instead heeded the counsel of their oldest men, whom he termed priests. "I believe," he ventured, "they give them some commandments to observe, because there is no drunkenness, sodomy, or human sacrifice among them, nor do they eat human flesh, or steal."[9]

Yet no conquering Spaniard in an official capacity, much less the Franciscans, would have likened any Pueblo Indian tradition to their own true Roman Catholic faith—or grasped that the Natives' way was as all-encompassing and rich in ceremony as their own. Pueblo religion, as Coronado surmised, did have much to do with weather control, bringing rain in right quantities at right times to nurture maize and other crops, and also with fertility and the health of people, plants, and animals. Each Pueblo community's sphere of influence extended outward from a symbolic hole in the earth's surface, the place where the first ancestors emerged from the underground, to all the cardinal directions, and upward to a celestial plane.

Sacred features, mountains for example, marked the outer bounds of the earthly plane. Shrines abounded at springs and other significant places. The Pueblo people kept in harmony with their cosmos through correct behavior. This included precise ritual dance dramas featuring *kachinas,* elaborately masked representatives of spirits, and sacramental elements—blessed, finely ground corn meal, feathered prayer sticks, and effigies of animals—which they used daily.

Although fighting men from all six Zuni-speaking pueblos had joined unsuccessfully to defend their province in 1540, each community, the Spaniards would learn, governed itself. Such independence prevailed throughout the Pueblo world, where various clusters of towns spoke a half-dozen different languages. A hundred miles more west than north of Cíbola, the Hopi people occupied islands of habitation amid dramatic red, buff, and gray canyonlands. East of Cíbola some seventy-five miles, just over the Continental Divide into the Rio Grande drainage, the seemingly impregnable pueblo of Acoma nested on an isolated, 360-foot, sheer-sided mesa, "so high," reckoned Castañeda, "that it would require a good musket to land a ball on top."[10]

Three days farther east on horseback, Capt. Hernando de Alvarado came upon the broad valley of the Rio Grande in the vicinity of today's Albuquerque, with the hump-backed, bluish Sandia Mountains rising beyond. A verdant bosque of cottonwoods obeyed the meandering course of the river's flow from north to south. Alvarado named the life-giving stream the Río de Nuestra Señora, because it was September 7, 1540, eve of the Blessed Virgin's birthday. Here, he thought, among the dozen or so better supplied pueblos of a province he called Tiguex, the army could winter more comfortably than at Cíbola.

Taos, upriver a hundred miles at an elevation of seven thousand feet, capped the Pueblos' world in the north. En route, Spaniards would pass by Keresan- and Tewa/Tano-speaking towns and, up a tributary to the west, the belligerent, mountain-dwelling Jemez people. East over other mountains, with more than two thousand inhabitants and the same Towa language as the Jemez, citadel-like Cicuique, known later as Pecos, served as principal gateway and trade center between pueblos and plains.

South of Tiguex for another hundred miles, Piro-speakers occupied intermittent pueblos on terraces above the river, and east across a lower extension of the Sandias, similar people of Tiwa or Tompiro speech congregated near arroyos and springs in a province Spaniards would name Las Salinas, for its numerous shallow saline lakes.

Coronado's invasion, at least for a time, upset the prevailing Pueblo Indian

Zuni shalako winter solstice ceremonial. *From* Century *(February 1883)*.

Taos Pueblo, north house block, by John K. Hillers, 1879. *Courtesy of the Museum of New Mexico, no. 16096.*

balance of power. Living in a mostly semiarid and fragile environment subject to fickle weather patterns, the Pueblo peoples for uncounted generations had shifted for survival, competing with each other, at times violently, for control of water, cultivable land, wood, hunting areas, and other resources. Pecos, or Cicuique, wrote Pedro de Castañeda,

> is a pueblo containing about 500 warriors. It is feared throughout that land.
> . . . The people of this town pride themselves because no one has been able
> to subjugate them, while they dominate the pueblos they wish.[11]

This proud community had sent a peace delegation to Coronado at Cíbola, then asked Spaniards to join them as allies against neighbors with whom they were presently at war. For generations, the Jemez had been pushing aggressively from the northwest into territory occupied by Keres. Such tensions between Pueblo groups, as well as the endemic factionalism within individual towns, explained the pragmatism of those Pueblo Indians who sought alliance with Spaniards against

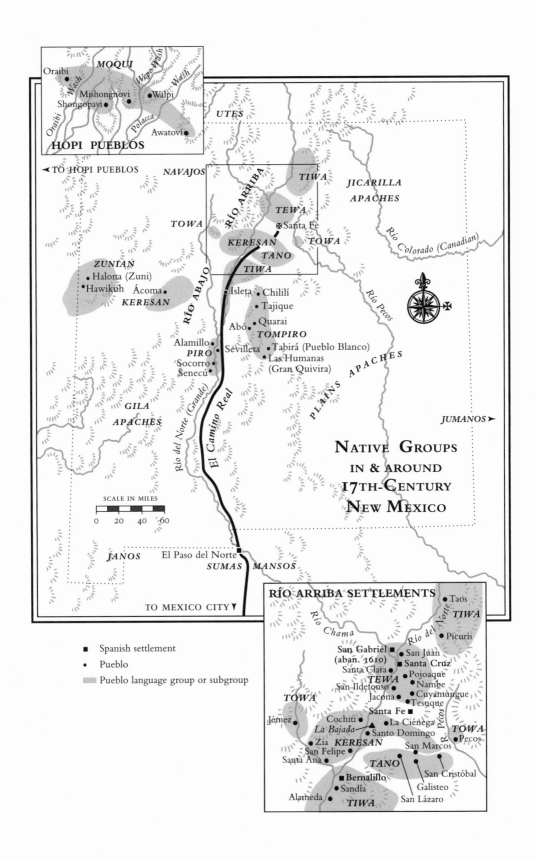

HOPI PUEBLOS

MOQUI

Oraibi

Mishongnovi
Shongopavi •Walpi

Awatovi

◀ TO HOPI PUEBLOS

NAVAJOS

UTES

JICARILLA
APACHES

TIWA

RÍO ARRIBA

TOWA

TEWA

⊛ Santa Fe

Río Colorado (Canadian)

KERESAN

TOWA

TANO

RÍO ABAJO

TIWA

ZUNIAN

Halona (Zuni)
Hawikuh   Ácoma•

KERESAN

• Isleta • Chililí

• Tajique

Abó • Quarai

TOMPIRO

Alamillo
PIRO   Sevilleta   • Tabirá (Pueblo Blanco)

Socorro   • Las Humanas
Senecú   (Gran Quivira)

Río Pecos

PLAINS APACHES

GILA

APACHES

JUMANOS ▶

Río del Norte (Grande)

El Camino Real

NATIVE GROUPS
IN & AROUND
17TH-CENTURY
NEW MEXICO

SCALE IN MILES

0   20   40   60

JANOS   El Paso del Norte

SUMAS MANSOS

TO MEXICO CITY ▼

■ Spanish settlement

• Pueblo

Pueblo language group or subgroup

RÍO ARRIBA SETTLEMENTS   • Taos

TIWA

Río Chama

Río del Norte

• Picuris

San Gabriel ■   ■ San Juan
(aban. 1610)   ■ Santa Cruz
Santa Clara •   • Pojoaque
TEWA   • Nambe
San Ildefonso •   • Cuyamungue
Jacona •   • Tesuque

Santa Fe ■

TOWA

Jémez •   Cochiti •   • La Ciénega
La Bajada   ▲ • Santo Domingo   Pecos R.

TOWA

• Pecos

• Zia   KERESAN
San Felipe •   San Marcos •
Santa Ana •

■ Bernalillo   San Cristóbal •
• Sandía   Galisteo •
Alameda •   TIWA   San Lázaro •

TANO

other Pueblo Indians. For their part, the invaders grasped and exploited Pueblo disunity again and again to have their way.

More than any other member of the Coronado expedition, the crusty,
indomitable, short-tempered fray Juan de Padilla personified the lasting grip of
Reconquista mentality. He was utterly obsessed. And when the mortified fray
Marcos de Niza took first opportunity to return to New Spain from Cíbola, fray
Juan became ranking chaplain. A native of southern Spain and veteran missionary,
Padilla visualized himself as the heroic mortal who would, by God's grace, reunite
Christendom with the long-lost Seven Cities of Antilia.

In the year 714, according to widely held belief, as the forces of Islam swept
over the Iberian Peninsula, seven Portuguese bishops had embarked with their congregations and sailed westward. On an unknown island or continent, they had
founded seven utopian cities that had grown enormously wealthy. Father Padilla,
with every ounce of his being, meant to find them.

He volunteered for every side expedition. Group after group of Pueblo Indians,
subjected to his intense questioning by sign and gesture, disappointed the driven friar.
His disposition worsened. He seemed to take pleasure in openly rebuking soldiers
for cursing or immoral acts. Still, in the tradition of the first twelve Franciscan apostles
invited to New Spain by Cortés in 1524, fray Juan saw to it that his subordinates set
up substantial crosses in numerous pueblos. "We taught the natives to venerate them,"
Padilla boasted, perhaps mistaking Pueblo rites of exorcism for veneration,

> and they offered them their powders [sacred corn meal] and feathers, some
> even the blankets they were wearing. They did it with such eagerness that
> some climbed on the backs of others to reach the arms of the crosses to put
> plumes and roses [feather rosettes] on them. Others brought ladders, and
> while some held them others climbed up to tie strings in order to fasten the
> roses and feathers.[12]

A more genial Spaniard among the Indians in 1540 was curious, wide-eyed professional man-at-arms Juan Troyano, an artilleryman attached to Capt. Hernando
de Alvarado's company. He relished the adventure. Young Juan had left his village
in the Spanish province of Valladolid in 1511 "to the curses of his father," soldiered
in Italy, and gained passage in the same fleet that brought Viceroy Mendoza and
Francisco Vázquez de Coronado to New Spain in 1535.

Words in different Native languages fascinated Troyano, and he enjoyed fraternizing with Indians. At some point, in fact, he formed a lasting union with a local
woman, probably from one of the pueblos, and years later in Mexico City congratulated himself for bringing back the only female from Tierra Nueva. Troyano, like
Padilla, always rode with the vanguard.[13]

Both men and nearly two thousand fellow invaders suffered through the long, frigid winter of 1540–41 at Tiguex and witnessed its bloody consequences. Trekking over from Cíbola in late fall, the boisterous, unkempt first wave had demanded that the residents of a large pueblo vacate their homes. Spaniards then moved in.

More than a thousand horses and pack animals, as well as sheep, cattle, and pigs, overran Native maize fields, consuming every dry stalk. To stay warm and fed, the unwelcome intruders demanded levies of blankets, buffalo robes, firewood, and foodstuffs. There were rapes. On every level, relations festered. One eruptive incident, recounted later in an investigation of Coronado's dealings with the Natives, brought open war closer.

Captain Alvarado, with Father Padilla, Juan Troyano, and others, had been guests at Pecos and been taken, wonder-struck, onto the near plains among herds of buffalo. Of greater interest to Padilla were hints of a rich and civilized land farther on called Quivira. Willingly, the friar believed the boasts and gestures of El Turco, a roguish Plains Indian the Spaniards thought looked like a Turk. Ysopete, another Plains Indian, consistently demurred.

The leaders at Pecos allegedly possessed a gold bracelet and other valuable artifacts from Quivira but refused to produce them. To get at the truth, Alvarado seized El Turco and Ysopete, along with two principal Pecos men—the elderly Cacique, of commanding presence, and Bigotes, who wore an uncharacteristic mustache— and marched the four in chains to winter camp at Tiguex.

There, evidently on Coronado's order but not in his presence, Pedro de Tovar set his dogs on Bigotes to elicit the facts. Bitten on the leg and arm, the Indian confessed what his tormentors wanted him to. "He admitted to having at Cicuique," Troyano remembered, "a gold bracelet, a dog, an earthenware flask, and other jewelry." Father Padilla had been certain of it.

News of what the Spaniards had done to Bigotes traveled throughout Tiguex, adding to Native grievances. Finally, some of the emboldened Tiwa men killed more than forty horses and pack animals, an act of defiance they must have known the Spaniards could not ignore. Then they holed up in a pueblo they hoped would prove impregnable. It did not.

The besiegers broke holes in the walls and lighted smudge fires. When the choking defenders, having received a seeming safe-conduct by sign of the cross, emerged unarmed one or two at a time, Spaniards herded sixty or seventy of them together into don García López de Cárdenas's tent. A hurried conference between Coronado and López de Cárdenas, probably with fray Juan de Padilla present, resulted in a brutal sentence without trial. While workers dug holes and set up stakes, guards brought the Pecos prisoners to witness and learn from this ghastly scene. Three years later, Juan Troyano offered the following testimony:

> Don García López, who at that time was maestre de campo, ordered that some posts be set in the ground and that some Indians be bound to them two at a time until fifty Indians had been so secured. These were from the group that had come from the pueblo in peace and had been placed in the tent under assurance of safety. Then the Spaniards set fire to them and burned all of them alive. The rest of the Indians, who had remained in the tent, when they saw that the Spaniards were taking their comrades out and tying them to posts . . . rose up and fortified themselves in the tent and defended themselves with poles and stakes they took from the tent. Then the Spaniards killed all of them by lancing and stabbing.

Word of the Spaniards' dreadful duplicity convinced the defenders of another pueblo not to surrender, "although they were summoned repeatedly by Francisco Vázquez. The Indians said that the Spaniards were dishonest people and did not respect the truth."[14]

Most surviving Tiwa families fled, dispossessed for the duration of the Spaniards' stay, abandoning a dozen towns, which the invaders sacked to assure that they would not return and fortify them.[15] No one compiled a body count of combatants killed in the vicious Tiguex war, which lasted from December 1540 into March 1541. In its wake, however, hundreds of widows and orphans huddled as slaves in the camps of Spaniards and Mexican Indians.

Coronado had dealt militarily with a potential enemy at his rear, and now, to Father Padilla's delight, he resolved to lead a migration eastward to the land of Quivira. El Turco, who knew some Mexican Nahuatl words, had given his captors to believe that passage to Quivira might lead them to "the richest prize found in the Indies": a river two leagues (five or six miles) wide; fish big as horses; canoes with sails and more than twenty oarsmen on a side, nobles seated under canopies, and golden eagles at the prow. The contrast with the shallow, brown Rio Grande could scarcely have been greater.

"The lord of that land," wrote Castañeda, putting El Turco's tale in words,

> took his siesta under a large tree from which hung numerous golden jingle bells, and he was pleased as they played in the wind. He added that the common table service of all was generally of wrought silver, and that the pitchers, dishes, and bowls were made of gold.

A mix of artifacts, gestures, and phrases in three or four languages had raised participants to this eager level of communication. Testing the canny Indian, Spaniards had presented him with utensils made of tin. He smelled them and pronounced them neither gold nor silver, for he knew those metals well and much preferred them.[16]

The first Plains people Coronado met east of Pecos were nomadic, tepee-dwelling hunters, and they were not alarmed at the enormous, straggling caravan of strange beings. "These people," Castañeda marveled, "were so skillful in the use of signs that it seemed as if they spoke. They made everything so clear that an interpreter was not necessary." These were western Plains Apaches, Querechos in the earliest Spanish accounts, and as they moved off, medium-sized, shaggy dogs harnessed to two-pole travois dragged their belongings behind.[17]

Snaking eastward, Coronado's loosely jointed column of people, animals, and baggage receded into the landscape: the hauntingly flat terrain of the Llano Estacado; endless buffalo herds moving across it like dark, woolly blankets; hailstones so big they beat down tents, bruised horses, dented helmets, and broke pottery water jugs. Finally, the expedition dropped over the multihued caprock into *barrancas,* or canyons, several hundred feet deep.

The fear of being swallowed up, led on by El Turco indefinitely until provisions gave out, forced a decision. Ordering the bulk of the army back to Tiguex, Coronado chose thirty horsemen, including Juan Troyano, and a few footmen. With Ysopete as guide, the general made ready for a reconnaissance to Quivira. Fray Juan de Padilla, as always, volunteered. El Turco was going too, but in chains.

Near where the camp divided, arguably in Blanco Canyon, about a hundred miles more south than east of today's Amarillo, El Turco had confessed. Ysopete had tried all along to unmask the wily adviser. Now, Teyas, another dog-powered, hunting people—competitors and enemies of the Querechos, but likely also Apaches—confirmed that Quivira lay north, not southeast, and comprised not prosperous, multistoried cities, but grass lodges.

The Teyas favorably impressed the travelers. One Teya archer, according to Castañeda, shot an arrow through both shoulders of a buffalo bull, "which would be a good feat for an arquebus. These natives," he went on,

> are an intelligent people. Their women are well treated, and through modesty they cover their whole bodies. They have shoes and buskins of tanned hides, and wear blankets over their short underskirts, made of skins tied at the shoulders, and a sort of short tunic . . . with small fringes reaching to the middle of the thighs.[18]

Other Spaniards in Coronado's band described how Querechos and Teyas utilized practically every part of the buffalo, eating its flesh in various forms and drinking the blood and stomach juices, and how expertly they tanned hides and skins, trading surpluses for maize, blankets, and pottery among the Pueblos.

On June 29, 1541, having followed buffalo trails north, the smaller party reached the Arkansas River in present-day central Kansas. Crossing to the north bank, the explorers found themselves in Quivira among Caddoan-speaking Natives

Plains Apaches with burden-bearing dogs, by Roy Andersen. *Courtesy of the artist and Pecos National Historical Park.*

that later Europeans called Wichitas. The well-traveled Capt. Juan Jaramillo thought this lush, sweet-smelling country had "a fine appearance," finer even than Spain, Italy, or France.

> It is not a hilly country, but one with mesas, plains, and charming rivers with fine waters, and it pleased me, indeed. I am of the belief that it will be very productive for all sorts of commodities.

Had Father Padilla allowed himself, he would have cursed. The populous villages they passed through showed not a sign of contact with the Seven Cities, unless it was the copper ornament the huge Native chief had around his neck. His two hundred male companions, who wore feather headdresses and carried bows and arrows, were otherwise scantily clad in breechclouts.

"The houses of the Indians there," Jaramillo observed matter-of-factly,

> were of straw . . . most of them round, the straw hanging to the ground like a wall. Superimposed on the outside they had a sort of chapel or sentry box with a doorway where the Indians were seen either seated or lying down.[19]

Again confronted, El Turco confessed further. The people of Pecos, he admitted, had prevailed upon him to mislead the invaders until their horses weakened and died. Then, when Coronado and any survivors straggled back afoot, Pecos warriors could finish them off. That revelation cost El Turco his life. In a Spanish campaign tent at night, several men restrained the manacled prisoner, garroting him by tightening a cord around his neck with a key. Coronado ordered Ysopete, as reward for his presumed loyalty, released among his own people.[20]

The curious interlopers, supplied with maize and guides by the Wichitas, now struck a more direct route back to the Rio Grande Valley and Tiguex, still a journey of nearly six hundred miles. The plan was to come back to Quivira the following spring and press onward to whatever lay beyond. By the cross erected in the principal village—the base of which bore a carved inscription testifying that Francisco Vázquez de Coronado had come this far—Father Padilla swore to return.

Because the Coronado venture was a military one and the product of a rigid and well-defined patriarchy, the documents made little mention of females. Undoubtedly, dozens of unnamed women, some with children, had accompanied Spanish and Mexican Indian men as servants and slaves, cooks and laundresses, in the male view, as chattel.

Only three wives of soldiers earned individual recognition: nurse María Maldonado, wife of Juan Gómez de Paradinas, tailor and quartermaster; the Señora Caballero, Indian wife of Lope de Caballero; and Francisca de Hozes, wife of Alonso Sánchez, an indebted Mexico City cobbler. Hozes, who with her husband and a grown son had risked all the dangers of the expedition, dreaded the months-long journey back to New Spain. And she made no secret of it.

A second, bitterly cold and boring winter in the abandoned Tiguex towns had broken the will of the majority, including Coronado, who yearned to go home. The general had been kicked in the head when he fell from his horse during a race, and he never quite recovered. According to Francisca de Hozes, first of fourteen witnesses at Coronado's trial in 1544, some sixty Spaniards wanted to stay and make their homes in Tierra Nueva. Coronado, she swore, threatened to hang them if they persisted.[21]

The Spaniard who did stay was, of course, fray Juan de Padilla. He had vowed by God to return to Quivira. The prickly friar convinced the general to leave with him a select, multicultural party. Lucas and Sebastián, his Tarascan Indian catechists, went wherever he did. They wore the knee-length gray tunic and knotted Franciscan cord of *donados,* lads entrusted to and raised by the friars. Portuguese gardener Andrés do Campo would interpret at the court of the Seven Cities. Unnamed, a free black man and a mestizo were also going. A half-dozen Natives from Quivira would guide the obsessed Padilla back to their villages.[22]

Elderly fray Luis de Ubeda, humble lay brother and carpenter, who had been a companion to Bishop Zumárraga, stayed as well, keeping with him Cristóbal, a black slave boy given to him by Capt. Juan Jaramillo.

Before the hundreds of Spaniards, Mexican Indians, and their swarms of menials decamped, Coronado ordered the release of all Natives acquired in Tierra Nueva. This included the captive Tiwa women, a number of them surely pregnant, and children. An exception, Juan Troyano's *compañera* never left his side. A few Mexican Indians, encountered by subsequent expeditions forty years later, had deserted or chosen for whatever reasons to live on among the Pueblos. Finally, in April 1542, like a receding dark cloud, the rest vanished from sight, except for Padilla's little band.

Fray Luis, hoping to baptize sick children and with his chisel and adze to fashion more crosses, stayed in Pecos with young Cristóbal, whom he hoped would learn the language. A Spaniard who took the friars some sheep reported seeing residents of Pecos leading the friar away to some unknown destination. Where, when, and how he and Cristóbal died no Spaniard ever found out. Fray Juan de Padilla, in contrast, did not fade away so meekly. He left witnesses.

The spellbound Franciscan did make it back to Quivira. Not content to work there as a Christian missionary with Ysopete and his race, fray Juan journeyed on, lured by his vision of the Seven Cities. Then abruptly, his quest ended. Pierced by numerous arrows, he expired somewhere in today's Kansas, assuredly, in Roman Catholic terms, protomartyr of the Great Plains. Lucas and Sebastián, who may have buried the corpse, escaped and turned up later in New Spain.

Andrés do Campo, fleeing for his life on horseback, also got away, only to fall captive for another ten months. Bolting again, he found his way miraculously via Pánuco in 1543 back to Mexico City.[23]

Thus ended face-to-face contact for more than a generation. The Coronado expedition, along with a support group that sailed up the Gulf of California, had brought the reality of awesome invaders into the lodges, rooms, and tepees of the culturally diverse Native peoples who occupied, though sparsely, lands that stretched from the Colorado River delta to central Kansas, across half a continent. Yet Coronado's Spaniards did not settle. Given the mid-sixteenth-century technology and markets of their empire, they discovered no animal, mineral, or vegetable they could grow, extract, or cultivate. Hence, for the time being, tens of thousands of potential laborers remained beyond the reach of Europe's world system.

The marvels the explorers had experienced were simply not exploitable. In an immediate, material sense, the enterprise had failed. Still, Viceroy Mendoza, intent on assessing the data for himself and blocking access by agents of Cortés and others, decreed that participants in the Coronado expedition remain silent. But how could they?

García López de Cárdenas and his detachment, traveling in November 1540 across a high plateau "covered with low and twisted pines," had gasped at the brink of the Grand Canyon. For three days, they looked for a way down, finally sending their two lightest, most agile men, Capt. Pablo de Melgosa and Juan Galeras, over the edge. The climbers descended only a third of the way. From that point, the Colorado River appeared as mighty as the Indians had said.

Peering from the top, the others could make out part way some rocks that appeared to be the height of a man. But "those who went down and who reached them swore that they were taller than the great tower of Seville." In comparison, the famed Giralda, standing 320 feet, made a humble measuring stick.[24]

And who could ever forget the plains alive with buffalo? "I want to tell, also," Pedro de Castañeda would write,

> about the appearance of the bulls, which is likewise remarkable. At first there was not a horse that did not run away on seeing them, for their faces are short and narrow between the eyes, the forehead two spans wide. Their eyes bulge on the sides, so that, when they run, they can see those who follow them. They are bearded like very large he-goats. When they run they carry their heads low, their beards touching the ground. From the middle of the body back they are covered with very woolly hair like that of fine sheep. From the belly to the front they have very heavy hair like the mane of a wild lion. They have a hump larger than that of a camel. Their horns, which show a little through the hair, are short and heavy. . . . They have short tails with a small bunch of hair at the end. When they run they carry their tails erect like the scorpion.[25]

While Coronado had led his army beyond the pale, with a man assigned to count human paces across the plains, the Natives of Nueva Galicia, the nearer northwest, chose to rise in great numbers. Intermittent hostilities had characterized the entire region terrorized by Guzmán's regime, but never on this scale. The so-called Mixtón War of 1540–42, taking its name from a steep-sided, rocky mountain, or *peñol,* where one of the final battles took place, grew into a frenzied, religiously inspired, revitalization movement pitting tens of thousands of Indians on a side. It had scared Mendoza into taking personal command in the field.

Spanish accounts told of messengers of the devil, shamans from wild, unconquered tribes infiltrating the submissive Cazcán and other peoples in the broken highlands north of Guadalajara and turning them violently against Spaniards and Christianity. Hearing of the fighting, the rash don Pedro de Alvarado, adelantado of Guatemala, who was readying a fleet of discovery on the Pacific in a joint venture with Mendoza, had determined to quash the uprising.

On June 24, 1541, feast day of San Juan Bautista, when Christians said it would rain in New Spain, hell-bent Alvarado attacked the peñol of Nochistlán with a hundred armed Spaniards on horseback, a hundred on foot, and five thousand

Indian allies, only to fall under his horse in a muddy, ignominious retreat and die ten days later.

The warfare spread. Coronado's lieutenant governor, don Cristóbal de Oñate, a level-headed Basque who had sailed for New Spain in 1524, found himself besieged in Guadalajara. The delirious attackers, numbering a reported fifty thousand, nearly overran the place. Already, Viceroy Mendoza was en route from Mexico City at the head of several hundred Spaniards, some cannons, and an estimated thirty thousand Aztec and Tlaxcalan auxiliaries. By special concession of the viceroy, the Native leaders rode horses and carried Spanish weapons.

The hard-fought campaign, a series of sieges and assaults on the fortified peñoles, broke active resistance. As the dispirited Governor Coronado, carried on a litter, made his way back through the war zone later in 1542, signs of Native dislocation were everywhere, but most of the fighting was over.[26]

Even as Viceroy Mendoza encouraged the development and stability of Nueva Galicia, granting large spreads of agricultural and grazing lands to Spaniards and encouraging Franciscan missionary efforts, he kept an eye on the far horizon. Heir to the fleet of his deceased partner, Pedro de Alvarado, the viceroy eagerly promoted Pacific exploration. He would dispatch one fleet up the mainland's west coast and another out across open ocean toward the setting sun and the Spice Islands.

To command the first group, he recalled from Guatemala a much experienced fighter, entrepreneur, and shipowner who had been closely associated with Alvarado, one Juan Rodríguez Cabrillo, and instructed him to navigate north beyond California.[27]

As long as ships relied only on sails or occasionally oars, this would be a terrible voyage, running against currents, winds, and heavy seas, close by fog-blanketed, perilously rocky shores. Yet there were compelling reasons to attempt it. A strait was thought to slice back eastward through North America, a lane connecting South and North Seas, Pacific and Atlantic. If Spain failed to secure this Strait of Anián, foreigners would surely slip through it into the Pacific. Beyond the strait, too, the shore might trend to China, opening for Spain the cities and trade of the Orient.

Cabrillo's square-rigged flagship, the *San Salvador,* which he owned and probably had built, was a slim galleon of high sterncastle and lower forecastle measuring about a hundred feet, with a carrying capacity of two hundred tons. Incredibly, she crawled with nearly a hundred people: four officers, twenty to thirty sailors, about as many black and Indian slaves, two or three cabin boys, twenty-five soldiers, Augustinian fray Julián de Lescano, and a few merchants.

Smaller and shorter, the round-bellied carrack *La Victoria,* also square-rigged, carried a hundred tons and fifty to sixty men. Finally, the launch *San Miguel,* with

European caravels of the sixteenth century, by Theodore de Bry in Girolamo Benzoni, *Americae pars quarta* (1594).

single lateen sail and thirteen pairs of oars, served to tow the other ships in and out of port and ferry men and supplies back and forth.[28]

On June 27, 1542—as Coronado, Juan Troyano, and Francisca de Hozes dragged back from Tierra Nueva—Cabrillo's crews cleared the west coast port of Navidad and rode smartly out to sea in three very small vessels. Within two months, they had sailed higher up the outside shore of the dry California peninsula than any other Spaniards. An additional month brought them to a "closed and very good" anchorage. Because the day was September 28, eve of the feast of archangel San Miguel, they gave the broad, sheltered harbor that name, pleasing the crew of the miniature *San Miguel*. Sixty years later, sailing in on a different saint's day, another explorer would call it San Diego.

Natives who came out to the ships in canoes "said by signs," according to a surviving summary of the log,

> that in the interior men like us were travelling about, bearded, clothed, and armed like those of the ships. They made signs that they carried crossbows and swords; and they made gestures with the right arm as if they were throwing lances, and ran around as if they were on horseback. They made signs that they were killing many native Indians, and that for this reason they were afraid. These people are comely and large. They go about covered with skins of animals.

Since Pacific coast gatherers, like these Yuman-speaking Ipais, had long traded seashells with inland peoples who carried or passed them eastward across the Colorado River and the Pueblo world out onto the Great Plains, it was natural that news of Coronado's conspicuous brutalities would get back to them.[29]

Navigating now along pleasant and thickly populated shores, the sea-borne Spaniards noted smoke hanging in the air from controlled fires set by the Indians to facilitate acorn and grass seed harvests and regenerate the browse for wild animals. Almost too eagerly, Natives clambered up from their canoes onto the unfamiliar floating houses, offering quantities of fresh sardines and accepting strings of glass beads and other small gifts. Often, Cabrillo rode ashore in a longboat to take ritual possession in the name of the king. Two prominent islands the explorers named for their other ships: San Salvador, later Santa Catalina, and La Victoria, later San Clemente.

Living by the bounty of land and sea, the coastal peoples gathered, fished, and hunted but grew no maize. Their villages of large, round, pole-frame and reed-covered dwellings encircled spacious central enclosures that bristled with mast-sized poles on which there were paintings. "We thought that they worshipped them, because when they dance they go dancing around the enclosure." Of many language groups, "they have bitter wars with one another." True or not, such statements provided a familiar rationale for European conquest—to pacify warring Natives.

Observing beds of kelp, with broad, slippery, yellow-brown leaves floating in immense patches on the water's surface; herds of animals on shore, apparently pronghorn antelope; magnificent level valleys and wooded hills, these first Spanish visitors to southern California concluded that "the country appears to be very fine."[30]

But then the elements turned ugly.

> So great was the swell of the ocean that it was terrifying to see, and the coast
> was bold and the mountains very high. . . . When sailing along near the land,
> it seemed as if the mountains would fall upon the ships.

The *San Salvador,* separated from its consorts in a lashing storm, fought up the coast to the vicinity of today's Russian River, missing both Monterey and San Francisco bays, then turned back. Battered but reunited, the three ships made for the protection of Santa Catalina Island, there to weather the numbing winter that would cost Juan Rodríguez Cabrillo his life.[31]

The island's Native inhabitants resented these haggard Spaniards' rude and persistent demands for food, wood, and fresh water. "All the time the armada was in the Isla Capitana," sailor Francisco de Vargas recalled, "the Indians there never stopped fighting us."

Near Christmas 1542, Juan Rodríguez Cabrillo personally hastened to relieve a shore party under attack. "As he began to jump out of the boat," according to eyewitness Vargas, "one foot struck a rocky ledge, and he splintered a shinbone." The wound was nasty and quickly gangrenous. Don Juan called for his chief pilot, Bartolomé Ferrer, and ordered him to take command and continue the voyage. On January 3, 1543, Cabrillo died. His crews buried him on the island and a couple of weeks later again put out to sea.[32]

Ferrer tried. He pressed farther north than before, probably to near forty-two degrees north latitude, the border today between California and Oregon. Mountainous waves toyed with the ships, sending torrents breaking over the decks. Driving rains, dense fogs, and dark, ominous tree trunks floating offshore contributed to their peril. Fervently imploring the Virgin of Guadalupe, the men vowed to make pilgrimages. Most would get their chance.

At last, in April, weather-beaten but spared, they put back into Navidad. En route home, they had abducted two Native boys to serve as future interpreters, a common practice excused by law. But again the hoped-for flush of discovery and profit—an island of Amazons, northern cities, a Strait of Anián, or China—had eluded Mendoza and the other investors.

Their second fleet fared worse. Captain Ruy López de Villalobos had sailed in early November 1542, with half a dozen ships and some eight hundred men of all classes, including pilot Ginés de Mafra of the *San Juan de Letrán*. As a sailor twenty years earlier, Mafra had been among the western islands with Ferdinand Magellan. Other Spanish survivors, rumors had it, were still living on Cebu trading with the Chinese for gold and gemstones. But nothing went right for don Ruy.

Clashes with Portuguese, mutiny, and frustrated efforts to sail back condemned the effort. If nothing else, before dying on Amboina allegedly in the company of Francisco Xavier, archetype of Jesuit missionaries, Ruy López de Villalobos made a contribution. He named the archipelago for the Spanish Prince Felipe—*las Islas Filipinas,* the Philippines.[33]

Costly, high-risk ventures all, the expeditions of Coronado, Cabrillo, and López de Villalobos left sponsors muttering. Whether Viceroy Mendoza took any pleasure in the equally bad luck of his rival Hernando de Soto, he offered asylum in 1543 to the survivors of Soto's expedition, barely half the army that had set out from Cuba in 1539.[34]

Anchoring close by the eastern shore of Florida's spacious Tampa Bay, in Timucua Indian territory, Soto's ships had disgorged most of 237 horses and 513 soldiers, along with nameless and numberless European, African, and Indian support people, war dogs, and lots of pigs. One early captive, hardly distinguishable from the Natives, turned out to be Juan Ortiz of Sevilla, missing in an attempt to find Narváez years before. He knew the Timucuas' language.

Cursing mud flats, sloughs, timbered marshes, and there-and-gone Timucua bowmen, the passionate Soto slashed and splashed his way north and west against fierce, intermittent resistance as far as Anhaica, principal town of the agricultural Apalachee chiefdom, on the site of today's Tallahassee. Here, the invaders helped themselves to maize, squash, beans, and dried fruits, wintering amid determined hostility.

Rapes were common, and hardly anyone mentioned them. A foiled attempt early on, however, suggested that some Native women, like their European counterparts, risked death rather than submit. Doubtless, too, on occasion Native women consented willingly and enjoyed sexual encounters with the invaders.

One Timucua woman—who unknowingly avenged the celebrated rape of a Carib sister by Columbus's friend nearly fifty years before—proved too tough. Young Pedro Díaz de Herrera, lagging behind his companions, had pulled her into the bushes, untied his pants, and exposed himself. Instead of complying, the woman grabbed his genitals, squeezed with all her might, and hung on. Only Pedro's pitiful screams brought help.[35]

Despite steady losses of personnel and animals in frequent ambushes and a few

De Soto sets sail from Spain to conquer Florida, J. W. Orr, New York, 1858. *Courtesy of the Library of Congress.*

notable major battles, the expedition cut a violent, zigzag path through Southeastern chiefdoms in today's Georgia, Alabama, Mississippi, and Arkansas, passing two more winters among Natives who would willingly have annihilated them.

Soto did not survive. Evidently brought low by typhoid fever, he died on May 21, 1542. To keep the Natives from learning of the immortal leader's death and to prevent desecration of the corpse, his own men dug it up, stuffed it into a hollow log, and sank it in the middle of the Mississippi more than a hundred miles downriver from present-day Memphis. Another singular death had taken one of the few recorded women participants, pregnant Francisca de Hinestrosa, burned to death in an Indian attack on the Spanish camp.

In the same way the dying Cabrillo had bidden Ferrer to carry on, Soto had released his command to Luis de Moscoso Alvarado, who now led the sorry fewer than four hundred expeditionaries westward again across present-day southern

Arkansas and deep into the Caddo Indian country of east Texas. Fate, meanwhile, led a young Indian woman, who had escaped from the Coronado expedition on the plains a year earlier, into Moscoso's camp. What was this she tried to get across about other metal men to the west? Refusing to believe her, the Spaniards trekked back to the Mississippi, constructed seven makeshift boats, and, weather permitting, coasted all the way to Pánuco. Coincidentally, in July 1541, Soto and Coronado had come within three hundred miles of each another, the former then in Arkansas, the latter in Kansas.[36]

Don Hernando, forty-two when he died, had accrued a great deal more experience as conquistador than thirty-year-old don Francisco. Acknowledged by peers as an especially ferocious and skilled warrior on horseback, Soto evidently enjoyed running down and lancing Indians. He was blunt, short-tempered, and rapacious, seemingly more so than Coronado. Still, the attitudes and actions of the rank and file who followed the two men varied little. Differences resulted not so much from their leaders' perceived ferocity or restraint as from the notably contrasting human and physical environments in which the two expeditions operated.

Soto repeatedly faced more numerous, better-organized fighting forces than did Coronado. The Southeast supported a far denser population than the Southwest. Paramount Southeastern chiefs could and did call up thousands of tributary vassals as warriors. Without pack animals, Soto's raiders forced chains of Indian captives to serve as burden bearers, a constant irritant. Moreover, bogs and swamps, rivers, and tangled and rugged woodlands impeded not only the free run of horses in a cavalry charge, but also daily progress, month after month. Merciless humidity and parasites, too, sapped the energy of the young Spaniards, typically from semiarid Extremadura.

Coronado, questing in higher, drier country, relied on a larger cavalry force, more and healthier animals, and his ever-intimidating contingent of Mexican Indian allies. Soto may have been a nastier man than Coronado, but it was the luck of the draw, not don Hernando's character, that dealt his expedition a crueler destiny.[37]

Although three of the four commanders had perished in the field, the explorations of Soto, Cabrillo, López de Villalobos, and Coronado cast Spanish claims across the vastness of North America and the Pacific. For a variety of reasons, colonization would follow later, north from the Caribbean and north and west from New Spain. Viceroy Antonio de Mendoza, meanwhile, met challenges closer at hand.

Chief among them was reaction to the so-called New Laws of 1542, which struck at the economic well-being of the conquerors. Hernán Cortés had gone to Spain in 1540 to protest Mendoza's encroachment on his privileges, but it was the indomitable fray Bartolomé de las Casas who swayed the Council of the Indies. By legislation drawn up in the mother country, the government meant simultaneously to rein in the conquerors and set the Indians free. It might as well have outlawed bread and wine.

Judiciously staying enforcement of the New Laws until appeals could reach Spain, Mendoza avoided violence. In Peru, however, protest erupted into civil war, and that colony's first viceroy was assassinated. Appalled, don Antonio readied an army under his son Francisco and Cristóbal de Oñate, but when the insurgents capitulated, he recalled and disbanded it.

Having proven himself an extraordinary administrator, Antonio de Mendoza, although in poor health, now found himself appointed second viceroy of Peru. He departed Mexico City in 1551, only to die in Lima the following year. Mendoza's legacy of stability at the core along with far-ranging reconnaissance would underlie expansion by future generations and, along with it, continued disruption and resistance of Indian peoples on the periphery.[38]

Francisco Vázquez de Coronado outlived his patron. Despite probable concussions sustained at Cíbola and Tiguex, he continued to function but not as before. The *residencia,* or judicial review, of his governorship in Nueva Galicia resulted in charges against him, a fine, and loss of that office. Don Francisco did, however, resume his position on the council of Mexico City, to which he had first been named in 1538. But his health worsened. In June 1554, he petitioned the crown to appoint as substitute his daughter Isabel's fiancé. And in September, he died.

That the audiencia of Mexico, presided over by Mendoza, had acquitted Coronado of all charges stemming from the expedition to Tierra Nueva, including alleged acts of cruelty to Indians, came as no surprise. The verdict, rendered in 1546, reflected the Mixtón War scare and the colonists' anger over the New Laws. Yet someone had to pay.[39]

The reformers, whose influence was always stronger in the mother country, settled for don García López de Cárdenas, Coronado's second-in-command, who had returned to Madrid. Embellishing the testimony recorded in New Spain, the prosecutor for the Council of the Indies arrayed graphic charges of unjustifiable savagery toward Indians. Proceedings dragged on until 1551, when the Council handed down a second, lightened sentence: one year's forced military service, a fine of two hundred gold ducats, and banishment for ten years from the Indies. If don García did not scoff at the final provision, he should have.[40]

Other veterans of the far north got on with their lives. Bartolomé Ferrer, who had brought Cabrillo's ships back in 1543 and then been sent to Peru with a cargo of horses from Mendoza's farms, became a lesser entrepreneur, trading up and down the coast.[41] Tristán de Luna y Arrellano, who had led the main army back to Tiguex while Coronado rode for Quivira, and later put down uprisings of Zapotec Indians in southern New Spain, was named governor and captain general of Florida by Luis de Velasco, Mendoza's successor. Aging expeditionaries from both the Soto and Coronado ventures joined Luna's abortive, hurricane-racked 1559 colony on Pensacola Bay. After Coronado's death, too, certain of his former retainers went in 1561 with his nephew, don Juan Vázquez de Coronado y Anaya, to conquer the central plateau of Costa Rica, a more lasting enterprise than that of Luna y Arrellano.[42]

Some famed conquerors died in Spain, while seeking to clear their names, gain redress, or further their ambitions: Cortés in Castilleja de la Cuesta near Sevilla on December 2, 1547; Cabeza de Vaca in Valladolid between 1556 and 1559; and Nuño de Guzmán also in Valladolid in 1558.

The Franciscan fray Marcos de Niza, who may have been the first white European to look upon Cíbola and who endured the curses of Coronado's men, did not immediately retire in shame. He marched, in fact, during his tenure as Franciscan provincial, with Viceroy Mendoza in the Mixtón War. The tone of a note he addressed to his abiding friend Bishop Zumárraga several years later, however, hinted that by then fray Marcos felt ostracized, like an orphan. He begged that the bishop send him some wine, to which Zumárraga replied kindly. The bishop's death in 1548 deeply saddened him. By 1554, when Franciscan historian fray Gerónimo de Mendieta met him in Jalapa, the old friar was sorely crippled in hands and feet, probably from arthritis. Not long after, possibly in 1558, fray Marcos breathed his last.[43]

The era of contact had resulted in no lasting European presence in the far north. In Pueblo Indian communities, as mixed-blood babies grew to adulthood and Mexican Indian deserters assimilated, open conversation in councils returned less and less to the trauma of metal-clad destroyers. Yet the people did not forget. An anxiety remained. When, they meditated, might the raiders return? A drama unfolding late in the 1540s in the shadow of a singular, hump-backed mountain, only 350 miles northwest of Mexico City, presaged the answer: not for a lifetime.

3 A Mestizo Captain

In the hope of seeing in my time another spiritual conquest like that of this land, I set out from this city [Mexico] in the company of two other religious, now more than two years ago, in search of the new Mexico, of which there has been word, although unverified, ever since we came to this land. . . . We traveled 150 leagues . . . to where there is a great difference of peoples. They are at war with the Spaniards. I do not know if it is a just war. I do know that they came to see us and to beg that we go baptize their children, appearing very content with us.

—FRAY CINTOS DE SAN FRANCISCO TO FELIPE II, MEXICO CITY, JULY 20, 1561

Some twenty-five days ago I arrived at the mines of Santa Bárbara, in this jurisdiction, very worn and tired after traveling for more than a year, in which I covered eight hundred leagues, examining and exploring the provinces of New Mexico.

—ANTONIO DE ESPEJO TO THE ARCHBISHOP OF MEXICO, VALLEY OF SAN BARTOLOMÉ, OCTOBER 1583

Seeking shelter amid the excited swirl of miners drawn to Zacatecas in 1548, an unmarried Native Chichimeca woman gives birth. This is not a rape case. The dark child is wanted and the father, peninsular Spaniard Pedro Caldera, is well known.

The couple's squalling mestizo baby is baptized Miguel. Not many years later, when his Indian mother dies, his father arranges that Miguel be raised by Franciscans at the local *convento*. He grows up "tall of body, of fine and healthy appearance." And for the next half-century, Miguel Caldera epitomizes the perilous, rough-and-tumble advance of New Spain's northern frontier.[1]

Had Spanish explorers discovered a mountain of silver on the Arkansas in 1541, alert investors would have scrambled to open a supply port on the Texas coast, and

Illuminations from a sixteenth-century map of northern New Spain. Redrawn by Jerry L. Livingston. *From Kessell,* Kiva, Cross, and Crown.

Tulsa would be Spanish-speaking today. Instead, the flat failure of Coronado's grand enterprise and the fright of the Mixtón War had collapsed such far-reaching hopes. Providentially, the mountain of silver lay closer at hand. Some 350 miles northwest of Mexico City, at first by no direct road, the hill called *la Bufa,* with its distinctive greenish, bare-rock crest, became the landmark for New Spain's richest silver bonanza.

Zacatecas took its name from Zacateco Indians, a Chichimeca people, some of whom in 1546 had shown chunks of ore to members of a typical armed prospecting party of Spaniards and allied Indians. Assay proved promising. Basque mine and town developers, enterprising men like Cristóbal de Oñate, Juan de Tolosa, Miguel Ibarra, and the latter's nephew Diego, provided capital and incentive. During 1548, the year of Miguel Caldera's birth and the town's formal founding, miners struck all three of the Zacatecas district's major veins, into which their laborers picked and hammered shafts and tunnels.

Competition was frantic. Lesser miners kept opening and abandoning holes in hopes of better finds. They jumped claims, failed to register their diggings, and evaded taxes on yield. Merchants and peddlers swarmed in and undercut each others' prices. Tricksters, gamblers, blacksmiths, and whores showed up. By 1550, fifty mine owners operated busy stamp mills and ore refineries, employing swarms of black slaves and salaried Indian *naborías.* The town had five churches.[2]

The reality of how starkly different—in terms of landscape and Native peoples —the environment of Zacatecas was from sedentary, town-dwelling, watered central New Spain dawned slowly on intruders so bent on quick profits. For some, revelation came en route to or from Mexico City. Crawling along a new track through the *despoblado,* a monotonous, prickly, high desert basin, lulled by the heavy heat of July 1551, travelers in a wagon train owned by Cristóbal de Oñate and Diego de Ibarra could scarcely keep their eyes open. Suddenly, all was a noisy blur. Ferocious, naked, painted wild men had jumped out of the chaparral. They were everywhere, unleashing stone-tipped arrows with deadly accuracy. Amid the screaming, a

Portuguese wagon master, two blacks, and five Indians died. The survivors never again took this place for granted.[3]

But mines multiplied, supported wherever the environment permitted by live-stock ranches, farms, and roisterous camps, luring wave after wave of intrusive out-siders and the bawling herds that followed them. And war spread, not all at once but unevenly, frighteningly, over the *Gran Chichimeca,* that vast, dry country of maguey, mesquite, nopal cactus, and all manner of spiny underbrush stretching from south of Zacatecas five hundred miles northward and broadening between Sierra Madre Occidental and Sierra Madre Oriental. Forays for Chichimeca slaves stiffened Native resistance. While raw silver moved over lonely roads from mines to government mints, containers of mercury, a crown monopoly, were freighted back for use in the amalgamation process, which in the 1550s greatly increased production by extend-ing the range of ores that could be profitably worked.

At first, Spaniards and Indian allies went out on search-and-destroy missions meant to punish Chichimeca raiders who more often than not faded into formidable, waterless country they knew better than their pursuers. In an effort to protect travel on the government inland highway, the *Camino Real de la Tierra Adentro,* the viceroy authorized small salaried garrisons, or *presidios,* set out at intervals.[4] Generous grants of land to stockraisers and licenses to innkeepers sought to attract protection in num-bers. By the 1560s, the outsiders were fortifying everything: towns, churches, rural estates, even experimental wagons.

But the enemy grew bolder and more hated. The Spaniards, by their use of the generic term *Chichimecas,* reduced numerous culturally distinct groups—among them Pames, Guamares, Guachichiles, and Zacatecos—to naked, rootless, relentlessly war-ring, unspeakably cruel, and barbarously wild people.[5] Presented with such a dehu-manized, irredeemable foe, even churchmen and legalists joined the cry for a just war by fire and blood, *guerra a sangre y a fuego.* Chichimeca males over twelve years of age could be hunted down and killed, their heads tallied for bounty payment, and their families sold profitably into slavery. Trouble was, the policy did not work.

The more pressure Spaniards applied, the more fearsome their desert enemies grew. Those with any tendency to plant maize or beans, offering fixed targets, gave it up in favor of nomadism. Native groups consolidated and war parties swelled in size to hundreds, and thus newly emboldened, attacked not only travelers and livestock but also towns and haciendas. Once they had eaten their fill of the first horses and mules they captured, the Chichimecas emulated their enemies and learned to ride, splendidly enhancing their speed of movement.

Spanish veterans of the Chichimeca war, which dragged on from 1550 to 1590, remembered best and loathed most the stories of their antagonists' devilish, drunken *mitotes,* or victory celebrations, and the exquisite forms of torture the Natives invented to prolong the agony of captured victims. Both sides cut and mutilated body parts of living prisoners. Chichimeca archers, who some soldiers conceded must be the best in the world, awed Spaniards with their precision and the penetrating power of their arrows. "It has happened," recalled one,

> that an arrow hit a horse on which a soldier was fighting and the arrow passed through the horse's crownpiece (which consisted of a very strong leather and metal piece), his head, and came out through the neck and entered the chest, a thing which, if it were not known to be certain, seems incredible.[6]

Even though some Spaniards attributed the Natives' fearlessness in battle to fermented cactus juice or peyote, it is doubtful that Chichimeca fighting men impaired their aim with drugs. Those they left for the mitote.

While Miguel Caldera took up soldiering against Chichimecas in the 1560s, 1570s, and 1580s, staying alive and earning his enemies' respect, the viceroyalty of New Spain expanded east and west. Captain Caldera would never see St. Augustine, Florida, or Manila in the Philippines, but as he fought and parleyed in the dry interior, these distant ports came into being. Both resulted from European imperial rivalry on a global scale. The first parried a brazen thrust by French Protestants to inhabit Florida; the second challenged the Portuguese monopoly in the Orient by opening trade across the Pacific. And both sprang from the grit and daring of Spanish seamen.

Born on Spain's north coast in 1519, the year Cortés launched his conquest, heroic mariner Pedro Menéndez de Avilés first proposed a fortified guard station on Florida's Atlantic shore in 1555. During the succeeding decade, Spain suffered not only the growing assertiveness of French and English privateers in the Caribbean, but also the wrecks of colonization schemes and treasure ships. In 1565, the bold Menéndez stepped forward as heir to half a century of ill success, signing an adelantado contract to discover, pacify, and settle Florida from the Gulf Coast around the peninsula's tip and on up the Atlantic shore as far as Newfoundland.

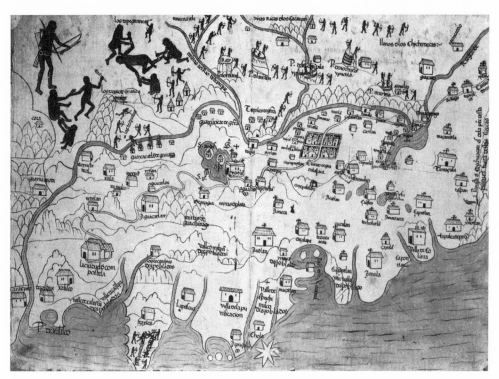

A sixteenth-century map of New Spain west and north of Mexico City, showing Guadalajara, the "rich mines of Zacatecas" (top center), and the ferocious Chichimecas. *Courtesy of the Ministerio de Educación, Cultura y Deporte, Archivo General de Indias (Sevilla, Spain), Mapas y Planos, México, 560.*

When news came that heretical French Huguenots had actually landed and built Fort Caroline, Felipe II contributed to the venture and made their elimination don Pedro's first priority.

That Menéndez achieved with gusto. Then, from his municipality of St. Augustine—a Timucuan village site hastily appropriated in September 1565 and fortified—the adelantado threw himself into Indian diplomacy meant to ease distribution of more than a thousand colonists. Another half-dozen little coastal settlements took temporary hold, from Tampa Bay around to present-day Port Royal Sound, South Carolina, where on Parris Island in 1566, Menéndez ordered his capital laid out.

From there, the visionary Spaniard reckoned, he could mount a search for the elusive strait across North America and open a road to Zacatecas. Menéndez had written to Felipe II that he meant to expand Florida to "fix our frontier lines here, gain the waterway of the Bahamas, and work the mines of New Spain." Twice in the late 1560s, tough Capt. Juan Pardo headed Spanish columns into the woodlands in the direction of Zacatecas, but they got no closer than the Tennessee Valley.

Though Menéndez's other foundations soon succumbed to Indian resistance,

Pedro Menéndez de Avilés. A late-eighteenth-century engraving. *Courtesy of the Library of Congress.*

hurricanes, and dissension among poorly provisioned colonists, St. Augustine endured, the oldest permanent European town in the future United States. A government-subsidized coastal presidio, it came to serve also as supply base for missionaries to disease-thinned Native communities as far west as Apalachee province on the Gulf Coast. Above all, it proved up Spain's claim to a strategic corner of the continent.[7]

Another far-flung Spanish claim, to the archipelago already named the Philippine Islands, appeared laughable so long as Spaniards who ventured out could not find their way back. *El tornaviaje,* the return trip, they called it. In Havana, in 1566, Pedro Menéndez de Avilés met the man who figured it out.

Andrés de Urdaneta was no mere theoretician. As a teenaged seaman in the 1520s, he had been out to the Philippines on an ill-starred Spanish follow-up to Magellan. After years of adventure in the Moluccas and a return around the Cape of Good Hope to Spain, he had emigrated to Guatemala and from there to Nueva Galicia with Pedro de Alvarado.

Life as district governor, or *corregidor,* had not provided the rewards Urdaneta sought, so don Andrés became fray Andrés, entering the Augustinian order in 1552. Even then, people remembered his seamanship. Called upon during preparations for yet another attempt to consummate Spain's claim to the Philippines, this time under fellow Basque Miguel López de Legazpi y Gurruchátegui, fray Andrés had charted a conjectural tornaviaje and sailed in 1564 as advisory pilot.

Applying what he knew about Atlantic winds and currents, which invited sailing from Europe to the Indies in lower latitudes and coming back high, Urdaneta proposed that by first navigating north of the Philippines to a point off Japan, even though the return voyage would be considerably longer, a ship might get back through more northerly waters. He was right. This news, in fact, fray Andrés was carrying in person to the court of Felipe II when he talked in Havana with Menéndez de Avilés. As for the uncharted strait across North America, Urdaneta speculated that it lay at a latitude much farther north than the Bahía de Santa María, today's Chesapeake Bay.[8]

In the South Pacific, meanwhile, López de Legazpi despaired. "The Philippines," he wrote to the viceroy of New Spain, "ought to be considered of little importance, because at present the only article of profit which we can get from them is cinnamon." Pursuing a more diplomatic than military, island-by-island conquest, the governor in 1571 moved Spanish administrative headquarters from Cebu to Manila. Sensing the enormous potential of commerce between the empires of China and Spain, López de Legazpi's successor crowed to Felipe II, "We are stationed here at the gateway of great kingdoms. Will your majesty aid us with the wherewithal so that trade may be introduced and maintained among many of these nations?"[9]

And His Majesty did. From the 1570s on, the king obliged his viceroy of New Spain to provide subsidies, *situados,* to royal officials and garrisons at Manila as well as St. Augustine. Hence, oriental luxury goods, traded for silver from New Spain and Peru and transshipped at Manila, started flowing annually on great, lumbering galleons, eastward across the North Pacific and down to Acapulco, thence up to Mexico City by human and animal bearers and over by wagon to Veracruz, and from there on smaller ships pushed by the Gulf Stream through the Straits of Florida out across the Atlantic to Spain.

But Urdaneta's tornaviaje was a killer. The voyage from Manila to Acapulco, vowed one passenger, was

> the longest and most dreadful of any in the World, as well because of the vast Ocean to be cross'd, being almost the one half of the Terraqueous Globe, with the Wind always a-head; as for the terrible Tempests that happen there, one upon the back of another, and for the desperate Diseases that seize People, in 7 or 8 Months, lying at Sea sometimes near the Line, sometimes cold, sometimes temperate, and sometimes hot, which is enough to Destroy a Man of Steel, much more Flesh and Blood, which at Sea had but indifferent Food.[10]

The prices people in the Americas and Europe were willing to pay for fine Chinese fabrics, porcelain, gems and jewelry, tea, spices, and objects of ivory, teakwood, and jade, even Chinese mercury, supplied the motive. Much more cargo came as contraband than was declared and registered. "This profit," observed fray Sebastián Manrique, "made all hardships and dangers appear as nothing."[11]

So the great galleons, called "China Ships" in New Spain, with burdens of as many as two thousand tons, plied their relatively swift, three-month passage out and their labored, six- to nine-month tornaviaje, finally raising the coast of North America in the vicinity of Cape Mendocino. The prospect of a port of haven for the returning Manila galleon set Spaniards thinking once again of upper California.

When the flamboyant, Protestant Englishman, Francis Drake, rounded the tip of South America late in 1578 and drove up the Pacific coast, plundering coastal towns and taking prizes as he came, Viceroy Martín Enríquez, preoccupied with the Chichimeca war, responded too late. Stuffed with booty from a Peruvian treasure ship, Drake's *Pelican,* later renamed the *Golden Hind,* needed careening. That task Drake's men saw to in midsummer 1579 on the California coast, of which he took symbolic possession as Nova Albion. From there, the Englishman sailed out across the Pacific and around the world so quickly, dropping anchor off Plymouth in September 1580, that certain of his Spanish enemies drew a faulty conclusion. El Draque must have found the Strait of Anián and run home eastward through it.[12]

Seventeenth-century Spanish galleons like those of the Manila trade, by Rafael Monleón. Museo Naval, Madrid. *From Cook,* Flood Tide of Empire.

The heretical Drake and the terrifying Chichimecas were twin scourges laid by God upon the Spaniards of New Spain for their mistreatment of the sedentary Indians—so sermonized the prophet and Franciscan chronicler, fray Gerónimo de Mendieta. Calling for repentance, not defeat, Mendieta also advocated war by fire and blood. Not all Franciscans agreed. As early as the 1550s, an elderly conqueror-turned-lay brother had ventured north with two other friars to the Chichimeca frontier and found the Natives receptive.

Fray Cintos de San Francisco had come to the Indies as Jacinto "Sindos" de Portillo about 1515, fought alongside Cortés, and received Indian tributaries. Seeing the error of his ways, he had entered the Franciscan order in the late 1520s as a lay brother and served humbly for years as porter of the mother house in Mexico City. Transferring later to the Franciscan custody of Zacatecas, he died in 1566 or 1567 at a very advanced age.

Writing to Felipe II in 1561, fray Cintos had urged peaceful conquest. Among the first to use the term *the new Mexico,* if only in a vague and hopeful sense, he wanted the killing, slaving for profit, and forced Indian labor stopped. Instead, he suggested, by underwriting expenses for the friars and a hundred god-fearing soldiers, the crown would hasten the conversion of tens of thousands of heathens. A judge of the Mexican audiencia, Alonso de Zorita, stood ready to command. Another Spaniard who had actually been there, Coronado's veteran artilleryman Juan Troyano, volunteered to serve as general protector of the Indians.[13]

But their timing was off. For another two decades, the mood of the colony dictated war. Not until the Chichimecas had proven too tough militarily did alternate proposals of peace by purchase gain support. Skeptics had only to ask the scarred, much touted, Zacatecas-born mestizo Captain Caldera. By the late 1580s, he was escorting gawking delegations of Chichimeca headmen to Mexico City for audiences with the viceroy, gifts, and assurances of amnesty, foodstuffs, lands, and protection. A dry cycle and attrition of their fighting men offered the Natives further incentives to end their resistance.

Caldera and other captains who had fought Chichimecas now became their provisioners and protectors. It was cheaper. Great quantities of maize, meat and hides and tallow, beans, salt, axes, copper kettles, ropes, hats, blouses, and cloth of bright colors, charged to the treasury's peace account, came to far less than the expenses of war, not to mention the savings in human lives. Moreover, the Viceroy Marqués de Villamanrique had banned slaving unequivocally in 1586, although from continuing allegations, a good many slavers must have kept at it.

Villamanrique's successor, Luis de Velasco II, authorized royal funds to transplant model communities of agricultural Tlaxcalans in the north and to subsidize Franciscan missionaries. The entire program would have greatly pleased fray Cintos.[14]

As Spaniards and their Indian allies campaigned against and then bought off Chichimecas, the mining frontier advanced, supported by livestock spreads of grand proportions and farms in fertile pockets. Mining towns strung out like beads on rosaries as Zacatecas (1548) begot San Martín, Sombrerete and Avino (1550s), then Nombre de Dios and Durango (1563), which begot Indé and Santa Bárbara (1567). Dozens of rowdy camps came into being, but none farther north than Santa Bárbara.[15]

Although its ores assayed well, Santa Bárbara did not immediately prosper. The community's remoteness in present-day extreme south-central Chihuahua, resistance by local Conchos Indians to slaving roundups, and the difficulty of keeping laborers made for discontent. Its core population of *vecinos,* citizens or householders, in the mid-1570s numbered no more than thirty. The usual motley crews worked for them.

People talked a lot at Santa Bárbara about rumors of Indians to the north who lived in towns, farmed, grew cotton, and wore clothes. One eager listener, Pedro de Bustamante, admitted later that such talk recalled to his mind "the information in Alvar Núñez Cabeza de Vaca's book about his travels from Florida to this land of New Spain."[16]

Franciscans, too, heard the rumors. Successors of fray Cintos, they, by virtue of the division of New Spain among religious orders, laid claim to the Gran Chichimeca and unknown north. When lay brother Agustín Rodríguez secured the viceroy's permission "to preach the holy gospel in the region beyond the Santa Bárbara mines," nine Indian-fighting prospectors signed up. Rodríguez, two Franciscan priests, and servants brought the party to hardly thirty. Setting out in the dry heat of early June 1581, they were gone ten months. Not everyone returned.

Ailing Francisco Sánchez Chamuscado, senior member of the armed escort, bled by his men with a horseshoe nail, died en route back. Pueblo Indians followed and dropped a big rock on one of the Franciscan priests who had left the party early to report the civilians' greed and insubordination. The blessed prospect of martyrdom inspired Rodríguez and his remaining Franciscan companion to stay among the Tiwas of Puaray, near today's Bernalillo, New Mexico. Only bravado, firearms, and the residual fear instilled by Coronado forty years earlier saved the others.[17]

The Pueblo world and the name New Mexico now came together. *Mexica* tradition placed Nahua origins in the far north. After more than a generation of fighting wild Chichimecas, Spanish frontiersmen conceded that, by contrast, the settled Pueblos seemed like another, or "new" Mexico. Sánchez Chamuscado had called the populous land San Felipe to honor the king, while his associates, particularly the ambitious Hernán Gallegos, intent on magnifying their discovery, proclaimed it the New Mexico.

A nasty sequel to Rodríguez-Chamuscado, the fast-moving, alleged rescue operation under would-be mine developer Antonio de Espejo, got off from Santa Bárbara late in 1582. Its members verified the martyrdom of the two friars at Puaray, prospected far and wide, and made it back in September the following year. They, too, had bullied the Pueblos. When the Indians of Pecos refused them provisions, recalled slaver Diego Pérez de Luján, "six armed men entered the pueblo, determined to burn it, and the people were so frightened that they gave us the food against their will." Of the two young Pecos men the Spaniards abducted, only one got away.[18]

The other would serve his captors. Taken to Mexico City by Espejo and entrusted to fray Pedro Oroz, Franciscan commissary general for New Spain, this Pecos Indian, described later as "intelligent and amiable," would learn Nahuatl at the friars' famed Indian college of Santa Cruz de Tlatelolco, then teach Mexican Indians his own native Towa language. Thus, when Espejo reentered New Mexico, he would have a staff of interpreters. In recommending Espejo to Felipe II on April 22, 1584, Father Oroz commented that "the land he discovered is very extensive, exceeding fourteen hundred leagues in length from the so-called Strait of Anián to the tip of Labrador."[19]

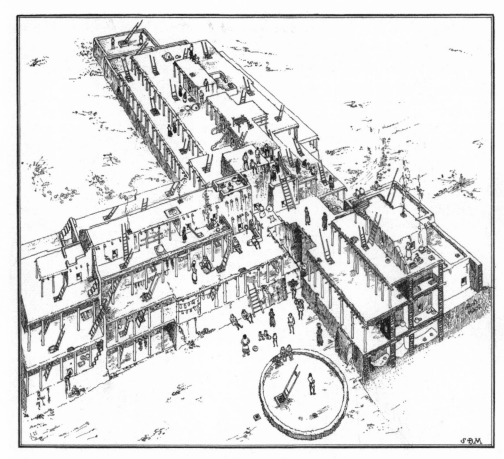

Southwest corner of Pecos pueblo's main plaza, by S. P. Moorehead. *From Kessell,* Kiva, Cross, and Crown.

No stranger to exaggeration, Felipe II had already decreed the pacification of New Mexico, directing his viceroy of New Spain to enter into a contract with "the most suitable person who may present himself, someone in whom you have the greatest confidence, to accomplish it without a thing being expended from my treasury."[20]

Again hope prevailed. Time had shrouded Coronado's experience. Hernán Gallegos and Antonio de Espejo submitted rival bids, but neither was rich. Suitability came down to investment capital, along with good lineage, experience, and influence. In their minds, that characterization fit more than one of the silver frontier's mining and ranching moguls, *los hombres ricos y poderosos*. So several competed.[21]

In matters of birth and breeding, society held two of these men apart; age, accomplishments, and mutual respect brought them together. By order of Viceroy Velasco, they had joined in 1592 to found the mining town of San Luis Potosí. On this occasion at least, the frontier made them almost equals. Yet don Juan de Oñate, son of Cristóbal, had been born with a Zacatecas silver spoon in his mouth, while Miguel Caldera was the illegitimate son of a Chichimeca. Don Juan had married elite Isabel Tolosa Cortés Montezuma, while Miguel remained single, fathering a natural daughter whose sons would inherit his property.

That he had property at all spoke well of Caldera. More important as a legacy, however, was the Chichimeca peace. Repeatedly on later frontiers, when faced by similar, unyielding Native peoples, Spaniards offered gifts and provisions, peace and alliance, whether or not they had heard of Miguel Caldera.

The mestizo captain had aided Franciscans as they evolved ways of ministering to nonsedentary Indians reduced to artificial communities, anticipating the missions of Texas and California. He did duty as soldier, presidial commander, provisioner, and protector of Indians. In 1597, seeking medical help and audience with a new viceroy, the ailing Caldera rode again for Mexico City. Death, however, overtook him en route.[22]

As for don Juan de Oñate, his destiny lay farther north.

4 Don Juan's Misfortune

*Finding myself helpless in every respect, because I have used up on this expe-
dition my estate and the resources of my relatives and friends, amounting to
more than six hundred thousand pesos, and anxious that the fruits of so many
expeditions and of more than eleven years of labor should not be lost . . . I find
no other means . . . than to renounce my office [as governor of New Mexico],
which resignation I am sending your excellency.*

—JUAN DE OÑATE TO THE VICEROY, SAN GABRIEL, AUGUST 24, 1607

Juan de Oñate and Miguel Caldera may have discussed in 1592 the prospect of paci-
fying New Mexico. They must have known about the pending proposal of Juan
Bautista de Lomas y Colmenares, flush and unscrupulous lord of Nieves, a hundred
miles north of Zacatecas. In return for colonizing New Mexico, Lomas had asked
in 1589 for the moon: a virtual principality with forty thousand Indian vassals, the
title *marqués* or *conde,* full civil and criminal jurisdiction, monopolies, the governorship for six lives in succession, a personal estate of more than 100,000 acres, and on
and on.

Felipe II, it turned out, did not want New Mexico so badly. The Council of
the Indies considered Lomas's terms insolent and preposterous, and the king agreed.
His viceroy must find someone else. Luis de Velasco chose Francisco de Urdiñola,
whose blood purity, astuteness, and enterprising nature had attended his rise from
soldier to founder of Saltillo and land baron. Unhappily, the rejected Castilian
Lomas hated his Basque neighbor Urdiñola with a passion.

Just as don Francisco and the viceroy were about to sign a contract for the pacification of New Mexico, the vengeful Lomas, who had sons-in-law on both the
audiencias of Mexico City and Guadalajara, arranged that his rival be charged with
a heinous crime. Urdiñola, paid accusers swore, had murdered his wife and her

Viceroy Luis de Velasco, viceroy of New Spain, 1590–95 and 1607–11. *From Manuel Rivera Cambas, Los gobernantes de México (1872).*

lover. Guilty until proven innocent, don Francisco languished in jail, while the viceroy summoned his next choice, don Juan de Oñate.[1]

The 1595 contract between Oñate and the Spanish crown in the person of Viceroy Velasco adhered scrupulously to law. Replacing the word *conquest* with the word *pacification,* however, would not, in the experience of the Pueblo Indians, make Oñate a gentler master than Coronado. Nevertheless, in 1573, Felipe II had reiterated the crown's theoretical doctrine of human rights in a general compilation of Ordinances for New Discoveries, occasioned in part by Spanish occupation of the Philippines. There, thanks less to law than to the native Filipinos' previously acquired immunity to the Euro-Asian disease complex, pacification had come at a far lower cost in human lives.

Already, in 1590–91, a desperate, would-be Cortés had tested the Ordinances for New Discoveries by invading New Mexico without license. Down on his luck, Gaspar Castaño de Sosa, lieutenant governor of Nuevo León, southeast of New Mexico, had transported an entire community of some two hundred men, women, and children, with loaded carts, cattle, goats, and dogs, up the Rio Grande and Pecos rivers into the midst of the Pueblo Indians.

Sadly, don Gaspar and his unauthorized colonists found no treasure to share with the crown, and Viceroy Velasco dispatched an armed party to remove them. The quixotic Castaño de Sosa, punished by exile to the Philippines, died in a mutiny of Chinese galley slaves on a voyage to the Moluccas. Acquittal came too late. Some of his former retainers, meanwhile, cast about in Mexico City.[2]

In that teeming, smelly, flood-prone viceregal capital built in Lake Texcoco and surrounded by snow-capped volcanos, for men and women who looked fit and able, swore they were free of debts or servitude, and were willing to risk uncertainty for a new start in life, there were in the mid-1590s several options: New Mexico, California, or the Philippines. Recruiters for all three vied to attract them.

A trade, skill, or family was desirable, but racial mixture hardly mattered. Only vagabonds and fugitives dared relocate in the Spanish empire without license. Because of the celebrated Inquisition trial and burning of Luis de Carvajal, accused for the second time of secretly practicing Judaism, fellow crypto-Jews became likely recruits. On later occasions, when willing colonists for remote frontiers were too few, authorities screened prisoners and orphans who appeared healthy enough.[3]

Evidently encouraged by what they had seen in New Mexico in 1590–91, certain of Castaño de Sosa's evacuees signed on with the new proprietor. Doña Inés, the Pueblo Indian woman Castaño had taken from Tano-speaking San Cristóbal, had no choice. Oñate hoped she would prove "a second Malinche," referring to Cortés's indispensable interpreter. Colonizer Oñate had contracted to recruit, outfit, transport, and settle two hundred soldier-colonists and their families in New Mexico.

The unauthorized Castaño de Sosa entrada, 1590, by Roy Andersen. *Courtesy of the artist and Pecos National Historical Park.*

At first, harkening to recruiters' fife and drum in Mexico City, Zacatecas, and elsewhere, too many volunteered. Later, after a run of costly, unanticipated delays and, in Oñate's words, "a flood of vexations," when finally the unruly mob mustered at Santa Bárbara in January 1598, an inspector officially counted only 129 men. To guarantee restoration of the 71 missing, the consortium had to post bond.[4]

Taken together, the larger first contingent and the subsequent group mustered at Santa Bárbara in 1600—which exceeded Oñate's shortfall of soldier-colonists by ten—must have numbered at least six hundred, from nursing babies to mulatto muleteers. Mostly, the adults were young and married, in their late teens, twenties, and thirties. Single men far outnumbered single women. Colonists elaborated in the musters, males for the most part, came almost equally from Spain and the Indies, although a large number of them had lived on the northern frontier. Oñate wrote of his many relatives, close and distant, and their retainers and friends, along with comrades on Chichimeca campaigns, drawn to the venture by his leadership.[5]

Other incentives were several. In don Juan, adelantado once he took possession of New Mexico, resided authority as New Mexico's first governor and captain general to grant his colonists title, lands, and Indian tribute. For their part, to earn these rewards, they had to remain in the new land for five years.

The title *hidalgo* (literally, son of something, that is, possessing inherited property), or member of the lowest rank of Spanish nobility, carried with it the honor of being addressed as don or doña, freedom from commoners' taxes, and other advantages before the law. It alone was worth the risk. If one endured five years as conqueror and first settler, earned his title, then discovered that neither lands nor Indian tribute yielded as handsomely as anticipated, he could petition as an hidalgo to withdraw. From the date of muster, however, anyone, regardless of status, who left without license was subject to death.

Some, like twenty-year-old Bartolomé de Herrera, medium-built native of Sevilla, declared, "I have nothing to manifest because the governor, my lord, is giving me the arms, horse, and everything else." Of those who did have items to manifest, Asensio de Archuleta, twenty-six, from Eibar in the Basque country, was average. He owned armor, a harquebus, sword, one mailed glove, a shield, ten horses, two mules, some horse armor, two saddles, and a half-dozen pairs of horseshoes with nails. He had a black beard and a small scar on his forehead. A fighter, he would see more action than he wanted.[6]

Eight Franciscan priests and two lay brothers were going, attended by Native catechists and helpers. The crown was expected to cover not only their travel expenses but also the cost of maintaining them in New Mexico. Back in 1593, Viceroy Velasco had nudged the miserly Felipe II, reminding him that

> to avoid a contract with such outrageous conditions as those asked by Juan Bautista de Lomas, some expense may be unavoidable, such as the cost of the friars who will take part in the expedition, since your Majesty invariably provides whatever is needed for them in such explorations.[7]

Striking due north across the entire present-day Mexican state of Chihuahua and its daunting desert, Oñate's advance party reached the near bank of the Río del Norte, or Rio Grande, here flowing southeast, some thirty miles downriver from today's El Paso. The whole cavalcade, proceeding in detachments a few days apart to let water holes refill, had straggled in by the end of April—eighty carts and wagons, hundreds of culturally Hispanic and racially mixed people, thousands of head of livestock. Although Oñate called it an army, this was a migration. As such, in form and intent, it contrasted notably with Coronado's entrada fifty-eight years before.

Settlement had eclipsed exploration. Now they drove not only reserve war horses but breeding mares, not only pack animals but wheeled vehicles freighting heavy crates of building tools and mining equipment. The ratio of female helpmates and squealing children to men was far higher. The numerous Mexican Indians among them, neither segregated nor arrayed for battle, came as servants, not as a military force. In boxes and bundles, the Franciscans had brought not only tools to erect crosses but also the liturgical furnishings for churches. This time, the invaders had come to stay.

To quizzical *ranchería* Indians, Sumas or Mansos, who crept through the chaparral and dared come close, the aliens held out ample inducements: strands of glass beads and earrings, shoemaker's needles, hawk's bells, butcher knives, combs, mirrors, even scissors. The encampment was astir. These oddly overdressed, gesturing strangers seemed to want the Natives to watch. By the Christian calendar, it was April 30, 1598, feast of the Ascension. Don Juan de Oñate was about to take formal possession of New Mexico. At a culminating moment in the heavily ritualized ceremonial, the adelantado,

> observing the requirements of the law, personally nailed on a living tree the holy cross of our redeemer, Jesus Christ, which had been prepared for this purpose. Turning toward it, his knees on the ground, he said: "Cross, Holy Cross that thou art, divine gate of heaven, altar of the only and essential sacrifice of the body and blood of the son of God, way of the saints and the attainment of His glory, open the door of heaven to these heathens, establish the church and altars where the body and blood of the son of God may be offered, open to us the way to security and peace for their preservation and ours, and give to our king, and to me in his royal name, peaceful possession of these kingdoms and provinces for His blessed glory. Amen.[8]

From here on, the highs and lows of Oñate's decade-long proprietorship would be marked by formal rites. By performing them properly, don Juan meant to maintain what he perceived as a right relationship with his universe—his god, worldly lords, subordinates, and environment—and, at the same time, awe non-Christians into embracing the Spanish way. As colonizers, few Spaniards would ever recognize that the Pueblo Indians, through their equally elaborate and symbolic rites, sought a similar harmony. But invaders always want more. Whatever they called it, conquest or pacification, they willed to dominate.[9]

A peculiar idea possessed one of Oñate's officers. Capt. Gaspar Pérez de Villagrá, born in New Spain but educated at the University of Salamanca, had read the classics. A romantic, he sensed the drama of Oñate's enterprise. Not only did Pérez de Villagrá cast himself in the tumultuous acts to come, taking notes, but he also survived to pen and see published in Spain in 1610 his own epic poem, the 11,877-line *Historia de la Nueva México*. Whereas Cabeza de Vaca had recounted the unmaking and transformation of a conquistador, Pérez de Villagrá, his cultural biases intact, pridefully dwelt on the heroics of the victors. Not captured by Indians or forced to get to know them as brothers, don Gaspar never stood among them naked.[10]

Capt. Gaspar Pérez de Villagrá. *From his* Historia de la Nueva México *(1610)*.

Bard Villagrá, average Archuleta, and most everyone else had parts in another animated, day-long ceremonial on the Blessed Virgin's birthday, September 8, 1598. Oñate's colony had labored up the Rio Grande through Piro, Tiwa, and Keres communities and come to rest at the Tewa pueblo of Ohke near the river's confluence with the Chama. Here don Juan made headquarters.

Renamed San Juan Bautista for the proprietor's patron saint, Ohke, at an elevation just over six thousand feet, seemed a pleasant, almost secure place in late summer. Shady green cottonwoods lined the water's meandering course, while tan, piñon- and juniper-dotted hills and high, blue-gray mountains beyond gave the valley definition. Yet already, certain disillusioned colonists whispered of desertion, risking the death penalty.

For now, Oñate suspended justice. He needed them. Fifteen hundred Pueblo workers, alleged volunteers who outnumbered the immigrants three-to-one, were digging an irrigation ditch. At the Spaniards' direction, Indian women—if traditional Pueblo gender roles prevailed—laid up in two weeks New Mexico's first temporary church, probably of poles and sun-dried mud. Its dedication provided the occasion. Hundreds of Pueblo Indians crowded in to watch don Juan preside in the manner of feudal lord, his various clients and underlings responding on cue.

The friars were a sight. Their ornately embroidered vestments, shining chalices, sung mass, and processions inspired among non-Christian onlookers a restrained wonder. As on Ascension Day, Spaniards performed a simple morality play composed especially for the event. Then they showed off their splendid control over animals in feats of horsemanship and bull baiting. Finally, bringing to life their crusade-affirming Reconquista, they put on a version of *Los Moros y Cristianos,* featuring a sham battle between Moors and Christians.

A delegation from distant Acoma, according to Pérez de Villagrá, carried back to that imposing fortress the intelligence that Spanish firearms

> were no more than fright alone, A clamorous noise, fearful horror, And, finally, all sound, for their lightnings, If thus you wish to call them, wounded not A single one of those who walked about Amid their frightful thunderings.

The Acomas did not yet know that in celebrations the invaders fired black powder only, without ball. "Slain" Moors got up laughing.[11]

For several months, Oñate galloped around his proprietorship with clanging escort, gathering ore samples and putting Pueblo leaders through symbolic acts of obedience to Felipe II. At the assembly of northern Pueblo leaders he called at Ohke, he relied on a polyglot corps of interpreters: gray-bearded Juan del Caso

Baraona, who knew Nahuatl; Mexican Indian Juan de Dios, a Franciscan catechist taught Towa in New Spain by Pedro Oroz, the abducted Pecos who had since died; Tomás, another Mexican Indian, who had come with Castaño de Sosa and stayed; and Juanillo, an otherwise unidentified Indian. The adelantado

> told them that he had come to this land to bring them to the knowledge of God our Lord, on which depended the salvation of their souls, and to live peaceably and safely in their countries, governed justly, safe in their possessions, protected from their enemies, and that he had not come to cause them any harm.[12]

Once they had undergone this ritual, any who took up arms against their new overlords, spurned reconciliation, and fell into Spanish hands risked summary trial, guilty verdict, and ten or twenty years as slaves, which was often fatal. Accused instigators risked prompt execution. The interpreters, who may have known some of the words but few of the concepts, were at pains to render them. Nevertheless, and tenuously at best, European civil and ecclesiastical justice now overlay the Pueblo world.

By terms of the *patronato real,* or royal patronage, the Spanish crown administered the Roman Catholic Church in Spanish America. Juan de Oñate, as founding adelantado and governor, exercised vice patronage to put the Franciscans in exclusive charge of the church in his jurisdiction. Considering that

> Franciscan friars discovered it and already three have died for its spiritual well-being at the hands of these natives . . . I do concede, grant, designate, and entrust, the Lord as my witness, from now for all time binding to the aforesaid sacred order of St. Francis and its Friars Observant present and future . . . the following provinces, pueblos, and Indian doctrinas with full faculty and license to build in each of them the churches and conventos they deem necessary for their residence and the better administration of Christian doctrine.[13]

To Pecos, don Juan and the Franciscan superior assigned fray Francisco de San Miguel, a humble man in his sixties, along with catechist Juan de Dios. Vicente de Zaldívar, younger of Oñate's two nephews, and some sixty men-at-arms gave the missionary an escort and straightaway spurred for the plains to contact Apaches and hunt buffalo.

Taking in the endlessness of the scene, they gaped as openly as Coronado's men, then fell back on detail, marveling at the quality of the nomads' bright red and white tents. Zaldívar traded for one. Watching the Apaches' "medium-sized, shaggy dogs," he found it both interesting and amusing to see them traveling along, one after the other, dragging the ends of their [travois] poles, almost all of them with sores under the harness. When the Indian women load these dogs, they hold their heads between their legs, and in this manner they load them or straighten their loads.

It was, of course, the slow-moving, numberless buffalo that interested the Spaniards more. A seemingly inexhaustible resource, could these weird cattle not be raised as easily as those of New Spain? The experiment was over almost before it began. They built a big corral of cottonwood logs in three days. "It was so large," reported Zaldívar, "and had such long wings that they thought they could enclose ten thousand head." But as horsemen drove the plodding buffalo toward the corral, they turned and stampeded furiously. There was no use, "because they are stubborn animals, brave beyond praise, and so cunning that if one runs after them, they run, and if one stops or moves slowly, they stop and roll, just like mules, and after this rest they renew their flight."

Zaldívar's men tried "a thousand ways" to round them up, none to avail. Even the calves they captured, some tied by the tail and others draped across horses, all died quickly of rage. So, despite the Spaniards' agreement that the meat, hides, and fat of these animals were of high quality, henceforth, they would come to the buffalo, not the other way round.[14]

Nothing seemed to work out as Oñate hoped. Not only was he himself a mine developer, but the art of metallurgy had advanced notably since Coronado's day. Yet time and again, assay reports proved disappointing. Dependent on levies of food from glum Pueblo Indians, his colonists cursed their lot. Pursuing four deserters, Captain Pérez de Villagrá's party caught up with and slit the throats of two. Fear gripped the camp.

But Oñate, accompanied by his only son, Cristóbal, evidently in his midteens, rode off again with dozens of the men, touring first the southern pueblos and saline flats east of the Rio Grande, then spurring westward toward the Pacific, where he hoped a supply port might succor his colony. He sent for his older nephew, Juan de Zaldívar, second in military command, to bring thirty more men and overtake the expedition. Zaldívar, however, halted at Acoma to exact provisions and unwisely accepted the Indians' invitation to climb up to the pueblo.

Only days before, Captain Pérez de Villagrá, eager to report on the deserters, had passed by Acoma brash and alone. Unsuspecting, he and his mount fell into a horse trap. Afoot, with only his dog as companion, the dazed Spaniard pushed on, bragging later of his ingenuity. To confuse Acoma war parties, he put his boots on backward. Unless he carried the dog, it was not much of a ruse.

Before an eleventh-hour rescue by some of Oñate's soldiers searching for strayed horses, the numbed and starving Pérez de Villagrá thought he was going to die. His desperate decision to kill and eat his dog later found poignant memory in the poet's words. He had struck the animal twice, probably with a rock.

> Whining in friendly sort and crouching down,
> My badly wounded friend came back to me,
> Licking the blood that he poured out.
> And, though in pain and wounded sore,
> To please me in something if he but could,
> He also licked my hands, till they
> Were stained and well-bathed with his blood.
> I looked at him then, lord, and much ashamed
> That I had treated him and wronged him thus,
> With such crass ignorance as not to see
> That I did lack a fire to cook his flesh,
> I lowered my sad eyes and, beginning,
> Repenting of my deed, to caress him,
> He lay dead at my feet.[15]

To the west, Oñate took guarded pleasure in the readiness of Zunis and Hopis to swear allegiance and in reports of a splendid saline and alleged precious minerals farther on. But winter had come, and snow blanketed ridge and mesa. The Pacific must wait. Doubling back past the pool and campsite at El Morro, don Juan met urgent riders dispatched from San Juan.

The news could hardly have been worse. His nephew and namesake, the maestre de campo, Juan de Zaldívar; two captains; eight soldiers; and two servants, cleverly separated on the peñol by Acomas offering foodstuffs, had died in combat. Another five had thrown themselves over the edge. Pedro Robledo, "his flustered brains knocked out / Among the rocks, came down losing both eyes," but the others landed in dunes blown up against the base and, unbelievably, survived.

What had possessed the Acomas? Had their headmen, only weeks before, not "replied with spontaneous signs of pleasure and accord that they wished to become vassals of the most Christian king our lord, and . . . render at once obedience and vassalage for themselves and in the name of their nations"? The adelantado had the document to prove it, duly executed on October 27, 1598, and witnessed by his son and other officers. No challenge to the invaders' authority could have been clearer.[16]

The Franciscans concurred. Hastily summoned from their posts, they joined in council at San Juan. Their superior, fray Alonso Martínez, who suffered the periodic agony of gout, framed the declaration. A Christian prince, fray Alonso averred, was just to wage war against delinquent vassals so long as his intention was "to secure and preserve peace . . . and not through ambition to rule nor for mortal vengeance, nor for the desire for the property of others." In the case of rebellious subjects, however, once humbled, their property and their persons were to "remain at his will and mercy."[17]

Years later, questions arose about the adelantado's choice of Vicente de Zaldívar to command the punishment of Acoma. As the murdered Juan's brother, surely he "would be dominated by passion."[18] So much the better, anxious noncombatants at San Juan must have thought as the young *sargento mayor* and his heavily armed column of seventy-odd mounted men trailed off into the cold gray of mid-January 1599. Although Captain Pérez de Villagrá rode with them, he later heard how the women, whose presence was regularly noted only among men's chattel, rallied to defend San Juan against attack.

One of the women, doña Eufemia, wife of the vain Francisco de Sosa Peñalosa, had already caught the poet's eye. "Extremely beautiful," displaying a fiery courage and spirit any man could admire, she was, moreover, "unusual For splendid, quick and clear mentality." Back in the dark days of delay at Santa Bárbara, doña Eufemia had harangued the men who considered desertion. Now, with the women and children's fate hanging on the outcome of the Acoma campaign, she took charge, organizing the wives into guard details. Oñate approved. Caught up in the moment, at least two dozen women enlisted, among them Ana Pérez de Bustillo, bride of Asensio de Archuleta, and "With gallant spirit they did promenade / The roofs and lofty terraces."[19]

From atop the towering peñol of Acoma, Zaldívar's horsemen, circling the base and shouting the required offers of peace and amnesty, looked singularly puny. The defenders hurled back insults, shooting arrows and throwing down rocks and heavy chunks of ice. Raucously belligerent, these excited, gesturing Natives never imagined what three days would bring.

The larger force of Spaniards, by cunning design, assembled to attack by the main trail up, drawing the Indians to that side of the rock, while Zaldívar, Pérez de Villagrá, and ten others scaled the opposite side. By the time the Acomas caught on, it was too late to dislodge the assailants. The date, by chance, was Zaldívar's saint's day, January 22. Eventually, the attackers hauled up with ropes two culverins, small, swivel-mounted cannons.

Eyewitness Pérez de Villagrá described the action in epic terms, endowing memorable Acomas with imaginary names—Zutacapán, Milco and Polca, Mompil, Chumpo, and Bempol—and noble qualities, if only to make them worthy opponents for the nobler Spaniards to vanquish. Dashed heads, severed limbs, and spilt entrails attested to the fury of the battle.

In the confusion, Asensio de Archuleta shot a charge of four balls through the

The peñol and pueblo of Acoma, by William Henry Jackson. *Courtesy of the State Historical Society of Colorado, no. 15032.*

torso of his dearest friend, the red-bearded Lorenzo Salado de Rivadeneyra. The fatally wounded man, as Pérez de Villagrá remembered it, cried out for God's forgiveness; he had not confessed to a priest in two years. Staggering to his feet and resisting the devil's temptation to jump, he made his way down to the chaplain's tent where he confessed, received absolution, and died.[20]

The fighting raged, with intermittent lulls of exhaustion, for the better part of two days. The Spaniards did not admit the number of their casualties, but the terrible carnage among the Acomas told of the outcome. How had it happened? Who, the poet made old Chumpo ask, were the fierce, invincible Castilian warrior on a white horse and his radiant woman companion "More beautiful than the sun or the heavens"? No need for further search of the smoldering pueblo. Santiago and the Blessed Virgin Mary, their mission accomplished, had returned to their celestial homes.[21]

As word of the Spaniards' miraculous victory spread over the Pueblo world, Oñate rode south to populous, centrally located Santo Domingo to congratulate the returning Zaldívar, whose men on horseback flanked a forlorn and stumbling procession of Acoma prisoners, hundreds of them, mostly women and children. The adelantado meant to put them on trial for all the Pueblos to see.

After brushing aside the plea of their court-appointed Spanish defender, Oñate handed down a brutal and resounding sentence. Each of the two dozen men who looked to be the legal age of twenty-five or older was to have a foot severed and to serve twenty years as a slave. Males twelve to twenty-four and women over twelve would also serve twenty years. Younger children, to be raised as Christians, were separated from their relatives and entrusted to Spaniards, the boys to Vicente de Zaldívar, the girls to Father Martínez. Two Hopi captives would suffer loss of their right hands; thus mutilated and released, they could carry a warning to their distant pueblos.[22]

Only one brief mention in the record testified that Oñate's punishment was carried out. Elsewhere in colonial Spanish America, on similar occasions, while the conqueror maintained his stern countenance, churchmen knelt at his feet to beg that he show paternal mercy and commute so harsh a sentence. "In this manner," Oñate himself had instructed Zaldívar before the battle, the Acomas would "recognize the friars as their benefactors . . . and come to love and esteem them, and to fear us."[23] The absence of any subsequent reference to a one-footed Acoma slave, *un cojo,* raises doubt that Spaniards wielding axes or swords indeed followed through.

Inspiring fear bought the adelantado only temporary relief. In midsummer 1599, when Zaldívar demanded a levy of maize from the Jumano pueblos east of the mountains, the Indians gave him stones. Next, according to an unsympathetic, secondhand witness, Oñate himself appeared with "a large force . . . to punish their insolence toward the sargento mayor, his nephew." The attack left half a dozen Indians dead from gunshot wounds and three hanged. Retaliating some months later, Jumanos killed two or three Spanish travelers. Vicente de Zaldívar, at the special request of the friars, then led a second punitive strike against the Jumanos, resulting in a bloody five- or six-day siege. This time, the invaders killed or captured hundreds, and don Vicente came away with a broken arm.[24]

Ironically in the end, waging war and peace with the Pueblos proved not so critical to Oñate's enterprise as the mood of his own colonists. Many hated New Mexico: the extremes of heat and cold; the uncertainty of food supplies; the fixed, unfriendly looks of their Tewa neighbors; the plagues of bedbugs, mice, and lice; and the suffering of their children. Evidently in 1600, the adelantado, seeing the community swollen by Acoma slaves, moved headquarters from Ohke, or San Juan Bautista, across the river to the west-bank, four-hundred-room pueblo of Yunge, which he ordered remodeled and called San Gabriel. Conditions did not improve.

Another winter came, and on Christmas Eve 1600, don Juan received at San Gabriel the second wave of colonists, who ranged in station from married doña Francisca Galindo, with her trunks of satin, silk, and taffeta court dresses, to Isabel, a free mulatta and single head of household. Among supplies were listed quince and peach preserves. The energetic, balding Gaspar Pérez de Villagrá, who had gone to Mexico City with dispatches from Oñate, was supposed to lead the reinforcements north from Santa Bárbara. Instead, in a quarrel with Juan Guerra de Resa, the adelantado's kinsman and chief financial backer, he had sought asylum in the church of the Franciscan convento. Never again did Oñate's poet-captain return to the scene of his epic.[25]

Yet the drama continued. On June 23, 1601, don Juan led forth from San Gabriel an expedition of discovery. With Vicente de Zaldívar, more than seventy chosen men, hundreds of horses and mules, eight wagons, four pieces of artillery, and dozens of servants, the adelantado would claim the great kingdoms of the plains. As he mounted up, don Juan admonished the colonists who remained in San Gabriel to hold the fort. Some smirked.

With Oñate gone, the undercurrent of resentment surfaced. Debate was bitter. Factions coalesced rapidly around captains and friars who swore that God and king would be better served by abandoning San Gabriel and others who swore as formally that, without specific orders, no one should leave. Families split.

Capt. Alonso Gómez Montesinos, who had served as defense attorney for the Acoma prisoners, recorded this conversation with supply master Diego de Zubía, who was pressing him to join the exodus.

> This witness answered: "Mr. Purveyor, even if we were not in the service of the king our master, could we show a greater cruelty than to abandon the governor and his forces in the interior and leave them without refuge or shelter on their return? Even if I am left here all alone, I am going to wait for him." To this the purveyor replied: "Mr. Captain, what we are doing is not cruelty but the work of men as honorable as your grace. And I swear to God that your grace and your companions deserve to be beheaded for issuing the order not to abandon the land. By refusing to leave, you, my father-in-law, are rendering the king a poor service." To which this witness replied: "Well, I swear to God and your grace that if we were on an equal footing I would settle this question, but your grace has sixty men and I have only eight, but some day we will meet before the royal audiencia, where the one who deserves it will be punished."[26]

Where the bold doña Eufemia stood, without an admiring poet to record it, no one said. Her husband, the anguished Francisco de Sosa Peñalosa, found himself caught in the middle. Admonished as lieutenant governor by Oñate, he now presided over formal meetings of both factions. Asensio de Archuleta acted as secretary for the smaller group that vowed to stay. Damning the consequences, most of the others—at least four hundred men, women, and children packing what they could carry and heading up their animals—merged into a long, noisy refugee column and were gone. Lucky for them, they reached Santa Bárbara in Nueva Vizcaya before Vicente de Zaldívar caught up.

This pathetic backwash of humanity from New Mexico actually reinvigorated the Santa Bárbara frontier. When authorities dropped the charges of desertion against them in 1602, on the grounds that these were not so much soldiers engaged in war as civilian colonists, many settled nearby in the jurisdictions of Valle de San Bartolomé, Todos Santos, and Atotonilco. Had New Mexico proven the bonanza of Oñate's illusions, the rush north might well have depopulated the province of Santa Bárbara. Instead, it worked in reverse, and the colonists' flight south doomed don Juan's proprietorship on the Rio Grande.[27]

No matter that Zaldívar went on to Mexico City and then to Madrid as advocate for his uncle; the volume of testimony from disgruntled former colonists deploring Oñate's harsh rule, abuse of Pueblo Indians, and misrepresentation of a sterile land weighed against the proprietor's every petition for additional aid from the crown. A new, less-decisive king now ruled. The deliberate, storied Felipe II, in whose name Viceroy Luis de Velasco had negotiated Oñate's original contract, had died on September 13, 1598, just days after New Mexico's first settlers, half a world away, celebrated the consecration of that remote colony's first Christian church.

More prone than his father to leave details to others, Felipe III did sign the decree put in front of him at Burgos in 1603 authorizing Zaldívar to recruit in Spain "as many as forty experienced musketeers and skilled ship carpenters" for New Mexico. A few of the latter seem to have reached the colony in 1606 with don Vicente's thin reinforcements, and one at least so impressed the Indians of Pecos with woodworking that a group of them became the carpenters of colonial New Mexico.[28]

Although his contract authorized Oñate to bring two ships a year "free of taxes and import duty" to New Mexico, the adelantado still had not traveled to the coast and identified a harbor. That challenge he met at last between October 1604 and April 1605, while the fifty or so colonists left all winter at San Gabriel told stories by the fire, made love, and wondered if the ocean had swallowed him up. To prove that it had not, a member of the party inscribed deeply in the sheer sandstone wall behind the pool at El Morro: "Adelantado don Juan de Oñate passed this way on the 16th of April 1605 returning from the discovery of the South Sea." "I discovered a great harbor," he wrote apprehensively to a new viceroy, "and clarified the reports of extraordinary riches and monstrosities never heard of before."[29]

The Viceroy Marqués de Montesclaros was no fool. "I cannot help but inform your majesty," he wrote to Felipe III later in 1605, "that this conquest is becoming a fairy tale. If those who write the reports imagine that they are believed by those who read them, they are greatly mistaken."

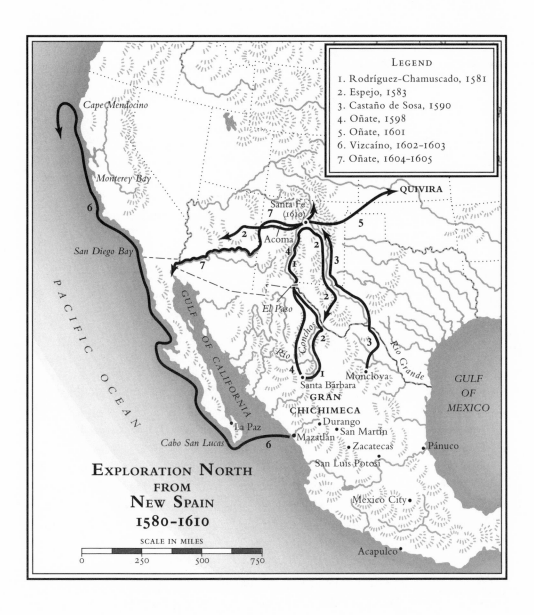

LEGEND

1. Rodríguez-Chamuscado, 1581
2. Espejo, 1583
3. Castaño de Sosa, 1590
4. Oñate, 1598
5. Oñate, 1601
6. Vizcaíno, 1602-1603
7. Oñate, 1604-1605

Cape Mendocino

Monterey Bay

PACIFIC OCEAN

San Diego Bay

GULF OF CALIFORNIA

QUIVIRA

Santa Fe
(1610)

Acoma

El Paso

Rio Conchos

Rio

Monclova

Rio Grande

GULF
OF
MEXICO

Santa Bárbara

GRAN
CHICHIMECA

Durango
San Martín

Zacatecas

Pánuco

San Luis Potosí

La Paz

Cabo San Lucas

Mazatlán

Mexico City

Acapulco

EXPLORATION NORTH
FROM
NEW SPAIN
1580-1610

SCALE IN MILES

0   250   500   750

Fray Francisco de Escobar, the expedition's chaplain, had diverted himself, visualizing the fantastic beings evoked by a willing Colorado River Native informant the Spaniards called Otata. The men of one tribe, gestured the wide-eyed Otata, possessed virile members so long that they wound them four times around their waists. Curious, even amusing, thought the king's viceroy, yet "all that has been discovered thus far are naked people, some pieces of inferior coral, and a handful of pebbles, all of which I am forwarding to your majesty."[30]

Miguel de Cervantes, whose ageless *El ingenioso hidalgo don Quijote de la Mancha* appeared in Madrid early the same year, would have chortled. Juan de Oñate was don Quijote. There he stood, stiff and prideful, having traversed impossibly rugged terrain to a beach on the Gulf of California impossibly far from San Gabriel, obeying the urge to take formal possession. "So, fully dressed and armed, with a shield on his arm and sword in hand," wrote fray Alonso de Benavides thirty years later, "he gallantly waded into the water up to his waist, slashing the water with his sword and declaring: 'I take possession of this sea and harbor in the name of the king of Spain, our lord.'"[31]

The South Sea had greatly interested Viceroy Velasco. He, in fact, envisioned California and New Mexico as related enterprises. Occupation of both might secure at once the mouth and near shore of the Strait of Anián. In 1587, English corsair Thomas Cavendish had dramatically underscored the need, too, of a way station for returning, Acapulco-bound Manila galleons.

Unburdened by the weight of cannons so that merchants and passengers might cram aboard every possible ounce of Oriental luxury goods, the seven-hundred-ton *Santa Ana* had raised the northern California coast in the fall of 1587 and then plowed southward. As she came near Cabo San Lucas at the tip of Baja California, her lookouts had sighted two ships closing. The much smaller, more maneuverable *Desire* and *Content* showed respectively eighteen and ten cannons. Yet the battle had lasted six hours. Tossing up grappling hooks, the Englishmen boarded, were beaten off, and reboarded. A Spaniard on the *Desire* yelled at the people crowding the China ship's littered deck to give up and beg for mercy. They did.

Put ashore, the castaways could only watch as foreigners swarmed over and thoroughly pillaged the *Santa Ana,* a task requiring six days. The booty they stole amounted in value to hundreds of thousands of pesos, considerably more than the entire investment of Oñate's consortium in New Mexico. Venting his Protestant spleen, Cavendish watched as Father Juan de Almendrales, canon of Manila, swung, neck broken, from the mizzen arm of the *Desire*. At the same time, he provided the people on shore with food and wine, firewood, sailcloth for tents, and planking for a boat. After the Englishmen had taken their merry leave, the smoking hull of the galleon had drifted to shore, where survivors made of it a giant raft and saved themselves.[32]

In 1595, during the final months of his first term as viceroy, Velasco had negotiated not only the New Mexico contract, but also a deal for further exploration of California. Its author, a fast-talking speculator and former soldier, Sebastián Vizcaíno, had put together a loose and quarrelsome partnership to exploit the gulf's pearl fisheries. After a dizzying series of maneuvers, Vizcaíno finally sailed from Mazatlán in August 1596, early in the term of the Viceroy Conde de Monterrey. He had three ships, fewer than two hundred men after desertions, four Franciscans, dozens of wives and children—among them seven-year-old Juan, his son—a few horses, and supplies enough, he swore, for eight months.

Vizcaíno's two makeshift settlements, one on a cove close by Cabo San Lucas and another up the inside coast at La Paz, did not last eight months. Ill-prepared, the colonists begged to withdraw, judging the hostile peninsula too sterile for survival and the Natives too primitive for conversion. Storms heightened their misery.

Exploring on up the gulf, Vizcaíno's parties clashed with Indians, and nineteen armed men drowned when their launch capsized. A fire, whipped by wind, consumed half the thatched huts at La Paz. Before the end of 1596, everyone had left. Apologizing to viceroy and king, the glib promoter set about planning a successful reprise. Future colonists would enjoy hidalgo status, Native tribute, and tax exemptions. But Felipe II died and so did the proposal.[33]

Ever resourceful, Vizcaíno rebounded. Viceroy Velasco, in response to a royal order of 1593, had identified Sebastián Rodríguez Cermeño, veteran pilot on the ill-fated *Santa Ana,* as the mariner most likely to find a safe harbor for the China ships. Commanding the cargo-laden galleon *San Agustín,* homebound from Manila with a Philippine longboat on deck, Rodríguez Cermeño ordered the big ship anchored in Drake's Bay in the lee of Point Reyes, where coast Miwoks came out in canoes and invited the Spaniards to land. Those who did noticed the Natives' painted faces and long, straight hair and their tule-covered, partly dug out lodges. Given gifts, they watched the foreigners' rites of taking possession and readying the longboat for coastal charting.

Then on November 30, 1595, with little warning, biting winds rose and dashed the *San Agustín* onto the shore. Hence, their longboat became the crowded lifeboat that returned passengers and crew to New Spain. Once there, with the officers blaming one another for the disaster, the Conde de Monterrey suggested in retrospect that "to all practical men" a better plan would be to dispatch from Acapulco a ship or ships of light burden to chart California's outer shore as far north as Cape Mendocino. With customary élan, Vizcaíno volunteered.[34]

Again, as with Rodríguez Cabrillo sixty years before, the ships were three: the

Viceroy the Conde de Monterrey, viceroy of New Spain, 1595–1603. *From Manuel Rivera Cambas,* Los gobernantes de México *(1872).*

San Diego, General Vizcaíno's flagship, towing a longboat; the *Santo Tomás,* used earlier in trading on the coast of Peru; and the small frigate *Tres Reyes,* newly built at Acapulco. With shore batteries booming, the crews, in all perhaps 130 men, set sail on May 5, 1602. Young Juan again accompanied his father. Chief Pilot Francisco Bolaños had survived the wreck of the *San Agustín.* Three Carmelite friars, one per vessel, and a hallowed statue of Our Lady of Carmel supplied divine comfort and protection.

The Vizcaíno expedition, in accord with Monterrey's minute instructions, would bestow saints' names on ports along the way but not change existing names. How the general was to comply, without precise records of previous voyages, the viceroy did not say. So, calendar in hand, Vizcaíno renamed practically everything. The frequent need to take on fresh water and firewood amid coastal Natives, and the pilots' struggle against wind and current to keep the ships within sight of each other, made for slow going. Not until November 12, feast of San Diego, more than six months out of Acapulco, did Vizcaíno's flota rest at anchor inside Cabrillo's bay of San Miguel.

In a hut hastily built on shore, the Carmelites celebrated a mass in honor of San Diego, whose name the port still bears. One detail went in search of water, another for wood. Vizcaíno aboard the frigate supervised sounding the bay. Later, with a shore party, he hailed some Indians armed with bows and arrows. Only a weepy old woman approached. According to a diarist of the voyage, she appeared to be more than 150 years old. The general consoled her with some beads and food. "This Indian woman," the diarist went on graphically, "from extreme age, had wrinkles on her belly which looked like a blacksmith's bellows, and the navel protruded bigger than a gourd."[35]

Naming the Santa Barbara Channel and renaming Santa Catalina Island, which Cabrillo had called San Salvador, the Spaniards marveled at the Natives' quickness in their plank canoes. One came alongside, the diarist remembered, "so well constructed and built that since Noah's Ark a finer and lighter vessel with timbers better made has not been seen." Four men rowed, with an old man in the center, the latter chanting and the others responding. The elder handed up a flask of fresh water and some acorn porridge in a willow basket, indicating to the visitors that they must land and making himself "so well understood by signs that he lacked nothing but ability to speak our language." When the Spaniards hesitated, "as a greater inducement he said he would give to each one of us ten women to sleep with. This Indian was so intelligent that he appeared to be not a barbarian but a person of great understanding."[36]

By mid-December, they had rounded a rocky point and anchored off a sandy white beach partway along a great sweeping arc of coastline. Inland, blanketing the mountains, stretched endless stands of stately, deep blue-green pines. Too hastily, the exhausted Vizcaíno proclaimed this "bay of Monterrey" the ideal port for

> protection and security of ships coming from the Philippines: In it may be repaired the damages which they may have sustained, for there is a great extent of pine forest from which to obtain masts and yards, even though the vessel be of a thousand tons burden, very large live oaks and white oaks for ship-building, and this close to the seaside in great number. There is fresh water in quantity and the harbor is very secure against all winds. The land is thickly peopled by Indians and is very fertile, in its climate and the quality of the soil resembling Castile, and any seed sown there will give fruit, and there are extensive lands fit for pasturage, and many kinds of animals and birds— as is set forth in the report.[37]

So many of his men lay terribly sick, and supplies had run so low, that Vizcaíno dispatched the *Santo Tomás* back to New Spain from Monterrey carrying the infirm and word of the discovery in letters, reports, and charts. Together, over the years they would give rise to the myth of a magnificent, sheltered bay at Monterrey. Eventually, overland parties searching for it would pass by, unable to reconcile Vizcaíno's description with this roadstead gaping open to the northwest. They would discover instead the bay of San Francisco, finest harbor on the Pacific Coast, which, because of fog, the narrowness of the Golden Gate, and fear of offshore rocks, Cabrillo, Vizcaíno, and everyone else had failed to spy across the water.

Crewmen judged healthy enough to proceed northward aboard the *San Diego* and *Tres Reyes* cursed their lot. Separated on leaving Monterrey, neither ship saw the other again during the entire voyage. Tossed about by frighteningly high, cold seas, each attained more or less forty-two degrees north latitude. "The pitching was so violent," reported the diarist on the *San Diego,* "that it threw both sick and well from their beds and the general from his. He struck upon some boxes and broke his ribs with the heavy blow."

Worse was the scurvy. The sick lay in their bunks moaning, "although there was neither assistance nor medicines nor food to give them except rotten jerked beef, gruel, biscuits, and beans and chick-peas spoiled by weevils." It hardly mattered. "The mouths of all were sore, and their gums were swollen larger than their teeth, so that they could hardly drink water, and the ship seemed more like a hospital than a ship of an armada."[38]

A third of his men died, but Vizcaíno was a hero. He had charted the California coast and recommended a port. That Spanish strategists chose not to occupy Monterrey (later Monterey) for 166 years was no fault of his.

For another two decades, don Sebastián kept busy, always with an eye for adventure, profit, and the Pacific. He opened a supply road across the Isthmus of

Tehuantepec, operated confidently as first European ambassador to Japan, searched midocean for the illusory islands of Rica de Oro and Rica de Plata, repulsed Dutch pirates on the coast of Colima, and governed Acapulco, finally retiring in 1619 to Mexico City, where he died in 1623 in his seventy-fifth year. Too bad neither Felipe III nor Felipe IV thought to grant Sebastián Vizcaíno the title "Marqués del Mar Pacífico."[39]

Surprisingly, don Juan de Oñate outlived Vizcaíno. Viceroy Montesclaros had heaped coals on the heads of both. Felipe III in 1606, on the basis of incriminating reports, decreed a halt to the New Mexico enterprise and recalled Oñate. The paltry aid and the few people delivered to San Gabriel that year by Vicente de Zaldívar sank the colony in gloom.

Spartan Oñate pretended that he could endure, but the disillusioned soldier-colonists were sick of waiting. "Nor do I find myself able," confessed the proprietor in late summer 1607, "to restrain them, for they are as exhausted, hard pressed, and in need of help as I am helpless to furnish it." With that, having estimated his consortium's losses at more than 600,000 pesos, Oñate resigned his governorship. If they had heard nothing from the viceroy by June 1608, he told the colonists they were free to leave.[40]

Capt. Juan Martínez de Montoya, a tall, handsome, black-bearded Castilian in his forties, had come with the reinforcements of 1600, bringing fancy suits, silk stockings, cordovan shoes, two bags of soap, and a man servant. Although credited with plenty of action on his service records, he had not gone with Oñate to the South Sea, acting instead at San Gabriel as secretary of government and war and local magistrate of the town council. Martínez, it seems, also had some part in relocating people to the site of a proposed new villa and capital already known in 1608 as Santa Fe. Evidently he was a good leader, and that reputation accompanied fray Lázaro Jiménez who carried Governor Oñate's resignation to Mexico City.

Neither anticipated the moment, but the viceroy who accepted Juan de Oñate's resignation was none other than the friend who had signed the original contract with him in 1595, Luis de Velasco, back for a second term after distinguished service as viceroy of Peru. Velasco ordered that no one relocate. Until word arrived from Spain—which could take a year or more—don Juan was to remain in the colony.

As interim governor, the viceroy appointed Martínez de Montoya; the colonists, however, refused to accept him, claiming that he was not a soldier. There were, as well, "other objections they did not wish to make public." Having earned hidalgo status, Martínez de Montoya left New Mexico for the viceregal capital in 1608 and never returned.[41]

Oñate must have had a hand in the colonists' rejection of Martínez. For a dozen

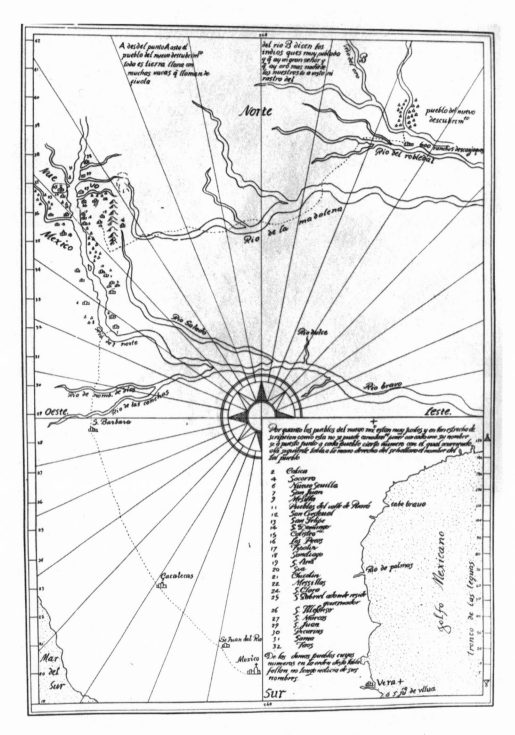

Enrico Martínez's sketch map of New Mexico, c. 1602, reflecting Oñate's exploration of the plains. *From Kessell,* Kiva, Cross, and Crown.

years, the adelantado had exercised life-and-death authority over them. Showing their deference, the men of the colony in open meeting reelected don Juan. When he declined, they chose his son Cristóbal, now in his twenties. Even if the crown decided to transform New Mexico from proprietary to royal colony, the Oñate family might still retain the governorship. But that was not the royal will. Early in 1609, Felipe III appointed a salaried bureaucrat, don Pedro de Peralta, to a three-year term.

The decision whether to abandon unprosperous New Mexico rested on the number of Pueblo Indian baptisms that had taken place. Jurists, theologians, and professors from the University of Mexico were asked to consider the most appropriate means, in the king's words, to "preserve the Indians who have been converted to our holy Catholic faith, but at the least possible cost to my royal treasury." Previous estimates put the number at four to six hundred, including Acoma slaves and people baptized at the point of death who had recovered. Surely removal of that number in the event of withdrawal from New Mexico would not be costly, but would it not harden the hearts of unconverted relatives left behind? The debate became moot, however, when the Franciscans took the initiative.

Fray Lázaro Jiménez, who had ridden once to Mexico City and returned to New Mexico as the viceroy's emissary, suddenly reappeared in the capital late in 1608 with a report that, marvelous to relate, "more than seven thousand persons had been baptized and so many others were ready to accept baptism." By their self-serving claim, the friars insured continuation of their New Mexico ministry. Neither viceroy nor adelantado challenged the inflated figure. Given such a bountiful harvest of souls, their failed proprietorship looked not so bleak.[42]

With deeply mixed emotions, the undone adelantado, accompanied by his son and nephew and their entourage, rode out of New Mexico early in 1610. The new governor had taken over. Settlers with no good reason to leave, like Asensio de Archuleta and Ana Pérez de Bustillo, provided continuity. They had become New Mexicans.

For Oñate, prospects were not promising; he knew that sooner or later he must face the criminal charges of his accusers. Tragedy struck first. In 1612, his son Cristóbal died. His patron Luis de Velasco embarked for Spain that year as well. During the term of Velasco's successor, the Marqués de Guadalcázar, a thirty-count indictment was brought against don Juan.

Judged guilty on twelve counts—ranging from the unjust hanging of two Acomas on hearsay, the exercise of great severity in battle and trial against the Acoma people, adultery with women of the camp, and swearing falsely about New Mexico's potential—Oñate learned his punishment in May 1614: He could never return to New Mexico; he was banished for four years from Mexico City; and he must pay a fine of six thousand ducats and court costs. These were matters of honor, not causes for distress, and don Juan appealed the convictions almost immediately.

In 1621, after the death of his wife, Oñate carried his case to the court of young Felipe IV. There, after several rebuffs, he won back his fine. The king, moreover, appointed the old adelantado inspector general of mines in Spain. He died while on duty underground in a flood-damaged mine, about June 3, 1626, at the age of seventy-five or seventy-six.[43]

The northward advance of New Spain, like Juan de Oñate's life, had begun in the mining district of Zacatecas. It had occasioned war and peace with the Chichimecas and generated new interest in town-dwelling Native peoples farther on. Adventurers less glamorous than Coronado had sought another—new—Mexico. Concurrently, Spaniards annihilated Frenchmen in Florida and opened the Manila trade, enabling Oñate's successors who occupied Santa Fe's mud-built governor's palace to eat oysters on Chinese porcelain plates.

In 1607, as don Juan resigned from the enterprise of New Mexico, Englishmen of the Virginia Company cursed and sweat to construct a three-sided palisade in a foul, marshy place along the James River. Far north of them, on the grand and more salubrious St. Lawrence, Frenchmen in 1608 built a fur-trading post at Quebec.

Although defending their empire against European rivals in North America always figured in Spanish reasoning, the primary justification for maintaining New Mexico at government expense throughout the seventeenth century was religious, not material. Foreigners scoffed. But as anyone who had been there understood, New Mexico bore no resemblance to Mexico, its rich namesake. Instead, the poverty-bound colony represented a missionary obligation Their Most Catholic Majesties could not in conscience evade.

Among Englishmen and Frenchmen, however, the myth of New Mexico's great wealth persisted. Oñate would have curled his lip. When Capt. John Stevens published his Spanish-English dictionary early in the eighteenth century, the entry for New Mexico read:

> Nueva México, New Mexico, a large Province of North-América, to the North of New Spain, its Bounds not well known; but its principal City is Santa Fe, its Air Temperate, Pleasant and Wholesom, its Soil Fruitful, and Rich in Mines of Silver.[44]

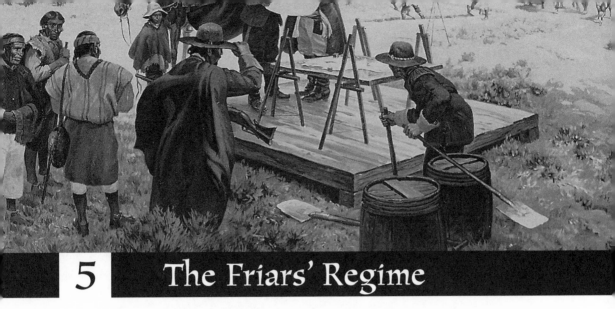

5 | The Friars' Regime

Would to God the Devil were coming instead of that Friar.

—Gov. Pedro de Peralta, Santa Fe, c. 1611

In royal councils, they referred to it as the kingdom and provinces of New Mexico. Fitting only as vague claim to half a continent, so grand a title poorly represented reality. Distant and meager, the settlement passed from semifeudal Oñate estate to Franciscan city of God on the Rio Grande, from proprietary to royal colony, at a cost to the Spanish crown during the seventeenth century of nearly two million pesos. Royal expenditures in support of the missionary regime exceeded revenues by a ratio of ninety to one.

Neither imperial security—as in the case of Florida, guarding the homeward passage of treasure fleets—nor commercial advantage—exemplified by Manila in the Philippines—figured prominently in Felipe III's decision to subsidize New Mexico. Here, the cardinal motive was religious.[1]

"Governor don Pedro de Peralta is warned," read an admonition from Viceroy Velasco, "that whatever disservice, miscarriage, or delay that may result to the lofty aims of his majesty will be at his risk." A veteran of previous government service, the salaried don Pedro reached San Gabriel with escort, eight more Franciscans, and a twenty-wagon supply caravan late in 1609.

Juan de Oñate and his replacement must have conferred, however stiffly. Don Juan, from the beginning, had intended to found a Spanish villa, or chartered municipality, and call it San Francisco, but circumstances had not favored the project.[2] Oñate's depleted colony had congregated instead in the laps of Tewa Pueblo Indians because the colonists were of no mind to build, plant, and harvest for themselves. Yet by 1607 or 1608, some of the proprietor's people, led by rejected interim governor Juan Martínez de Montoya, had begun a second settlement downriver

on a more centrally located site unoccupied by Pueblo Indians. It lay along a pleasant southwestward-flowing tributary of the Rio Grande with fields nearby, abundant grazing land, and wood for fuel and building. They were calling the place
Santa Fe.

Wasting no time, the new governor early in 1610 accepted the site previously
chosen and presided over the formalities that made Santa Fe, after St. Augustine
(1565), the oldest European town within the present-day United States. Because
certain families had already begun constructing homes on the more suitable south
side of the Santa Fe River, Peralta chose to mark off the broad, rectangular plaza
on the swampy north bank. Although the notarized founding documents were
destroyed, lost, or stolen, Viceroy Velasco's instructions, a reflection of the
Ordinances for New Discoveries of 1573, have survived.[3]

In accordance therewith, all legitimate heads of household, men and women,
along with other males twenty-five and older, but neither servant nor slave, became
vecinos, citizens of the new corporation. They in turn elected, under the governor's
eye, a four-man town council, or *cabildo,* who then chose two local magistrates, the
alcaldes ordinarios, to serve with them. Because Santa Fe, the seat of royal authority
and governor's residence, stood alone as seventeenth-century New Mexico's only
chartered municipality, its cabildo acted also as advisory council to the governor and,
depending on his will or whim, functioned or did not function.

Cabildo and governor assigned vecinos their town lots for house and kitchen
garden, fields with river or ditch frontage for crops and orchards, as well as grazing land. Understandably, they favored prominent members of the community,
the so-called captains and previous grantees of lands and Indian tribute. The more
common citizens also received their parcels, likely by lottery.

Because of constant building and rebuilding, it has been impossible, even for historical archaeologists, to determine accurately Santa Fe's original plan. Evidently, it
was neither neat nor tidy. By the early eighteenth century, the adobe *casas reales* (town
hall) and governor's palace occupied the north side of the plaza. The church and
attached convento, the Franciscan residence, stood by that time at the east end. House
lots facing on the remaining two sides of the plaza went to important citizens.

Some of the colonists breathed easier after Oñate left but not for long. Although
Peralta and his successors lacked quite the proprietor's utter dominance, they exercised near totalitarian civil authority in their capacity as chief executive, legislative,
judicial, and military officer. Not that they went unchallenged. The power to rule
remote New Mexico was, in fact, singularly polarized.

On the ecclesiastical side, because there were no Roman Catholic priests other
than Franciscans, the friars enjoyed an intimidating spiritual monopoly. They could
administer or withhold the sacraments of the Church. Their superior, who func-

tioned also as ecclesiastical judge ordinary for a distant bishop and often, after 1626, as local agent of the Holy Office of the Inquisition, could complement or oppose the governor with a similarly fused authority. Peralta and the saintly Father Alonso Peinado, who had arrived with him as Franciscan superior, seemingly cooperated as the viceroy intended. In contrast, the zealot who replaced Peinado wanted the governor's hide.

Fray Isidro Ordóñez, veteran New Mexico missionary who had accompanied fray Lázaro Jiménez to Mexico City with the report that saved New Mexico for the Franciscans, meant to run the colony as he saw fit, royal governor be damned. Reappearing as overseer of the mission supply caravan of 1612, fray Isidro falsely proclaimed himself Franciscan superior. Next, he thrust at Peralta a viceregal decree allegedly permitting any colonist to leave New Mexico at will. When the governor protested, choosing to invoke the familiar ritual that allowed lesser officials to set aside superior mandates for the local good—"*Obedezco pero no cumplo,*" "I obey but do not comply"—the friar proclaimed the order anyway, and a number of families picked up and left.[4]

Don Pedro was beside himself. Who did this friar think he was? Who was he to question whether Indian laborers summoned in relays from the pueblos for public works in the new villa were being properly fed? How dare he countermand the governor's orders to colonists on official business merely to enforce pretended compliance with Roman Catholic ritual? As the two men clashed, each testing the limits of his perceived authority, Ordóñez struck a mean blow, excommunicating Peralta and posting notice on the church door.

Scandalized, Asensio de Archuleta—who had chosen not to desert the colony in 1601 or 1612—his wife Ana Pérez de Bustillo and their children, and her parents, brothers, and sisters, found themselves caught in the crossfire. Because Asensio de Archuleta considered himself devout and because he was among the colony's literate minority, he had accepted employment from the Franciscans as ecclesiastical notary. When Governor Peralta ordered him to provide a statement incriminating the friars, Archuleta refused and was jailed. Ana feared for his life. Death threats sounded from both sides.

In this charged atmosphere, Peralta, grudgingly absolved by the friars, strode across the plaza toward the church with his nervous entourage one Sunday in July 1613, only to find that his chair had been tossed out onto the dirt. Motioning his men to pick it up, he had it placed in the back near the baptismal font among the Indians. There he sat.

At one point in the service, Asensio de Archuleta, who had been released in the interim, read aloud an edict threatening excommunication and stiff fines for any colonist who dared carry a dispatch to Mexico City without first notifying

Gov. Pedro de Peralta surveying the site of Santa Fe, 1610, by Roy Grinnell. *Courtesy of the artist and the School of American Research, Santa Fe.*

Father Ordóñez. The passionate prelate himself next mounted the pulpit and hurled a personal challenge.

> Do not be deceived. Let no one persuade you with vain words that I do not have the same power and authority that the Pope in Rome has, or that if his Holiness were [here] in New Mexico he could do more than I. Believe [me] that I can arrest, cast into irons, and punish as seems fitting to me any person without any exception who is not obedient to the commandments of the Church and mine. What I have told you, I say for the benefit of a certain person who is listening to me and who perhaps raises his eyebrows. May God grant that affairs may not come to this extremity.[5]

But come they did. During an altercation at the Franciscan convento, the governor discharged his pistol, wounding armorer Gaspar Pérez and lay brother Jerónimo Pedraza, the community's medical practitioner. Furious, Ordóñez ordered the Santa Fe church closed and services suspended. At the mission at Santo Domingo, which would serve for much of the century as the friars' headquarters, he argued ardently before his brethren that the governor should be arrested. When the cabildo balked, fray Isidro, fraudulently claiming deputation by the Inquisition, enlisted some of the leading colonists. On the night of August 12, an armed party surprised Governor Peralta, who had just set out for Mexico City to report in person to the viceroy.

With his adversary in chains in the convento at Sandia Pueblo, Father Ordóñez bullied the colony for nine months. "Excommunications were rained down," according to his harshest critic, "and because of the terrors that walked abroad the people were not only scandalized but afraid . . . existence in the villa was a hell."[6]

In time, another governor appeared. Peralta left in 1614 and afterward governed Acapulco. The stormy Ordóñez was summoned to Mexico City two years later. Two unyielding men, Governor Peralta and Father Ordóñez, had set a malignant precedent. At base lay the poverty of the colony and the obscene, recurrent competition for access to its one readily exploitable resource—the Pueblo Indian people.

Before 1680, some 250 Franciscans labored as missionaries in New Mexico. The first were predominantly *peninsulares* from Spain, joined by a growing number of Spanish *criollos* born in the Indies. Except for a few lay brothers, all were ordained priests ranging in age from their midtwenties to midseventies. All could read, write, and quote biblical scripture and Church fathers, and all fervently believed in the gift of eternal salvation offered through conversion to Spanish Catholicism. The way they went about imposing their faith, however, varied greatly.

Some, insecure or suspicious, tried to regiment the Pueblo Indians, coincidentally demanding that every perceived vestige of their former "idolatry" be smashed or burned. Others, for whatever reason, exhibited a notable tolerance for and desire to learn about Native ways, possibly hoping to persuade their wards by example. A few of the missionaries clearly were scoundrels, men like fray Nicolás Hidalgo, accused of practicing sodomy and forcing his charges to perform unwanted sexual acts, or the sadistic fray Salvador de Guerra who reportedly took pleasure in cruel whippings. But most, despite what competing governors, colonists, and aggrieved Pueblos said to discredit them, went about their lonely ministries in deep, if at times clumsy, devotion.[7]

No one chronicled the Franciscan ideal in New Mexico more enthusiastically than fray Alonso de Benavides, propagandist par excellence. Born on San Miguel in the Azores just before Spanish annexation of the Portuguese empire and schooled by his order in Mexico City, fray Alonso presented his credentials at Santa Fe early in 1626. Since 1616, the missions of New Mexico had been grouped in a Franciscan administrative unit called a custody—the custody of the Conversion of St. Paul—dependent on the Franciscan province of the Holy Gospel in Mexico City. The superior of a custody was known as the *custos*.

Benavides had come to New Mexico not only as father custos but also as the colony's first legitimate agent of the Inquisition. In the latter capacity, the Franciscan, by a formal edict of the faith read in church, urged every member of the ingrown, mixed-blood Hispanic community to report antisocial acts: everything from suspected Jewish practice, heresy, and sorcery to bigamy, blasphemy, and solicitation of sex by a priest in the confessional.

Empowered to hear, record, and forward testimony to the tribunal in Mexico City, the local agent of the Inquisition could, upon receipt of a warrant, order the arrest, confinement, and transportation of a colonist—even a governor or priest—to the viceregal capital for trial. Only unbaptized persons and mission Indians, considered minors in the Catholic faith, were exempt. Although some of his successors swung the power of the Inquisition ferociously as a club over the heads of perceived enemies, fray Alonso concerned himself more with preaching to Indians.[8]

He was tireless. Not only did he install the first missionaries in several Pueblo communities, but he also sought, largely in vain, to make converts among southern Athapaskan-speaking Apaches and Navajos, whom he described as "very spirited and belligerent." Since Oñate's time, these peoples who surrounded the Pueblos on all sides had run off horses and other livestock. They had begun to ride. Whether on the eastern plains, in the mesa and canyon country northwest of Santa Fe, or in the mountains of the headwaters of the Gila River, horses widened the spheres of Apaches and Navajos. Ever more frequently now, as raiders or traders, they broke into the valley worlds of Pueblo Indian farmers and Hispanic stockgrowers.[9]

No megalomaniac, fray Alonso nevertheless held a cherished ambition. He wanted to be a bishop, perhaps New Mexico's first. Although he energized the missionary program in the field during his three-year tenure, it was through his writings after he left that Benavides put New Mexico on the map. So persuasive was he that his superiors dispatched him to court in Madrid as a lobbyist. There in 1630, fray Alonso's breathless *Memorial* was published at government expense. Even the young king, fun-loving Felipe IV, read it. Still the ebullient Benavides, now in his mid-fifties, kept his eye on a bishopric. Toning down the affirmation of New Mexico's fabulous mineral potential and relating in greater detail miraculous conversion stories, the headstrong friar carried a lengthier, unpublished version to the Vatican in 1634 for Pope Urban VIII.[10]

The window provided by Father Benavides on seventeenth-century New Mexico is in some places difficult to see through, as where he seeks to edify by Christian metaphor, and in others remarkably clear, where he simply reports what he observes. That Pueblo women built houses, Pueblo men wove, and Apaches mutilated their adulterous women can be verified by other ethnographic evidence; that Franciscans had converted half a million Indians in New Mexico cannot. On the other hand, the friar's estimate of converts group-by-group adds up to fewer than fifty thousand, not an improbable figure.[11]

Always the public-relations man, Benavides in Spain arranged an interview with a reluctant celebrity, a stately, twenty-nine-year-old Franciscan abbess. Fray Alonso had written previously about the hunger for conversion inspired among the Jumano Indians of the south plains by the mysterious visits of a beautiful young woman in blue. María de Jesús de Agreda confessed to Benavides her numerous miraculous flights to lands across the ocean where during the early 1620s she had implored Natives in their own languages to seek baptism. He knew it. Addressing an excited letter to his New Mexico brethren, he enclosed the endorsement of Mother María de Jesús for their labors. Surely this was an unmistakable sign of God's special blessing on the Franciscans in New Mexico.

Fray Alonso de Benavides never rejoined them. He secured instead appointment as auxiliary bishop of Goa, the Portuguese trading colony on the Arabian Sea. Booking passage from Lisbon and dropping from sight, he may have died during the voyage out. As for the mystical Mother María de Jesús de Agreda, she became at the king's invitation a frequent and trusted correspondent of Felipe IV. Investigated by the Inquisition, she received praise, not censure. Later, however, her book *Mystical City of God*—a minutely detailed autobiography of the Blessed Virgin dictated to María in ecstasy and published posthumously in 1670—embroiled professors at European universities in heated debate.[12]

No one at the time appeared to take particular note of Father Benavides's novel suggestion to recruit English-speaking Irish Catholic priests for New Mexico to counter the pernicious influence of English and Dutch Protestants.

María de Jesús de Agreda writing. *From Hodge, Hammond, and Rey,* Benavides' Revised Memorial of 1634.

Fearing that from Virginia and the islands of North America, through the navigation of the English and Dutch, heresy might be introduced into New Mexico, which borders on those places . . . the said Father Benavides notes that it is necessary to establish a mission of Irish fathers who know the English language. Thus they may not only convert the heathens of those places to the Catholic faith, but also the heretics who have come from England and Holland and have increased in large numbers, taking Indians for wives, and together might convert the heathen already perverted, and hinder the propagation of heresy in New Mexico.[13]

Someone should have listened. Already by the 1630s, the swelling Protestant migration to the Massachusetts Bay Colony and tobacco production in Virginia had drawn to North America's eastern seaboard a hundred times more European colonists than had settled in New Mexico. That their descendants would someday encroach on Santa Fe would not have surprised the prophetic friar; that it would take them two centuries might have.

Within a dozen years after Benavides left New Mexico in 1629, Franciscans had fully overspread the Pueblo world. From the Piro communities in the south up the Rio Grande more than two hundred miles to Taos, and in the east from Pecos Pueblo and the Tompiro and Tiwa towns over the mountains three hundred miles west to the farthest Hopi pueblos, friars had moved in and directed construction of churches and adjoining conventos. The regimen in their missions, termed more properly *doctrinas,* or Native congregations, was rigorous and thoroughly paternal. By assuming the key role in sacred control of life rhythms, healing, production, and weather, and by close scheduling of religious and technical-vocational instruction, ceremonial events, and work, the missionary fathers sought to supplant the Pueblo way with the Spanish Catholic way.[14]

During the 1620s and 1630s, in the early stages of conversion, the friars may even have built kivalike structures within the conventos of their missions. Although Father Benavides did not mention such an effort specifically in New Mexico, Franciscan practice elsewhere and the local archaeological record suggest that the missionaries did indeed seek to incorporate architecturally a facsimile of Pueblo sacred space.[15]

Nowhere did the friars succeed fully. Nor did they fail without a trace. Instead of replacing Pueblo culture, which proved more resilient than any of them anticipated, they modified it, mostly by consent of their mission children. At first, almost everyone accepted the visual pleasures of the beautiful Virgin Mary, shimmering vestments, and silver chalice, and the unfamiliar sounds of console organ, trumpet, flageolet, and polyphonic chant. Favored men embraced the delegated authority and honors of a new layer of community officials, and who could not see the utility of metal tools, flocks of sheep, and grapes? Offered religious, political, and economic innovations, the Pueblos were selective. When on occasion a Franciscan pushed too hard or demanded too much, especially at a pueblo far from Santa Fe, his neophytes rose up and killed him.

One Lenten Sunday in 1632, the ardent fray Francisco Letrado, ministering at the Zuni pueblo of Hawikuh, noted that his people were late for mass. All right, he would round them up, by God. Met by an angry crowd, "they attacked him in a body," related Father Benavides, "smashing his head with their clubs in order to prevent him from preaching the word of God to them any longer." The missionary crumpled and bled to death, reportedly clutching a crucifix. His adversaries scalped him, then disposed of the body and defiantly celebrated with their trophy. Other Zunis put to death a second Franciscan a few days later and took refuge atop foreboding *Dowa Yalanne,* or Corn Mountain.

Within a month, Spaniards of a punitive expedition camped at the foot of El Morro, en route, says the mute inscription, "to avenge the death of Father Letrado." In that, they failed. Eventually, when offered amnesty, the Zunis came back down, and other friars revived Letrado's ministry. Far from dissuading the more impassioned Franciscans, martyrdom—to die in the line of sacred duty—promised a blessed fame and sure salvation. "As a result," Benavides avowed, "we can assure ourselves of marvelous fruits."[16]

None of the seventeenth-century governors of New Mexico who bought the office and received an annual salary of two thousand pesos was less subtle than Luis de Rosas. Rough and ready, he would make his investment pay or be damned. Both happened. During his profitable administration from 1637 to 1641, violent schism rent the colony. In 1642, don Luis was murdered in a Santa Fe cloak-and-dagger plot, and in 1643, the new governor had eight prominent New Mexicans beheaded behind closed doors, then publicly declared a general amnesty.

Rosas simply went too far. Evidently accepting a bribe, not an uncommon practice, he manipulated his predecessor's residencia and let him off easy, to the Franciscans' dismay. To facilitate his own extortions, he rigged cabildo elections, turning out former members and replacing them with other men eager to do his bidding and earn favors. Through them and their extended families, he challenged the friars' hold on the colony's means of production. He demanded big cuts of all items of Indian tribute and trade, amassing foodstuffs and goods for export: captives, hides and skins, locally woven wool and cotton cloth, salt, and piñon nuts. In his bustling, dark, and dirty textile workshop at Santa Fe, unfree Apaches toiled alongside purported orphans and levies of Pueblo Indian laborers.

Naturally, the friars protested. But their feisty veteran, fray Esteban de Perea, then

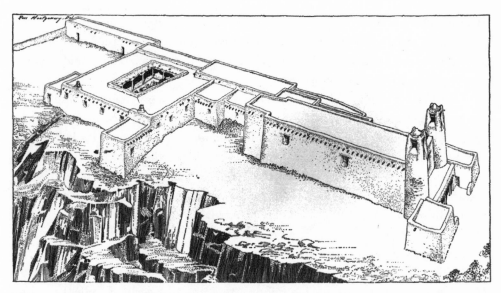

Mission church constructed in the 1630s at the Hopi pueblo of Awatovi, by Ross G. Montgomery. *From Montgomery, Smith, and Brew,* Franciscan Awatovi.

serving as agent of the Inquisition, had grown old and feeble; he died in the winter of 1638–39. Unafraid, the pro-Rosas cabildo accused the Franciscans of mean and arbitrary use of their monopolistic church authority, unsavory economic practices, and enrichment at the expense of mission Indians, even the hoarding of weapons. The friars had grown "so powerful," the cabildo complained to the viceroy, "that, while enjoying the quiet and ease of their cells and doctrinas, they are able to disturb and afflict the land and to keep it in [a state of] continuous martyrdom."[17]

One wonders how much Capt. Juan de Archuleta remembered about his father's part in the strife between Governor Peralta and Father Ordóñez a generation earlier. Peralta had ordered Capt. Asensio de Archuleta arrested in 1613. Unrepentant, the elder Archuleta had continued his close association with the Franciscans, acting as their syndic, or business agent, in the 1620s. Although he was dead by 1626, his son Juan remained a staunch partisan of the friars. When a foul-mouthed slanderer who enjoyed Rosas's favor was murdered early in 1640, the governor had Juan arrested as a suspect, but soon released him in response to a public outcry.

By then, New Mexico's Hispanic community, probably not many more than a thousand people, had split into two armed camps. At Santa Fe, where the Franciscans had shut the church, convento, and chapel of San Miguel, Rosas installed in the casas reales a shadowy, turncoat friar who, despite excommunication, continued ministering to the governor and his party. Downriver at Santo Domingo, Custos Juan de Salas called an urgent meeting, summoning the missionaries from their posts. Signatories to a manifesto of grievances against the governor included citizens Juan de Archuleta and his brother-in-law Antonio Baca.

When Rosas, the king's representative, actually struck with a cane and blood-ied the heads of two friars who ventured to Santa Fe as emissaries, calling them liars, pigs, traitors, heretics, and the like, any hope of reconciliation vanished. Each side blamed the other for the dismal state of the colony and the discontent of the Indians. The Taos people murdered their missionary, and another was killed among the Jemez, perhaps in an Apache attack. A deadly epidemic in 1640 carried off three thousand Pueblo Indians, more than 10 percent of the population.

Morale could hardly have been worse in the spring of 1641 as the heavy, mule-drawn, covered wagons of the triennial mission supply service crawled northward over the camino real accompanied by armed riders and the retinues of replacements for Rosas and Salas. Gov. Juan Flores de Sierra y Valdez was sick. Trying to super-vise the residencia of Luis de Rosas, he accepted the counsel of the former gover-nor's enemies. Cabildo elections, meanwhile, brought outspoken critics Francisco de Salazar and Juan de Archuleta to power as *regidores* and Antonio Baca as an alcalde ordinario. Then Sierra y Valdez died, and the anti-Rosas cabildo, outmaneuvering Lt. Gov. Francisco Gómez, assumed all interim governmental powers. Now they had Rosas just where they wanted him.

A young soldier, Nicolás Ortiz, became their dupe. Born in Zacatecas, he had first appeared in Santa Fe about 1634 as a teenaged member of an armed escort; he stayed on and married María de Bustillo, niece of Antonio Baca. Again employed to do escort duty, Nicolás had departed for Mexico City in 1637 with the return-ing caravan that had brought Rosas, not to reappear until 1641 in the train con-veying Sierra y Valdez. His wife, however, was visibly pregnant. Later she would testify that she had been Governor Rosas's mistress for four years. Yet Ortiz with-held his rage for several months, while Antonio Baca confined Rosas, seized his property, recorded the discovery of María in a chest under don Luis's mattress, and left town for the Zuni-Hopi country on an Apache campaign.

It was a cold January 25, 1642, by coincidence the patronal feast of the Franciscan custody, when the cuckolded Ortiz finally avenged his shame. Out of the darkness with a party of masked men, he burst into the house where Rosas was being held and dispatched the notorious ex-governor with a dozen thrusts of his sword. When Baca returned from his campaign, he presided over the murderer's acquittal and sent him with the proceedings to Mexico City. Taken into custody en route and retried by the governor of Nueva Vizcaya in Parral, the hapless Ortiz was condemned to be hanged, after which his severed head and sword hand were to be displayed on the gibbet. But he escaped.

Antonio Baca did not. Along with brother-in-law Juan de Archuleta and six other relatives and associates in the anti-Rosas clique, the incredulous Baca found himself in the summer of 1643 confined by order of Gov. Alonso Pacheco y Heredia. Even though Custos Hernando de Covarrubias insisted on administering the last rites to the eight men, surely the governor, who had issued a general pardon, was not thinking of summarily executing them. But he was. Armed with secret and detailed instructions from unbending Bishop-Viceroy Juan de Palafox y Mendoza, who considered the friars and their faction guilty of treason, Pacheco had resolved to carry out the harshest article against the lay leaders, "to get rid of them by a brief and exemplary punishment."[18]

Father Covarrubias and the New Mexicans who carried out the gory business on the morning of July 21 must have experienced conflicting emotions. Self-serving or not, these men had stood by the Franciscans, and their executioners were kin. Covarrubias reported that when Francisco de Salazar's punishers tried to behead him with his own dagger, they made a bad job of it. "For God's sake," he screamed, "sharpen that thing and put me out of my misery." Then, marvelous to relate, Salazar's severed head recited the entire true and essential creed of the Roman Catholic faith.[19]

The crowd summoned to the plaza that afternoon included Juan de Archuleta II and other relatives of the victims. Governor Pacheco addressed them gravely, reiterating the pardon, revealing his secret instructions from Mexico City, and announcing the executions. A mute warning, Antonio Baca's head was nailed to the gibbet. The governor also told the assembled people that he had ordered the traitors' property seized; the proceeds would pay for a peacekeeping force of thirty men enlisted that very day. And when governors and friars clashed violently again during the 1650s and 1660s, Juan de Archuleta II sided with the former.

Hispanic New Mexico was forever a colony of cousins. With the exception of a few soldiers, muleteers, or prisoners recruited in the south who jumped the supply caravan, or an occasional peddler or vagabond, few outsiders immigrated to the distant kingdom. Increase was primarily local, not only by birth but also by adopting Apache, Navajo, and Pueblo orphans, and other Indian children into Hispanic extended families.

At its peak in the 1660s, New Mexico's nonaboriginal population probably numbered no more than twenty-five hundred souls. These included *españoles, castas,* Mexican Indians, and other integrated Natives—everybody regardless of blood mixture or origin living in a manner more Spanish than Indian, nominally Roman Catholic and Spanish-speaking, and not a resident member of an Indian community. That compared with a 1667 estimate of fifteen to sixteen thousand in the city of Zacatecas alone.[20]

Not only cousins by blood and marriage but also in economic, political, and social affairs, New Mexico's fifteen or so tightly interwoven leading families ran the colony: the Gómez Robledo, Lucero de Godoy, Anaya Almazán, Baca, Durán y Chaves, Romero, Montoya, Archuleta, González Bernal, Márquez, Martín Serrano, Domínguez de Mendoza, and their kin. Although strong governors or Franciscan superiors—outsiders who came and went—sometimes set them at each others' throats, their shared parochial sense as New Mexicans belonging to a difficult and unique place deepened generation after generation.

Accepted racial designation and lightness of skin counted in New Mexico, but not so much as in Zacatecas or Mexico City. Castas, mostly mestizos but occasionally mulattos, could and did become lesser officials, joining the ruling españoles. From numerous contemporary allusions to them, persons of African blood seem to have maintained a significant presence in the seventeenth-century colony, perhaps as high as 10 percent. If there were fifty to sixty thousand Pueblo Indians during Oñate's time and only twenty thousand in 1680, they still outnumbered the Hispanic community eight to one.

Living day by day amidst so many Pueblo Indians, it is surprising that seventeenth-century New Mexicans did not come to look more like them. They were influenced to be sure, as were the Pueblos, exchanging foods, cures and curses, items of wearing apparel, words in their languages, household appliances and techniques, and certainly blood. Yet for the most part, babies fathered by culturally Hispanic men with Pueblo Indian servant women grew up in either the Indian community or Spanish households, becoming members of one or the other. Thus, while openly acknowledging certain individuals as mixed-bloods, the two ethnic groups maintained their distinctive and mutually reassuring cultural identities.

New Mexico was poor, not destitute. Ready locals generated revenue from three sources: Pueblo Indian tribute; livestock, mainly sheep; and trade with Pueblos and other tribes. Food crops were used mostly for subsistence. The Pueblos, as sedentary, agricultural vassals of the Spanish crown, owed annual tribute. From Oñate on, New Mexico's seventeenth-century governors made grants of *encomienda* in the king's name to leading citizens, *encomenderos,* authorizing them to collect and benefit from such tribute. Initially, the grants were intended to last three lifetimes.

Not surprisingly, avaricious governors like Luis de Rosas bent encomenderos to their will by threatening to reassign their grants. Aggrieved citizens, in fact, prevailed upon Rosas's successor to restore all titles, offices, and encomiendas nullified by the ex-governor.

The recipient of an encomienda, for his part, agreed to formal citizenship in the villa of Santa Fe, theoretical responsibility to protect and attend to the Christianization of his tributaries, and willing response to the governor's summons to military

Pack train at Taos Pueblo, by Henry R. Poore. *From Elbridge S. Brooks,* The Story of the American Indian *(1887).*

service, providing his own arms and mounts. As men-at-arms, the encomenderos, whose number was limited in the 1630s to thirty-five, became the officer corps of the colony's militia, which was composed of every able-bodied man, as well as leaders of Pueblo auxiliaries. Only the royal armorer received a salary.

Standard encomienda tribute in New Mexico was a *fanega* of maize (something less than three bushels, and valued at four *reales,* or half a peso) and a *manta* of cotton cloth (a piece less than six feet square and worth the equivalent of six reales), to be collected from each Pueblo Indian household, the cloth in May, the foodstuffs in October. Substitutes in kind, depending on a pueblo's location or harvests, included animal skins, salt, piñon nuts, and other tradable commodities. Labor arrangements in lieu of goods, although illegal, also seem to have been common.

A grant of encomienda was not a grant of land, even though most encomenderos held *mercedes de tierras* as well.[21]

Land grants, also made by the governor in the king's name, were separate and by law were not to encroach on lands used by Pueblo Indians or those previously granted to other third parties. Naturally they did, and litigation was constant. Large ranches up to several thousand acres, most often termed *estancias,* predominated in pre-1680 New Mexico, especially in the Rio Grande Valley south of La Bajada; below this descent a dozen miles southwest of Santa Fe, the land flattened out and the growing season was longer. Once he had been granted a modest piece of land with water, wood, and pasture nearby, an *estanciero* might expand his spread by simply appropriating a much larger area and claiming customary use.[22]

Never as sprawling or as diversified as the classic farming-ranching-mining haciendas of northern New Spain, the estancias of land-owning New Mexicans provided work for a majority of the Hispanic community. Horses, mules, and cattle were of greater value, but in the mesa country of New Mexico sheep did best, lean and rangy little *churros* that grew relatively long-stapled, greaseless wool ideal for home weaving. Their tasty meat, although a little tough when roasted, made an especially pleasing stew.

As a bloc, the missionary friars of New Mexico ran more sheep on their scattered estancias and harvested more maize than any colonist. They also controlled the colony's only regular supply service. By a 1631 agreement with the viceroy, the Franciscans were given an annual lump-sum payment for the purchase of everything from sacramental wine to mule shoes. Their business agents made all the necessary purchases and ran a caravan of wagons to the distant colony every third year.

Not the picturesque, shrieking, two-wheeled oxcarts used for short hauls, these were heavy-duty freight wagons with four iron-rimmed wheels capable of carrying two tons and pulled by eight mules. Normally, the train consisted of thirty-two such vehicles, escorted by armed men and accompanied by livestock on the hoof. The usual round-trip took a year and a half—six months out, six months to distribute and unload supplies, and six months for the return.

Outbound, the wagons carried not only friars and their considerable gear but also new government officials, occasional settlers, baggage, mail, and private merchandise. Anyone or anything going to New Mexico joined the caravan. Coming back, the empty wagons often were commandeered or leased by the governor or by private citizens engaged in freighting and commerce.[23]

In an almost exclusively barter economy, everybody traded, whether as a matter of subsistence—a metal hatchet for ten loads of firewood—or a nonessential swap of an ornate scarlet coat for a captive Navajo girl, or a venture transaction of three hundred *belduques* (trade knives) on credit with a merchant in Parral. Nodes of wider economic and social exchange, tying New Mexico to Nueva Vizcaya, its closest neighboring colony, moved progressively closer: first, Santa Bárbara; then after the silver strike of the 1630s, Parral; and finally, in the early eighteenth century, Chihuahua.

The Spaniards' presence in New Mexico greatly stimulated the exchange of goods not only among neighbors in the Rio Grande Valley, but also with surrounding Native peoples on all sides, most conspicuously the plains. And although the colony lay on the farthest northern periphery, mundane and even luxury goods bumped along over fifteen hundred miles, binding New Mexico to the busy network of markets, production centers, and resources to the south.

In the summer of 1660, Capt. Diego Romero, a rugged, barely literate, second-generation New Mexican and contemporary of Juan de Archuleta II, flattered himself. A big man, with curly black hair and beard, Romero, the leader, stood in his stirrups and looked back at the train of pack animals strung out behind him. The counterbalanced bundles slung across their backs contained trade knives, beads, and other goods on consignment for Gov. Bernardo López de Mendizábal. A dozen jovial mixed-bloods kept the animals headed up. Afoot and led by their impressive headman Carpintero, a party of Pecos Pueblo Indians, longtime trade partners of the Plains Apaches, completed the motley cavalcade. Romero seemed impatient.

Setting a purposeful course eastward across the grassy expanse, they had traveled for weeks, covering 200 leagues (at 2.6 miles per league, some 520 miles) to a river Romero identified as the Colorado, perhaps today's Red River forming the Texas-Oklahoma border. He knew where he was. Keeping to the river's bank, the traders soon made out dozens of colorful, scattered tepees at the semipermanent Apache "ranchería or pueblo of don Pedro."[24]

Here at last, Romero revealed his ulterior motive. His deceased father, Gaspar Pérez, a blond armorer from Flanders, had told stories about how Apaches at a similar rendezvous a generation earlier had bestowed on him the honorary title of chief captain of the Apache nation. Now it was the younger man's turn.

Carried in festive procession facedown on a buffalo robe, feted in a calumet ceremony, and given the place of honor for a mock battle, Romero eagerly awaited what he considered the culmination: his night in a specially prepared tepee with a young virgin. He had vowed to leave a son among the Natives, as his father had. No one said whether the burly New Mexican met his Apache half-brother. The Apaches put a band with a white feather on Romero's head. Thereafter, he wore the feather on his hat. He could not have been prouder.

Three years later, in the grim chambers of the Inquisition in Mexico City, a contrite and dispirited Diego Romero would hear the prosecutor describe that white feather as evidence

Plains Apaches, after
an eighteenth-century
painting on hide,
Segesser I, Museum
of New Mexico.
Detail redrawn by
Jerry L. Livingston.
From Kessell, Kiva,
Cross, and Crown.

that proved a covenant or union according to heathen rites. The defendant,
possessed by greed, made himself the object of such sacrilegious and superstitious acts to gain better advantage in the trading.[25]

The memory of Romero's adventures among the Plains Apaches might not
have outlived his raucous bragging for long had the Franciscan agent of the
Inquisition not shown an interest. Captain Romero was unconcerned; he enjoyed
the protection of both ex-governor López de Mendizábal, who in 1662 remained
in Santa Fe during his residencia, and the brash new governor, don Diego de
Peñalosa. Besides, had he not served as sargento mayor, third in command of military affairs and recruiter of militia; alcalde ordinario of Santa Fe; and *protector de
indios,* defending Indians accused of crimes? Did he not hold half of the pueblos of
Cochiti and Zia in encomienda? Was he not the son-in-law of Pedro Lucero de
Godoy, lieutenant governor of the kingdom?

In the end, none of this mattered. The Franciscans, fully recovered from their humiliation in 1643, had regained the upper hand. Through hundreds of pages of incriminating testimony, given by aggrieved missionaries or fearful New Mexicans and remitted to the tribunal of the Inquisition in Mexico City, they had built formidable cases against former governor López de Mendizábal and his associates. As a consequence, Diego Romero, three other leading citizens, the ex-governor, and his cosmopolitan wife, doña Teresa Aguilera y Roche, were arrested in the name of the Holy Office and held in close confinement at Santo Domingo to be shipped ignominiously south in the returning supply wagons for trial.

López de Mendizábal, weakened by the ordeal, died during the proceedings, and the Inquisition released doña Teresa. Romero's cousin, Francisco Gómez Robledo, whose physical exam proved that he possessed no devilish little tail, successfully defended himself, paid court costs out of his embargoed possessions, and went free. No one in Santa Fe expected to see the prisoners again, but Gómez Robledo, whose deliverance his family considered a miracle, took back his encomiendas, properties, and offices—among them mayordomo of the religious confraternity of Nuestra Señora del Rosario—and got on with his prominent life.[26]

Bluffing at first, the rustic Romero gradually broke down. Charges against him included espousing such false doctrines as conjugal duty between men and their concubines, joining in a heathen Apache marriage rite, incest with Juana Romero whom he insisted was not his cousin, "incredible hatred" toward the Franciscans, and lying to officers of the Inquisition. Apparently on the counsel of his court-appointed defense attorney, the frightened New Mexican began to confess even his most outrageous sexual perversions as a youth. He went on to implicate his fellow prisoners and, finally, to beg for mercy.

As was customary in response to contrition, the inquisitors commuted Romero's harsh sentence of convict labor on Philippine ships to a ten-year banishment from New Mexico. Once a free man, however, he weakened again. Even though Catalina de Zamora, his New Mexican wife, refused to join him in Parral, he should not have married mestiza María Rodríguez in Guanajuato. Somehow the Inquisition found out. Pronounced guilty again, this time as a bigamist, Romero suffered a public lashing astride a burro in the streets of Mexico City and was condemned to six years' unpaid service aboard the Atlantic fleet. Deeply depressed by the consequences of his antisocial behavior and wishing he had escaped to the plains to live among the heathens "in their manner," the ill-starred chief captain of the Apache nation died one Sunday in 1678 in a dank cell in Veracruz.[27]

Figuratively speaking, a black cloud hung over New Mexico in the late 1660s and early 1670s, but it did not rain. Fray Juan Bernal, newly arrived agent of the

Inquisition, reported graphically to the Holy Office on April 1, 1669, predicting the colony's rapid demise. Two calamities had transpired. "The first," wrote the alarmed Franciscan,

> is that the whole land is at war with the very numerous nation of the heathen Apache Indians, who kill all the Christian Indians they encounter. No road is safe. One travels them all at risk of life for the heathens are everywhere. They are a brave and bold people. They hurl themselves at danger like people who know not God, nor that there is a hell.

Hispanic New Mexicans had reaped the wind. For three generations they had abducted Apache women and children, who as a commodity brought the equivalent of thirty or forty pesos, about the price of a good mule. It was a just war, they claimed, mounting punitive strikes one after another, each in retribution for previous Apache raids. Now drought and famine, the second of Father Bernal's calamities, had settled over pueblos and plains, intensifying the vicious cycle. "For three years," the friar insisted,

> no crop has been harvested. Last year, 1668, a great many Indians perished of hunger, lying dead along the roads, in the ravines, and in their hovels. There were pueblos, like Las Humanas, where more than 450 died of hunger. The same calamity still prevails, for, because there is no money, there is not a fanega of maize or wheat in all the kingdom. As a result the Spaniards, men as well as women, have sustained themselves for two years on the cowhides they have in their houses to sit on. They roast them and eat them. And the greatest woe of all is that they can no longer find a bit of leather to eat, for their livestock is dying off.[28]

A native of Mexico City where earthquakes, floods, and tumults made people fatalistic, Father Bernal may have been a born doomsayer. Still, under conditions half as pathetic, who could fail to notice? To some Pueblo Indians, it appeared that their traditional gods had lost patience with them over the place Christianity had taken in their lives. The case of don Esteban Clemente, the most Hispanicized, notable, and trusted Pueblo Indian in all the kingdom, portended trouble to come.

Don Esteban, who affected proudly the "don" Spaniards bestowed on allied Indian leaders, was Native governor of the Salinas and Tano pueblos and "very capable interpreter of six languages of this kingdom." Raised at the Tompiro-speaking pueblo of Abó, he was among the boys taught by the friars to read and write Spanish, which skills he retained. He also ran a profitable business employing his sons and others, trading with Apaches in the Siete Ríos area near present-day Artesia. Don Esteban's pack trains at times conveyed goods for New Mexico's governors. He had, in fact, entered a private claim as creditor during former governor López de

Mendizábal's residencia. By then, however, the Franciscans had enlisted the Indian's service.

Missionaries ill-served by López de Mendizábal had accused him and his cohorts of encouraging the Pueblo Indians to renew their kachina ceremonials, saying that these dances were wholesome entertainment, not idolatrous devil worship at all. The friars especially hated the irreverent Nicolás de Aguilar, branding him the "Attila of New Mexico." Aguilar, who served López de Mendizábal with relish as *alcalde mayor* (district officer) of the Salinas pueblos, had been arrested with Diego Romero and tried in Mexico City. Before that, in 1660, young fray Diego de Santander, apostolic notary for agent of the Inquisition and Custos Alonso de Posada, had asked don Esteban Clemente to denounce Aguilar and kachina dances in writing. Clemente had complied.

Later, as drought and famine fastened themselves upon the Salinas pueblos, don Esteban, "very conversant in Spanish, intelligent, and a good Christian," recanted. Secretly, he began plotting the Spaniards' overthrow. "He ordered the Christian Indians," one colonist recalled, "to drive all the horse herds of every district into the mountains, so as to leave the Spaniards afoot, and on Maundy Thursday night . . . to consume the entire body of Christians, sparing not a single friar or Spaniard."

But somehow they found out. And they hanged don Esteban. "When the property of said Indian was seized," the colonist continued, "there was found in his house a great quantity of idols and whole pots of idolatrous powdered herbs, feathers, and other disgusting things."[29]

The planned uprising of don Esteban Clemente, foiled about 1670, might have made a greater impression on the Spaniards had it stood alone. But calamities abounded. Eastern Apaches overran the pueblo of Las Humanas at harvest time in 1670, sacked the church, killed eleven people, and dragged away thirty-one captives. Measles, smallpox, or typhus struck again in 1671. Within a few years, half a dozen Piro and Salinas pueblos had been deserted. To the west in 1672, during their deadly assault on Hawikuh, Gila Apaches laid hands on fray Pedro de Ayala in the church, wrestled him outside, ripped off his habit, tortured him with stones and arrows, then smashed his head with a heavy bell.[30]

As the apocalypse dawned, governors and friars began to cooperate. The Holy Office in Mexico City admonished its agents in New Mexico to get along with the colony's civil officials. In 1675, fray Francisco de Ayeta, overseer of Franciscan supply, carried to the viceregal capital a fervent plea from Gov. Juan Francisco de Treviño and the cabildo. Without aid, New Mexico was doomed. The edgy Treviño, meantime, authorized a fateful witch-hunt among the Tewa pueblos northeast of Santa Fe.

Superstitious old fray Andrés Durán of San Ildefonso swore that Pueblo sorcerers had called down bodily illness upon him, as they had upon numerous others, often with fatal consequences. In response, Governor Treviño sent Capt. Francisco Javier, his secretary of government and war, with a column of armed men into the pueblos to round up alleged medicine men and bring them to Santa Fe for trial. They apprehended forty-seven. Three were found guilty and hanged, one each as a warning at Nambe, San Felipe, and Jemez; another hanged himself. Some were whipped. Then unexpectedly, a grim-faced party of more than seventy armed Pueblo warriors showed up at the casas reales offering gifts but demanding release of the prisoners. The exchange was tense. "Wait a while, children," Treviño is supposed to have stalled, "I will give them to you and pardon them on condition that you forsake idolatry and iniquity." With that, he let them go.[31]

Plainly, the Pueblo Indian population had not collapsed physically or psychologically. The high, dry uplands of New Mexico, unlike humid Florida and the Gulf Coast, continued to support Native peoples despite their heavy losses to disease, drought, and warfare. Back in 1638, fray Juan de Prada, Franciscan commissary general for New Spain, had reckoned the number of Pueblo Indians at around forty thousand. Although more than sixty thousand must have been baptized over the previous four decades, he thought, the numbers had declined "to that extent on account of the very active prevalence during these last years of smallpox and the sickness which the Mexicans called *cocolitzli* [general epidemic or typhus]."[32]

If during the four decades after 1638 the Pueblos declined to twenty thousand more or less, there were still many more of them than Hispanic colonists. That fact, along with the lash marks across his back and a loathing of Spanish persecution, set one of the released Tewa medicine men to plotting. A native of San Juan Pueblo, he moved farther from Santa Fe north to Taos, a community known for resistance. So secretive were his intrigues that no New Mexican ever identified him in the records by his Christian name. They would know him only as Popé.

Father Ayeta, meanwhile, had proven an apt beggar. From viceregal authorities he secured a number of concessions to struggling New Mexico: fifty convict soldiers, a hundred harquebuses, a thousand horses, and other gear. Named custos, fray Francisco—in company with a new governor, don Antonio de Otermín, and the mission supply train—left Mexico City at the end of February 1677. With detachments of the additional men-at-arms, provisions, and refugees from the abandoned Salinas and Piro pueblos, governor and custos collaborated to reestablish defensive outposts at Galisteo and Senecú.

The tireless Ayeta, reappearing in Mexico City with the wagons in 1678, now urged that a royal presidio of fifty men, like the one in Sinaloa, be authorized at government expense for Santa Fe. That proposal, forwarded to Spain, would languish until news of Popé's revenge jolted the Council of the Indies.[33]

In his late forties, of "medium stature, [with] protruding eyes, thick, partly gray beard, [and] wavy, chestnut-colored hair," Capt. Francisco de Anaya Almazán II had seen it all, everything this God-forsaken colony had to offer. Rancher, trader, former alcalde mayor, he and his flamboyant older brother Cristóbal were characterized by Custos Juan Bernal as men "of little shame and without fear of God." Widowed when his first wife, Gerónima Pérez de Bustillo, died, Francisco, already the father of a girl and boy, married Francisca Domínguez de Mendoza, daughter of the prominent Capt. Tomé Domínguez de Mendoza and a sister of Cristóbal's wife.[34]

With small warning, the events of Saturday, August 10, 1680, feast of San Lorenzo, shattered the provincial world of Anaya Almazán and his family. Francisco was lucky he did not die that morning. Foreman of a small detail guarding a drove of horses near the Tewa pueblo of Santa Clara, he heard the shouting. The Santa Claras had gone crazy. Painted and armed for war, the usually peaceable men of the pueblo rushed the New Mexicans. "They caught all of them," Governor Otermín learned, "attacking them treacherously under promise of safety." Marcos Ramos and Felipe López fell dead in the fighting, as Anaya Almazán and the others spurred hell-bent for Santa Fe.[35]

The fury at Santa Clara was not unique. Popé and dozens of collaborators had seen to that. Invoking the names of Pueblo deities in several languages, the embittered Tewa medicine man had appealed through the network of caciques and war captains to even the farthest communities of Zunis and Hopis. He bid them all to join him in nothing less than an unconditional war of purification to rid their world of Spaniards forever. Some hesitated, even warning their Hispanic neighbors. But as the appointed time drew near, runners carried knotted cords out to the pueblos, where by untying a knot each day local headmen coordinated the countdown. When two of the messengers fell into Spanish hands with their cords, the leaders advanced the day. Their plan came off stunningly.[36]

In response to the first frantic, eyewitness news of Pueblo violence, Otermín dispatched his lieutenant governor and maestre de campo—resurrected Inquisition prisoner Francisco Gómez Robledo—with a heavily armed squadron to assess the damage. His report could scarcely have been more foreboding.

Everywhere, the Pueblos were killing Hispanic New Mexicans, whole families in their homes and fields, not even sparing the friars, several of whom had already died horrible deaths. They had carried off Francisco de Anaya Almazán's wife and children. Later, an Indian would testify that he had seen doña Francisca's naked body in a field, her head bashed in, a very small baby dead at her feet. South of Santa Fe, at the pueblo of Galisteo, among confirmed fatalities was Anaya Almazán's son, Francisco.[37]

Thirsty, scared, and confused, fathers and mothers and whimpering children who jostled for a sheltered corner with their animals inside the barricaded casas reales could hear the piercing war cries and chanting of their Pueblo Indian besiegers. How had they offended God so grievously to deserve what was happening to them? By word and deed, the Pueblos answered. "They were saying that now God and Santa María were dead . . . and that their own God whom they obeyed never died."

Juan, a trusted, Spanish-speaking Indian resident of Santa Fe, was sent by Governor Otermín to go among and calm his indecisive Tano kin in the Galisteo Basin. Instead, he returned on horseback at the head of an attacking horde, wearing "a sash of red taffeta which was recognized as being from the missal of the convent of Galisteo, and with harquebus, sword, dagger, leather jacket, and all the arms of the Spaniards."[38]

Persuaded to parley with Governor Otermín and asked why he had gone over to the rebels, Juan answered that now with the father custos and so many Hispanic New Mexicans dead, there was no turning back. He offered the governor a choice: accept the white banner and lead the Spaniards out under safe conduct, or accept the red one and die. Otermín refused. It was not too late, he told Juan; despite their atrocities, if they would but lay down their arms and renew their vows to God and king, he would pardon them all. With that, Juan rejoined the attackers, who threw themselves with unaccustomed vengefulness into ransacking and burning the Mexican Indian barrio of Analco and the church of San Miguel across the Santa Fe River.[39]

More and more Pueblo besiegers converged on Santa Fe. They cut the ditch that carried water into the casas reales and overran the church and private houses around the plaza. Fierce localized fighting and ominous lulls took turns. "What grieved us most," offered Otermín, "were the dreadful flames from the church and the scoffing and ridicule which the wretched and miserable Indian rebels made of the sacred things, intoning the alabado and the other prayers of the church with jeers." Stray survivors who broke through swelled the sorely distressed crowd inside the casas reales to nearly a thousand. Days passed.

"Surrounded by such a wailing of women and children, with confusion everywhere," Otermín and the desperate colonists still able to bear arms burst out at dawn on August 20 and broke the siege. Next day, despite two arrow gashes on his face and a gunshot wound in the chest, the royal governor of the kingdom and provinces of New Mexico evacuated his capital. "I trusted in divine province," he wrote eighteen days later,

> for I left without a crust of bread or a grain of wheat or maize, and with no other provision for the convoy of so many people except four hundred animals and two carts belonging to private persons, and, for food, a few sheep, goats, and cows.[40]

Popé, maquette of a statue by Clifford Fragua of the Pueblo of Jemez to represent New Mexico in the National Statuary Hall of the U.S. Capitol. *Photo by Clifford Fragua, reproduced courtesy of the New Mexico Statuary Hall Commission.*

And the Pueblos let them go. They watched as the pathetic, slow-moving stream of refugees, mostly New Mexico-born, plodded southward through the narrows of the Rio Grande downriver from San Felipe Pueblo. Eighty-two summers had passed since their Pueblo forefathers, from the same heights, wondered at Juan de Oñate's caravan of strangers. Among the tiny figures, Francisco de Anaya Almazán, who had lost his entire immediate family, braced for further torment. The low-built, adobe ranch headquarters belonging to his older brother Cristóbal lay just ahead. "It was found to have been robbed," read Otermín's official proceedings, "the cattle and all his other property stolen, and he, his wife, six children, and other persons, to the number of twelve, all dead and their bodies stripped, were found lying at the main door."[41]

Farther south, Governor Otermín's doleful procession finally overtook the fifteen hundred exiles who had retreated ahead of it from the Río Abajo. Inaccurate early reports that the governor and everyone upriver had been slain had already reached the outpost and mission of Nuestra Señora de Guadalupe on the opposite bank at El Paso, the river crossing.

Fray Francisco de Ayeta had just arrived there again with dozens of heavy-laden freight wagons. Dismayed but clear-witted, he oversaw the election of an interim governor and organization of a relief party. Later, a dozen miles above the customary ford, the assertive Franciscan almost drowned when he ordered six spans of mules harnessed to the lead wagon and, flanked by Indian swimmers, rode it into the roiling Rio Grande.

When at last the friar and governor embraced tearfully on the near bank at La Salineta, a broad, dry expanse of chaparral, they compared the magnitude of their sins. Otermín had already bemoaned in a letter to Ayeta "the lamentable tragedy, such as has never before happened in the world, which has occurred in this miserable kingdom and holy custodia, His divine Majesty having thus permitted it because of my grievous sins." Stunned by the first dire news, Ayeta had written to the viceroy that "the contingency has arrived, through my great sins, of our experiencing the total ruin and resultant loss of these extensive provinces of New Mexico."[42]

Not as critical as the Mixtón War of 1541–42 in numbers engaged, casualties, or proximity to New Spain's core, nor as disruptive economically as the Tepehuan rebellion of 1616–20 in Nueva Vizcaya, the Pueblo uprising of 1680 nevertheless rocked the empire. Nowhere else had Native peoples taken back a province. In six weeks, the Pueblo Indians had reduced Hispanic New Mexico to the sorry muster of 1,946 exiles camped at La Salineta. They had rained death on 21 of 32 Franciscan missionaries and 380 or more Hispanic New Mexicans, nearly 15 percent of the colony.

During the exodus of his people, Governor Otermín had interrogated don Pedro Nanboa, a Pueblo elder.

Asked for what reason the Indians of this kingdom have rebelled, forsaking their obedience to his Majesty and failing in their obligation as Christians . . . he declared that the resentment which all the Indians have in their hearts has been so strong, from the time this kingdom was discovered, because the religious and the Spaniards took away their idols and forbade their sorceries and idolatries; that they have inherited successively from their old men the things pertaining to their ancient customs; and that he has heard this resentment spoken of since he was of an age to understand.[43]

Publicly, earnestly, both Otermín and Ayeta confessed. Both had sinned. Yet neither related his unspecified personal sins against God to oppression of the Pueblo Indians. The devil, not they, had made the Pueblos rebel. Their actions to bend these Indians to the will of the Spanish Christian God and king had, in their minds, been too lax. Although they recorded Pueblo testimony, neither man, whose very identity depended on the colonial system, listened to what Pedro Nanboa and others said about religious persecution as cause. Both vowed to return, to humble the apostates and restore without delay the kingdom and provinces of New Mexico.[44]

But that, both would discover to their sore disillusionment, was apparently not God's will.

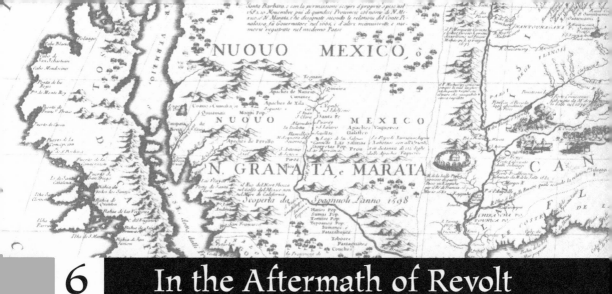

6 In the Aftermath of Revolt

If [El Paso] should be abandoned, this body of Christian Indians will be endangered, and, as a consequence, those of La [Nueva] Vizcaya and of the provinces of Sonora, for in all of them there is a multitude of Indian nations who are disposed to do the same thing that those of the provinces of New Mexico did.

—FRANCISCO GÓMEZ ROBLEDO, EL PASO, APRIL 5, 1681

The principal purpose of Sieur de la Salle in making this discovery was to find a port on the Gulf of Mexico on which could be formed a French settlement to serve as a base for conquests upon the Spaniards.

—MARQUIS DE SEIGNELAY, MINISTER OF LOUIS XIV,
ON LA SALLE'S DESCENT OF THE MISSISSIPPI IN 1682

Bushy-browed, intense Eusebio Francisco Kino, a Jesuit from northern Italy, entered Mexico City about June 1, 1681. In black cassock, he stood agog in the cavernous cathedral, whose countless darkened side chapels appeared like so many short mine tunnels exposing the veins of gold and silver altar screens. Here, a couple of months earlier, the viceroy of New Spain and his court had attended elaborate memorial services for the twenty-one Franciscan martyrs of New Mexico. The Pueblo revolt had occurred the previous August 10, Kino's thirty-fifth birthday.

Always the student, Father Kino had brought with him from Europe a 1668 cartographic field manual by one of his former professors, Adam Aigenler, which included tables for determining latitude, date, and location, and a map of the world. All by itself directly north of New Spain lay New Mexico, labeled by Aigenler "Nova Granada," a name dating from Coronado's time. North America was far too wide, but Baja California, to which Kino would soon be assigned as cosmographer and missionary, was shown correctly as a peninsula. La Florida occupied everything south of Virginia and east of New Mexico.[1]

Father Eusebio Francisco Kino. Composite pencil sketch by Frances O'Brien based on photographs of four generations of the Chini (Kino) family. *Courtesy of the Arizona Historical Society, Tucson, no. 44478.*

Considered hardship posts without exploitable resources—an image cultivated by their opportunistic residents—Spain's two occupied extremities in North America, New Mexico and Florida, had evolved differently. Given the seventeen hundred miles that separated the villa of Santa Fe and the older garrison town of St. Augustine, it is not surprising that virtually no contact occurred between the two. It was a notable oddity, disclosed in his Inquisition trial, that New Mexico's Nicolás de Aguilar had obtained a copy of fray Francisco de Pareja's Castilian-Florida Timucuan catechism, published in Mexico City as early as 1612.[2] Still, no Spanish colonial governor, lesser official, or missionary friar, it would appear, served time in both Santa Fe and St. Augustine.

After the adelantados had cut their losses and resigned, the Spanish government subsidized Florida and New Mexico as crown colonies. Justification resided in the same two motives—imperial defense and evangelization—weights that rose and fell as on a scale in the royal conscience. In Florida, military considerations outweighed missionary, and the crown used the friars; in New Mexico, the reverse obtained, and the friars used the crown.

As Father Kino knew, Jesuit missionaries had ministered and suffered in Florida, then withdrawn from it by the early 1570s, and Franciscans had replaced them. In New Mexico, the friars had no precursors. On Florida's strategic maritime frontier, vital to the safe transfer of riches from the Indies to the mother country, the royal treasury invested more heavily in the coastal presidio of St. Augustine than in the missions. True, the friars received a soldier's wage in kind along with other support. In return, however, Franciscan missionaries in the hinterlands contracted with Hispanicized leaders of Native chiefdoms to provide Indian labor levies and delivery of foodstuffs. This arrangement culminated, between 1672 and 1696, in the imposing fortress of Castillo de San Marcos.[3]

The fort would save St. Augustine for Spain but not the hinterlands. Carolina-based English traders and slavers with eager Native allies devastated missions and welcomed fleeing survivors into their growing sphere of influence. To the west, meanwhile, across Aigenler's deceptively blank map all the way to the Pacific, contests for empire intensified, bringing other Europeans and Natives into alliance and conflict.

Jesuits, expanding their missionary empire in northwestern New Spain, thought to cross the Gulf of California. The bold Frenchman Sieur de la Salle descended the Mississippi, claimed Louisiana, then foundered on the Texas coast, exciting Spanish parries by land and sea. And in El Paso, New Mexico's exiled colonists listened to Pueblo Indian emissaries who volunteered that a majority of their people upriver, fallen on hard times since 1680, would welcome Spanish restoration of the lost kingdom.

They swore to excel. Pope Paul III had given them his blessing in 1540. By the time Ignacio de Loyola, their zealous Basque founder, died in 1556, the highly centralized, rigorously trained, and intellectually exceptional Society of Jesus had nearly a thousand disciplined members. By 1626, there were more than fifteen thousand. Chosen for mental and physical toughness, good appearance and family, and fitness for active lives in education and mission, Jesuits wore the black cassock of the parish priest, rather than a distinctive habit. They were not friars. The Society's constitution required life tenancy of its superior, or general; periodic written reports from every unit; and a unique vow of obedience to the pope from professed fathers. Conversion of the nonbeliever, one of Loyola's passions, had from the beginning propelled Jesuits to the outer limits of Europe's world empires.

Menéndez de Aviles had invited them to Florida, where they fared badly. Eight were killed in 1571 in a foolhardy attempt to convert Algonquian-speaking Indians on Chesapeake Bay near the future site of Jamestown.[4] Redirected, Jesuits had landed in New Spain the following year and for the next two decades dedicated themselves to teaching the sons of the wealthy, ministering to Christianized Indians, and establishing profitable, tithe-exempt estates in support of their colleges.

Ardent Gonzalo de Tapia, assigned to found a Jesuit school for Indians at Zacatecas in 1590, had voiced other aspirations. He wanted to carry the light of the Christian gospel to fabled New Mexico, which, he learned grudgingly, lay by previous claim and martyrdoms within the Franciscan sphere. Instead, at the urging of Gov. Rodrigo del Río y Losa of Nueva Vizcaya, Tapia's superiors directed him to begin missionary work four hundred miles northwest of Zacatecas in the mesquite-covered brush country beyond Culiacán. Tapia and Father Martín Pérez reached the tiny inland villa of San Felipe y Santiago de Sinaloa in the summer of 1591. Again, Father Kino knew the story.

Giving gifts and working seeming wonders, the two black robes had brought together into mission communities hundreds of unconverted, Cahitan-speaking ranchería peoples. Two more Jesuit missionaries joined them; the number of reported baptisms climbed to six thousand. A ghastly epidemic of measles and smallpox followed in 1593. It was the devil's work not theirs, proclaimed the priests, pointing to Natives who chose, by God's grace, not to blame them. "They aver," wrote Father Juan Bautista de Velasco, "that they do not die because of us, for we run to help them in their illness, seeking them out and consoling them."[5] Some Native spiritual leaders who also did not succumb scoffed.

Hechiceros the black robes called them, benighted and resistant shamans enlisted by the devil, in the missionaries' view, to oppose the inevitable spread of Christianity. One called Nacabeba had grown increasingly resentful of the padres' widening intrusion. He and a small party surprised Tapia one evening in July 1594 and split open the priest's head with a macana, then decapitated him. This time, however, the Jesuits did not withdraw. Spurred on, dozens of keenly devoted missionaries of the Society of Jesus carried their attractive material benefits, faith, and talents northward up the western Sierra Madre from river valley to river valley, barranca to barranca, to disease-wary Mayos, Yaquis, Tarahumaras, Tepehuanes, and Lower Pimas, as if climbing a ladder.

A fifteen-year veteran of these missions, Jesuit chronicler Andrés Pérez de Ribas trumpeted the first half-century. His book, *Historia de los Triumphos de Nuestra Santa Fee* (Madrid, 1645), published fifteen years after Benavides's *Memorial* and in competition with it, also combined careful observation of Native ways, which the author judged in the main inferior to Christian ways, and disclosure of Jesuit strategies, not only to convert unbelievers but also to justify to civil and ecclesiastical authorities the order's northwest missionary empire. Although Pérez de Ribas—like the Natives he shepherded as infants toward mystical salvation—credited unseen, supernatural forces for good and bad effects in daily life, he also pondered the Indians' earthly origins. "Most likely," he surmised, "they entered the New World by land from the continent of Asia, by way of the north, crossing a narrow stretch of the sea that was easy to cross, which has yet to be discovered."[6]

Just as the *Historia de los Triumphos* appeared, Jesuits in northern Sinaloa uncovered a conspiracy to thwart further expansion of their missions. Don Pedro de Perea, mine developer, rancher, and longtime captain of the presidio of Sinaloa, had contracted with the viceroy in 1640 to settle the country beyond the Río Yaqui, which he was calling Nueva Andalucía, today's Sonora. Seemingly to circumvent entrenched Jesuits, Perea had traveled to Santa Fe, where he recruited a dozen men, eight from the Pérez Granillo family, with wives and children, and without authority negotiated for five or six Franciscans of New Mexico to join the venture as missionaries to the Opatas and Pimas. Ever since Oñate's time, when they had accompanied the adelantado on his probes toward the South Sea, the friars had considered the unmapped territory west and southwest of New Mexico, even California, their domain. Now the Franciscans of New Mexico accepted the chance to claim it.

In high dudgeon, meanwhile, Jesuit Pedro Pantoja dispatched a colleague to the Opata country to baptize every baby in sight before the Franciscans did. In a letter to the father custos of New Mexico, Pantoja "expounded on how the Jesuits would gladly receive the [Franciscan] religious as guests in their houses with hospitality and courtesy; but as ministers, no." The friar claimed never to have received the letter.[7]

Beginning in 1645 and continuing for six years, New Mexican Franciscans ministered in northern Sonora, baptizing, by one estimate, seven thousand Natives.

Yet Perea—who in 1645 fell ill on July 31, feast day of St. Ignatius of Loyola, and died on October 4, feast of St. Francis—did not survive to witness the convention signed at Arizpe in 1650 by superiors of both orders. By its terms, a dividing line between Jesuit and Franciscan territory was agreed upon, and the friars withdrew. "Although the Franciscans were skilled and experienced ministers, whom we respect as our own Fathers," crowed Pantoja, savoring alleged Jesuit superiority in Native languages, "and although they had made every effort to catechize the Indians well, it had all been done through means of interpreters."[8]

The next threat came from within the Society. Too few Jesuits were volunteering for foreign missions. Although the order's membership would exceed seventeen thousand by 1680, most black robes preferred the life of educators.[9] Others, as spiritual directors and confessors of Europe's nobility, relished the power. In an effort to staff its missions in New Spain, South America, and the Philippines, the Society's superiors prevailed upon the Spanish crown to grant passports to non-Spanish Jesuits, mostly men from specified Hapsburg countries of the Holy Roman Empire. The agreement permitted one third of any missionary contingent to be foreigners. Often, however, they exceeded the quota.

To get around the law, clerks had assigned Tyrolean Eusebio Francisco Kino a false name and birthplace. He crossed the Atlantic in 1681 as Eusebio de Chaves: "A native of Córdoba. 21 years old. Well-built, dark-complexioned, wavy black hair."[10] Born in truth in the mountain village of Segno near Trent in northern Italy on August 10, 1645, Kino was ten days older than Carlos de Sigüenza y Góngora, a native of Mexico City, who also attended Jesuit schools, excelled in science and math, and entered the Society. Eventually the two would meet and be at odds. Kino, continuing his formation as a Jesuit, turned down a university appointment and set out for overseas missions in 1678, while Sigüenza, expelled from the Society ten years earlier for curfew violations, won the chair of mathematics and astrology at the University of Mexico.[11]

The great comet of 1680 had awed both men. They discussed it the following year at Sigüenza's home in Mexico City. A self-proclaimed champion of reason, don Carlos had already demolished in print explanations he considered ludicrous superstitions. Then Father Eusebio, at the urging of fellow Jesuits, wrote a little book, reminding readers that, whatever else, comets were signs from God of ill omen, a self-evident truth, "unless," he added, "there be some dull wits who cannot perceive it."

Sigüenza was furious. The Jesuit had patronized him, so typical of high and mighty Europeans, who "think those of us who were born here by chance . . . walk on two legs only by divine dispensation." By then, however, Father Kino had joined Adm. Isidro de Atondo's acclaimed expedition to permanently occupy Baja California, a project that might have wished for a better omen.[12]

Carlos de Sigüenza y Góngora. *From his* Mercurio volante *(1693)*.

He had wanted China. So had fellow missionary Antonio Kerschpamer. They had drawn lots, and Kino lost. As cosmographer assigned to California, he had borrowed maps from Sigüenza before their falling out. From these charts, he evidently concluded that his European geography professor had erred. California was not a peninsula but an island, "in my opinion," he proclaimed in a letter to the duquesa de Aveiro y Arcos, patroness of Jesuit missions, "the largest island which the Orb contains."[13]

Having studied the *Historia de los Triumphos* as a missionary manual, Father Kino already had in mind a primitive cultural image of California's fishing, gathering, and hunting residents, the souls he meant to save. Provision had been made for gifts in the amount of six thousand pesos to assure that their pacification would succeed "not by force of arms, but rather by the gentle means of persuasion and evangelical preaching." On pain of death, no member of this expedition was to take pearls from any Native, the cause of repeated conflicts since the days of Cortés. Finally, the whole outfit—scarcely more than a hundred people, including Hispanicized Native workers from Sinaloa—crossed over in two small ships to the palm-lined bay of La Paz, where Atondo took possession on April 5, 1683.

All but naked, the Guaycura men, who at first approached threateningly with bows and stone-tipped arrows drawn, succumbed in minutes to the gifts. These Indians struck Kino as "of a very lively and friendly disposition, of good stature, strength, and health, and . . . very happy, laughing and jovial." Three months of contact soured relations. Provisions dwindled. The ship dispatched for supplies and horses never came back. A shooting incident left three Guaycura fighting men dead and others maimed. In mid-July, Atondo ordered all eighty-three intruders aboard the remaining ship and sailed back across the gulf. Natives scavenged the camp.

Ten weeks later, refitted and resupplied, they tried again, this time a third of the way up the gulf coast at a place they named San Bruno. With help from more willing Cochimí-speaking Indians, a rude, triangular, stone and adobe fort, as well as a storehouse, barracks, and church took shape. Kino's sketch showed two mission bells, two large, free-standing crosses, two swivel-mounted culverins, and a larger cannon on a carriage.

With horses and mules brought over from the mainland, the energetic admiral and the priest led a corps of discovery through arid mountains and grotesque vegetation to the Pacific, the first crossing of California by Europeans. The beautiful, bowl-sized abalone shells, unknown on the gulf shore, engaged Kino, and he picked up several as souvenirs. He loved exploring.[14]

Father Eusebio and two other Jesuits fell back on their ingenuity to learn the Native languages, unaware of how badly they misunderstood on occasion. As Kino recalled,

The western half of Vincenzo Maria Coronelli's map *America Settentrionale*, 1688.

We had to employ signs, gestures, act out the ideas, show them various objects and especially sacred images. It was even a harder and slower process to get across to them the expression of the Apostles' Creed "He rose from the dead." To learn the corresponding native term, we showed them some flies rendered unconscious by being held under water. Then we put them in the sun, sprinkling a bit of dust on them and thus brought them back to life. The Indians, on beholding the phenomenon, exclaimed "Ibimuhuegite," thus giving us the native equivalent of "He arose from the dead," the desired expression.

The Native Cochimí phrase, however, more properly *"ibi muhuet té,"* meant just the opposite: "It [the fly] has just died."[15]

Nothing else, meanwhile, did well at San Bruno, not crops, or animals, or people whose immune systems, fed brackish water and a poor diet, malfunctioned. Scurvy tormented most of them. Pitifully, they begged to leave the unfit site. Again, Atondo gave the order to pack up. Dejectedly, he watched early in May 1685 as Native workmen dismantled the fort.

Six months later, the viceroy sent urgent word to the admiral in Sinaloa to use his little California ships to warn the incoming Manila galleon of lurking pirates and escort her to Acapulco. Accepting the captain's invitation, Father Kino climbed aboard the China ship and rode it down the coast. In Mexico City, Atondo and Kino presented appeals to continue the enterprise of California, but Tarahumara troubles in Nueva Vizcaya and payment of an indemnity to France siphoned available funds. Hence, in 1686, the government dropped the project. Kino, characteristically, did not.

Four years later, he anxiously awaited a guest. Reassigned as first missionary to the Upper Pima Indians or O'odham of present-day northern Sonora and southern Arizona, Father Kino had transformed the ranchería of Bamotze into his *cabecera* (residence and head mission) of Dolores. He had taken the name from a fine painting of Our Lady of Sorrows presented to him by New Spain's popular mulatto artist Juan Correa. Pimas from surrounding rancherías had come to see the luminous canvas. The charismatic black robe had returned their visits, whence small chapels and shelters had risen at nearby *visitas* (preaching stations). All seemed to be going so well. Then came the allegations from Kino's Hispanic neighbors. Perplexed, the Jesuit provincial in Mexico City had dispatched an investigator.

Father Juan María de Salvatierra was no pushover, but he too was northern Italian. A blocky, decisive man who had served for a decade among Tarahumaras, Salvatierra dismounted at mission Dolores on Christmas Eve 1690. The recent assignment, at Kino's urging, of four more Jesuits to the Pimas had occasioned vehement opposition from mine and ranch owners. Kino had brought with him from the audiencia of Guadalajara confirmation of a royal decree exempting newly baptized Indians from the *repartimiento,* or labor levy, for twenty years. Reports had reached Mexico City that the Pimas despised and fled from their missionaries. To set Salvatierra straight, Kino orchestrated a tour early in 1691.

The two Italians got on famously. Welcomed by exuberant crowds in ranchería after ranchería, they accepted the invitation of Natives from a northern valley Kino had not yet visited. The January air was dry and exhilarating, the sun warm at noon. Crossing today's Sonora border into Arizona just west of Nogales, they kept at the head of pack animals and servants as eager guides beckoned them across mesas of broken red and brown rock, scrub mesquite, and cactus and down into the valley of the Santa Cruz River. Great gray cottonwoods, leafless in winter, marked the meandering course of the clear, shallow, northward-flowing stream. High purple mountains rose in the distance.

Amid a cluster of forty or more scattered, dome-shaped, brush and earth-covered houses flanked by open *ramadas,* the Pima residents, alerted and instructed by Kino's Yaqui or Opata foremen, had erected three shelters, "one in which to say Mass, another in which to sleep, and the third for cooking." The polysyllabic name of this place sounded to Europeans like Tumacácori. Headmen from farther north, Piman-speaking Sobaípuris, presented themselves. Jostling to touch the black robes, everyone appeared "so docile and so friendly."

Salvatierra was sold. Not one of the Jesuits would be removed from the Pimería. Moreover, another four would come, "and I, by Divine Grace," vowed Father Juan María, "shall try to be one of them."[16]

Kino had not forgotten his own earlier vow. "In all these journeys," he noted in his diary, "the father visitor and I talked together of suspended California, saying that these very fertile lands and valleys of this Pimería would be the support of the scantier and more sterile lands of California." Why not, in fact, build a boat in the desert, carry it in pieces west on muleback, and assemble it on the gulf coast? Encouraged by Salvatierra early in 1691, Kino hardly looked back. For the next twenty years, the irrepressible, northern-Italian Jesuit would explore, make maps, and propose plan after plan for Spanish expansion to which imperial strategists could only aspire.[17]

The very month Father Kino had begun his ministry at mission Dolores, March 1687, the bloody denouement of a French colonial project gone pitifully wrong played itself out a thousand miles east in the rain-soaked hill country of present-day east Texas. Bold, erratic, lecherous René-Robert Cavelier, Sieur de La Salle, with commission from Louis XIV, had visualized a settlement on the lower Mississippi but endured instead, as a consequence of faulty geographical reckoning, a hellish two years on the hostile Gulf Coast far to the west of that grand waterway.[18]

Now in March 1687, seventeen desperate survivors, each with grudges born

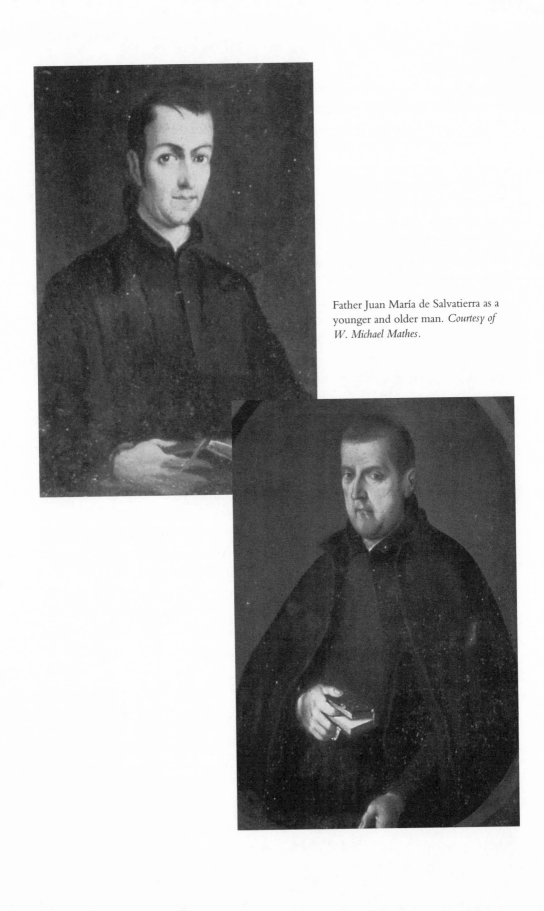

Father Juan María de Salvatierra as a younger and older man. *Courtesy of W. Michael Mathes.*

of unspeakable hardship, struck out from their forsaken Fort Saint-Louis near Matagorda Bay bound for New France. Apparently they reached today's Trinity River, where members of a hunting party quarreled. That night, the surgeon Liotot murdered La Salle's haughty nephew and two others with an axe while they slept. The rest conspired. When La Salle came to investigate, Pierre Duhaut's young servant Jean l'Archevêque acted in seeming disrespect, drawing LaSalle's attention. Duhaut fired, and the French explorer's "head was well-nigh blown away."[19]

The first warning the viceroy received regarding a French threat to northern New Spain had come in a royal decree of December 10, 1678. It said nothing of La Salle. Rather, Spanish intelligence at Versailles had learned of the traitorous activities of a well-born Peruvian rogue, former governor of New Mexico, and self-proclaimed count, don Diego Dionisio de Peñalosa Briceño y Berdugo. During his venal tenure at Santa Fe from 1661 to 1664, Peñalosa, a blasphemer who enjoyed making up dirty jokes about the friars, at one point held Custos Alonso de Posada prisoner in the governor's palace. Formal accusation against Peñalosa before the Inquisition in Mexico City ran to 237 articles. Pronounced guilty, subjected to an *auto de fé,* fined, forbidden in the future to hold any military or political office, and banished forever from New Spain and the West Indies, don Diego did not fade away.[20]

He traveled to London. When several years of vengeful scheming there proved unsuccessful, he moved to Paris, wed a French woman, and began ingratiating himself at the court of Louis XIV. His credentials included the fabricated diary of a grand expedition he professed to have led across the plains to Quivira in 1662. One "town" on an accompanying map bore the name Santa Fe de Peñalosa. His proposals were vicious: among them, to invade the Río Pánuco with infamous Michel de Grammont and twelve hundred pirates and seize the mines of Nueva Vizcaya. When La Salle, having successfully descended the Mississippi to its mouth in 1682, reached Versailles late the following year, Peñalosa envisaged a collaborative, two-pronged attack. The Frenchman, however, kept his distance.[21]

Spaniards in New Spain first heard specifically of La Salle's colony in 1685 from a half-dozen deserters captured aboard a pirate ship off Campeche. Homesick young Denis Thomas testified how "Monsieur de Salaz" had sailed from France in the summer of 1684 with four ships and more than 250 colonists, including missionaries, bound for the "Micipipi," a river his interrogators surmised must drain into the bay of Espíritu Santo, long presumed to exist by Spanish explorers. Wherever these intrusive Frenchmen had landed, they must be found. "His Majesty's prompt action is required," Spain's Council of the Indies admonished, "to pluck out the thorn that has been thrust into America's heart."[22]

Although the thorn disintegrated on its own, verification and discovery of the abandoned site required a series of deliberate Spanish probes, a half-dozen by sea

La Salle landing on the Texas coast. *From Louis Hennepin,* A New Discovery of A Vast Country in America *(1903)*.

La Salle's murder. *From Louis Hennepin,* A New Discovery of A Vast Country in America *(1903).*

and others by land. Most impressive by sea was the third, which departed Veracruz December 25, 1686, and returned July 3, 1687. The viceroy had ordered two shallow-draft boats custom built, piraguas with a large single sail and twenty oars on a side, for close coastal reconnaissance. Each carried sixty-five sailors and men-at-arms, a guide or interpreter or two, and a surgeon. Each vessel mounted six bronze swivel guns and towed canoes.

Coasting the low, sandy barrier islands well beyond the Rio Grande, known at its mouth as the Río Bravo, the Spaniards spied in a Native canoe assorted iron artifacts from a big ship, then, not far from the shallow entrance to Matagorda Bay, the sorry wreck of a smaller ship with three fleurs-de-lis carved on her poop. This was *La Belle,* a six-gun frigate Louis XIV had given La Salle as a gift. When she was driven ashore by a norther in the winter of 1685–86, La Salle, inland at the time, suspected that her skeleton crew had deserted with the ship. His only remaining vessel, *La Belle* had been the French colony's last hope of maritime supply or escape by sea.[23]

Gradually, strategists in Mexico City pieced together the story of the French ships, but what had happened to so many Frenchmen? Had all perished? Not until 1689, on the fourth land probe, would they find out for certain.

Intriguing clues, meanwhile, filtered through intervening Native peoples to Spanish settlements as widely distant as Monterrey in Nuevo León and Parral in Nueva Vizcaya. In June 1686, the Marqués de Aguayo, governor of Nuevo León, had word by a Pelón Indian, who had heard from Blanco and Pajarito Indians, that white men from a settlement to the north had come to the lower Rio Grande. Cíbolo and Jumano traders, traveling freely all across the southern plains between El Paso and east Texas, came with similar stories in 1687 and 1688 to Franciscan missionaries at La Junta, where the Río Conchos and Rio Grande flowed together. Foreigners with armor and long harquebuses who lived on the water in wooden houses were trading for horses and sex among the Tejas people and seeking allies for a strike up the Rio Grande against Nueva Vizcaya.

On orders from Gov. Juan Isidro de Pardiñas in Parral, Basque veteran Juan Fernández de Retana, first captain of the new presidio of San Francisco de Conchos, led a force across the Rio Grande to a meeting in March 1689 on the Pecos River with the wily, entrepreneurial Jumano governor Juan Sabeata, who was full of information. Coastal Indians, he related, had massacred all the Frenchmen, except for four or five who happened to be away trading with the Tejas. He had met these white men. Astonishingly, Sabeata carried wrapped in a lace neckerchief a few papers in French and the painting of a European warship.

In April, Sabeata and three other Native captains were escorted nearly four hundred miles to an audience with the governor at Parral, testifying through interpreters who translated their language into Nahuatl and then Spanish. The strangers, wearing steel breastplates and helmets, had come several times to rancherías on the lower Rio Grande and given gifts, befriending the Indians, and, declared Miguel, "not doing any evil or harm, but, on the contrary, they ran and danced with them." Did he not know that these Frenchmen were enemies of the Spaniards? Since in their eyes all white men looked alike, the Indians assumed they were "one and the same; furthermore he saw that they also had rosaries, and that they spoke to them of God, the same as the padres, and, since they took nothing from them, they took them to be good people."[24]

But now nearly all the Frenchmen were dead. When Muygisofac, a non-Christian Cíbolo in Sabeata's company, had recently visited rancherías near the intruders' settlement, the inhabitants "were still having dances in celebration of having killed the strangers." They proudly displayed their spoils. Later, he visited the site itself. The only signs of life he saw "were some pigs that were running around the fields. Inside the place where the strangers had lived," recalled Muygisofac, "there were many broken chests and some very large harquebuses (for it is thus that these nations describe pieces of artillery)." The Natives' testimony put Governor Pardiñas at ease, and he promptly recalled Fernández de Retana.[25]

Ten days later, other Spaniards finally poked for themselves through the wreckage of La Salle's deserted colony. The fourth overland expedition commanded by seasoned Gen. Alonso de León, son and namesake of a famed chronicler of Nuevo León, had brought along an unforgettable Frenchman. Jean Géry, having gone native several years earlier, had been persuaded to give himself up on León's previous foray north of the Rio Grande in 1688.

Dispatched by La Salle to pacify the Natives of the lower Rio Grande Valley, Géry, in the manner of the *coureurs de bois* of New France, had taken a Native wife, fathered a child by her, learned the language, and according to Spanish accounts, lived in a spacious buffalo-skin house and reigned as king over a ranchería of more than a thousand Coahuiltecan bowmen. Curious Spaniards had escorted the grizzled and tattooed Frenchman, who looked to be more than fifty years old, to the viceroy's palace in Mexico City, where he seemed bemused and gave rambling testimony, then brought him back to act as guide for León.[26]

Late in the 1680s, a decade that saw pirate hordes led by Frenchmen rape Veracruz, Campeche, and a dozen other Caribbean ports, Spaniards dreaded similar losses in the interior of the silver-rich north. In part as reaction to French overland encroachment, in part to resolve jurisdictional disputes between Nuevo León and Nueva Vizcaya, the ill-defined northern province of Coahuila had come into being in 1687, with Alonso de León as first governor. Arid and landlocked, Coahuila overspread the drainage of the Rio Grande east of the Big Bend, on both sides of the river known upstream as the Río del Norte and below as the Río Bravo, but did not extend to the Gulf. It was to Coahuila's capital, the presidial town of Monclova, that Jean Géry's escort had delivered him after his time in Mexico City.[27]

The presence of Juan Bautista Chapa, an elderly chronicler and family friend, on the 1689 entrada reflected Alonso de León's resolve to succeed on this fourth attempt. Its planning and supply had required half a year. Finally under way, the various segments formed into a raucous, bawling, mile-long base camp in motion: the governor and his staff, including an officer who understood French; eighty-some armed and mounted men drawn from the presidios of Nueva Vizcaya, Nuevo León, and Coahuila; two priests; a corps of muleteers, servants, and Indians; the pack train; two hundred beef cattle; a remuda of more than seven hundred horses and mules; and Jean Géry. From the wildly enthusiastic greeting staged in his honor at a ranchería just south of the Rio Grande, one might have thought that only Géry counted.

The two churchmen looked the other way. One was the secular priest of Monclova, Toribio García de Sierra, and the other an independent-minded Franciscan from the island of Majorca, fray Damián Massanet, representing a new missionary college. In response to the same shortage of missionary vocations that had prompted the Jesuits to import foreigners like Father Kino, Spanish Franciscans had obtained royal license for specialized New World colleges to encourage and train friars for work among non-Christian Native peoples and to provide a haven for retirees. Some two dozen recruits from Spain, including a clique of Majorcans, along with seven volunteers from the Mexican provinces had founded the missionary college of Santa Cruz at Querétaro in 1683.[28]

Massanet harbored an ulterior motive. Eager to advance the cause for canonization of the mystical Franciscan nun María Jesús de Agreda, fray Damián and his Majorcan brothers had vowed to gather evidence of her miraculous visits to Natives north of New Spain. Massanet had a copy of fray Alonso de Benavides's 1631 letter containing Mother María's exhortation. He would follow after her belatedly, baptizing the children of the Indians she had inspired. Searching for Frenchmen simply provided the impetuous Franciscan with the opportunity he sought.

Massanet disliked Jean Géry. Everywhere Indians greeted the nasty old Frenchman as if he were their friend. A skilled linguist, he obviously could communicate with them but hardly cared that they were not Christians. The friar, trusting only the two Native guides he had retained, thought Géry was purposely misleading the expedition. "I resented so much that the Frenchman should be given occasion to speak," admitted the Franciscan, "that I grew angry, and Captain Alonso de León said to me: 'Father, we are going wherever you wish.'"[29]

On Friday, April 22, a day that had dawned rainy, the party finally dismounted a hundred or so yards from the depressing remains of La Salle's temporary Fort Saint-Louis. "We went to see it," reads León's itinerary, and found all the houses sacked, all the chests, bottle-cases, and all the rest of the settlers' furniture broken; apparently more than two hundred books, torn apart and with the rotten leaves scattered through the patios—all in French. We noted that the perpetrators of this massacre had pulled everything [the colonists] had out of their chests, and divided the booty among themselves; and that what they had not cared for they had torn to pieces, making a frightful sack of all the French possessed. . . . We found three dead bodies scattered over the plain. One of these, from the dress that still clung to the bones, appeared to be that of a woman. We took the bodies up, chanted mass with the bodies present, and buried them. We looked for the other dead bodies but could not find them; whence we supposed that they had been eaten by alligators, of which there were many.[30]

General León ordered eight iron cannon, salvaged by the Frenchmen from the wreck of their storeship *L'Aimable,* buried in a common grave for safekeeping.[31]

Among the remnant of twenty-odd sick people, priests, women, and children La Salle had left at Fort Saint-Louis in 1687 was the redoubtable Madame Isabelle Planteau Talon, who had embarked from France with her carpenter husband Lucien and five children, giving birth to a sixth at sea. At Fort Saint-Louis, Lucien had turned up missing and Marie-Elizabeth, her elder daughter, succumbed to disease. Twelve-year-old Pierre Talon had set out with La Salle in 1687 to be left with young Pierre Meunier among the Tejas Indians to learn their language. Presumed a widow, Madame Talon had looked after the other children and survived smallpox, typhoid, and constant discomforts, only to die in the final assault, shot with arrows by Karankawas as the children watched.

Indian women prevented a worse atrocity. They wanted the children alive. Fifteen-year-old Marie-Magdelaine, her three younger brothers, and one other boy were adopted into scattered Native rancherías and tattooed; they later became objects of ransom by Spaniards. In 1690 and 1691, all, including Pierre, were recovered. Marie-Magdelaine had not been violated sexually. She and the others, in a change of scene almost beyond imagining, were plucked from the Karankawas and placed in the viceregal palace in Mexico City as wards of the viceroy's wife, childless doña Gelvira.[32]

Jean-Baptiste Talon, Isabelle's second son, testifying later in France, blamed La Salle for the massacre. The French colonizer had earned the Karankawas' undying hatred by stealing their canoes for his own desperate explorations. In addition to the children, half a dozen other colonists had survived because of their timely absence from the fort while fraternizing among the agricultural, Caddoan-speaking Hasinai confederation, whom the Spaniards called Tejas and the French Cenis. León, hearing of these men, dispatched an athletic Indian runner with a letter in French urging them to give themselves up. Two did.

Earlier, the literate one, Jean l'Archevêque, had scribbled notes in the margin of the ship painting delivered by Juan Sabeata to Governor Pardiñas at Parral. Risking Spanish imprisonment, he had begged for rescue. "We are sorely grieved," he wrote, "to be among the beasts like these who believe neither in God nor in anything. Gentlemen, if you are willing to take us away, you have only to send a message." Since no one in Pardiñas's circle read French, l'Archevêque's words had gone unheeded. Now, a message had come, not from Pardiñas, but from León.[33]

The Spaniards said the two Frenchmen—l'Archevêque and Jacques Grollet— were naked, meaning that they were dressed not like Europeans but in skins, and heavily tattooed. And they could converse in the Indians' tongue. One of them interpreted Father Massanet's earnest admonition to the Native governor of the Hasinais "that his people should become Christians, and bring into their lands priests who should baptize them, since otherwise they could not save their souls, adding that if he wished, I would go to his lands."[34] Whatever the Indian replied, fray Damián, his head full of utopian illusions, took it as a petition for missionaries. And true to his word, he returned the following year with León's company and three other priests from his college.

The strategy-minded Conde de Galve, viceroy of New Spain between 1688 and 1696 and husband of doña Gelvira, interrogated l'Archevêque and Grollet in Mexico City, bought them proper clothing, and sent them off to Spain as prisoners. Surprisingly, his path and theirs would cross again. In the meantime, after conferring with Father Massanet, the viceroy in council authorized funds for another entrada by Alonso de León; its purposes would be to search the bay area for other French refugees or new arrivals, burn the fort, and escort the Franciscans beyond to the country of the Hasinais. Jean Géry, who had apparently gone back to his Indian family, did not make the trip, which pleased Massanet no end.

On a blustery April 26, 1690, he and León again surveyed the ruins of the French outpost. The commander's itinerary of the year before provided a graphic description:

> The principal house of this settlement is in the form of a fort, made of ship's timber, with a second story [roof], also made of ship's timber, and with a slope to turn off water. Next to it, without any partition, is another apartment, not so strong, which must have served as a chapel where mass was said. The other five houses are of stakes, covered with mud inside and out; their roofs are covered with buffalo-hides. All are quite useless for any defence.[35]

With relish, fray Damián strode around among the buildings, putting them to the torch. "I myself set fire to the fort," he bragged, "and as there was a high wind— the wood, by the way, was from the sloop [storeship] brought by the Frenchmen, which had sunk on entering the bay—in half an hour the fort was in ashes."

L'Archevêque's note and ship drawing, 1689. *Courtesy of the Ministerio de Educación, Cultura y Deporte, Archivo General de Indias (Sevilla, Spain), Ingenios, 9, and the Texas State Historical Association.*

Afterward, the party rode the five miles downstream to an arm of the bay, where soldiers from inland Nuevo León excitedly took off their clothes and got in the water so they could say they had bathed in the sea. As proof, they collected samples of saltwater to take back to Monterrey, where "it was held a great favor to try and to taste, because it was seawater."[36]

Even though, according to Massanet, it rained hard for eleven days, breaking a dry spell, nothing about their reception among the Hasinais dampened the missionaries' zeal. Between celebrations, gift exchange, and fellowship, Spaniards had time to admire the Natives' cultivated fields, well-provisioned, round, pole-and-thatch houses, the hierarchical government of their chiefdom, and certain of their beliefs perceived to be compatible with Christianity. In less than a week, the first temporary mission church in today's east Texas, San Francisco de los Tejas, went up 240 miles northeast of Matagorda Bay in the reddish hill country of live oak and pine between the Trinity and Neches rivers.

The Spaniards treated the Hasinais to Roman Catholic pageantry on May 25, 1690, the feast of Corpus Cristi, and a week later at the consecration of the church.

The Natives joined in the processions with gusto and applauded each salvo fired as the host was elevated during mass and at other moments of drama. With due pomp, General León presented a cane of authority to the Indians' governor who accepted it with solemnity, offering his ritual obedience to the Spanish crown, whatever that meant to him. And just as don Juan de Oñate had bestowed religious jurisdiction on the Franciscans in New Mexico in 1598, so did León in Texas in 1690. Then, as time drew near for the expedition to leave, he and Massanet quarreled.

Men-at-arms stationed in or near missions always posed a quandary for missionaries. Would such guards not ravish neophyte women? Would they not curse, get drunk, and gamble? If of good character, on the other hand, might they not provide positive examples of civilized Christian behavior? Only when internal or external threats appeared sufficiently grave were missionary priests likely to demand a military presence.

León probably wanted to expand his own jurisdiction by founding a presidio. He claimed, however, that the friars needed protection. Massanet disagreed. The Hasinais seemed more than affable. Three soldiers of his choosing were quite enough, the Franciscan insisted, angrily rejecting Leon's plan to leave a garrison of fifty men under Capt. Nicolás Prieto—in Massanet's opinion "an incapable and undeserving old man." That was that. The friar prevailed.

Later the same year, when Father Massanet set down his lengthy account of the expeditions of 1689 and 1690 for Prof. Carlos de Sigüenza y Góngora, the viceroy's chronicler, he saved until last "the most noteworthy thing of all." It had occurred in early May 1689, when the governor of the Hasinais brought l'Archevêque and Grollet to the Spaniards' camp. The revered Native leader, in Massanet's version of the encounter, wanted the Franciscan to give him blue cloth for a burial shroud for his mother. No other color would do. "I then asked him," wrote Massanet,

> what mystery was attached to the blue color, and he said that they were very fond of that color, particularly for burial clothes, because in times past they had been visited frequently by a very beautiful woman, who used to come down from the heights, dressed in blue garments, and that they wished to be like that woman.

Had he himself seen her? No, but his mother and other old people had. That was good enough for Massanet. Here, to his mind, was clear proof that María de Jesús de Agreda had indeed come miraculously among the heathen tribes of North America, just as Father Benavides had reported sixty years earlier.[37]

According to another version, Spaniards, relying on a Native interpreter and the two Frenchmen, initiated the inquiry. Had the Indian per chance seen a woman in a habit like fray Damián's? Not personally, but he had heard from his ancestors that such a woman had appeared to them on several occasions. It mattered not to

La V. M. Maria de Iesus de Agreda. Predicando á los Chichimecos del Nuebo-méxico. Antt de Castro f.

María de Jesús de Agreda preaching. *From Alonso de Benavides,* Tanto que se sacó *(1730).*

Father Massanet whether others had put words in the Indian governor's mouth. He had his proof.[38]

While Franciscans in Texas and Jesuits in Pimería Alta made tentative territorial advances northward in the late 1680s, the New Mexico colony-in-exile stagnated near El Paso. The Pueblo Indians, united in their revolt of 1680, had expelled Spaniards from the Pueblo world, prevailing in the abrupt first round of a sixteen-year-long, three-round Pueblo-Spanish war. A decade of impasse between 1681 and 1691, the war's second round, revealed deep divisions on both sides. During the hard-fought final round, from 1692 to 1696, returning Spaniards would pull together while the Pueblos broke apart.[39]

For a time, however, they celebrated. Popé, instead of isolating himself in prayer and thanksgiving, put himself at the head of a victory tour, descending on one after another of the Rio Grande pueblos with a large entourage, much in the manner of a Spanish governor on his required inspection of the colony. Everywhere the Pueblo prophet proclaimed a return to the ways of their ancestors. "He ordered in all the pueblos through which he passed," remembered Pedro Naranjo, an Indian of San Felipe,

> that they instantly break up and burn the images of the holy Christ, the Virgin Mary and the other saints, the crosses, and everything pertaining to Christianity, and that they burn the temples, break up the bells, and separate from the wives whom God had given them in marriage and take those whom they desired. In order to take away their baptismal names, the water, and the holy oils, they were to plunge into the rivers and wash themselves with amole, which is a root native to the country, washing even their clothing, with the understanding that there would thus be taken from them the character of the holy sacraments.

If they would rebuild their kivas, fashion kachina masks, and restage their true, unadulterated ceremonials, blessings would surely follow: abundant harvests, good health, and leisure. But, the Native leader warned them, "he who might still keep in his heart a regard for the priests, the governor, and the Spaniards would be known from his unclean face and clothes, and would be punished."[40]

By ritual parody, Pueblo Indians had long taught lessons to the young and reinforced the boundaries of their culture. Popé, drawing on that rich tradition, mounted an elaborate burlesque at the pueblo of Santa Ana. He ordered a long table set with food prepared in the Spanish manner. Then he took his place at the head of the table and had the mixed-blood Alonso Catití, principal leader of the uprising in the Keres pueblos, sit at the far end, with their followers between. "He ordered to be brought two chalices, one for himself and the other for the said

Cliofi Arquero, Keres Pueblo Indian, by T. Harmon Parkhurst, c. 1935. *Courtesy of the Museum of New Mexico, no. 46990.*

Alonso, and both began to drink, ridiculing and scoffing the Spaniards and the Christian religion." Then Popé, playing the role of the Spanish governor, rose and offered a toast to Alonso, as if he were the Franciscan superior. "To your Paternal Reverence's health," he intoned. Whereupon, Alonso responded with mock solemnity, "Here is to your lordship's health, Sir governor."[41]

Violence accompanied parody. Yet the grandest act of Pueblo defiance went largely unrecorded in the Spanish record. It may also have happened during Popé's tour. The Indians of Pecos, refusing to take the blame for it, accused the Tewas. Only an extensive, telltale mound, noted by Spaniards in the 1690s, and imaginative deconstruction by historical archaeologists in the 1960s, recalled the event. With deliberate and vengeful fury, Pueblo Indians had demolished the most prominent architectural reminder of the Spanish regime, the Pecos mission church.

Dedicated about 1625, the year before Father Benavides reached Santa Fe, the church of Nuestra Señora de los Angeles dwarfed any other Spanish building in the colony; its inside dimensions were 41 feet across at the entrance by 145 feet from front door to apse. By one estimate, church and convento required 300,000 adobes. It was, Benavides had written, a "most splendid temple of singular construction and excellence on which a friar expended very great labor and diligence." Not every descendant of the Pecos people who had laid up the towering monument wanted to see it thrown down. Popé did.

It was no small feat. The wreckers must have heaped an enormous quantity of branches and brush inside to kindle the wooden choir loft and roof. The flames then sucked air through the broken-out transverse clerestory window, and the wounded structure, like a giant furnace, spewed ashes out the front door. When the burned roof collapsed, the Indians—Tewas or Pecos—probably climbed up and began prying loose and throwing down tens of thousands of adobes. The front wall, no longer supported by side walls, then toppled forward facade down, blanketing the layer of ash.[42]

Not everyone approved. Nothing in their tradition prepared them for a despotic Pueblo leader, one of their own who swaggered like a Spaniard, issuing orders and demanding tribute. While some Pueblo leaders joined Popé in flaunting Roman Catholic vestments and profaning sacred vessels, others hid religious items for the day the priests would surely return. Discerning Pueblos understood that Spanish New Mexicans, after three and four generations, considered the colony as much their home as the Indians did. Juan, a Tewa from Tesuque, testifying in 1681, expressed a common belief that eventually Spaniards "must come and gain the kingdom because they were sons of the land and had grown up with the natives."[43]

Downriver in the El Paso district, some of those sons, defying Governor Otermín's decree of death to deserters, waded and swam across to the river's right

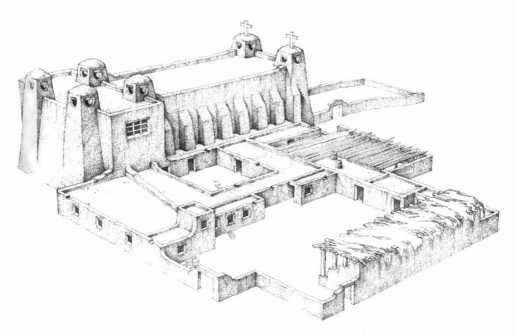

The massive mission complex at Pecos built in the 1620s. By Lawrence Ormsby. *Courtesy of Pecos National Historical Park.*

bank and kept going, seeking safer havens in Nueva Vizcaya. The rest, close to two thousand people, huddled for a year in makeshift refugee camps spaced six or eight miles apart downriver from the mission of Nuestra Señora de Guadalupe, suffering hardships and indignities, quarreling, and awaiting word of aid from Mexico City. Again, the tireless provisioner fray Francisco de Ayeta was man of the hour, riding to the viceregal capital, representing the colony's dire exile, and returning in September 1681 at the head of another relief caravan. He also brought authority for Otermín to enlist a fifty-man presidial garrison and lead a reentry into the lost province.

The Spanish governor attempted reconquest between November 1681 and February 1682, wherein he "burned" the abandoned southern pueblos and evacuated 385 Tiwas from Isleta. His bootless winter thrust intensified factions among Pueblos and Spaniards. The heavy-handed Popé had already been deposed in favor of Luis Tupatú of Picuris. In their own self-interest—in trade, protection, food supply, favors, and family relations—Pueblos who wanted peace with Spaniards began speaking up. In contrast, Alonso Catití, who decorated his house at Santo Domingo with finery from the looted church, tried to entice a column of Otermín's men, including Catití's half-brother Capt. Pedro Márquez, into a trap with feigned tears of joy and the sexiest Cochiti women.[44]

It broke Father Ayeta's heart. He had believed that only the Pueblos' leaders were responsible for the atrocities of 1680 and that the people would soon tire of their tyrannical rule and welcome the Spaniards back. "But they have been found," he reported during Otermín's entrada, "to be so pleased with liberty of conscience and so attached to the . . . worship of Satan that up to the present not a sign has been visible of their ever having been Christians." That was not all. Most of the Spaniards on the expedition were contentious. "Those who have horses," the friar asserted,

> have no regard for anything except their own convenience, although the heavens fall, they would not lend them to their own fathers, much less to the governor, for there is an epidemic of hatred in these parts toward any person who governs and commands.[45]

Ill and weary, Governor Otermín hated New Mexicans at least as much as they hated him. When he learned that the cabildo had dispatched an unauthorized delegation carrying charges against him to the viceroy in Mexico City, he begged Father Ayeta, also bound for the viceregal capital, "for the love of God and Saint Anthony as soon as you arrive in Mexico, do everything you possibly can to get me out of here."[46]

That took a year and a half. Otermín's replacement, the decisive don Domingo Jironza Petrís de Cruzate, assumed the governorship on August 29, 1683. He expedited his predecessor's residencia within the requisite thirty days. Evidently influenced by customary extralegal considerations, neither Jironza nor the dozen witnesses he interviewed lodged a single complaint against Otermín. He was free to go.

Not yet thirty-five, Domingo Jironza, an able and energetic Aragonese, had volunteered boastfully before leaving Mexico City that he would mount another entrada upriver at his own expense. Once he saw for himself the scattered clusters of huts and fearful, demoralized refugees, he ate his boast. There were more pressing matters. Hoping to lessen factionalism, Jironza dropped cases against Otermín's enemies. He formalized the presidio of San José and in 1683 thought briefly of elevating sorry El Paso to villa status as the capital of New Mexico in exile. A survey of both sides of the river convinced him that better sites for the half-dozen settlements existed upstream closer to El Paso. Even more urgent were Indian affairs, external and internal.

Ever-bolder Apaches kept running off the colony's horses. The unpredictable Mansos living at mission Guadalupe were in constant touch with their heathen kin and rancherías of Sumas, Janos, and Jocomes to the west toward Sonora. Rumors persisted that Pueblo Indians residing in the El Paso settlements—Piros, Tompiros, and sundry others who had drifted in during the 1670s, the additional 317 Piros who had accompanied Otermín in 1680, and the 385 Tiwas from Isleta—intended to rise and kill whomever they could.

Restive fray Nicolás López, left in charge as vice-custos and procurator by Father Ayeta, wanted more missions. If reentry among the Pueblos was delayed, he would find other fields. He envisioned an east-west axis below El Paso in Nueva Vizcaya, anchored on one side by mission La Soledad, ministering precariously to Jano and western Suma rancherías in the vicinity of Casas Grandes, 125 miles southwest. López himself took credit for revitalizing the mission at Ojito for eastern Sumas 30 miles south of El Paso. And in October 1683, when a big delegation of Jumanos led by Juan Sabeata reappeared at El Paso and invited Franciscans to come live with them in the vicinity of La Junta, 190 miles downriver to the southeast, López leapt at the prospect.

Governor Jironza interviewed Sabeata. The Indian leader, who claimed through an interpreter that he had been baptized at Parral, made no secret of his people's desire for Spanish protection from southward-moving Plains Apaches. Ten thousand Jumanos and Julimes awaited Franciscans at La Junta. Three dozen other nations interrelated by trade and diplomacy, including the Tejas and Quiviras, could also be brought within the Spanish sphere. Jironza, adding his own hyperbole in a letter to the viceroy, gave Father López license.

The friar's opportunistic cohort, Mre. de campo Juan Domínguez de Mendoza, son of old Tomé, wanted to be New Mexico's first Native-born governor. But that could wait. From December 1683 to July 1684, Domínguez was away from El Paso, taking with him López, some armed volunteers, dozens of extra hands, and several wagons. After dropping off a missionary or two near La Junta, he headed north past the Davis Mountains and east across the Pecos to the prime buffalo range where he had been with Diego de Guadalajara's expedition thirty years before. There, in grassy south-central Texas, while don Juan kept his eye on profit, alienating even Juan Sabeata, the men brought down and skinned six thousand of the big animals.[47]

Back in El Paso, eight jailed Christian Manso leaders confessed elaborate plans for an 1684 massacre of Spaniards. Jironza kept his head. He stayed the prisoners' execution to appease scared colonists, then moved the settlements upriver closer to El Paso. Yet in early May, like-minded Janos and Sumas rose at La Soledad, killing fray Manuel Beltrán, his Spanish bodyguard, and the latter's family. At Ojito, in the missionary's absence, Sumas put to death Juan de Archuleta and his family. The two friars at La Junta, although naked, miraculously escaped to Parral. From end to end, Father López's mission axis went up in flames.[48]

Whether such widespread outbreaks sprang from the unavenged Pueblo revolt of 1680, Spaniards believed they did. They visualized Native agitators, *tlatoleros,* flitting between Indian nations, stirring up resistance. Even the Opatas of the Sonora Valley, considered by neighboring colonists as the most loyal and compatible of

Indians, had been caught conspiring with Apaches in 1681. Indignant Spanish frontier officials swiftly executed the suspected organizers.[49] Then came the troubles of 1684.

Jironza cursed his predicament. He could not ignore Spaniards west of El Paso who were clamoring for protection. Yet the more men and munitions he sent to Casas Grandes to fight emboldened Janos, Jocomes, Sumas, Mansos, and Apaches, the longer the Pueblos upriver went unpunished. Fortunately for don Domingo, the Piros and Tiwas of San Antonio de Senecú, Corpus Cristi de la Ysleta, and Nuestra Señora de la Concepción de Socorro—names of upriver pueblos they had brought with them—did not join the Mansos but fought fiercely as auxiliaries alongside presidial soldiers and colonists. They also witnessed in August 1684 ten executed Manso corpses left dangling in the plaza.[50]

Poverty and disillusion persisted. A September census of 1,051 Hispanic residents revealed just how pathetic their condition had become. Still a prominent citizen, widower Francisco de Anaya Almazán was better off than most. His household consisted of four persons. "He has a small plot of maize. He does not know what it will yield, so they are eating the ears green. Their clothing is somewhat decent. He has five horses, a saddle, a harquebus, and a sword."[51]

Three times in 1684, the cabildo implored Governor Jironza to abandon El Paso; each time, knowing that Mexico City considered it the defensive pivot of the entire northern frontier, don Domingo refused. In 1685, he reported a lull in the fighting; no enemy ranchería remained in the El Paso district. If supplies from Parral arrived in time, the governor planned an entrada upriver to the Pueblos in October. Lucas, a Tiwa Indian who had ventured as far north as Santo Domingo, swore that Alonso Catití had dropped dead in his house and his people now recognized that they had been "very crazy."[52]

Meanwhile in Mexico City, Father López and Juan Domínguez de Mendoza, the latter having departed El Paso this time without license, lobbied to replace Jironza as governor. They were not alone. The very messenger don Domingo had sent to the viceregal capital in his behalf reappeared at El Paso in 1686 as governor. Pedro Reneros de Posada, a bachelor from Castile, had enlisted in 1681 as a common soldier in Otermín's presidio. By 1684, he had risen to the rank of captain. Now, from September 1686 until February 1689, the arrogant Reneros governed recklessly, as if he had friends in high places.[53]

While evidently shuffling accounts to embezzle the presidial payroll, the new governor led a scantly documented strike up the Rio Grande. His troop assailed the Keres pueblo of Santa Ana, took captives, and beat a hasty retreat to El Paso. On don Pedro's order, four of the prisoners, identified as leaders, died by summary execution. Accusing the other ten of murderous participation in the revolt of 1680,

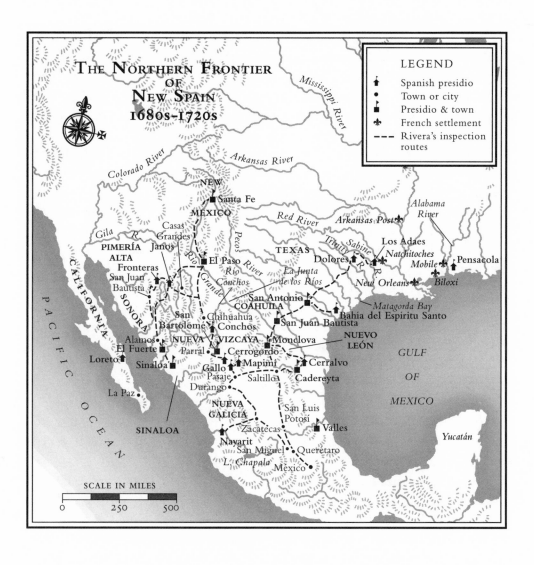

THE NORTHERN FRONTIER OF NEW SPAIN 1680s–1720s

LEGEND

↑ Spanish presidio
● Town or city
■ Presidio & town
⚜ French settlement
--- Rivera's inspection routes

Mississippi River

Colorado River

Arkansas River

NEW MEXICO
■ Santa Fe

Red River

Arkansas Post ⚜

Alabama River

Gila R.

PIMERÍA ALTA
Casas Grandes
Janos

Trinity R.
Sabine R.

Los Adaes
Natchitoches
Mobile ⚜

Pensacola ↑

Fronteras
San Juan Bautista ●

Río Grande

El Paso River ■
Río Conchos

Dolores ↑

La Junta de los Ríos

New Orleans ⚜
Biloxi ⚜

SONORA
CALIFORNIA

TEXAS

San Antonio ■
COAHUILA

Bahía del Espíritu Santo ↑

Matagorda Bay

P A C I F I C   O C E A N

San Bartolomé ●
Chihuahua ●
Conchos ↑

San Juan Bautista ■

NUEVO LEÓN

G U L F
O F
M E X I C O

Alamos ●
El Fuerte ■
Loreto ↑
Sinaloa ■

NUEVA VIZCAYA
Parral
Cerrogordo ↑
Mapimí ↑
Gallo ↑
Pasaje ↑

Monclova ●

Cerralvo ↑

Durango ●
Saltillo ●
Cadereyta

La Paz ●

NUEVA GALICIA

San Luis Potosí ●

Valles ■

Yucatán

SINALOA

Nayarit ↑
Zacatecas ●
San Miguel ●
Querétaro ●

L. Chapala
Mexico ●

SCALE IN MILES

0 — 250 — 500

he had them conducted brusquely to Nueva Vizcaya, sold for ten years' servitude, and permanently exiled. Except for this raid, apparently carried out in August 1687, Reneros accomplished little. The governor appointed to succeed him eighteen months later relished the moment. It was Jironza.

Having presented in Mexico City the accounts of his previous administration and accepted a settlement in his favor of 3,335 pesos, don Domingo took over again in February 1689. Reneros and his cabal departed for Zacatecas. Nothing, Jironza had vowed, would now stand in the way of his own military reconnaissance upriver. He scheduled its departure for the anniversary of the Pueblo revolt, August 10, a day commemorated emotionally by survivors every year since 1680. Now 80 men-at-arms and 120 Piros and Tiwas formed up with a support train and moved north.

Hundreds of Keres, remembering the fight at Santa Ana, waited defiantly at the fortified, hilltop pueblo of Zia. The invaders drew up in the dark and commenced their assault at first light on August 29. It lasted all day. Amid the yelling and acrid smoke, the carnage mounted, reminiscent of the battle of Acoma ninety years earlier. The claim that more than six hundred of Zia's defenders perished, many preferring death in the flames to surrender, suggests that Jironza had read Pérez de Villagrá's book. No other Spanish victory over insurgent Pueblo Indians, he implied, could exceed the heroics of his own action at Zia in 1689.

The king in council agreed. He would reappoint Domingo Jironza governor of New Mexico to carry out its reoccupation and would raise the El Paso presidial soldiers' annual pay from 315 to 450 pesos, granting as well to the victorious entrada's participants a one-time, 30-peso bonus.

Much of Jironza's confidence in the future derived from intelligence he obtained from a valiant prisoner of war who had fought the Spaniards almost to the death at Zia, then received Christian absolution and recovered. A Keres war captain, Bartolomé de Ojeda was literate, multilingual, commanding—and he had a change of heart. Henceforth, he would walk a difficult path. To save at least some of his people, he resolved to ease the Spaniards' inevitable reentry into the Pueblo world. In testimony before Governor Jironza, Ojeda described the state of the Pueblos' disunity and affirmed that a number of them would side with the returning colonists.[54]

Supplying a further motive—due punishment of heinous crimes against God—Ojeda related, in edifying detail, how tormentors had mocked and tortured seven of the Franciscan martyrs of 1680. At Acoma, they had stripped fray Lucas Maldonado and fray Juan de Bal naked, along with Ojeda's grandmother, Juana Maroh, a Christian mestiza. Then they roped the trio together and, with Juana in the middle, paraded them through the pueblo, whipping and stoning them. Finally, in the porter's lodge at the convento, they had finished them off with lance thrusts.[55]

Despite his undeniable successes, the seasoned Domingo Jironza was troubled. He had heard the rumors. Late in 1690, months before news of his reappointment reached New Spain, another appointee to the governorship of New Mexico, a personal acquaintance of the viceroy, had set out for the frontier. Although don Domingo probably expected to serve the customary full three-year term, as he had done previously, his 1689 appointment did not specify a set tenure, only that he would continue in office at the pleasure of king and viceroy. After his great triumph at Zia, replacing him now with a newcomer seemed not only bad policy but singularly unfair.

7 Tides of Empire

Innumerable tribes were brought back to the fold of the Catholic Church, and an entire realm was restored to the Majesty of our lord and king, Charles II, without wasting a single ounce of powder, unsheathing a sword, or (what is most worthy of emphasis and appreciation) without costing the Royal Treasury a single maravedí.

—CARLOS DE SIGÜENZA Y GÓNGORA, MERCURIO VOLANTE, 1693,
ON DIEGO DE VARGAS'S RITUAL 1692 RECONQUEST OF NEW MEXICO

The devil planted in their heads that we had brought the sickness to this land. When they saw that some 300 people more or less died . . . they convinced themselves further that we had killed them. Some wanted to kill us.

—FRAY FRANCISCO DE JESÚS MARÍA CASAÑAS, AUGUST 15, 1691,
ON A SMALLPOX EPIDEMIC AMONG THE HASINAI OF EAST TEXAS

But now, thanks to His Divine Majesty, through various expeditions . . . I discovered with all details, certainty and evidence, by means of a magnetic needle and astrolabe in my hand, that California is not an island but a peninsula or isthmus, and that in thirty-two degrees of latitude there is a passage by land to California.

—EUSEBIO FRANCISCO KINO, C. 1702

The 1690s were prologue. As competing Spanish, French, and English colonials schemed to impose their overlapping spheres of influence on shrinking but still vigorous Native American nations, more of North America became contested ground. Salient but tenuous, Spanish New Mexico had stood alone for most of the century. In the 1690s, however, in a series of previews, not only would Spaniards restore that colony, but they would also intrude among farming Hasinais in humid east Texas, cross the Sonoran Desert into present-day southern Arizona in Pima country, and gain a hold on the dry and daunting Baja California peninsula.

Because of confusing bends and twists in the multiple channels through the Mississippi Delta, La Salle had badly miscalculated the location of the river's mouth, above which he envisioned a French colony. Finally in 1699, Frenchmen, seeing that Spaniards had begun work the year before on a presidio at Pensacola, would find their way into the Mississippi from the Gulf and put up a temporary wooden fort at Biloxi. Farther east, Englishmen and Creeks all but annihilated Florida's remnant Apalachee and western Timucua mission populations.

During this same decade, for reasons of their own, some Indians collaborated. Others, not surprisingly, took up arms to resist. Yet the outsiders, with their gospel, firearms, and glass beads, kept coming. Mostly creoles or castas, they often still took orders from well-born Europeans.

"He is a young man," the witness stated, "of average stature, broad face, and straight hair, who lisps to the point of not being able to pronounce certain words." Diego José de Vargas Zapata Luján Ponce de León y Contreras, son of an illustrious but thoroughly indebted noble family of Madrid, had missed his turn as *menino,* or page in the royal household, because of his speech impediment. His father Alonso before him and his son Juan Manuel grew up as meninos. Don Diego compensated through boldness. Proudly he paraded in the uniform of the palace guard. In 1672, preparing to sail as royal courier to the viceroy of New Spain, he executed legal proof that he was the sole, legitimate, surviving male heir of Capt. Alonso de Vargas, who had died several years earlier in Guatemala leaving a considerable estate.[1]

In New Spain, Diego de Vargas earned a reputation as a tough and able administrator. In 1688, through an agent in Spain, he paid the requisite contribution to the royal treasury for a future on the governorship of New Mexico. His fellow *madrileño,* the Conde de Galve, activated Vargas's appointment in 1690, after forwarding news of Domingo Jironza's victory at Zia to Spain but before receiving the king's response.

Insincerely lamenting his self-exile "to this kingdom, at the ends of the earth and remote beyond compare," don Diego kept his eye on the prize. Plagued for more than a year by similar difficulties of supply, factionalism, and constant campaigning as his predecessors had been, Vargas could write in April 1692 to his son-in-law back home that he was about to restore the colony. "I am prepared," he boasted, "to carry out the invasion this summer on the feast day of St. Lawrence, the same day the kingdom was lost in 1680."[2]

More an armed reconnaissance than an invasion, Vargas's audacious, four-month tour of the Pueblo world late in 1692 hung repeatedly on his personal boldness. The

Don Diego de Vargas. The only known portrait, Capilla de San Isidro, Madrid. *Courtesy of J. Manuel Espinosa.*

men who followed him and the Pueblo Indians with whom he dealt learned to take don Diego at his word. When he quixotically threatened the unsubmissive Tano and Tewa occupants of Santa Fe with a siege, they yielded. They opened the gates on Sunday, September 14, feast of the Exaltation of the Holy Cross, and let him swagger in with the royal standard and preside over a ceremonial repossession. The Indians kneeled to receive absolution. They saw that these fewer than two hundred armed Spaniards and Pueblo auxiliaries were not prepared to move back in; they had not brought their women and children.

Despite his arrogance, owing more perhaps to station than to character, Diego de Vargas treated Pueblo Indian leaders as heads of dependent nations. He did not scruple to embrace them. Repeatedly, as his three Franciscan chaplains baptized the hundreds of Native children born since 1680, don Diego stood as godfather to sons and daughters of the principal men, making these dignified personages his compadres, in Roman Catholic terms—something he did not let them forget.

When strategies of war dictated, Vargas took women and children hostage, destroyed crops, and angrily executed unrepentant enemies. He also used restraint. When the Pecos people defied the Spanish governor's order and scattered into the hills, don Diego gave them a second chance. A year later, when he desperately needed their aid, Pecos fighting men swelled the Spaniards' ranks.

No one questioned don Diego's daring. Once, during his tenure as district officer at the mining town of Teutila in the mountains of Oaxaca, he had dashed into a burning church to save the holy images. Restoring New Mexico, he knew, was of far greater moment. All his predecessors had failed. What might he expect as reward? Halfway through the tour, Vargas wrote to his son-in-law, Ignacio López de Zárate, a ranking royal bureaucrat only three years his junior. He craved early word of the court's reaction to part one of his triumphal campaign journal. "It will be easy for Your Lordship to find out in the office of the Secretary of the Indies. . . . Once I know with certainty what they tell Your Lordship, I can consider my possibilities for advancement."[3]

The column found Zia in ruins in 1692. Yet the walls of its houseblocks and church, "which my predecessor . . . had razed," noted Vargas disapprovingly, still stood. Its survivors had joined with others from Santo Domingo and Santa Ana, under the leadership of the elderly Antonio Malacate, and were living in a defensive pueblo atop the Cerro Colorado. Vargas wanted them to come back down and rebuild. Calmed by Keres spokesman Bartolomé de Ojeda, they received the new Spanish governor peaceably on the mesa. "They all had crosses in their hands," Vargas dictated to his secretary,

> and on most of the houses of the cuarteles of the plaza, where they had prepared a ground-level room for me. With the people of the pueblo on the

plaza, I told them through the Indian Bartolo, who acted as interpreter, about my coming and took possession for his majesty, as in the other pueblos. The reverend fathers absolved and baptized them, as is stated. I, the governor and captain general, was godfather to Antonio Malacate's child, whom I named Carlos, in honor of the king, our lord (may God keep him), and to many others. . . . 123 of all ages, male and female, were baptized.[4]

The special courier dashed for Mexico City from El Paso. Don Diego de Vargas, boldly surviving fractious Hopis and a ferocious early winter, had returned his expedition in order in December 1692. If he doubted the sincerity of the Pueblos' verbal pledges of obedience, he kept the reasons to himself. He had reconquered New Mexico. His patron, the Marqués de Galve, rejoiced. With the first news, he had ordered the vast cathedral illuminated with thousands of candles. Bells pealed in all parts of the city. The viceroy asked don Carlos de Sigüenza, his court chronicler, to laud Diego de Vargas in print. The rousing, thirty-six-page *Mercurio volante,* or "news flash," summarizing Vargas's campaign journals, appeared in 1693. Don Diego was the toast of the capital.[5]

Galve, whose preoccupations ranged from St. Augustine to Manila, took particular interest in New Mexico. Restoration of the lost colony figured importantly in his overall protectionist strategy. He dictated personal thanks to Vargas and his men, vowed to inform the king, and authorized immediate expenditures from the strained royal treasury for a proper recolonization. Leaving nothing to chance, don Diego rode as far south as Zacatecas to expedite payments for recruiting and supply from lethargic treasury officials.

It was not that he distrusted Galve. He simply wanted to make sure that his bold deeds reached the king's ear. Dictating a lengthy memorial to Carlos II from Zacatecas on May 16, 1693, don Diego suggested his own reward: a noble title of Castile, marqués, "and in order to continue serving your majesty, the post of governor and captain general and president of the kingdom of Guatemala"—or the Philippines, or Chile, or Buenos Aires and the Río de la Plata. Vargas knew that response to a petition sent from New Mexico via Mexico City and Veracruz to Madrid, even with the best land and sea connections and prompt action by the bureaucracy, could take two years. Meanwhile, he appealed for more colonists—five hundred families in all.[6]

The viceroy helped. Galve believed that a better class of people—artisans and tradesmen—would ensure greater permanence than convicts and debtors. Capt. Cristóbal de Velasco, ironically a convict sent to New Mexico with Father Ayeta in 1677, and veteran fray Francisco Farfán, handled provisioning, housing, and outfitting the recruits and their families in the viceregal capital. Although they hoped for more, sixty-some family units volunteered, giving up the lives they had known

Viceroy the Conde de Galve, viceroy of New Spain, 1688–96. *From Manuel Rivera Cambas,* Los gobernantes de México *(1872).*

for the usual incentives of new settlers. Categorized as españoles, they came mostly from urban Mexico City and Puebla.

The men's occupations varied almost as much as their looks: barber, blacksmith, cabinetmaker, cartwright, chandler, filigree maker, coppersmith, cutler, miller, mining amalgamator, musician, painter, paver, stone and brick mason, and weaver.

Many were related by family ties or membership in craft guilds or religious lay brotherhoods. Once they reached New Mexico in the summer of 1694, these people would stick together, intermarry, and for generations maintain their social networks.[7]

Three of the prospective colonists were an afterthought, a conspicuous trio of tattooed Frenchmen listed after all as convicts: Pierre Meunier of Paris, Jacques Grollet of La Rochelle, and Jean l'Archevêque of Bayonne. Their adventures, told with French accent, rivaled don Quijote's. Seemingly the cleverest, l'Archevêque, who became Juan de Archibeque among Spaniards, possessed a joie de vivre that transcended culture.

Back when his father's import business was failing, young l'Archevêque had made his way from the port of Bayonne to the French West India Company's Caribbean colony on the west end of Española. There, at Petit Goave, Jean assured himself further excitement, contracting in 1684 as indentured servant to merchant Sieur Pierre Duhaut, one of the few people of means among La Salle's transient, low-life colonists. L'Archevêque had survived the ghastly ordeal on the Texas coast while most of the others died.

Later, while living at one of the Hasinai farming villages in the east Texas hills, he and his friend Grollet had allowed themselves to be tattooed, a painful process wherein the Indians cut tiny incisions in the skin, then introduced a dye made of crushed walnuts. The resulting black lines had marked their faces and other parts of their bodies for life, despite all efforts to erase them. Although compelled by circumstances not unlike Cabeza de Vaca's to stay with the Hasinais for two years, neither Jean nor Jacques wished to live out his life as a white Indian.

A dubious answer to their prayers, Alonso de León had ransomed them in 1690. Because Spanish authorities were already considering the occupation of east Texas to Christianize the agricultural Hasinais and forestall further French encroachment, the Conde de Galve himself had interrogated the French survivors in Mexico City. L'Archevêque and Grollet were then shipped off to Spain as prisoners, confined for thirty months, brought back in chains, and finally, to prevent their escape to France with damaging intelligence, banished to distant New Mexico. Meunier, meanwhile, had served as translator and language teacher to the friars in east Texas. In New Mexico, against all odds, the three striped Frenchmen would flourish, especially the zestful Juan de Archibeque.[8]

The persistent shadow of France, falling across the Gulf Coast and lower Mississippi Valley, all but assured government support of Franciscan missionary operations in east Texas. Writing on September 4, 1690, at mission San Francisco de los Tejas, fray Miguel de Fontcuberta had addressed a letter to the father custos of New Mexico and entrusted it for delivery to Jumano captain Juan Sabeata. The

Texas friar had misunderstood Sabeata and supposed that the distance between the province of the Hasinais and El Paso was "no more than five days' journey."

Fray Miguel related that he, two other priests, and a catechist, all from the missionary college of Querétaro, in the company of three soldiers, had been left by fray Damián Massanet, their superior, whom they expected to return with supplies and more missionaries in six or seven months. An Indian had just reported white men to the north. "We believe," Fontcuberta stated nervously, "that they are Frenchmen." He thought they might be vengeful. Since he reckoned that the march from El Paso was so short, he appealed for soldiers to come and learn the foreigners' intent. Given the critical nature of this intelligence, the Franciscan explained, he would have reported directly to the viceroy but for "the large rivers and the never-ceasing rain."[9]

Fray Miguel might have saved himself the trouble. Sabeata, who had his own business to attend to, did not deliver the missionary's letter for almost two years, and then not to El Paso but to Parral and his old acquaintance, Governor Pardiñas. By that time, Fontcuberta had died of a fever, and his brethren were hard pressed to persuade worried Natives that baptism was not killing them.

Fray Francisco de Jesús María Casañas tried European logic. He asked them

> if they had killed Father fray Miguel de Fontcuberta and the soldier who had died soon after arriving in their land. All answered that they had not. I told them that they spoke very well . . . that God had killed the two, that when God wills. . . . He kills Spaniards too, just as He is now killing the Indians, and we must therefore accept everything God does as well done. . . . All were amazed.[10]

The minor novelties brought by these alleged holy men paled quickly. The Hasinais, capable enough of feeding, defending, and supplying themselves with horses and other commodities through Native trade, had little need of Spaniards. Besides, these intruders brought sickness. And if, as the unbending Father Casañas seemed to say, the Christian God's holy will was to strike down individual Spaniards one at a time and Hasinais by the hundreds, why tolerate such an arbitrary presence?

A third Spanish expeditionary force had penetrated the lands of the Hasinai confederation in the scorching summer of 1691. En route, in the vicinity of present-day San Marcos, its members had happened upon a great fair or rendezvous of two to three thousand Indians, many on horseback using saddles and stirrups in Spanish form—Jumanos, Cíbolos, and others from the south and west come to hunt buffalo and deal in bows and arrows, bags of salt, shells, feathers, and turquoise, along with European hunting knives, scissors, and mirrors.

First to hold concurrent appointment as governor of Coahuila and Texas, seasoned Domingo Terán de los Ríos, who had most recently administrated Sinaloa and Sonora, distrusted the Indians' haughty captains. Ubiquitous Juan Sabeata, who took advantage of white men every chance he got, proposed that Terán give them instruments of safe conduct similar to those allegedly granted them by the authorities of Nueva Vizcaya and New Mexico. The Spaniards held their breaths as these proud men, with Sabeata in the lead, paraded in columns two abreast before them. Father Massanet noted with satisfaction that several held aloft the banners of the Virgin of Guadalupe he had presented in 1690.[11]

Such communications across the south plains between La Junta, Parral, and El Paso to the west and the Hasinai confederacy in east Texas—personified by Juan Sabeata and his concourse—were about to be cut. Fiercer mounted hunters migrating south, Apaches first, then Comanches, would eventually dominate this range. By about 1700, the Jumano nation, as defined in Spanish documents, would cease to exist as its remnant bands merged with Apaches, Hasinais, or other less distinguishable elements of the frontier populace.[12]

The relatively low cost of mission startups and maintenance, combined with Massanet's guarantee that the Tejas were apt for Christian conversion, had convinced Galve to occupy east Texas by missionary initiative. The viceroy's cost-effective design called not only for strengthening ties to the Hasinai confederation, but also for binding with additional Franciscan missions the related, Caddo-speaking Kadohadacho confederation farther north and east. Massanet volunteered priests from the college of Querétaro, and Galve, to Governor Terán's keen displeasure, had put the imperious Franciscan in overall charge of the 1691 entrada.

From the onset, the plan went wrong. Massanet blamed Terán's incompetence, his oversexed Spanish soldiers, and the weather. After an arduous winter excursion to Kadohadacho country, Terán formed up his army in January 1692 to withdraw from Texas; six of Massanet's dispirited priests, including fray Francisco de Jesús María Casañas, elected to abandon the field as well. Soon after they left, the swollen Neches River swept away mission Santísimo Nombre de María, founded by Casañas in 1691 five miles northeast of San Francisco de los Tejas. Another epidemic struck, and God let many Hasinais and one more missionary die.

When a resupply detachment under the new governor, Gregorio de Salinas Varona, showed up briefly in June 1693, two more friars opted out. That left only the embittered Massanet, fray Francisco Hidalgo, "three catechists, two boys, and eight soldiers, along with another lad who also stayed, making us sixteen in all." Returning to Coahuila, Salinas Varona carried a letter from Father Massanet to Viceroy Galve.

Massanet had joined the skeptics. Having lived among the Hasinais, he now had nothing good to say about them. Insolent, deceitful, hopelessly idolatrous,

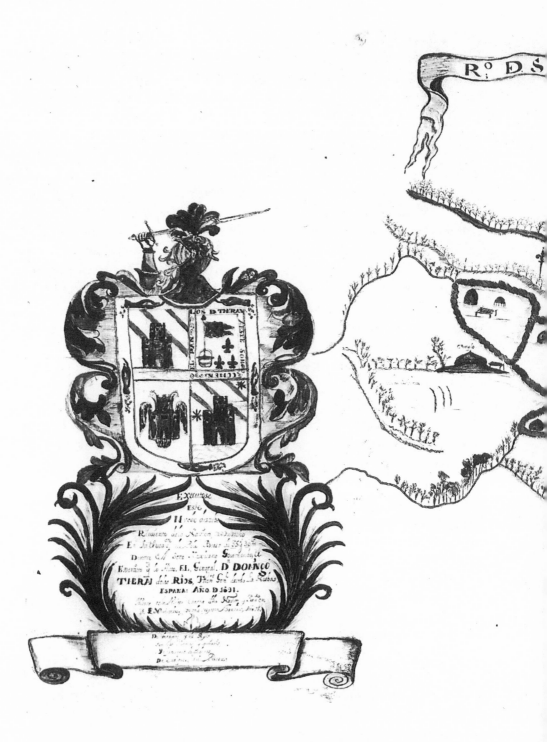

Gov. Terán de los Ríos map of the Kadohadacho communities, 1691. *Courtesy of the Ministerio de Educación, Cultura y Deporte, Archivo General de Indias (Sevilla, Spain), Mapas y Planos, 90, and Robert S. Weddle.*

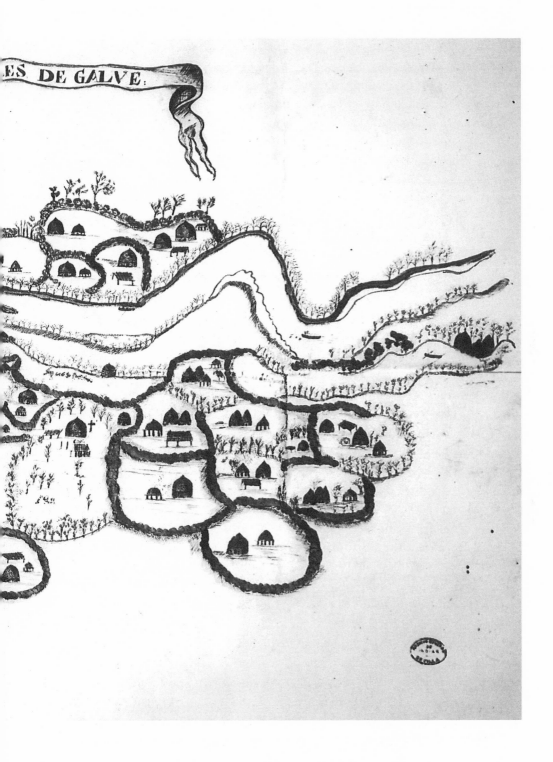

constantly plotting to murder their missionaries, interested only in material benefits, and unwilling to congregate in mission towns, these Natives would have to be
forced to convert. After supplying ten reasons why, the missionary suggested three
expedients: soldiers, distant relocation, and concentration.

Galve's chief legal advisor, the royal *fiscal,* Dr. Juan de Escalante y Mendoza,
blanched. Such violent measures, he sputtered, conformed with "neither good the-
ology nor the resolutions of sacred councils."[13]

No one except Father Hidalgo cared to recall the pomp and good feelings of
May 1690. Massanet, certain now that he and his fellow outsiders were about to
be killed, resolved to slink away into the woods. Burying stone mortars, supplies,
and mission bells and setting fire to the church to avoid its desecration, the evacuees abandoned San Francisco de los Tejas on October 25, 1693, carrying vestments and silver vessels with them. Whoever trailed them for days chose not to
catch up. Two soldiers deserted and lagged behind, unburying the cache and dis-
tributing surplus goods to the Indians.

Between the Colorado and San Marcos rivers, "God willed for my sins,"
Massanet lamented, that the little flock wander lost in a dense forest, the Monte
Grande, for a biblical forty days. Their number shrank again as another two soldiers
turned back. Of the deserters, fifteen-year-old José de Urrutia found special favor
among the Hasinais, rose in their ranks, and led them and their allies in battle against
Apaches. Seven years later, in 1700, the irrepressible Urrutia, by then a white Indian
thoroughly schooled in his adoptive peoples' ways and words, reappeared among
Spaniards and reembraced their culture, eventually becoming a presidial captain.[14]

The remaining fugitives did not drag into Monclova until February 17, 1694.
Father Massanet wrote the viceroy the same day. He wanted no more to do with
Hasinais. Politely, young fray Francisco Hidalgo dissented. He would advocate for
twenty years a return to east Texas, and when that finally came to pass, he would
be welcome. Until then, however, only Urrutia and a few other wild irregulars
represented Spain in the interior.[15]

Over on the coast, in an effort to preempt known bays before Frenchmen did,
Viceroy Galve had dispatched into the gulf a two-ship reconnaissance in 1693.
Galve's choice of personnel showed his involvement. Admiral Andrés de Pez commanded, and the chief cosmographer of New Spain, Prof. emeritus don Carlos de
Sigüenza, who had never been to sea before, was in charge of sounding, mapping,
and scientific observation. Ashore on Pensacola Bay, which he renamed Santa María
de Galve, Sigüenza extolled the inexhaustible pine forests, then swooned at the
magnolias' heavy fragrance. A fine chart resulted, but no Spanish town or presidio
during Galve's lifetime.[16]

In contrast, the news from New Mexico resonated throughout the empire. Diego de Vargas extolled the restoration in battle of the former colony's capital at Santa Fe. Certain details, however—the execution of seventy male Pueblo defenders by Spanish firing squads and distribution of about four hundred women and children as servants among the colonists—exercised Dr. Escalante y Mendoza.

Citing the long-delayed, 1681 *Recopilación de leyes de los reynos de las Indias,* Escalante y Mendoza reproached Vargas for excessive use of force. Ordering the death of so many Pueblo men struck the fiscal as "more like desolating than chastising. To restrain by example and terror the rest of the pueblos and nations . . . ," he reasoned,

> it would have been enough to render justice upon eight or ten of those who were the heads and leaders in the uprising. . . . He could have made the rest prisoners and inflicted upon them some other kind of punishment. In this way, fear would touch all, but punishment few, until account could be given to your excellency.

Nor did Escalante y Mendoza trust Vargas not to make slaves of the women and children. "In no way," he warned, "can the Indians be distributed as property without a royal order, under penalty of a 1,000-peso fine for such governors as may do otherwise."[17]

As a matter of routine, Viceroy Galve summoned a junta of audiencia judges and leading advisors, listened to his fiscal's opinion, then, often in precisely the same words, dispatched directives to appropriate officials in the field. On this occasion, however, Galve took the part of his bold governor. From the viceroy's vantage, Vargas's campaign journal and letters fully justified his actions. Galve held that

> With this understanding, and bearing in mind the governor's conduct in the first conquest, the reality of the deceit the Indians practiced is proved. The violence was not on his part; rather it was the defense necessary for the restoration. Everything that he did for that defense is approved.[18]

In Santa Fe, Tano and Tewa Indians had built a pueblo right over the former governor's palace. Work details of the newly restored colonists huddled in the cold against its lower walls. With picks and crowbars, they broke openings through the adobe for doors and windows, covering them with hides and skins and crowding their families into tight corners out of the icy wind and snow. Despite his largesse in assigning one or two mute, fearful Indian women and children to bring water and firewood to their families, many returnees harbored deep animosity toward their conceited, lisping governor.

Diego de Vargas had brushed aside the counsel of experienced New Mexicans who voted against moving the recolonizing caravan out of El Paso as late as

October, predicting it could not possibly reach Santa Fe before winter closed in. They had been right.

The trek of over a thousand people of all ages, with their livestock and household goods, had lasted the entire fall of 1693. It reversed the exodus of 1680 but had proven equally traumatic, as wagon axles broke, herds strayed, and provisions ran low. The camino real, alternately washed out or overgrown, had tested their will every league of the way. Don Diego, his officers, and members of the cabildo, along with the eighteen blue-robed Franciscans, tried keeping spirits up with frequent hymns and vows to La Conquistadora, the much-venerated little statue of the Virgin Mary they were returning in a chapel on wheels to her throne in Santa Fe.[19]

Children and babies died of malnutrition and exposure in the encampment outside the walls of Santa Fe, while their parents endured endless, numbing days of negotiations between Governor Vargas and the increasingly obdurate Pueblo Indians inside. More than once, however, it appeared that fighting could be avoided. Indian leaders had allowed Vargas and his captains to inspect the ruined chapel of San Miguel, but they objected to reroofing it in midwinter as a home for La Conquistadora. They suggested instead that the large kiva jutting out like the base of a tower from a corner of the first plaza be converted into a temporary Christian church.

Vargas had liked the idea. He entered the structure through the trap door and descended the ladder into the dimness. If the Indians would whitewash the interior —a suggestion that there might have been kiva murals—break open a door through the wall, and construct an altar of adobes, the Spanish governor saw no reason why the building should not serve. Fray José Díez, a founder of the missionary college at Querétaro and one of its eight volunteers for the recolonization of New Mexico, also liked the idea.

But Díez, assigned to Santa Fe as priest, had overstepped his authority. Fray Salvador de San Antonio, aged and ailing Franciscan custos who had ministered in New Mexico as early as the 1660s, disapproved vehemently. "He said mass could not be celebrated there," Vargas later reported to Viceroy Galve, "because it had been the place of their idolatries and diabolical gatherings for their dances." Other reasons the old friar kept to himself. Unwilling to waste time arguing, don Diego arranged to use another room "a musket-shot's distance from the villa." Still, he wanted the last word.

> I did, however, tell the father that the main cathedrals of Spain had been Moorish mosques. . . . He said in reply that they had driven off the Moors so that those mosques could be churches. I responded that there was a big difference, because those [Indians] who were living nearby were Christians, and the reverend father had absolved them . . . and their children had been baptized in 1692.[20]

The battle had erupted on December 29 and 30, 1693. As Governor Vargas told it, Spaniards, provoked beyond endurance, joined by 140 Pecos fighting men, stormed the snow-covered houseblocks. They burned the main gate, raised ladders on the walls, and occupied one plaza and then the next, engaging the defenders in a hard-fought, room-by-room assault. When Vargas entered the stronghold, he noted with rage that residents had broken to bits the holy cross in the main plaza and hacked with macanas a little statue of the Virgin Mary. He prayed that his hard-hearted sentence would take the fight out of the Pueblo resisters, but it did not.

No year of the Pueblo-Spanish war, with the possible exception of 1680, turned as bloody as 1694. Thanks to the unfailing don Bartolomé de Ojeda, the Keres of San Felipe, Santa Ana, and Zia kept their vows of obedience. The dominant Pecos faction led by don Juan de Ye, and the Tewas of Tesuque, mostly because of their proximity to Santa Fe, also allied themselves with the recolonizers.

The rest of the Pueblo world fought back. Abandoning their communities in the valleys, thousands of them chose displacement, carrying possessions and food to the top of steep-sided mesas, where they restored old fortified defensive sites. From these they swept down in guerrilla raids and dared the Spaniards and their weak-willed allies to dislodge them.

Accepting the dares, Vargas campaigned almost without rest. On a hot July day, he ordered Sebastián Rodríguez, his African herald, to beat the drum in the villa's two plazas and proclaim another military action. Because of previous hostilities, the colonists had been unable to plant in the spring, and food supplies were all but exhausted. A month earlier, the two hundred or so new recruits gathered in Mexico City, including the three Frenchmen, had reached Santa Fe with fray Francisco Farfán. The resultant crowding had caused bad feelings. Not only did the midsummer operation promise captured maize and other foodstuffs, but also temporary relief of the pressures inside close-built Santa Fe.

The noisy column moved out on Wednesday, July 21: ninety presidial soldiers, most enlisted by don Diego from the mining towns of northern New Spain; thirty New Mexican militiamen; a trio of Franciscan chaplains; muleteers, cooks, and drovers. Not until the next day did Governor Vargas share with his officers their objective—the formidable Jemez refugee pueblo of Ahtiolequa.

Vargas counted on surprise, knowing the Jemez would not expect his forces back in the field so soon after a recent raid on Taos Pueblo. Before noon on Thursday, they entered the abandoned pueblo of Santo Domingo, where they rested. An Indian courier delivered a letter to Vargas from Ojeda:

> Lord governor, my compadre,
>
> I advise your lordship that yesterday morning many Navajo Apaches, Tewas, and people from Cochiti and Jemez attacked Zia. They killed four

of us, and we killed one of them, a Jemez captain. Nothing more; may God
keep your lordship for many years as I wish.

Bartolomé de Ojeda[21]

The Keres were split, with a faction of Cochiti under Antonio Malacate and
most of Santo Domingo joining the Jemez in active resistance. As the Spanish
horsemen and field train crossed the shallow Rio Grande, Ojeda met them and
expressed to Vargas his gratitude that the Spaniards had come so quickly to avenge
the attack on Zia. The Keres leader swore to rally the men of San Felipe, Santa
Ana, and Zia for the coming assault.

On Friday after food and rest at Santa Ana, the column formed up again by 4:00
P.M. and advanced along the banks of the Jemez River. A storm raging over toward
the Jemez pueblos helped conceal their approach. About seven o'clock, they were
outside Zia. Here, in council with Ojeda and other Keres war captains, don Diego
learned of a second steep trail up the north face of the promontory and decided to
divide his forces. Capt. Eusebio de Vargas (no relation to the governor), accompanied by twenty-five Spanish soldiers and a hundred-plus men of Zia and Santa Ana,
would climb this back way to the top. The rest of the Spaniards and the Keres of
San Felipe were to go directly to the abandoned pueblo of Pahtoqua on the mesa
below and ascend the main trail from there.

Around 1:00 A.M. on Saturday the twenty-fourth, Eusebio de Vargas and his
Keres auxiliaries split off in the dark. The main column waited in anxious silence
behind a hill until the morning star appeared. Passing by deserted Pahtoqua, still
apparently unseen by Jemez scouts, don Diego and a small party halted at the bot-
tom of the narrow trail as the rest moved on in semidarkness. Sgto. mayor and captain of the Santa Fe presidio Antonio Jorge led the charge up the trail, despite the
rain of arrows and rocks. Eusebio de Vargas and the men of Zia and Santa Ana
were already on top. Caught between two swarms of invaders, the Jemez scattered,
many taking refuge in the pueblo's stone building.

Seeing that no Jemez could escape down the main trail, Governor Vargas
climbed up to find both his divisions assaulting the houses, where, in his words,
the Jemez were "defending themselves with great bravery." The attackers set fire
to whatever would burn. When a Jemez and an Apache were captured and ordered
shot, the latter asked to be baptized. Fray Juan de Alpuente, who always volunteered for chaplain duty, obliged, baptizing both before their execution.

It was now past noon. While his troops secured Ahtiolequa room by room, the
exultant don Diego went back down to Pahtoqua, ordering the 361 captive Jemez
women and children to be brought along. By four o'clock, the battle was over.

So full were the storerooms of Ahtiolequa that it would take the women and
young girls nine days to carry down and shell the tons of dried maize. In addition,

the attackers confiscated 172 head of sheep, some horses, and countless spoils. Vargas made sure his Keres allies received their fair share of everything, thanking and praising everyone. Looking up from the river below and marveling at the near impregnability of Ahtiolequa, the Spaniards beheld their victory as a miracle.

Three years later, bidding for knighthood in the Military Order of Santiago, don Diego recalled in a letter to son-in-law Ignacio López de Zárate the great triumph of July 24, 1694, eve of the glorious feast of "the patron saint and universal advocate of the armies and kingdoms of Spain, the Apostle Santiago." But his bid failed, not for lack of valor but because López de Zárate procrastinated in presenting it and two of Vargas's mortal enemies turned thumbs down.[22]

Later in 1694, Governor Vargas struck a calculated bargain with the Jemez survivors of Ahtiolequa. He would return their women and children on condition that they joined forces with him to assault Black Mesa, symbol and citadel of Tewa and Tano resistance. They kept their part and so did don Diego. By such pragmatic diplomacy and violence, Diego de Vargas presided over the last phase of the Pueblo-Spanish war. He did not, however, win the hearts and minds of the Jemez people.

Texas veteran fray Francisco de Jesús María Casañas could feel their animosity two years later. Another of the Querétaro volunteers, the pensive Casañas had been installed at the mission of San Diego de los Jemez on one of Vargas's inspection tours. As rumors of new Pueblo rebellions circulated in the spring of 1696, he had withdrawn to Bernalillo and joined in the friars' debate about what was worth dying for. Was it true martyrdom, which advanced the Christian faith, or stupidity to accept blindly the risk of death from insolent apostates? "If they say that not all of the pueblos are bad, that some are peaceful, like the one that I administer," fray Francisco offered, "I say that when the occasion arrives . . . as when they crucified Jesus Christ . . . if anything is expected of them, it will be manifest deceit." Yet if ordered to return, he vowed, "I am very ready to obey and to give up my life if necessary for the salvation of souls and to carry out my holy obligation."[23]

Necessary or not, when Jemez, Tanos, and Tewas erupted in early June 1696, five Franciscans, including Casañas, and twenty-one colonists died at their hands. "In the pueblo of San Diego de Jemez," reported Custos fray Francisco de Vargas, "they killed the apostolic father preacher fray Francisco de Jesús," along with a Spanish militia captain, three adults, and three children. Soldiers who fought their way into the pueblo several weeks later found that the missionary's body "had been consumed by animals, but they gathered some of the bones, which they carried away and buried in the church at Zia."[24] As protomartyr of the college of Querétaro, the fastidious fray Francisco de Jesús María was eulogized by pious chroniclers as the ideal missionary.[25]

The revolt of 1696 also tore at the entrails of the once-formidable fortress pueblo of Pecos, the only other Towa-speaking community besides those of the Jemez. Seeking to incite the acknowledged rebel faction at Pecos, the elders of San Diego de los Jemez dispatched Luis Cunixu with a trophy proclaiming the death of Father Casañas, the Franciscan's "eight-sided gilded brass reliquary containing various relics, among them a piece of wood of the cross and an ecce homo." But Cunixu and the Tewa agitator who accompanied him walked right into a trap set by the pro-Spanish governor of Pecos, don Felipe Chistoe, with prior approval of Diego de Vargas.

Feigning sympathy for the cause, Chistoe invited the two tlatoleros, their leading Pecos sympathizers, and enough trusted representatives of his own faction to join him in a Pecos kiva to take counsel about the uprising. Pecos cacique Diego Umbiro, "old and principal personage of this nation," spoke in favor. The Indians who had rebelled were their brothers. To kill Spaniards was good. Spaniards were, after all, "of a different flesh. . . . And the rest of his following, Cachina and the others, answered in like manner."

What Chistoe was about to do, the equivalent of murder at the altar of a Christian cathedral, betrayed the intensity of Pecos factionalism. It also set his pueblo on a 140-year downward spiral to eventual abandonment. He stood and, raising his governor's staff for all to see, exclaimed gravely, "Here we are the king's men!" On that signal, Chistoe's men leapt up and overpowered the five leaders of the opposition, hanging four of them in the act. The fifth, a younger man known as Caripicado ("Pockface"), escaped, only to be shot dead by Chistoe some weeks later.

As evidence of his purge, Chistoe and a Pecos delegation appeared at the governor's palace in Santa Fe with Caripicado's severed head, hand, and foot. "All the citizens of the villa saw them," dictated Governor Vargas, "marveling at the loyalty of this Indian. I thanked him and gave him a gift, as well as the others."[26] It did not occur to the Spanish governor that Chistoe's "loyalty" might have been more self-serving, more the case of a native leader consolidating his sway over the Pecos people. Vargas would hardly have cared. Either way, the result served Spanish ends.

No less determined than in 1680, the Pueblo Indians who took the lives of friars and colonists in 1696 saw whatever advantage they had gained lost to disunity. Fighting lasted until year's end, but Governor Vargas, relying on bravado, unforgiving diplomacy, and the toughness of combined Hispano-Pueblo field units, at last prevailed. Most of the resisters came down off the mesas and resumed life in their old pueblos.

Although the majority of Pueblo Indians had been, in the rhetoric of Diego de Vargas, "reconquered" in this third and final stage of the Pueblo-Spanish war, they did not assimilate, disperse, or wither. They rode out the trauma and, despite the Spaniards' will to dominion, kept themselves culturally more Pueblo than Hispanic.

Restored kiva, Pecos National Historical Park. By Fred E. Mang, Jr. *Courtesy of Pecos National Historical Park.*

The colonists, meanwhile, clamored for greater security. Few who survived the constant food rationing, fighting, hard winters, and sickness of the mid-1690s wanted to stay in isolated New Mexico. Yet the risks associated with desertion were so great that not many tried it. Prominent New Mexico-born citizens like Sgto. mayor Francisco de Anaya Almazán, sixty, nostalgic, and married for the third time, pieced their lives back together; they accepted offices and revalidated land grants—and discriminated against post-1693 immigrants, most of whom cursed the place.

From their first day, all the newcomers were forced to endure wartime conditions. They had arrived in three waves: Vargas's rough, mixed-blood recruits for the Santa Fe presidio in 1693; the intermarried, sixty-odd artisan families of *españoles mexicanos* who came in June 1694; and another forty-four alleged families of castas thrown together in the vicinity of Zacatecas by the governor's agent Juan Páez Hurtado and escorted by him to Santa Fe in May 1695. The previous month Governor Vargas had tried to make room for the latter group by moving the españoles mexicanos twenty miles north to the new villa of Santa Cruz de la Cañada; this had set in motion the uprising of 1696. Now the citizens of Santa Cruz begged for a safer, more compatible site.

Appealing to Viceroy Galve's successor late in July 1696, Vargas reminded the central government that recruitment for New Mexico's recolonization had fallen 276 families short of the 500 he required. He wanted instant replacements for 58 deceased soldiers and male colonists. Better, he urged, send 200 men, from jails if necessary, each with two riding mules; 200 harquebuses; 4,000 flints and lead; 2,000 head of mature cattle; and 3,000 fanegas of maize. In one respect, the 1696 revolt served the colony. It roused authorities in Mexico City who, aware of recent English and French gains in North America, unanimously rejected another withdrawal to El Paso.

Although the ailing Conde de Galve, Vargas's friend, had retired early in 1696 and would die upon reaching Spain, the interim viceroy, Bishop Juan de Ortega Montañés, also knew and esteemed don Diego. His fiscal, don Baltasar de Tovar, reviewed the appropriate laws in the *Recopilación* and endorsed all Vargas's actions to date in suppressing the revolt. Tovar also cautioned him not to embark on new conquests, but instead to defend the existing Spanish communities of Santa Fe, Santa Cruz, and Bernalillo. Although replacements for the fallen presidial soldiers would be provided, Vargas could not count on more colonists at government expense.[27]

Don Diego, who regularly styled himself "restorer, reconqueror, and settler here," waited daily for news of honors from Spain. Through agents in Mexico City, he tried to block assignment of a successor until he had received word of a promotion. Under Galve, he might have succeeded, but the next viceroy, the Conde de Moctezuma y Tula, did not know him.

If lower-born don Pedro Rodríguez Cubero carried to New Mexico no grudge against the strutting reconqueror, he found cause for one immediately. Don Diego, compelled to turn over the governorship to his legally appointed successor in July 1697, allegedly connived to obstruct an orderly transition. Even though he had already been in office sixteen months longer than his allotted five-year term, Vargas believed that by right of conquest the colony belonged to him until the crown rewarded him with reappointment or a better post.

Still, Rodríguez Cubero held the upper hand. Many vocal colonists already hated don Diego and his privileged circle. Others recognized that don Pedro now wielded the life-and-death authority of governor and readily answered summons to testify against Vargas. As charges of graft, favoritism, misgovernment, and immorality mounted, Rodríguez Cubero dared place the reconqueror under house arrest, seizing his personal belongings and selling them at public auction. "My slaves, mules, and clothing, and even that of the members of my household have been sold," the disbelieving Vargas protested.[28]

His confinement dragged on for nearly three years, from October 1697 to July 1700. Don Diego, scion of the house of Vargas of Madrid, languished five months in leg irons. "I am as good as dead," he scrawled to his son-in-law on pages torn from a book and smuggled out of Santa Fe in 1699. In reality, Diego de Vargas had five more years.[29]

He would live to put his accounts in order and defend himself in Mexico City. Blacklisted by the Order of Santiago, New Mexico's restorer would receive the greater honor of a noble title of Castile—first Marqués de la Nava de Barcinas, a consummation that had eluded both Juan de Oñate and Francisco Vázquez de Coronado. Another friend of the family, the Duque de Alburquerque, viceroy from 1702 to 1711, would exonerate Diego de Vargas and expedite his reappointment as governor and captain general of New Mexico.

He would also suffer the greatest grief of his life when his dashing son and heir to his title, cavalry Capt. Juan Manuel de Vargas Pimentel, who had ventured to New Spain to know his father, died of a respiratory illness on the return voyage. Don Diego himself would die in April 1704, in his sixty-first year, campaigning against Faraón Apaches in the middle Rio Grande Valley, ten thousand miles from home. The proud campaigner succumbed not to wounds inflicted by the enemy, as he might have preferred, but seemingly to dysentery.[30]

Born in Spain in 1670, Capt. Juan Mateo Manje heard in Sonora about the unexpected death of New Mexico's reconqueror. In 1692, the well-educated young Manje, summoned from Spain by his uncle, Gen. Domingo Jironza, had carried Carlos II's decree offering don Domingo knighthood in one of the three military orders and reappointment to the governorship of New Mexico. But Viceroy Galve had already set Diego de Vargas en route to El Paso; Jironza therefore accepted appointment as alcalde mayor and military governor of Sonora. When he assumed his new post at the real of San Juan Bautista in 1693, his nephew had stood at his side.

Since then, Captain Manje, Jironza's lieutenant alcalde mayor, had become the assigned military companion and trusted friend of missionary explorer Eusebio Francisco Kino. Together, they had made nine expeditions. Manje lauded the Jesuit. Reporting in 1702 how Kino had spread word of the Roman Catholic faith far across Pimería Alta, Manje vouched for the accuracy of his maps and descriptions of the country and its peoples. The captain had seen the livestock ranches Father Kino boasted of. "To all this I can testify as an eyewitness during the past nine years," Manje insisted, "when I accompanied his Reverence on various explorations."

> On each of these expeditions with his Reverence, I traveled from 200 to 300 leagues, or a total of 3,100 leagues, as is more fully evident from the diaries, notes, and reports which both Father Kino and I compiled. . . . I can testify . . . that the said Pimas, numbering more than 16,000 . . . have been progressively won over to the obedience of his Majesty. They live along good rivers and valleys, where they cultivate productive and fertile lands. Four missions were recently added to the one founded originally. The Pimas' territory borders on the Gulf of California, which I reached at three different points.[31]

Not everyone praised Kino. After the congenial Christmas inspection by Father Visitor Juan María Salvatierra in 1690, half a dozen more Jesuits, mostly non-Spaniards, had come to labor in Pimería Alta; none but Father Agustín de Campos had stayed. In October 1694, after orienting idealistic young Francisco Javier Saeta, a Sicilian, and supplying him with animals and provisions, Kino had personally installed the new priest at Caborca, 110 miles straight west of mission Dolores, where Kino had his own residence. He told Saeta how close the seashore lay and about his plans for building a boat.

Eager to parry the rumors that arid Pimería Alta was uninhabitable and its Native peoples were as indomitable as Apaches, Kino started for Mexico City late in 1694. General Jironza, however, who now orchestrated warfare from the west against enemies he already knew well from his El Paso years—Jocomes, Janos, Sumas, and Apaches—asked the influential Jesuit not to go. As peacemaker and provider of Pima auxiliaries, Father Kino, in Jironza's estimation, was more valuable than an entire presidio. Bloody raids by soldiers and armed citizens accompanied by Pima and Opata bowmen had occasioned strikes by hostile bands and vice versa throughout 1694, and no end was in sight. Jironza asked for Kino's help.

On Good Friday, April 1, 1695, Saeta dashed off a warning to Kino that a

Jocome war party had assaulted mission San Pedro de Tubutama in the valley of the Río Altar fifty miles northwest of Dolores. Father Daniel Januske had survived by being absent, but two of his servants and other Indians had not. Unknown to Saeta, the violence had escalated. Aggrieved Pimas now rose at Tubutama; they murdered Father Januske's Opata mission overseers and, inciting relatives as they went, surged toward Caborca.

They shot Saeta repeatedly with arrows, a cruel, unknowing play on his name, which meant *arrow,* and for several months Pimería Alta echoed with the cries of revolt. Once Father Kino and Lieutenant Manje had reassured enough of the Pima leaders that they were safe again in their rancherías, the Jesuit set about writing an impassioned biography of Father Saeta and defense of the Pima missions.[32]

As his detractors inside and outside the Society of Jesus worked to remove Kino from Pimería Alta, the embattled missionary gained an audience in Mexico City with Viceroy Galve, who was about to retire and to whom he presented a copy of the Saeta biography. Another went by mail to the Jesuit general, Father Tirso González, in Rome. Kino wrote persuasively of imperial expansion, of productive Pimería Alta missions supplying a renewed occupation of California, of access from the southwest to the apostate Hopi pueblos, and of new discoveries. He thoroughly convinced Galve. But it was the Jesuit general's unconditional endorsement that rocked Kino's critics.

Writing three letters from Rome on July 28, 1696, Father González lectured Juan de Palacios, the Society's new provincial in Mexico City. "The rebellion of the Pimas, in which Father Francisco Javier Saeta met with such a glorious death," González admonished, "would cause us to fear for the very existence of those new missions if we listened to the gloomy reports of some persons." These doomsayers claimed the Pimas were of unstable character, hated the missionaries, and refused to settle in civilized communities, and now they had conspired to recall Father Kino to a desk job at provincial headquarters.

González would have none of it. Kino's success in Pimería Alta, where he had toiled "with untiring zeal and boundless enthusiasm," had been so great that Palacios was to permit him to return immediately, unless the California enterprise again beckoned. The Jesuit general then reviewed and dismissed the only two charges brought against Kino.

> The first is that, carried away by his enthusiasm and zeal, he is superficial in his work, hurrying as he does from one task to another. It is said that he baptizes the natives without sufficient instruction in their obligations as Christians. If we consider how much Saint Francis Xavier attempted in such a short span of time, we must admit that saints use quite a different yardstick from the one applied with such caution by ordinary mortals; for them the might of God

has no limits. I am convinced that, if superiors do point out some specific
fault to Father Kino, he will amend it and follow their instructions.

Just as forcefully, the general demolished the second charge, that Kino was
"excessively severe on his fellow workers." That simply did not accord with the
data reaching Rome. No one had ever complained about him before. "There is
scarcely anyone in all the foreign missions," González continued, "who speaks with
greater deference and respect of other missionaries." No one showed greater kindness than Father Kino. Since neither count held up, Palacios was to put Kino back
in the Pima field. "You will let him work there, inasmuch as 'the just man is not
to be hemmed in by any law.' I am convinced," concluded the Jesuit general, "that
Kino is a chosen instrument of Our Lord for His cause in those missions."[33]

But Kino never let go of California. On his busy 1695–96 map, "Theater of the
Apostolic Labors of the Society of Jesus in North America," which identified settlements from Mexico City north to New Mexico but featured mainly the Jesuits'
northwest missionary empire, the painstaking cartographer drew the Californias as
one giant island, narrow at its southern tip but swelling greatly northward to latitudes beyond Cape Mendocino and on around an imaginary, ragged north end. A
long, slender strait, the Sea of the Californias, separated it from the mainland.

Early in 1697, Juan María Salvatierra had word from the viceregal government
that the Jesuits' offer to repossess California in the king's name, financing the entire
enterprise themselves, had been accepted. Already en route south to join Salvatierra
in the new California enterprise, Kino was overtaken by a courier with a letter
from Father Provincial Palacios, who wrote, "The Señor Viceroy has requested
me to leave your Reverence with your dear Pimas, and so you must care for them,
because in other places they fear a general uprising." Jironza had raised such a
clamor over Kino's reassignment that Viceroy Moctezuma had intervened. Father
Salvatierra, rather than wait any longer for the designated substitute, shoved off for
California in mid-October 1697 alone.[34]

Not quite alone. Also aboard the slim, shallow-draft galliot *Santa Elena* were
nine men and a boy; crates, bundles, and bags; two stanchion-mounted, smooth-
bore swivel guns; a statue of Our Lady of Loreto; and a few head of sheep, goats,
and pigs. A third of the way up Baja California's long inside coast, they put in near
the ruins of Kino's San Bruno and dragged their gear across the beach up onto a
rise, the future site of the presidio and community of Loreto.

The Natives were curious. Word spread that the strangers had food, and for
several weeks the crowd grew, until one day Salvatierra and his tiny force found
themselves fighting off several hundred arrow-shooting, rock-throwing California
Indians. Failing to overrun the makeshift compound and the deadly swivel guns,
the attackers faded away at sunset.

Despite so unpromising a revival, the Society of Jesus would cling to and expand its corporate hold on Baja California for another seventy years. Drawing on a well-managed endowment established by Salvatierra and Father Juan de Ugarte—the notable, enduring Pious Fund of the Californias—they met all expenses, choosing and paying officials, soldiers, and colonists who knowingly came to work for the missionaries.[35]

On the mainland, Father Kino redoubled his efforts to aid his friend Salvatierra. Driving cattle south for weeks and shipping them across to Loreto, however, would cost a fortune. There had to be an alternative. Overland Native trade in lustrous abalone shells, the kind Kino had collected only on California's Pacific coast, suggested that the Californias might not be an island after all. If a land passage existed, he vowed to find it. When Salvatierra returned to the mainland early in 1700 to establish a closer port at Guaymas, he rode on north nearly two hundred miles to Dolores, arriving with an escort of California Indians and a banner of Our Lady of Loreto.

The desert northwest of Caborca was ablaze in early March with so many wildflowers, Kino rejoiced, "that it seemed as if nature had placed them there to welcome Our Lady of Loreto." At the outset, the caravan proceeded in vociferous anticipation. "Almost all day, we were saying and chanting various prayers and praises of Our Lady in different languages—in Castilian, in Latin, in Italian," even in a California tongue. Two weeks of waterless, spiny terrain, rock-strewn wastes, and sand dunes silenced everyone. But they made the coast above today's Puerto Peñasco, recited a blessing, and looked across at California. To the north, the mountains on both sides of the water seemed to converge, but a ridge obstructed the view.

The party split. Manje went south with the played-out animals and thus missed the climax. Scrambling with the banner up a rocky peak above their campsite at sunset, the two priests cried out in exultation at the vista, embraced, and "sang the Lauretanian Litanies to Our Lady as a sign of thanksgiving." Clearly, they could see "that the half arch of sierras of California whose end had been concealed from us by the spur of the mountains kept getting constantly closer together and joining with other hills and peaks of New Spain."

Kino was back exploring before the end of the year, this time riding south along the east bank of the Colorado River toward the head of the gulf with his Pima entourage through the country of Yuma and Quíquima peoples. When his only non-Indian servant ran away in fear, the fifty-five-year-old black robe kept on. His greatest thrill this time was crossing the Colorado seated in a big, watertight basket on a raft pushed by Quíquima swimmers to meet Natives on the California side. He remembered floating across "very comfortably and pleasantly, without the least risk, taking with me only my Breviary, some trifles, and a blanket in which to sleep, afterwards wrapping up some branches of broom weed in my bandanna to serve me as a pillow." In 1702, he descended to the Colorado River delta and watched the sun rise over an expanse of tidewater at the head of the gulf. Plainly, the Californias were not an island.[36]

As he challenged that huge myth, Father Kino perpetuated a lesser one. Happily but erroneously, he blamed the Protestant Francis Drake for popularizing California's insularity. His Jesuit brethren, congratulating Kino, shared in the fun. Crowing from the Tarahumara missions, Father Visitor Wenceslaus Eymer proclaimed, "Away now with British temerity, with her English Drake, and let him keep silent who boasts that he has circumnavigated California, as if, by a foolish fiction, California were the Atlantis of the West."[37]

Father Kino did not live to see a single cow or letter delivered safely across his perilous land passage to Salvatierra in Baja California, nor did the Spanish crown ever implement his proposal, seconded by Manje, to found a Spanish villa at the junction of the Gila and Colorado rivers—where Yuma, Arizona, now sprawls. Nevertheless, he contributed signally to a clearer knowledge of North America's geography.

On maps he drew between 1701 and 1710, Lower California began to reshape itself as an elongated but still too bulky peninsula, greater in length than Italy; Upper California hove firmly to the mainland. Significant islands, among them Tiburón and Angel de la Guarda, appeared in the Gulf of California. West of the Continental Divide, the Jesuit was first to trace the Gila-Colorado drainage in easily recognizable detail, which enabled him to put the Rio Grande in proper perspective and direct its flow southeastward toward the Gulf of Mexico. Kino's cartography also helped remove from European maps the mythical kingdoms writ randomly across terra incognita since Coronado's time.[38]

But maps, he insisted, meant less to him than souls. As missionary contact man for his Christian faith, Father Kino excelled, so much so that Roman Catholic churchmen at the turn of the twenty-first century, following Father General González's ancient lead, are pursuing his cause for sainthood. A restless, charismatic man, Kino chose to serve on frontiers, lavishing material gifts, preaching, and glorying in the awe he saw reflected in the Natives' eyes. "And I showed them on the map of the world," he exulted,

> how the Spaniards and the Faith had come by sea to Vera Cruz, and had gone into Puebla and to Mexico, Guadalaxara, Sinaloa, Sonora, and now to . . . Dolores del Cosari, in the land of the Pimas, where there were already many persons baptized, a house, a church, bells, images of saints, plentiful supplies, wheat, maize, and many cattle and horses; that they could go and see it all, and even ask at once their relatives, my servants, who were with me. They listened with pleasure to these and other talks concerning God,

heaven, and hell, told me that they wished to be Christians, and gave me some infants to baptize.[39]

Crowding around him, the Quíquimas of the lower Colorado marveled especially at the vestment he wore while celebrating mass, "at its fine embroidery representing Spring, and its skillfully woven flowers of different beautiful colors; and they would ask us to keep it on so that those who continually came to visit us might have the pleasure of seeing it."[40]

He knew the importance of first impressions and how pervasively news spread. "Hence," he cautioned, "it is so imperative not to offend or displease any one of them." Natives, even at great distances, asked about a missionary, "inquiring what he does, what he says, what he gives, what he carries with him, what he teaches, how he speaks, and so on." On this basis, they decided which of the priests was good or generous and which one they would take their children to for baptism. "On journeys to very distant regions," related Kino admiringly, "I was met by Indians I had never seen; they would come up to me and say that they already knew me. That would happen to me even as I kept traveling farther from home."[41]

Back at mission Dolores, there was always something going on. By driving livestock, making adobes, planning for new explorations, or receiving Native delegations from other parts, Kino succeeded in keeping his mission Indians busy and bound up in his vision. Different challenges faced missionaries at a second- or third-generation reduction on a stagnant frontier, cursed by persistent and repugnant Native practices, epidemics, high infant mortality, and runaways. Kino, herald of Christian paternalism, recognized his advantage. "Many of these poor people," he observed,

> despite their humble condition, on seeing and experiencing kind treatment will come to rely on the missionary with deep attachment, sharing with him the best of their possessions and food. Gradually they will place themselves and their families at the disposal of the missionary. These newly converted Christians, with striking simplicity and with less reluctance than other Indians and older Christians, hold in high esteem and awe what they had not heard before, such as the more extraordinary doctrines of our faith: for example, the resurrection of the dead, the never-ending torture of hell for the wicked, the ever-lasting happiness of heaven given in reward to the good, the divine creation of the universe—all men, the sun, moon, heaven, earth, and all else.[42]

By the turn of the eighteenth century, New Spain's far northern frontier had come into clearer focus. Reconquered by force of arms, New Mexico no longer stood alone. Precedents had been set in Texas on the eastern flank. To the west, Kino and Manje were putting Pimería Alta on the map, as Salvatierra hung on in

Eusebio Francisco Kino's culminating 1710 map showing Baja California as a peninsula. Bibliothèque Nationale, Paris. *From Kessell,* Friars, Soldiers, and Reformers.

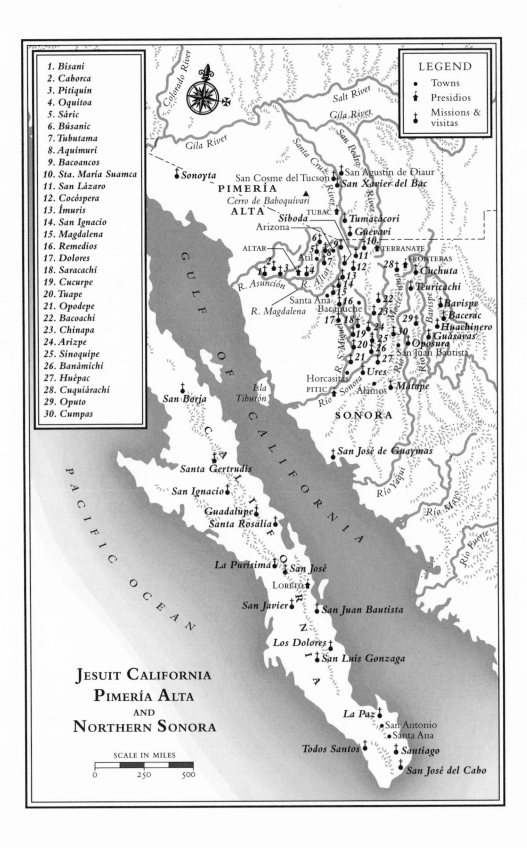

Legend
- Towns
- Presidios
- Missions & visitas

1. Bisani
2. Caborca
3. Pitiquín
4. Oquitoa
5. Sáric
6. Búsanic
7. Tubutama
8. Aquimuri
9. Bacoancos
10. Sta. María Suamca
11. San Lázaro
12. Cocóspera
13. Ímuris
14. San Ignacio
15. Magdalena
16. Remedios
17. Dolores
18. Saracachi
19. Cucurpe
20. Tuape
21. Opodepe
22. Bacoachi
23. Chinapa
24. Arizpe
25. Sinoquipe
26. Banámichi
27. Huépac
28. Cuquiárachi
29. Oputo
30. Cumpas

Colorado River
Salt River
Gila River
Gila River
Santa Cruz River
San Pedro

Sonoyta
PIMERÍA
ALTA
Cerro de Baboquívari
Arizona
Síboda
ALTAR
Atil
R. Asunción
R. Altar
Santa Ana
R. Magdalena
Bacapuche

San Cosme del Tucson
San Agustín de Oiaur
San Xavier del Bac
TUBAC
Tumacácori
Guevavi
TERRANATE
FRONTERAS
Cuchuta
Teuricachi
Bavispe
Bacerac
Huachinero
Guásavas
Oposura
San Juan Bautista
Ures
Horcasitas
PITIC
Río Sonora
Álamos
Matape
SONORA

Río Yaqui
Río Mayo
Río Fuerte

GULF OF CALIFORNIA
Isla Tiburón

San Borja

Santa Gertrudis

San Ignacio

Guadalupe
Santa Rosalía

La Purísima
San José
LORETO
San Javier
San Juan Bautista
Los Dolores
San Luis Gonzaga

PACIFIC OCEAN

San José de Guaymas

La Paz
San Antonio
Santa Ana
Todos Santos
Santiago
San José del Cabo

JESUIT CALIFORNIA
PIMERÍA ALTA
AND
NORTHERN SONORA

SCALE IN MILES
0   250   500

Baja California. And while each of these four nonconnected colonial projections drew personnel and supplies almost exclusively from the south—and initiative from Mexico City—a few interesting if feeble associations began forming between them.

Spaniard Domingo Terán de los Ríos, former first governor of the failed Texas colony, who met Jumano mogul Juan Sabeata in 1691 en route to the Hasinais, led reinforcements from Nueva Vizcaya to Pimería Alta during the rebellion in 1695; he sickened and died there, far west of Sabeata's range.[43] Hasinais and Hopis, widely separated peoples who had rid themselves of Europeans once, became objectives again to outsiders—Spaniards and Frenchmen, Jesuits and Franciscans—whose vying to restore them created linkages.

In 1700, Spain's last Hapsburg, Carlos II, about to die, had named as heir seventeen-year-old Duke Philip of Anjou, second grandson of Louis XIV. That arrangement united Spain and France against England and her continental allies for the duration of hostilities. At war's end in 1713, Felipe V kept his throne on condition that the Bourbon crowns of Spain and France never rest on the same head. In New Spain, meantime, Viceroy Alburquerque looked the other way as French colonials in Louisiana took full advantage of his inattention.

That suited fray Francisco Hidalgo, obsessed with a return to the Hasinais. As Spaniards once again moved among Native woodland peoples in east Texas, their uneasy but beneficial association with French Louisiana deepened. The simultaneous founding of Spanish San Antonio and French New Orleans in 1718, on either side of the Hasinais, gave partisans of both empires easier access to the region.

In contrast, the apostate Hopis' geographical isolation and undesirable environment afforded them greater protection from renewed European intrusion. It hardly mattered that Father Kino sent a cross and letter to them in 1697, "inviting them to our friendship and their reduction, and urging that they reconcile themselves with our Holy Mother Church, returning to our holy faith." He understood that there were Hopi *indios ladinos* who could write in response, but none did.[44]

From the New Mexico side, Governor Rodríguez Cubero, Vargas's interim successor and nemesis, looked westward in 1699, installing Franciscans at the newly designated *congregación* of San José de la Laguna and at Acoma and Zuni. Later that year, the principal Hopi leader Espeleta proposed by messengers to the Spanish governor a peace treaty granting his people freedom to practice their own religion. Softening his diplomacy the following year, Espeleta came to Santa Fe in person with a new offer: if nonresident priests would appear at one pueblo each year for six years, the Hopis would reconvert to Christianity. But Rodríguez Cubero turned a deaf ear.

Evidently, the Hopis were deeply at odds. When the people of Awatovi, farthest east, welcomed absolution and the baptism of their young people by fray Juan

The Hopi pueblo of Walpi, by Ben Wittick, c. 1895. *Courtesy of the Museum of New Mexico, no. 102064.*

de Garaycoechea of Zuni and rebuilt the Franciscan convento in 1700 or 1701, other Hopis exterminated the community. Rodríguez Cubero's expedition to punish them failed utterly. Thus, while Jesuits of Pimería Alta and Franciscans of New Mexico crossed paper swords over the honor of bringing these apostates back into the Christian fold, the independent Hopis, while holding out the prospect from time to time, took counsel on their own terms to bid or not for Spanish aid.[45]

At century's end, on the Gila River above its junction with the Colorado, Lieutenant Manje recorded what he believed was a sighting of the mystical Franciscan nun María de Jesús de Agreda, much as fray Damián Massanet had in east Texas a decade earlier. Father Kino demurred. The widely read Manje appeared fascinated by New Mexico, the colony his uncle Domingo Jironza had twice governed. He had brought chronicles from Mexico City to Sonora with him, and he married into the local branch of the Pérez Granillo family, kin to Diego de Vargas's childless lieutenant governor, Mre. de campo Luis Pérez Granillo. Not only did the cultured Manje recall María de Agreda's miraculous ministry from the 1630 Benavides *Memorial,* but like Vargas in New Mexico, he also had access to the *Mística Ciudad de Dios,* Mother María's life of the Virgin Mary.[46]

Unable to confirm the "monstrosities" described by fray Francisco de Escobar, chaplain on Juan de Oñate's exploration west from New Mexico in 1604 and 1605, Manje and Kino did coax from Yuma oral tradition in 1699 the memory of armored Spanish soldiers on horseback. Their informants, they reckoned, must have been eighty years old. Manje attested,

> And they added (without our having asked them), that, when they were boys, a beautiful white woman, dressed in white, gray, and blue to her feet, with a cloth or veil covering her head, came to their land. Carrying a cross, she spoke to them, shouting and haranguing them in a language they did not understand. The tribes of the Colorado River shot her with arrows and left her for dead twice, but, she, coming back to life, vanishing into the air, without their learning where she lived.[47]

The devil, offered Manje, must have addled their memories. Surely God, who had arranged the greater miracle of María's appearance in such remote parts, would have given her the lesser gift of tongues. Because they had collected essentially the same story five days earlier from Piman-speaking Natives, the two Europeans paid special heed. Rumors had cast the Yumas as fierce cannibals, yet camped among them, they felt perfectly safe. Lieutenant Manje attributed their friendly reception to the influence of the Franciscan nun.

Perhaps, allowed Father Kino. But Jesuits could take care of their own. "Others," he pointed out, "have been of the opinion that the blessed blood of the venerable father Francisco Javier Saeta is fertilizing and ripening these very extensive fields."[48]

8 The Inspector General

I have never seen so much want, misery, and backwardness in my life. I suspect this land was better off before the Spaniards came.

—Gov. Francisco Cuervo y Valdés to the king, Santa Fe, 1705

The soldiers of New Mexico . . . are only sufficiently trained for the Indians and not for other enemies who may not be of this kind, such as may be considered the English, French, or any other foreigners.

—Gov. Manuel San Juan de Santa Cruz
to the viceroy, Parral, December 11, 1719

Duteous, sixty-year-old Brigadier Pedro de Rivera Villalón carried out the first general inspection of New Spain's northern frontier with all the documented authority of later Bourbon reformers but with little of the punch. He rode eight thousand miles and spent three and a half years at it, but he got the job done.[1]

Rivera's tour from 1724 to 1728 demonstrated a dawning awareness among Felipe V's viceroys and their advisers. By the 1720s, they had begun to visualize New Spain's outer marches as a single imperial entity, not merely a scattering of salients pushed up from the south. The peso-pinching, reform-minded Rivera visited twenty-three government-subsidized garrison towns in New Mexico, Pimería Alta, and Texas, as well as in the nearer northern *gobiernos*. He did not inspect the peculiar presidio of Loreto in Baja California, because there Jesuit priests, not soldiers, held sway.

Holding fast to the perverse California peninsula stretched the Jesuits' famed resourcefulness to the limit. Father Juan María de Salvatierra and his successors struggled to mount and supply, through their precarious beachhead at Loreto, a

Indian man and woman, Baja California. After a drawing by missionary Ignacio Tirsch, S. J., 1762–67. Watercolor by Joanne Haskell Crosby. *Courtesy of Harry W. Crosby and the artist.*

missionary offensive to the strong-willed, stone-age Natives of the place, while at the same time they vigorously defended the Society's extraordinary proprietorship. They promised the crown a harbor on the Pacific side, which would serve as a port of haven for the Acapulco-bound Manila galleon; then, with calculated self-interest, they dragged their feet while Salvatierra requested supplemental royal funding to assure the survival of the enterprise.

Demonstrating his rarely shaken resolve, Father Salvatierra rejoiced at the arrival in February 1698 of a half-dozen more volunteers: four Spanish soldiers, a mestizo, and a Yaqui Indian. "These reinforcements," he exulted, "so entirely unexpected, overwhelmed all of us with joy. We encouraged one another, and were ready to do battle with the whole of Hell."

Hell could wait. Previously, another Jesuit had crossed over from the mainland, the conspicuously tall, blond, blue-eyed Sicilian Francisco María Piccolo. Together, the two missionaries drove their helpers to heroic labors and, largely with maize and meat ferried from the opposite shore between storms, attracted some of the curious or hungry Cochimí-speaking California Indians.

Everything the Jesuits did was meant to instruct. When Father Juan María penned a note in the Monquí dialect to Father Francisco María from a few miles away, he purposely first read it aloud to the bearer, a headman named Pablo, then sent him off to Loreto. There, Piccolo read it again before Pablo. According to

A mule driver and his wife deliver cloth to a Baja California mission. After a drawing by missionary Ignacio Tirsch, S. J., 1762–67. Watercolor by Joanne Haskell Crosby. *Courtesy of Harry W. Crosby and the artist.*

Salvatierra, "When he heard the padre, paper in hand, repeating what I had previously said he was amazed. And thus all the Indians became aware of the power of letters."[2]

Such novelties appealed, but it was the constantly steaming iron pots of *atole,* a maize gruel, that brought Native families to Loreto to build walls, clear fields, and observe the black robes' unintelligible ceremonials. More and more of them chose to interrupt their year-round mobility through the parched and spiny mountains and valleys that had previously sustained their lives. They risked the ire of their shamans but, at the same time, made allies of these strange newcomers against old enemies. Infectious diseases, by God's grace, held off for a decade, as Indians came and went. Put simply, the missions offered an alternative.

Some of the Jesuits' imported helpers, meanwhile, suffered disenchantment. Not only was the climate trying but also the missionaries' demands. A person could hardly relieve himself without Salvatierra's permission. The irregular presidio's second captain, Spaniard don Antonio García de Mendoza, a veteran soldier and miner, found his ambitions thwarted. He had not signed up to run errands for two cocksure Italian priests.

García complained to the viceroy. These Jesuits, he charged, forbade any sort of development that would profit the crown (and people like him, he might have added). They pampered mission Indians, sparing the rod, which emboldened other

Natives. Yet, with little concern the two padres regularly ordered small detachments of soldiers out into the hostile countryside to explore or return runaways.
"In order to stop these rash acts," don Antonio fumed,

> I am not able to find any remedy other than to give the story to the Most
> Reverend Father Provincial of the Sacred Company of Jesus, asking that he
> remove from here the two *religiosos* and put them where they will receive
> the punishment they merit, and he may put me in a tower with a strong
> chain [as an example] so that my successors will not allow themselves to be
> led into similar fates.

When García resigned and washed his hands of the peninsula in 1701, seventeen
soldiers went with him, leaving the Jesuits' presidio with a muster of twelve.[3]

It was never easy, but the black robes hung on. By 1721, they had dedicated
nine peninsular missions and another at the supply port of Guaymas on the mainland. But since none of the California establishments was self-sufficient, they represented an ever-greater drag on the mission resources of Pimería Alta, Sonora, and
Sinaloa. Indians in mainland communities, watching so much of their livestock,
grain, and labor flow across the gulf by order of their missionaries, grew resentful,
especially Mayos and Yaquis.[4]

In 1706, Juan de Ugarte, missionary at San Francisco Xavier de Biaundó, deep
in a canyon fifteen miles inland from Loreto, took advantage of forty Native fighting men sent over from the missions of the Río Yaqui and set them to clearing
rocks from fields and building irrigation works. Whether they had volunteered or
not, their dependents and other members of their home communities resented their
absence. Such incidents happened repeatedly. When Yaquis and Mayos finally
united in their ferocious uprising of 1739, a major complaint was the forced export
of food and manpower to California.[5]

Father Salvatierra, even while soliciting government funds and defending Jesuit
authority to hire and fire the captain and soldiers of the presidio at Loreto, always
held up California as a gift from the Society of Jesus to the Spanish crown. If he
was discouraged by the smallpox epidemic of 1709, which carried off half their
converts, or a five-year drought that settled upon the peninsula the same year,
Salvatierra got over it. When a new viceroy, the Marqués de Valero, asked that he
come to Mexico City in 1717 to discuss the California project in person, the old
missionary agreed. Sixty-eight and suffering from kidney stones, he died en route.
The dream of California did not.

Still, Valero put the pressure on. In 1719, while agreeing to unfreeze eighteen
thousand pesos and keep on paying Loreto's twenty-five soldiers, he delighted in
broadcasting a royal decree calling for settlement of California as far north as San
Diego and Monterey. That galvanized Father Juan de Ugarte.

Father Juan de Ugarte. *Courtesy of W. Michael Mathes.*

With superhuman energy, Ugarte and English mariner Guillermo Strafford found lumber in localized mountain stands of white-barked giant poplar and built a ship, *El Triunfo de la Cruz*. Then in 1720, they sailed her up the gulf to the mouth of the Colorado River, reporting, as Father Kino had, that California was not an island. As before, influential people scoffed.[6]

In Pimería Alta, the tireless Kino predeceased his friend Salvatierra. Supply of California weighed on him until the end. Late in 1709, fifteen months before he died, Kino had written to the Jesuit supply officer:

> Father Rector Juan María de Salvatierra gives me to understand that by dis-position of our Father General my principal obligation is to succor California, and I am now sending thither also a goodly quantity of provi-sions and cattle, which is what they are asking of me.[7]

While his pride in the surpluses produced with Pima labor on his own mission and ranches suggests a flourishing agropastoral business, Kino's plans for similar operations in the Santa Cruz Valley of today's southern Arizona had withered. The two young Jesuits who had come to manage San Gabriel de Guevavi and San Francisco Xavier del Bac in 1701 were not as hardy as Kino. They got sick; one withdrew and the other died.

After that, the black robe who kept the Pimas of those orphaned missions on the northward-flowing Río Santa Cruz interested lived one drainage away and a few days south at San Ignacio del Cabórica on the Río Magdalena. He visited them on occasion and they him. He spoke their language better than any other of the white-skinned shamans. Born in Spain, temperamental Father Agustín de Campos had begun his ministry at San Ignacio in 1693 as a twenty-four-year-old Kino pro-tégé and served more than forty years, toward the end of which he suffered a men-tal breakdown. Neither geographer nor cartographer, Campos nevertheless knew the trails.[8]

Just before his mentor died in 1711, Father Campos was the object of a scan-dal that embarrassed them both. He was accused in a paternity suit. Certain of the provincial entrepreneurs who competed with Jesuits—men like Gregorio Alvarez Tuñón y Quiroz—enjoyed any discomfort the missionaries suffered. Others came to their defense. Testifying in writing in June 1710, Capt. Juan de la Riva Salazar, who had profitable dealings with Jesuits in Sonora and California, swore under oath that Campos's supposed, ten- or eleven-year-old son Agustín looked nothing like the missionary. Moreover, according to the witness, the boy was of pure Pima blood. Campos apparently was cleared.[9]

Kino, despite the odds, did not die on the trail. When Father Campos invited him to dedicate a chapel in Magdalena to San Francisco Xavier, Kino's personal patron, the older priest could not refuse. But he was stricken while singing the mass. At age sixty-five, he was painfully arthritic. Campos begged him to rest more comfortably, but he refused. "His death bed, as his bed always," wrote Father Luis Velarde, "consisted of two calfskins for a mattress, two blankets such as the Indian use for covers, and a pack saddle for a pillow."

Charles W. Polzer, S. J., contemplating the mortal remains of Eusebio Francisco Kino, S. J., Magdalena de Kino, Sonora, 1971. By Ed Ronstadt. *Courtesy of Charles W. Polzer.*

Eusebio Francisco Kino breathed his last just after midnight on March 15, 1711.[10] His uncompromising dreams of expansion, although never fully realized, did not expire with him, and his maps endured. In 1711 or 1712, scarcely missing a beat, Campos conveyed to his superiors the Hopis' preference for Jesuits over Franciscans. Yet in 1719, when the cavalier royal decree promulgated by Viceroy Valero bid the Society of Jesus to extend its ministry from Pimería Alta to the land of the Hopis, the black robes were in no position to do so.[11]

Although he never visited Franciscan New Mexico in person, Father Kino delineated the colony on his final map of 1710, dotting the Rio Grande Valley with settlements, among them the villa of Alburquerque, founded only four years earlier in 1706.[12]

Blustery Francisco Cuervo y Valdés, from the Spanish province of Asturias and a knight of the Military Order of Santiago, was a well-traveled, twenty-five-year veteran of the northern frontier when the viceroy Duque de Alburquerque appointed him as New Mexico's interim governor to succeed Diego de Vargas. Cuervo bragged about giving the new villa

> the spiritual and temporal patrons that I have chosen: namely, the ever glorious Apostle of the Indies, San Francisco Xavier, and Your Excellency, with whose names the town has been entitled Villa de Alburquerque de San Francisco Xavier del Bosque.[13]

Even though this verdant stretch of cottonwoods and willows had been known before as the Bosque Grande de San Francisco Xavier, naming New Mexico's newest chartered municipality for so Jesuit a saint cannot have gladdened the Franciscans. Cuervo smiled. Francisco Xavier was his name saint. And he favored Jesuits, having first served in America in Sonora, then among friars as interim governor or governor of Nuevo León, Coahuila, and New Mexico. When he died in Mexico City in 1714, a Jesuit confessor attended him.[14]

Ironically, Cuervo y Valdés had offended the viceroy by his choice. He had founded the town too casually, without prior approval from Mexico City; meanwhile, the Duque de Alburquerque had received royal orders that the next villa incorporated should honor King Felipe V's name saint. Informed of that, confused locals alternated for seventy years between San Felipe and San Francisco Xavier, until finally San Felipe Neri prevailed. In the interim, the governor of adjacent Nueva Vizcaya took advantage of the indecision, naming his new mining villa in 1718 San Felipe el Real de Chihuahua.[15]

Like Diego de Vargas, widower Cuervo y Valdés shared bed and board with a single woman, fathering children out of wedlock with her. Unlike Vargas, who housed his companion comfortably in Mexico City and never brought her to New Mexico, Cuervo met his young lover in Santa Fe.

María Francisca de las Rivas, in her early twenties, was less than half the governor's age. In 1694, she had come to New Mexico as a girl of ten or eleven among the españoles mexicanos, with her parents, brother, and three sisters. During Cuervo's twenty-eight-month tenure in Santa Fe, María Francisca bore him a son, then in 1707, accompanied him back to Mexico City with her parents. There, a year before don Francisco's death, she presented him with a daughter and later sued for a fair share of his estate.[16]

As governor, Cuervo y Valdés did not break with tradition. He damned what his predecessors had done, then set about trying to do the same thing: strengthen the Hispanic community, defend the Pueblo Indians with their help against the surrounding less-settled peoples, entice the Hopis, turn a profit, and enhance his reputation. His deeply felt need to win regular royal appointment set him on a highly visible course.

Throughout the Pueblo-Spanish war of the 1680s and 1690s, Athapaskan-speaking groups of Apaches, including Navajos, had struck ever more frequently at the preoccupied farming and ranching peoples of the valleys. Cuervo meant to reverse the trend. In late summer 1705, the governor incited a force of presidial soldiers under slim, dark-complexioned Capt. Roque Madrid, the most battle-tested leader in the colony, backed by more than a hundred Pueblo auxiliaries, to penetrate the fastness of Navajo country northwest of Santa Fe. They won a bloody encounter, took women and children captive, tore up and burned maize in the field, and forcibly restored apostate Pueblo Indian refugees. Another strike followed, and Navajos took heed.[17]

At the same time, however, Shoshonean-speaking Utes and Comanches intruded—Great Basin peoples migrating south and east to the plains in pursuit of horses. Ute traders and war parties had entered northern New Mexico before 1680, but the earliest surviving Spanish mention of Comanches did not appear until 1706, during the term of Cuervo y Valdés. Almost matter-of-fact, it hinted that New Mexicans had met them before. Regardless, no one could have anticipated in 1706 the terror Comanches would someday strike into the hearts of their grandchildren.[18]

Cuervo y Valdés cultivated Pueblo Indians by design. He employed not only their willing war captains and men as allies-at-arms, but also a council of Pueblo leaders to petition for his retention in office. When a messenger arrived in Santa Fe in 1706 from don Lorenzo of Picurís, claiming that he and dozens of his people were being held against their will by the Plains Apaches of El Cuartelejo (literally, The Far District or Barracks), Cuervo organized a rescue party. En route, its members heard the Taos and several bands of Apaches express fears of attack by Utes and Comanches.

The cavalcade of armed horsemen, pack train, and extra mounts, wending north from Santa Fe and east onto the plains in July 1706, mirrored as usual the colony's mixed heredity. In command of the twenty-eight presidial soldiers, dozen militiamen, and one hundred Pueblo Indians rode Sgto. mayor Juan de Ulibarrí, a military man of renown. Born in San Luis Potosí in 1670, Ulibarrí's steady hand and exploits under Vargas during the reconquest had erased the memory of his birth, probably to a mulatto slave woman. Bold actions and the esteem of one's superiors could in special cases lift the burdens of casta status.

The principal Pueblo war captain José Naranjo was an indio ladino at home among Spaniards; he was about the same age as Ulibarrí, in his midthirties, and also seemingly of mixed race. He could converse in many languages. On such fast-moving expeditions, Naranjo's Indian auxiliaries went mounted like everyone else, yet at day's end they made their own camp a little way off.

Mounted Pueblo auxiliaries battle unidentified Apaches, after an eighteenth-century painting on hide, Segesser I, Museum of New Mexico. Detail redrawn by Jerry L. Livingston. *From Kessell,* Kiva, Cross, and Crown.

The participation of tattooed French expatriate Juan de Archibeque, by now an established trader and respected family man in Santa Cruz de la Cañada, signaled Spanish officialdom's continuing concern with rumored French activities on the plains. From Vargas on, New Mexico's governors got the attention of Mexico City by reporting every such rumor.

When the column arrived at El Cuartelejo, Archibeque identified a telling artifact, a long French musket the Apaches claimed they had taken recently from a bald white man and his pregnant wife, both of whom they had killed. In the gestures of the Apaches, as they cursed "other" white men who put guns in the hands of their Pawnee enemies, Spaniards saw the shadowy figures of impious French voyageurs.

But this time they had come to rescue the Picuris. A decade earlier during the troubles of 1696, Vargas had caught up with and forcibly returned only part of the northern Pueblo Indians emigrating in haste to asylum among Plains Apaches. Earlier discontents from Taos had set the precedent. In seasonal Apache farming rancherías dependent on streams north of the Arkansas River, these displaced Pueblo Indians had built little houses in their manner. But now, disillusioned by the idea of permanent adoption by Apaches, a number wanted to go home.

Ulibarrí said don Lorenzo and the families with him wept for joy at the reunion. For whatever reasons, the Cuartelejo Apaches consented to the Pueblos' departure, calling in others from nearby rancherías and from hunting parties; among them was young don Juan Tupatú, son of the late headman Luis Tupatú. Fray Pedro de Mata, the chaplain, counted sixty-two in all, souls who had been lost and "living as apostate slaves."

Although the Apaches were unchurched to Spanish eyes, they wore Christian crosses, medallions, and rosaries from New Mexico. "We knew they were very old," read the campaign journal, "because the crosses are covered with perspiration and the girdles or chamois bags in which they carry them are very grimy and have been repaired." Why, asked the Spaniards, did they bother? They claimed that during battle, when they grew tired, "they remember the great Captain of the Spaniards who is in the heavens and then their weariness leaves them and they feel refreshed."

Whatever members of Ulibarrí's party thought, they left a tall cross set up in the principal Cuartelejo ranchería, presented a baton of authority as chief captain of all the Apachería to a fit young war leader, and took symbolic possession in the name of Felipe V. Concluding the rite, they shouted three times in unison "Long live the king!"—whereupon the royal ensign cleaved the air with his sword in the four cardinal directions and signaled for a salvo. "After throwing up our hats and making other signs of rejoicing, the ceremony came to an end."[19]

Frenchmen were out there, scheming and trading among the tribes. The governors who succeeded Cuervo y Valdés kept hearing the rumors. But even though an expedition from somewhere in New France had set a course westward to verify the rich mines of New Mexico as early as 1703, no Frenchman of record appeared in Santa Fe for more than a generation after that. To the southeast, however, much less distance separated the colonials of Bourbon Spain and Bourbon France.

During his previous tenure as governor of Coahuila between 1698 and 1703, Francisco Cuervo y Valdés had promoted expansion northward to the lower Rio Grande, forwarding from Monclova to Mexico City word of Frenchmen trading long muskets to the Hasinais of east Texas. Cuervo knew personally the thrown-together cast of characters who would in the second decade of the new century reestablish a Spanish presence in Texas by willing chicanery with French agents: astute, profit-minded Diego Ramón, first captain and patron of the thirty-man presidial garrison stationed next to mission San Juan Bautista on the west side of the Rio Grande; fray Francisco Hidalgo, who refused to forget the Hasinais; and the hardy young chameleon José de Urrutia, reemerging from east Texas in 1700 after his seven memorable years as a white Indian.

That same summer, Urrutia found himself in the viceroy's palace interpreting for two of the Caddoan-speaking Hasinais who had brought to him at San Juan Bautista news of the near incursion of thirty Frenchmen.[20] These were no mere shadows. They had names. One in particular, Canadian Capt. Louis Juchereau de Saint-Denis, already looked forward to displaying his wares for Captain Ramón and Father Hidalgo.

Momentum favored Saint-Denis. Renewal of La Salle's Mississippi enterprise by the Sieur d'Iberville, the rival interest of Englishmen out of Charles Town, and Spain's belated project to occupy the bay extolled by Carlos de Sigüenza in 1693 begot in rapid succession a Spanish coastal presidio of pine logs at Pensacola (1698) and makeshift French posts on Biloxi Bay (1699), the lower Mississippi (1700), and Mobile Bay (1702).

While Europe's War of the Spanish Succession ran its course, binding Spain to France in the first Bourbon Family Compact, Frenchmen in America took advantage of this convenient alliance. Aided by local Indians, they found their way into the Mississippi from the Gulf and then, in dugout canoes and on foot, quickly penetrated bayous, woods, and Native villages all over the lower Mississippi Valley.

French Jesuit missionary Paul Du Ru, during Holy Week in 1700 at Fort du Mississippi, "celebrated Mass here in the midst of the forest as well as if we had been in the Cathedral at Paris." His congregation was hardly Parisian. "There are all sorts of people here," he marveled, "voyageurs, soldiers, French, Canadians, sailors, filibusters, and others like them."

Saint-Denis knew them all. Louisiana became his world. With consummate bravado, he lived La Salle's dream. On his water-logged probe westward in 1700—reported by the two Hasinais and Urrutia in Mexico City—Saint-Denis had with him the now-grown Pierre and Robert Talon, survivors of Indian captivity, Spanish ransom, the viceroy's palace, and several transatlantic crossings.

The party reached the Kadohadachos, just short of Hasinai territory in east Texas. The Talons' Caddo was rusty, and Saint-Denis misunderstood the Indians to say that mounted Spaniards had been among them recently. The spokesmen, however, were using a past tense. Governor Terán de los Ríos had withdrawn eight winters before.[21]

Hot, dry summer winds blew over the Spaniards' actual location five hundred miles more west than south on the opposite bank of the Rio Grande (some thirty miles downriver from present-day Eagle Pass). There, Capt. Diego Ramón's garrison endured. So did the Franciscan college of Querétaro's three Coahuiltecan missions, visited in 1706 by the horror of smallpox.

Early in 1707, when Coahuila's governor Martín de Alarcón ordered Ramón to punish suspected Indian raiders on the other side of the river—and bring back to the missions any new blood he could—five Hispanic women rode along as far as the crossing, "motivated by love of husband or by feminine curiosity." Their men campaigned no farther than the Nueces River, attacking en route the camp of perceived enemies in a thunderstorm and rounding up for the missions several dozen Natives, willing and unwilling.[22]

They also fished. Among their catch from the Rio Grande were big yellow catfish. Chaplain fray Isidro Félix de Espinosa explained the name *piltontes,* "which in Mexican language means boys, because the fish is as big as a boy." The priest later claimed that a soldier brought him one "tied by the gills with a rope to the horn of a horse's saddle and its tail was dragging on the ground."[23]

Natural history that favored Spanish expansion interested Espinosa. The pragmatic Franciscan kept the diary of a Spanish reconnaissance in 1709 that marked a new trail via the San Antonio River to today's Colorado River of east-central Texas. No Spaniards of record had visited the region since the flight of Fathers Massanet and Hidalgo fifteen years before. Espinosa raved about the pecan crop and the abundance of deer, buffalo, and wild turkeys. He observed too, with deep regret, that the Hasinais had not migrated westward to the Colorado in hopes of new Spanish missions among their people. They still lived where Massanet and Hidalgo had left them.[24]

Father Hidalgo despaired of official sanction for his Hasinai project, so, with unFranciscan bravado, he wrote in Latin to the governor of French Louisiana. Would not Roman Catholic Frenchmen aid Spaniards in returning these apostate Indians to the Church's fold? Dated January 17, 1711, the letter was more than two years in transit to Mobile. When he read it, Antoine de La Mothe, Sieur de Cadillac, smiled. Saint-Denis laughed. With pleasure he would carry Cadillac's reply west to the Rio Grande.

Capt. Diego Ramón acted surprised when the visitors appeared. Still, he made them welcome: Saint-Denis, the Talon brothers, and Hasinai headman Bernardino. Luckily, the presidial paymaster spoke French. Now what? Ramón wrote at once to the viceroy in Mexico City for instructions and to Father Hidalgo in Querétaro for an explanation. It was now midsummer 1714.

As frontier gentlemen and businessmen, Saint-Denis and Ramón understood each other perfectly. The suave, thirty-four-year-old French bachelor noticed the Spanish captain's stepgranddaughter, seventeen-year-old Manuela Sánchez Navarro. Don Diego nodded. For months, while awaiting word from Mexico City, the household was entertained, and Saint-Denis learned essential phrases in Spanish.

The Talons, meanwhile, slipped back across the Rio Grande to inform

Louis Juchereau de Saint-Denis. From Ross Phares, *Cavalier in the Wilderness: The Story of the Explorer and Trader Louis Juchereau de St. Denis* (1952). *Courtesy of the UT Institute of Texan Cultures at San Antonio.*

Governor Cadillac in Mobile. "The sieur de Saint-Denis writes that he will be here by the end of the month," Cadillac reported to the French home office, "but, as he must marry a Spanish girl, one may believe that he is amusing himself there. . . . he loves his comforts, is given to vanity, and is not sufficiently zealous for the king's service."

Strained relations between France and Spain following the War of the Spanish Succession did not seem to concern Ramón or Saint-Denis. Their own family compact did. Incredibly, the smooth-mannered Frenchman had ridden to Mexico City under guard and persuaded the viceroy Duque de Linares to authorize a new Spanish entrada into east Texas. Moreover, Saint-Denis, indifferent to any traitorous implications, would serve as the expedition's salaried supply officer. The wedding festivities that united him and Manuela early in 1716 lasted three days.

Domingo Ramón, son of don Diego and uncle of Saint-Denis's young bride, would command the entrada. Manuela was not going, however; already pregnant, she would stay and have her baby at San Juan Bautista. At least seven soldiers took their families, the first Spanish women and children to make homes in Texas. Had they known the fate of Madame Talon and the other French dependents of La Salle's colony, they too might have stayed behind.[25]

A half-dozen missions and one presidio set out among the Hasinais in 1716 and 1717 did not bring on the millenial kingdom. Father Hidalgo, who had waited so long to resume his ministry, now sounded like Massanet. The Indians, despite what the Franciscan first read as assurances, refused to muster their scattered lodges around his church or give up their idols. The Hasinais' numbers had fallen from an estimated forty-five hundred in 1693 to fewer than two thousand. While delighting in the tangible gifts, they hated Christianity. Hidalgo noted on November 4, 1716, that "their repugnance to baptism from past times is well known, for they have formed the belief that the water kills them."[26]

The Indians' attitude grieved Father Hidalgo, but it did not stop Saint-Denis. Taking his Spanish kinsman Diego Ramón II with him to Mobile, he and a group of trading partners outfitted a pack train to carry French hardware and textiles, via his post at Natchitoches and Domingo Ramón's presidio on the Neches, back to San Juan Bautista. He rode ahead. The caravan, not far beyond the Colorado, was attacked by Apaches who made off with twenty-three reserve mules and a woman muleteer, a rowdy mulatta.

The goods that made it through, he argued, were not contraband. His wife and infant daughter were Spanish after all, and he himself wished to become a Spanish citizen. Escorted again to Mexico City, the Frenchman in 1717 faced a different viceroy, the stern Marqués de Valero, who sized him up, detained him, then let him go with a warning to stay out of Texas.

Louis XIV's death in 1715 had stiffened Spanish resolve against French incursions from Louisiana into east Texas. The former governor of Coahuila, Martín de Alarcón, reappointed in 1716 as governor of Coahuila and Texas, ordered an investigation into the Ramón family's questionable dealings with Frenchmen. Although nothing came of it, Manuela held her breath. In 1718, Spaniards moved to occupy San Antonio and Frenchmen founded New Orleans. The concurrence was no accident.[27]

With maps spread out before them, the Marqués de Valero and his top military adviser, don Juan Manuel de Oliván Rebolledo, ran their fingers over North America. On the left side, Manila galleons, raising the coast at Cape Mendocino, descended to Acapulco. Oceangoing Englishmen, who fancied a base on shore, posed the greatest threat in that sector. To thwart them, the entrenched Jesuits of Baja California must be pushed to secure the bays of San Diego and Monterey, long ago claimed by Spain. Jesuits farther inland might also redouble their efforts, fanning out northwestward to the peoples of the Gila and Colorado rivers and northeastward to the Hopis, as Father Kino had proposed.

The right side of the map appeared more congested. A lone Spanish flag still waved above walled St. Augustine, cut off from its former hinterland by English and Indian competitors. By dragging a finger westward across north Florida and along the Gulf Coast, one came first to reoccupied San Marcos de Apalachee and then to lonely Pensacola, where its captains watched French activity with alarm. The chance to dislodge Frenchmen from the lower Mississippi Valley had passed. Now they were spreading up its tributaries, especially the Red River toward the country of the Hasinais. Funds must be allotted, Oliván insisted, to keep Spaniards in east Texas.

Reluctantly, Valero acknowledged France's success. French colonials had bisected North America at midcontinent. Tracing an arc from the Saint Lawrence Valley through their posts on the Great Lakes and down the Mississippi, Frenchmen moved freely back and forth through Native nations from the North Sea, or Atlantic, all the way to the Gulf of Mexico. And from upper Louisiana, major rivers like the Missouri and Napestle, or Arkansas, gave access across the plains to Santa Fe. Viceroy Valero was not blind. Let the governor of New Mexico beware.

The most clever of Diego de Vargas's Spanish-born lieutenants who competed for local control after the reconqueror's death was Antonio de Valverde Cosío. Interim governor of New Mexico since 1716, he received regular royal appointment in 1718. As a *montañés,* a native of the northern Spanish province of Santander, Valverde availed himself of a tight and mutually beneficial circle of his countrymen. His connections, reinforced by a self-serving trip to Spain in the late 1690s, extended through Parral and Mexico City to Madrid.

Nearer, he had developed New Mexico's most lucrative farming, wine-producing, and stockraising property, the hacienda of San Antonio de Padua, downriver from El Paso. In his late forties, unmarried, and the proud father of three daughters and a five-year-old namesake, don Antonio ruled the district. He held titles as captain-for-life of the El Paso presidio and alcalde mayor of the district. Foremen and agents saw to business during his tenure in Santa Fe.[28]

A brief war in Europe, resulting from the plan of Felipe V and his Italian second wife to annex Sicily and Sardinia, recast France as enemy in 1719 and encouraged Valverde to dramatize the French threat to New Mexico. That year, the governor in person led an unusually large concourse of Hispanos and Indians—six or seven hundred in all—on a search-and-destroy mission against raiding Utes and Comanches, whom they failed to engage. Apaches, however, provided rumors of Frenchmen, and Valverde set out to find them.

The passage was not easy. Eight days east and a little north of Taos, the expedition's diarist reported that some of the men broke out in rashes "from an attack of an herb called ivy, caused strangely by lying down upon it or being near it. Those affected swelled up." The governor ordered Antonio Durán de Armijo, a barber and medical practitioner familiar with bloodletting, to look after them.

The diarist dwelled on Valverde's generosity. When Cristóbal Rodarte of Santa Cruz fell desperately ill, the governor had him brought to his tent, "giving him medicines that appeared proper for his case (these medicines and others he carried as a precaution)." Rodarte recovered. On the eve and feast of Saint Francis, October 3 and 4, 1719, don Antonio tapped a keg of his rich El Paso brandy and a larger cask of wine, with which governor and officers toasted the health of Franciscan Juan George del Pino, missionary at Pecos and the expedition's chaplain.

That same day of Saint Francis, men of the expedition killed a mountain lion and a wildcat. Then, a great bear boar plunged into the Pueblo auxiliaries' camp, and with much commotion they managed to kill it. An even bigger boar crossed the column's path a couple of days later. When a mounted lancer stabbed it "up to the middle of the shaft," the wounded animal turned on him, flailing at his horse. Another soldier rode into the fray. His lance also found the mark. "The bear, seizing the horse by the tail, held him down and, clawing viciously, tore a piece of flesh off the rump." Only after others had roped the beast were they finally able to finish it off.

Not until he reached the Arkansas River did Valverde hear reports of Frenchmen. If he understood his Apache informants correctly, these insolent white men had built two pueblos as large as Taos, where they lived with the Apaches' enemies and supplied them with long guns and pistols. But it was already late October. The governor, who had suffered the unforgiving winter of 1696 on Vargas's trek to El Cuartelejo, decided to double back, returning his numbed force to Santa Fe in good order before the end of November.[29]

The colony's next thrust onto the plains, smaller and under the command of don Pedro de Villasur, Valverde's lieutenant governor, would not be so fortunate. On June 15, 1720, the day before they had set out from Santa Fe, Valverde acknowledged orders from the viceroy that "either I, personally, or my lieutenant-general should make the journey I had promised to reconnoiter the French in the region where they are situated."

They had camped in tall grass near the confluence of the Platte and Loup rivers in present-day eastern Nebraska, six hundred miles northeast of Santa Fe. The force numbered forty-some presidial soldiers, sixty Pueblo auxiliaries, and a few citizens and servants, all well outfitted. Villasur had taken no silver to trade with Frenchmen, only service for his own use: cups, plates, saltcellar, forks and spoons, candlestick, and inkhorn. Mules carried their provisions and gifts of tobacco, cloth, knives, and hats to influence willing Natives.

A message in French drafted by Archibeque had brought unintelligible scribbling in response. The populous camp of Pawnees, Otos, and others whose tracks the Spaniards had picked up, appeared not especially welcoming, so the Spanish column had turned back.

According to angry critics later, Villasur made careless decisions that determined the expedition's fate: he chose an indefensible site for the camp; pastured the horses at some distance, which left his people afoot; failed to post sentries; and went to sleep as casually as if they had reposed in Santa Fe. At sunrise on August 13, while the men were busy catching their unsaddled horses, a horde of gaudily painted Natives who had silently encircled the camp fell screaming upon it.

Writing to Viceroy Valero from Santa Fe on October 8, 1720, Valverde professed that his heart was broken.

> When I contemplate those fields with the spilt blood of those who were the most excellent soldiers in all this realm, and who sacrificed their lives in the service of God and the king, my master, at the hands of the impious barbarousness of the enemies of our holy Catholic faith, I am persuaded that some were heretical Huguenots.

They had not even spared the life of the chaplain, fray Juan Mingues.

Villasur was dead. A veteran officer in Nueva Vizcaya, he had been Valverde's close associate in El Paso, his friend and unquestioning subordinate. Juan de Archibeque was dead; when the prosperous expatriate had remarried the previous summer, Valverde had stood as witness. Two shrewd and ambitious men, they greatly admired each other. Chief of scouts José Naranjo was dead, as well as dozens more. Only thirteen Spaniards and some forty Pueblo auxiliaries escaped.[30]

What is most notable today about Villasur's last stand is a busy, colorful, contemporary painting, 17 feet long by 4½ feet high, on buffalo or elk hide, probably by a mission-trained artist informed by survivors. Neither the person who commissioned it nor the reason for doing so is known.

The action depicted is frantic. A knot of presidial soldiers, dressed in their *cueras*—protective, thigh-length, leather vests—and flat, broad-brimmed hats is surrounded by circling Indians on foot, wielding bows, tomahawks, spears, or swords. The Spaniards' musket fire seems to have little effect.

Just outside his tent lies the slain Villasur in the bright red jacket of an officer's uniform. Father Mingues, cross in hand and a couple of arrows in his backside, runs toward the fallen commander, holding the skirt of his blue habit up over his tonsured head, exposing light-colored, knee-high stockings. Frenchmen appear interspersed among the attackers neatly attired in long uniform coats and tricorn hats, firing unwieldy muskets that the artist has greatly elongated to exhibit the dastardly advantage taken by these cowards.

Years later, perhaps through the agency of Miguel de Archibeque, trader son and heir of don Juan, the rolled-up mural passed into the possession of Jesuit missionary Felipe Segesser von Brunegg in Sonora, who shipped it in 1758 to his brother in Switzerland. To bring the Villasur massacre scene back home to New Mexico, state officials in 1988 purchased this telling artifact from descendants of the Jesuit's family. It is now displayed in the Palace of the Governors at Santa Fe.[31]

French chroniclers neither gloated over this signal Spanish defeat in 1720 nor bestowed credit for it on specific French voyageurs. Peace had been restored in Europe the same year. Pensacola and east Texas, briefly occupied by Frenchmen, were returned to Spaniards. While survivors of Villasur's expedition agreed that some of their attackers had used firearms, they disagreed about the actual presence of French technical advisers. Spanish authorities, meanwhile, looked to assign blame.

They were still looking in May 1726, when the inspector general, Brigadier don Pedro de Rivera, and his entourage reined up at El Paso. Don Antonio de Valverde made them welcome with cask and keg. Putting off inspection of the El Paso garrison until later, the brigadier ordered the former governor to accompany him to Santa Fe. Besides routine inspection duties, Rivera had several exceptional matters to attend to in New Mexico, among them completion of a judicial investigation of the Villasur disaster.

The two major charges against Valverde—that he did not personally lead the expedition of 1720 and that he entrusted it to an incompetent—resounded in the

Details of Pedro de Villasur's last stand, 1720, an eighteenth-century painting on hide, Segesser II, Museum of New Mexico. Photographs by Blair Clark. *Courtesy of the Museum of New Mexico, nos. 149804 and 158345.*

governor's palace. Don Antonio deftly parried both. He had been occupied with other royal business, and to the contrary, his friend Villasur was an experienced military officer with a distinguished service record.

When the Viceroy Marqués de Casafuerte finally absolved Valverde in 1727, he instructed only that the former governor pay 50 pesos for masses for the dead soldiers' souls and 150 toward chalices and vestments for the Franciscan missions of La Junta de los Ríos. On December 15, 1728, don Antonio, iron-fisted *patrón* of El Paso, died, leaving an estate valued in the tens of thousands of pesos.[32]

Rivera, meanwhile, rather enjoyed rude Santa Fe, staying on through the summer of 1726, from early June until late August. While his cartographer and military engineer, Francisco Alvarez Barreiro, with armed escort surveyed the surrounding countryside for one of several stylized maps, Rivera set about correcting certain "pernicious abuses." Although nepotism surprised no one, Gov. Juan Domingo de Bustamante, Antonio de Valverde's nephew, had entitled all manner of relatives and lackeys as reserve officers with salaries from the royal treasury. The inspector's remedy—cutting twenty positions from the Santa Fe presidio—struck at the capital's chief industry. When they found out, affected locals, from governor to tavern keeper, howled in protest.

Rivera's logic was flawed. He had seen Sigüenza y Góngora's *Mercurio volante* touting Vargas's alleged bloodless reconquest of 1692 and had taken it literally. If a hundred recruits, poorly armed and inexperienced, had pacified the whole kingdom back then, reasoned the brigadier, surely eighty veterans could defend it now. Besides, more than six hundred families lived in the vicinity. Hence, he concluded, "the fears and improbable dangers alleged by the missionary fathers can therefore be dismissed."

As if slashing the presidial roster were not enough, Inspector Rivera also recommended cutting the men's annual salaries by more than 10 percent, from 450 pesos to 400. "The presidio should remain as follows: 77 soldiers at 400 pesos, a lieutenant at 430 pesos, an alférez at 420 pesos, and a sergeant at 415 pesos." Subtracting his proposed total of 32,065 pesos from the current 45,000, Rivera beamed. The savings amounted to 12,935 pesos.[33]

To foil venal captains and governors who habitually overcharged their soldiers for equipment and supplies, deducted questionable fees from the men's salaries, and pocketed excessive profits, Rivera suggested a schedule of fixed prices. Hence, with a guaranteed real salary of 400 pesos annually in kind, an enlisted man would be considerably better off. Nevertheless, most of these soldiers, who had signed on for one or more ten-year enlistments, would remain debtors to the company store because of the mandated prices in New Mexico: required protective leather jacket at the equivalent of 40 pesos; musket at 30 and sword at 15; a horse, cow, or heavy

Campeche blanket at 12; a hat, 4; the standard fanega measure of maize, 3½; a pound of ordinary chocolate, 1½; and ten cakes of soap at 1. And since most of them had families, let the brigadier try to outfit himself, feed and clothe his wife and children, and have a good time on 400 pesos.[34]

If Rivera did not know before that the frontier officer corps was inbred, he found out soon enough as he continued his tour of inspection. At El Paso, where the garrison passed muster in good order, José Valentín de Aganza, the captain-for-life who had succeeded Valverde, was also husband to don Antonio's eldest daughter, Antonia.[35]

To the west at Janos, Capt. Antonio Becerra Nieto presided ably over a fifty-man company. Becerra's daughter, María Rosa, wed Juan Bautista de Anza, lieutenant of Janos and soon to be captain at Fronteras. Their children, including Juan Bautista de Anza the younger, would also choose spouses within the tight family circle of officers, landowners, and entrepreneurs, mostly Basques in Sonora.[36] As long as these officers were a credit to the royal service, Rivera did not object.

Six days farther west, at the presidio of Fronteras on the southeastern frontier of Pimería Alta, the inspector met an officer he deemed an utter discredit. Captain-for-life don Gregorio Alvarez Tuñón y Quiroz, who had collected a commander's salary for more than twenty years and openly defied governors and Jesuit priests, lived two days' hard ride to the south at his mining hacienda with a personal body-guard of six. The remainder of his indebted, demoralized troops hardly ventured from the vicinity of the presidio. As his debtors, the captain did not want them out on campaign where they might get killed. Rivera reported that "they were a total disgrace." The blame lay not with the soldiers, however, but with their wily, insubordinate, absentee commander.[37]

During his inspection at Fronteras, the brigadier accepted the hospitality of Jesuit Father Ignacio de Arzeo of the neighboring Opata mission San Ignacio de Cuquiárachi. Arzeo also served as chaplain of the unkempt presidio. Rivera stayed a month.

Tuñón y Quiroz showed up at the presidio to welcome him. After formal writ and response, the inspector, as was customary, ordered captain and officers to withdraw during interrogation of the men. Fifteen testified. Evidence of malfeasance mounted. After summoning don Gregorio again and recording his testimony, Rivera sorted the heap of irregularities into fifteen counts.

The captain's defense struck him as specious. Passing summary judgment on two counts, the inspector found Tuñón y Quiroz guilty of habitually embezzling the salaries of phantom soldiers. Since the captain showed no "signs of mending his ways or hope that he might," Rivera removed him from command, pending the viceroy's decision. Proceedings of the entire investigation would be forwarded to Mexico City. As courier, Rivera chose an interested observer who despised don Gregorio. Juan Mateo Manje, elder spokesman for an aggrieved faction of Sonora citizens, believed that the captain's greedy, nonmilitary preoccupations had emboldened Apache raiders and imperiled the future of the province. Before leaving the vicinity of Fronteras on December 2, 1726, Rivera appointed as interim captain the unstained Lt. Juan Bautista de Anza, who had escorted him from Janos.

The fate of Gregorio Tuñón y Quiroz, passionately argued by his attorney in Mexico City, was decided by the viceroy who had dispatched Inspector Rivera in the first place. The Marqués de Casafuerte, acting on the unequivocal advice of don Juan Manuel de Oliván Rebolledo, sacked the lifetime captain of Fronteras. Scapegoat or scoundrel, by early summer 1728 the cunning don Gregorio had died.[38]

En route in August 1727 to the farthest presidio of east Texas, Rivera cursed the "insufferable swarms of venomous mosquitoes." He and his party rested only one day at the presidio of San Antonio de Béxar, then pushed on east-northeast.[39]

Spanish settlements in Texas had proliferated during the previous decade. Gov. Martín de Alarcón and crusty fray Antonio de San Buenaventura Olivares of the Querétaro College, who disliked each other, had taken credit for founding the humble cluster at San Antonio in May 1718: the mission San Antonio de Valero, the presidio of San Antonio de Béxar, and the so-called villa of Béxar. While Alarcón pointed to the trades represented among his several dozen settlers and soldiers—weaver, carpenter, stonemason, blacksmith, and stockman—Olivares saw them as "mulattoes, lobos, coyotes, and mestizos, people of the lowest order, whose customs are worse than those of the Indians."[40]

When the short-lived French hostilities of 1719 chased Spaniards from east Texas to San Antonio, fray Antonio Margil de Jesús of the college of Nuestra Señora de Guadalupe of Zacatecas had used the confusion to inaugurate mission San José y San Miguel de Aguayo early in 1720. Olivares had objected. The Indians at his mission of San Antonio de Valero, he claimed, were enemies of the ones at Margil's. Clever Margil, however, had outmaneuvered old Olivares. His flattering petition had found favor with the new governor, the Marqués de San Miguel de Aguayo.

Something of a frontier don Quixote, Aguayo owed title and fortune to his wife, who had inherited estates that sprawled across Coahuila and into Nueva Vizcaya. Like Diego de Vargas thirty years before him, Aguayo had sent recruiters for soldiers and colonists to Zacatecas and other mining districts. A reported five hundred, many with families, crowded Monclova in the fall of 1720, moving with household goods and thousands of mules, horses, cattle, sheep, and goats toward San Juan Bautista and the Rio Grande.

Crossing the swollen river, more than a musketshot wide, took almost all winter, from December to March, according to diarist fray Juan Antonio de la Peña. Fifty Indian swimmers roped to rafts in the frigid water dragged and swam people, animals, gear, and unprecedented tons of provisions across day after day. Despite brandy, chocolate, and plentiful rations of meat and maize, many sickened. Yet when it came to logistics, few colonizers compared to the Marqués de Aguayo.

The governor knew that peace had been signed in Europe between Spain and France the year before. Still, when word reached him at San Juan Bautista that Louis Juchereau de Saint-Denis was parleying with Texas Indians, he had dispatched more than a hundred men to protect San Antonio. On July 31, 1721, Aguayo met Saint-Denis face to face. The cunning forest entrepreneur now commanded the French post at Natchitoches near the Red River, where Manuela and their children had joined him. In past encounters with high-ranking Spaniards, Saint-Denis had more than held his own, charming one viceroy and confounding another. But the Marqués de Aguayo stood up to him.

Saint-Denis grandly offered to observe the peace that now prevailed between their two countries. Not only that, countered Aguayo, but every Frenchman must withdraw at once from Texas. The Río Hondo between Los Adaes (at today's Robeline, Louisiana) and Natchitoches, not twenty miles apart, would henceforth be the boundary between French Louisiana and Spanish Texas.

Saint-Denis then wanted to know why, if a truce existed, the marqués was ordering the construction of a log fort for a one-hundred-man garrison and provincial capital at Los Adaes? Aguayo pointed out the obvious: fray Isidro Félix de Espinosa, fray Antonio Margil de Jesús, and other Franciscans reinstalled among the Hasinai would need protection from enemy tribes.

Aguayo had previously sent Capt. Domingo Ramón, the uncle of Madame Saint-Denis, to secure Matagorda Bay for Spain. He relocated the captain's former presidio of Nuestra Señora de los Dolores to near the Angelina River, named for a durable Hasinai woman who had learned Spanish at San Juan Bautista and returned to interpret for a succession of Spaniards, including Aguayo.

Venturing back out from San Antonio to La Bahía himself in early spring 1722, the governor experienced no greater satisfaction during his entire reoccupation of east Texas than when, on April 6, he stepped off the plan for an octagonal Spanish presidio right on top of La Salle's Fort Saint-Louis. Workers digging the foundations turned up French gun parts, nails, and other debris.

Balancing, if unevenly, military and missionary foundations at La Bahía, Aguayo also directed construction of Mission Espíritu Santo de Zúñiga across Garcitas Creek from the presidio. Meant to serve local Coco, Karankawa, and Cuján Indians—some of whom must have witnessed the massacre of La Salle's colonists thirty-five years earlier—the unlikely mission would soon be moved inland, along with the garrison.

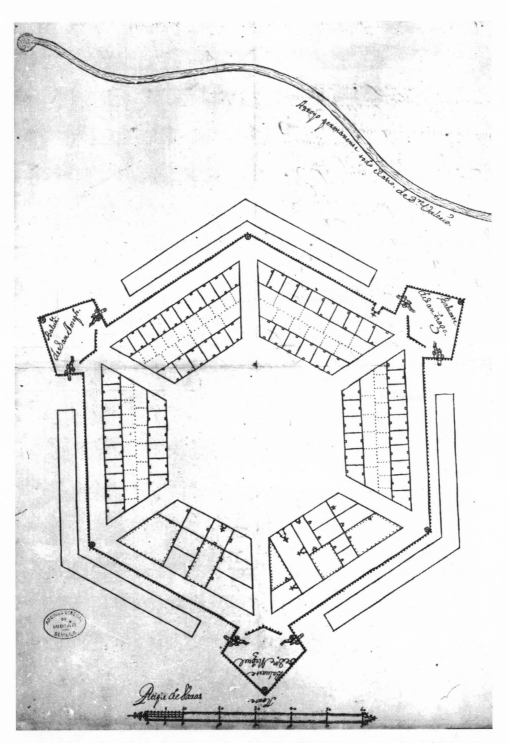

Proposed plans of the Marqués de Aguayo's Texas presidios of Los Adaes (1721) and La Bahía (1722), the latter on the site of La Salle's Fort Saint Louis. *Courtesy of the Ministerio de Educación, Cultura y Deporte, Archivo General de Indias (Sevilla, Spain), Mapas y Planos, 113 and 115, and Donald E. Chipman.*

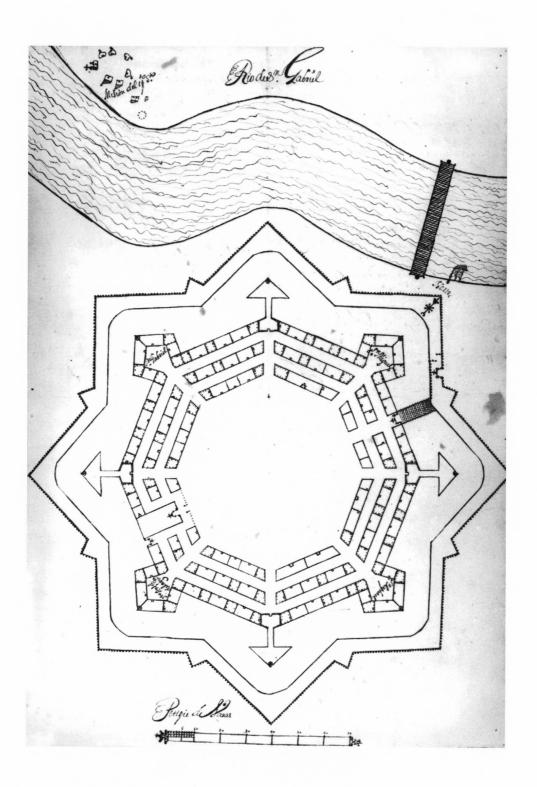

Rio de S.ᵗ Gabriel

The Marqués de Aguayo left Texas later that spring, returned to Monclova, and retired from government service. The adventure was over. Where only San Antonio had stood in 1719, Spanish Texas now held ten Franciscan missions, four presidios, and a total of 268 soldiers.[41]

But why so many soldiers? demanded Pedro de Rivera. When finally he reached Los Adaes, the humid capital of Texas, the brigadier did not linger. He carried out his inspection in September 1727, in only eleven days. Allegedly because of ill health, Gov. Fernando Pérez de Almazán had withdrawn to San Antonio. Rivera faulted him for appointing too many officers and charging the men exorbitant prices at all four Texas forts.

The presidio of Los Adaes, surrounded by a log stockade, and its neighboring three missions, at which no Indians resided, did at least serve to mark the extent of Spanish territory. An hour's ride east through the woods stood Saint-Denis's French fort, with a company of twenty-five, where people from Los Adaes went regularly to fraternize and trade for maize, beans, and fancy goods.

Rivera predicted that if war with France broke out again, Frenchmen would attack "with a formal army led by experienced officers brought in from Mobile or Canada." A hundred Spanish presidials would be no match. Hence, he recommended cutting the roster at Los Adaes to sixty. Besides, the inspector admitted, "French firearms are effective from a long range, whereas our arquebuses have only short-range capability."[42] That belief, widely held by Spanish colonials—that French manufactured goods, including guns, were superior to those made in Spain—assured a quick, unpreventable contraband trade.

Rivera doubled back to the southwest the way he had come to inspect the three remaining Texas presidios. He judged the twenty-five-man company of Dolores, or los Tejas, wholly dispensable. It should be eliminated. The presidio of La Bahía, along with its attendant mission, had been moved in 1726 about twenty-five miles inland to the Guadalupe River to get away from the independent Karankawas and a marshy locale. Its founding captain, Domingo Ramón, had died of an infected stab wound in the chest resulting from an altercation with an enraged Karankawa. Its garrison numbered ninety. Forty would do.

Rivera praised the location of San Antonio de Béxar, noting the rich, irrigable land and the potential for stockraising, even while he pared the garrison from fifty-four to forty-four. He wanted at least twenty-five civilian families brought in to colonize the lands around the presidio and the two missions nearby on the San Antonio River. Because of the expense, however, he opposed Aguayo's earlier plan to recruit for Texas hundreds of families from Galicia in Spain, the Canary Islands, or Cuba.[43]

Once back in Mexico City in the summer of 1728, Pedro de Rivera hastened to compose for Viceroy Casafuerte a scrupulous, three-part report, his *proyecto*.

First, presidio by presidio, he detailed how he had found things; second, how he had left things; and third, what he proposed for the future. His considered reforms would reduce the annual cost of defending western North America from 445,000 pesos to 284,000, a savings of 161,000, or 36 percent.

The resulting *Reglamento* of 1729, decreed by Casafuerte on March 2 and approved by the crown on July 30, 1731, unsettled the frontier military only momentarily. Men displaced by elimination of one Texas presidio found enlistment at another, where—more likely than not—the commander continued skimming the payroll. Overall costs resumed their spiral upward.[44]

But from the 1720s on—because Rivera had taken the field and Alvarez Barreiro had mapped so much of North America—increasingly professional bureaucrats in Mexico City and Madrid knew better what they were dealing with. Transfer in 1721 of imperial oversight from the antiquated Council of the Indies to the new Ministry of the Navy and the Indies also helped.

Not for forty years did Spaniards launch another general inspection of New Spain's northern frontier. Despite intervening Native uprisings, new settlements, and embarrassing defeats, conditions in the 1760s would not have surprised Valero, Casafuerte, or Oliván Rebolledo.

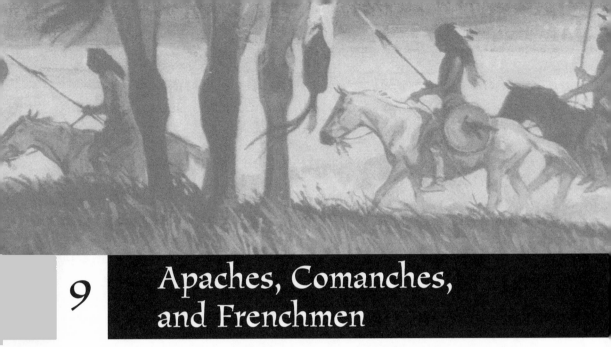

9 Apaches, Comanches, and Frenchmen

*I suggest to your Excellency that if every proposal for the foundation of presidios
. . . were acceded to, the treasury of Midas would not suffice.*
—Brigadier Pedro de Rivera to Viceroy Marqués de Casafuerte,
El Paso, September 26, 1726

No one knew exactly where the Comanches came from. An ancient tradition, related to Brigadier Pedro de Rivera in 1726, placed their origin in a land called Teguayo, hundreds of miles northwest of Santa Fe, seemingly the Great Basin. By the mid-eighteenth century, they thrived on the plains, numbering perhaps ten thousand, and were rich beyond compare in horses.

Although Comanches moved continually, "wandering like the Israelites," their tribal solidarity gave them an advantage over other Plains peoples. "They dominate with the power of arms all the nations who live in that region," Rivera had heard, "because they terrorize them with the ferocious war which they make."

The Jicarilla Apaches' sudden and transparent desire to embrace Roman Catholicism was no mere coincidence. And although Inspector Rivera did not formulate strategies in the mid-1720s to turn the rising tide of the Comanche nation, he sensed that it was a force to reckon with.[1]

Frenchmen thought so too, but they first tried to enroll Plains Apaches as allies. In 1720, impetuous Etienne de Véniard, sieur de Bourgmont, had negotiated in Paris a contract with the Duc d'Orleans, regent of France, by which he stood to gain letters of nobility in turn for "making peace among all the Indian tribes between Louisiana and New Mexico in order to open a safe trade route and by establishing a post, which will shield the mines of the Illinois from the Spaniards."

During the winter of 1723–24, Bourgmont had supervised construction of Fort d'Orleans on the north bank of the Missouri River, two hundred miles upstream from its juncture with the Mississippi. His abiding hope was to bring within the expanding French sphere the Padoucas, or Plains Apaches of present-day western Kansas, apparently the ones Spaniards called Cuartelejo Apaches.

Bourgmont finally met them in mid-October 1724. Overcoming sickness, the vagaries of transportation, and the nervousness of his Missouri, Osage, Kansa, Oto, and Pawnee escort, he rode to a point east of El Cuartelejo and laid out for the Padoucas an unbelievable array of goods, all free for the taking—muskets, sabers, axes, red and blue Limbourg cloth, mirrors, Flemish knives, shirts, scissors, combs, awls, needles, kettles, hawkbells, vermillion, beads, rings, and brass wire.

Awed, the head chief of the Padoucas accepted from Bourgmont with high courtesy the French king's gift of a white flag with fleur-de-lis. At one point, Bourgmont, his ten-year-old, half-Missouri son, and several others were conveyed on a buffalo robe to the Apaches' camp. Trader Diego Romero of New Mexico had experienced a similar welcome among Plains Apaches during his memorable summer of 1660.

After speeches that challenged the interpreters' skills, feasting, and assent with the calumet to a new peace on the plains, these Apaches entertained the French soldiers, "gave them a thousand caresses, and offered them their daughters." The Apache chief assured them that should Frenchmen wish in the future to travel on and trade with the Spaniards of New Mexico, the Padoucas would escort them, the journey beyond El Cuartelejo requiring only twelve days. Spaniards, who refused to trade guns to them, came every spring with horses, "a few knives and some awls and inferior axes, but they are not like you, who give us a quantity of merchandise, such as we have never seen before."

But Bourgmont never passed that way again. He shepherded a Missouri chief and his daughter, along with leaders from the Illinois, Osage, and Oto nations, down the great rivers and across the ocean to Paris, where even King Louis XV, then fifteen, received them. Elevated to the French nobility, Bourgmont retired to a small estate in Normandy and died in 1734.

The peace he had achieved with his gifts a decade earlier did not last. Comanches, who almost immediately began disrupting the Plains Apaches, saw to that. Their furious raids on the spring and summer camps of Cuartelejos, Jicarillas, and others drove a wedge between French suppliers and Apaches.

A savage, uncustomary nine-day battle in 1725 between Comanches and Apaches was reported in Spanish sources; whether it actually took place, it symbolized stark reality. During the 1720s, hard-riding Comanches came to dominate the prime buffalo range east of New Mexico, scattering Plains Apaches like chaff on the wind.[2]

Before the settlers of San Antonio ever met a Comanche, they felt their distant presence as Apaches shifted southward before the advancing foes. Several Spaniards who strayed too far fell victim to Apache war parties; then in August 1723, Apaches struck at the San Antonio presidio's horse corral, making off with eighty head. Its first captain, the illiterate former private Nicolás Flores y Valdés, retaliated with unusual success. Tracking the raiders with thirty soldiers and as many Coahuiltecan mission Indians for more than three hundred miles, he surprised an Apache camp, killing the chief and thirty-some men, capturing twenty women and children, and rounding up 120 horses and other spoils of war.

Fray José González of Mission San Antonio de Valero, who claimed angrily to have sent the Indian contingent on condition that Flores y Valdés approach the Apaches peacefully, had the captain removed from command for a year. Viceroy Casafuerte forbade a second campaign in 1725. Venerable fray Francisco Hidalgo, then in his midsixties, wanted to end his days as a missionary among the Apaches, but death overtook him at San Juan Bautista in September 1726. Still, until 1731, Texans and Apaches observed a cautious truce.[3]

Proposals and counterproposals, meantime, echoed between Madrid and Mexico City. One called for four hundred families from Spain and the Canary Islands to people towns in Texas. After years of argument, the paltry result amounted to no more than fifteen or sixteen such families, a majority of whom began their assisted migration at Santa Cruz de Tenerife late in March 1730. Some fifty-five exhausted *isleños* finally crowded into San Antonio one year later.

Quarrels began overnight. The Canary Islanders questioned why the San Antonio missions—now five in number after the recent relocation of three more left unprotected in Hasinai country by Inspector Rivera's elimination of the Presidio de los Tejas—should be permitted so much of the good land along the river? They wrangled about where to locate their new villa, agreeing finally to a site between presidio and river. It was the first chartered municipality in Texas.

Capt. Juan Antonio Pérez de Almazán supervised closely. In July 1731, employing sundial, fifty-*vara* measuring cord, plow, stakes, and stones, the Canary Islanders laid out the plaza, parcels for church and casas reales, house lots, and pasturelands. The captain then appointed their tempestuous leader, Juan Leal Goraz, first councilman along with five associate members of the cabildo.

Full of himself, Leal Goraz insisted on riding all the way to Mexico City, carrying a petition from the isleños. They wanted the spent, government-issued horses they had left at San Juan Bautista to be given to them. Irked, Viceroy Casafuerte reprimanded Captain Pérez de Almazán for allowing Leal or any other Canary Islander to leave the colony, but he let them have the horses.

Yet these immigrants were not horsemen. They were farmers, fishermen, and laborers forced by their new circumstances to adapt to the horse culture of San

Antonio. Nevertheless, they considered themselves superior to the earlier settlers. They had been given the usual subsidies and incentives as recruited colonists, or pobladores, and they looked forward pridefully to being addressed as hidalgos.[4]

A contentious lot, they cursed everybody. An official in Mexico City despaired that

> these families from the Canary Islands complain against the reverend fathers of the five missions, against the Indians that reside therein, against the captain of the presidio, and against the other forty-nine families settled there, so that it seems they desire to be left alone in undisputed possession. Perhaps even then they may not find enough room in the vast area of the entire province.[5]

Formal incorporation of the huffy Canary Islanders in 1731 completed the greater San Antonio conglomerate—villa of San Fernando, presidio of Béxar, and five Franciscan missions—situated in a band of watered prairie that looked out upon a vastness of open brush country ideal for raising cattle. The colony's capital, however, remained at Los Adaes in a dank forest five hundred miles east-northeast, opposite Natchitoches. The French post's proximity encouraged contraband.

Meanwhile, the swelling of San Antonio in 1731 invited further Apache response. Why a war party of hundreds, engaged with presidials from Béxar in September of that year, suddenly broke off hostilities and withdrew when it was plainly capable of wiping out the Spanish detachment, Captain Pérez de Almazán did not understand.

Neither did old José de Urrutia, the white Indian who in the 1690s had led a Native coalition in east Texas against Apaches. After reemerging into the Spaniards' world, Urrutia had married a daughter of Capt. Diego Ramón. Appointed to command at San Antonio in 1733, don José was surprised to hear that Jumanos and Pelones had joined with their former Apache enemies.

Urrutia parried Apache thrusts, took captives, bore the friars' wrath, tried to make peace, and sympathized with the community's terrified residents. "Their timidity does not surprise me (although I do not let them know it)." Apaches, he admitted, "who can enter a presidio at night as far as the center of the plaza and who without being heard can safely remove the horses from the corral in which they are tied to the doors of the houses are to be feared."[6]

Although he never met the savvy casta Captain Urrutia, criollo Juan Bautista de Anza, commanding the presidio of Fronteras seven hundred miles west-northwest of San Antonio, shared his counterpart's profound respect for Apaches.

While Urrutia dealt with Eastern or Plains Apaches, most often Lipanes, Anza did battle with Western Apaches, often Gileños. The latter, who suffered no Comanches pressing them against Spanish frontiers, also quickened their warfare in Sonora and Pimería Alta during the 1720s. Inspector Rivera had instituted at

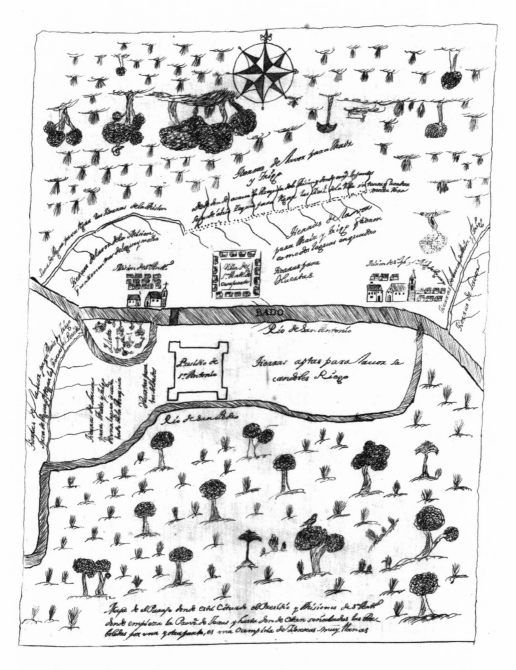

The Marqués de Aguayo's error-prone map from memory of San Antonio de Béxar, 1730. The San Antonio River bends the wrong way, the presidial irrigation ditch is incorrectly placed, and Mission San José appears on the opposite bank of the river. Archivo General de la Nación, Mexico City, Provincias Internas, 236. *Courtesy of the UT Institute of Texan Cultures at San Antonio.*

Fronteras in 1726 a set of twenty-one regulations for interim Captain Anza and had urged constant vigilance when passing through Apache territory, "being careful of the ambush which the cunning ones use."

The inspector noted the advantage Apaches wielding long lances had over presidial soldiers armed with short, broad swords, or *espadas anchas*. He had ordered that the soldiers arm themselves with and learn to use lances, but not so long as to impede their horsemanship.

Rivera knew, too, that because of the lax command of Anza's predecessor and the enemy's cleverness, Apaches had "committed continuous thefts of horses, cattle and other things penetrating right to the presidio itself." Hence, a squadron should be in the field at all times patrolling the passes by which the enemy entered the province. When scouts warned of Apaches in the interior, Anza was to cooperate with Janos in joint operations.

During his month at Fronteras, the inspector had anticipated every detail of supply, training, and discipline, down to a uniform dress code, including black hats. "Soldiers," furthermore, "must try to be clean and neat, for slovenliness in a soldier makes him a coward in spirit." Godliness counted too. The men should, above all, hear mass on days of obligation, comply with the annual precepts of the Church, and "pray the rosary every day in the guard room."[7]

Anza received formal royal appointment as captain at Fronteras in 1729. He never lacked confidence in his ability to deal with Apaches or any other Indian group. He had bragged to Rivera of his previous campaigns among the indomitable, poison-arrow-shooting Seris, a nonagricultural fishing and foraging people along Sonora's coast of the Gulf of California two hundred miles southwest of Fronteras. Hence, the inspector had given Anza a special charge to pacify the Seris "in case they become agitated." "In doing this," the *Reglamento* of 1729 warned, "the Captain should be careful not to neglect the defense of his own borders from the [Apache] enemy."[8]

He must also facilitate expansion beyond. A sworn ally of the Jesuits, Captain Anza took the missionaries' part. Their plan was to reoccupy the valley of the mainly northward-flowing Río de Santa María, today's Santa Cruz of southern Arizona, which had been without resident priests since the days of Father Kino. Based there, Father Agustín de Campos asserted, Jesuits could reach the Hopis.

That prospect also appealed to the twelfth bishop of Durango, don Benito Crespo. On an unprecedented visitation of New Mexico in 1730, the bishop severely criticized the Franciscans of that custody. They did not maintain the quota of missionaries for which they received annual stipends, they did not minister effectively or lovingly to the Pueblos, and worse, they did not know the Native languages. These friars, moreover, lacked the zeal to convert neighboring peoples, content instead simply to trade with them.[9]

Crespo grieved for the apostate Hopis. Since he imagined that their isolated mesas lay nearly equidistant from Franciscans in New Mexico and Jesuits in Pimería Alta, the bishop urged the Society of Jesus to bring the Hopis back within the Christian fold. He also seconded the Jesuits' appeal for ministers to man the northern Pimería, recalling a colorful delegation of headmen that Father Campos had led southward to meet him in 1726 at the Sonoran mining camp of Motepori.

In October 1731, three Jesuit missionaries-to-be—an Austrian, a Moravian, and a Swiss—reached Cuquiárachi, closest mission to Anza's presidio of Fronteras. Their superiors, Father Visitor Cristóbal de Cañas and Father Rector Luis María Gallardi, awaited them. Captain Anza and the two eldest missionaries of Pimería Alta, the Spaniards Campos and Velarde, were there too.

While the three recent arrivals underwent internships with veterans at established Pima missions and begged for supplies and animals, Captain Anza and a troop from Fronteras visited the rancherías of Santa María Soamca, San Gabriel de Guevavi, and San Xavier del Bac, and set Pimas of each to constructing shelters and planting wheat for the missionaries they were about to receive.

Later, Anza and don Eusebio Aquibissani, namesake of Kino and Native captain general of the Pima nation, presided over a gala ceremonial at Guevavi on May 4, 1732, before a reported one thousand Pimas. On signal, the presidials tossed their black hats in the air.

The tall, pock-marked Austrian Juan Bautista Grazhoffer at last found himself *entre infieles,* among heathens. As resident missionary at Guevavi with visitas at Sonoita, Arivaca, Tumacácori, and Tubac, he did not last long. When Father Felipe Segesser von Brunegg, the Swiss from Lucerne whom Anza had placed at San Xavier del Bac, rode south through Guevavi a year later, he found Grazhoffer gravely ill. On May 26, 1733, the Austrian died in Segesser's arms. Segesser accused the Pimas of poisoning him, "a fact which they later admitted."

Reassigned to Guevavi himself, Father Segesser now became the object of Pima scorn. The Natives along this river had grown used to the occasional festive visits of Father Kino or Campos who passed back and forth, always with gifts. Those black robes did not overstay their welcome. But Grazhoffer and Segesser did, along with Opata or Yaqui foremen who bossed the Pimas around. These resident missionaries challenged their hechiceros and forbade plural wives, transvestites, and ceremonial bacchanals with fermented cactus juice.

At least Father Segesser had a sense of humor. Once, after he ordered the Natives of his visita at Sonoita, half a day's ride northeast, to come help clear additional land for planting at Guevavi, their failure to appear perplexed him. When he investigated, he found them drunk, celebrating with gusto their annual rain ceremonial just before the summer planting. Brazen, they bid him to join them.

"Father, what do you say! Taste the wine, how sweet it is. It is certainly a fine drink." Thereupon some Indians brought a gourd dish filled with wine, to propitiate me. Since I wished to have nothing to do with the intoxicated Pimas, I sat cautiously to horse so as to be ready any instant for flight. Thereupon the magistrate [headman] called his companions to greet me, according to the custom of the region. Then one should have seen the capers they cut! Some, who could not even walk on their quaking knees, were dragged up by the others, and all shouted very tearfully: "Father, the drink is good! Get off your horse and join us, the wine is good!"

I did not consider it advisable to tarry longer with those drunkards. So although I could hardly contain my laughter I turned to the magistrate and said, very earnestly, "Tomorrow, we will look into the matter."[10]

Segesser and the others recorded routinely more burials than baptisms in the sacramental registers of their missions. To replace river Pimas who died, the missionaries invited desert-dwelling Pápagos, or Tohono O'odham, to move in. More and more came each winter, worked for food, and let their children be baptized, then left in the summer, thereby incorporating a stay at the missions in their seasonal migrations.

Of the three Europeans installed in the Santa Cruz Valley in 1732 by Anza, it was the tough Moravian Ignacio Javier Keller who endured longest and who accepted the challenge of the apostate Hopis. He served as long as he lived, until 1759. Like Kino, Keller was a loner. Unlike Kino, he drank too much.

Just as he and Segesser were about to observe the feast day of the Jesuits' founder, July 31, 1734, all the Pimas of Soamca, Guevavi, and Bac deserted. Rumors, planted allegedly by Spaniards who resented the missionaries' lock on Pima laborers, said that Captain Anza planned a slaughter. Instead, with the captain's assistance the black robes negotiated the return of their neophytes.

Always open to them, Anza's house at Fronteras saw a steady stream of Jesuits. When Segesser took violently sick at Guevavi for a second time—again he suspected the malignant influence of his neophytes—doña María Rosa, señora de Anza, nursed him back to health at the presidio.

She was six months' pregnant when her husband took in the elderly, overwrought Father Campos, whom, don Juan assured the Jesuit provincial, "with much joy and charity I will attend in my home until his death, for in his present state of health he has not much longer to live." In midsummer, doña María Rosa gave birth. No one said whether Father Agustín was fit to attend the baptism of Juan Bautista de Anza the younger on July 7, 1736. Campos had lost his mind the previous April and had fortified himself at his visita of Imuris with hundreds of armed Pimas, swearing to fight his removal to the death. Anza's offer of asylum had defused a highly explosive situation. The old missionary then left the Anzas'

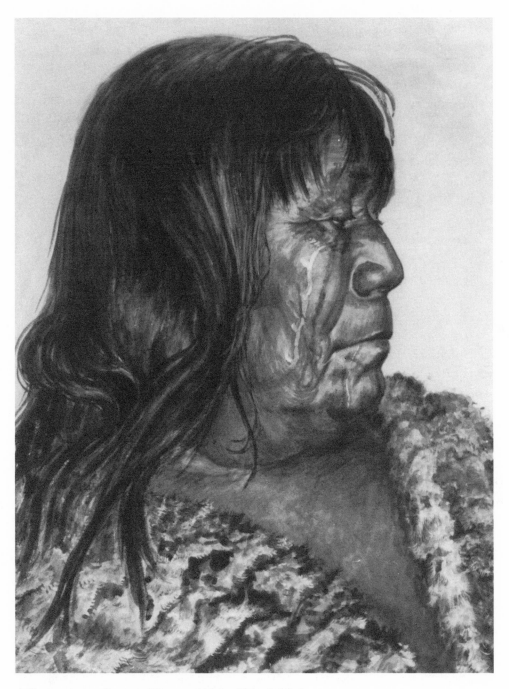

A Piman woman. *Courtesy of Tumacacori National Historical Park.*

home for his order's community in Chihuahua. He died at Baserac en route on
July 24.

Although the Society of Jesus had no third order of sworn laymen, the previous provincial had admitted the captain of Fronteras as a Jesuit "brother," a most
unusual acknowledgment of the order's esteem for Juan Bautista de Anza.[11]

Encouraged by Anza, Father Keller organized an expedition later in 1736 and
followed the Santa Cruz all the way northwest to its junction with the Gila. He
inquired about the Hopis. Captain Anza wanted to trace the Gila westward to the
Colorado and, like Kino, cross over to California. Both hoped that any royal share
of the phenomenal *planchas de plata,* chunks of virgin silver found in 1736 not far
from a small settlement called Arizona, would be invested in expansion.[12]

Though he would try again in 1743, with an escort from the new, nearer presidio of Terrenate, Keller, confronted by Apaches, never did reach the Hopis, nor
Anza California. After Father Jacobo Sedelmayr's 1744 effort also aborted, the Jesuits
quietly excused themselves from the enterprise of the Hopis, turning their attention back toward the Gila and Colorado rivers.

Their heroic friend, Juan Bautista de Anza the elder, spurring toward Fronteras
from Keller's mission of Soamca on May 9, 1740, had got ahead of the column.
He failed to sense the ambush. Toppled from his horse, Anza died of arrow wounds,
while Apaches cut away the crown of his scalp. No one could believe it, least of
all the numbed Father Keller.[13]

Across the gulf in California, where the exclusive Jesuit regime had produced
thirteen missions by the late 1730s, troubles had erupted in the south.

Late in 1720, some months before Father Visitor Juan de Ugarte sailed his
Triunfo de la Cruz to the head of the gulf and the Colorado River, he had loaded
aboard Aragonese Father Jaime Bravo, armed helpers, and supplies for another
Spanish attempt at occupying the broad Bay of La Paz. Bravo fought the odds at
Mission Nuestra Señora del Pilar until 1728, when the Scotch Jesuit Guillermo
Gordon took over.

The mission the Jesuits had been promising for three decades—near the very
tip of the peninsula as an aid station for returning Manila galleons—at last took
shape in 1730, thanks to an extra donation of ten thousand pesos by don José de la
Puente, Marqués de Villapuente, who contributed heavily to Jesuit missions in
California and the Far East. He wanted it dedicated to his name saint, hence Mission
San José del Cabo, situated just back from the Bay of San Bernabé.

As always, dozens of crewmen and passengers aboard *Nuestra Señora del Pilar de
Zaragosa* lay about suffering scurvy and malnutrition as the galleon rode endlessly
down the coast in January 1734. When at last she anchored in the shallow Bay of

San Bernabé, veteran Father Nicolás Tamaral wasted no time in providing *pitahaya* fruit and fresh meat. Most of the sick recovered quickly.

The galleon's elite had evidently not hoarded food or medicine for themselves during the passage, because the captain and an Augustinian superior traveling back to Mexico City from the Philippines also remained too weak to reboard. For two months, Tamaral tended them at the mission. When they had regained strength, he arranged their passage all the way to the viceregal capital, assigning Santiago Villalobos, the one soldier of his mission guard, as escort. The Jesuits capitalized on the story. Future galleons should count on succor at the Bay of San Bernabé.

A year later, don Mateo de Zumalde, unable to anchor the *San Cristóbal* because of high winds and waves, managed to secure the vessel nearby in the Bay of San Lucas. Longboats took the sick ashore and a detail to dig for fresh water. Eight sailors who had landed earlier and five more went for Father Tamaral.

When the men sent to find the missionary did not return, Gerónimo, a clever, Spanish-speaking headman, made excuses. Zumalde became suspicious. Ordering the people on shore back on board, the captain arrested Gerónimo and three others not quick enough to jump over the side. Hundreds of Pericúes now appeared on the beach and let fly a shower of arrows.

Under interrogation, Gerónimo confessed. Months before, they had bludgeoned, mutilated, and burned Father Tamaral. Father Lorenzo Carranco, his two servants, and don Manuel Andrés Romero had met similar ends. Short of women, the Natives had taken as captives María, wife of the absent Santiago Villalobos, her sister, and the couple's two daughters.

The Pericúes, occupying the far southern end of the peninsula and several off-shore islands, had not welcomed Jesuits among them. Ever-competing, disease-racked bands had joined in 1734 to destroy missionaries and soldiers. Syphilis had killed so many of their women that surviving males fought for mates. Their leaders and shamans resented whippings for showing disrespect or having plural women. Among them, too, were restless outsiders, in the words of Father Tamaral,

> a number of *coyotes, lobos,* and others of mixed background left by the English or Dutch ships that had long frequented those coasts. These people of vile, mixed blood are the ones who disturb and agitate the local people. They are the ones who domineer the populace and lead them astray.[14]

No friend of the Jesuits, Viceroy-archbishop don Juan Antonio de Vizarrón y Eguiarreta delayed sending a punitive expedition to avenge the deaths. He brushed aside their plea the next year that Juan Bautista de Anza of Fronteras be named commander of an expeditionary force and instead chose Sinaloa-Sonora's first governor, Manuel Bernal de Huidobro, who despised Jesuit privilege as much as the viceroy did.

Mission San José del Cabo, Baja California, with the Manila galleon arriving with food supplies. After a drawing by missionary Ignacio Tirsch, S. J., 1762–67. Watercolor by Joanne Haskell Crosby. *Courtesy of Harry W. Crosby and the artist.*

Belatedly in 1736, Bernal de Huidobro crossed to the peninsula with soldiers and armed citizens from Sinaloa, some of them relatives of California presidials. He went to learn what he could about the closed operation of the Jesuits as much as to pacify the Native peoples. Missionaries on the mainland had recruited and sent across a hundred Yaqui fighting men, so-called volunteers.

The governor stayed a year and a half, largely ignoring the Jesuits' advice, belittling locals who answered to them, and attempting to negotiate peace with rebel bands. Just before he left, he got tough and seized twenty-six alleged rebel leaders, then exiled them to the mainland. Others gave up.

Bernal de Huidobro challenged the Jesuit enterprise of California as no one had before him. On the viceroy's order, he had set up in 1736 an independent, thirty-man presidio at San José del Cabo. Not until 1740 could the Society of Jesus exert enough pressure in Madrid and Mexico City to force Viceroy Vizarrón to reverse himself and again acknowledge Jesuit oversight.

Violence, meantime, shifted to southern Sonora. A searing drought followed by torrential downpours in 1739 set the scene. As famine settled over the land, Jesuit insistence on supplying the usual foodstuffs and cattle to dependent California heightened tensions.

A Baja California soldier and his daughter. After a drawing by missionary Ignacio Tirsch, S. J., 1762–67. Watercolor by Joanne Haskell Crosby. *Courtesy of Harry W. Crosby and the artist.*

Yaqui veterans of the recent lackadaisical California venture laughed with contempt at Bernal de Huidobro and his Spanish worthies. Joined in the Yaqui revolt of 1740 by Mayos and Lower Pimas, thousands of Natives went on a sporadic, two-year rampage against their Jesuit missionaries and the colonial regime. They attacked missions, mines, and ranches, and the governor fled. Although not that many people died, the disruption of mining, ranching, and commerce won for the Yaquis a hearing of their grievances.

They wanted specific overbearing Jesuits and their arrogant mixed-blood foremen removed. They wanted to carry their traditional weapons. They wanted pay for work in the missions, supervision of their own elections, recognition of their plots of land and subsistence crops, and the right to sell their produce and seek work outside the missions. In short, they wanted less interference in their communities and their lives. From the early 1740s on, under such pressures, Jesuits in Sonora and Baja California found themselves increasingly on the defensive.[15]

Nevertheless, from Madrid came a decree in 1744 urging the shaken black robes to extend their missions into Alta California. Escorted by soldiers, they could move north from Sonora and Pimería Alta, convert the Natives along the Gila and Colorado rivers, then cross over. "This refers," the decree proclaimed, "to our having discovered and ascertained that the province of the Californias is not an island, as was commonly believed, but is land bordering upon New Mexico along its upper regions, or to the north."[16]

No one in New Mexico at the time gazed westward toward California. They were looking in the opposite direction, from whence a party of eight or nine audacious Frenchmen had actually made it across the plains to Santa Fe in July 1739.

Received as miraculous foreign visitors, not enemies, Pierre and Paul Mallet reveled in cordial confinement. Lodged in the homes of Santa Fe's leading citizens, they and their men stayed nine months while a courier carried southward Gov. Gaspar Domingo de Mendoza's plea for instructions from the viceroy. Should these Frenchmen be detained? Yes and no, came the reply. They should be encouraged to become New Mexicans, but not by force. Two did.

Louis Morin or Moreau, renamed Luis María Mora, married Juana Muñiz. Accused later of sorcery and stirring up Pueblo Indians, he met his death in one of eighteenth-century New Mexico's rare cases of capital punishment. The other, a barber named Jean, or Juan Bautista Alarí, wed María Francisca Fernández de la Pedrera, a young widow, and dutifully raised a large family.

With no alternative to high-priced manufactured goods from the south via Chihuahua, a good many New Mexicans favored commerce across the plains with French Louisiana. Vicar Santiago Roybal, New Mexico's first native-born Hispanic priest, who was trained in New Spain and installed by Bishop Crespo, took the lead. Writing from Santa Fe to his counterpart in New Orleans, Roybal listed items he wanted, assuring French merchants of the profits to be made, "because we are not farther away than 200 leagues from a very rich mine, abounding in silver, called Chihuahua, where the inhabitants of this country often go to trade." The Mallets delivered the letter.

Even though the elaborate expedition mounted in response by the Sieur de Bienville, governor of French Louisiana, aborted, small parties of Frenchmen, chancing passage through Comanche country, occasionally straggled in through Taos or Pecos during the 1740s and 1750s. They could never predict their reception. Dynastic wars in Europe sometimes cast France and Spain as allies, other times as foes. Individual governors of New Mexico, too, had their prejudices.

When Pierre Mallet and three fellows, despoiled of most of their trade goods by Comanches, reappeared in November 1750 with letters from the governor and merchants of Louisiana, local officials took them into custody, hustling them down to El Paso, where Gov. Tomás Vélez Cachupín awaited. He showed no sympathy but seized the Frenchmen's remaining possessions and sold them at auction. With the proceeds, Vélez Cachupín dispatched the four under guard to Mexico City.

Jean Chapuis and Louis Feuilli, who showed up in 1752 with silk garters, ivory combs, dry goods, and hardware, suffered the same fate. Such treatment discouraged others.[17]

On the close border between Louisiana and east Texas, meanwhile, Frenchmen and Spaniards all but lived together. Nearly constant exchange, quarrels, and intimacy bound neighboring Los Adaes and Natchitoches, where the irrepressible Louis Juchereau de Saint-Denis still ruled. Without French foodstuffs, the presidial garrison of Nuestra Señora del Pilar de los Adaes could not have survived.

Passing back and forth, Spanish Franciscans baptized and married the French commander's own children and grandchildren. Seventeen-year-old Victoria González, daughter of the Spanish presidial captain, fell in love with one of Saint-Denis's soldiers, taking him as her husband in Natchitoches on April 8, 1736. Although the common people of the two communities grew used to daily intercourse, officials on both sides hastened to express nationalistic loyalties to their superiors.

When Saint-Denis died in June 1744, Texas Gov. Justo Boneo y Morales showed proper restraint, and he and Father President Francisco Vallejo put on sad faces at the funeral. A few days later, however, reporting to Viceroy Conde de Fuenclara, Boneo as good as rejoiced at Saint-Denis's demise. At last, he implied, Spaniards in Texas could breathe easier.[18] The viceroy was not so sure. Frenchmen trading among the thinned Caddo peoples, even their selling firearms to Plains nations, paled before the looming menace of England's ever more populous North American colonies.

Stretching northward from the gulf port of Tampico, lately sacked twice by Englishmen, lay the so-called Seno Mexicano, an uninhabited, four-hundred-mile arc of coastline. Given the dangerous precedent of Georgia, founded in 1733 on the Atlantic with a sea-to-sea claim, what was to prevent a similar English initiative in the Gulf of Mexico? The vacant shores opposite Nuevo León and Texas tempted foreign rivals.

Inland, across the flat coastal plain and back into rugged mountain canyons, unreduced ranchería Indians moved about at will—surviving gatherers and hunters joined by resentful runaways from Franciscan missions in the formidable Sierra Gorda to the south and from the slavelike *congrega* system of Nuevo León. Their raids on neighboring ranches and towns gave Spaniards a second, more immediate cause for action.

No one who went to sleep in 1747 and awakened in 1757 would have believed it. The militia colony of Nuevo Santander sprang into being during that decade, overspreading the vastness between the Río Pánuco in the south and the Nueces

River to the north and from Nuevo León and Coahuila eastward to the Gulf. Inspector José Tienda de Cuervo in 1757 reckoned the colony contained eight thousand *gente de razón;* eighty thousand cattle, horses, and mules; and three hundred thousand sheep.

No relocation of people and resources from New Spain to the northern frontier was ever better planned. And one man, contemporaries agreed, deserved the credit: don José de Escandón, Conde de Sierra Gorda, who laid out the project in exacting detail. Then, relying on the extraordinary authority given him by Viceroy Conde de Revillagigedo, his own keen organizational skills, and his personal wealth from extensive landed estates, don José oversaw the entire operation and paid half the cost himself, evidently well over fifty thousand pesos.

A detachment from undermanned Texas took part in the initial 1747 reconnaissance, wherein seven distinct columns from bordering jurisdictions penetrated the region in a coordinated sweep to identify healthful, watered sites and intimidate Natives. Gov. Francisco García Larios sent twenty-five men from Los Adaes to La Bahía to join Capt. Joaquín de Orobio y Basterra's twenty-five. Their discovery that the Nueces did not empty into the Río Grande, but directly into the Bay of San Miguel Arcángel on the Gulf, surprised some of the veterans.

When early in 1748 captain and governor attended solemn rites mourning Felipe V and hailing Fernando VI, La Bahía on the Guadalupe River, with its ninety-man garrison, was the strongest military base in Texas. At Escandón's bidding, the whole community moved westward a year later to another inland site on the lower San Antonio, later Goliad, but the colonizer's proposed coastal town at the mouth of the Nueces, where Corpus Christi now rises, did not soon materialize.

Still, the phenomenal colonization proceeded, with Governor Escandón founding two dozen villas or villas-to-be all over Nuevo Santander. While some fifteen missionary reductions attended the occupation, most run by Franciscans from the college of Nuestra Señora de Guadalupe in Zacatecas, it was neither traditional missions nor presidios that distinguished Escandón's effort, but civilian towns. At each, a militia captain appointed by the governor served as mayor.

Hundreds of volunteer families rallied first in Querétaro, then in Nuevo León and Coahuila. Crop failures in central New Spain had doubled the price of maize, rendering more attractive the incentives offered by Escandón—bonuses up to two hundred pesos, moving expenses, allotments of land, and exemption from taxes for ten years—while at the same time driving up costs for him and the government.

Settlement spilled into the lower Rio Grande Valley mostly on the near side where Camargo and Reynosa took primitive form in 1749. Revilla (Guerrero) and Mier followed, and on the far bank Dolores, which faltered, and in 1755 Laredo, which lasted. Laredo's location on the Rio Grande alongside the Paso de Jacinto

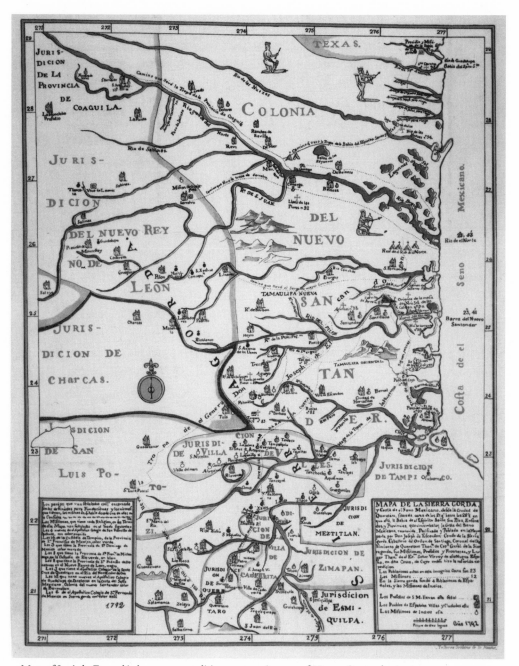

Map of José de Escandón's seven-expedition reconnaissance of Nuevo Santander in 1747.
Archivo General de la Nación, Mexico City. *From Chipman and Joseph,* Notable Men and Women.

de León—where the most direct route to Texas from Nuevo León and Coahuila crossed—assured its growth. Lured by broad grazing grants, the stockmen from Coahuila and Nuevo León who became founding captains of these isolated ranching communities bore family names still prominent in the area: Cantú, Garza Falcón, Guerra, Vásquez Borrego, Sánchez.

Laredo in 1757, ten years before its charter as villa, boasted eleven families and four single men, eighty-five souls in all. Capt. Tomás Sánchez de la Barrera y Garza and wife doña Catalina Uribe headed the largest household with nine children and seven servants. Later censuses of criollos, mestizos, and mulattos residing in the villa and its district would put Laredo's population at 200 in 1767, 700 in 1789, and 1,418 in 1819. Fares on the town's ferry, free to locals, were set at two reales per head and one per package.[19]

Before Laredo, most travelers crossed to Texas eighty miles upriver at the old Paso de Francia near San Juan Bautista. None splashed over with more gusto than Capt. Felipe de Rábago y Terán, a handsome and vainglorious lecher en route in 1751 to found a presidio and scandalize the Franciscans at their unprosperous, multiethnic San Xavier missions on the San Gabriel River, some 130 miles northeast of San Antonio.

Emboldened by wealth from Zacatecas mines, don Felipe was evidently one of those charmers who could get away with murder. Such outrageous behavior as his, however, unchecked by self-restraint or peers, could bring down an upper class.

Willingly or not, the pretty young wife of tailor Juan José Ceballos fell easy prey. Don Felipe had her in his bed in an instant. Rábago flaunted his sexual misdeeds. When challenged by Ceballos and the friars, the captain went berserk. According to hostile testimony, he ordered the tailor shackled to a wall, had a cot set up, and proceeded to rape the woman while her husband watched.

She was not his only victim. Rábago's soldiers procured Indian women for him and for themselves, to the point that fray Miguel Pinilla in February 1752 excommunicated the entire garrison. When in May the cuckolded tailor and fray José Francisco de Ganzábal were found dead, Rábago was implicated in the double murder.

As an officer and gentleman of means, Felipe de Rábago y Terán had recourse to lawyers and relatives. Testimony in the case, too, was rife with inconsistencies. Transferred as captain to the presidio of Santa Rosa del Sacramento in Coahuila, Rábago underwent eight years of investigation and occasional confinement, finally winning acquittal on appeal and, incredibly, reassignment to another Texas presidio. Although the Franciscans in San Antonio blanched at his return, don Felipe was a changed man.[20]

No don Juan, veteran Diego Ortiz Parrilla swaggered as famously as Rábago and like him always seemed to be in the wrong place at the wrong time. Calamity stalked don Diego: in 1751, 1758, and 1759. But he always blamed others and got on with his career.

Late in 1751, Lieutenant Colonel Ortiz Parrilla, former captain of dragoons in Veracruz and commandant of Puebla de los Angeles, was feeling rather smug about his recent appointment as governor and captain general of Sinaloa-Sonora. He had waged with some success the all-out war against the Seris that reformer Rafael Rodríguez Gallardo believed wrongly would crush their resistance forever. He had also orchestrated the destruction of Seri missions on the Río San Miguel, the exile of adult prisoners to the Caribbean, and invasion of the Indians' refuge on Tiburón Island. The last feat was accomplished with the assistance of more than four hundred Upper Pima fighting men under their charismatic leader Luis Oacpicagigua, whom Ortiz Parrilla, without consulting the Jesuit missionaries, had designated Native captain general of Pimería Alta.

Like the trusted Esteban Clemente, who turned on the Spaniards of New Mexico about 1670, Luis Oacpicagigua of the Pima ranchería of Sáric also used his position to advantage. He attracted an entourage. Mirroring Spanish behavior, he became a planter and stockman, a patrón who employed other Pimas as dependents and displayed lavish generosity. He gave gifts and hosted feasts and ceremonials.

On his way in 1751 to join in the fall Apache campaign with soldiers from Terrenate—one of two Sonora presidios founded in the wake of the 1740 Yaqui uprising—don Luis rode tall in the saddle, sporting a Spanish uniform jacket, mounted on a fine horse, and brandishing musket and sword. At Guevavi, the jovial Father José Garrucho feted him and his men as heroes of the Seri wars. Luis loved it. He and his spirited party then continued south up the river to Soamca, where the crusty Father Keller may have been drunk. Whatever the circumstances, Keller was alleged to have gravely offended don Luis—by one account calling him a Chichimec dog better suited to wearing coyote skin and loincloth and to chasing rabbits and rodents in the hills.

When the Upper Pimas rose in rebellion several weeks later, killing two Jesuit priests and a hundred or more mission sympathizers, destroying property, and fleeing to the hills, Ortiz Parrilla blamed the Jesuits and the Jesuits blamed him. Partisans of both sides gave scathing testimony of their opponents' abuses. Although they later thought of countless reasons why an uprising was bound to occur—most notably, the excessive honors the governor had heaped on Luis and his men—Jesuit correspondence on the eve of the revolt demonstrated that the missionaries had no clue that it was about to happen.

Pima discontent with a rising tide of Spanish livestock growers and small-scale miners across their territory, the resentment of mission Indians punished or asked to work by Jesuits, and episodes of drought and disease probably came together to create a climate of unrest. The spark, however, was the pride of Luis Oacpicagigua. With a vengeance, don Luis transfigured himself into the "Enemy of Adobe Houses."

Hastily mobilizing presidial troops and militiamen, Governor Ortiz Parrilla nevertheless showed restraint. He offered amnesty. Once Pima combatants had suffered a humiliating defeat at Arivaca, they began reappearing at the missions. Even Luis gave up, coming in alone at sunset on March 18, 1752, to Tubac on the Santa Cruz River, a visita of Guevavi. There a year later, workers would construct Sonora's newest Spanish presidio.[21]

Diego Ortiz Parrilla's next assignment took him to Texas, where at least there were no Jesuits. Although local Franciscans had long clashed with presidial captains over how best to pacify the Lipan Apaches, certain of the friars saw Ortiz Parrilla as an ally. He was essential to their special project.

Back in the summer of 1749, just as don Diego acceded to the governorship of Sinaloa-Sonora, the friars, soldiers, and settlers of San Antonio had assembled for an elaborate, three-day peace ceremonial. Four Lipan chiefs had taken part, driven by Comanches and their French-supplied brothers-in-arms to seek open alliance with Spaniards.

Subsequent expeditions had identified a comely site for the Franciscans' long-anticipated mission to the Lipanes, an irrigable plain with protective bluff along the San Sabá River, about 135 miles northwest of San Antonio. Mineral deposits purportedly lay nearby. This country was more arid, like the plains. Because of doubts about jurisdiction, the viceroy directed the undertaking, not the governor of Texas.

Fray Alonso Giraldo de Terreros, stiff-necked former superior of the missionary college of Querétaro, had lobbied in Mexico City for the project. When fray Alonso's cousin, mining magnate and philanthropist don Pedro Romero de Terreros, volunteered to pay all expenses of three missions for three years, viceregal authorities consented to support a nearby, hundred-man presidio.

By early 1757, Colonel Ortiz Parrilla had brought the remnant of Rábago's garrison of San Xavier de Gigedo to San Antonio, where the autocratic Father Terreros soon reminded him of Jesuits he had known. The friar let no one forget his status as coequal commander of the venture.

The colonel foresaw trouble, but it would not be his fault. Having observed members of a Lipan delegation, whose attention seemed not to extend beyond the gifts they were receiving, Ortiz Parrilla wrote to the project's benefactor in Mexico City, cautioning him. "The state in which we have found the Apaches is so different from what I expected that I assure you the method of their pacification is a

NOBILISSIMUS EQUIDEM VIR,
Cujus egregias animi dotes,
In Deum pietatem,
In Divos reverentiam,
Vitae integritatem, avitum majorum splendorem,
Nulla unquám aetas debet oblitterare,
Tanti ergo Heróis
Temporum injuriâ grata ne pereat memoria.

El Sr. D. Pedro Romero de Terreros Ochoa
y Castilla Primer Conde de Regla,
Caballero profeso en la orden militar
de Calatrava, Fundador del Real Monte de
Piedad de la Ciudad de Mexico &. Varon
distinguido por el zelo de la propagacion
de la fe Católica, por el servicio del Rey,
y por el del Público.

Lit. Martinez y Cª

Pedro Romero de Terreros, patron of the San Sabá mission project. *From* Biografía de D. Pedro Romero de Terreros *(1851). Courtesy of the Benson Latin American Collection, University of Texas at Austin.*

major concern to me." Father Terreros fumed over what he perceived as Ortiz Parrilla's delaying tactics. When at last in April 1757 the two of them stood on the banks of the San Sabá, the arthritic friar resented the colonel's smugness. Not a single Apache showed up to greet them.

No matter. The half-dozen Franciscans vowed to get on with raising their first mission, Santa Cruz de San Sabá, on the river's south bank near a grove of welcoming oak trees. Woodcutting, hauling, digging, and building by hired artisans, laborers, and a small corps of Tlaxcalan Indians enlisted by Terreros in Saltillo, took their minds off the omnipresent chiggers and ticks and absent Apaches.

Three miles upstream to the west on the opposite bank—far enough, the friars calculated, to keep soldiers and Apache women from fraternizing—the momentarily resigned Colonel Ortiz Parrilla oversaw the first phase of military construction. With a strong log and earth stockade, gun platforms, and rows of rude barracks of jacal and thatch construction, the presidio of San Luis de las Amarillas came to house perhaps four hundred people, more than half of them women and children.

Still no Apaches; then in mid-June, overnight, hundreds of bright tepees stretched away outside the mission complex. The friars estimated three thousand people. If indeed they were determined to continue northward on their seasonal buffalo hunt, would the hunters at least leave their women and children at the mission? They would not.[22]

The missionaries hung their heads. Four gave up and withdrew; another came. Terreros anguished in letters to his cousin. He had begun to feel sorry for himself, lamenting that "This writing is upon the trunk of an oak tree, surrounded by others. I remain with a pain in the shoulder which catches my whole arm and has put my fingers to sleep. I believe it is rheumatism of some severity." Although he judged himself a poor manager of the project, he would not allow his cousin's investment to be wasted. "I commit myself," he swore, "to protect all, to gorge the ticks, and suffer rheumatism. For our Divine Majesty I wish to do it, for it coincides with the benefit of eternal life." Discomfited in mind and body, he endured the fall and a vicious winter.[23]

The Lipanes, if Spanish veterans assessed the Indians' strategy correctly, had worked to encourage enmity between Comanches and Spaniards. Raiding Comanche camps, these Apaches would purposely leave behind items of Spanish manufacture while they stole Comanche artifacts to plant during their own raids on Spaniards.

At about midnight on February 25, 1757, unidentified Indians attacked and stampeded the San Sabá presidio's horse herd, confirming rumors that Comanches and their northern allies were gathering for war. A vain pursuit and an attack on a squad going for escort duty followed. Smoke signals rose menacingly from the hills to the north and east.

When the fatalistic Terreros flatly rejected Ortiz Parrilla's written plea that he and thirty-some others at the mission take refuge in the presidial compound, the commander went in person to appeal to the friar's better judgment. It was no use. Therefore, what happened the next day, March 16, 1758, was not Ortiz Parrilla's fault. As proof, the colonel requested later that fray Miguel Molina, who had lived at San Sabá only six weeks, give an eyewitness account.

The sun had barely risen. Father Terreros had just finished saying his mass, and fray José de Santiesteban was about to begin. Molina, hearing commotion outside the stockade, ran to warn the other two priests. Hundreds, maybe thousands, of Indians, shouting and firing their muskets, had surrounded the mission and were calling for the people inside to open the gate. Asensio Cadena, corporal of the mission guard, heard words in Spanish and recognized some Hasinais, presumed to be friends. He convinced the friars to let their visitors in.

Whereupon, from the courtyard Fathers Terreros and Molina looked out upon a scene that stuck terror in their hearts. "[I was] filled with amazement and fear," Molina remembered,

> when I saw nothing but Indians on every hand, armed with guns and arrayed in the most horrible attire. Besides the paint on their faces, red and black, they were adorned with the pelts and tails of wild beasts, wrapped around them or hanging down from their heads, as well as deer horns. Some were disguised as various kinds of animals, and some wore feather headdresses. All were armed with muskets, swords, and lances, and I noticed also that they had brought with them some youths armed with bows and arrows, doubtless to train and encourage them in their cruel and bloody way of life.[24]

The friars practically fell over themselves trying to distribute gifts to the horde that pressed in. Molina handed four bunches of tobacco to an Indian, "whom the others recognized as their great chief. He was of the Comanche nation," Molina learned.

> This Indian was ceremonially dressed in vestments of war, with a red coat from a French uniform, and was well armed. Of a horrible countenance, he was extremely serious; indeed, he accepted the handfuls of tobacco I offered with a sneer and too much circumspection, without dismounting or making any gestures of gratitude.

Now they began carrying off everything they could lay hands on: pots from the kitchen, clothing, the horses from the corral. A Hasinai leader asked Father Terreros for a written permit to enter the presidio, and the scared friar consented. When that did not open the fort, the Indian came back for Terreros.

In the tense moments that followed, the Franciscan got on a horse and someone

Comanche war leader, by Roy Andersen. *Courtesy of the artist and Pecos National Historical Park.*

shot him. That set the mob on a rampage. Outside the stockade, Indians lighted the wood and brush they had piled against all four sides. Molina, who crouched in a room with others firing through embrasures, reckoned the number of their attackers must have grown to over two thousand, more than half carrying firearms.

They turned back the detachment sent by Ortiz Parrilla from the presidio and kept on sacking the mission. Somehow, gathered in the church amid smoke and mayhem, Father Molina and a majority of the defenders survived, escaping about midnight. Six mission residents had died, along with the other two Franciscans, Terreros from gunshot wounds and a lance thrust, Santiesteban from decapitation.

The terrified Molina, whose chest stung from the wound of a ricocheting musket ball, made his way to the south "away from the unfortunate mission, constantly searching for hidden paths and trails." On the second day, he doubled back and reached the presidio; he found it "on the alert and expecting an attack from the Indians, because they were still in the vicinity, to the east and north." His own deliverance, the friar knew, was a miracle.[25]

A few days later, surveying what was left, Ortiz Parrilla kicked at blackened boards and smoldering debris in what had been the mission warehouse. Barrels of flour, crates of chocolate, tobacco bales, and crocks lay smashed or strewn over the floor. Sacred images and paintings, priestly vestments, and altar furnishings intended for the project's next two missions had been hacked and torn to pieces. The colonel's men, covering their noses and mouths, rolled human body parts onto blankets and buried them. Not even the mission cats had survived.[26]

Vengeance—the desire to restore the honor of Spanish arms by defeating the tribes of the north in their own country—drove Ortiz Parrilla, if not the majority of his unkempt force. Finally in September 1759, seventeen months after the annihilation of mission Santa Cruz de San Sabá, more than five hundred men took to the field, counting presidial soldiers, militia irregulars, mission Indians, and Apache guides and scouts.

A victory too easily won, at a Tonkawa camp 160 miles northeast of San Sabá, where they claimed to have killed 55 and captured 149, made them cocky. Pressing on another hundred miles, they approached the Red River, about fifty miles east of today's Wichita Falls.

The presidials of the vanguard, drawn forward in a skirmish with the enemy, rubbed their eyes. Before them stood a Taovaya, or Wichita, village, "formed of large huts of oval shape, enclosed by a stockade and a moat," in the words of their commander. Above, provocatively, waved the flag of France.

Not only Taovayas, but also Comanches and people of other nations of the north, had gathered here, the same confederation that had thrown down the gauntlet at San Sabá. Ortiz Parrilla knew that the hour of reckoning had come.

The destruction of
Mission San Sabá.
Painting by José de
Páez (?), c. 1763.
Photo by Arturo
Piera. *Courtesy of the
Museo Nacional de
Arte, Mexico City,
and the Texas State
Historical Association.*

But the enemy fort was too strong. There were too many of them, and, he admitted, "they have the advantage in arms and determination." After four hours of fighting, the Spanish commander ordered his two small cannon brought up. At each of eleven rounds, the defenders jeered. He was forced to withdraw, having suffered 10 percent casualties. Ortiz Parrilla blamed his ill-disciplined, untrained militia—what could he expect of shepherds, tailors, laborers, cigar dealers, shoemakers, mine workers, and the like?

Nevertheless, by acknowledging the bravery, military preparedness, and unprecedented firepower of the nations of the north, he provided valuable intelligence to Spanish imperial ministers. Furthermore, he believed these enemies were not only supplied but also directed by Frenchmen. Bidding for promotion, Diego Ortiz Parrilla assured the Spanish king that he had served with "zeal, valor, and exemplary conduct . . . in inflicting punishment on the enemy."[27]

Later, as governor at Pensacola in 1764, Colonel Ortiz Parrilla directed the town's evacuation as England took possession of Florida—an event undeniably not his fault.[28]

Despite the costly reverses, Spaniards refused to abandon the presidio of San Sabá, but kept men-at-arms and civilian workers under the reformed Capt. Felipe de Rábago y Terán at that advanced post for another decade. To get there, Rábago struck directly north from San Juan Bautista, leaving San Antonio and his harshest critics far to the east.

During an active command at San Sabá, don Felipe rebuilt the fort with quarried limestone and rearmed its garrison, spending liberally of his own money. Viceroy Marqués de Cruillas wanted him to open a route to New Mexico. The reconnaissance he sent west to the Pecos, however, proved that the distance was far greater than the viceroy's advisers reckoned and that warring Native peoples made the way impracticable.[29]

While Captain Rábago tried to redeem himself at isolated San Sabá, don Pedro Romero de Terreros in Mexico City commissioned a mural-sized oil painting to memorialize his martyred Franciscan cousin. This was not a primitive frontier sketch on hide, but a monumental, 83 by 115-inch easel painting by professional artists, probably associated with Miguel Cabrera's famed studio. Again, as in the cruder depiction of the Villasur massacre thirty-eight years before, the action is furious.

At the center of the canvas, flanked by two giant, stereotypical, bloodied figures of fray Alonso Giraldo de Terreros and fray José de Santiesteban, the mission compound is being overrun. More than three hundred separate figures dash about, engaging each other or cowering. Puffs of gunsmoke issue from the attackers' French muskets. On close examination, red letters reveal that what appears to be the frozen frame of one violent moment is actually eighteen sequential vignettes, each identified in the extensive key, each based on details from accounts of the pillaging. Fearful disobedience has reentered the garden.[30]

During the three decades between Brigadier Pedro de Rivera's keen observations in the mid-1720s and the obliteration of mission Santa Cruz de San Sabá in 1758, the Comanches and their chosen allies had become the dominant power on the south plains. Spanish horses had been there for the taking. Plentiful French guns in the hands of these deft horsemen rendered them virtually unbeatable in their own element. Yet as much as they terrified colonists who ventured beyond San Antonio or Santa Fe, Comanches posed only one of the knotty challenges that absorbed Spanish imperialists as the 1760s dawned.

10 Visions and Realities

I praise God because it seems that in our times that ancient Spanish enthusiasm for discovering and taking possession of new lands lives again, sacrificing lives and fortunes in this enterprise for the gain of such precious pearls as souls.

—FRAY FRANCISCO GARCÉS, 1776

The Spaniards accuse the Indians of cruelty. I do not know what opinion they would have of us: perhaps it would be no better.

—BERNARDO DE GÁLVEZ, C. 1785–86

Two singular world events guaranteed that the three decades from 1760 to 1790 would be the most eventful yet on New Spain's far northern frontier. France lost the Seven Years' War, and Carlos III ascended the Spanish throne. Visions and realities commingled.

Ever-confident Diego Ortiz Parrilla, briefing Viceroy Marqués de Cruillas late in 1760, quoted a letter from veteran fray José Francisco Calahorra y Sáenz at the east Texas mission of Nuestra Señora de Guadalupe de los Nacogdoches. The Franciscan had learned that "the English hasten in their war with the French. It is said that they have taken Quebec, which is in Canada, and that five thousand English are marching to the Illinois. They occupy the lower part of this river."[1]

Yet before English soldiers could capture New Orleans, diplomats more than doubled the British empire in North America. At peace talks in Paris in 1763, Great Britain negotiated Florida from Spain—returning conquests in Cuba, principally Havana, and in the Philippines, principally Manila—and from France took Acadia, Canada, Cape Breton, and Louisiana east of the Mississippi. Representatives of France, to compensate their ally in a losing cause, had already ceded to Spain all of

Louisiana west of the Mississippi. While most Frenchmen stayed on in Spanish Louisiana, the elimination of French sovereignty at midcontinent drew the contending colonies of England and Spain into close and present confrontation. Now only the Mississippi separated them.

More obvious to imperial staff members in Europe than to colonists in the field, England's huge advantage in population north of the thirtieth parallel cast an ominous shadow westward across their maps toward the Pacific. The Spaniards' response was not to cower. Energized by an able young king, they instead set about defending their claims with vigor.

Women and children, dependents of the garrison, along with families of settlers who lived in and about the royal presidio of San Ignacio de Tubac, gawked on a December day in 1766 as the highest-ranking officer ever to visit Sonora and Pimería Alta reined up before Capt. Juan Bautista de Anza the younger.

The zealous Marqués de Rubí, his keenly observant chief engineer, his cartographer, aides, servants, and heavily armed escort had come from Spain, it was said, by direct order of the king to inspect the entire northern frontier of New Spain, a theater notably changed since the general inspection of Brigadier Pedro de Rivera forty years earlier. In Rivera's day, there had been no presidio at Tubac. As an effect of the Pima uprising in 1751, Gov. Diego Ortiz Parrilla had activated a company of fifty men in Sonora on April 1, 1752. A year later, they moved to Tubac.

The presidio's first captain, the Basque Juan Tomás Belderrain had fallen ill and sought out Father Francisco Javier Pauer, his Jesuit compadre at Guevavi eighteen miles south. He died there on September 7, 1759, only weeks after the birth of his last daughter. The next captain was Anza. Rubí had already heard of him. Fatherless by the age of four, the younger Anza had come up the privileged way, enlisting as an unpaid, teenaged cadet in the company of famed Capt. Agustín de Vildósola, his brother-in-law, and making lieutenant by nineteen. Already, his service record shone with deeds of great bravery against Seris, rebel Pimas and Pápagos, and Apaches. And he was only thirty.

Rubí stayed two weeks at Tubac. Like Rivera's, his methods were scrupulous. Interviewing ten men and conducting an audit, the king's inspector could scarcely believe Captain Anza's honesty. Anza was a rich man, the owner of properties, herds, and mining shares, but unlike the typical presidial commander, he did not gouge his men at the company store. In fact, he sold them supplies and equipment at lower prices than those set by Rivera before he was born. Soldiers at Tubac paid 40 pesos, not 50, for their cueras, and 2 reales, not 2½, for liturgical calendars on fine paper.

Lt. José de Urrutia (a peninsular Basque not closely related to San Antonio's deceased captain) drew a plan of each presidio they inspected based on measurements he took in the field. Washed in shades of red-brown and yellow-green, these handsome aerial views contained keys that identified important structures by letter. Tubac appeared less than imposing.

The captain's house, for which Anza had paid Belderrain's widow one thousand pesos, enclosed a patio with a gate that faced south. Some paces to the west lay a "church begun at the Captain's expense," with cemetery in front. Until it was finished, families continued to seek baptism, marriage, and burial by grace of the Jesuit at Guevavi.

Soldiers' and settlers' humble, one-story, flat-roofed homes stood scattered about, a number along the track south labeled "Road from Tumacácori." The main irrigation ditch, taken out of a bend in the fickle Santa Cruz, or "Río de Tubac," bowed to the west and north then rejoined the river, enclosing a patchwork of cultivated fields. No hint of defensive works enhanced the picture. "All construction at this presidio," Urrutia noted dryly, "is of adobe."

At the time unmarried, Anza had brought doña María Rosa, his widowed mother, to live with him at Tubac; but she soon died and was buried beneath the altar steps in the Guevavi church next to Captain Belderrain. She had missed seeing her son wed by less than a year.

Don Juan had courted and won Ana María Pérez Serrano; they were married on his saint's day, June 24, 1761. Because of his devotion to elderly Jesuit Father Carlos de Rojas, who had baptized him twenty-five years before, Anza traveled to Arizpe for the ceremony. Ana María's brother, don José Manuel Díaz del Carpio, a secular priest, had agreed to serve as chaplain at Tubac, but he reneged and rarely visited.

By 1766, the community had grown to between five and six hundred souls, counting the garrison. The Marqués de Rubí thought the settlers numerous enough to defend themselves and would suggest relocating the presidio. This occurred in 1776–77, when soldiers and dependents removed to Tucson, a visita of San Xavier del Bac.

Even though Rubí recognized Tubac presidio's dependence on the neighboring Jesuit missions for beef, he ordered Anza to stop guarding the horses belonging to San Ignacio, Guevavi, and Bac. His soldiers had complained that not only were they required to wrangle the presidial herd and some of the settlers' animals, but also hundreds owned by the Jesuits.

The captain tried to explain. Soon after implementing the order, he asked Father Custodio Ximeno of Guevavi to provide thirteen head of cattle, to comply with another Rubí order that each man should have a quarter of beef every fifteen

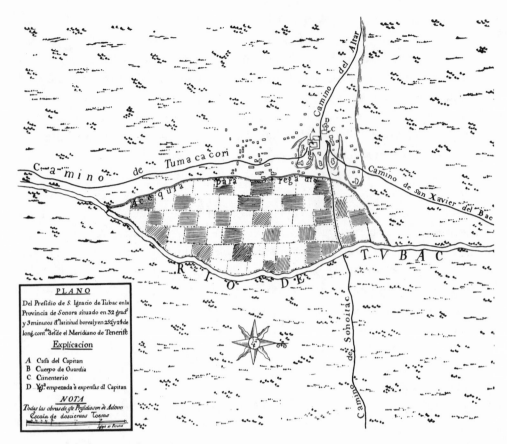

Lt. José de Urrutia's plan of the Tubac presidio, 1766. British Museum, London. *From Kessell,* Mission of Sorrows.

days. The priest refused. Then thieves ran off Ximeno's mares, his mission's most valuable possession. The missionary's "greatest worry now," Anza explained to Gov. Juan Claudio de Pineda,

> is that the same thing will happen to his herd of riding horses, which by order of the Marqués he separated from ours. But in order to save it, as well as to prevent them from stealing the soldiers' herd from me along with it, I am of a mind to have him bring his herd back and put on a couple of Indians to look after it.

Regulations had their place, but neighbors tended to work things out between them.[2]

On January 5, 1767, Rubí and his entourage left Tubac, riding west by the "Road from Altar" en route to the presidio of that name. They were moving faster than Rivera had. In just over ten months, Rubí's inspection team had traveled via Durango, Chihuahua, and El Paso to Santa Fe, thence from one presidio to another through San Buenaventura, Janos, Fronteras, and Terrenate to Tubac. After Altar, Horcasitas, and Buenavista in Sonora, the party recrossed Nueva Vizcaya and made for Texas, no longer a buffer against French encroachment.

After crossing the Rio Grande in mid-July fifteen miles above present-day Eagle Pass, they hastened north in eight days to San Sabá, where, with a cautious eye on distant Comanche smoke signals, the marqués ridiculed Captain Rábago's limestone fort. Its two bastions were "badly built" and "ill-aligned with their opposed angles." In short, "this is a fortification . . . as barbarous as the enemy who attacks it." He would recommend abandonment.

Rubí's picturesque descriptions of the natural world were intended as a trail guide. On the way from San Sabá to San Antonio, he wrote typically,

> we marched through elongated hills of greater than medium height that exposed many step-like strata of stone, and frequent vales in which four very fresh, clear creeks flowed. It appeared that their origin was only a short distance away in the same hilly range. These creeks had varieties of wild plums, grapes, and other delicious fruit growing along their banks—and the same has been true of all the creeks of the past days.

A few days earlier, he had marveled at the wild game. "This day we found enormous numbers of small bison herds, to which we gave chase and killed four. Also, a bear was roped and caught alive, and three wild turkeys [were taken], all of which was a great bounty for the convoy." Why they chose to rope and capture a bear alive, the marqués did not say.

Capt. Luis Antonio Menchaca's twenty-one-man San Antonio garrison turned out for the Marqués de Rubí in the most bizarre attire, each man wearing his choice of colors and insignias, silver buttons, silk handkerchiefs, and lace. A less serious inspector would have laughed. But Rubí decreed that henceforth all would conform to the dress code in every detail. He, of course, never returned to verify compliance.

At the Nacogdoches mission, they found a Franciscan but no Indians, and at Natchitoches, a leftover contingent of Frenchmen now in the service of Spain. The presidio of Los Adaes, no longer strategic, was a sorry staked-pine enclosure with three bastions, "badly constructed and in worse condition," and as useless, in Rubí's opinion, as San Sabá. Nor did the water-logged, dysentery-plagued presidio of San Agustín de Ahumada de Orcoquisac and its nearby mission, both built in 1756 near the mouth of the Trinity River to parry French influence, now serve any good purpose.

Passing through and inspecting the presidio of La Bahía, where they noted malaria and scurvy, the Rubí column kept on to Laredo, where men and equipment crossed in canoes. The climate was dry again. Engineer Nicolás de Lafora, Rubí's

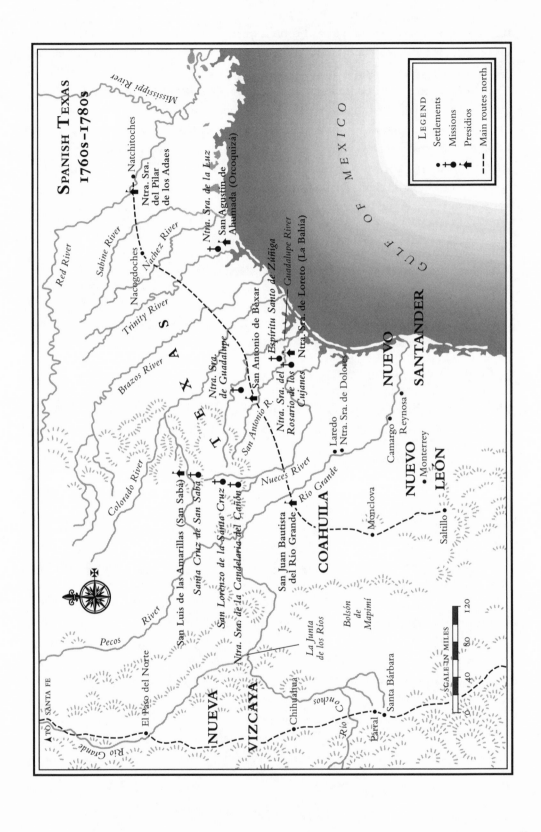

SPANISH TEXAS
1760s–1780s

Mississippi River

Red River

Sabine River

Natchez River

Nacogdoches

Trinity River

Natchitoches

Ntra. Sra.
del Pilar
de los Adaes

San Agustín de
Ahumada (Orcoquizá)

Ntra. Sra. de la Luz

Brazos River

T E X A S

Ntra. Sra.
de Guadalupe

San Antonio de Béxar

Espíritu Santo de Zúñiga

Guadalupe River

Ntra. Sra. de Loreto (La Bahía)

San Antonio R.

Ntra. Sra. del
Rosario de los
Cujanes

San Luis de las Amarillas (San Sabá)

Santa Cruz de San Sabá

San Lorenzo de la Santa Cruz

Ntra. Sra. de la Candelaria del Cañón

Nueces River

Ntra. Sra. de Dolores

Laredo

NUEVO
SANTANDER

Camargo
Reynosa

NUEVO
LEÓN

Monterrey

Rio Grande

Colorado River

COAHUILA

San Juan Bautista
del Río Grande

Monclova

Saltillo

Pecos River

El Paso del Norte

La Junta
de los Ríos

Bolsón
de
Mapimí

NUEVA

VIZCAYA

Chihuahua

Río Conchos

Parral

Santa Bárbara

Río Grande

TO SANTA FE

GULF OF MEXICO

LEGEND
Settlements
Missions
Presidios
Main routes north

SCALE IN MILES
0   40   80   120

fellow diarist, hated insect-infested Texas, especially the endless dismal, wet, and boggy forests bordering on Louisiana.[3]

Reentering Mexico City on February 23, 1768, after two years and seventy-five hundred miles, the travel-weary Rubí, who longed to return to Spain, now faced the daunting task of digesting all the information he had gathered and proposing a tidy solution to Spain's defense of western North America. He confessed his "lack of practice in laying out projects, which is not my profession," then wrote a report that profoundly affected Spanish policy until the end of the colonial period.

Much as the lines on Lieutenant Urrutia's overall map took shape, so did Rubí's key distinction between real and imaginary domains. Pimería Alta—with functioning presidios and Jesuit missions that shielded the mines of Sonora from Apache raids—was real; east Texas—where the two presidios of Los Adaes and Orcoquisac and four empty Franciscan missions no longer served—was imaginary. Abandon the latter, consolidate and strengthen the former, he urged.

Moreover, one could draw a line between the real and imaginary. By eliminating some presidios and relocating others, a readily defensible cordon of fifteen posts, spaced a hundred miles or so apart, could stretch roughly along the thirtieth parallel across the shortest distance between the Gulf of California and the Gulf of Mexico. A commandant-inspector would coordinate their operations. Santa Fe and San Antonio, too well established to withdraw, would remain as salients. "These," Rubí explained for the benefit of expansionists, "will be the two original points from which we go forth to extend and advance the whole of our line."

The Lipan and Gila Apaches, whom Rubí saw as immediate and perfidious foes, should be the object of relentless pursuit and total reduction. The more formidable Comanches and nations of the north, "whose generosity and bravery make them quite worthy of being our enemies," might instead be seen as allies. Such willingness to join in alliance with non-Christian Native nations reflected the dawning pragmatism of the enlightened Carlos III.

The marqués made clear that neither his inspection nor his cordon included the Jesuit-supervised presidio of Loreto "in the island (or maybe peninsula, it matters little to me) of California." Yet when he categorized the occupation of Monterey Bay and settlement of Alta California as foolhardy, Rubí crossed swords with the most intense reformer in New Spain, minister extraordinary José de Gálvez.[4]

Gálvez personified the king's program. This brilliant, somewhat unstable minor nobleman from Andalucía owed his sudden appointment as visitor general to one man's dodge and another's death. He relished the authority, greater for his purposes than even the viceroy's. He would increase revenues from New Spain.

Arriving in 1765, he threw himself at once into implementing new taxes, additional royal monopolies on playing cards, salt, gunpowder, and tobacco, and a more efficient collection of the tribute from free commoners. The sluggish Marqués de Cruillas, who plainly could not keep up, was succeeded as viceroy by the Marqués de Croix.

Together in 1767, Gálvez and Croix, with rare élan, put into practice in New Spain Carlos III's most drastic reform. The precision and secrecy of the operation testified to the success of Spain's enlightened Bourbon kings in modernizing their civil and military bureaucracies at home and overseas.

Following the lead of Portugal (in 1759) and France (in 1764) and the doctrine of eighteenth-century regalism, yet "locking away in his royal breast the reasons for his decision," Carlos III decreed an abrupt end in his empire to the all-powerful Society of Jesus. Arrest every Jesuit, demanded the king, and confiscate the Society's every property, enterprise, and hoard. The fiat reached New Spain by stealth.

Deliberately planned in Mexico City for the night of a holiday—the feast of St. John the Baptist, June 24, 1767—the government takeover of the order's main house proceeded flawlessly. To justify the seizure and head off popular reaction in favor of the Jesuits, José de Gálvez used propaganda to discredit them.[5] The Society of Jesus was a parasite on the social body. Jesuits had profited mercilessly from the sweat of hacienda workers and mission Indians. In a vain effort to exhibit ill-gotten Jesuit treasure, Gálvez ordered even the cesspool probed, yielding, one Jesuit recalled, no more than "an unbearable smell in the house and raging dispositions on the part of the commissioners."[6]

A courier's illness set back the schedule three days in Sonora. Portly Governor Pineda sweat to make up the time, writing out instructions in his own hand for the presidial captains who would physically round up the Jesuits from their missions and escort them to the church at Mátape where an official would read them the king's decree. He relied on Juan Bautista de Anza, who reacted in disbelief.

Pineda dispatched Tubac's captain to Arizpe, hoping that Anza's lifelong relationship with Jesuit superior Carlos de Rojas might help ease the expulsion. Anza obeyed. "After all," he mused to the governor, "the king commands it and there may be more to it than we realize. The thoughts of men differ as much as the distance from earth to heaven."[7]

Like every other Jesuit, Custodio Ximeno, a Spaniard in his midthirties, had felt the envy with which others viewed the Society. He knew, too, of powerful enemies at court. But when soldiers from the presidio of Altar rode into Guevavi, took his keys, and told him to speak to no one, he was dumbfounded. Then, courteously, they led him away.

What the three hundred Pimas of Guevavi and its visitas thought about their missionary's sudden departure no one bothered to record. On a whim, Andrés Grijalva, assigned as civilian overseer, gave them the keys to the granaries. Captain

Anza reported that at Tumacácori the people in a frenzy consumed alarming quantities of maize and meat. He was afraid

> everything would have been finished off within a few days. For this reason
> I have on my own initiative taken back the keys, leaving out enough pro-
> visions for their normal needs . . . until such time as the comisario appears,
> when I shall warn him not to proceed in such a disorganized manner.

José de Gálvez hated disorganization. He and Teodoro de Croix, the viceroy's nephew, had negotiated with the ranking Franciscan in New Spain for missionary replacements. The order's colleges in Querétaro and Mexico City would supply fifty-one gray-robed friars, its provinces dozens more in their characteristic blue habits.[8]

In cities like Guanajuato and San Luis Potosí where crowds gathered to protest the Jesuits' expulsion, Gálvez ordered hundreds of people hanged, whipped, or imprisoned. No one challenged the king's special envoy without swift response.

Isolation delayed the expulsion in California, a Jesuit fief, where there had been no royal governor before the appointment in 1767 of thirty-year veteran Capt. Gaspar de Portolá. His troop of twenty-five Catalonian Volunteers displayed New Spain's increasingly professionalized military.

They sailed from Matanchel, the Jesuits' roadstead due west of today's Tepic, on the Jesuit schooner *Lauretana*. Subjected to six typical weeks of alternate squalls and calms, they finally stumbled ashore on November 30, 1767, not at Loreto but on the long beach of San Bernabé near San José del Cabo. Ten days' travel overland, through the driest, rockiest, thorniest environment he had ever seen, disabused Governor Portolá of Gálvez's obsession that the Society of Jesus had quietly amassed great treasure in fabled California.

The Jesuits came in from their missions voluntarily. Obeying his orders in the main, the sympathetic Portolá permitted the exiles a final mass. On February 3, 1768, after dark to discourage an audience, he directed that the sixteen missionaries embark. Writing later in Germany, a nostalgic Father Benno Ducrue, their superior, relived the event.

> As we walked down to the shore, behold we were surrounded on all sides
> by the people, the Spanish soldiers among them. Some knelt on the sand to
> kiss our hands and feet, others knelt with arms outstretched in the form of
> a cross, publicly pleading for pardon. Others tenderly embraced the mis-
> sionaries, bidding them farewell and wishing them a happy voyage through
> loud weeping and sobbing. This sad spectacle moved the Governor to tears.[9]

No one recalled José de Gálvez shedding a tear. Yet, as the visitor general drove himself to implement his grand design for the northwest, the lingering legacy of

The "governor" and his wife, dressed for a public occasion, and a soldier, Baja California. After a drawing by missionary Ignacio Tirsch, S. J., 1762–67. Watercolor by Joanne Haskell Crosby. *Courtesy of Harry W. Crosby and the artist.*

Jesuit successes haunted him. The black robes had offered not only the sacraments but also social services, jobs, agricultural produce, markets, and some measure of security. His reforms, by God, would offer more.

Gálvez always had a vision. In the interest of turning traditional, paternalistic, government-subsidized frontier missions toward more profitable forms of production, he advanced Native rights. His Franciscan replacements would be allowed to minister in spiritual matters only; economic affairs and secular government would remain in the hands of select, less-oppressive laymen. The friars knew such a division would not work.

Beyond mission reform, Gálvez would make over the Jesuits' former economic empire in his own image. But first he had to suppress the Seris, then drive back the Apaches. Simultaneously, he would restore Antigua California and launch the occupation of Nueva or Alta California, thereby thwarting rival designs by Englishmen and Russians, a project long promised but unrealized by Jesuits.

In May 1768, the visitor general inspected the port of San Blas, chosen on his order as headquarters of a new naval department and supply base, 140 miles west of Guadalajara. Despite sweltering tropical heat, mangrove swamps, and whining clouds of mosquitoes that made life all but intolerable from June through October,

A Spanish woman, attended by a Moorish and an Indian servant, walks in her garden in Baja California. After a drawing by missionary Ignacio Tirsch, S. J., 1762–67. Watercolor by Joanne Haskell Crosby. *Courtesy of Harry W. Crosby and the artist.*

this site, Gálvez convinced himself, offered greater protection from storms than nearby Matanchel.[10]

Six hundred miles up the mainland coast, the Sonoran port of Guaymas witnessed an unusual volume of traffic. Coastal vessels offloaded uniformed troops and mountains of supplies for Gálvez's war on the Seris. Some of the Franciscan missionary surrogates arrived by sea. And finally, after nine months of confinement, the fifty Jesuit exiles of Sonora found themselves crowded aboard the empty packet boat *Príncipe* at Guaymas for transportation down the coast to San Blas.

Twenty-four days later, tossed about by contrary winds and low on food and water, the ship made an unscheduled call for repairs and provisions at Puerto Escondido, south of Loreto. Few of the passengers even cared; most wanted to die. The locals took pity. They notified the asthmatic, sometimes irascible, fifty-four-year-old fray Junípero Serra, father president at Loreto of sixteen Franciscans from the college of San Fernando in Mexico City, who had come to take over the missions of California. Serra went fifteen miles down to the beach where the Jesuits lay, offering what consolation he could.[11]

Gálvez, meanwhile, put his decisive Seri campaign under joint command of Col. Domingo Elizondo and Sonora's Governor Pineda. By one count, 705 presidial soldiers, along with 150 Yaqui and Pima auxiliaries, were positioned to converge on the water holes and campsites of an estimated two hundred families in the inhospitable desert rock pile known as the Cerro Prieto.

Their object was to kill or capture every Seri and rebel Pima. Pineda put a bounty on their heads, decreed the death penalty for anyone who harbored one of them, and instructed priests to pray for victory. When Gálvez learned that field operations had not succeeded—hampered by enemy thefts of livestock, ambushes, and the ferocity of the terrain—he vowed to take personal command.[12]

But first California. The visitor general and his large armed retinue had crossed from San Blas, landing on the scorched south coast early in July 1768, seven months behind Portolá, three behind Serra. Not by coincidence, Gálvez rode straight for the silver mining camp of Santa Ana, seat of private enterprise on the peninsula, where for the duration he appropriated the buildings of entrepreneur Manuel de Ocio. The poverty of the place stunned him, but he was confident he would set things right.

Details crowded his mind. The larger issues—economic development of the backward peninsula and Spanish occupation of San Diego and Monterey—intermingled with the small ones such as shade trees for Santa Ana's dirt streets. Such a welter demanded his attention: relocating California's pathetic Indian remnant; redistributing mission lands and water rights; appointing a mine inspector and a tax collector; providing a school and secular priest; mustering militia companies—and on and on. "So infinite is my business," Gálvea protested, "so many are the things to be seen to by me at one time that even though my ardor rises with my difficulties, my days not merely are consumed, but in great part my nights!"[13]

Galvez's year of micromanagement may actually have hindered his self-proclaimed sacred expedition by land and sea to Nueva California, but no one dared say anything. The visitor general himself insisted on inventorying and packing crates of supplies, many of them requisitioned with no thought for the chronic scarcity of goods and foodstuffs on the peninsula.

Requesting by letter that Father Serra comment on the instructions he had composed for the new missions, Gálvez professed modesty, "for I am very far removed from self-love and my labors are sufficiently bad to prevent their author from falling in love with them." Already he had taken back mission temporal matters from the newly appointed soldier-administrators and again entrusted them to the friars.[14]

In January 1769, before the refitted packetboat-turned-flagship *San Carlos* hoisted anchor in the Bay of La Paz to sail for Nueva California, José de Gálvez, Father Serra, Capt. Vicente Vila, and other dignitaries went aboard for the blessing. The deck was crowded. Gálvez gave a speech. For God, king, and viceroy, they were about to embark for heathen lands with the banner of the holy cross.

"He gave us with his natural eloquence," a witness recalled, "the most fervent exhortation which filled us with faith and firm intentions to give up our lives before failing in this noble enterprise."[15] Weeks later, with a similar sendoff, El Príncipe, alias San Antonio, commanded by Capt. Juan Pérez, sailed from San Bernabé.

Governor Portolá, who would lead the larger overland party, had looked upon Capt. Fernando Javier de Rivera y Moncada with some suspicion. Rivera had served the Jesuits of California for twenty-five years and was the black robes' last commandant of the Loreto presidio. Yet like Captain Anza, he stoically obeyed and did his part to expel the Jesuits. No one knew the California peninsula better.

Gálvez ordered Rivera to take twenty-five of his rough California presidials and muleteers and reconnoiter a land route from Loreto to the Bay of San Diego, a distance of more than six hundred miles, then find the way on to Monterey, another four hundred. Portolá and company would follow a few weeks later.

Father Serra, who had to be lifted by two men onto his mule because of a painfully infected foot and leg, should never have gone, but "Even though I should die on the way," he swore, "*I shall not turn back*." As the cavalcade neared the sea in the vicinity of present-day Ensenada, the little Franciscan, despite his pain, gloried in the creation around him. To his diary he confided,

> the thorns and rocks of [Antigua] California are now behind us, for these very high mountains are of pure earth. Also there are many flowers, and beautiful ones. . . . today [June 21, 1769] on arriving at our resting place, we encountered the queen of them all, the rose of Castile. As I am writing this, I have before me a branch of rose bush, with three petals opened, others in bud, and more than six unpetaled. Blessed be He who created them.[16]

Reunited July 1 on the Bay of San Diego, expeditionaries present from both ships and both land parties embraced and thanked God to be alive. Not all were. The sea cohort had fared worse. All the sailors aboard the San Carlos but one had died terribly, along with several of the soldiers, from scurvy. Most of El Príncipe's crew lay sick and incapacitated. Surgeon Pedro Prat had no rest.

Even before July 16, 1769, when Serra blessed the brush huts of Nueva California's first mission among the naked men and clothed women of the Ipai nation, talk was of an alternate route for colonists and supplies overland from Sonora and Pimería Alta via the crossing of the Colorado River. That had been the counsel of Father Kino in 1709 and of the elder Captain Anza in 1739. Soon, the latter's son would act on their proposal.

El Príncipe departed for San Blas conveying letters and pleas for more men and provisions. Captain Vila remained aboard the San Carlos. Governor Portolá and seventy-some men, with chaplain and diarist fray Juan Crespí, headed north along the coast range for Monterey. One of several earthquakes, half as long as an "Ave María," hurried their progress.

On August 15, with little warning, Natives attacked the few soldiers and hands left at the mission, killing one of Serra's servants who had come with him from Loreto. Several of the assailants died or sustained gaping wounds from Spanish musket balls; after that experience, they chose to tolerate the intruders.

The weary Portolá and his men returned from their northern reconnaissance in January 1770, "smelling frightfully" of the mules they had eaten. When Serra learned that they had discovered San Francisco Bay by land, but failed to recognize that of Monterey, the Franciscan quipped unkindly, "You come from Rome without having seen the pope."

Shortages at San Diego grew critical and morale gloomy. To decrease the number drawing rations, a column set out on the long journey by land back to Loreto. The *San José,* another packetboat built and outfitted at San Blas in support of Nueva California, never showed above the horizon and was presumed lost with all aboard. *El Príncipe,* however, returned from San Blas and saved the day. It was sighted on March 19, feast of San José, patron saint of the expedition and of José de Gálvez.

Gaspar de Portolá did recognize the open harbor of Monterey on his second try in May 1770, but surmised that, during the 168 years since Sebastián Vizcaíno had gushed about the bay, the towering sand dunes on its eastern shore had reclaimed much of it. Father Serra, arriving there by sea aboard *El Príncipe,* wrote about his momentous liturgy of Pentecost Sunday, June 3, held under a venerable oak tree near the beach. "A very beautiful statue of Our Lady . . . stood on the altar," loaned to him by José de Gálvez for the occasion. Once he had folded his vestments and made his thanksgiving,

> the officers conducted the ceremony of taking possession of that land in the name of His Catholic Majesty, setting up again and waving the royal standard, pulling up grass, removing stones, and conducting the ceremonies prescribed by law, accompanied by the shouts of "Viva!," the clangor of bells, and musket shots. After this we all ate together along the beach and walked along it during the afternoon. Then the members of the land expedition returned to their [encampment at] Carmel and we to the bark. With this, the day's function came to an end.

Symbolic acts of possession were satisfying but easy. Juan Rodríguez Cabrillo had first claimed this coastline for Spain in 1542; actual settlement had waited until 1769–70.

No other accomplishment, real or imagined, of the many that José de Gálvez took credit for thrilled him more. The ports of San Diego and Monterey defied Russian sea-otter hunters working down from Alaska and Englishmen questing for a Northwest Passage. The Jesuits had fallen short, but he had not. His vision of Nueva California was now a reality.[17]

Gálvez did not let up. From Antigua California, seeking to resolve the stalled Seri war, he wrote to fray Mariano Antonio de Buena y Alcalde, father president of the Franciscans from the college of Querétaro assigned to the former Jesuit missions in Pimería Baja and Pimería Alta. He wanted fray Mariano to get word to the Seris—without revealing Gálvez's part in it—that all would be forgiven if they surrendered upon the visitor general's arrival.

Recrossing the gulf, the visitor general set up at the mining town of Alamos in extreme southern Sonora, where from mid-May to early September 1769 he labored in quixotic fervor to revitalize that province. He established a branch of the royal mint, a diocese of Sonora, and commercial fairs, reduced prices of mercury and black powder to stimulate mining production, and issued dozens of regulatory ordinances. The role of creator suited him.

Certain of Gálvez's decrees dealt with the categories, measurement, and taxation of lands. Others allotted mission commons to individuals, purportedly elevating Opata, Lower Pima, Yaqui, and Mayo Indians to the status of tribute-paying citizens. Their combined effect, however, enlarged private estates and transformed more and more erstwhile Jesuit mission wards into peasants and migrant laborers for Spanish haciendas and mines.[18]

Father Buena, after polling his friars in Pimería Alta, asked for an audience with the visitor general in Alamos. The new regime, in which missionaries had no say in material or disciplinary affairs, was destroying the frontier missions. Buena, a former missionary in Texas and Coahuila, saw after scarcely two weeks at Tubutama that his neophytes were ignoring him. "They live," he had reported to the superiors of his college,

> in perpetual idleness, wandering through the backcountry and from one mission to another. Because of this, since we cannot reprimand them, only the ones who feel like it come to catechism, without according us so far even the slightest recognition or more attention than a stranger might get in their pueblo.

Worse still, Apaches took full advantage of the redeployment of military resources against the Seris and raided the weakened missions at will. Given the circumstances, Gálvez retreated again from his original stance, as in California. On June 3, 1769, the visitor general dispossessed the civilian administrators, entrusting to Buena's Franciscans the temporal management of their missions. Later, as he passed through the mission of San Miguel de Ures in central Sonora, an ailing, melancholy Gálvez, at Father Buena's urging, reinstated the missionaries as disciplinarians, thereby overturning Indian civil rights. And the severity of his instructions shocked Buena.

Mission Indians, *chicos o grandes,* who failed to attend daily Christian instruction or carry out work assignments were to receive twenty-five lashes the first time and fifty the second. They must stop thinking and acting like heathens, favor the Spanish language, and give up their Native surnames. Although he meant these spontaneous orders to be provisional pending more study, the visitor general himself had put Franciscans back in charge.

Because José de Gálvez envisioned a mission for Seris who accepted amnesty, he asked Father President Buena, pastor of Ures at the time, to accompany him north to Pitic (present-day Hermosillo), where the visitor general intended to command a final offensive against holdouts in the Cerro Prieto.

Governor Pineda and Colonel Elizondo could see that he was not well. Suffering from malaria, he appeared unusually morose and erratic. Then, at 2:00 A.M. on October 14, Gálvez snapped. Bounding out of bed, he ranted that St. Francis had come to him in a dream foretelling total victory over the Seris. Before members of his staff could contain him, the deranged commander-in-chief was noisily rousing soldiers from their sleep, shaking their hands and promising them fabulous bonuses.

Gálvez's personal physician him bled five times over the next three days; he diagnosed the visitor general's malady as megalomania. When Father Buena offered to nurse him at Ures, no one had a better suggestion. Hence, for five months the Franciscan father president served José de Gálvez as psychotherapist and protector. One stretch of dementia lasted a biblical forty days. The friar censored Gálvez's mail, withholding the depressing news of the latest failed Seri campaign. Although the Marqués de Croix feared that the visitor general would not recover, he did.

When the patient was able, Father Buena insisted on accompanying him as far as Chihuahua. Later, as a gesture of gratitude, Gálvez sent from Mexico City a supply of oil for the altar lamp at Ures.[19]

At the request of Minister of the Indies don Julián de Arriaga, an elite, worldly-wise group of five met in midsummer 1772 at the elegant home in Madrid of former viceroy the Marqués de Croix. José de Gálvez seemed composed. Field marshal Antonio de Ricardos, a member of the military mission to New Spain, greeted Alejandro O'Reilly, whose imposition of Spanish rule on Louisiana all had toasted previously. And because of the unusual geographical span of his experience, even Col. Diego Ortiz Parrilla was there.

Their main topic, already much discussed by Gálvez and other experts, had

José de Gálvez. *From Kessell,* Kiva, Cross, and Crown.

been published provisionally by Croix the previous year—the Marqués de Rubí's recommendations, or "Dictamen" of 1768. Arriaga had the group's commentary on it in a matter of days. On September 10, the final form of the new regulations for New Spain's presidial line was promulgated by Carlos III—the *Reglamento* of 1772. Rubí, at home in Barcelona, may have smiled. Almost all the ideas were his.[20]

The man they all counted on to put Rubí's realigned cordon of presidios on the map, wage a coordinated war against Apaches, and enforce the new regulations was O'Reilly's younger cousin, Dublin-born, thirty-seven-year-old bachelor Hugo O'Conor, who had served with energy and distinction in New Spain since 1764. Along with cousin O'Conor, two nephews of men at that summer cabinet in Madrid in 1772—Teodoro de Croix and Bernardo de Gálvez—as able and ambitious as their uncles, would carry the reforms even further.

O'Conor had left Ireland young, one of the self-styled Irish "wild geese" aspiring to church or military careers in the service not of Protestant England but of a Catholic monarch. On a difficult special assignment, don Hugo had found himself in 1765 in east Texas, where he became commander and interim governor, serving in that dual capacity at Los Adaes during Rubí's inspection. Inspired, O'Conor composed a new schedule of prices for his men. "The fairness of it," Rubí had thought, "gives the greatest honor to the disinterest of this official, and I doubt that it could be improved upon."[21]

The Marqués de Croix, before retiring to Spain in mid-1771, had named Hugo O'Conor commandant-inspector of the entire northern frontier. The job was immense and eventually it broke his health. Yet for five years between 1772 and 1777, don Hugo devoted himself in the field to carrying out the *Reglamento* of 1772, inspecting and lining up the presidios, and mounting general campaigns against Apaches. His successor, accorded even greater authority, gave O'Conor little credit.

As early as 1768, José de Gálvez had conceived of a virtual northern viceroyalty. Carlos III approved. When Gálvez took over as minister of the Indies in 1776, he instituted the *Comandancia General de las Provincias Internas,* the General Command of the Interior Provinces.

Gálvez's choice as first commandant general was Teodoro de Croix. Independent of Viceroy Antonio María Bucareli in Mexico City, who took measured offense, Croix assumed overall command of the Californias, Sonora, Nueva Vizcaya, New Mexico, Coahuila, and Texas. Their governors, along with the commandant-inspector, would henceforth answer to him. Rather than take orders from Croix, O'Conor quit. Reassigned despite his poor health to the governorship of Yucatán, the Irishman died there in 1779 at age forty-four.[22]

Although the six united northern fringe colonies lacked the wealth to support a viceregal court, an archbishop, or a university, the commandant general, like a viceroy, functioned as superintendent of the treasury and vice-patron of the church in the Provincias Internas. Croix's primary duty, however, was imperial defense, first against the ubiquitous *indios bárbaros,* second against European rivals.

Fewer than two thousand salaried troops, manning fifteen presidios along the eighteen-hundred-mile Rubí-O'Conor cordon, could not realistically mount the all-out war of extermination against Apaches envisioned in the *Reglamento* of 1772. So Croix requisitioned another two thousand, relocated several of the presidios again, implemented special light forces, reorganized militia units, and sought Indian alliances.

Then the winds shifted. In 1779, José de Gálvez conveyed to Croix a royal order in which Carlos III echoed Felipe II's Ordinances for New Discoveries of 1573: he wished to be remembered not as a conqueror, but as a humanitarian. Since Spain—in a bid to retake Florida, Minorca, and Gibraltar—was going to war with England on the side of France and the rebel British American colonies, resources must be reallocated from the northern frontier to the Mississippi Valley and Gulf Coast. Hence, with slim hope of military victory over the numerous, wily Apaches, don Teodoro must give up his offensive war, defend existing settlements, and offer peace through gifts, trade, even firearms. Former enemies would grow used to Spanish commodities. Such dependency had pacified the Chichimeca frontier in the 1570s, 1580s, and 1590s.[23]

Apparently, his nephew Bernardo had influenced José de Gálvez. Don Bernardo, serving as governor of Spanish Louisiana, had noted how efficiently Frenchmen dealt with the Indian nations. Friendly commerce, he explained to his uncle, put in the hands of Indians "sundry conveniences of life of whose existence they previously knew nothing, and which now they look upon as indispensable."[24]

Later, Bernardo de Gálvez found himself in a position to expand upon and impose this "peace by deceit," meant to render Native peoples economically dependent on Spanish suppliers. When Matías de Gálvez, his father, yielded the viceroyalty of New Spain to Bernardo in 1785, his uncle José put the Provincias Internas back under viceregal jurisdiction.

Viceroy Bernardo de Gálvez brought together a remarkably cogent synthesis of reform policy since 1768, his *Instructions* of 1786 to Com. Gen. Jacobo Ugarte y Loyola. Commanders in the field accepted it not only because of its clarity, but also because it came from someone who had fought in the early 1770s and been scarred on the Apache frontier of Nueva Vizcaya. More than any previous viceroy, don Bernardo knew what he was talking about.

While he recommended continuing relentless but smarter war "against the Apaches who have declared it," Bernardo de Gálvez coolly calculated the spiraling costs and advocated peace, however imperfect, with any tribe that asked for it.

> By proceeding unceasingly against the declared enemies it will be pos-
> sible to punish, restrain, and intimidate them to the point that they will
> depart from our frontiers or solicit peace; by conceding peace to them they
> may be attracted gently to the advantages of rational life and to necessary
> dependency on us by the interesting means of commerce and by discreet
> and opportune gifts. If peace is broken by the fickleness of the Indian or
> because of his intolerably bad faith, we should rightly return to incessant and
> harsh war, alternating war and peace as often as the haughty or humble
> behavior of the barbarous Indians requires.

At the same time, he urged officers in the Provincias Internas to "employ the
ancient hatred, factional interest, and inconstancy and perfidy of the heathen tribes
to their mutual destruction," to fan the enmity between Lipan and Mescalero
Apaches, Navajos and Gila Apaches, Comanches and Apaches.

Gálvez's "discreet and opportune gifts" went beyond the usual livestock, foodstuffs, tobacco, hardware, and dry goods—he wanted to addict former hostiles to
alcohol. This cynically argued proposal, however, did not catch on, most likely
because supplies of brandy and mescal in the colonial Provincias Internas never
exceeded the thirst of gente de razón.

Acknowledging the Indians' advantages with bow and arrow and their illogi-
cal preference for firearms, Viceroy Gálvez urged that they be given long, clumsy,
weakened but gaudily decorated inferior guns, thereby decreasing their effective-
ness in war and increasing their dependence on Spaniards for powder, lead, and
repair. Fellow veterans agreed.

By spelling out the alternatives of war and peace, emphasizing the latter, and
by trusting not only field commanders but also Indian leaders to choose between
the two, Bernardo de Gálvez offered something to everyone. Warriors on both
sides could still pick their battles, but now the benefit of goods and services could
be had by not fighting.[25]

Although the younger Gálvez died that same year, 1786, conditions over the
next generation favored a greater mutual desire for peace than for war. The reality of his vision for the Provincias Internas lived on, until the gifts gave out.

The friars, meanwhile, refused to pass from the scene. Despite threats by secular absolutists like José and Bernardo de Gálvez, missionaries stood out on New
Spain's contested northern frontier as boldly in the late eighteenth century as they
ever had. And anyone with pen and ink or a penchant for figures knew why.
Missions were cheap.

Dotted across the landscape, they also demonstrated the Spanish crown's abiding concern to convert non-Christian Native peoples, even while offering avowed

heathens peace, aid, and comfort. Thus, with wave after wave of military reform breaking over the Provincias Internas, missionary friars, operating with less bluster on annual stipends of 330 or 450 pesos, continued their everyday, symbiotic relationship with presidios and towns.

From Matagorda Bay to the Santa Barbara Channel, Franciscans from the provinces and colleges (and Dominicans after 1772–73 in Antigua California) administered the sacraments, produced surpluses in good years, called up auxiliary fighting men, served as Indian agents and explorers, and on occasion gave their lives. Some, as in the past, abused their privileged status and took improper advantage of the people who depended on them.

In midsummer 1768, a pair of peninsular Spanish friars from the Querétaro college had begun their ministries at the farthest missions of Pimería Alta, Los Santos Angeles de Guevavi and San Xavier del Bac. Port authorities had described the two as they sailed from Cádiz: fray Juan Crisóstomo Gil de Bernabé, "tall, slender, round-faced, swarthy, with heavy black beard, curly hair of the same color, and small eyes," and fray Francisco Garcés, "of average build, sparse beard, not overly swarthy, with black eyes and black hair."

Although he was a cultured ascetic, like Father Serra, and practiced self-mortification, the demonstrative fray Juan Gil had rather deliver hell-and-brimstone sermons before Tubac's sinning gente de razón than preach through interpreters to a few dozen seemingly unmoved Pimas. Openly, he prayed for a heavier cross. On the other hand, quiet and unassuming but strong-willed in his own way, Father Garcés rejoiced that he had no Spaniards in his care. "There are plenty of Indians," he wrote from San Xavier. "I like them and they like me." He embarrassed his superiors at Querétaro by reporting that curious Natives lifted the skirt of his habit to see for themselves whether he was man or woman. A more urbane friar reasoned that "God has created him, as I see it, solely for the purpose of seeking out these unhappy, ignorant, and rustic people." Ironically, both Gil and Garcés would die martyrs.

The earthy, intrepid Francisco Garcés, escorted only by Natives, ventured north and west to the rancherías of the Gila and Colorado rivers—Kino's territory seventy years earlier. Gil accepted the call as second father president of the Querétarans. With it came the unfinished drama of the Seris.[26]

Colonel Elizondo, recalled by the Marqués de Croix to confront the English threat, had promised Seri prisoners of war a mission at Pitic before he decamped in 1771. While politicians fought over that project, Seri headmen Cazoni and Tumuzaqui invited Spaniards to found a mission for them at a sandy, alkaline, bone-dry site opposite Tiburón Island. Here was the heavier cross. Gil took it up.

Requesting government surplus mules and a launch for a salt works and fishing

Fray Juan Crisóstomo Gil de Bernabé. A stylized, eighteenth-century martyrdom painting. *From Kessell,* Friars, Soldiers, and Reformers.

industry, the Franciscan had camped uncomfortably at Carrizal in November 1772 with only his acolyte. Three months later, Cazoni showed up at Pitic with two severed heads. They belonged, he alleged, to disgruntled Seris who had stoned to death fray Juan Crisóstomo Gil de Bernabé.

By 1780, don Pedro Corbalán, José de Gálvez's appointee as experimental intendant of Sonora, pronounced the Seris incorrigible one more time. He favored genocide. Either kill them in the field, he urged, or exile them, "the males twelve years and older to Havana and the women and children to the Californias." From Madrid in 1782, Gálvez concurred. Even Carlos III had lost patience. "His Majesty," the minister of the Indies announced,

> believes that to chastise the Seris and their relatives of Tiburón Island it would be advisable as soon as possible [that is, when the war with Great Britain was over] to mount a vigorous and well-planned expedition against this island in an effort to annihilate all its perfidious inhabitants capable of bearing arms.[27]

On occasion, lessons from the not-so-distant past seemed lost on José de Gálvez.

At San Xavier del Bac, Father Garcés commemorated the martyrdom of fray Juan Gil and redoubled his own efforts. His correspondents now included the viceroy of New Spain. Prodded from Madrid, Antonio María Bucareli developed a keen interest in Nueva California, soliciting information from Sonora, Pimería Alta, and New Mexico about retaining that newest and most distant colony. Reports by certain Franciscans held out the prospect of further colonization and supply overland. It made perfect sense, Garcés wrote to Bucareli, "that a poor friar should involve himself in these matters, since they all pertain to the preservation of my pueblos and to the service of both Majesties which we all should promote."

Captain Anza scowled. This falsely humble Franciscan bragged about his rapport with Indians and meddled regularly in affairs of empire that should not have concerned him. How dare he recommend transferring the Tubac garrison north a hundred miles to the junction of the San Pedro and Gila rivers? It was a wonder that this friar's foolhardy solo excursions had not stirred up an uprising or got him killed. Still, Anza had to admit that communication with Nueva California by tracing the Gila to the Colorado and crossing there with help of the Yuma Indians— a dream of his father—appeared feasible, even more so when Sebastián Tarabal, a runaway Cochimí Indian from Mission San Gabriel in California, appeared at Altar having come that way.

A partner of convenience, Garcés joined the column. Strenuous though it was, the thousand-mile round trip from Tubac to San Gabriel in 1774—crossing the Sonoran Desert, skirting the dunes west of the Colorado River, and negotiating the San Jacinto Mountains—took the three dozen riders only twenty weeks. En route back from a visit to Monterey, Anza had met Father Serra.

His pathfinding feat earned the captain of Tubac a hero's reception at the viceregal palace in Mexico City. Anza accepted promotion to lieutenant colonel and command of a touted migration of families from Sinaloa and Sonora over the same route to California. The plan was to people the splendid harbor of San Francisco, still known only from shore.

It was August 1775 before a Spanish ship, the San Blas packetboat *San Carlos* under command of Juan Bautista de Ayala, finally followed its longboat in through the Golden Gate to chart the outspread bay within. Not even Bucareli questioned its strategic import.

Garcés favored a more northerly route to California up the Colorado River and via the Hopi pueblos of New Mexico, which he rightly reckoned lay at near the latitude of Monterey but wrongly placed farther west than they actually were. The friar won over Sonora's energetic new governor, Spanish career officer Lt. Col. Francisco Antonio Crespo. Why not conquer the Hopis militarily, Crespo asked Bucareli, and open a road between Sonora and New Mexico, thereby facilitating communication between those provinces and Nueva California? Let Anza convey the colonists the only way he knew. Crespo gambled on a new route.[28]

Franciscans in New Mexico, through their superiors in Mexico City, also conferred with Viceroy Bucareli. One in particular, zealous, young fray Silvestre Vélez de Escalante, took it upon himself to visit the Hopi pueblos and inquire about the way west. The experience shook him to the core.

Just after midday on July 2, 1775, as an uneasy guest in the castellated Hopi pueblo of Walpi, he had sensed a commotion and, without thinking, hastened outside. "I had already heard," he admitted later, "about the idolatrous abominations associated with their most solemn dances." Now, the blue-robed friar became a reluctant eyewitness.

Deep, resonant drumming filled his ears. Native women, their dark hair in characteristic swirls, amid children and old men, lined the street and flat roofs watching. Ceremonial masked dancers, males all but naked, cavorted before them. The friar noted in rapt disgust that each one wore at the end of his penis "a small and delicate feather subtly attached." He felt a profound nausea.

> The frightful and gloomy painting of their masks and the height of indecency with which they ran in view of many people of both sexes were very clear signs of the foul spirit who has their hearts in his power. . . . This horrifying spectacle saddened me so that I arranged my departure for the following day.

Vélez de Escalante understood perfectly well that the preferred method of bringing non-Christian peoples into the fold, or returning apostates, was friendly persuasion. Yet these proud, obstinate Hopis had repeatedly repulsed such overtures. Since 1680, owing largely to the isolation of their craggy mesas, they had maintained a haughty independence, accepting visits, aid, and offers of alliance from Spaniards only when it suited their purposes.

Chagrined by the episode, fray Silvestre delayed six weeks before sending his Hopi diary to Mexico City. Bucareli addressed a copy to Garcés who, because of his wanderings, did not get it for a year. By then, fray Francisco could empathize. The viceroy also forwarded the governor of Sonora's Hopi plan to the governor of New Mexico. The latter wanted to know what Father Vélez de Escalante thought of it. Yes, came the answer; he agreed with Crespo. By force of arms, let the Hopis be brought down off their heights "to a flat and convenient site. And let all other steps be taken that may be considered necessary to hold them in due subjection."

The Franciscan might as well have called for a gentle, soaking rain. Few people in embattled, eighteenth-century New Mexico shared the missionary's evangelical concern. Year after year, defending homes and crops from Gila Apaches and Comanches, the fatalistic Hispano and Pueblo Indian farmers and stockraisers of the Rio Grande Valley could have cared less about distant Hopi apostates. Moreover, don Pedro Fermín de Mendinueta, the colony's veteran governor, protested that any show of force against the Hopis would scare off Navajos and Utes inclined to peace. "My feeling is that three or four missionaries, known and chosen for their ability and truly apostolic zeal," should go with trade goods as gifts for Hopi chieftains "who (as sons of their own interests) would permit them to teach the mysteries of our religion."

The governor's words stung. As if the friars, repeatedly and at the risk of their lives, had not tried to do just that. Rather than confront Mendinueta directly, Vélez de Escalante complained in confidence to his superiors from the colony's isolated, westernmost mission of Zuni. Not all laymen were such insensitive boors as the governor.[29]

No more engaging personality rode out from Santa Fe to confer with Father Escalante at Zuni than the jaunty retired Capt. don Bernardo de Miera y Pacheco, long-term resident of the colony, former district officer, wholesaler, and maker of maps, paintings, and religious images. Although Vélez de Escalante was only half Miera's age and not as well born, kinship grew between them. Both men were *montañeses* from the green mountains and valleys of Santander in the far north of Spain.

Had the priest heard about the viceroy's letter to Governor Mendinueta inquiring if there were pelicans in New Mexico? If there were, the governor was to capture and cage some of the big, gangly birds, then send them to Mexico City for transshipment to the royal zoological gardens in Madrid. Pelicans raised again the pressing issue of a road to California.

The distance from Santa Fe to Monterey had to be at least four hundred leagues, more than a thousand miles. Since Governor Mendinueta wanted to coddle the stubborn Hopis and there were warring tribes west of them, it made better sense to strike north and west up into the mountainous country of the heathen but friendly Utes to a latitude as high or higher than Monterey, thence straight into the setting sun.[30]

The opportunity came in mid-1776 with the arrival in Santa Fe of a high-level Franciscan inspector. He was to investigate reports reaching the Convento Grande from New Mexico for more than a decade of matters that had distressed the governing superiors. A dozen years earlier, the colony had witnessed a notorious outbreak of witchcraft. Women, thought to have been possessed by the devil, had destroyed the Franciscans' library and archive. Several friars faced charges of soliciting sex in the confessional. Others allegedly drank too much, hoarded material goods, or fraternized raucously with laymen. If anyone could get at the truth and apply remedies, it was the incorruptible, meticulous, urbane fray Francisco Atanasio Domínguez.

If the thirty-six-year-old fray Francisco felt any inferiority as a criollo, he disguised it with cultured show and wit at the table of Governor Mendinueta. Confident to a fault, he extolled the marvels of Mexico City, in his words, "the delightful and alluring cradle of my birth, for which no praise is ever adequate."

The Franciscan, who also carried instructions regarding a road to Monterey, asked Mendinueta to envision the bounteous harvest of souls that would result were the way opened between New Mexico and Nueva California. The governor demurred, pondering out loud how Father Domínguez could propose new spiritual conquests when his order lacked priests enough to supply the extant missions of New Mexico. Had he heard don Pedro correctly? Such an attitude, muttered the friar, would certainly "chill a spirit ardently burning to win souls."

Summoned from Zuni by the father visitor, Vélez de Escalante reached the Franciscan convento in Santa Fe late on June 7. By pact that night, the two Franciscans vowed to make the journey to Monterey. They would set out on July 4, 1776.[31] The departure, was postponed, however, because a Comanche war party hit La Ciénega just southwest of Santa Fe, killing ten people; fray Silvestre went as chaplain of the pursuing soldiers and consequently fell ill. Meantime, a rider from Zuni delivered to Santa Fe a startling letter from fray Francisco Garcés, dated at the Hopi pueblo of Oraibi on July 3, 1776.

The headstrong Garcés had agreed to go with Anza's second overland expedition to California as far as the Colorado River. That exodus of 240 people had left Tubac on October 23, 1775. No fewer than 167 were women and children. The first night out, the wife of Vicente Félix died giving birth. Garcés buried her at San Xavier while a companion baptized the baby.

Garcés's Franciscan companion later stayed on among the Yumas, while Anza led the colonists for San Francisco west and fray Francisco explored down the Colorado. He said he would return, but did not. Instead, he found his way again to mission San Gabriel, stayed only briefly, then set out on his own initiative to test the route eastward from Nueva California via the Colorado River to New Mexico.

Relying on a succession of Indian guides and unaccompanied by other Europeans, the trusting Franciscan on muleback had ridden an uncharted course into the southern San Joaquin Valley, across the Tehachapi Mountains, Mojave Desert, and Colorado River, and through the canyonlands to the Hopis, who, one year to the day after offending Father Vélez de Escalante, made Garcés even less welcome. They gave him neither water nor shelter. On July 2, 1776, "before the sun rose, the cacique proclaimed that he did not want anyone to become Christian, that he would punish anyone who went near the father." Garcés, hunkered down in a plaza "full of rubbish and ordure, etc.," tried for hours to get someone, some mother or child, to accept a gift from him. None would.

Before turning back the way he had come, the lone explorer wrote to his Franciscan brother at Zuni, whose name he did not know, entrusting the hasty note to a Native of Acoma called Lázaro. "I would gladly have gone that way [i.e., to New Mexico]," Garcés assured the recipient, "but since these Moquis are displeased, it would be necessary to return with troops and Christian Indians and to bring gifts. Therefore I should have had to wait for a reply from the lord governor."[32]

Receipt of the letter from Garcés only confirmed their choice of route. The little corps of discovery finally left Santa Fe on July 29. Twelve members in all, led by Father Domínguez, with Father Vélez de Escalante as diarist and Captain Miera as cartographer, they rode northwest along the pleasant Río Chama past Abiquiu. Then the scene swallowed them up.

Ushered again into Governor Mendinueta's presence on January 3, 1777, they had a story to tell. In their wanderings, they had traced an enormous, irregular, eighteen-hundred-mile circle around today's Four Corners of New Mexico, Colorado, Utah, and Arizona. Moving through some of the most rugged and dramatic country in North America, they saw landscapes beyond the Gunnison River and met Native peoples no Europeans had before. They did not see Monterey.

In the wild and desolate country of west-central Utah, on the feast day of Santa Brígida, October 8, they had suffered a falling-out. It had snowed heavily. A bitter north wind swept over them, and the distant mountains showed white. None of the bearded Utes they encountered had heard of Spaniards beyond. For these good reasons, the friars decided to turn back, but Miera protested. Knowing nothing of

Santa Fe, July 1776, by Wilson
Hurley, based on Lt. José de
Urrutia's map of the villa in
1766. *Courtesy of the artist*.

Juan Bautista de Anza's second California expedition departs Tubac, October 1775, by Cal N. Peters. *Courtesy of Tumacacori National Historical Park.*

the Sierra Nevada, he had convinced himself that another ten days would bring them to Monterey, and he only "came along very peevishly."

Three days later, to quell the growing dissension, Domínguez proposed casting lots about whether to go forward or back. All agreed, and the two friars prayed for strength to do God's will. Luck fell to them; the party would return to Santa Fe.

All but starving, they had at last found a place to cross Glen Canyon, chipping out steps with axes and lowering gear and surviving animals down the slickrock by ropes and slings. The spot, known later as the Crossing of the Fathers, today lies 550 feet under the surface of Lake Powell. "We got down to the canyon," Vélez de Escalante recalled calmly,

> and after going a mile we reached the river and went along it downstream for about as far as two musket shots, now through the water, now along the edge, until we came to the widest part of its currents where the ford appeared to be. One man waded in and found it all right, not having to swim at any place. We followed him on horseback, entering a little farther down, and in its middle two mounts which went ahead missed bottom and swam through a short channel. We held back, although with some peril, until the first one who crossed on foot came back from the other side to lead us, and we successfully passed over without the horses on which we were crossing ever having to swim.[33]

Garcés hated the commandant general's austerity. The Franciscan had promised missionary fathers to the Gila Pimas and a dozen other nations. He had counted on Spanish presidios at the junctions of the San Pedro and Gila and the Gila and Colorado. What he got satisfied neither him nor the Indians. Yet he volunteered to participate.

Teodoro de Croix was strapped. Faced with a redirection of the war effort from Apaches in the Provincias Internas to Englishmen on the lower Mississippi and Gulf of Mexico, the commandant general made concessions. Because the Franciscans' quixotic wayfaring in the Great Basin had discouraged movement in that direction, Croix knew he must hold the Yuma crossing of the Colorado. To that end, he left the old Tubac garrison at Tucson but pulled back both Terrenate and Fronteras, which O'Conor had moved beyond the defensible line with disastrous results.

Instead of transferring the presidio of San Miguel de Horcasitas to the Colorado, at an annual cost of 18,998 pesos, 6 reales, Croix proudly came up with a money-saving alternative: two small military colonies that would share four Franciscans, twenty-two men on detached duty from existing presidios, and twenty families of colonists at a total cost of 4,774 pesos a year.

If the Yumas remained "constant in their docile reduction," the commandant general predicted in his annual report for 1781 to José de Gálvez,

> not many years will pass until the banks of the Río Colorado may be them-
> selves covered with grain fields, fruits, and herds, and settled with faithful
> vassals of the king, who may augment the forces of Sonora, and who will
> attend to their reciprocal defense and aid California.

Such a vision existed only in Croix's mind. That summer, tensions mounted on the Colorado.

At two intrusive settlements on the California side, one opposite today's Yuma and the other a dozen miles upriver, two hundred demanding, irritable foreign men, women, and children along with hungry livestock had taken up residence amid the rancherías of possibly three thousand Yuma Indians.

Fray Francisco Garcés and three Franciscan companions were at pains trying to keep a thankless peace. The Yumas had wanted gifts of food, cloth, and weapons. Following in the footsteps of numerous Native delegations from the northwest—Yaquis, Pimas, and Seris—Juan Bautista de Anza had escorted Yuma headman Olleyquotequiebe (The Wheezy One) to Mexico City in 1777. Anza had stood by the Indian's side at a glittering reception in the viceroy's palace, then as his god-father in the colossal cathedral when they baptized him Salvador Palma. The authorities willed that the Native leader see such incomprehensible power and might with his own eyes. When, finally, Spaniards had come to the Colorado in

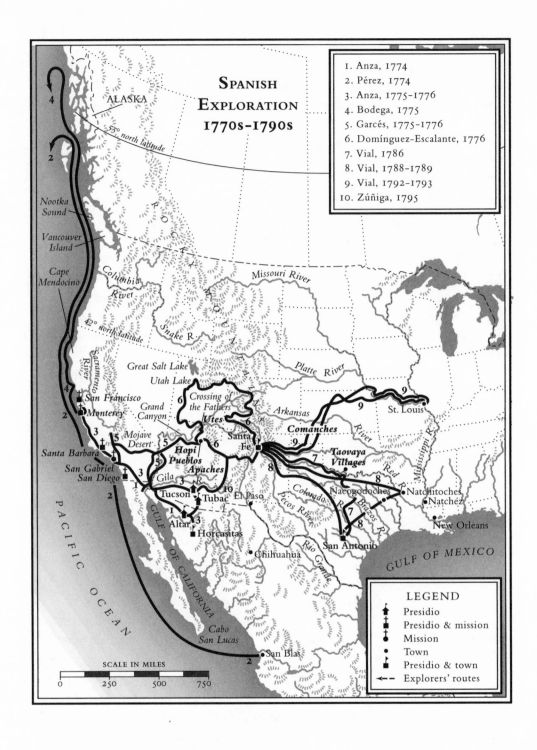

SPANISH
EXPLORATION
1770s–1790s

1. Anza, 1774
2. Pérez, 1774
3. Anza, 1775–1776
4. Bodega, 1775
5. Garcés, 1775–1776
6. Domínguez-Escalante, 1776
7. Vial, 1786
8. Vial, 1788–1789
9. Vial, 1792–1793
10. Zúñiga, 1795

ALASKA

55° north latitude

Nootka
Sound

Vancouver
Island

Cape
Mendocino

ROCKY MOUNTAINS

Columbia
River

Missouri River

42° north latitude

Snake R.

Platte River

Great Salt Lake
Utah Lake

Sacramento River

San Francisco
Monterey

Crossing of
the Fathers
Utes

Grand
Canyon

Arkansas

St. Louis

Comanches

Mojave
Desert

Hopi
Pueblos
Apaches

Santa
Fe

Taovaya
Villages

Santa Barbara

San Gabriel
San Diego

Gila R.

Tucson
Tubac

El Paso

Nacogodoches

Natchitoches
Natchéz

Altar
Horcasitas

Colorado R.

Pecos River

Brazos R.

Red R.

Mississippi R.

New Orleans

PACIFIC OCEAN

GULF OF CALIFORNIA

Chihuahua

Rio Grande

San Antonio

GULF OF MEXICO

Cabo
San Lucas

San Blas

LEGEND
Presidio
Presidio & mission
Mission
Town
Presidio & town
Explorers' routes

SCALE IN MILES
0   250   500   750

the winter of 1780–81, their ragged appearance and unfriendliness mocked Salvador Palma's memories of Mexico City.

Almost concurrently, two other similarly unkempt columns of soldier-colonists and their families, mustered at Alamos, inched north. One crossed to Loreto and moved up the California peninsula; the other came via Tucson and the Colorado River. These were to be first citizens of the pueblo of Los Angeles. "Thus, by sea and land," Croix boasted, "I have supported the new establishments of California." En route were fifty-nine presidial recruits, sixteen male settlers, sixty-five women, and eighty-nine boys and girls. The unyielding Captain Rivera y Moncada, who in California had held his own in jurisdictional duels with the equally unyielding Father Serra, reported to Arizpe to receive his orders from Croix in person. The commandant general liked Rivera. He recommended him to Gálvez and the king and approved his request to retire at the end of this assignment.

With forty soldiers and their families, a thousand head of horses and mules, and the supply train, Rivera was nearing the Colorado. Croix knew that he might winter there to strengthen the horse herd, sending mules and families ahead to San Gabriel. "In any event the expedition, already beyond the risk of enemies, has conquered the greatest difficulties and the important supplies are very close to New California where they are needed."

Yet before Croix could dispatch his general report to José de Gálvez, a courier from Tucson brought dire news. Hastily, the commandant general added a marginal note: "With the greatest treachery the Yuma[s] have murdered the religious missionaries, troops, and settlers." And alongside his commendation of Rivera y Moncada, Croix placed another:

> Beaten to death like all the unfortunate others who were on the Colorado, Captain Moncada, a sergeant, and six soldiers of the presidios of the Colorado died. When the misfortune occurred, the families, recruits, and the rest were safe in the mission of San Gabriel with the exception of 257 horses and mules that could not continue the march.

Details came later. Long-suffering and held in contempt by the intruders, Yumas had overrun the two settlements on July 17, 1781. Next day, across the river, they wiped out Rivera and his camp. At first they spared Father Garcés and a companion, but on the third day, at the goading of a former servant and interpreter, they put the priests to death.

Following Croix's orders, Lt. Col. Pedro Fages negotiated the ransom of seventy-four captives, most of them widows and fatherless children, had the friars' remains put in two boxes, and compiled a list of 104 dead. Fages and his men neither punished nor subdued the Yumas. By a resounding act of unwillingness, Salvador Palma's people had closed the road to California.[34]

Fray Francisco Garcés and fray Juan Antonio Barreneche, Yuma martyrs. *From Kessell,* Friars, Soldiers, and Reformers.

Few residents of the northwest lamented Teodoro de Croix's departure in 1783. The Franciscans applauded. They blamed Croix for the massacre on the Colorado; in turn, the commandant general denounced Anza and the deceased Garcés for misrepresenting the area's resources and the docility of the Yuma nation. José de Gálvez and Carlos III upheld Croix, promoting him to the highest post in the Indies, viceroy of Peru.

Although no more colonists or supplies for Nueva California floated or swam the Colorado, by the 1780s programs were in place from the Gulf of Mexico to the Pacific presaging a generation of greater peace and prosperity. Not surprisingly, as Spaniards on New Spain's far northern frontier learned to exploit their physical and human environment more efficiently, the interest of their colonial rivals quickened.

The *norteños* themselves contributed. When Spain allied its empire with rebel British colonists against England, even presidial soldiers at Tucson donated or had their salaries assessed 459 pesos. Citizens of New Mexico gave 3,677 and Californians 4,216. Texans drove beef cattle to Louisiana.[35]

Polished young Francisco Rendón had dined with George Washington and conducted business with Robert Morris. A royalist through and through, the astute Spanish agent at Philadelphia during the American Revolution sensed the vibrant confidence of these new republicans. It scared him.[36]

The Treaty of Paris in 1783 ended the war between England and its breakaway North American colonies, France, and Spain. The latter recovered the Floridas but now bordered the United States up the Mississippi. England kept Canada, and even though Englishmen maintained a presence at St. Louis, St. Augustine, and New Orleans, and challenged Spaniards to defend their claims to the north Pacific coast, they posed little threat to the occupied Provincias Internas. England's former colonists, however, brashly calling themselves Americans, coveted whatever lay to the west.

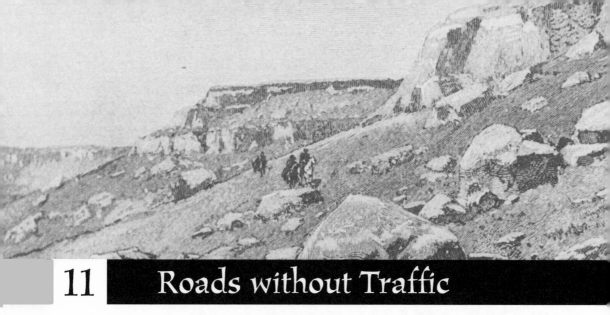

Roads without Traffic

Now I am going to open this road to Santa Fe in order that the Spaniards of San Antonio may cross through the Comanche country and that those from Santa Fe may pass from there to San Antonio, since they are all friends. And if on my return I see that you Taovayas are quiet, I will take you to San Antonio before the Spanish captain, and you will see that he is a kind-hearted man to you as soon as you promise him not to do harm.

—PEDRO VIAL, VILLAGE OF THE TAOVAYAS AND WICHITAS,
DECEMBER 28, 1786

At 11:45 A.M. on a still winter's day, January 26, 1779, the rolling volley of musketry announced a rare public execution in Santa Fe's main plaza. Two Keres Pueblo Indian women from Cochiti, a mother and daughter both named María, had been found guilty of murdering the younger woman's husband. They died before a firing squad for lack of a professional hangman. Now their lifeless bodies hung from the gallows.

The colony's famed new governor, Lt. Col. Juan Bautista de Anza, had carried out a superior order. If fray Juan José Llanos of the Santa Fe parish appealed for clemency on the basis of the condemned pair's race or gender, the act went unrecorded. Although capital punishment outside warfare was uncustomary in the Spanish empire, these women had confessed to parricide, killing a close relative, a man at that. They had bloodied the sanctity of the patriarchal family in Hispanic tradition.

Father Llanos did request at 3:00 P.M. that the corpses be taken down and carried to the church, which Anza approved. After the priest performed the Christian burial service, he had the women interred inside, where the ground was not frozen. Ironically, six years earlier to the day, while serving as missionary at Nambe, fray

Juan José had married María the daughter and Agustín, the murdered man, a Tewa of Tesuque. From alleged crime to punishment, the proceedings against the two Marías had lasted five years and nine months and had perplexed two governors.

Most criminal cases consisted of three parts: the fact-finding *sumaria;* an often haphazard *juicio plenario,* wherein the parties offered judicial proofs of their positions; and the *sentencia* proclaiming acquittal or punishment. Even though the initial sumaria was, in theory, supposed to be impartial, in practice it served to gather incriminating evidence against the accused, who was presumed guilty until proven innocent.

Alcalde mayor José Miguel de la Peña of the Cochiti district, having word of the crime in mid-April 1773, had gone with two corroborating witnesses to the pueblo of Cochiti to investigate. The Native governor, lieutenant governor, and a third Cochiti man testified to the discovery and burial of the body, with Peña's lieutenant alcalde mayor, Nerio Antonio Montoya, acting as interpreter.

María Josefa, mother, and María Francisca, daughter, had openly confessed, recounting through the same interpreter in grizzly detail their premeditated murder of Agustín, the former's son-in-law and the latter's husband. They admitted luring Agustín from the pueblo with an invitation to join them on an excursion into the hills to dig squawbush root for dyeing cloth. They had waited until the rest of the people had gone out to clean the irrigation ditch, then left by way of the Cañada de Peralta to be less conspicuous.

Sitting under a pine tree, María Francisca told her husband she would delouse his long hair. While lying on her skirt, the victim had fallen asleep. Swiftly, the younger woman picked up the band Agustín had worn to tie up his hair and slipped it around his neck. She held one end while calling to her mother to take the other. Then they pulled. With Agustín half choked, his wife told her mother to grab the digging knife and stab him. When the point hit bone just beneath the cavity at the base of the neck, she plunged the old blade into his throat. Then, lifting his jacket, she stabbed him in the side. Later, as evidence, someone traced the weapon in the margin of the court record. Agustín's body, exhumed for examination, bore the two gruesome wounds that verified the women's testimony.

Why had they done it? Agustín was an angry, stingy, unloving husband, and he was planning to take María away from Cochiti, which he had promised never to do. For that reason, María Josefa, who at first opposed her daughter's plan, consented to take part. Theirs, after all, was a matrilocal society.

The proceedings had continued in Santa Fe. Gov. Pedro Fermín de Mendinueta, who reheard the women's confessions, appointed Pedro Tafoya as legal guardian of the daughter, who appeared to be a minor, and Julián de Armijo as her mother's defense counsel. Beyond reiterating Agustín's nasty qualities and his intention to remove María from her pueblo forever, Tafoya and Armijo had no further defense.

Citing the women's ignorance as rustic, neophyte Indians, both counselors entered pleas for mercy. The two Marías, meanwhile, remained in jail in Santa Fe.

Considering the seriousness of their crime, Mendinueta had forwarded the proceedings in June 1773 to a legal adviser in Chihuahua. In his absence, the matter was referred to Durango, where in November, Lic. Rafael Vallarta responded. Vallarta counseled Mendinueta to correct a couple of irregularities. Because all Indians, regardless of age, were considered minors in the eyes of the law, both Marías should have had legal guardians. The more important point, however, concerned María Francisca's exact age. Neither María knew the daughter's age. She appeared to be between sixteen and eighteen, and her mother about forty. If she was not seventeen at the time of the murder, María Francisca's sentence would have to be mitigated; on the other hand, if she was between seventeen and twenty-five, mitigation would be at the judge's discretion. Therefore, her age must be certified.

If with these amendments nothing requiring further legal advice should be discovered, and if the governor deemed such a delay detrimental to public vengeance, he could sentence the two women to death. Depending on María Francisca's age, she would either die with her mother or, having witnessed María Josefa's public hanging, serve ten years in a women's prison. Before carrying out the sentence, however, the governor should consult the appropriate audiencia for confirmation or modification of its terms.

Mendinueta had complied during the spring of 1774. He renamed María Josefa's defender her guardian; presided as the defendants ratified their declarations without change; and determined María Francisca's age. A baptismal entry at Cochiti showed that she was twenty-two when she plotted the crime. The governor then sent the amended proceedings back to Vallarta, who replied, this time from Guadalajara, on December 30, 1774.

Now the case was clear. The women's open confessions left no doubt of their treachery in the deceitful, premeditated murder of a defenseless man. Vallarta stood by his previous opinion. Mendinueta could sentence both to death as parricides, but first, they might be given two hundred lashes while led through the streets of Santa Fe in the customary manner. This was Vallarta's legal opinion, not a sentence, and there is no evidence that the two Marías were ever whipped.

For another four years, they were kept in jail. Mendinueta next directed the case to the viceroy, who also served as president of the audiencia in Mexico City. For whatever reason, Viceroy Bucareli took no action for two years. Finally, on the recommendation of an adviser, he ordered it sent to Com. Gen. Teodoro de Croix, under whose jurisdiction New Mexico by then resided. Croix, of course, turned the matter over to his legal adviser, Pedro Galindo Navarro, who did not pronounce an opinion until August 8, 1778.

Galindo agreed fully with his colleague Vallarta. So heinous was the women's crime that their punishment should be conspicuously severe. To that end, Galindo endorsed the gallows. Moreover, he urged,

> the cadavers should be left hanging there for an interval of several days so that those who did not attend and see the sentence carried out may have this time after the fact to see and convey the news to their pueblos, where it is likely to produce the salutary effect of terrifying and restraining wrongdoers.

This, he added, would be especially fitting in a thinly garrisoned frontier area subject to uprisings.

Late in 1778, Anza assumed the governorship of New Mexico. It fell to him to pronounce sentence, which he ordered interpreted for the two Marías in January 1779. They were made to understand and, as a customary sign of submission, to hold the document above their heads. Three days later, they were dead.[1]

Continuing his envied climb to prominence, the frontier-born Lieutenant Colonel Anza served for a year as military governor of Sonora, then became governor of New Mexico while in Chihuahua, where Commandant General Croix administered the oath of office. Croix had summoned Anza and his predecessor Mendinueta, along with other governors, officers, and influential citizens to a series of high-level councils of war in midsummer. Conducting his initial inspection of the frontier, the commandant general had already held lesser meetings in Monclova, Coahuila, and San Antonio, Texas.

He was not optimistic. "It is evident," he had complained on June 29 to José de Gálvez,

> that with small, poorly arranged forces scattered over great distances, and troops vice-ridden and maladjusted, advantageous operations of war could not be undertaken nor can an extensive country of unhappy and sparse settlements be defended.

If the two thousand reinforcements he requested were not provided, no cumulative offensive could be carried out against the Apaches, and those garrisons moved by O'Conor to Rubí's outer line should be pulled back. Previous peace agreements with Apache bands, regardless of group affiliation, had proven unenduring and counterproductive.

When others estimated the number of Apache fighting men at five thousand, Anza and Mendinueta took issue. There were many more. Besides, they argued,

> to these should be added an equal number of women, who, if they do not make war in the same way as the men, aid it in whatever actions the Apaches undertake, as has been observed in fact. Thus they form regularly a reserve

corps, round up the horses while the men attack our troops, and, finally, even when they serve no other purpose than to make the parties larger, the enemy succeeds, by increasing the number of individuals, in creating the well-founded idea that they are more formidable.

Council members had discussed Rubí's old idea of alliance with Comanches and other nations of the north against Apaches. Most agreed. Comanches, true buffalo people whose lives centered on the plains, had no intention of seizing Spanish territory. The strategy would be to turn their audacious raids—even to the gates of San Antonio and Santa Fe—against common Apache enemies.

Anza had never met a Comanche. Despite former Governor Mendinueta's depressing recital of Comanche depredations, he was in no wise intimidated. He listened intently to the minutes of Croix's meeting in San Antonio. Texans had already opened talks with Comanche leaders, and he must do the same when he arrived in New Mexico.[2]

Don Juan Bautista and doña Ana María Pérez Serrano, still childless after seventeen years of marriage, along with relatives and retainers from Sonora, Franciscan replacements from Spain, and a heavily armed escort did not reach El Paso until September 1778. Their numbers strained the resources of that poor community for more than a month, while Anza reorganized the local Spanish and Indian militias.

At last they directed their trunks and furnishings into the governor's palace in Santa Fe, displacing interim Lt. Gov. Francisco Trébol Navarro and his family. Certain locals resented this Basque invasion from Sonora. Not a peninsular Spaniard like previous governors, the famous Anza, dutiful agent of Bourbon reformers, would try to change their lives. One of his first public acts authorized the belated execution of the two Marías. Anza also set don Bernardo Miera y Pacheco to drawing a new map of the province documenting the dispersed nature of Hispanic settlement and the Comanche threat.

That winter the new governor gathered from colonists every detail he could about Comanches. Many remembered the efforts of Tomás Vélez Cachupín, the colony's brash, two-term governor from 1749 to 1754 and 1762 to 1767. Don Tomás had shown the courage not only to meet Comanches in battle but also to sit with them face to face and discuss the advantages of peace and trade.

After his first term, Vélez had tried in vain to impress upon his successor that

> it is necessary, when the Comanches come to Taos to trade, that your grace present yourself in that pueblo surrounded with a suitable guard and your person adorned with all splendor possible. The first measure your grace must take must be to provide security and protection for their ranchería. Prohibit anyone from entering it when the fair is not open and your excellency not present.

A late nineteenth- or early twentieth-century portrait said to be Juan Bautista de Anza. *From Kessell, Kiva, Cross, and Crown.*

He had explained further that the governor should assign an officer and soldiers to guard the Comanches' horse herd, a courtesy that set them greatly at ease. He should upon arrival call the chiefs to counsel and smoke with them. After that,

> your grace will make them understand that they are welcome. . . . This should always be done with an appearance of pleasure and agreeableness, which they also esteem highly. Exterior acts and circumstances of one's looks influence considerably the idea that they ought to form. You should introduce your-self with skill and with expressive words maintain in your looks a mien, grave and serene. . . . With these necessary exaggerations which are required to make them cling to peace . . . permit their familiarities and take part in their fun at suitable times, all of which is necessary with this kind of people. I have done so and have been able to win the love they profess for me.[3]

No one had to tell Anza about such protocol; it was second nature to him. As appealing as Vélez Cachupín's peace had been, a more timid successor had let it unravel. Comanches had shown so little respect for defense-minded Governor Mendinueta that they assaulted even the outskirts of his capital.

A name Governor Anza heard over and over was Cuerno Verde, "Green Horn," fiercest of Comanche war leaders and cruelest scourge of the colony. The strategy to follow seemed obvious: go after Cuerno Verde and defeat him in battle.

No one could remember a New Mexican expedition half as big. Horses requested by Mendinueta and delivered after his term by the government made it possible. Together, presidial troops, Pueblo auxiliaries, and Hispano militiamen numbered nearly six hundred. En route, two hundred Utes and Jicarilla Apaches joined them. Anza insisted on a policy of dividing spoils in equal shares. Heading out in the heat of mid-August—season of harvest among farming peoples, not warfare—the decorated, forty-three-year-old commander sought the element of surprise. Their route contributed. The column wound its way directly north from San Juan Pueblo, passing by Ojo Caliente, then west of San Antonio Mountain. Leaving it behind, silhouetted like a giant, upside-down bowl, the eager, polyglot expeditionaries made their way along the west side of the San Luis Valley by night, forded the Río Napestle, today's Arkansas, and stole through the Front Range of the Rockies, turning back south. Scouts ranged ahead.

About halfway between today's Colorado Springs and Pueblo, Anza delivered his surprise. It was August 31, 1779. Hundreds of unsuspecting Comanche men, women, and children, tying up the conical pole frames of their tepees, only had time enough to catch their horses and gawk in disbelief at the Spaniards and their allies "drawn up in a form they had never before seen." Then they bolted for the emptiness of the plains. Anza's men gave chase and after seven or eight miles began to catch up. Of the Comanche warriors who wheeled round to give battle, eighteen died. The invaders took dozens of women and children captive, collected more spoils from the half-made camp than a hundred pack animals could carry, and rounded up more than five hundred of the enemies' horses.

When Governor Anza learned that the Comanche campsite was to have been a rendezvous for Cuerno Verde after a raid on New Mexico, he recrossed the Arkansas, "to see if fortune would grant me an encounter with him." Fortune did. Neither chief, Spaniard nor Comanche, lost face. The final action, within sight of 12,349-foot Greenhorn Mountain, drew Anza's praise for his enemy. The Spanish governor's tactics to draw Cuerno Verde's light cavalry into a tightening circle inspired in his foe a defiant, barefaced temerity.

Caught in an arroyo, Cuerno Verde and his staff arrogantly defied the odds. "There without other recourse," wrote Anza, "they sprang to the ground and, entrenched behind their horses, made in this manner a defense as brave as it was glorious." All died fighting.

As trophies, the triumphant Lieutenant Colonel Anza wrapped and sent to Commandant General Croix the distinctive headdress of Cuerno Verde and that of Jumping Eagle, his second-in-command. Eventually, Carlos III would promote Anza to colonel. News of the defeat, meanwhile, traveled throughout the Comanche nation. Yet alliance waited.[4]

Anza took little rest. Croix wanted action on two old proposals: winning back the Hopis and opening commerce between New Mexico and Sonora.

During his Comanche campaign, the governor had heard that a natural calamity had befallen the Hopis. A shriveling, two-year drought gripped the people. Many had descended from their mesas to forage in small groups. Rather than starve, some were reportedly selling their children. Anza advised Croix that now was the time to force the Hopis down from their mesas. He applauded Father Vélez de Escalante's earlier proposal, enclosing copies of the friar's letters. If the commandant general approved their removal by force of arms, the governor could make it look like a survey for the road to Sonora or an Apache campaign. To succeed, however, such a stratagem had to be kept from the Franciscans, who surely would reveal it.

Once on level ground, the Hopis could either be resettled as Christians in their own country or in the depopulated Rio Grande Valley at El Sabinal and other sites south of Albuquerque. Anza strongly favored the latter, but he awaited Croix's orders. By no means, came the reply, would Carlos III condone the use of force. Anza should reacquaint himself with the attached royal orders of 1774, 1777, and 1779. Moreover, if such a military operation failed, the apostate Hopis would likely join an enemy alliance of Gila Apaches, Navajos, and Utes, forever dooming their salvation. If, on the other hand, the governor wished to extend humanitarian aid to the drought-stricken pueblos, he might consider taking Father Vélez de Escalante with him. When in September 1780 Anza did mount a relief expedition, it was too late. The ailing Vélez de Escalante had died at Parral the previous April on his way to Mexico City for medical attention. He was not yet thirty.

Anza found the Hopis in "dark desolation." Famine, combined with Navajo and Ute raiding, had reduced the population from the almost eight thousand estimated by Vélez de Escalante in 1775 to fewer than eight hundred. Although the caciques wished to die in their pueblos, they gave their people permission to leave with the Spanish governor. Some did.

Governor Anza later bragged of attracting two hundred Hopis to the Rio Grande pueblos, where they added to a number of previous voluntary exiles. Reporting again to Croix in November 1781, he lamented that for five months the remnant population of the Hopi pueblos had been invested with smallpox. The governor's informants convinced him that this epidemic "will almost result in the final extermination of this unhappy nation." To the contrary, those who hung on in their own country survived, increased, and by the grace of their own gods, maintained their proud tradition of independence.[5]

Disease in its various forms regularly caused much higher death tolls in frontier communities, Indian and Spanish, than did the habitually reported and more newsworthy armed combat and occasional homicide. Burial entries for the pueblo of Pecos, for example, between the years 1695–1706 and 1727–1828, showed clusters of dying every ten to fifteen years: in 1696 (fever), 1704, 1728–29 (measles), 1738 (smallpox), 1748, 1759, 1780–81 (smallpox), 1800 (smallpox), 1816 (smallpox), and 1826. None exceeded the severity of North America's smallpox pandemic of 1779–81.[6]

At Tumacácori in the Santa Cruz Valley of Pimería Alta, fray Baltasar Carrillo, during five weeks in mid-1781, buried one in ten of his Piman neophytes. Similar decimation spread from mission to mission in Antigua California.[7]

Even on the distant northern Pacific coast, fur traders in the mid-1780s believed that a Spanish seaborne expedition had brought the smallpox that ravaged the local Native people. An unnamed contagion had indeed broken out aboard the *Princesa,* anchored in Bucareli Sound in May 1779, and the sick had been carried ashore on today's Prince of Wales Island. At that very time in central New Spain, smallpox with its burning fever and odious skin eruptions was spreading furiously. Anza on May 1, 1781, put the number of adults, boys, and girls who had succumbed in New Mexico alone at 5,025, about a quarter of the colony's sedentary population.[8]

Just as the disease reached New Mexico, Governor Anza returned from a frustrated attempt to open a direct road between Santa Fe and Sonora. He and Croix had imagined supplying New Mexico not through Chihuahua, where merchants took advantage and extralegal trading abounded, but instead through Arizpe, Croix's headquarters. Since the distance would be shorter, they calculated, the people of New Mexico "could buy effects from Europe more reasonably." But

Arizpe, Sonora, in the late eighteenth century. *From Kessell,* Friars, Soldiers, and Reformers.

New Mexicans doubted it. Rumors that silver production in Sonora had declined, depressing the economy, made them skeptical. Besides, they loathed Anza and questioned anything he promoted.

Anza's expedition, which departed Santa Fe on November 9 and entered Arizpe on December 18, 1780, had more success as an Apache campaign than as a trade caravan. Two concurrent forces, one from Nueva Vizcaya and another from Sonora, failed to join with Anza's as planned; instead, they upset Gila and Chiricahua bands who imagined they were safe in their rugged fastness.

Anza apologized and swore that he would find a better way on his next try. Meanwhile, travelers continued to use the well-worn but rough caminos reales, north-south down the Rio Grande into Nueva Vizcaya and east-west to and from Sonora, precisely the route taken to Arizpe early in 1780 by angry New Mexicans intent on laying before Commandant General Croix their grievances against the cocksure Juan Bautista de Anza.[9]

Anza should have known that he would meet resistance when he proposed consolidating the colonists into defensible walled compounds. Mendinueta had warned him in Chihuahua in 1778 that New Mexicans were surly and resistant to authority. Spread out along the colony's meager watercourses, their farms presented a constant invitation to raiders. The former governor had suggested that these free-spirited subjects be made to congregate in such compounds, yet he had not dared effect the plan himself lest the colonists become ungovernable.

Miera's map of 1779 justified the program. A lengthy headnote, lamenting New Mexico's sorry state of disorder, urged New Mexicans for their own preservation to obey Governor Anza's remedial order,

building their ample square plazas of at least twenty families each in the form of redoubts, the small ones with two bulwarks, and the large with four, between the ramparts, for the range of the short firelocks that are in use. It is not wise to build large towers in the old style, for the enemy takes cover below them, pierces them, and sets fire to them, as has been learned by experience.[10]

Evidently, in 1779 locals had accepted consolidation projects at Albuquerque, Taos, and several other scattered Hispanic communities. But when Governor Anza proposed drastically restructuring Santa Fe, he went too far. A hundred and seventy years after the fact, he thought he could correct Gov. Pedro de Peralta's mistake.

The higher barrio of Analco south of the Santa Fe River had always been more defensible than the low-lying plaza. Anza wanted to relocate its *genízaro* residents— mostly acculturated descendants of ransomed or captured Plains Indians, Apaches, and Navajos—then raze their humble dwellings and lay out on the site a new plaza, administrative center, and proper presidio with barracks for the garrison.

Successors of the seventeenth-century's Mexican Indians, these genízaros worked for the Hispanos of the capital. Did Anza honestly believe their employers would allow him to transfer them to defensive sites on the frontier, much less to remove the nucleus of town from among the homes their families had occupied for generations?

It fell to Croix to rein in his overly enthusiastic governor. The commandant general met with the mutinous New Mexican colonists in Arizpe and agreed to suspend the program of consolidation.[11] Next, Anza incensed the colony's Franciscans.

Since midcentury, governors and friars had often quarreled. Because it fell annually to the colony's chief executive to certify how many missionaries had earned their 330-peso royal stipend, any question about their services naturally put them on the defensive. Repeatedly, governors noted the friars' failure to learn Pueblo languages or to compose primers. And on occasion, they suggested the government economize by paying fewer stipends. More than any other matter over which they clashed, that issue set don Juan Bautista and the Franciscans at odds. Again, calamity suggested reform to Anza.

Considering the 25 percent drop in the colony's population caused by the smallpox epidemic of 1780–81, the governor thought it reasonable to reduce proportionately the number of subsidized missionaries from twenty-six to twenty. Smaller Pueblo congregations would be attached as visitas to larger ones, thus requiring fewer priests. Croix liked the idea. And long after Anza left, Franciscans would remember him as the governor who not only reduced their numbers but also enforced the long-ignored ban on Indian personal labor in the missions. They had trouble forgiving him.[12]

Anza's finest hour in New Mexico came while a dark cloud hung over him. Croix's successor as commandant general, peevish but clever Felipe de Neve, despised the touted Basque criollo. Apparently, while serving as governor of the Californias between 1775 and 1782, Neve, a peninsular Spaniard from Andalucía, had formed a bad opinion of the man who opened the overland road from Sonora. He may also have associated Anza with Jesuits and the old order. Whatever rankled him, Neve did not forget his grudge.

Late in 1783, the second commandant general listened with satisfaction to a delegation of New Mexicans who had sought an audience with him. Anza interfered in every aspect of their lives. As loyal and long-suffering subjects, they wanted him removed from office. Neve gave them good reason to hope. Without further investigation, Felipe de Neve wrote from Arizpe on January 26, 1784, to José de Gálvez urging Anza's dismissal. Moreover, Neve recommended that Anza be forced to erase from his service record his two most prominent deeds: opening the road to California and defeating Cuerno Verde.

But Anza persevered. While the Council of the Indies set aside Neve's vain bid to alter the record, the king did appoint don Manuel de Flon governor of New Mexico on October 16. By then, however, Neve had died, and Flon took up the interim governorship of Nueva Vizcaya instead.

Two years later, Com. Gen. Jacobo Ugarte y Loyola commended Juan Bautista de Anza profusely. The serving governor of New Mexico had achieved, by his "skillful direction of these delicate affairs," another notable feat.[13]

By the mid-1780s, Comanches had begun to consider seriously the advantages of peace with Spaniards. Spanish agents in Texas, like cunning former French trader Athanase de Mézières, had supplied and armed the Wichita nations of the north, directing their warfare first against Apaches and then Comanches. Smallpox may have thinned Comanche camps. Raids on Anza's New Mexico were becoming riskier and less gainful.

When four hundred Comanches showed up at Taos in July 1785 volunteering to ally themselves with New Mexicans, Governor Anza procrastinated. That October at the Taos fair, Comanches turned over two captives without ransom and left two of their own men as a sign of good faith. In spite of these gestures, Anza insisted there could be no formal alliance until every branch of the Comanche nation agreed. In response, representatives of all but the two most distant groups met on the Arkansas River in November 1785 and elected as spokesman Ecueracapa (Leather Cape), by all accounts their most distinguished chief. He accepted the honor of talking with Cuerno Verde's conqueror.

Emissaries, lavishly entertained by both parties, carried messages back and forth. They arranged to meet at Pecos for negotiations, which was in itself a sign of Comanche willingness to suspend hostilities. Since the 1730s, their war parties had viciously assaulted that exposed pueblo, traditional ally of their Plains Apache enemies.

In February 1786, a hungry, difficult time to travel, they came in peace, hundreds of them, putting up their tepees across the field that spread below the pueblo to the east. Ecueracapa and his mounted staff, in their winter finest, filed through the mountains to Santa Fe, where Anza awaited them with as much pomp as Santa Fe could muster.

Solemn but demonstrative, the Comanche leader rendered homage to Anza, and according to a contemporary account, "His harangue of salutation and embrace of the governor on dismounting at the door of his residence exceeded ten minutes." Inside, the exaggerated diplomacy continued. Anza, exercising the influence he had won on the field of battle, proposed to the Comanche delegation a difficult condition: peace with the Utes, fellow Shoshonean-speakers but sworn enemies for a generation. "After several accusations and apologies by both parties," according to the same source, "this was achieved and formalized in their manner, chiefs and attendants exchanging their garments with their counterparts."

The Spanish governor was gambling. He must not favor Comanches in the eyes of previously established Ute allies. By regaling equally Ecueracapa and Moara, the Ute chief, he maintained the requisite aura of lordly impartiality. Then on February 28, he accompanied them to Pecos, where the ceremonial of treatymaking entered a more hectic, egalitarian stage. Two hundred Comanches gathered around him. "All, one by one, came up to embrace him with such excessive expressions of affection and respect that they were by no means appropriate to his rank and station." Anza took no offense.

Shared food, speeches, gifts, and a ritual burying of warfare marked the process.

A Comanche village, by George Catlin, 1834. *From George Catlin,* North American Indians *(1926).*

Tosapoy, third-ranking war captain of the Cuchanec division of the Comanche nation, climaxed an impassioned oration by presenting to Governor Anza a Spanish youth from Santa Fe, Alejandro Martín, captive among them for eleven years. Martín, who had lived the Comanche way, would profit from his experience. For the rest of his life, he would serve as a government-salaried Comanche agent and interpreter.

The treaty permitted Comanches to move closer to New Mexico, granted them access to Santa Fe and free trade at Pecos, and confirmed them as allies in a relentless war against Apaches. It bound all divisions of the Comanche nation to ratify the terms and endorse Ecueracapa as preeminent captain general. On him, Anza bestowed a sword and banner and agreed that his own staff of office be displayed to Comanche leaders not present at Pecos.

Next day, March 1, Ash Wednesday on the Christian calendar, heavily bundled heathen Comanches and Utes voluntarily joined the Spanish governor at the imposition of ashes. They had agreed that day to inaugurate the new era with an off-season trade fair, over which Anza exercised firm control. Cautioning Hispanos and Pueblos that none of their familiar swindles would be tolerated, he had Vélez Cachupín's 1754 list of fair values posted with two changes, both favoring the non-Christian Indians. For each buffalo hide they were to receive two trade knives, not just one, and for an average horse, thirteen.

Traders faced one another along a corridor marked on the ground by two parallel lines inside which both parties openly displayed their offerings until agreements were struck. Designated monitors looked over their shoulders. Soldiers stood by. Never had the ritual of exchange proceeded so smoothly.

Within the month, Governor Anza, accompanied by a Comanche observer, entered into similar personal diplomacy on New Mexico's western frontier with representatives of the widely dispersed Navajos. At a meeting on the Río Puerco arranged by the alcaldes mayores of Zuni, Laguna, and Jemez, he elevated two headmen whom he named don Carlos and don José Antonio to token governorship and lieutenant governorship. He promised them medals and hired with their approval an interpreter as Navajo agent. Like the Comanches, Navajos would again be welcome to trade with New Mexicans. For their part, they swore to gird up their loins and make war on Gila Apaches.[14]

Because there had been such agreements before, many New Mexicans remained skeptical. Yet conditions were changing, if imperceptibly. On the Spaniards' side, the cumulative intent of repeated royal orders, especially that of 1779, culminated in 1786 in Viceroy Bernardo de Gálvez's bold *Instructions* for peace by purchase. The end of war with England in 1783 made available increased appropriations for gifts. And for particular reasons of their own, various heathen nations now favored alliance and trade with colonists.

Before Anza and his Sonora household packed up and departed New Mexico for Arizpe in the fall of 1787, he could boast of the kingdom's four allied tribes: Jicarilla Apaches, Utes, Comanches, and Navajos. Their people had recourse not only to New Mexico's trade but also to annual gifts from the government warehouse in Santa Fe. Comanches, through their agents, sent tally sheets of enemy Apaches killed. And despite Commandant General Ugarte y Loyola's desire that these buffalo nomads become town-dwelling farmers—an illusion tested and abandoned at the so-called pueblo of San Carlos on the Arkansas River in 1787—they kept the peace.[15]

Juan Bautista de Anza was weary. Ugarte y Loyola thought he should be appointed governor of Texas to solidify the work of elderly Gov. Domingo Cabello y Robles, but Viceroy Manuel Antonio Flores thought not. Instead, with headquarters in Arizpe, Anza once again found himself directing military operations against the Apaches of Sonora. On October 1, 1788, it was proposed that he be transferred to Spain with rank and salary of colonel.

But on December 19, at the age of fifty-two, Anza died. In the hulking parish church of Arizpe, his relatives buried the northwestern frontier's most prominent native son, and doña Ana María applied to the government for a widow's pension.[16] That same month, Anza's king, Carlos III, most effective of the Spanish Bourbons, also breathed his last.

Eager to test Anza's Comanche peace, Commandant General Ugarte had taken under advisement in mid-1786 a bold offer conveyed to him by Governor Cabello of Texas. Pedro Vial, a self-assured but semiliterate Frenchman of Lyon and Louisiana, who had lived illegally with Taovayas and Wichitas as an armorer and gunsmith, bragged that he could travel alone in safety from San Antonio to Santa Fe. Let him try, urged Ugarte.

Vial had brokered the deal in October 1785 at San Antonio between eastern Comanches and Spaniards, with help from Taovayas and Wichitas. Although competent enough in the Native languages, the Frenchman had welcomed assistance from Francisco Javier Chávez, captured as a child in New Mexico by Comanches, then traded by them to Taovayas.

When Vial rode out from San Antonio de Béjar on October 4, 1786, bound for Santa Fe, he took with him as companion and servant one Cristóbal de los Santos, a *bejareño*. Sickness, diplomacy en route, and winter weather combined to greatly delay their progress and lengthen their route. But guided as always by Natives, they made it. Escorted via Pecos by a party of Comanches, Vial proudly presented the Spanish flag he carried to don Manuel Delgado, commanding officer of the Santa Fe presidio, on May 26, 1787.

In his diary Vial explained in labored French why his course had not been the shortest. His unnamed but lingering sickness, whose cure he had entrusted to Tawakoni healers, had cost him weeks. Furthermore, Governor Cabello had ordered him to detour to his former village of Taovayas and Wichitas and straighten out the chiefs, who had let their young men run wild on raids for horses even to San Antonio.

According to Vial, he minced no words. Gathered in the smokey closeness of Chief Corichi's grass lodge, the elders heard him out. He reminded them how valuable the Spaniards' gifts and commerce had been to their survival. If they offended their suppliers, they might as well give themselves up as slaves to their enemies, who carried English guns and steel axes. Impugning not only their wisdom, but also their manhood, he hurled a challenge.

> If you wish to make war on the Spaniards, the men do not need to go; send the women, which will be the same. You have for enemies the Osages and Apaches, who are killing and taking your horses every day, while none of you has the courage to go take a scalp.

Somber, they admitted he spoke the truth. They would take the proper remedies.

Governor Anza had congratulated Vial on his mission. But New Mexico's chief executive intended to find a more direct route from Santa Fe to San Antonio. That challenge he placed in the hands of spry, near seventy-year-old José Mares, retired squad leader with the Santa Fe garrison and Hispanic resident of Pecos. Cristóbal de los Santos, returning home to San Antonio, went with him. Former captive

Alejandro Martín, the Comanche-speaking youth given to Anza the year before at Pecos, drew pay as interpreter, and Domingo Maese as servant. They set out on July 31, 1787.

The Mares party moved faster than Vial had, but outward bound, diverted by Comanches to the Taovaya and Wichita village, they hardly improved on the Frenchman's route. Returning to Santa Fe early in 1788, however, Mares reckoned they cut off 48 leagues, or 125 miles. In spite of both journeys, since poor San Antonio had little that anyone in Santa Fe wanted, and vice versa, no regular traffic developed between the two.

Vial, meanwhile, was enjoying Santa Fe and applied to make it his home. Again, he boasted. Given permission, he could open a road eastward all the way to Natchitoches in western Louisiana. And Juan Bautista de Anza believed him. In July 1787, the month before his designated successor, Lt. Col. Fernando de la Concha, arrived in Santa Fe, Anza had forwarded Vial's latest proposal to the commandant general. Again, Ugarte concurred: thank Vial for his previous service, outfit him for the trip to Natchitoches, but order him to return afterward to San Antonio. Accordingly, on June 23, 1788, Pedro Vial led another small party out through Pecos onto the plains, while Governor Concha begged the commandant general for license to make the Frenchman a legal resident of Santa Fe.[17]

While Concha nurtured peace with the Comanches, Ugarte imagined linking Santa Fe through Natchitoches with New Orleans, Spain's busy entrepôt on the Gulf of Mexico. Hence, the commerce envisioned by Louisiana's former French governors might finally begin flowing.

Bound for Natchitoches, Vial knew firsthand the shifts that had taken place in the region over the past fifteen years, ever since the forced evacuation of east Texas. The *Reglamento* of 1772, which gave the Marqués de Rubí's judgment the force of law, had withdrawn presidial soldiers, settlers, and missionaries from Los Adaes and vicinity. San Antonio had become official capital of Texas in 1773. Don Juan María Vicencio, Barón de Ripperdá, the province's governor between 1770 and 1778, set the removal in motion. Yet he sympathized with the evacuees, compelled on short notice to leave their homes amid the moss of east Texas and endure a killing, three-month trail of tears to semiarid, unwelcoming San Antonio.

The governor, in fact, gave leave to a successful forty-four-year-old Native and opportunist of Los Adaes, rancher and trader Antonio Gil Ybarbo, along with a neighbor and an Indian leader, to carry in person their plea to Viceroy Bucareli. In Mexico City, they earned a compromise that infuriated Commandant-Inspector Hugo O'Conor, who while residing at Los Adaes had ordered Gil Ybarbo's arrest for smuggling and meant to see that the place remained abandoned indefinitely. Thanks to an alleged shortage of suitable lands around San Antonio, however, Gil

Pedro Vial's map, 1787: Santa Fe left center, St. Louis right center, New Orleans lower right. *From Kessell,* Kiva, Cross, and Crown.

...dro. Vial taixo tranzitau

...1787.

Ybarbo had gained viceregal authority to lead surviving east Texas families back, but no closer than a hundred leagues (about 260 miles) west of Natchitoches. Their precarious civil settlement, named—to recall Los Adaes and the viceroy—Nuestra Señora del Pilar de Bucareli, was located where the road from San Antonio crossed the Trinity River; it lasted only from 1774 to 1779. Comanches and floodwaters convinced Gil Ybarbo and his fellows to risk an unauthorized move farther east.

Nacogdoches, the town they founded in 1779 next to the deserted mission, thrived. A multiracial fait accompli deep in dense woods, it served several purposes that came together in Gil Ybarbo's resourceful person. In recognition, Governor Cabello named him lieutenant governor of Texas, administrator of annual gifts to allied Indian nations, and militia captain. No one better understood the ever-changing kaleidoscope of Indian commerce and war in the late eighteenth-century colony. It was a complex business in horses, deerskins, and delivery of gifts by the bale orchestrated by the likes of Paris-born Athanase de Mézières, at one point the son-in-law of Louis Juchereau de Saint-Denis and associate of his son and name-sake. These dealings took place against a backdrop of relentless Native population decline. Observers accused even former Governor Ripperdá of profiting illegally from the trade.

By the time of his successor, Domingo Cabello y Robles, the Spanish government of Texas was providing gifts to twenty-one recognized friendly Native peoples, with the addition of Comanches after 1785. Because the colony spread physically along the Gulf Coast and across deserts, woodlands, and plains, the recipients could hardly have been more varied.

The hundreds of boxes and bundles that reached San Antonio on August 22, 1786, in Gil Ybarbo's pack train, had come from core to periphery by sea, river, and road. This wide array of textiles, tools, and sundries from Europe had been offloaded and transshipped at Veracruz for New Orleans, thence carried by boat up the Mississippi and, when the water rose high enough, in big canoes up the Red River as far as Natchitoches. There they were lashed on horses and mules for the trip via Nacogdoches to the capital. Within days of the ritual distribution, these items graced the wooden-pole, grass, or skin lodges of Spain's Native North American allies.

The lively trade center at Natchitoches, whose polyglot population in August 1788 he reckoned at twenty-seven hundred to three thousand, favorably impressed literate Francisco Javier Fragoso. A native of Guadalajara and longtime veteran of the Santa Fe presidio, Fragoso had volunteered to keep a diary in Spanish of Pedro Vial's journey to Natchitoches and return via San Antonio.

Louis de Blanc, commandant at Natchitoches, feasted his visitors from New Mexico and hastily sent word to Gov. Esteban Miró of Louisiana, enclosing Fragoso's diary. The way to Santa Fe now lay open, "a road very passable in all seasons and with no risk other than that from the Osages, since the Comanches are already very peaceful and are our friends."

After ten days, Vial's little party left Natchitoches for San Antonio as ordered, traveling by the camino real to the southwest a distance of nearly four hundred miles. Fragoso commented as they passed Rancho Lobanillo, a large property owned by Antonio Gil Ybarbo. At Nacogdoches, the diarist estimated eighty or ninety wooden houses and 200 to 250 assorted Spaniards and Frenchmen.

Neither Fragoso nor the three young New Mexicans who had accompanied Vial liked the climate. All but the Frenchman "were attacked by chills and fevers," probably malaria. Even in drier San Antonio, they remained intermittently ill until San Juan's day, June 24, 1789. On the twenty-fifth, they struck for home. Pedro Vial, who had been out with Francisco Javier Chávez delivering presents to Comanche chiefs, joined the others on July 1. After refusing his request earlier, higher authorities had reversed themselves and granted him license to live in Santa Fe.[18]

Studying the map, Commandant General Ugarte had traced desirable routes not only southeastward from New Mexico's capital across the Comanchería to New Orleans, but also southwest to Sonora and west even as far as Monterey in California. Again, Juan Bautista de Anza, only months before his death, had received the call. With no general peace in the western Apachería, the mission demanded a reconnaissance in force toward New Mexico, more campaign than exploration.

From Arizpe in late summer 1788, Anza orchestrated the union of four hundred men from the presidios of Nueva Vizcaya and Sonora. He delegated command to Capt. Manuel de Echeagaray of Santa Cruz, directing the force to ascend the Gila to the Mogollon Mountains and Río de San Francisco; from its headwaters it was not far to the pueblo of Zuni.

Echeagaray thought they had reached the passes leading to Zuni and Acoma, which Miera y Pacheco had learned about on campaign in 1747 and had drawn on several of his maps. Had Miera not died in Santa Fe on April 11, 1785, he might have shown them the way. But their horses were too weak to go on, and they stopped short of opening a road between Sonora and New Mexico.

As an Apache campaign, Echeagaray's operation resounded: 54 Apaches killed, 125 captured, and 55 enlisted as scouts and allies. The latter statistic, however, perplexed acting Viceroy Manuel Antonio Flores, a no-nonsense official who had followed the lamented Bernardo de Gálvez in 1787 and retained supervision of the Provincias Internas. Flores disavowed Gálvez's deceitfully soft policy of accepting peace overtures from Apaches, no matter what the circumstances. Henceforth, the viceroy decreed in 1788, all Apaches who surrendered as a result of military action were to be considered prisoners of war and deported. Only those who came in voluntarily might be admitted to peace.

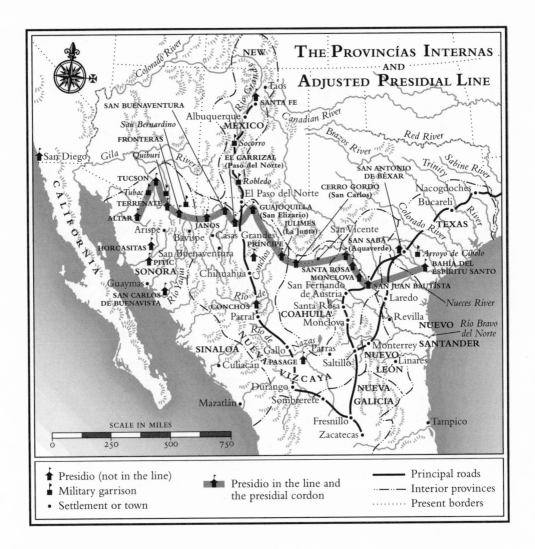

THE PROVINCÍAS INTERNAS
AND
ADJUSTED PRESIDIAL LINE

NEW

Colorado River

Rio Grande

Taos
•SANTA FE

SAN BUENAVENTURA

Albuquerque•
MEXICO

Canadian River

Brazos River

Red River

San Bernardino
•Socorro

FRONTERAS

Gila

San Diego•

Quiburi

River

EL CARRIZAL
(Paso del Norte)

Trinity

Sabine River

SAN ANTONIO
DE BÉXAR

Nacogdoches•

TUCSON
•Robledo
Tubac

El Paso del Norte

CERRO GORDO
(San Carlos)

Bucareli

TERRENATE

GUAJOQUILLA
(San Elizario)

Colorado River

TEXAS

ALTAR

JANOS

JULIMES
(La Junta)

San Vicente

Arispe•

Bavispe•

Casas Grandes

PRÍNCIPE

SAN SABA
(Aquaverde)

Arroyo de Cíbolo
BAHÍA DEL
ESPÍRITU SANTO

HORCASITAS

San Buenaventura

C A L I F O R N I A

PITIC

SONORA

Chihuahua•

Conchos

SANTA ROSA
MONCLOVA

San Juan Bautista

Guaymas•

San Fernando
de Austria•

Laredo•

Nueces River

SAN CARLOS
DE BUENAVISTA

Río Yaqui

Río de

CONCHOS

Santa Rosa
COAHUILA
Monclova

Revilla•

NUEVO Río Bravo
del Norte

Parral•

Río de

SINALOA

Gallo•

Nazas

Parras•

Monterrey **SANTANDER**

•Culiacán

N U E V A

PASAGE

Saltillo•

NUEVO
LEÓN

•Linares

V I Z C A Y A

Durango•

NUEVA
GALICIA

Mazatlán•

Sombrerete•

Fresnillo•

•Tampico

Zacatecas•

SCALE IN MILES

0   250   500   750

Presidio (not in the line)

Military garrison

• Settlement or town

**Presidio in the line and
the presidial cordon**

Principal roads

Interior provinces

Present borders

There had been desertions and other troubles at the Chiricahua Apache peace camp at Bacoachi, southwest of the presidio of Fronteras. Regardless, Echeagaray owed his success to Chiricahua scouts, especially El Compá and El Chacho, who joined him in the field. So Commandant General Ugarte looked the other way, and by late 1789 more than two hundred Chiricahuas lived at Bacoachi. A year later, Ugarte reported that they had petitioned for a Christian missionary.[19]

The next viceroy and the next commandant general, the second Conde de Revillagigedo and Brig. Pedro de Nava, favored Gálvez's peace by purchase, lending their support to subsidized Apache *establecimientos de paz* near presidios on the Nueva Vizcaya and Sonora frontiers. They also nurtured the previously authorized Native infantry garrisons of Opatas and Pimas commanded by Hispanic commissioned and noncommissioned officers.

One such Indian unit, the eighty-man Pima company of San Rafael de Buenavista, moved in 1787 to the old presidio of Tubac, whose Spanish garrison had left in 1776–77 for Tucson by order of Commandant-Inspector O'Conor. The company's acting commander, Spaniard Nicolás de la Errán, received promotion to lieutenant and full command in 1788. The annual payroll for an Indian company of eighty men, 13,098 pesos, amounted to only two-thirds of what the fifty-man Spanish garrison had cost in 1776.

Pimas from nearby Tumacácori and elsewhere signed on for the standard ten-year tour, taking their families with them and depleting further the mission's sparse population. These Pimas, who fought mostly on foot with bow and arrows, light lance and shield, and surplus muskets, got the equivalent of 3 reales a day, 137 pesos annually, or less than half of the current 290 for a regular presidial soldier. Few spoke Spanish, none had uniforms, and in battle they went stripped from the waist up.

Apache raiding, disease, and runaways had reduced Tubac's neighboring mission of San José de Tumacácori to a single village. One by one, the visitas of Guevavi, Sonoita, and Calabazas had fallen away, the latter in 1787.

Not overly energetic, fray Baltasar Carrillo watched it all happen. During his fifteen-year tenure, during which he neither learned the Piman language nor replaced the cramped and deteriorating adobe church left by the Jesuits, the missionary buried a third more of his charges than he baptized, identifying most of them—when he chose to provide an ethnic affiliation—as Pápagos.

Infant mortality hung like a pall over the missions of Pimería Alta. At Tumacácori, of 164 persons Carrillo buried, 35 died before age two, 29 from two to fifteen, and the rest between sixteen and eighty. Of newborns he baptized, not one in three lived two years, and only about half of the survivors reached adulthood. In less than a year, one Indian couple lost four children between the ages of six days and five years.

Father Carrillo also served as chaplain at Tubac. Because the Pima presidio and his mission lay not three miles apart, both on the west bank of the Santa Cruz, the two communities grew together socially and economically. Gente de razón who settled nearby regularly stood as godparents to Indian children.

As civil magistrate of the Tubac district, Lieutenant Errán was authorized to make land grants. In 1789, he bestowed on one don Toribio Otero a town lot and four farming lots near the river ford north of the presidio. The stipulations were standard. The grantee swore to maintain horses and weapons for militia duty, build a house within two years, live on the land for four to gain title, plant fruit trees, and never sell to the church.

Ironically, as Apache warfare in Pimería Alta wound down, the valley of the northward-flowing Santa Cruz in present-day southern Arizona was better defended than ever before. The regular garrison originally founded at Terrenate and moved twice with dire results had finally come in 1787 to reside at the abandoned mission site of Santa María Soamca, just below today's U.S.-Mexico border.

About as far to the north downriver from Tubac, a half-day's ride, stood the presidio of San Agustín de Tucson, commanded between 1777 and 1786 by the imperious Spanish swashbuckler Pedro de Allande y Saavedra. His veteran successor, Capt. José de Zúñiga, former commander of the garrison at San Diego in California, led an armed column up the Gila and San Francisco rivers toward the pueblo of Zuni in western New Mexico, attempting to achieve in 1795 what Manuel de Echeagaray had not done in 1788—connect Sonora and New Mexico. Among his 150 men were 25 Pimas of Tubac.

With Apache scouts and Echeagaray's diary to guide him, Zúñiga actually reached Zuni and dispatched riders ahead with a letter to the governor in Santa Fe proclaiming his feat. After waiting a week for a reply that never came, he led his tired column back to Tucson. Again, two colonies had been linked but by a road too long and too difficult to maintain. Like the trails of Pedro Vial, Zúñiga's saw no regular traffic, no pack trains, and no mail couriers.[20]

In 1792, two years after Pedro de Nava took the reins as commandant general, the Spanish government reunited, trimmed down, and restored autonomy to the Provincias Internas. The general command's vastness had dictated previous divisions into sectors. Effective in 1793, Nuevo León and Nuevo Santander to the east and the Californias to the west reverted to the viceroy's jurisdiction. Nava, released from viceregal supervision, henceforth exercised direct control over Coahuila, Texas, Nueva Vizcaya, New Mexico, and Sonora. Their governors looked to him.

It made sense to return the neglected Californias to the viceroy. They remained one colony until 1804, with the governor in Monterey after 1777 and the lieutenant governor at Loreto. Once the Yuma uprising of 1781 had shut off Anza's overland road from Sonora, the Californias depended exclusively on supply by sea.

Zuni Pueblo Indian scouts. *From* Century *(May 1883)*.

Orders from Mexico City, conveyed by rider through Guadalajara to the port of San Blas and by government-owned packet boat up the outer coast, could reach Monterey twice as fast as mail from Nava's Chihuahua headquarters, which went by road across to Arizpe and down to Guaymas, by boat to Loreto, and then over the killing trail up the peninsula. The same held for a chalice, a barrel of black powder, or an orphan recruit. Moreover, the viceroy, as patron of the Manila trade, took greater interest in pressing Spain's claim up the Pacific rim as far as Alaska and foiling the Russians.[21]

José de Gálvez, who had a half-dozen young naval officers transferred to San Blas for the purpose, inspired three voyages of remarkable daring between 1774 and 1779. The first, commanded by Juan Pérez with Esteban José Martínez as second officer, actually left before the six new men reported for duty. Although Pérez was later criticized for failing to land and take possession or to describe the coastline in greater detail, he and Martínez pushed the 225-ton, 82-foot-long San Blas frigate *Santiago* as high as fifty-five degrees north latitude, just above the present-day Canada-Alaska boundary.

Their journals graphically portrayed north coast Haida Indians, with whom they traded knives, cloth, beads, and pieces of copper for beautifully tanned skins, resplendent sea-otter pelts, and white Chilkat blankets decorated with fanciful creatures and finished with long fringe. About the latter, chaplain fray Juan Crespi observed wryly:

> Some of the sailors who bought cloaks passed a bad night, for having put them on, they found themselves obliged to take to scratching, on account of the bites they suffered from the little animals these pagans breed in their clothing.

Yet it was the day-after-day, mountainous swells, impenetrable fog, damp cold, and the cursed sores of scurvy that rendered these months-long voyages a monotonous, constantly moving up-and-down hell. Pérez died at sea the next year.

Lima-born Juan Francisco de la Bodega y Quadra, a commander twice as courageous, in the *Sonora,* a schooner less than half as big as the *Santiago,* took Spain's claim even farther north in 1775, above fifty-eight degrees, into the labyrinthine straits, sounds, and glacial fjords off today's Juneau, Alaska. Assisted by iron-nerved, twenty-year-old Francisco Antonio Mourelle y la Rúa as pilot, a boatswain, and a couple of cabin boys, Bodega had only fourteen sailors, ten of whom were vaqueros who had never been to sea before. Their feat became all the more extraordinary in light of what happened halfway up the Washington coast. Lookouts aboard the *Santiago,* their larger consort commanded in 1775 by Bruno de Hezeta with Juan Pérez as first pilot, were too far away to notice.

A day of friendly trading with men who came out in big canoes from a summer village visible from their anchorage put the Spaniards at ease. Next morning,

July 15, 1775, a chief brought his wife aboard the *Sonora*. All seemed well for six of the sailors to go ashore for fresh water, a new topmast, and firewood. Because the ship's boat was so small, one would bring it back for Bodega, Mourelle, and the empty water casks.

Instead, as the captain watched through a spyglass, the boat swamped in heavy surf. As the crew struggled to pull it onto the beach, about three hundred Native males wielding long lances and bows and arrows emerged screaming from the brush. Two seamen swam frantically toward the ship but disappeared. Fire from the ship's swivel gun and muskets fell short. The attackers smashed the boat to pieces and dragged several corpses into the woods, leaving the beach deserted. There was nothing Bodega could do but go in search of the *Santiago*.

Hezeta provided him with five seamen and a mate along with a boat from the larger ship. Bodega's little schooner then lost contact on July 29; the two ships were not reunited until October 7 in Monterey Bay. Everyone aboard the *Sonora* was suffering from scurvy; Bodega and Mourelle had to be carried off.

By coincidence, the supply ship *San Carlos* also was at anchor in the harbor, and Father Serra and ten friars had gathered at mission San Carlos on the Carmel River. They attended the ailing mariners with fresh fruit and vegetables, meat, and milk. "In truth," Mourelle confessed in his diary, "we could not possibly have so soon recovered from our distressed situation, but by their unparalleled attentions to our infirmities, which they removed by reducing themselves to a most pitiful allowance."

At mission San Carlos, all the men of the sea knelt before La Conquistadora, Nuestra Señora de Belén, the statue that José de Gálvez had sent with Serra. A traditional patroness of mariners, she had interceded six times, the Franciscans believed, to save the crew of the *Sonora* from oblivion. Bodega remembered.

While Gálvez in Spain tried concurrently to keep Spanish voyages into the north Pacific secret and learn what he could of foreign designs through his king's ambassadors at London and St. Petersburg, Nueva California had grown by spurts.[22] Mainly from the cradles of their birth in Sonora and Sinaloa, some 450 people had migrated with Anza via the Yuma crossing of the Colorado in 1776, with former Gov. Rivera y Moncada over the same route in July 1781, and with Afz. José de Zúñiga up the peninsula in August 1781.

Families from the first wave had founded San Francisco, the upper colony's third presidio, in 1776, and San José, its first civilian town, in 1777. Heads of household from the Zúñiga and Rivera entradas became first citizens of Los Angeles in 1781 and first enlistees at the fourth and final presidio of Santa Barbara in 1782. Notably fertile and blessed with a low rate of infant mortality, these *californios,* joined by a few shipborne immigrants, multiplied handily, nearly doubling their numbers from 990 in 1790 to 1,800 in 1800.

Their proliferation had made Father Serra uneasy. The first father president,

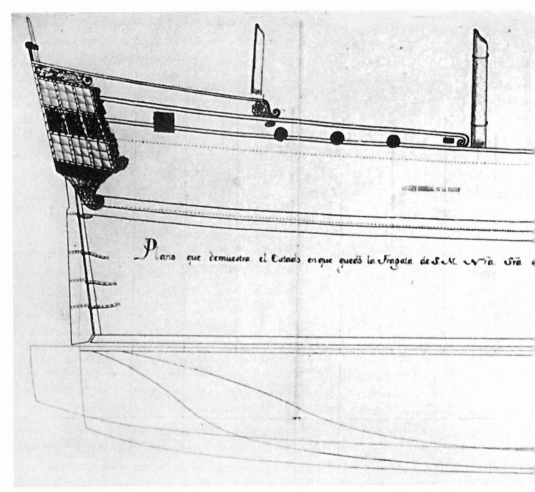

Drawing of the 193-ton frigate *Nuestra Señora de los Remedios,* alias *La Favorita,* reconfigured at El Callao, Peru, in 1778 under the supervision of Juan Francisco de la Bodega y Quadra for exploration of the north Pacific coast. *Courtesy of the Santa Barbara Trust for Historic Preservation.*

who advocated segregation of gente de razón and mission Indians, saw Nueva California primarily as a government-subsidized Franciscan ministry. Felipe de Neve, who had taken over as governor at Monterey in 1777, disagreed. He viewed the colony as a military and civilian outpost of empire.

Neve had taken part in the expulsion of the Jesuits, seizing their properties in Zacatecas in 1767. But he had ignored the lessons of 1768 in Antigua California and Pimería Alta, where the pragmatic José de Gálvez restored to their Franciscan replacements the traditional economic and disciplinary control over their neophytes. In Nueva California, bureaucrat Neve, dancing to the secular tune of Teodoro de Croix, had tried again to emasculate the missions.

Serra fought him every step. Neve represented the Enlightenment view—

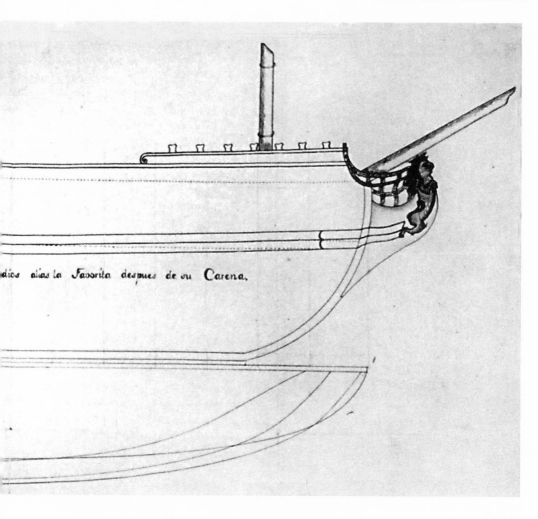

dios alias la Favorita despues de su Carena.

subordinate churchmen, allow only one per mission, take temporal authority from him, let Indians come and go, and never whip them—and Serra was a pre-Enlightenment, scholastic, paternalistic missionary. The governor's new set of regulations, drafted in 1779 and promulgated in 1781, and the friars' noncompliance with them mirrored the clash.

When Neve, acting as patron of the church, demanded that the father president produce the document authorizing him to administer the sacrament of confirmation, Serra resisted. Neve ordered him not to perform it, but the friar kept on. A heated, two-year-long correspondence between mission San Carlos, Monterey, Mexico City, and Arizpe ensued. In 1781, the governor finally backed down when Croix ordered him to do so.[23]

Fray Junípero Serra. The Mosqueda-Herrera copy of a portrait now lost, once at the Franciscan Colegio de Santa Cruz, Querétaro. *Courtesy of the Santa Barbara Trust for Historic Preservation.*

As in seventeenth-century New Mexico, the collective population and wealth of the missions far exceeded those of the colonists, an imbalance that increasingly favored the Franciscans until the end of the Spanish colonial period in 1821. Everyone depended in one way or another on the missions to produce or consume. Hence, no genuine reform of the traditional missionary establishment occurred in Nueva California.

When Father Serra died in 1784, eighteen friars from the College of San Fernando in Mexico City ministered by their count to 4,650 Indians at nine missions set in fertile coastal basins and ranges from San Diego to San Francisco. Sensibly, they had delivered the struggling former Jesuit stations in Antigua California to Dominicans a dozen years earlier.

After Felipe de Neve had become commandant general and moved to Arizpe, even he, taking some of the credit, praised Serra's band. "In a word," he concluded in 1783,

> they have brought to those establishments that state of progress they enjoy today, compared to which there are no other missions like theirs in all these provinces. They have made fertile and fecund a portion of land which they found uncultivated wastes.

Ignoring the enormous ecological advantages of temperate Alta California, Neve criticized the Dominicans' efforts in Baja California and urged that Franciscans repossess those missions.

The busy, self-assertive first bishop of Sonora, Sinaloa, and the Californias, fray Antonio de los Reyes, a Franciscan himself, would have had it the other way round. Consecrated in 1782, Reyes noted that Franciscans in the Provincias Internas—from Texas to the Californias—answered to three different provinces and three different apostolic colleges. Hence, he proposed creating four Franciscan custodies. When his brethren protested, Reyes vindictively thought of giving both Californias to the Dominicans. But nothing came of his proposal.[24]

Life for Natives in California's artificial Franciscan mission communities did not change all at once. For years, traditional rancherías existed alongside the simple palisade structures of mud-plastered wood. Indians from outside, voluntarily or by coercion, brought their babies in for whatever power baptism might convey. Those inside obtained permission to visit their kin from time to time and join in hunts or wild food harvests.

Even as cultivated wheat, maize, barley, and beans came to replace gathered acorns, grasses, and berries, and beef and mutton supplanted meat from hunted animals, Indian women within their mission quarters kept on preparing and cooking foods in their customary ways. They continued to make fine baskets, increasingly incorporating European designs.

Bone whistles used by shamans, along with crystals and other seemingly sacred paraphernalia later excavated by archaeologists hinted that Native religious practice also endured within mission walls. Other forms of resistance ranged from occasional warfare and frequent desertion to work slowdowns and dirty jokes about the friars.

The most violent outbreak during Father Serra's tenure had taken place at San Diego, in a zone of Ipai discontent where the mission had been moved four miles away from the presidio. The causes seemed to have included rape of Native girls by soldiers and, more immediately, fear of whipping on the part of mission leader Carlos and his brother Francisco for alleged theft.

About one o'clock in the chill, moonlit morning of November 5, 1775, hundreds of armed Natives had sneaked up on the mission. The guards were asleep. Before crackling flames awakened the two friars, the attackers had cowed the mission's neophytes and removed the statues of the Immaculate Conception and St.

Mission San Carlos Borromeo, Carmel, Nueva California, by Henry Chapman Ford, 1883. Honeyman Collection, no. 0917:18. *Courtesy of The Bancroft Library, University of California, Berkeley.*

Joseph from the church, passing them to a horde of women stationed to carry off the loot.

Father Vicente Fuster's fearful description of mortal combat and the firing of buildings was reminiscent of Medina's at San Sabá, although not as many residents of the California mission died. Just before dawn, the raiders withdrew, and fray Vicente stumbled around looking for his companion, fray Luis Jayme. He discovered a mutilated body, then fainted. The figure was naked except for underpants, the face disfigured beyond recognition: "Finally I recognized him as Father Luis only insofar as my eyes noted the whiteness of his skin and the tonsure of his head."[25]

Almost all the missions except San Diego produced surpluses. The colony grew self-sufficient in European livestock and foodstuffs. No longer required to haul such cargos, the annual supply ships in the 1780s now brought fancy church furnishings, tools, textiles, and luxury items like fine brandy, tropical fruit preserves, and snuff.

As the initial palisade structures gave way in the 1780s and 1790s to more permanent and spacious stone and adobe complexes, the numbers of Indians on mission census roll rose steadily. Recruiting gangs ranged farther and farther, eventually into the great central valley where the Yokut peoples lived. But more and more mission Indians died. After entering the missions, they lived on average scarcely a dozen years. A less diversified diet, crowding, unsanitary conditions, diseases like measles and syphilis, along with the psychological trauma of losing the elders and being put into unfamiliar family and work patterns—all contributed to early death.

Concurrently, neophytes took part in the pageantry and play of feast days. Some learned animal husbandry or were apprenticed to a carpenter, blacksmith, or shoemaker. Most accepted regular meals, board, and a variety of gifts—clothing, blankets, glass beads, and needles—and a few dozen married gente de razón.

By one rough estimate, between 1769 and 1800 the total Native population of Nueva California's occupied coastal zone, where the Chumash of the Santa Barbara area were most numerous, fell from sixty thousand to thirty-five thousand. If the benefits they anticipated were found wanting, and they did not die, they could always resist, which they often did. Yet because more and more Native peoples were enticed or coerced to join mission congregations, the neophyte population of Nueva California kept rising.[26]

While Spanish officials, unable to attract desirable artisan families to California, considered accepting orphans, convicts, prostitutes, and debtors, Pedro Vial of Santa Fe—in 1790 a town of 4,346 souls—went trailblazing again, this time destined for St. Louis in the Illinois country of upper Louisiana.

Because a couple of years in Santa Fe had not improved Vial's written Spanish, Governor Concha instructed him to keep his diary in French. Upon Vial's return, the governor would have it translated in the Frenchman's presence. He would travel again in the style to which he was accustomed, with only two young companions from Santa Fe, José Vicente Villanueva and Vicente Espinosa, each to be paid thirty pesos for the round trip.

After a day at Pecos arranging their packs, the trio rode into the rising sun on May 23, 1792. Two days out, they chanced to meet Vial's old friend Francisco Javier Chávez of San Antonio traveling with a Comanche party to visit his parents in Santa Fe. Elated, Chávez and the Comanches insisted that Vial ride with them back to the Pecos River. "Consequently," reads the diary, "that day's march was lost."

One lost day turned out to be nothing compared to what followed: Vial's ten-day sickness at one camp; a frightful seven-week stay with Indians he identified as Kansas, who robbed and all but killed them; and delays as the French traders who rescued them in a pirogue hunted for deer and bear along the banks of the Missouri.

They did not reach St. Louis until the night of October 3; their journey had taken more than four months.

Vial's scarcely less eventful, two-stage return to Santa Fe the next year, ascending by boat higher up the Missouri and then being escorted overland by Pawnees, actually took slightly longer. Yet as Governor Concha boasted, the French pathfinder had definitively shown the way. Moreover, after consulting the travelers, don Zenon Trudeau, commander and lieutenant governor at St. Louis, had reported to Gov. the Baron Carondelet in New Orleans that with better luck the trip could be made in twenty-five days. That left Spanish officials to ponder.[27]

As reverberations of the 1780s—of United States independence, the death of Carlos III in Spain, and eruption of the French Revolution—sounded across the nineties from Louisiana to California, a growing number of foreigners chose to test the Spanish frontier. More than a few had already made contacts or homes in the northern borderlands among Hispanic and Indian inhabitants. And who was to prevent them?

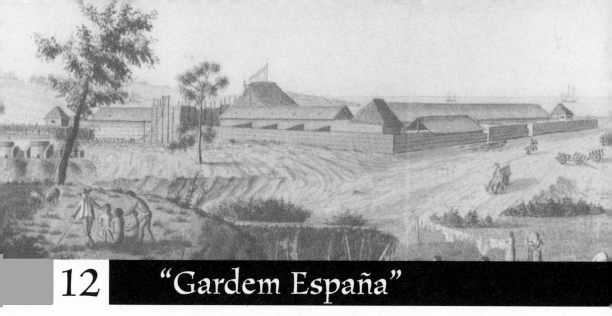

12   "Gardem España"

*[The Anglo-Americans] introduce themselves in the thickness of the forests, like
the Indians. . . . First they become acquainted with the Indians, trade with
them, and afterwards engage in contraband trade with the natives of Mexico.
Some stay in the territories. . . . They are settled in sufficient numbers so that
they will establish their customs, laws, and religion. They will form independent states, aggregating themselves to the Federal Union, which will not refuse
to receive them, and progressively they will go as far as the Pacific Ocean.*

—GOV. MANUEL GAYOSO DE LEMOS OF LOUISIANA
TO THE VICEROY, LATE 1798

A decade earlier, in the 1780s, citizens of the United States—dubbed *americanos* by
Spaniards on the northern frontier—had already introduced themselves in the
Pacific and along its coasts. And sailors from Great Britain and other nations had
preceded them.

As instructed, crews of the Hezeta-Bodega expedition in 1775 had enacted formal rites of Spanish possession, leaving sturdy crosses protruding from cairns of
rocks at four points along the north coast between forty and fifty-eight degrees.
These proved not enough.

When British hero Capt. James Cook sailed from Plymouth in July 1776 on his
third and fatal voyage of Pacific exploration, one of his goals had been to navigate
any Northwest Passage from Pacific to Atlantic and claim Parliament's twenty-
thousand-pound prize. José de Gálvez knew about his voyage almost immediately.
By the time Spanish ships weighed anchor in 1779 to intercept Cook, however, the
captain had already called. Having effaced a Spanish inscription on Tahiti and discovered the Hawaiian Islands, he had raised today's Oregon coast in March 1778
and set course northward.

At Nootka Sound on the west side of Vancouver Island, Cook's crew eagerly

traded trinkets for fifteen hundred sea-otter pelts, admiring their shimmering soft-
ness but unaware of the price they would bring in China. Cook never found out;
he was killed upon his return to the Hawaiian Islands. His men did. In Macao or
Canton, one dark, northern sea-otter pelt might bring as much as a hundred Spanish
pesos. The Northwest Passage could wait.

In belated response, two newly constructed Spanish frigates, just under two
hundred tons each, had coasted Alaska in 1779 to above 60 degrees, higher than
any previous Spanish voyage. The *Princesa* was commanded by Ignacio de Arteaga,
and the *Favorita* had steel-nerved Juan Francisco de la Bodega y Quadra as captain
and Francisco Antonio Mourelle as first officer. Taking possession on Hinchinbrook
Island and the Kenai Peninsula, they reported no sign of Cook or other foreigners. And apparently at this time the Russians had not expanded their fur-hunting
operations beyond the Aleutians.

Zestful John Ledyard, a footloose Connecticut Yankee who had sailed with
Cook, finally in 1783 let the seamen of Boston and Salem in on the potential of a
sea-otter boon. In *A Journal of Captain Cook's Last Voyage to the Pacific Ocean,* Ledyard
enthused about Nootka Sound, claiming, "Skins which did not cost the purchaser
sixpence sterling sold in China for 100 dollars."

Even though the voyage around Cape Horn took a year, in September 1788
two American ships entered Nootka Sound, the 212-ton *Columbia Rediviva,* Capt.
John Kendrick commanding, and the 90-ton sloop *Lady Washington,* with Robert
Gray as captain. No one aboard had any idea that Spaniards, especially intent on
thwarting British and Russian projects, had already launched a feigned colonization of Nootka Sound.

To ignore these Americans, Viceroy Manuel Antonio Flores warned late in
1788, was sheer folly. "Republican and independent," the former British colonies
of North America likely aspired already to a safe port on the Pacific. Furthermore,
he added prophetically, the United States might

> try to sustain it by crossing the immense land of this continent above our
> possessions of Texas, New Mexico, and the Californias . . . and, in truth, it
> would obtain the richest trade of Great China and India if it were to suc-
> ceed in establishing a colony on the west coasts of America.

And that was precisely how John Ledyard saw it: cross the continent to the
Pacific above Spanish territory. Ledyard had, in fact, described his vision to an interested Thomas Jefferson, then United States minister in Paris.

Wintering in the vicinity of Nootka, the two American skippers Kendrick and
Gray found themselves front and center in July 1789 for the encounter between
erratic, quick-tempered subjects of Europe's two great imperial powers. The experience rather invigorated them.

Rocky beach with sea otters, 1803–1807. Honeyman Collection, no. 1035. *Courtesy of The Bancroft Library, University of California, Berkeley.*

Testy veteran Esteban José Martínez, a nephew of Viceroy Flores, carried specific instructions from his uncle. With clarity and firmness he was to demonstrate to any English interloper how Spanish discoveries antedated Captain Cook's. What clearer documentation than Cook's own reference to bartering with Natives in 1778 for the pair of silver spoons stolen from Martínez himself during Juan Pérez's initial visit to Nootka four years earlier?

On June 24, 1789, the proud Spaniard presided over a festive repossession of Nootka with Americans, Englishmen, and other foreigners as witnesses. Fifteen-gun cannonades rumbled from the *Princesa, San Carlos,* and the hastily constructed little wooden fort, San Miguel. At Martínez's bidding, Chief Ma-kwee-na described the Spanish banner flown by the first European ship to call at Nootka.

Eight days later, the trading ship *Argonaut,* outfitted in Macao and flying the British flag, brought to Nootka's shore the impudent Capt. James Colnett, who imagined himself governor of the English port of Nootka. Martínez sensed rightly that Colnett bore no commission from his king, only instructions from a private commercial firm. Americans Kendrick and Gray, having convinced the Spanish commandant that they posed no such threat to Spanish sovereignty, watched with interest.

At the height of an argument in Martínez's cabin aboard the *Princesa* on July 3, 1789, Colnett allegedly placed "his hand two or three times on his sword" and blurted out "the evil-sounding and denigrating words 'Gardem España' ['Goddamn Spain']." Arresting the Englishman forthwith, Martínez seized the *Argonaut* and, ten days later, the British sloop *Princess Royal*.

With prize crew and Colnett aboard, Martínez dispatched the *Argonaut* for San Blas before dawn on July 14, carrying also the Spanish commandant's version of the confrontation. Other correspondence went as well. Disillusioned fray Severo Patero, one of four Franciscans sent with Martínez allegedly to convert the Nootka people, saw little hope. "We expect the Russians from one day to the next, and some other English vessels, so that if Spain does not take strong resolves on the particular, these coasts and our establishments are in imminent danger."[1]

The court of vacuous Carlos IV appeared incapable of taking strong resolves. And Great Britain, still sore over losing its North American colonies, had no intention of letting the Nootka incident pass. British propagandists screamed for revenge. The timing put Spain at grave disadvantage.

The very day Martínez's prize weighed anchor from Nootka, a mob in Paris assailed the Bastille and murdered the governor. France's Louis XVI, with deepening troubles at home, had no energy to aid his Bourbon cousin in Madrid as war threatened. So, after mutual recriminations, Spain backed down. In 1790, by the first Nootka Convention, the government of Carlos IV not only agreed to restore British property taken at Nootka in 1789, but also to allow navigation, fishing, trade, or settlement on the Pacific Coast by British subjects "in places not already occupied." That meant, in the minds of those subjects, any place north of San Francisco.[2]

Although no great rush to the Pacific Northwest ensued, Spain's concession that its claims as high as Alaska were not exclusive marked a turning of the tide. Title based on earliest European discovery, symbolic acts, and sturdy wooden crosses no longer sufficed. Occupation had become the measure. Yet to the citizens of isolated Monterey, Santa Fe, or San Antonio—most of whom resented their government's policy forbidding foreign intercourse—not even Spanish occupation of an area assured impenetrable sovereignty over it.

The very success of the Bourbon reforms, especially peace by purchase, had made California, New Mexico, and Texas safer and more prosperous. These sparsely defended, peripheral colonies naturally appealed to would-be intruders, especially Anglo-Americans and erstwhile Frenchmen seeking new lands, goods, and markets. As barriers, official Spanish pronouncements against free trade did little to stem the extralegal flow.

Viceroy Flores in 1788 had predicted Lewis and Clark (1803–1806), and Governor Manuel Gayoso de Lemos of Louisiana in 1798 would prophesy the Treaty of Guadalupe Hidalgo (1848). Few foreign intruders on New Spain's far northern frontier after 1790 arrived unforeseen.

Philip Nolan, an unbridled young Irishman from Belfast and Kentucky who took oaths to Spain and engaged in questionable ventures with the governors of Spanish Louisiana, epitomized such intruders. He dealt in wild Texas horses, broken and sold in Louisiana, and kept a place and mistress at Nacogdoches. She was rumored to be Gertrudis de los Santos, twenty years his senior and wife of his business partner, Antonio Leal.

During the 1790s, Spanish officials alternately issued passports to Nolan and ordered his arrest. All the while, he gathered information for his scheming former employer, U.S. Gen. James Wilkinson, who forwarded whatever suited him to the vice-president, Thomas Jefferson.

Governor Gayoso of Louisiana, a former associate of Nolan, by 1799 had turned fiercely against him. Writing to Commandant General Pedro de Nava, he branded the mustanger the most dangerous American of all. Nolan was astute and devious, and Gayoso cautioned:

> It would be advisable to seize this man and send him far away, so well guarded and so secretly that his whereabouts would never again be learned, because I have more than good reason to suspect that he is commissioned by General [James] Wilkinson to make a complete reconnaissance of the country.

In 1800, Nolan, this time without passport, led twenty-seven formidably armed men into central Texas. Nava issued orders for the invaders' arrest. Oddly, the American and his band hunkered down and built shelters on the Brazos River near today's Waco. There they wintered, traded with Comanches, and collected horses. In March 1801, surrounded by a much larger force under Lt. Miguel Francisco Músquiz of the Nacogdoches garrison, Nolan chose to die fighting.

Another Irishman watched. William Barr, a naturalized Spanish citizen, had ridden out with Músquiz as interpreter. He and his partners in the House of Barr and Davenport, on contract with the Spanish government, supplied promised goods to friendly tribes. These and other non-Spaniards already held large tracts of Texas land. "Moved by his well-known love for the king," Barr volunteered to carry Nolan's severed ears to Texas Gov. Juan Bautista de Elguezábal, who sent the trophies on to the commandant general.

Whatever his shorter-term profit motives, Philip Nolan, who admitted that he had tired of wild horses, seemed to have had bigger things in mind. A fellow American, testifying some years later, recalled a prophetic boast. Nolan is supposed

Monterey presidio, Nueva California. Drawing ascribed to José Cardero, 1791. Honeyman Collection, no. 1310. *Courtesy of The Bancroft Library, University of California, Berkeley.*

to have exclaimed, "I look forward to the conquest of Mexico by the United States; and I expect my patron and friend, the General, will, in such an event, give me a conspicuous command."

The prospect of such a conquest loomed so menacingly that Spanish officials cracked down on American sympathizers in Texas. Seven of Nolan's men were Hispanic, including a brother of Gertrudis de los Santos. She and Antonio Leal were deported from Nacogdoches for their alleged part in the Nolan intrigue and put conspicuously on trial in San Antonio.

The commandant general, judging Gertrudis and Antonio, Santiago (Jesse) Cook, and Pedro "Big Foot" Longueville guilty of secret association with Nolan, recommended exiling them to the interior of New Spain. But because Longueville had a useful trade, he was encouraged—as so often happened with foreigners in Spanish territory—to remain in San Antonio, where he opened a bakery, married, and eventually took up ranching.

The nine Americans of Nolan's party who survived waited five years in jail in Chihuahua for a royal order regarding their fate. When it came, it commanded that someone must die for having fired on the king's men. Forced to roll dice to determine who it would be, the lucky eight commiserated with Ephraim Blackburn, oldest member of the party, who finally was hanged November 11, 1807.[3]

Plaza of the Monterey presidio, Nueva California. Drawing ascribed to José Cardero, 1791. Honeyman Collection, no. 1308. *Courtesy of The Bancroft Library, University of California, Berkeley.*

Although Santa Fe lay hundreds of miles deeper west in North America than San Antonio, Commandant General Nava kept Gov. Fernando de Chacón constantly informed of foreign threats to New Mexico: French, British, and American. He passed on as well a Spanish version of the tumult in Europe.

France had erupted. Frenzied factions of French republicans had brought down the monarchy, plunged that country into bloody civil war, and early in 1793 executed Louis XVI. Carlos IV, his scheming queen María Luisa, and their young favorite and chief adviser Manuel Godoy shuddered in horror. France, meanwhile, declared war on Austria, Great Britain, Holland, and Spain.

Agents of French revolutionary regimes operated in North America, conniving to recover Louisiana and convince Spaniards that the Mississippi Valley, if once again in French hands, could better contain Americans pushing westward and Englishmen trading south from Canada. Not for a moment, Nava warned Chacón. On January 6, 1795, he advised New Mexico's governor, "Just reasons have obliged Viceroy [the Marqués de] Branciforte to take the serious step of ordering the arrest and imprisonment of all Frenchmen in the viceroyalty."

Governor Chacón had only two to report. Domingo de Labadía, born in France and unaccountably in Santa Fe, had married Micaela Padilla nearly thirty years earlier and fathered at least a dozen children. Under an exception for Frenchmen married to Spanish, casta, or Indian women, Chacón inventoried Labadía's property and told him to confine himself to his residence.

Although French-born Indian agent Pedro Vial took an oath of loyalty to the Spanish king, the governor still had his doubts. He let Vial remain at home with "some of his children," but had his horses put in the public corral. Reiterating to Nava the Frenchman's previous good services, Governor Chacón hardly blinked before enlisting Vial to undertake another sensitive mission. There was no one else.

Spaniards feared rightly that American traders, ever eager to expand their business, meant to turn Indians of the trans-Mississippi West against their previous suppliers. The Pawnees, east of the Comanches, appeared especially vulnerable. So, in the summer of 1795, Chacón dispatched Comanche agent Vial from Santa Fe to make peace between Comanches and Pawnees.

Lt. Gov. Zenon Trudeau of upper Louisiana reported Vial's success from Spanish St. Louis on July 4. Arriving among the Pawnees on the Kansas River, Vial had met up with traders from St. Louis. Once he had regaled the Pawnee chief with a medal, a complete set of clothing, and other gifts and brokered the peace, the Frenchman led the St. Louis traders on westward to the Comanche nation. He invited them to Santa Fe, but because of more immediate interests, they declined.

Vial said that he had traveled east from Santa Fe to the Pawnees in eight days. St. Louis traders, going west by water, regularly reached the Pawnees in ten days. Hence, reasoned Trudeau, the distance between St. Louis and Santa Fe could not be very great. For trailwise Pedro Vial, it never was.

The errant Frenchman, branded a deserter by Chacón in 1797, seems to have left his debts in Santa Fe and operated in upper Louisiana for several years. By 1803, however, he was back, again on salary as Indian agent, again trying to woo the Pawnees, and again enjoying the amenities of Santa Fe.[4]

New Mexico's capital was the largest urban settlement in the western borderlands. By the 1790s, San Antonio's population had stabilized at around two thousand, and neither Tucson nor Monterey counted half that number. But in Santa Fe, baptisms per year had increased more than threefold since midcentury, to an average of about 150. Still, with about five thousand inhabitants in 1800, the villa boasted no cathedral, printing press, or university. But there was a so-called governor's palace, fronting on the town plaza with military barracks behind; a well-attended primary school attached to the presidio; three churches, soon to be four; several active religious confraternities; and no beggars.

Santa Fe also had a doctor, don Cristóbal de Larrañaga, surgeon of the garrison, who in 1804 vaccinated hundreds of children against smallpox with vaccine that had arrived from New Spain in the arms of inoculated boys. The practice had been inaugurated in Europe by Edward Jenner in 1796.[5]

The wealthier families of the capital—the Ortiz, Pino, Archuleta, Sena, and

Delgado clans—according to the governor, enjoyed putting on airs, dressing up and strutting. Based more on their social position than blood, these *ricos* considered themselves españoles, as did most of the ordinary people they looked down on.

Toward the end of the eighteenth century, New Mexico's culturally Hispanic society had grown more rigid. Early on, Juana Hurtado, illegitimate daughter of an español and a Zia Pueblo woman, was able to parlay her mixed ethnic connections and land grant into economic and social prominence. Like several other contemporary, independent, and unwed matriarchs, Juana "La Galvana" passed on español status to her several children.

Such cases were rare by late century. The relative economic prosperity following peace with the Comanches and other non-Christian nations led to a hardening of rico class lines as fewer men and women married outside them.[6]

Because so many *santafecinos* were related, church officials routinely conducted prenuptial investigations. Judging from these records, as well as the civil and criminal proceedings filling the archive, the populace of Santa Fe rarely lacked deviant behavior to gossip about. Not uncommonly, women accused priests of soliciting sex in the confessional. It was the same in San Antonio, Tucson, and Monterey.

While censuses enumerated artisans and tradesmen—tavern and shopkeepers, carpenters and wheelwrights, blacksmiths, barbers, tailors, shoemakers and saddlers, teamsters, and the like—most everyone else, including a good many of the soldiers of the Santa Fe presidio, farmed and raised stock.[7]

In 1798, because farm and grazing land around Santa Fe was filling up so fast, Lorenzo Márquez and fifty-one heads of family in 1798 petitioned Governor Chacón for a community land grant about fifty miles southeast at the uninhabited ford of the Pecos River. They called their settlement San Miguel del Bado. To earn title, the law required them to make improvements and occupy the land for five years. In 1803, don Pedro Bautista Pino, Santa Fe's district officer, rode out to supervise measurement of ditch frontage and its allocation to each family by lottery. Several women received parcels as heads of household. Then he put them in final possession.

The process took several days, and Pino evidently enjoyed himself. A prosperous man about fifty, widowed and remarried, don Pedro presided over extensive lands, commercial interests, and a big family of children and stepchildren. Yet he professed to understand what small farms and commons meant to these poorer folks. "Upon taking leave of them," he remembered,

> (refusing the recompense they offered me for my work), my heart was filled with the most profound joy I had ever experienced. Parents and small children encircled me, and all with tears in their eyes thanked me for the land I had given them for their livelihood.[8]

Governor Chacón reckoned that the people's livelihood would have been better assured had they known more about agriculture. Upon royal order, he compiled a brief report on the colony's economy in 1803 and requested that books about agricultural subjects be sent

> illustrating for the residents everything pertaining to planting; methods of controlling insects which greatly reduce the harvests; the method of planting trees and grafting; the treatment of different illnesses affecting cattle, sheep, and horses; knowledge of the use of herbs; or other innumerable things, etc., all of which they have here only the remotest idea.[9]

Responding to the same royal order for an economic assessment of his jurisdiction, Capt. José de Zúñiga wrote in 1804 from Tucson, farthest settlement of Pimería Alta. Zúñiga, leader of the 1795 expedition as far as Zuni, had turned back because of tired horses and want of an invitation from Governor Chacón in Santa Fe. For nearly a decade since, however, no one of record had ventured that way again.

Geography still forbade direct intercourse between Texas, New Mexico, Pimería Alta, or California. All were bound commercially to points south. The coarse New Mexican woolen or cotton cloth Zúñiga mentioned in his report had to be packed south to Chihuahua, then west to Arizpe, then north to Tucson, accruing handling fees en route.

Unlike Santa Fe or San Antonio, Tucson was neither capital nor chartered municipality but a presidial town of 1,015 soldiers, settlers, Indians, and dependents. According to the captain, it desperately needed "a leather tanner and dresser, a tailor, and a shoemaker"—and even more, a saddlemaker. Since no one connected to the presidio paid taxes, Zúñiga thought immigrant artisans and tradesmen could make a good living there. The resident population he considered lazy.

Settlers within five miles of the presidio held their house lots and farmlands under terms of the military *Reglamento* of 1772. And while they owed no taxes to church or state, they were obligated to serve as a militia, providing their own firearms and horses. They did not pay to support a parish priest, having recourse instead to fray Pedro de Arriquibar, an energetic Basque Franciscan who served for decades as presidial chaplain.

Of 300 beef cattle slaughtered annually at Tucson, 130 were consigned at government expense, along with sugar and tobacco, to Apaches who came and went at the peace camp downriver from the presidio. Although Apache warfare had decreased notably since the 1790s, soldiers and settlers still sallied forth on joint campaigns with the Pima garrison of Tubac.

Fear lingered. Zúñiga listed the named places along the Santa Cruz River, beginning with the presidio of that name ninety-five miles south, and still characterized

A *Soldado de cuera* by Ramón de Murillo, c. 1803. Part of a reform proposal that would have cut the protective thigh-length *cuera* down to jacket size. *Courtesy of the Ministerio de Educación, Cultura y Deporte, Archivo General de Indias (Sevilla, Spain), Uniformes, 81.*

most of them as deserted—the ranches of Divisadero, Santa Bárbara, San Luis, and Buenavista, as well as the former mission rancherías of Guevavi and Calabasas.

At Tumacácori, a stubborn and manipulative Spanish Franciscan, fray Narciso Gutiérrez, ministered on his terms to the combined community of mission and nearby Pima presidio at Tubac, about six hundred men, women, and children in all, counting Indians and gente de razón. The friar had watched the laying of a massive, river-boulder-and-mud foundation for a new church at the mission, but the job languished.

Neither did Gutiérrez take much interest in the grand project for mission expansion proposed by his brethren at the College of Querétaro. Two dozen missionary recruits had arrived from Spain in 1790. The superiors wanted to put two friars in each of the eight missions of Pimería Alta and assign others to Pápagos, Gila Pimas, and Cocomaricopas. Captain Zúñiga had provided an escort for Father Visitor Diego Miguel Bringas in October 1795. The friar meant to sample for himself the mood of the Natives who lived along the middle Gila. His enthusiastic description echoed Father Kino's a hundred years before.

The Gila Pimas, Bringas had sworn in a letter to Commandant General Nava, were not like "those heathens who barely have the use of reason." Industrious farmers, they begged for Christian missionaries. Moreover, he added,

> they have acted as faithful allies. They have conducted their own campaigns against the barbarous Apaches. . . . These new missions, Señor, will soon unite the peoples of New California with those of New Mexico. What great benefits will result from this mutual communication!

But nothing came of the Franciscan's vision. No compelling reason convinced the financially burdened commandant general to invest in such an enterprise. No foreigners threatened Pimería Alta. No Kino, Anza, or Garcés stood ready to sacrifice himself. Hence, in a century, the frontier had not moved beyond Tucson.

A singular feat of architecture, however, had arisen nearby. Two dedicated Franciscans had built at Mission San Xavier del Bac, ten miles southwest of the presidio, a soaring church meant to attract Natives from far beyond. Fray Juan Bautista de Velderrain, borrowing seven thousand pesos on the mission's wheat futures, oversaw in the 1780s most of the construction. His successor, fray Juan Bautista Llorens, finished the job in the 1790s except for the dome of the right tower, seemingly left off intentionally.

At pains to describe the church in 1804, Captain Zúñiga considered it the only public work in the Tucson area worthy of mention. "Other missions here in the north should really be called chapels, but San Xavier is truly a church." Built entirely of fired brick and lime mortar, the cruciform structure had cost an estimated thirty to forty thousand pesos.

> The ceiling is a series of domes. The interior is adorned with thirty-eight full-figure statues, plus three 'frame' statues dressed in cloth garments, and innumerable angels and seraphim. The facade is quite ornate, boasting two towers, one of which is unfinished.

Father Llorens had discussed with the captain the friars' rationale for building it. Zúñiga explained.

> The reason for this ornate church at this last outpost of the frontier is not only to congregate the Christian Pimas of the San Xavier village, but also to attract by its loveliness the unconverted Pápagos and Gila Pimas beyond the frontier. I have thought it worthwhile to describe it in such detail because of the wonder that such an elaborate building could be constructed at all out here on the farthest frontier. Because of the consequent hazard involved, the salaries of the artisans had to be doubled.[10]

Recruiting artisans for Nueva California proved even more troublesome. Manuel Carcaba, in charge of the effort in Mexico City during the 1790s, managed to sign up only a few. Their contracts obligated them to terms of two to six years. José Reyes, a chairmaker, agreed to take his wife and family and teach his trade to California Indians for three years. His daily wage of ten reales would commence the day he set out, and he and his wife would receive military rations for the round trip.

Whether blacksmith, carpenter, mason, tailor, tilelayer, or weaver, almost invariably these skilled tradesmen refused to renew their contracts and remain in California. Blacksmith José Faustino Arriola asked instead for early termination.

Frustrated, Carcaba turned to orphanages. While he subscribed to the viceregal authorities' exclusion of blacks and mulattos, he urged that girls as well as boys be considered. Having gathered some twenty-one orphans, ages seven to twenty-two, and spent a thousand pesos on their upkeep, officials accepted merchant Francisco Barrón's bid of 3,600 pesos, or just over 170 each, to chaperon them from Mexico City to California. The oldest female, poor but literate María de Jesús Torres, reluctantly agreed to look after the other eleven girls for a minimal salary.

One orphan died at sea during the voyage from San Blas to Monterey. The rest, with María de Jesús, disembarked from the frigate *Concepción* on August 24, 1800, to be "distributed like puppies," as seven-year-old Apolinaria recalled later. Some stayed in Monterey, but others were taken in by families of Santa Barbara, Los Angeles, and San Diego. Owing to the patronage of Archbishop Francisco Antonio Lorenzana of Mexico City, the orphans became known collectively as Lorenzanas. Most of the females eventually married presidial soldiers, as the planners hoped they would. The cost, however, had proven too great, and no more orphans arrived at government expense.

Recruiter Carcaba believed that robust convicts who had wives but no bad habits might willingly trade sentences of hard labor at Veracruz or Havana for resettlement in California. To be considered, the prisoners' women had to petition judges and swear to accompany their men.

María Antonia Sandoval, wife of Juan Antonio Hernández and mother of his many children, begged that her husband's ten-year sentence in Havana be commuted to time in California. The families' five girls, she stressed, might marry in that colony, adding to its population. Although the couple's oldest daughter ran away just before the family boarded the *Concepción,* the others reached Monterey. Hernández, however, was a notorious drunk and caused more trouble than he was worth. After putting in his ten years, he wanted a license to leave with María Antonia and part of the family, a request gladly granted.

Convict relocation was not the answer either. Raimundo Carrillo of the Monterey presidio had no use for the convicts. "The conduct of those sent is scandalous," he complained. "The majority of them brag about their ugly crimes and even worse, do so without thinking seriously about reform."[11]

Mission San Xavier del Bac, by H. M. T. Powell, 1849. *Courtesy of The Bancroft Library, University of California, Berkeley.*

So, as in Texas, New Mexico, and Pimería Alta—while Native Indian populations, except for the Pueblos, declined—the number of Hispanic residents grew mainly not by immigration but from the abundant fertility of their families. An unusually low infant mortality rate (100–150 deaths per 1,000 births) permitted californios to nearly double again between 1800 and 1821, from approximately 1,800 to 3,200.[12]

And a lively lot they were. Seaborne foreign visitors to California ports, whose calls had increased notably since the first Nootka Convention of 1790, commented

gleefully. When two British warships, *Discovery* and *Chatham,* sailed into Monterey Bay late in 1792, their officers and men expected not a fight but a party. No one was disappointed.

Capt. George Vancouver, sent by London to implement the terms of that treaty, found his counterpart, don Juan Francisco de la Bodega y Quadra, at Monterey. Though neither man spoke the other's language, the two had become fast, gentlemanly friends during their recent negotiations at Nootka. At don Juan's bidding, the locals entertained their English guests with gusto. Parties, excursions

A Monterey presidial soldier and the wife of a Monterey presidial soldier, 1791, by José Cardero. Museo de América, Madrid. *From Cutter,* California in 1792.

into the countryside, a grizzly bear hunt, and a bullfight preceded the culminating fiesta hosted by Gov. José Joaquín de Arrillaga. The women, who delayed their appearance until nearly ten, utterly enchanted Surgeon Archibald Menzies, who wrote in his journal,

> Most of them had their Hair in long queues reaching down to their waist.
> . . . even in this remote region they seemed most attached to the Spanish
> exhilarating dance the *Fandango,* a performance which requires no little elas-
> ticity of limbs as well as nimbleness of capers & gestures.

The couples danced wickedly close, "wheeling about, changing sides & smacking with their fingers at every motion." It took the Englishman's breath away. They proceeded, he gasped, "with such wanton attitudes & motions, such leering looks, sparkling eyes & trembling limbs, as would decompose the gravity of a Stoic." Vancouver reciprocated by asking the two Hawaiian girls he was returning to the islands if they would exhibit "their manner of singing and dancing, which," according to Menzies, "did not appear to afford much entertainment to the Spanish Ladies, indeed I believe they thought this crude performance was introduced by way of ridiculing their favorite dance the *Fandango,* as they soon afterward departed."[13]

Fandangos added undeniable spice, but it was California's thriving and accessible agrarian economy, driven by mission surpluses, that attracted most foreigners at the turn of the nineteenth century. Neither sales to presidios and towns nor occasional exports on returning supply ships kept pace with mission production of foodstuffs, cowhides, and tallow. The friars laid hands, as well, on more than a few sea-otter pelts.

Coastal California's benign climate, populous reserve of Native peoples, and fray Fermín Francisco de Lasuén's encouraging tenure as father president had combined to raise that colony's Franciscan missions to levels unprecedented in New Spain's far north. Between 1784, when Father Serra was buried at Carmel, and 1803, when Lasuén was laid beside him, the missions had multiplied from nine to eighteen.

According to the friars' own bookkeeping, the number of Indians living at the missions, despite a relentless decline in the overall Native population, had risen from 4,646 in 1784 to 18,185 in 1803. It would peak at more than 21,000 in 1821. Because of heavy infant and elderly mortality, the large majority of surviving neophytes was of laboring age, from nineteen to forty-nine.

Production figures concurred. Crops were up from 15,796 fanegas to 48,003, and cattle had multiplied from 5,384 to 77,578. Mission flocks of sheep by the end of 1803 had swelled to 117,736 head.

George Vancouver took Father Lasuén to be much older than he really was—about seventy-two, the Englishmen reckoned when they had met at Carmel in

1792. Prematurely gray, Lasuén was only fifty-six at the time. The second father president elicited almost uniform praise from visitors and missionaries alike. In contrast to the testy Serra, they found Lasuén pleasant, gracious, and sweet of temper. Probably tolerant as well, Lasuén as superior recognized the difficulties of marketing mission produce legally and may have looked the other way. Certainly, his successors did.

In 1806, fray José Señán, who hoped to built a new church for the Chumash at mission San Buenaventura, expressed his frustration in 1806 at dealing with an agent in Mexico City. The short, stout Señán had shipped from nearby Santa Barbara quantities of tallow, cowhides, and sheepskins, but the agent had not settled the mission's account in two years.[14]

It was not surprising therefore that when William Shaler, skipper of the *Lelia Byrd* out of Salem, Massachusetts, showed up along the California coast with trade goods for immediate transaction, he found ready customers in certain of the Franciscans. He wanted all the sea-otter pelts they had. On several visits, Shaler came away with not only furs but also promissory notes signed by the friars. "For several years past," Shaler vowed in an account published in 1808,

> the American trading ships have frequented this coast in search of furs, for which they have left in the country about 25,000 dollars annually, in specie and merchandize. . . . At present, a person acquainted with the coast may always produce abundant supplies of provisions. All these circumstances prove that, under a good government, the Californias would soon rise to ease and affluence.[15]

Providentially, Thomas Jefferson headed the good government Shaler had in mind. Like the captain of the *Lelia Byrd,* most Americans of the early nineteenth century believed their republican form of government far superior to any other, especially when they pondered the turmoil in Europe.

After the French National Convention had abolished the monarchy and executed Louis XVI, the festering revolution spawned a reign of terror at home and victories abroad by French armies, which invaded northern Spain. Fearful of further losses, Manuel Godoy, acting for Carlos IV, made peace in 1795, bartering Santo Domingo in the Caribbean for French withdrawal from Spain.

Imperial-minded Gen. Napoleon Bonaparte, while acknowledging a shadow French republic, had emerged by the end of 1799 as the most powerful arbiter of European affairs. In 1800, he prevailed upon Spain's weak king to trade Louisiana to France for the Italian throne of Parma, which the Spanish queen wanted for her brother. Napoleon had assured Spanish negotiators that France would never transfer

Louisiana to another nation. But a slave revolt in French Haiti and the need to keep the United States neutral in his struggle with Great Britain caused the European strongman to change his mind. In 1803, Napoleon sold Louisiana to President Jefferson's United States.

Earlier that year, the president had already secured an appropriation from Congress and commissioned his private secretary, Capt. Meriwether Lewis, to lead a corps of discovery across the continent to the Pacific.[16]

"Gardem España" indeed.

13 Mexico's Problem

I have instructed myself from the conversations of the town that the Anglo-Americans will come, and of the facility with which they will make themselves owners of this province, without observing displeasure in the people or hearing expressions of animosity from them or willingness to risk their lives to guard their homes.

—Gov. Joaquín del Real Alencaster of New Mexico
to the Commandant General, Santa Fe, April 15, 1807

Like waves, they had rolled westward across North America every twenty years, in 1763, 1783, and 1803—momentous shifts in sovereignty that favored the Anglo-Americans.

The first wave was a result of the French and Indian War; by the happy outcome of that conflict, Great Britain extended its sway at the expense of France to the banks of the Mississippi. Two decades later, through another peace treaty signed at Paris, United States citizens parlayed their newly won independence just as far. Then in 1803, their expansion-minded president bought the west bank and an unknown portion of the continent beyond.

Thomas Jefferson, by sponsoring the expedition of Meriwether Lewis and William Clark, meant to find out. Its members would ascend to the Missouri River's headwaters and, if practicable, cross the Rocky Mountains to the Pacific. To the south and west, Jefferson thought that his Louisiana Purchase might as well include West Florida and Texas and extend as far as the Rio Grande. Spain thought not.

In May 1804—the same month Lewis and Clark's party of some fifty men began poling up the Missouri—Com. Gen. Nemesio Salcedo at Chihuahua relayed Spain's concern about American intrusion to the governor of New Mexico, don Fernando Chacón. High time, it seemed to Chacón.

For more than a year, Anglo-Americans had been showing up in Santa Fe, and while most of them bore French names, the St. Louis merchants and traders who employed them were all U.S. citizens. In the manner of the earlier French voyageurs of the 1740s and 1750s, these calculating, nineteenth-century trespassers gambled on quick wits, useful talents, and desirable trade goods. One Juan or José, whose misspelled surname hid his Philadelphia Presbyterian roots, by 1803 had fallen in with Pedro Vial. The old plainsman called him José Jarvet.

Jarvet's experiences paralleled Vial's. He had fraternized for years with Plains Indians, repairing their guns and boasting of at least one Pawnee son. With Vial in 1803, he escorted five Pawnee chiefs to Santa Fe to meet with Governor Chacón.

Spaniards rightly feared that Lewis and Clark would enroll northern plains tribes to spread the influence of the United States among Pawnees, Comanches, and other Native nations grown used to accepting Spanish medals, gifts, and supplies. In turn, Spaniards utilized the services of double-dealing James Wilkinson, ranking U.S. general and first American governor at St. Louis. Cautioning his Spanish contacts never to use his name, only the number "13," Wilkinson urged that Salcedo and Chacón dispatch a large enough armed force "to intercept Captain Lewis and His party who are on the Missouri River, and force them to retire or take them prisoners."

The Spaniards tried. At least four counterexpeditions rode northwestward from Santa Fe between August 1804 and June 1806 in hopes of challenging the American party of Captain "Merri." Vial and Jarvet led the first three and may have accompanied the fourth. Midway in the series, stiff Lt. Col. Joaquín del Real Alencaster took over as governor from the ailing Chacón.[1]

Real Alencaster meant to set New Mexico's house in order. No longer would regulations be ignored. Yet when he tried to prevent the men of San Miguel and San José del Bado from trading with Comanches, they rioted. Proceedings against their leaders turned up other grievances: limits on what New Mexicans could export to Chihuahua in the annual caravan; a ban on selling sheep to Navajos; forced collection of grain from the poor of the Río Arriba to feed the Santa Fe garrison.[2]

In this climate of unrest, Real Alencaster ordered out the third probe for Lewis and Clark. Vial and Jarvet's two previous failures did not endear them to the new governor, but who else did he have? He liked Vial's idea of building a fort on the Arkansas in today's eastern Colorado and also agreed that salaried Hispanic interpreter-agents should be assigned to live with the Comanches, Pawnees, and others. Most of all, he wanted the commandant general to send more regular troops.

A singularly irregular force, meanwhile, took the field. In late April 1806, Vial and Jarvet struck north and west with a reported three hundred men, mostly militia and Indians. Four weeks later, Vial and Jarvet were back. Their men had deserted. So Real Alencaster opened more legal proceedings.

New Mexico *cibolero,* or buffalo hunter. Redrawn by Jerry L. Livingston. *From Kessell,* Kiva, Cross, and Crown.

Remarkably, Commandant General Salcedo had heard the New Mexico governor's plea. Sixty dragoons on detached service under the blocky Lt. Facundo Melgares reined up in the plaza at Santa Fe in late spring 1806. Now, the governor boasted to Salcedo, he could plan the fourth probe, a genuine reconnaissance in force. He would send forth Melgares in the direction of the Missouri with 105 regular soldiers, 400 militiamen, 100 Indian allies, more than 2,000 horses and mules, and rations for six months—numbers that recalled Governor Anza's campaign against Cuerno Verde in 1779.

The Melgares reconnaissance trailed out of Santa Fe in midsummer 1806; it relied heavily on the militia, five hundred poor Hispanos and Pueblos who were leaving their crops unharvested in the fields. Whether or not they encountered Lewis and Clark, there appeared little prospect of spoils.

Somewhere en route, the militiamen had the gall to complain. A spokesman presented Melgares a petition in behalf of two hundred of his fellows. They wanted to go home. The young Spanish commander exploded. Straightaway, he ordered a gallows built and mustered the entire force, dividing the petitioners from the rest. He had their leader stripped and given fifty lashes. Any man who objected would die on the gallows. The grumbling ceased, and the expedition proceeded. Ill feelings turned inward.

With roughly half his men—still outnumbering Lewis and Clark's party six to one—Lieutenant Melgares ventured as far east as a large Pawnee village on the Republican River in present-day southern Nebraska. By then, it was late August or early September. A few days later, not 150 miles farther east on the Missouri, homeward-bound Lewis and Clark floated by. Unaware, Melgares had begun his return to Santa Fe.

The likelihood of war between Spain and the United States loomed in 1806. Early that year, a U.S. column had convinced the thirty-man garrison at Los Adaes in east Texas to give up the post without a fight. Everywhere the commandant general looked, Americans pressed in on the dominions of his king. They appeared by April to be massing troops "without question of expense," Salcedo warned Texas Gov. Antonio Cordero,

> to hold by force their spoils. They are also intriguing with the Indians, have built a storehouse at Natchitoches and have filled it with gifts for them. It has not been possible for us to oppose them in force, but in order to counter-act their influence among the Indians I have dispatched expeditions to the various tribes, our dependencies—some to the far Northwest.

In July, Capt. Francisco Viana had led a Spanish force from Nacogdoches across to the Red River and turned back the flatboats of American surveyor Thomas Freeman and Dr. Peter Custis, who with less fanfare than Lewis and Clark had meant to run that river to its headwaters.[3]

Within weeks of the Spaniards' departure, a U.S. military officer addressed the Pawnees at the same village Melgares had visited:

> My Brothers; Here is an American Flag which I will present to you—but it must never be hoisted by the side of that Spanish one which I desire in return. . . . You cannot have two Fathers. . . . after next year we will not permit Spanish officers, or soldiers; to come into this country to present medals or Flags—as all those marks of Distinction must come through your American Father.

Arrogant, handsome, and either inept or unlucky, a regular officer of the U.S. Army in irregular dress, twenty-seven-year-old Lt. Zebulon Montgomery Pike later told his Spanish captors that he had gotten lost. Governor Real Alencaster doubted the story.

Pike and his men, dispatched by General Wilkinson to explore the southwestern reaches of the Louisiana Purchase, had left the Pawnee village in October 1806 and dropped down to the Arkansas. From that point, the American lieutenant professed to be looking for the headwaters of the Red. Riding southwest, the small

American party splashed instead across the upper Rio Grande in the San Luis Valley of today's southern Colorado. There, he and fifteen or so of his frost-bitten men survived the fierce winter of 1806–1807 in a stockade they built five miles up the Río Conejos. A Spanish patrol brought them half-frozen into Santa Fe on March 3.[4]

Descending the hill into town on horseback and looking over the single-storied adobe dwellings, Pike recalled that the capital of New Mexico

> struck my mind with the same effect as a fleet of flat bottomed boats, which are seen in the spring and fall seasons, descending the Ohio river. There are two churches, the magnificence of whose steeples form a striking contrast to the miserable appearance of the houses.

American lieutenant and Spanish governor made themselves understood in French. The Americans should not consider themselves prisoners of war, Real Alencaster assured Pike. Still, they were not exactly free to go. They would proceed to Chihuahua with the returning Lieutenant Melgares and his sixty dragoons. Commandant General Salcedo awaited them. At Pike's request, he and his men retained their weapons and ammunition.

While in Santa Fe, Pike met a couple of fellow Americans who were truly prisoners. Sad-hearted Zalmon Nicolás Coley (or Cole), a tailor from Connecticut, had been captured in Texas with Philip Nolan's band and sent to New Mexico to work at his trade. James Purcell (or Pursley) of Kentucky, finding his way to Santa Fe in 1805 and detained as a carpenter, bragged that with a two-hour lead he could escape them all.

Midday dinner at the governor's palace, Lieutenant Pike had to admit, was

> rather splendid, having a variety of dishes and wines of the southern provinces, and when his excellency was a little warmed with the influence of cheering liquor, he became very sociable. . . . After dinner his excellency ordered his coach; captain D'Almansa [Nicolás de Almanza], Bartholemew [Bartolomé Fernández] and myself entered with him, and he drove out 3 miles. He was drawn by six mules and attended by a guard of cavalry. When we parted his adieu was "remember Allencaster, in peace or war."

En route south of Albuquerque to Chihuahua, the two gentlemen lieutenants, Zebulon Pike and Facundo Melgares found that they liked one another. They, too, considering the Spaniard's superior education, probably conversed in French, with occasional retreats into English and Spanish. Pike observed generously that the high-born, thirty-two-year-old don Facundo, possessed

> none of the haughty Castillian pride, but much of the urbanity of a Frenchman; and I will add my feeble testimony to his loyalty, by declaring that he was one of the few officers or citizens whom I found, who was loyal

to their king, felt indignant at the degraded state of the Spanish monarchy; who deprecated a revolution or separation of Spanish America, from the mother country; unless France should usurp the government of Spain.

Wined, dined, feted at fandangos, and taken by the beauty of the young women he met, the American officer delighted in his guided tour of New Spain's rustic borderlands. Although he said nothing to his friend, he took as a sign of corrupt Spanish discipline that a mere lieutenant could travel the way Melgares did, "having eight mules loaded with his common camp equipage, wines, confectionery, &c."[5]

They made Chihuahua in a month. Commandant General Salcedo, "a middle sized man," according to Pike, "apparently about fifty-five years of age, with a stern countenance," confiscated the small trunk containing the American's papers but graciously allowed him to retain letters from his wife Clarissa. Salcedo assigned Pike to board with Lt. Juan Pedro Walker, formerly of New Orleans, a military engineer and cartographer in Spanish employ.[6]

Thanks to Melgares and his father-in-law, Lt. Col. Alberto Maynez—who would serve as interim governor of New Mexico in 1808 and again between 1814 and 1816—the American lieutenant savored Chihuahua society for three weeks, dining a number of times with Salcedo. Pike pleaded in vain for the release of Nolan's men still alive, borrowed a thousand pesos, and studied Spanish. Cautioned by Melgares, he held forth on politics and religion only when asked.

When he left for lower Louisiana on April 28, 1807, escorted part way by Lieutenant Melgares, half of Pike's "Dam'd set of Rascals" had not yet reached Chihuahua. Salcedo said he would send them on, but instead, he detained them for thirty months. One individual, who had killed a fellow expeditionary in a quarrel, the Spaniards kept until 1820.

Pike's "involuntary tour" now dipped south, bending around the dry, formidable Bolsón de Mapimí, down to Guajuquilla, across to Monclova, and back up to the Presidio del Río Grande, the old San Juan Bautista, where the party dismounted June 1.

The first day out of Chihuahua, Lieutenant Melgares had "changed color," ordering the American to cease his note taking. Resisting his first impulse, Pike bowed

> assent with a smile, and we proceeded on our route, but had not proceeded far before I made a pretext to halt—established my boy as a vedet, and sat down peaceably under a bush and made my notes, &c. This course I pursued ever after, not without some very considerable degree of trouble to separate myself from the party.

As further precaution, Pike tore up a fine shirt, wrapped pieces of it around his notes, and stuffed them down the barrels of his mens' muskets. He would later

Zebulon Montgomery Pike, by Charles Willson Peale. *Courtesy of Independence National Historical Park.*

applaud his ingenuity in a letter to General Wilkinson, admitting, however, that he faced the difficult task of sorting his observations into categories, "as military, political, moral, trade, clime, soil, &c."

At Guajuquilla, today's Ciudad Jiménez, Melgares had turned the escort over to Capt. Mariano Varela, bound for command at the Presidio del Río Grande. "At night," Pike observed, perhaps under his moral category, "the officers gave a ball, at which appeared at least sixty women, ten or a dozen of whom were very handsome." Bidding the gallant Melgares "an eternal adieu," Pike prayed that they would not meet "in the field of battle as the most deadly enemies, when our hearts acknowledge the greatest friendship."

They did not. On July 1, 1807, in time to celebrate the Fourth, Zebulon Montgomery Pike once again beheld the American flag waving at Natchitoches. At last, his exploration was over.[7]

Pike's recollections of Texas remained especially vivid. Honoring him at a dinner in San Antonio on June 8, 1807, Texas Gov. Antonio Cordero had proposed a toast to the president of the United States. In turn, Pike toasted "His Catholic Majesty." Someone then, directing himself to the Americans, offered, "Those gentlemen; their safe and happy arrival in their own country—their honorable reception, and the continuation of the good understanding which exists between the two countries."

Eight months earlier, no loyal Spaniard would have uttered those words. War threatened, and a clash along the contested border between U.S. Louisiana and Spanish Texas had seemed certain. Commandant General Salcedo dispatched Lt. Col. Simón de Herrera, governor of Nuevo León, to Texas with reinforcements. By June 1806, nearly nine hundred Spanish men-at-arms had deployed in the Nacogdoches area to repel an expected U.S. invasion.

But General Wilkinson, hastening to Natchitoches, had adopted a face-saving compromise. He would pull U.S. forces back east of the Arroyo Hondo if Herrera would keep his Spanish troops west of the Sabine. Herrera, disobeying his superiors, had agreed on November 4, 1806. The resulting thirty-mile-wide Neutral Ground, beyond either country's jurisdiction, kept the peace but attracted all manner of conniving cutthroats.

Nearing home, Pike and his diminished party had enjoyed Texas, despite the mosquitoes and horseflies that molested them on the road from the Rio Grande to San Antonio. They met several units of troops returning south from their detached duty in east Texas. Just south of town, they halted at mission San José y San Miguel de Aguayo, where the priest greeted them warmly.

The two governors, don Antonio Cordero and don Simón de Herrera, came

Fandango, by Theodore Gentilz. *Courtesy of the Daughters of the Republic of Texas Library at the Alamo.*

out in a coach to meet the American lieutenant. Cordero could not have been more gracious. Pike took him to be about five feet, ten inches, and fifty years old; of fair complexion and blue eyes, "he wore his hair turned back, and in every part of his deportment was legibly written 'The Soldier.'"

That evening in the plaza, don Antonio and don Simón joined in the dancing. Pike learned that his host had been in New Spain since the time of José de Gálvez, served all over the north, and become "by far the most *popular man* in the *internal provinces.*" As governor of Coahuila and acting governor of Texas, Colonel Cordero had moved from Monclova to San Antonio after the United States purchased Louisiana to better "apply the remedy to any evil which might arise from the collision of our lines."

Cordero and Herrera surprised the young American with their knowledge of the United States, its government, and regions. The dark-complected, black-eyed don Simón had even been in Philadelphia and met George Washington.

Pike shared Nolan's earlier fascination with the abundance of Texas lands and wild horses, anticipating waves of future American immigrants. He guessed the colony's settled population in 1807 at about seven thousand, probably twice the actual number. Their religion, of course, was Catholic "but much relaxed."

Like Real Alencaster in New Mexico, Cordero tried to regulate Texans' easy access to the plains. The governor, according to Pike,

> by restricting (by edicts) the buffalo hunts to certain seasons, and obliging every man of family to cultivate so many acres of land, has in some degree checked the spirit of hunting or wandering life, which had been hitherto so very prevalent, and has endeavored to introduce, by his example and precepts, a general urbanity and suavity of manners, which rendered St. Antonio one of the most agreeable places that we met with in the provinces.

He further offended descendants of the still dominant, interrelated Canary Island families by summarily reducing the cabildo from nine to five members and largely ignoring them.[8]

Pleasant as the town appeared to Pike, San Antonio would soon be ravaged. Shock waves from Napoleon's Europe and revolutionary New Spain would turn its plaza from dance ground to war zone.

Pike, meanwhile, rose rapidly in rank. He was cleared of possible involvement in the Aaron Burr conspiracy to detach U.S. territory or invade New Spain. His ill-organized journals appeared in print in 1810, but the imminent War of 1812 with Great Britain temporarily deferred his countrymen's interest in Santa Fe or San Antonio. Pike died a brigadier general, leading the assault on Toronto in 1813.[9]

The allegation that the Louisiana Purchase extended as far south and west as the Rio Grande struck Spanish officials as preposterous but worrisome. Admonished by Carlos IV for not halting Lewis and Clark, Commandant General Salcedo welcomed Governor Cordero's plan to reconnoiter the plains in force between San Antonio and Santa Fe. Some two hundred mounted men, eight hundred horses, and unspecified wheeled vehicles formed up under stalwart, nearly seventy-year-old Francisco Amangual, former captain of La Bahía presidio. They did reach Santa Fe and return, although the round-trip took them most of 1808, the year events in Spain spun crazily out of sync.

Carlos IV was tired. Menaced more by the continental armies of Napoleon than the naval might of England, he had gone along with Manuel Godoy in trying to appease France, but part of the cost, in October 1805 at the battle of Trafalgar, was the best of Spain's navy. Yet they dared not say no to Napoleon when, early in 1808, he asked to march French armies across northern Spain to invade Portugal, England's ally.

Protesting Spaniards looked to Fernando, the king's twenty-four-year-old son, to save Spain. With mobs in the streets, Godoy advised Carlos and María Luisa to retire from Madrid to Sevilla, for a possible escape to Mexico City. French troops occupied Madrid on March 23.

Both father and son, Bourbon rivals for the Spanish crown, now hastened to lay their claims before Emperor Napoleon at Bayonne just over the border in southern France. Napoleon, however, fancied a Spanish house of Bonaparte. Forcing the two Bourbons to abdicate, he confined each to a plush French estate and named his brother King José I of Spain.

On May 2, 1808, as Francisco Amangual's hunters brought down buffalo in the hilly country along the Colorado River in west-central Texas, French soldiers fired on crowds in Madrid, affording court painter Francisco Goya an indelible moment and the Spanish people a ringing battle cry against the invaders.

Napoleon's dethroning of the Bourbons between 1808 and 1814 caused a monumental crisis of authority. Local juntas sprang up all over Spain. José I ruled only by force. English troops landed and commenced the Peninsular War to drive Frenchmen out of Portugal and Spain. The Spanish people's dogged, hit-and-run warfare against French armies of occupation gave rise in English to the word *guerrilla*. The resulting confusion in Spanish America encouraged rival foreign governments to press their territorial claims, adventurers to take every advantage, and receptive colonial citizens to rally around the idea of independence.[10]

The thought that colonists in the Spanish Indies would actually sever their ties with the mother country struck some peninsular Spaniards as preposterous. Yet in Mexico City, prominent criollos, bidding for power in the name of Fernando VII, who languished against his will in France, talked Viceroy José de Iturrigaray into joining them. Other Spaniards, also in Fernando's name and supported by the audiencia judges, countered with their own bid in favor of Sevilla's caretaker central junta in Spain. Arresting and deposing Iturrigaray, the peninsulares installed two successors, neither of whom lasted a year. Finally, the central junta's appointee, Francisco Javier de Venegas, became viceroy in September 1810.

But his timing was unfortunate. That very month, Miguel Hidalgo y Costilla, passionately liberal priest of Dolores, 170 miles northwest of Mexico City, got word that a pro-independence conspiracy implicating him had been discovered. Impetuously, he raised the "Cry of Dolores" on September 16, commemorated still as Mexico's independence day.

The rash curate's appeal for social justice and good government, again in the name of Fernando, quickly got out of hand. Disadvantaged Indians and castas swarmed to the banner of the Virgin of Guadalupe, overrunning towns and committing indiscriminate acts of ghastly violence on people of property. Yet inexplicably, within sight of Mexico City, Father Hidalgo turned his hordes away.

Defeat came on January 17, 1811. Royalist troops and a raging grass fire near Guadalajara at Calderón Bridge set Hidalgo fleeing northward toward the Provincias Internas, still the domain of Nemesio Salcedo.

The commandant general did not waiver. He damned Hidalgo's insurrection, decreed the arrest of suspected sympathizers, and authorized twenty thousand pesos shipped under heavy guard to Texas to buy weapons from manufacturers in the United States.

Don Nemesio's young nephew now governed Texas. Because of the Napoleonic Wars, Manuel María de Salcedo, his wife and daughter, a chaplain, and servants had disembarked from Spain in 1808 at New Bedford, Massachusetts, and toured the United States en route via Natchitoches to San Antonio, where don Manuel took urgent counsel with Antonio Cordero.

After nine months in office, Gov. Manuel de Salcedo had convinced himself that Texas, with "its prodigious space and beautiful lands," fewer than four thousand overwhelmingly poor people—most in San Antonio, La Bahía, and Nacogdoches—and nearness to the United States, deserved greater consideration from his uncle. Rebuffed by him, the governor had appealed to the citizens of Texans for donations to keep nearly a thousand men-at-arms in the field.

Both sides, royalists and revolutionaries, wanted access to the United States. After their fiasco in central New Spain, Father Hidalgo and his advisers thought their best chance to win aid from the United States or France lay in capturing the Provincias Internas. Texas was the key.

Governor Salcedo called upon officials at Nacogdoches, Laredo, and the Presidio del Río Grande to close Texas borders to foreign travelers and seditious literature. He bound José Erasmo Seguín, postmaster for San Antonio, to hold all mail for inspection. Texans must remain in the vicinity of their homes. And in secret, he sent his own family east.

The five-day festival of the Immaculate Conception and Virgin of Guadalupe, from December 8 to 12, was drawing near, with its bazaar, bullfights, dancing, and drinking. The governor issued a lengthy edict. Should a disturbance of the peace require him to suspend the customary fun, he wanted the people of San Antonio to understand.

> The desire I have to contribute to the satisfaction of the settlers cannot be the cause of my neglecting my sacred obligation to preserve this province from the fatal destruction of the revolution which has engulfed certain settlements in the viceroyalty. It may be justly feared that the revolutionary leaders may have some partisans here, although I do not believe that any such perditious monster can be found among us because of the loyalty of the inhabitants of this province.

The monster already resided among them. Juan Bautista de las Casas, former militia captain in Nuevo Santander, had acquired a passport the previous August to cross into Texas. His business was not really horses, but ousting Spanish royalists.

Quietly, Las Casas had gone about lining up a small group of disgruntled members of the Canary Island families, men like Francisco Travieso and Gavino Delgado, and together they influenced common folk and soldiers of the Villita barracks.

People all over New Spain were hearing similar arguments from committed revolutionaries who, like Las Casas, often showed up in their communities from somewhere else. Why should we who have made our homes for generations in these parts be governed by haughty Spaniards who never have taken our best interests to heart? Remember how former governor Domingo Cabello y Robles was more concerned about the loss of a cook than the welfare of poor Texas herders. Cabello had hired his cook in Cádiz as he left Spain. When don Domingo was named governor of Texas and they were still in Mexico City, the cook

> was told so many things about this place . . . that he came to believe that the Indians would eat him, for which reason he resigned from my service. And the same thing happened with my manservant and a secretary, so that I am reduced to the most deplorable state. Although I recognize that they did right, because this [place] is worse than Siberia and Lapland.

Governor Salcedo was no different. The coup orchestrated by Juan Bautista de las Casas on January 21, 1811, on the surface succeeded splendidly. In a simultaneous assault on government buildings, aroused Hispanic Texans seized Governor Salcedo, Lieutenant Colonel Herrera, and a dozen other officers. Outsider Las Casas, who assumed command of a provisional Texas government, showed his nasty side when he insisted on publicly humiliating Salcedo, Herrera, and the others before sending them off to Monclova in chains. Coahuila also, after the capture of Governor Cordero, had fallen to revolutionaries.

The swiftness of a counterrevolution in San Antonio, however, revealed the bejareños' localized self-interest and ambivalence. Understandably, most of them—buffeted by hard times economically, threats of Indian raiding or invasion from the United States, and the swirling uncertainty of a wider independence movement—cast their lot with whatever faction offered at the time the best hope of peace and stability.

The unpopular Las Casas, who had no clear program of reform or means of enforcing his rule, quarreled with supporters. Within weeks, a better prospect seemed to reside in the person of native son and secular priest Juan Manuel Zambrano. Hence, on March 2, Zambrano and other leaders of the community swore an oath to Fernando VII, appointed a local governing junta, and arrested Las Casas. To the south, royalists freed Governor Salcedo. Before returning to San Antonio, Salcedo and others, including Pike's friend Capt. Facundo Melgares, riding the antirevolutionary tide, ambushed and took as prisoners Father Hidalgo and his entire demoralized staff.

Having jailed twenty-seven rebel leaders in the royal hospital at Chihuahua, once the Jesuit college, Manuel de Salcedo saluted his stern uncle. Straightaway, the commandant general named a seven-man military tribunal to try the revolutionaries, with the younger Salcedo as president. Found guilty of treason, all save Hidalgo met the customary ignominious death, shot in the back by firing squad. Their leader, a defrocked priest, merited special treatment. On July 30, 1811, he faced his executioners alone and was shot dead.

The following month, officials at San Antonio opened a box containing a grizzly trophy, the head of Juan Bautista de las Casas pickled in brine. Gov. Antonio Cordero, restored in Monclova, wanted it displayed in the military plaza. Commandant General Salcedo rewarded the undecided people who had overthrown Las Casas and elevated the municipality from villa to *ciudad,* or city, the only one in New Spain's far north.[11] For San Antonio, however, the worst was yet to come.

In 1810, Com. Gen. Nemesio Salcedo had distributed to governors in the Provincias Internas an invitation from the central junta in Spain to send delegates to an extraordinary *cortes,* or parliament, at Cádiz. The junta was soliciting unprecedented representation from throughout the Spanish Indies.

Ignoring the proviso that their representative be a native son, the San Antonio council had voted to send Manuel de Salcedo, a nice way to get rid of their governor. But when the audiencia of Guadalajara, which heard cases from the Provincias Internas, overturned the election, confusion regarding qualifications and travel costs snarled the process. Texas missed its chance to be represented. Instead, Coahuila's delegate, the avid liberal Miguel Ramos Arizpe, spoke for it, and Salcedo, to his grief, stayed on in Texas.

At the villa of Arizpe, capital of Sonora, Gov. Alejo García Conde had seen to the election of Lic. Manuel María Moreno as that province's representative. Thirteen years earlier in 1797, Moreno had inspected the missions and presidios of Pimería Alta for the bishop of Sonora. Whether anyone from that far district had cast a vote for him, at least Moreno, unlike any governor or bishop, had actually been there.

Californios, even farther distant, voted for no one. Viceroy Venegas, whose office superintended California as a remote military colony, simply disqualified them. They would have no representation in the cortes because they were too few, too poor, too far away.

New Mexicans belatedly did send a delegate. From a slate of three chosen in August 1811 by ten leading men designated as electors, the lot fell to popular and influential, sixty-year-old don Pedro Bautista Pino, who agreed to pay his own way and that of a wide-eyed, eleven-year-old grandson and two menservants. They set out from Santa Fe in late October. The trip took ten months.

By the time New Mexico's representative was seated in August 1812, the assembly had already debated and published the progressive Spanish Constitution of that year. Pino nevertheless presented to his fellow delegates—who nicknamed him "The Abraham of New Mexico"—his memorable, fifty-one-page *Exposición sucinta y sencilla de la Provincia del Nuevo México,* also issued by the government printing office in Cádiz in 1812.

His European readers turned most eagerly to what don Pedro had to say about wild—that is, non-Christian—Indians. The Gila Apaches he characterized as "a traitorous people, cruel, thieving and always naked." No other Apache group, not even the Mescaleros, were as bad. Out of respect, Pino reserved his fullest description for "the honorable Comanches."

Enlightened Europeans equated civility with dress. Comanches wore modest clothing of tanned animal hides exquisitely embroidered with porcupine quills in animal and floral designs. Pino commented on the Comanches' religion, government, hunting, funeral practice, and their firm alliance with Spaniards since Anza's defeat of Cuerno Verde. A party of Comanche warriors visiting Coahuila had even joined in the capture of Father Hidalgo.

Navajos had resumed warfare with New Mexicans at the turn of the century and only recently had sued again for peace. On orders from Commandant General Salcedo, a force from Sonora had penetrated Canyon de Chelly, the very heartland of Navajo country, in the dead of winter, January 1805. Seasoned Lt. Antonio Narbona of Fronteras, who had trekked to Zuni a decade earlier with Captain Zúñiga, sallied forth in the snow from that western pueblo with presidial regulars, Opata auxiliaries, Zunis, and New Mexican militiamen under Lorenzo Gutiérrez, Bartolomé Baca, and Antonio Armijo. Their hard-won, two-day fight on the floor of the eight-hundred-foot-deep, red-walled chasm had broken Navajo resistance, at least for a time.

Besides Indians, what held the attention of his fellow delegates in Cádiz was don Pedro's ringing exposé of New Mexico's spiritual backwardness. Pino likely exaggerated to make his point. Admitting that the population was not precisely known, he guessed it to be forty thousand. A mere 22 Franciscan friars and 2 secular priests ministered to all of them: residents of the El Paso district and the 3 upriver villas (Santa Fe, Santa Cruz de la Cañada, and Albuquerque); 26 Indian pueblos; and 102 scattered defensive plazas. That made each pastor responsible on average for the care of 1,667 souls.

None of them had seen the bishop of Durango's face in more than fifty years, not since the visitation of don Pedro Tamarón in 1760. Hence, ecclesiastical requirements had been ignored. "No one born in the last 50 years," Pino avowed,

> has been confirmed. And the poor who wish to marry relatives and need a dispensation cannot get it, owing to the high cost of traveling the more than

EXPOSICION

SUCINTA Y SENCILLA

DE LA PROVINCIA

DEL

NUEVO MÉXICO:

HECHA

POR SU DIPUTADO EN CÓRTES

Don Pedro Baptista Pino,

CON ARREGLO Á SUS INSTRUCCIONES.

CÁDIZ:

IMPRENTA DEL ESTADO-MAYOR-GENERAL.

Año de 1812.

Title page of Pedro Bautista Pino's *Exposición* (1812). *From Kessell,* Kiva, Cross, and Crown.

400 leagues to Durango. Therefore, it happens that many people moved by
love, form a family and live in sin. . . . Even I, who am over 50 years of age
did not know how a bishop dressed until I came to Cádiz.

Like fellow propagandist fray Alonso de Benavides in 1630, Pino begged for a
diocese of New Mexico. The annual tithe on the colony's agricultural produce,
nine or ten thousand pesos, could go to support not only a bishop at Santa Fe but
also a missionary college for twelve trainees. Benavides would have smiled. Since
the people of New Mexico had grown so used to the sight of the Franciscan habit,
don Pedro thought no other would be welcome. Hence, the first bishop and dozen
missionary recruits should all be Franciscans.

New Mexico's economy also needed fixing. The delegate pointed to the
province's unfavorable balance of trade: exports worth 60,000 pesos; imports,
112,000. Freight costs of goods shipped from Spain or Mexico City north to
Chihuahua doubled prices. New Mexicans lived and died in debt to Chihuahua
merchants. Again like Benavides, Pino wanted the government to open a port on
the Texas coast. Through it and Guaymas in Sonora, he believed New Mexico
could be supplied more reasonably.

Lamenting the lot of the province's brave and burdened militiamen, don Pedro
dreamed on. They should be paid, and there should be uniform regulations.
Moreover, five regular presidial garrisons from Nueva Vizcaya and Sonora, where
they were no longer needed, should be moved north, four to be relocated on the
Rio Grande between El Paso and Taos and one at San Miguel del Bado on the
Pecos. To seek judicial remedies, New Mexicans should not have to travel to
Guadalajara; an audiencia should be established in Chihuahua. There should be
money for public-school teachers and more than one doctor. And on and on.

Sometime after don Pedro finally returned home, locals composed a ditty that
summed up dryly what the delegate from New Mexico had accomplished: "*Don
Pedro Pino fue, don Pedro Pino vino* (Don Pedro Pino went, don Pedro Pino came
back)." Still, a native-born New Mexican had traveled to Spain and told an imperial congress how he felt about conditions in his homeland. He was not without
pride for having done so.

And if he stretched the truth, it was for a purpose. "The way to bring peace
once and for all to New Spain," he advised, "consists in giving everyone landed
property, as has been done in my province." As a result, New Mexico was spared
the vagrants and beggars who swarmed other parts of the viceroyalty like ants.

Subtly, Pedro Bautista Pino anticipated independence. His point of view dif-
fered notably from that of Spaniards sent out to the colonies to govern. Joaquín del
Real Alencaster, for one, had disparaged New Mexicans in 1807, presupposing that
they would not even defend their homes against encroaching Americans. While

agreeing that the United States posed a grave threat, Pino staunchly upheld the loyalty of his fellow citizens. Had they not resisted the blandishments of Pike and subsequent traders?

> The New Mexicans are so honest that despite their poverty and need, which is their usual condition, none was willing to buy so much as one-half of a *real*'s worth of [goods] from these foreigners. Everything confiscated was turned over to the . . . commandant [general], including the arrested merchants.

According to Pino, race was another issue that set New Mexicans apart. Spaniards who governed the colony were wont to comment unkindly about its numerous mestizos, mulattos, and other mixed-bloods. To counter that slur, don Pedro lied, swearing that no one of African descent had ever lived in New Mexico. Compared to Veracruz or Havana, cities he had passed through, New Mexico's percentage of African blood truly paled, but it had never faded away. Pino's assertion that all forty thousand New Mexicans were either Spaniards or pure Pueblo Indians revealed the mindset of a New Mexican rico, not the truth.

Pino had wanted to favorably impress the cortes. He knew that self-interested peninsular members of that body had adopted a formula in 1811 excluding people of color in Spanish America and the Philippines from the population counts that determined representation. Still, despite any personal prejudices don Pedro may have harbored toward castas, it would appear that in New Mexico, social acceptance and economic station meant more than blood. Beyond español or indio, racial designations—except to curse an adversary—hardly mattered.[12]

While Pedro Bautista Pino took in Spain, Manuel de Salcedo grudgingly resumed the governorship of Texas. His previous experience had shaken him. Besides Simón de Herrera, serving again in Texas, whom could he trust? Relying on his military council on public safety, Salcedo sought to identify and isolate revolutionary sympathizers. The case of retired Capt. José Menchaca, found guilty of sedition, illustrated the confusion in the minds of many colonists.

Menchaca belonged to a numerous, old-line cattle-raising and soldiering clan. Like many upper-class criollos, he could not decide about independence. He had corresponded with insurgents but then helped capture Father Hidalgo. Still, he disliked and had often clashed with the high-handed Spaniards sent to govern Spanish Texas.

In the summer of 1811, Menchaca had aided revolutionary Bernardo Gutiérrez de Lara to escape to Natchitoches. A former blacksmith, rancher, and trader, Gutiérrez claimed to officially represent the revolutionary government of Mexico in the United States. Buoyed after meeting in Washington, D.C., with Secretary of State James Monroe and President James Madison, he ardently set about to lib-

erate Texas. Menchaca, disgusted by the rabble rallying for an invasion, again abandoned the cause of Mexican independence in hopes of a royal pardon. Instead,
judged guilty in San Antonio, he ended up in a Chihuahua prison.

Dozens of U.S. citizens, meanwhile, joined Gutiérrez, none more enthusiastically than twenty-four-year-old Bostonian Augustus William Magee. A West
Point graduate who resigned his commission in 1812, Magee accepted military
command of Gutiérrez's "Republican Army of the North." To interest other
Americans, Gutiérrez let Magee offer forty dollars a month and a league (4,428
acres) of Texas land for joining up. Even James B. Wilkinson, the general's son,
signed on.

As special agent of the U.S. State Department at Natchitoches, William Shaler
of Bridgeport, Connecticut—who had dangled ill-defended California before his
American readers in 1808—blessed Gutiérrez and Magee's shady undertaking.
Extraofficially in October 1812, Shaler shared his pleasure with Secretary Monroe.
"The volunteer expedition," he bragged,

> from the most insignificant beginning is growing into an irresistible torrent,
> that will Sweep the crazy remains of Spanish Government from the Internal
> Provinces, and open Mexico to the political influence of the U.S. and to
> the talents and enterprize of our citizens.

Not knowing what to expect, most of the polyglot people of Nacogdoches
welcomed the Republican Army, while those members of the garrison remaining
loyal to Spain fled eastward. The big but hardly defended stone presidio at La Bahía
(later Goliad) fell next in November 1812 to Gutiérrez's invaders, swollen now to
nearly a thousand. Here they hunkered down and withstood a four-month siege
by a force under the command of Governor Salcedo and Simón de Herrera. Magee
at one point met with the governor to discuss terms under which the Republican
Army of the North would withdraw from Texas, but they could not agree. Finally,
it was Salcedo who withdrew to San Antonio. Early in February 1813, Magee died.
Gutiérrez later excoriated him as a cowardly traitor for "promising to sell me to
Salcedo for fifteen thousand pesos and the position of colonel in the Royalist ranks."

A month after lifting their siege of La Bahía, regulars and militia under
Lieutenant Colonel Herrera flowed out from San Antonio on March 28 to meet
Gutiérrez's advancing army at Salado Creek, some thirteen miles southeast of town.
The invaders won easily, routing Herrera's indecisive array in twenty minutes.
Governor Salcedo surrendered Texas a few days later. Savoring his accomplish-
ment, Gutiérrez could or would not restrain his filibusters (*filibusteros* or freeboot-
ers), who drank, raped, and pillaged.

Empowering a local junta, on which sat several vindictive Menchacas, the revolutionary regime condemned to death Salcedo, Herrera, and a dozen other royal

La Bahía, from Francis Moore, Jr., *Map and Description of Texas* (1840). *Courtesy of the UT Institute of Texan Cultures at San Antonio.*

officers. When some of the Americans and *tejanos* cried foul, Gutiérrez appeared to relent. He charged bejareño Antonio Delgado of the militia and sixty or more armed men to remove the prisoners, each with his hands tied behind him. Only when Delgado returned a few days later, by one account boasting that he had evened the score with Salcedo for executing his father and brother, did the townspeople shudder in horror.

Earlier at the battle site, Delgado had ordered the bound captives unhorsed and cruelly taunted. His men then drew their knives, stabbing, mutilating, and slitting the throats of all without exception. Their work done, the assassins rode back to San Antonio, leaving the corpses where they lay. Thus, ignominiously, died the royal governor of Texas, nephew of the commandant general.

News of this bloody act galvanized royalist authorities. Later in 1813, Viceroy Félix María Calleja, hardened victor over insurrectionists in the south, decreed the division of the Provincias Internas into eastern and western departments based in Monterrey (Nuevo León) and Durango respectively. As commandant general in the east, he named tough Col. Joaquín de Arredondo, former governor of Nuevo Santander, who relished the mission. He would revenge Governor Salcedo, rout the murdering rebels, and restore Texas to the empire. Nothing else mattered. Let the mob have its moment.

Styling himself President Protector, Bernardo Gutiérrez de Lara proclaimed Texas an independent republic for the first time. But again tempers flared as an irregular government headed by an outsider tried to impose itself on the ambivalent tejano community of San Antonio. Four months later, in early August 1813, a flashy Cuban rival outmaneuvered Gutiérrez and took over. The deposed first president hastened to Natchitoches and lived to fight another day. Remarkably, under an independent Mexico, Gutiérrez himself ascended in the mid-1820s to the rank of commandant general of the Provincias Internas del Oriente.

By their quarreling with one another, the ethnically diverse revolutionaries of San Antonio made Arredondo's job easier. Their straggling Republican Army took the field in mid-August and engaged Arredondo's advance party on the Río Medina. Thinking this was the whole force, the republicans rushed across the river only to be confronted by the main royalist army.

There may have been two thousand on each side. After battling four hours across oak-studded hills, the revolutionaries broke and ran for San Antonio. Young Wilkinson died in the fight. Colonel Arredondo stayed on in Texas for several weeks, effecting a counterrevolutionary reign of terror that exceeded Gutiérrez's. He showed little mercy, ordered hundreds of males suspected of antiroyalist sentiment herded into stifling, makeshift holding pens. His firing squads had no rest. Women, torn from their children, faced rape and slave labor cooking for the occupying army.

Members of leading families fled east toward Louisiana to escape the purge. Wide-open Nacogdoches practically evaporated. Arredondo's cavalry under Lt. Col. Ignacio Elizondo intercepted a caravan of San Antonio refugees at the Trinity River, turning back some and shooting others, among them the notorious Antonio Delgado. At that, several notable bejareños accused of collaborating with insurgents, among them the irrepressible José Erasmo Seguín, cleared themselves and pieced their lives back together.[13]

Although Colonel Arredondo kept Texas Spanish, he all but ruined it. Confiscations of livestock and land broke up once-prosperous ranching operations, as heads of families died or dispersed. Lawlessness prevailed in the countryside, particularly in east Texas. Armed bands lived off the land, scavenging for whatever food or spoils they could uncover. Indians, responding to the interruption of gifts and trade, fell back on raiding. The province's Hispanic population dropped by half to about two thousand. No wonder that once the United States gave up its territorial claim to Texas in the Adams-Onís Treaty of 1819, Gov. Antonio María Martínez listened to Moses Austin's offer the following year.

For two hundred thousand acres of Texas land, the *empresario* contracted to bring into the colony and settle three hundred American families. By early 1821,

Entierro de un ángel, by Theodore Gentilz. *Courtesy of the Daughters of the Republic of Texas Library at the Alamo.*

even Commandant General Arredondo approved. He had convinced himself that Texas stood to gain "important augmentation, in agriculture, industry, and arts, by the new emigrants." From a tiny trickle.[14]

Texas, plainly, lay too close to the United States, California too far from anywhere. With England and Spain locked in war against Napoleon, czarist Russia looked to expand its operations in North America. Generations of hunting had depleted sea-otter herds at higher latitudes. And once Spain abandoned Nootka in 1795, no rival European settlement existed north of San Francisco.

Hence, New England skippers, who had ships capable of sailing to China, and agents for the Russian-American Company, who commanded flotillas of Aleut Indian hunters in skin *bidarkas,* struck a clever, mutually lucrative deal. Who was to prevent them from harvesting otter along hundreds of miles of California's unoccupied coast? Sovereignty be damned.

When Russian aristocrat Nikolai Petrovich Rezanov, having bought the *Juno* from a Rhode Islander, sailed into San Francisco Bay in April 1806, he was of course received as a gentleman by Capt. José Darío Argüello, commandant of the Spanish presidio. During a pleasant six-week stay, the suave, forty-two-year-old widower

La cocina, by Theodore Gentilz. *Courtesy of the Daughters of the Republic of Texas Library at the Alamo.*

proposed marriage to Argüello's comely fifteen-year-old daughter Conchita, a situation reminiscent of Louis Juchereau de Saint-Denis and Manuela Sánchez at San Juan Bautista on the Rio Grande ninety years earlier.

Because Nikolai was Russian Orthodox, however, the couple would have to await royal and papal dispensations. The Russian swore to obtain them and return. Without questioning Rezanov's romantic interest, his German doctor, Georg Heinrich von Langsdorff, suggested a baser motive. Perhaps Rezanov had "conceived the idea that through a marriage with the daughter of the Commandante . . . a close bond would be formed for future business intercourse between the Russian-American Company and the province of Nueva California."

Neither union ever happened. Although he advocated a Russian settlement at Bodega Bay just north of San Francisco, Nikolai Resanov died en route back to St. Petersburg when he fell through the ice of a river in Siberia. Conchita never knew his fate. Waiting endlessly, she spurned other suitors and finally became a nun, enshrined thereafter in one of Spanish California's most enduring love stories.

Russians, meanwhile, took advantage of the colony's meager defenses. Thirty miles up the coast from Bodega Bay, Ivan Kuskov in 1812 traded blankets, tools, and beads to Kashiya Pomo Indians for a commanding site on which he oversaw construction of a sturdy, redwood-plank stockade and settlement. He called it Rossiya, to Americans Fort Ross.

Kuskov also posted men to the Farallon Islands, a source of seal and sea-lion meat, skins, blubber, and oil. Since the rocky, kelp-choked coves inside San Francisco Bay teemed with otter, lines of bidarkas entered along the far shore at the outer range of the presidio's guns.

California's Gov. José Joaquín de Arrillaga could only watch. No orders came for him to mount an overland campaign and expel the Russians, nor were armed vessels available to catch the mother ships or bidarkas at sea. So he looked the other way as Russians and californios traded hardware, hides, and foodstuffs.

When the order finally did arrive in 1818 for him to eliminate Fort Ross, don Pablo Vicente de Sola, California's last Spanish governor, could not comply. He simply lacked the means.[15]

Russian designs on California appeared the least of Fernando VII's worries when, following Napoleon's defeat in 1814, he finally assumed the Spanish throne. What was this Constitution of 1812? Authority emanated from him, not from the people. Finding enough support among the old guard, he scrapped the document, persecuted its audacious liberal authors, and reinstalled traditional Bourbon absolutism.

While negotiators for the United States muttered in private about decadent Spain's relapse, at least now they had a legitimate government with which to discuss boundaries in North America. And they enjoyed an enormous advantage. Preoccupied with revolts in core areas of his New World empire, Fernando VII had little energy to devote to its northern periphery.

John Quincy Adams, eminent nationalist and secretary of state in President Monroe's cabinet, represented the United States in the subsequent negotiations. Don Luis de Onís, longtime Spanish minister in Philadelphia and Washington, spoke for Fernando VII. He knew his handicap. Writing to Madrid in 1818, Onís confessed,

> If His Majesty can't get the support of any Power, and hasn't sufficient forces
> to make war on this country, then I think it would be best not to delay mak-
> ing the best settlement possible, seeing that things certainly won't be better
> for a long time.

So Spain gave up indefensible East and West Florida in hopes of a favorable boundary at midcontinent. Adams wanted Texas as well, and if the president, cabinet, and triumphant Gen. Andrew Jackson had rallied behind him, the United States might have had it. Instead of the Rio Grande, however, the chief American diplomat settled for the Sabine, today's border between Louisiana and Texas.

The proviso of the Adams-Onís Treaty of 1819 that made it truly the Transcontinental Treaty detailed a boundary between the Louisiana Purchase and

San Francisco, 1806. Honeyman Collection, no. 1021. *Courtesy of The Bancroft Library, University of California, Berkeley.*

the Provincias Internas that resembled three giant northwesterly stair steps across North America. The line relied on rivers, parallels, and meridians: up the Sabine to the thirty-second parallel, north to the Red, along it upriver westward as far as the one hundredth meridian; thence north to the Arkansas and up to its source; and last, north to the forty-second parallel and a thousand miles west to the Pacific. That, at least on paper, kept U.S. territory several days north of Spanish San Antonio, Santa Fe, Tucson, and Monterey. Yet no one relaxed.[16]

Diplomacy did not replace preparedness. The month before he signed the Transcontinental Treaty, don Luis de Onís alerted Spanish officials to another probable U.S. invasion of New Mexico. Already don Alejo García Conde, commandant general in Durango, had dispatched Capt. Facundo Melgares to Santa Fe, just as Nemesio Salcedo had done a dozen years before. This time, Melgares stayed on. Appointed governor in 1818 and promoted to lieutenant colonel, don Facundo meant to defend New Mexico. He asked the commandant general for reinforcements, the people for food to mount campaigns against Navajos, and scouts for news of Americans and their influence among the Plains Indians.

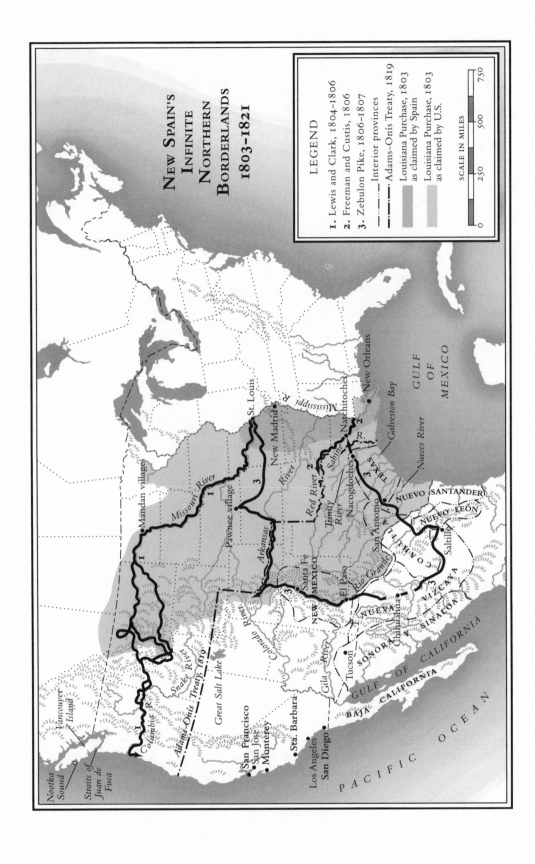

NEW SPAIN'S
INFINITE
NORTHERN
BORDERLANDS
1803–1821

LEGEND

1. Lewis and Clark, 1804–1806
2. Freeman and Custis, 1806
3. Zebulon Pike, 1806–1807

⋯⋯ Interior provinces
—··— Adams–Onís Treaty, 1819
▧ Louisiana Purchase, 1803
 as claimed by Spain
▨ Louisiana Purchase, 1803
 as claimed by U.S.

SCALE IN MILES

0   250   500   750

PACIFIC OCEAN

Nootka Sound
Vancouver Island
Straits of Juan de Fuca
Columbia R.
Snake River
Adams-Onis Treaty, 1819
Great Salt Lake
San Francisco
San Jose
Monterey
Sta. Barbara
Los Angeles
San Diego
BAJA CALIFORNIA
GULF OF CALIFORNIA
Gila River
Colorado River
Tucson
SONORA Y SINALOA
Chihuahua
NUEVA VIZCAYA
El Paso
Rio Grande
Santa Fe
NEW MEXICO
Arkansas
Pawnee village
Missouri River
Mandan villages
St. Louis
Mississippi R.
New Madrid
Red River
Arkansas River
San Antonio
COAHUILA
Saltillo
NUEVO LEÓN
NUEVO SANTANDER
TEXAS
Nacogdoches
Trinity River
Sabine R.
Natchitoches
New Orleans
Galveston Bay
Nueces River
GULF OF MEXICO

While Melgares's king delayed ratification of the Transcontinental Treaty—hoping in vain for a U.S. pledge to deny recognition to emerging nations that declared independence from Spain—the governor of New Mexico sent a party well north of the line into present-day Wyoming. He called on old hand José Jarvet to lead it. Pedro Vial, trailsman without peer, was gone. A lifelong bachelor, Vial had bequeathed his seven-room house in Santa Fe to María Manuela Martín on October 2, 1814, and died by the following summer.

In 1819, Jarvet and fifteen men who could survive by hunting reconnoitered the Yellowstone River, a tributary of the upper Missouri. Maj. Stephen H. Long's touted Yellowstone expedition of the same year, trusting in a fire-belching steamboat to ascend the Missouri and awe the Mandans, got nowhere near as far, and Jarvet reported no sign of Americans.[17]

A different Long, meanwhile, crossed the line into Spanish territory. The rash James, merchant of Natchez, determined to fix by force of arms his country's failure to gain Texas by treaty. With republican slogans on his lips and Texas lands on his mind, Long incited roughly three hundred irregulars, among them the previously failed revolutionary Bernardo Gutiérrez de Lara.

Their occupation of Nacogdoches in June 1819 was too easy. Flushed by success, Long galloped off to Galveston to enlist pirate Jean Laffite. In his absence, riders under Texas cattleman Lt. Col. Ignacio Pérez, a steady royalist, routed these latest invaders and temporarily swept the area clean of foreign squatters. No more than a temporary reverse, swore Long.

Back again in 1821, this self-styled freedom fighter led another mob of filibusters from Bolivar Point on Galveston Bay inland to La Bahía, leaving on the coast his wife Jane, niece of Gen. James Wilkinson, pregnant with the couple's third child. This time around, Pérez had the pleasure of capturing Long. By December, when Jane gave birth to Long's daughter, Mexico had declared its independence. The American had been taken as a prisoner to Mexico City, where in April 1822 he was shot dead by a guard.[18]

Events in Spain had again intruded. In the same way that Napoleon's takeover had inflamed revolutionaries, Fernando VII's harsh restoration had given clear advantage back to the royalists. In most of New Spain, the king's men prevailed. Yet in pockets of rough terrain, bands of individuals willing to die for independence fought on.

As late as 1817 and 1818, presidial rolls in Pimería Alta belied the government's assurance that the insurrection was dead. A third of the Pima infantry company of Tubac still served on detached duty in Sinaloa and Sonora fighting insurgents. Besides bonuses, they earned double service time on their military records.[19] In

The abandoned mission church at Tumacácori, by H. M. T. Powell, 1849. *Courtesy of The Bancroft Library, University of California, Berkeley.*

1819, Viceroy Juan Ruiz de Apodaca reassured the king that no further reinforcements were needed in New Spain; Bourbon rule was safe. The viceroy had offered to pardon surviving revolutionaries who would lay down their arms.

Buoyed, the unpopular Fernando VII now resolved to reconquer the breakaway colonies of South America. That, however, had set off a mutinous reaction in Spain. Troops assembled at Cádiz joined a revolt that in 1820 forced the reluctant king to reinstate the Constitution of 1812. Out again went the call for delegates to the cortes. In far-off New Mexico, a dozen electors looked to don Pedro Bautista Pino for a second time. And again he packed his trunk. But while he waited at Veracruz for passage, Mexican independence invalidated his credentials.

To the privileged classes of New Spain—high-ranking army, church, and government officials, along with wealthy business people, mine owners, and landed gentry—it appeared that their king, once the prisoner of Napoleon, had now fallen prey to the liberals he had so viciously persecuted. Reforms in the mother country

again threatened the status quo. Hence, in an effort to protect their interests, members of the colonial elite began to shape an independent Mexico in their own image.

Still on the side of the king, Viceroy Ruiz de Apodaca directed an army led by Agustín de Iturbide, a cunning criollo officer in royalist ranks, to humble the insurgents of revolutionary Vicente Guerrero. Envisioning a higher destiny, Iturbide joined Guerrero.

Their compromise Plan of Iguala, on February 24, 1821, proclaimed three ringing guarantees: immediate independence of a Mexican monarchy temporarily guided by Spain's Constitution of 1812, equality of Mexican criollos and Spanish peninsulares, and full protection of the Roman Catholic Church. While large segments of the populace seemed indifferent, hardly anyone wanted more fighting, and acceptance of independence on these terms spread quickly.

Yet not one of the Spanish-born military men who governed Texas, New Mexico, Sonora, and California leapt to Iturbide's banner. Throughout the spring of 1821, they waited, heeding the viceroy's pleas to remain loyal to Spain. Only after word reached Texas that Iturbide's proponents had forced Ruiz de Apodaca from office early in July did Gov. Antonio María Martínez yield. Knots of cautious officials in the plazas of San Antonio and La Bahía swore on July 19 and 23 to uphold the Plan of Iguala.

Lt. Col. Facundo Melgares of New Mexico, who had been aware of Iturbide's treason since April, abided through the summer. Commandant General García Conde, who had moved his headquarters north from Durango to Chihuahua, imagined the western Provincias Internas as a separate and independent republic. Then in August, Durango went overwhelmingly for Iturbide, and García Conde took his cue.

The commandant general's orders to Melgares, dated late the same month, instructed New Mexico's governor to accept unequivocally the Plan of Iguala. El Paso's town fathers complied on September 8, 1821, and don Facundo and a large crowd in Santa Fe on the eleventh. Regardless of how he truly felt about independence, Melgares was still governor.

In receipt of the same orders a few days earlier, single-minded veteran Col. Antonio Cordero, intendant and governor of Sonora, refused and resigned. Others pointedly ignored his example. Lt. Col. Antonio Narbona, in command of the Arizpe garrison, swore the oath, and at distant Tucson, Lt. Col. Manuel Ignacio de Arvizu did the same.

On September 27, 1821, Gen. Agustín de Iturbide's cavalcade entered Mexico City to the orchestrated cheers of the crowd. By previous agreement, don Juan O'Donojú, last viceroy of New Spain, had bowed to Mexican independence.

At Monterey in California the following January, white-haired Gov. Pablo Vicente de Sola still considered Iturbide and independence a joke. Finally however, when told to do so in April, he presided as soldiers lowered the Spanish flag over the plaza for the last time, catching it before it hit the ground. The assembled californios just watched. "They do not cheer," don Pablo explained, "because they are unused to independence."[20]

In Mexico City, Iturbide reached for the golden ring. Selecting the feast of Spain's patron saint, July 25, 1822, he had himself crowned Agustín I, emperor of Mexico. His reign lasted not a year. Further struggle ensued, as factions convulsed the new nation's center and ignored its periphery.

The same year Mexico achieved independence, Missouri became a state. Anticipating the coincidence, two of Missouri's more enterprising citizens in 1821 had crossed the Transcontinental Treaty line to negotiate business in the capitals of Mexican Texas and New Mexico.

California Indians dancing in front of Mission Dolores, San Francisco. By Louis Choris, artist on the Russian expedition of Otto von Kotzebue, 1816. *Courtesy of the Yale Collection of Western Americana, Beinecke Rare Book and Manuscript Library, Yale University.*

Stephen F. Austin, heir to his deceased father Moses's colonization contract, reconfirmed its terms in San Antonio with Governor Martínez. By December 1821, American families had begun arriving. By the end of the decade, they would outnumber Hispanic Texans.

In mid-November 1821, semiliterate William Becknell, about twenty other men, and their pack train of goods from Franklin, Missouri, had reined up in Santa Fe. Governor Melgares made them welcome. If we believe Becknell, soldiers and citizens of Santa Fe who had evidently stashed away coins gave them gladly for his American merchandise. The following year he would be back with wagons.

Even though Facundo Melgares had formally acknowledged the independence of Mexico in September 1821, he had provided no fitting public display to mark the momentous event. In late December, he received orders to do so. His subsequent, high-blown description of the festivities, published in Mexico City's *Gaceta Imperial* the following March, was apparently meant to cover up an earlier lack of enthusiasm.

Melgares chose the day of Epiphany, January 6, 1822. Previously, such ceremonials had marked royal accessions, marriages, or births. Trusting in the old ways—soaring rhetoric, poems of praise, painted stage sets and bunting, allegorical skits, processions and church services, music, volleys of gunfire, clanging bells—Santa Fe gave new allegiance to

> make the tyrants see that although we inhabit the most northern point of
> North America we love the Holy Religion of our fathers, that we love and
> defend the longed-for union between Spaniards of both hemispheres, and
> that at the cost of our last drop of blood we will sustain the sacred
> Independence of the Mexican Empire.

Despite bad weather, crowds were large. After mass, a triumphal parade formed up behind the governor, town council, and two lines of prominent citizens between which came

> all the little children in sight . . . uniformed in white clothing, sashes of sky
> blue, green laurel encircling their brows, and across their breasts a tricolor sash
> with the inscription: "Long live the Independence of the Mexican Empire."

The dance in the plaza by Pueblo Indians of Tesuque lasted until one o'clock. People scattered next to a variety of public games. A much anticipated dramatic presentation, announced by salvos of artillery, unfolded on the makeshift stage, followed by a ball in the governor's palace "attended by all persons of distinction." Pleasing decorations greeted guests, refreshment flowed lavishly, and the party spun on until

> four-thirty in the morning as merrily as it had begun at eight in the evening.
> The occasion was so ineffable and outstanding that even the governor, the
> senior alcalde, and the chaplain happily presented themselves to perform an
> entertainment between dances.[21]

William Becknell missed the celebration. So eager was he to get back to Franklin and reoutfit himself for the Santa Fe trade that he and his men departed in haste. Another American party attended, however, having arrived on December 1.

Opinionated Thomas James, a hard-luck merchant who gambled with John McKnight to carry ten-thousand-dollars worth of goods to Santa Fe in 1821, had not counted on handing over so much of their merchandise to Comanches en route. While they readily sold what remained, the journal James kept of the venture was ruined when his trunk fell in a river. Two decades later, relying on faulty memory, he recalled with virulent anti-Mexican bias the observance of independence in Santa Fe.

James alleged that the local planning committee had put him in charge of erecting a liberty pole. Aroused to direct the raising of an improvised flag, he found don Facundo and others standing around in a quandary. When he suggested to the governor that the honor belonged to him, Melgares shot back, "Oh do it yourself . . . you understand such things." Thus, according to the American, "I raised the first flag in the free and independent State of New Mexico."

Cannons boomed and men and women came running. Their passionate, non-stop gaming at dice and faro tables set up around the plaza had especially offended James, who expected his readers to believe that

> No Italian carnival ever exceeded this celebration in thoughtlessness, vice and licentiousness of every description. . . . I saw enough during this five days of revelry to convince me that the republicans of New Mexico were unfit to govern themselves or any body else.[22]

The swelling population of the United States by the early 1820s had passed ten million. Of Mexico's six million, hardly fifty thousand lived in Texas, New Mexico, Pimería Alta, and California. U.S. citizens like Thomas James and William Shaler, who looked out across Mexico's northern marches to the Pacific, believed themselves in every way superior to Mexicans.

In the quarter century between 1821 and 1846, Anglo-Americans, who had begun infiltrating Spanish territory as early as the 1780s, redoubled their efforts. Agents in the lucrative hide-and-tallow trade took up residence in Mexican California, acquired sprawling rancho grants, and wrote to relatives in Boston and Philadelphia about how abundant this land would be in the hands of an enterprising people.

The Santa Fe trade reoriented New Mexico's and then Chihuahua's economy to Missouri and the United States. Hispanic New Mexicans readily entered the commerce and sent their children to learn English in St. Louis. American mountain men who bothered could now get licenses from the Mexican governor in Santa Fe to trap beaver on the upper Rio Grande and Gila. Taos became their haven.

Ambitious Mexicans like Manuel Armijo, born of a rico family in the Albuquerque district, for the first time could aspire to the governorship and to making deals with Anglo-Americans. Home rule in the provinces grew naturally out of the Mexican central government's paralysis.

Not imperceptibly, the Mexican far north gravitated into economic dependence on the United States. Few doubted that when a sufficient excuse presented itself, the U.S. flag would follow the dollar. By then, a good many descendants of the Hispanic men, women, and children who had originally braved the northern frontier with don Juan de Oñate nine or ten generations before favored U.S. sovereignty. That was Mexico's problem.

In 1848, at the end of the war Mexicans called the North American invasion, the Treaty of Guadalupe Hidalgo stripped their nation of half its territory. Texas, which had broken away in 1836 to spend a decade as an independent republic, had joined the United States at the very end of 1845. In 1850, the U.S. Congress dealt

An Anglo-American trade caravan approaching Santa Fe. *From Josiah Gregg,* Commerce of the Prairies *(1844).*

with the enormous Mexican Cession, granting California immediate statehood and creating the two huge, horizonal territories of New Mexico and Utah. In 1863, Arizona became a separate territory from New Mexico, but not until 1912—mainly because of their diverse populations—did either achieve statehood.

Thus was completed the metamorphosis from the unjoined but vital northern periphery of the Spanish empire to the U.S. Southwest, "this most exotic of our national regions."[23]

ABBREVIATIONS

CC1   David Hurst Thomas, ed. *Columbian Consequences*. Vol. 1. *Archaeological and Historical Perspectives on the Spanish Borderlands West*. Washington, D.C.: Smithsonian Institution Press, 1989.

CC2   David Hurst Thomas, ed. *Columbian Consequences*. Vol. 2. *Archaeological and Historical Perspectives on the Spanish Borderlands East*. Washington, D.C.: Smithsonian Institution Press, 1990.

CC3   David Hurst Thomas, ed. *Columbian Consequences*. Vol. 3. *The Spanish Borderlands in Pan-American Perspective*. Washington, D.C.: Smithsonian Institution Press, 1991.

CE   Ramón A. Gutiérrez and Richard J. Orsi, eds. *Contested Eden: California before the Gold Rush*. Berkeley: University of California Press, 1998.

CETN   Richard Flint and Shirley Cushing Flint, eds. *The Coronado Expedition to Tierra Nueva: The 1540–1542 Route across the Southwest*. Niwot: University Press of Colorado, 1997.

CG   Donna J. Guy and Thomas E. Sheridan, eds. *Contested Ground: Comparative Frontiers on the Northern and Southern Edges of the Spanish Empire*. Tucson: University of Arizona Press, 1998.

JAR   *Journal of Anthropological Research*

NMHR   *New Mexico Historical Review*

NV   Robert H. Jackson, ed. *New Views of Borderlands History*. Albuquerque: University of New Mexico Press, 1998.

SCSH   Nunis, Doyce B., Jr., ed. *Southern California's Spanish Heritage*. Los Angeles: Historical Society of Southern California, 1992.

SWHQ   *Southwestern Historical Quarterly*

NOTES

PREFACE

1. The most comprehensive treatment of the Spanish colonial period in North America, covering both the Southeast and Southwest of the present-day United States, is David J. Weber's *The Spanish Frontier in North America* (New Haven: Yale University Press, 1992). Weber's first chapter, "Worlds Apart," implies that Europeans and Native Americans had inherent trouble understanding one another.

For the vast literature about Spain's experience in North America, the reader is referred to Weber's notes and bibliography. See also the chapter-length description of the Southwest by Weber, "The Spanish-Mexican Rim," in Clyde A. Milner II, Carol A. O'Connor, and Martha A. Sandweiss, eds., *The Oxford History of the American West* (New York: Oxford University Press, 1994), 45–77. Other recent surveys include Bernard L. Fontana, *Entrada: The Legacy of Spain and Mexico in the United States* (Tucson: Southwest Parks and Monuments Association, 1994), and Iris H. W. Engstrand and Donald C. Cutter, *Spanish Settlement in the Far Southwest: Arizona, California and New Mexico, 1530–1821* (Golden, Colo.: Fulcrum Publishing, 1996).

Among general studies that look at New Spain's moving northward frontier from the south are Peter Gerhard, *The North Frontier of New Spain,* rev. ed. (Norman: University of Oklahoma Press, 1993), and Oakah L. Jones, Jr., *Los Paisanos: Spanish Settlers on the Northern Frontier of New Spain* (Norman: University of Oklahoma Press, 1979, 1996). Two recent essay collections are *CG* and *NV*.

2. Eleanor B. Adams, ed., *Bishop Tamarón's Visitation of New Mexico, 1760* (Albuquerque: Historical Society of New Mexico, 1954), 49.

3. A helpful map showing areas of Spanish colonization west of Texas is "The Southwest" (Washington, D.C.: National Geographic Society, 1982).

CHAPTER 1

The first of the opening quotations is translated by Rolena Adorno, "The Negotiation of Fear in Cabeza de Vaca's *Naufragios,*" in Stephen Greenblatt, ed., *New World Encounters* (Berkeley: University of California Press, 1993), 68. The second is from Lawrence A. Clayton, Vernon James Knight, Jr., and Edward C. Moore, eds., *The De Soto Chronicles: The Expedition of Hernando de Soto to North America in 1539–1543* (Tuscaloosa: University of Alabama Press, 1993), 1:134.

1. Regarding Ponce de León and his activities in the Caribbean, see Troy S. Floyd, *The Columbus Dynasty in the Caribbean, 1492–1526* (Albuquerque: University of New Mexico Press, 1973); Robert S. Weddle, *Spanish Sea: The Gulf of Mexico in North American Discovery, 1500–1685* (College Station: Texas A&M University Press, 1985); Samuel Eliot Morison, *The*

European Discovery of America: The Southern Voyages, A.D. 1492–1616 (New York: Oxford University Press, 1974); and Weber, *Spanish Frontier.*

2. Morison, *Southern Voyages,* 52–65.

3. Quoted by Morison, *Southern Voyages,* 112.

4. Irving Rouse, *The Tainos: Rise and Decline of the People Who Greeted Columbus* (New Haven: Yale University Press, 1992), 5. Kathleen A. Deagan, "Sixteenth-Century Spanish-American Colonization in the Southeastern United States and the Caribbean," in *CC2,* 233–34. Kathleen A. Deagan and José María Cruxent, "From Contact to *Criollos:* The Archaeology of Spanish Colonization in Hispaniola," *Proceedings of the British Academy* 81 (1993), 71–72. See also Carl Ortwin Sauer, *The Early Spanish Main* (Berkeley: University of California Press, 1966), 37–69.

5. Floyd, *Columbus Dynasty,* 20–22; Morison, *Southern Voyages,* 116–17.

6. Kathleen A. Deagan, "La Isabela, Europe's First Foothold in the New World," *National Geographic* 181:1 (January 1992), 40–53; José María Cruxent, "The Origin of La Isabela: First Spanish Colony in the New World," in Thomas, *CC1* , 251–59; and Deagan and Cruxent, "From Contact to *Criollos,*" 78–87. Sauer, *Early Spanish Main,* 72–77.

7. Regarding the transfer of a stripped-down "conquest culture" from Spain to the New World, see George M. Foster, *Culture and Conquest: America's Spanish Heritage* (Chicago: Quadrangle Books, 1960).

8. Quoted by Cruxent, "Origin of La Isabela," 257.

9. Floyd, *Columbus Dynasty,* 23–24, 48; Morison, *Southern Voyages,* 118–19.

10. Deagan, "La Isabela," 48.

11. Floyd, *Columbus Dynasty,* 44; Deagan, "La Isabela," 52.

12. Floyd, *Columbus Dynasty,* 51–59, 73, 82. See also Vicente Murga Sanz, *Juan Ponce de León, fundador y primer gobernador del pueblo Puertorriqueño, descubridor de la Florida y del Estrecho de las Bahamas* (San Juan: Universidad de Puerto Rico, 1959), who includes a rather complete genealogy of don Juan's Caribbean family and a number of transcribed documents.

13. Floyd, agreeing with Murga Sanz, believes that Las Casas greatly exaggerated Ponce de León's brutality toward the Natives, depicting him instead as remarkably diplomatic and fair. Other scholars, for example, Morison and Weddle, take Las Casas literally. Citing Morison and Las Casas, Hugh Thomas, *Conquest: Montezuma, Cortés, and the Fall of Old Mexico* (New York: Simon and Schuster, 1995), 80, characterizes don Juan as "that brave and swashbuckling bully." Henry Raup Wagner and Helen Rand Parish, *The Life and Writings of Bartolomé de las Casas* (University of New Mexico Press, 1967), 1–13.

14. Floyd, *Columbus Dynasty,* 95–106.

15. A good description of the office of adelantado is found in Eugene Lyon, *The Enterprise of Florida: Pedro Menéndez de Avilés and the Spanish Conquest of 1565–1568* (Gainesville: University Presses of Florida, 1976), 1–5. Floyd, *Columbus Dynasty,* 139. Murga Sanz (*Juan Ponce de León,* 100–102) paraphrases the details of the 1512 contract between the crown and Ponce de León.

16. Morison, *Southern Voyages,* 506–12 (Antonio de Herrera quotations, 507, 510). Weddle (*Spanish Sea,* 40–47) downplays the fountain of youth as motivation and discounts entirely the notion that Ponce de León discovered the north coast of Yucatán en route back to Puerto Rico. Thomas (*Conquest,* 57, 80–81, 87, 88, 516) embraces both.

17. Floyd, *Columbus Dynasty,* 106, 156–57; Morison, *Southern Voyages,* 503; Murga Sanz, *Juan Ponce de León,* 133.

18. Quoted by Weddle, *Spanish Sea,* 48. Floyd, *Columbus Dynasty,* 227–28.

19. Weddle, *Spanish Sea,* 48; Floyd, *Columbus Dynasty,* 230.

20. Sauer, *Early Spanish Main,* 200–206; Floyd, *Columbus Dynasty,* 189–93; Thomas, *Conquest,* 340, 443–46. The Caribbean demographic collapse is set in broader context by Alfred W. Crosby, Jr., *The Columbian Exchange: Biological and Cultural Consequences of 1492* (Westport, Conn.: Greenwood Press, 1972), 45–48, and *Ecological Imperialism: The Biological Expansion of Europe, 900–1900* (Cambridge: Cambridge University Press, 1986), 198–201.

21. Deagan and Cruxent, "From Contact to *Criollos*" (quotation, 67). See also Kathleen A. Deagan, ed., *Puerto Real: The Archaeology of a Sixteenth-Century Spanish Town in Hispaniola* (Gainesville: University Press of Florida, 1995).

22. Weddle, *Spanish Sea,* 55–108, 416–19; Sauer, *Early Spanish Main,* 215, 216; Thomas, *Conquest,* 79–80, 85–115, 152, 216–20, 231–32, 337–39.

23. Donald E. Chipman, *Nuño de Guzmán and the Province of Pánuco in New Spain, 1518–1533* (Glendale, Calif.: Arthur H. Clark, 1967), 1–83. Thomas, *Conquest,* 447–48, 549, 559, 583–85, 596. Some earlier scholars and writers made the Río de las Palmas the Rio Grande and placed the activities of Alvarez de Pineda and Garay there. Chipman (*Nuño de Guzmán,* 49–50) straightens out the confusion, and Weddle (*Spanish Sea,* 100–103, 420) strongly concurs.

24. Thomas, *Conquest,* 73, 77, 354–81, 443–46, 595.

25. Donald E. Chipman and Harriett Denise Joseph, *Notable Men and Women of Spanish Texas* (Austin: University of Texas Press, 1999), 1–21. About Cabeza de Vaca's published writings, principally the editions of 1542 (Zamora) and 1555 (Valladolid), see Henry R. Wagner, *The Spanish Southwest, 1542–1794,* 2 parts (Albuquerque: Quivira Society, 1937). There are several readily available English translations, among them Enrique Pupo-Walker and Frances M. López-Morillas, eds., *Castaways: The Narrative of Alvar Núñez Cabeza de Vaca* (Berkeley: University of California Press, 1993); Martin A. Favata and José B. Fernández, eds., *The Account: Alvar Núñez Cabeza de Vaca's "Relación"* (Houston: Arte Público Press, 1993); and Cyclone Covey, ed., *Cabeza de Vaca's Adventures in the Unknown Interior of America* (Albuquerque: University of New Mexico Press, 1983). Weddle, *Spanish Sea,* 185–207, offers a fine summary. Still the breeziest telling of Cabeza de Vaca's stranger-than-fiction adventures, not only in North America, but also later in South America, is Morris Bishop, *The Odyssey of Cabeza de Vaca* (New York: The Century Co., 1933). See also Rochelle A. Marrinan, John F. Scarry, and Rhonda L. Majors, "Prelude to de Soto: The Expedition of Pánfilo de Narváez," in *CC2,* 71–82.

26. Pupo-Walker and López-Morillas, *Castaways,* 42.

27. Nancy P. Hickerson explains "How Cabeza de Vaca Lived With, Worked Among, and Finally Left the Indians of Texas," *JAR* 54 (Summer 1998), 199–218, emphasizing the castaway's own resourcefulness and his keen ethnological observations.

28. Donald E. Chipman, "In Search of Cabeza de Vaca's Route across Texas: An Historiographical Survey," *SWHQ* 91 (October 1987), 127–48, and *Spanish Texas, 1519–1821* (Austin: University of Texas Press, 1992), 28–34. Earlier writers, more out of loyalty to Texas than to the documents, plotted for Cabeza de Vaca a trans-Texas route west. Chambers of commerce in New Mexico and Arizona have also claimed that the historic party passed through their states.

Daniel T. Reff, "Text and Context: Cures, Miracles, and Fear in the *Relación* of Alvar Núñez Cabeza de Vaca," *Journal of the Southwest* 38 (Summer 1996), 115–38, argues that the Indians' knowledge of the death and destruction wrought by Spanish slavers and disease among Native peoples farther south conditioned their responses to Cabeza de Vaca and his party.

29. Pupo-Walker and López-Morillas, *Castaways,* 107, 114.

30. Chipman, *Nuño de Guzmán,* 87–91, 141–43, 197–218.

31. Chipman, *Nuño de Guzmán,* 221–87. Tejo's story was recorded some years later by a chronicler of the Coronado expedition. George P. Hammond and Agapito Rey, eds., *Narratives of the Coronado Expedition, 1540–1542* (Albuquerque: University of New Mexico Press, 1940), 195–96. On Guzmán's conquest of Nueva Galicia and Cortés's failed colony in Baja California, see Gerhard, *North Frontier,* 42–46, 288–89. Pupo-Walker and López-Morillas, *Castaways,* 120.

32. Arthur Scott Aiton, *Antonio de Mendoza, First Viceroy of New Spain* (Durham, N.C.: Duke University Press, 1927).

33. Pupo-Walker and López Morillas, *Castaways,* 104.

34. Pupo-Walker and López Morillas, *Castaways,* 108. Adorno, "Negotiation of Fear," 69–76. Aiton, *Antonio de Mendoza,* 119. Herbert E. Bolton, *Coronado: Knight of Pueblos and Plains* (Albuquerque: University of New Mexico Press, 1949), 16–17.

35. Bolton, *Coronado,* 40–43. Paul E. Hoffman, "Hernando de Soto: A Brief Biography," in Clayton, Knight, and Moore, *De Soto Chronicles,* 1:421–59. A recent longer biography is David Ewing Duncan, *Hernando de Soto: A Savage Quest in the Americas* (New York: Crown Publishers, 1995).

36. The Soto contract is translated in Clayton, Knight, and Moore, *De Soto Chronicles,* 1:359–65.

37. Bolton, *Coronado,* 17–25. Mendoza's instructions and fray Marcos's report appear in Hammond and Rey, *Narratives of the Coronado Expedition,* 58–82, and in Spanish and English in Cleve Hallenbeck, *The Journey of Fray Marcos de Niza,* ed. David J. Weber (Dallas: Southern Methodist University Press, 1987). See also Fray Angélico Chávez, *Coronado's Friars* (Washington, D.C.: Academy of American Franciscan History, 1968), 10–11. Aiton, *Antonio de Mendoza,* 137. Gerhard, *North Frontier,* 94–95.

38. Hammond and Rey, *Narratives of the Coronado Expedition*, 75–77. The earlier quotation is on p. 64. Maureen Ahern, "The Cross and the Gourd: The Appropriation of Ritual Signs in the *Relaciones* of Alvar Núñez Cabeza de Vaca and Fray Marcos de Niza," in Jerry Williams and Robert Lewis, eds., *Early Images of the Americas* (Tucson: University of Arizona Press, 1993), 215–44. Bolton, *Coronado,* 25–39.

39. Hammond and Rey, *Narratives of the Coronado Expedition*, 145, 198–99.

CHAPTER 2

Initial quotation from Hammond and Rey, *Narratives of the Coronado Expedition,* 175.

1. Among English translations of the *Requerimiento* is Charles Gibson, ed., *The Spanish Tradition in America* (New York: Harper and Row, 1968). Colin M. MacLachlan, *Spain's Empire in the New World: The Role of Ideas in Institutional and Social Change* (Berkeley: University of California Press, 1988), 30–31.

2. "Traslado de las Nuevas," in Hammond and Rey, *Narratives of the Coronado Expedition,* 180, 181. Bolton, *Coronado,* 95–132. Although Bolton's 1949 narrative has remained the standard, another fast-paced account is A. Grove Day, *Coronado's Quest: The Discovery of the Southwestern States* (Berkeley: University of California Press, 1940). Janet LeCompte offers a judgmental review of the expedition, condemning Spanish arrogance, atrocities, incompetence, and insensitivity, in "Coronado and Conquest," *NMHR* 64 (July 1989), 279–304. Other accounts include Stewart L. Udall, *Majestic Journey: Coronado's Inland Empire* (Santa Fe: Museum of New Mexico Press, 1995), and *CETN.*

3. Hammond and Rey, *Narratives of the Coronado Expedition,* 78–79.

4. Chávez, *Coronado's Friars,* straightens out not only the number of Franciscans who went on the expedition, but also who they were.

5. Hammond and Rey, *Narratives of the Coronado Expedition,* 170, 208, 199. For a deft summary of the long, unresolved debate about whether fray Marcos ever saw Cíbola in 1539, see Weber's introduction to Hallenbeck, *Journey of Fray Marcos de Niza,* xix-xxvii. Accepting the friar's word that he did, Madeleine Turrell Rodack, "Cíbola, from Fray Marcos to Coronado," in *CETN,* 102–15, argues that the pueblo he first saw was Kiakima, not Hawikuh. The battle, however, likely took place at Hawikuh, as most historians have surmised. Zuni scholar Edmund J. Ladd, "Zuni on the Day the Men in Metal Arrived," in *CETN,* 225–33, agrees, explaining the summer-solstice ceremonial Coronado unknowingly interrupted.

About fray Marcos's text as a window on Native life, see Daniel T. Reff, "Anthropological Analysis of Exploration Texts: Cultural Discourse and the Ethnological Import of Fray Marcos de Niza's Journey to Cibola," *American Anthropologist* 93 (1991), 636–55.

6. Richard Flint, "Armas de la Tierra: The Mexican Indian Component of Coronado Expedition Material Culture," in *CETN,* 57–70. "The character of the Coronado expedition and its inventory of goods," Flint offers, "must have been decidedly Mexican Indian" (61).

7. Ann F. Ramenofsky, "The Problem of Introduced Infectious Diseases in New Mexico: A.D. 1540–1680," *JAR* 52 (Summer 1996), 161–84. The most comprehensive work about the Pueblo peoples is Alfonso Ortiz, ed., *Southwest,* vol. 9 of *Handbook of North American Indians,* gen. ed. William C. Sturtevant (Washington, D.C.: Smithsonian Institution Press, 1979), and about the region's non-Pueblo groups, Alfonso Ortiz, ed., *Southwest,* vol. 10 of the same *Handbook* (1983). More recent is Cárroll L. Riley, *Rio del Norte: People of the Upper Rio Grande from Earliest Times to the Pueblo Revolt* (Salt Lake City: University of Utah Press, 1995). General surveys include Bertha P. Dutton, *American Indians of the Southwest* (Albuquerque: University of New Mexico Press, 1983), and Stephen Trimble, *The People: Indians of the American Southwest* (Santa Fe: School of American Research, 1995). Two studies by Pueblo Indian scholars are Edward P. Dozier, *The Pueblo Indians of North America* (New York: Holt, Rinehart and Winston, 1970), and Joe S. Sando, *Pueblo Nations: Eight Centuries of Pueblo Indian History* (Santa Fe: Clear Light Publishers, 1992).

When referring to the people or to a proper place-name like Pecos Pueblo, I have capitalized Pueblo; otherwise, in describing their communities, I have left pueblo lowercase.

8. Hammond and Rey, *Narratives of the Coronado Expedition,* 175, 170.

9. Hammond and Rey, *Narratives of the Coronado Expedition,* 253.

10. Hammond and Rey, *Narratives of the Coronado Expedition,* 218.

11. Hammond and Rey, *Narratives of the Coronado Expedition,* 256–57. Jonathan Haas, "Warfare among the Pueblos: Myth, History, and Ethnography," *Ethnohistory* 44 (Spring 1997), 235–61.

12. Quoted in Chávez, *Coronado's Friars,* 51–52, and Hammond and Rey, *Narratives of the Coronado Expedition,* 184. Chávez discusses the testy Padilla's background and obsession with the Seven Cities of Antilia.

13. Richard Flint, "Great Cruelties Have Been Reported: The 1544 Investigation of the Coronado Expedition" (Ph.D. diss., University of New Mexico, 1999). For context, see Bolton, *Coronado,* 363–81.

14. Troyano's testimony in Flint, "Great Cruelties." Bolton, *Coronado,* 179–230.

15. Riley, *Rio del Norte,* 173–81, makes every effort to identify Tiguex towns with known archaeological sites.

16. Hammond and Rey, *Narratives of the Coronado Expedition,* 221, 290. The big river and its people as described by El Turco, if not the abundance of gold and silver, sounded a lot like the Mississippi and the populous chiefdoms then occupying its banks. Thus, Riley assumes (*Rio del Norte,* 196), El Turco's description was based largely on fact.

17. Hammond and Rey, *Narratives of the Coronado Expedition,* 235–36.

18. Quoted by Bolton, *Coronado,* 265, who revised slightly the translation of Hammond and Rey, *Narratives of the Coronado Expedition,* 239. There is still disagreement about who these Teyas were. Dolores A. Gunnerson, *The Jicarilla Apaches: A Study in Survival* (DeKalb: Northern Illinois University Press, 1974), 17–26, believes they were Apachean like the Querechos, pointing out that the two groups lived exactly alike, even though purportedly enemies. A more recent study, however, confirms Bolton's surmise that the Teyas were

probably ancestral Jumanos, a people who figured peripherally in the history of seventeenth-century New Mexico. Nancy P. Hickerson, *The Jumanos: Hunters and Traders of the South Plains* (Austin: University of Texas Press, 1994), 21–29. Bolton, *Coronado,* 256–69. Linguist Hickerson has also convinced archaeologist Riley, *Rio del Norte,* 190–91.

Although Bolton and others reckoned that the Coronado landmark barranca was Palo Duro Canyon, others still argue for more southerly gashes. Udall, *Majestic Journey,* 106–16, 122, discusses some of the alternatives. A loose concentration of artifacts from the period, including more than thirty copper crossbow dart tips, would seem to mark a Coronado campsite at the Jimmy Owens Site in Blanco Canyon, near present-day Floydada, Texas. What can be known and guessed about the expedition's route on the plains is the stuff of Part V of *CETN,* 280–385. See also John Miller Morris, *El Llano Estacado: Exploration and Imagination on the High Plains of Texas and New Mexico, 1536–1860* (Austin: Texas State Historical Association, 1997).

19. Hammond and Rey, *Narratives of the Coronado Expedition,* 305. Bolton, *Coronado,* 282–304.

20. Projecting his sympathy for invaded peoples, Riley (*Rio del Norte,* 197) lauds El Turco, whom he identifies as a proto-Pawnee. "Redefined in our own modern terms, Turk seems an authentic American patriot and hero with a vision that transcended narrow tribal boundaries to incorporate the greater good for his own culture world. Few of the Spaniards could claim such breadth of outlook and greatness of spirit."

21. Bolton, *Coronado,* 62, 318, 326–36, 377, 379; Hammond and Rey, *Narratives of the Coronado Expedition,* 12, 111. Flint, "Great Cruelties," challenges as apocryphal the story that Hozes gave birth to another child during the expedition, as Bolton believed.

22. Chávez, *Coronado's Friars,* 28–29, 41–43, 58–63; Bolton, *Coronado,* 335–42.

23. Chávez, *Coronado's Friars,* 64–74, sifting through the chronicles, weighs what others had to say about the deaths of Padilla and Ubeda.

24. Hammond and Rey, *Narratives of the Coronado Expedition,* 215–16.

25. Hammond and Rey, *Narratives of the Coronado Expedition,* 279.

26. For a brief and lively narrative of the Mixtón War, see Aiton, *Antonio de Mendoza,* 137–58.

27. Although Aiton (*Antonio de Mendoza,* 131) and many other scholars, following a mistaken chronicler, identify Cabrillo as Portuguese, Harry Kelsey, *Juan Rodríguez Cabrillo* (San Marino: Huntington Library, 1986), 3–21, demonstrates convincingly that he was a Spaniard, probably from Sevilla.

28. Kelsey, *Juan Rodríguez Cabrillo,* 70–76, 105–12.

29. "Relation of the Voyage of Juan Rodríguez Cabrillo, 1542–1543," in Herbert Eugene Bolton, ed., *Spanish Exploration in the Southwest, 1542–1706* (1908; repr. New York: Barnes and Noble, 1967), 23. Original logs of the Cabrillo voyage have been lost. Kelsey (*Juan Rodríguez Cabrillo,* 112–22, 168–70) describes how the surviving abbreviated summary came to be.

30. "Relation of the Voyage," 27, 28, 30. Kelsey, *Juan Rodríguez Cabrillo,* 141–63.

31. "Relation of the Voyage," 31, 32.

32. Vargas quoted by Kelsey, *Juan Rodríguez Cabrillo,* 158. According to the "Relation of the Voyage," 33, Cabrillo suffered a fall "from which he broke an arm near the shoulder."

33. William Lytle Schurz, *The Manila Galleon* (New York: E. P. Dutton, 1939), 21, 218. Morison, *Southern Voyages,* 456, 493. Aiton, *Antonio de Mendoza,* 134–35. Consuelo Varela, ed., *El viaje de don Ruy López de Villalobos a las islas del Poniente, 1542–1548* (Milan: Instituto Editoriale Cisalpino-La Goliardica, 1983).

34. For a full account of the Soto venture, vigorously told, see Duncan, *Hernando de Soto,* 215–425.

35. Duncan, *Hernando de Soto,* 295–96.

36. Chipman, *Spanish Texas,* 17, 40–41. Bolton, *Coronado,* 275–81, 303–304. Gloria A. Young and Michael P. Hoffman, eds., *The Expedition of Hernando de Soto West of the Mississippi, 1541–1543* (Fayetteville: University of Arkansas Press, 1993). Regarding the Soto landing site, see Jerald T. Milanich and Charles Hudson, *Hernando de Soto and the Indians of Florida* (Gainesville: University Press of Florida, 1993), 39–70, and on the expedition in general, Clayton, Knight, and Moore, *De Soto Chronicles;* the series of articles in *CC2,* 3–222; and Weddle, *Spanish Sea,* 208–33.

37. This comparison is suggested by Richard Flint, "The Coronado and de Soto Expeditions: A Contrast in Attitudes or Differences in External Conditions?" *El Viaje* (Coronado Trail Association Newsletter) 1:2 (April 1992), 4–8.

38. See Aiton, *Antonio de Mendoza.*

39. See Flint, "Great Cruelties."

40. Bolton, *Coronado,* 363–409.

41. Aiton, *Antonio de Mendoza,* 133–34, mentions that the ships and men were held in Peru. James Lockhart, *Spanish Peru, 1532–1560: A Colonial Society* (Madison: University of Wisconsin Press, 1968), 127, describes the activities of "a seaman like the Genoese Bartolomé Ferrer, who in 1547 had small commercial interests in various places on the coast from Mexico to Peru, owned a boat in Nicaragua, and accepted commissions from people in Trujillo to sell used clothes in Lima." Lockhart's identification of Ferrer as Genoese is at variance with Kelsey, who says "Ferrer was from the Levantine coast of Spain" (*Juan Rodríguez Cabrillo,* 112).

42. Paul E. Hoffman, *A New Andalucia and a Way to the Orient: The American Southeast during the Sixteenth Century* (Baton Rouge: Louisiana State University Press, 1990), 144–81, and Weddle, *Spanish Sea,* 251–84, set the Luna y Arrellano attempt in context. For Juan Vázquez de Coronado and the conquest of Costa Rica, see the sources cited by Robert M. Carmack, "The Spanish Conquest of Central America: Comparative Cases from Guatemala and Costa Rica," in *CC3,* 389–409.

43. Chávez, *Coronado's Friars,* 75–76. I owe to Richard Flint the reference to fray Marcos's presence with Mendoza's army during the Mixtón War; it is from Antonio Tello,

Crónica miscelánea de la Santa Provincia de Xalisco por fray Antonio Tello, Libro Segundo [c. 1650], 2 vols. (Guadalajara: Universidad de Guadalajara, 1968), 2:317.

CHAPTER 3

The opening quotations are from Joaquín García Icazbalceta, ed., *Nueva colección de documentos para la historia de México*, 5 vols. [1886–92] (Mexico City: Editorial Salvador Chávez Hayhoe, 1941), 2:217–28, and George P. Hammond and Agapito Rey, eds., *The Rediscovery of New Mexico, 1580–1594: The Explorations of Chamuscado, Espejo, Castaño de Sosa, Morlete, and Leyva de Bonilla and Humaña* (Albuquerque: University of New Mexico Press, 1966), 232.

1. Philip Wayne Powell, *Mexico's Miguel Caldera: The Taming of America's First Frontier, 1548–1597* (Tucson: University of Arizona Press, 1977), 3–11 (quotation, 95).

2. Peter J. Bakewell, *Silver Mining and Society in Colonial Mexico: Zacatecas, 1546–1700* (Cambridge: Cambridge University Press, 1971), 1–16. Philip Wayne Powell, *Soldiers, Indians, and Silver: The Northward Advance of New Spain, 1550–1600* (Berkeley: University of California Press, 1952), 3–15, and *Mexico's Miguel Caldera*, 12.

3. Powell, *Mexico's Miguel Caldera*, 23.

4. Thomas H. Naylor and Charles W. Polzer, eds., *The Presidio and Militia on the Northern Frontier of New Spain: A Documentary History, Volume One, 1570–1700* (Tucson: University of Arizona Press, 1986), offer analysis and documents illustrating the evolution of this conspicuous frontier institution.

5. For an informative discussion of how Spaniards used the term Chichimeca and why, see Charlotte M. Gradie, "Discovering the Chichimecas," *The Americas* 51 (July 1994), 67–88.

6. Powell, *Soldiers, Indians, and Silver*, 48.

7. Employing Lyon, *Enterprise of Florida;* Hoffman, *New Andalucia;* Weddle, *Spanish Sea;* and printed primary sources, Weber, *Spanish Frontier*, 60–71, offers a neat summary of Florida's founding. Menéndez's quote is from Lyon, *Enterprise of Florida*, 126–27. Entry for Saint Augustine (Amy Turner Bushnell) in Barbara A. Tenenbaum, ed., *Encyclopedia of Latin American History and Culture*, 5 vols. (New York: Charles Scribner's Sons, 1996).

8. Weber, *Spanish Frontier*, 71; Schurz, *Manila Galleon*, 220; and entries for Urdaneta (W. Michael Mathes) and López de Legazpi (Robert Himmerich y Valencia) in Tenenbaum, *Encyclopedia*.

9. Quoted by Schurz, *Manila Galleon*, 23, 26.

10. Gemelli Careri quoted by Schurz, *Manila Galleon*, 253.

11. The quotation is from the entry for Manila Galleon (William McCarthy) in Tenenbaum, *Encyclopedia*. See also Eugene Lyon, "Track of the Manila Galleons," and William M. Mathers, "*Nuestra Señora de la Concepción,*" *National Geographic* 178:3 (September 1990), 5–37 and 39–53.

12. W. Michael Mathes, *Vizcaíno and Spanish Expansion in the Pacific Ocean, 1580–1630* (San Francisco: California Historical Society, 1968), 11–12; Peter Gerhard, *Pirates of the Pacific, 1575–1742* (1960; repr., Lincoln: University of Nebraska Press, 1990), 60–77; Schurz, *Manila Galleon,* 303–305; and Powell, *Mexico's Miguel Caldera,* 64.

13. Flint, "Great Cruelties"; Ralph H. Vigil, *Alonso de Zorita, Royal Judge and Christian Humanist, 1512–1585* (Norman: University of Oklahoma Press, 1987), 213–21; and Powell, *Mexico's Miguel Caldera,* 69–70. Fray Angélico Chávez, ed., *The Oroz Codez* (Washington, D.C.: Academy of American Franciscan History, 1972), 273–77; García Icazbalceta, *Nueva Colección,* 2:xviii-xx; and Kieran McCarty, "Franciscans North from Mexico, 1527–1580," in Francisco Morales, ed., *Franciscan Presence in the Americas: Essays on the Activities of the Franciscan Friars in the Americas, 1492–1900* (Washington, D.C.: Academy of American Franciscan History, 1983), 253–54.

14. Powell, *Mexico's Miguel Caldera,* 105–46. Powell's listing of captains, including Caldera, who served as provisioners of Chichimecas in various localities (*Soldiers, Indians, and Silver,* 221) conveys an idea of the scope of the peace program.

15. On Santa Bárbara, see Chantal Cramaussel, *La Provincia de Santa Bárbara en Nueva Vizcaya, 1563–1631* (Chihuahua: Universidad Autónoma de Ciudad Juárez, 1990); also Gerhard, North Frontier, 236–38; Bakewell, *Silver Mining,* 23–30; and J. Lloyd Mecham, *Francisco de Ibarra and Nueva Vizcaya* (1927; repr., New York: Greenwood Press, 1968), 189–90, 230–31.

16. Bustamante quoted in Hammond and Rey, *Rediscovery,* 128.

17. Hammond and Rey, *Rediscovery,* 6–15, 67–150. The viceroy alludes to his permission on p. 123. Chávez, *Oroz Codex,* 336–40. Riley, *Rio del Norte,* 223–39, tries to sort out which Indian groups this and the succeeding Espejo party made contact with. Jerry R. Craddock offers a plea for "respectable editions of the original texts" in his "Philological Notes on the Hammond and Rey Translation of the '[Relación de la] Entrada que hizo en el Nuevo México Francisco Sánchez Chamuscado en junio de [15]81' by Hernán Gallegos, Notary of the Expedition," *Romance Philology* 49 (May 1996), 351–63.

18. Hammond and Rey, *Rediscovery,* 15–28, 153–242. Pérez de Luján's words are found on p. 206.

19. Oroz quoted in Hammond and Rey, *Rediscovery,* 236. Chávez, *Oroz Codex,* 17–18. The Pecos Indian, when baptized, took the name of his Franciscan guardian, Pedro Oroz.

20. Felipe II to the Conde de Coruña, Madrid, Apr. 19, 1583, Archivo General de Indias (AGI), Sevilla, Spain, Audiencia de México 1064.

21. The classic description of the northern moguls is Francois Chevalier, *Land and Society in Colonial Mexico: The Great Hacienda,* trans. Alvin Eustis, ed. Lesley Byrd Simpson (Berkeley: University of California Press, 1966), 148–84.

22. Powell, *Mexico's Miguel Caldera,* 178–86, 238–43, 255–66. It may be that Powell magnifies his subject's role. Still, he argues convincingly that Caldera epitomized his time and place. Marc Simmons, *The Last Conquistador: Juan de Oñate and the Settling of the Far Southwest* (Norman: University of Oklahoma Press, 1991), while emphasizing Oñate's part in the founding of San Luis Potosí, quotes Powell questioningly.

CHAPTER 4

The initial quotation appears in George P. Hammond and Agapito Rey, eds., *Don Juan de Oñate, Colonizer of New Mexico, 1595–1628,* 2 vols. (Albuquerque: University of New Mexico Press, 1953), 2:1042–43.

1. Vito Alessio Robles, *Francisco de Urdiñola y el norte de la Nueva España* (1931; repr., Mexico City: Editorial Porrúa, 1981), 191–98, 221–25; Chevalier, *Land and Society,* 157–58; Simmons, *Last Conquistador,* 55–58. Acquitted in 1599, Urdiñola went on to serve for a decade (1603-c.1613) as governor of Nueva Vizcaya, that sprawling jurisdiction that dated from 1563 and covered the present-day Mexican states of Durango and Chihuahua. See also Oakah L. Jones, Jr., *Nueva Vizcaya: Heartland of the Spanish Frontier* (Albuquerque: University of New Mexico Press, 1988), 75–80.

In addition to sources cited above regarding the Oñate expedition, see Carroll L. Riley, *The Kachina and the Cross: Indians and Spaniards in the Early Southwest* (Salt Lake City: University of Utah Press, 1999), 37–49, 260–63, and an Oñate theme issue of the *Colonial Latin American Historical Review* 7 (Spring 1998).

2. Hammond and Rey, *Rediscovery,* 28–48, 245–320; Albert H. Schroeder and Dan S. Matson, eds., *A Colony on the Move: Gaspar Castaño de Sosa's Journal, 1590–1591* (Santa Fe: School of American Research, 1965); Riley, *Rio del Norte,* 241–44; and Powell, *Soldiers, Indians, and Silver,* 193–94. The dramatic assault of Castaño's renegade corps on the pueblo of Pecos (December 31, 1590), and the temporary flight of its inhabitants, probably influenced the Pueblos' guarded but passive reception of Oñate in 1598. Castaño's description of Pecos is the best of any pueblo during the colonial period.

3. It is probable that some of New Mexico's first and subsequent colonists were indeed crypto-Jews. Circumstantial evidence also suggests the same of Castaño de Sosa and certain of his people. Stanley M. Hordes, "The Sephardic Legacy in New Mexico: A History of the Crypto-Jews," *Journal of the West* (October 1996), 82–90. The Viceroy Conde de Monterrey (February 28, 1696), quoted in Hammond and Rey, *Don Juan de Oñate,* 1:82–85, mentions the competition for colonist recruits. Simmons, in *Last Conquistador,* the standard narrative, does not speculate about crypto-Jewish recruits.

4. Hammond and Rey, *Don Juan de Oñate,* 1:199–308, 321, 375–82, 385, 542. Riley (*Kachina and the Cross,* 49) suggests that doña Inés might have been the Native American woman Juan Troyano had brought back from Tierra Nueva in 1542, who by 1598 would have been in her seventies.

5. Hammond and Rey, *Don Juan de Oñate,* 1:171. David H. Snow, *New Mexico's First Colonists: The 1597–1600 Enlistments for New Mexico under Juan de Oñate, Adelantado and Gobernador* (Albuquerque: Hispanic Genealogical Research Center of New Mexico, 1998). Carefully studying mostly published primary documents about the two contingents, Snow lists some 560 persons, named and unnamed, excluding religious personnel.

6. Hammond and Rey, *Don Juan de Oñate,* 1:269, 284–85, 293, 297. Although he is Arechuleta in the Oñate muster, his New Mexico family dropped the first e, becoming Archuleta.

7. Hammond and Rey, *Rediscovery*, 319.

8. Hammond and Rey, *Don Juan de Oñate*, 1:221, 335.

9. Ramón A. Gutiérrez, *When Jesus Came, the Corn Mothers Went Away: Marriage, Sexuality, and Power in New Mexico, 1500–1846* (Stanford: Stanford University Press, 1991), 47–49, 355 n. 28, interprets Oñate's 1598 entry as "conquest theater."

10. Gaspar Pérez de Villagrá, *Historia de la Nueva México, 1610,* ed. Miguel Encinias, Alfred Rodríguez, and Joseph P. Sánchez (Albuquerque: University of New Mexico Press, 1992). Simmons, *Last Conquistador,* 120–23.

11. Pérez de Villagrá, *Historia,* 234.

12. Hammond and Rey, *Don Juan de Oñate,* 1:343.

13. Oñate's concession quoted in John L. Kessell, *Kiva, Cross, and Crown: The Pecos Indians and New Mexico, 1540–1840* (Washington, D.C.: National Park Service, 1979), 79–80.

14. Quotations from Hammond and Rey, *Don Juan de Oñate,* 1:401–402. Jerry R. Craddock offers a reconciled Spanish text based on two manuscript copies of the lost original report in "Juan de Oñate in Quivira," *Journal of the Southwest* 40 (Winter 1998), 481–540.

15. Pérez de Villagrá, *Historia,* 180.

16. Act of obedience quoted in Hammond and Rey, *Don Juan de Oñate,* 1:355. Pérez de Villagrá, *Historia,* 212.

17. Fray Alonso Martínez quoted in Pérez de Villagrá, *Historia,* 223.

18. Hammond and Rey, *Don Juan de Oñate,* 2:1127.

19. Pérez de Villagrá, *Historia,* 75, 242. Fray Angélico Chávez, *Origins of New Mexico Families: A Genealogy of the Spanish Colonial Period,* rev. ed. (Santa Fe: Museum of New Mexico Press, 1992), 6. José Antonio Esquibel, "Doña Eufemia, La Valerosa: The Great Martesia of Oñate's Colony," *Herencia* 2:2 (April 1994), 19–28.

20. Pérez de Villagrá, *Historia,* 265–66. Simmons, *Last Conquistador,* 128–46. Nancy P. Hickerson, "The *Servicios* of Vicente de Zaldívar: New Light on the Jumano War of 1601," *Ethnohistory* 43 (Winter 1966), 130.

21. Pérez de Villagrá, *Historia,* 298.

22. Hammond and Rey, *Don Juan de Oñate,* 1:477–78. Not surprisingly, Gaspar Pérez de Villagrá chose not to mention in his *Historia* the trial and punishment of Acoma prisoners.

23. Hammond and Rey, *Don Juan de Oñate,* 1:459, 478.

24. Hickerson, "*Servicios* of Vicente de Zaldívar," 130–31, 134–40. Citing documentary and archaeological evidence, Hickerson places most of the action at the pueblo called Cueloce, later Las Humanas, and still later Gran Quivira. Ginés de Herrera Horta quoted in Hammond and Rey, *Don Juan de Oñate,* 2:650.

25. Hammond and Rey, *Don Juan de Oñate,* 1:514–79. *When Cultures Meet: Remembering San Gabriel del Yunge Oweenge, Papers from the October 20, 1984 Conference Held at San Juan Pueblo, New Mexico* (Santa Fe: Sunstone Press, 1987).

26. Quoted in Hammond and Rey, *Don Juan de Oñate,* 2:713.

27. Cramaussel, *La Provincia de Santa Bárbara,* 49–50. Hammond and Rey, *Don Juan de Oñate,* 2:672–739, 775–81.

28. Fray Angélico Chávez, "The Carpenter Pueblo," *New Mexico Magazine* 49 (September-October 1971), 26–33. Decree of Felipe III quoted in Hammond and Rey, *Don Juan de Oñate,* 2:994–95.

29. Quoted in Hammond and Rey, *Don Juan de Oñate,* 2:1007, 1:54.

30. Quoted in Hammond and Rey, *Don Juan de Oñate,* 2:1009–11, 1012–31.

31. Quoted in Frederick Webb Hodge, George P. Hammond, and Agapito Rey, eds., *Fray Alonso de Benavides' Revised Memorial of 1634* (Albuquerque: University of New Mexico Press, 1945), 61.

32. Mathes, *Vizcaíno,* 18–24; Schurz, *Manila Galleon,* 305–13; and Gerhard, *Pirates,* 81–94.

33. Mathes, *Vizcaíno,* 25–43. Although Schurz, Gerhard, and others placed Vizcaíno aboard the unlucky *Santa Ana* in 1587, Mathes (29–30 n. 14) concludes that he was not.

34. The Conde de Monterrey in Donald C. Cutter, ed., *The California Coast: A Bilingual Edition of Documents from the Sutro Collection* (Norman: University of Oklahoma Press, 1969), 99. Mathes, *Vizcaíno,* 44–53.

35. Diary of Vizcaíno in Bolton, *Spanish Exploration,* 82. Mathes, *Vizcaíno,* 54–92.

36. Diary of Vizcaíno in Bolton, *Spanish Exploration,* 87–88.

37. Vizcaíno in Cutter, *California Coast,* 107–9.

38. Diary of Vizcaíno in Bolton, *Spanish Exploration,* 96, 97.

39. Entry for Vizcaíno (W. Michael Mathes) in Tenenbaum, *Encyclopedia;* Mathes, *Vizcaíno,* 108–70.

40. Hammond and Rey, *Don Juan de Oñate,* 2:1032–39; Oñate quoted on p. 1042.

41. Velasco quoted in Hammond and Rey, *Don Juan de Oñate,* 2:1081. France V. Scholes, "Juan Martínez de Montoya, Settler and Conquistador of New Mexico," *NMHR* 19 (October 1944), 337–42. The documents upon which this article is based, in private hands when Scholes consulted them, in 1994 came into the possession of the Museum of New Mexico, Santa Fe. Hammond and Rey, *Don Juan de Oñate,* 1:542. Simmons, *Last Conquistador,* 180–82.

42. Velasco quoted in Hammond and Rey, *Don Juan de Oñate,* 2:1067; Felipe III quoted in Hammond and Rey, *Don Juan de Oñate,* 2:1039.

43. Simmons, *Last Conquistador,* 183–95. The documents are in Hammond and Rey, *Don Juan de Oñate,* 2:1109–57.

44. John Stevens, *A New Spanish and English Dictionary* (London: George Sawbridge, 1706).

CHAPTER 5

The lead quotation is from France V. Scholes, *Church and State in New Mexico, 1610–1650* (Albuquerque: University of New Mexico Press, 1937), 23.

1. France V. Scholes, "Civil Government and Society in New Mexico in the Seventeenth Century," *NMHR* 10 (April 1935), 71–111, and "Royal Treasury Records Relating to the Province of New Mexico, 1596–1683," *NMHR* 50 (January and April 1975), 5–23, 139–64. Regarding the chronology, personnel, and institutions of seventeenth-century New Mexico, the works of Scholes, most of which appeared singly or serially in *NMHR*, are basic. Other studies include Jack D. Forbes, *Apache, Navaho, and Spaniard*, 2d ed. (Norman: University of Oklahoma Press, 1994); Kessell, *Kiva, Cross, and Crown;* Gutiérrez, *When Jesus Came;* and Andrew L. Knaut, *The Pueblo Revolt of 1680: Conquest and Resistance in Seventeenth-Century New Mexico* (Norman: University of Oklahoma Press, 1995). Charles Wilson Hackett, ed., *Historical Documents Relating to New Mexico, Nueva Vizcaya, and Approaches Thereto, to 1773,* vol. 3 (Washington, D.C.: Carnegie Institution, 1937), is a rich potpourri of translated primary sources. And for a recent and comprehensive ethnohistorical analysis of the period and a critical review of pertinent scholarship, see Riley, *Kachina and the Cross.*

2. Hammond and Rey, *Don Juan de Oñate,* 1:323, 346 (Velasco's warning to Peralta is in 2:1102–103). Scholes, *Church and State,* 19–21. To date, little is known of Peralta's life or career before his appointment to the New Mexico post.

3. The viceroy's instructions to Peralta appear in Hammond and Rey, *Don Juan de Oñate,* 2:1087–91. Scholes, "Juan Martínez de Montoya," 341. See also Linda Tigges, ed., *Santa Fe Historic Plaza Study,* vols. 1–4 (Santa Fe: City Planning Department, 1990–92). Because the southside location soon became the so-called barrio of Analco, home to the Mexican Indian servant community, it may be that Martínez de Montoya, on Oñate's orders, settled Mexican Indians there from the beginning. In the Spanish hierarchy of settlements, a villa stood second, behind a ciudad, or city.

4. The prime source for the Peralta-Ordoñez clash is Scholes, *Church and State,* 19–68.

5. Quoted by Scholes, *Church and State,* 31.

6. Quoted by Scholes, *Church and State,* 34.

7. The existing documentary record does not support Gutiérrez's implication (*When Jesus Came,* 75–76, 114, 123, 127–28, 209) that sexual impropriety or cruelty were usual behaviors among New Mexico's seventeenth-century Franciscans.

8. On the establishment and functioning of the Inquisition, see France V. Scholes, "The First Decade of the Inquisition in New Mexico," *NMHR,* 10 (July 1935), 195–241; *Church and State;* and *Troublous Times in New Mexico, 1659–1670* (Albuquerque: University of New Mexico Press, 1942).

9. This vigorous interaction is described by Forbes, *Apache, Navaho, and Spaniard,* and by pertinent articles in Ortiz, *Southwest,* vol. 10.

10. Hodge, Hammond, and Rey, *Fray Alonso de Benavides' Revised Memorial.* Cyprian J. Lynch, ed., and Peter P. Forrestal, trans., *Benavides' Memorial of 1630* (Washington, D.C.: Academy of American Franciscan History, 1954), and Baker H. Morrow, ed., *A Harvest of*

Reluctant Souls: The Memorial of Fray Alonso de Benavides, 1630 (Niwot: University Press of Colorado, 1996).

11. Reminding his readers that Benavides's writings are "accounts of the Franciscan enterprise in New Mexico and not ethnographies per se," Daniel T. Reff, "Contextualizing Missionary Discourse: The Benavides *Memorials* of 1630 and 1634," *JAR* 50 (Spring 1996), 51–67, places them neatly in their cultural-historical contexts.

12. John L. Kessell, "Miracles or Mystery: María de Agreda's Ministry to the Jumano Indians of the Southwest in the 1620s," in Ferenc Morton Szasz, ed., *Great Mysteries of the West* (Golden, Colo.: Fulcrum Publishing, 1993), 121–44, and Nancy Parrott Hickerson, "The Visits of the 'Lady in Blue': An Episode in the History of the South Plains, 1629," *JAR* 46 (Spring 1990), 67–90.

13. Quoted by Hodge, Hammond, and Rey, *Fray Alonso de Benavides' Revised Memorial,* 197.

14. For a description of the Franciscan ideal, see, in addition to the contemporary Benavides *Memorials,* Ross G. Montgomery, Watson Smith, and John O. Brew, *Franciscan Awatovi* (Cambridge, Mass.: Peabody Museum, 1949). France V. Scholes and Lansing B. Bloom, "Friar Personnel and Mission Chronology, 1598–1629," *NMHR* 19 (October 1944), 319–36, and 20 (January 1945), 58–82. On the terms *mission* and *doctrina,* see the informative discussion of Amy Turner Bushnell, *Situado and Sabana: Spain's Support System for the Presidio and Mission Provinces of Florida* (New York: American Museum of Natural History, 1994), 21–23.

15. James E. Ivey, "Convento Kivas in the Missions of New Mexico," *NMHR* 73 (April 1998), 121–52.

16. Hodge, Hammond, and Rey, *Fray Alonso de Benavides' Revised Memorial,* 77–80, 300 n. 107. Scholes, *Church and State,* 107–108.

17. Scholes details the Rosas affair and its aftermath in *Church and State,* 115–91 (quotation, 129).

18. Quoted by Scholes, *Church and State,* 173. Chávez, *Origins of New Mexico Families,* 6, 10, 83.

19. Quoted by Scholes, *Church and State,* 176.

20. Gerhard, *North Frontier,* 159. Scholes, "Civil Government and Society," 96–98.

21. David H. Snow, "A Note on Encomienda Economics in Seventeenth-Century New Mexico," in Marta E. Weigle, ed., *Hispanic Arts and Ethnohistory in the Southwest* (Santa Fe: Ancient City Press, 1983), 347–57.

22. James E. Ivey, "Pueblo and Estancia: The Spanish Presence in the Pueblo, A.D. 1620–1680," in Bradley J. Vierra, ed., *Current Research on the Late Prehistory and Early History of New Mexico* (Albuquerque: New Mexico Archaeological Council, 1992), 221–26, points out the importance of Franciscan mission estancias, which appear to have outnumbered private estancias. Neither Marc Simmons, "Settlement Patterns and Village Plans in Colonial New Mexico," *Journal of the West* 8 (January 1969), 7–21, nor Malcolm Ebright, *Land Grants and Lawsuits in Northern New Mexico* (Albuquerque: University of New Mexico Press, 1994),

has much to say about the seventeenth century. Curiously, not a single pre-1680 land or encomienda title from New Mexico has yet come to light, although contemporary documents allude to their existence. The notion that all were destroyed in the Pueblo revolt of 1680 seems lame, since surviving refugees fleeing the colony likely carried such documents on their persons.

23. France V. Scholes, "The Supply Service of the New Mexican Missions in the Seventeenth Century," *NMHR* 5 (January, April, and July 1930), 93–115, 186–210, 386–404. See also Rick Hendricks and Gerald J. Mandell, "Juan Manso, Frontier Entrepreneur," *NMHR* 75 (July 2000), 339–67.

24. Since Pedro Lucero de Godoy held in encomienda twenty-four households in the pueblo of Pecos with its trading ties to the Plains Apaches, he may be the don Pedro for whom the settlement was named.

25. Quoted by John L. Kessell, "Diego Romero, the Plains Apaches, and the Inquisition," *The American West* 15 (May-June 1978), 14. Riley, *Kachina and the Cross*, 166–68.

26. Chávez, *Origins of New Mexico Families*, 36, 59–60, 87. Scholes, *Troublous Times*, relates in fascinating detail the circumstances of the Inquisition's cases against López de Mendizábal and the others. And Riley (*Kachina and the Cross*, 156–85) devotes a chapter to López's governorship.

27. Kessell, "Diego Romero," 16, and Scholes, *Troublous Times*, 172–78.

28. Quoted by Kessell, *Kiva, Cross, and Crown*, 212. Scholes, "Civil Government and Society," 84–85.

29. Diego López Sambrano, 1681, quoted by John L. Kessell, "Esteban Clemente, Precursor of the Pueblo Revolt," *El Palacio* 86 (Winter 1980–81), 16–17. Riley, *Kachina and the Cross*, 172–78, 214–15.

30. Kessell, *Kiva, Cross, and Crown*, 216, 219–21. Other sources offer variant details of fray Pedro's martyrdom. Forbes, *Apache, Navaho, and Spaniard*, 150, 168.

31. Declaration of Diego López Sambrano, 1681, in Charles Wilson Hackett, ed., and Charmion Clair Shelby, trans., *Revolt of the Pueblo Indians of New Mexico and Otermín's Attempted Reconquest, 1680–1682*, 2 vols. (Albuquerque: University of New Mexico Press, 1942), 2:300–301.

32. In Hackett, *Historical Documents*, 3:108.

33. Kessell, *Kiva, Cross, and Crown*, 223–24. Hackett and Shelby, *Revolt*, ixxix-ixxxv.

34. Chávez, *Origins of New Mexico Families*, 4; Bernal, 1669, in Hackett, *Historical Documents*, 3:270; Record and list of settlers, 1681, in Hackett and Shelby, *Revolt*, 2:115.

35. Otermín quoted in Hackett and Shelby, *Revolt*, 1:9.

36. The two-volume Hackett and Shelby, *Revolt*, with lengthy historical narrative and translations of the pertinent documents, is the standard work on the Pueblo revolt of 1680. Fray Angélico Chávez, "Pohé-yemo's Representative and the Pueblo Revolt of 1680," *NMHR* 25 (April 1967), 85–126, noting contemporary allusions to a strapping, yellow-eyed black man and the leadership role played in Pueblo society by assimilated mixed-bloods, hypothesizes that a mulatto named Naranjo, standing in the shadows behind Popé, master-

minded the uprising. A recent anthology, which includes the Chávez article, is David J. Weber, ed., *What Caused the Pueblo Revolt of 1680?* (Boston: Bedford/St. Martin's, 1999).

Pueblo Indian scholars are not agreed on whether Popé was primarily a religious or a military leader. Alfonso Ortiz of San Juan Pueblo ("Popay's Leadership: A Pueblo Perspective," *El Palacio* 86 [Winter 1980–81], 18–22) sees him as the former, while Joe S. Sando of the Pueblo of Jemez (*The Pueblo Indians* [San Francisco: Indian Historian Press, 1976], 137), emphasizes that Popé "was only one of a corps of leaders, probably one of the war captains who met secretly to plan the revolt of 1680." See also Riley's discussion, *Kachina and the Cross,* 216–19.

37. Chávez, *Origins of New Mexico Families,* 4. Hackett and Shelby, *Revolt,* 1:liv-lx, 10, 97.

38. Otermín in Hackett and Shelby, *Revolt,* 1:13.

39. Richard Flint has suggested in an unpublished paper that the Mexican Indians, who lorded their higher servant status over Pueblo Indians like Juan, were objects of special loathing.

40. Otermín in Hackett and Shelby, *Revolt,* 1:23.

41. Otermín in Hackett and Shelby, *Revolt,* 1:102.

42. Ayeta and Otermín in Hackett and Shelby, *Revolt,* 1:47, 94.

43. Otermín in Hackett and Shelby, *Revolt,* 1:60–61.

44. Daniel T. Reff, "The 'Predicament of Culture' and Spanish Missionary Accounts of the Tepehuan and Pueblo Revolts," *Ethnohistory* 42 (Winter 1995), 64–90, argues that "the missionaries represented the revolts as the work of the devil rather than as millenarian movements triggered by the devastating effects of Old World disease and Spanish colonialism" (64).

CHAPTER 6

The initial quotation is from Hammond and Rey, *Revolt,* 2:21, and the second from Robert S. Weddle, *Wilderness Manhunt: The Spanish Search for La Salle* (Austin: University of Texas Press, 1973), 15.

1. Aigenler's map is enlarged and handsomely reproduced in Ernest J. Burrus, *Kino and the Cartography of Northwestern New Spain* (Tucson: Arizona Pioneers' Historical Society, 1965), following p. 12. See also Ronald L. Ives, "Adam Aigenler's Field Manual," *Journal of Geography* 52 (October 1953), 291–99. Herbert Eugene Bolton, *Rim of Christendom: A Biography of Eusebio Francisco Kino, Pacific Coast Pioneer* (New York: Macmillan, 1936), 72–75.

2. Weber, *Spanish Frontier,* 108–109. Father Pareja's published linguistic works have, unfortunately, no known New Mexico counterparts. The same Franciscan author's revealing bilingual confessional guide has been translated in Jerald T. Milanich and William C. Sturtevant, eds., *Francisco Pareja's 1613 Confessionario: A Documentary Source for Timucuan Ethnography* (Tallahassee: Florida Department of State, 1972).

3. For an idea of how differently, when compared with high-desert New Mexico, the lives of Natives, Spaniards, and Africans intertwined on the circum-Caribbean maritime periphery of Florida in the seventeenth century, see Bushnell, *Situado and Sabana,* and her

"Republic of Spaniards, Republic of Indians," in Michael Gannon, ed., *The New History of Florida* (Gainesville: University Press of Florida, 1996), 62–77. On Franciscan mission endeavor in Florida, which varied in a number of telling ways from that in New Mexico, the works of John H. Hann are distinguished, especially *A History of the Timucua Indians and Missions* (Gainesville: University Press of Florida, 1996); *Apalachee: The Land between the Rivers* (Gainesville: University Presses of Florida, 1988); and "The Missions of Spanish Florida," in Gannon, *New History,* 78–99.

4. Weber, *Spanish Frontier,* 71–73.

5. Quoted by Peter Masten Dunne, *Pioneer Black Robes on the West Coast* (Berkeley: University of California Press, 1940), 32. On the epidemic of 1693 in Sinaloa, see Daniel T. Reff, *Disease, Depopulation, and Culture Change in Northwestern New Spain, 1518–1764* (Salt Lake City: University of Utah Press, 1991), 132–38. Reff, "The Jesuit Mission Frontier in Comparative Perspective: The Reductions of the Río de la Plata and the Missions of Northwestern Mexico, 1588–1700," in *CG,* 16–31, proposes that wonder-working Jesuit baptizers found such ready acceptance because Native peoples already lived in frightening disease environments.

6. Pérez de Ribas quoted by Reff, "Contextualizing Missionary Discourse," 63 n. 1. Reff, Maureen Ahern, and Richard K. Danford, have prepared a critical, English-language edition of Pérez de Ribas's *Historia de los Triumphos: History of the Triumphs of Our Holy Faith amongst the Most Barbarous and Fierce Peoples of the New World by Andrés Pérez de Ribas* (Tucson: University of Arizona Press, 1999). Writing of the same missionary field, twentieth-century Jesuit historians—W. Eugene Shiels, Peter Masten Dunne, John Francis Bannon, Ernest J. Burrus, and Charles W. Polzer—have been little less admiring than Pérez de Ribas.

7. Charles W. Polzer, ed., "The Franciscan Entrada into Sonora, 1645–1652: A Jesuit Chronicle," *Arizona and the West* 14 (Autumn 1972), 253–78 (Pantoja quotation, 267). Luis Navarro García, *Sonora y Sinaloa en el siglo XVII* (Sevilla: Escuela de Estudios Hispano-Americanos, 1967), 67–68, 249–54.

8. Quoted in Polzer, "Franciscan Entrada," 277. Navarro García, *Sonora y Sinaloa,* 252.

9. See Reff's "Critical Introduction: The Historia and Jesuit Discourse," in Reff, Ahern, and Danford, *History of the Triumphs,* 11–46.

10. Quoted by Burrus, *Kino and the Cartography,* 10 n. 15.

11. R. Douglas Cope, "Sigüenza y Góngora, Carlos de," in Tenenbaum, *Encyclopedia,* 5:110. Burrus, *Kino and the Cartography,* 3.

12. Bolton, *Rim of Christendom,* 77–83, 124 (quotations, 79, 81).

13. Quoted by Bolton, *Rim of Christendom,* 96. Kino also read the report of Oñate's overland trek from New Mexico to the South Sea in 1605, which further convinced him that California was an island. Burrus, *Kino and the Cartography,* 14–15.

14. Bolton, *Rim of Christendom,* 100–228 (quotations, 89, 111–12). Kino's plan of the fort at San Bruno and his handsome map of coastline and islands around the bay of La Paz in Baja California, which he still reckoned was the largest island in the world, were both drawn in 1683; they are reproduced in Burrus, *Kino and the Cartography,* following p. 36.

15. Burrus, *Kino and the Cartography,* 55 n. 28 (Kino's quotation, 41).

16. Quoted by John L. Kessell, *Mission of Sorrows: Jesuit Guevavi and the Pimas, 1691–1767* (Tucson: University of Arizona Press, 1970), 25. Bolton, *Rim of Christendom,* 233–35, 246–66.

17. Bolton, *Rim of Christendom,* 266, 277–80 (quotation, 266).

18. See Peter H. Wood, "La Salle: Discovery of a Lost Explorer," *American Historical Review* 89 (April 1984), 294–323.

19. Jean Delanglez quoted by Chipman, *Spanish Texas,* 84. In the sequel to his *Spanish Sea,* Robert S. Weddle, *The French Thorn: Rival Explorers in the Spanish Sea, 1682–1762* (College Station: Texas A&M University Press, 1991), 3–39, chronicles closely the endless reverses suffered by the La Salle colony. L'Archeveque's own description of La Salle's murder, as he related it to Henri Joutel, appears in William C. Foster, ed., *The La Salle Expedition to Texas: The Journal of Henri Joutel, 1684–1687,* trans. Johanna S. Warren (Austin: Texas State Historical Association, 1998), 197–99.

20. Scholes, *Troublous Times,* 107–244; Kessell, *Kiva, Cross, and Crown,* 198–208; Weddle, *French Thorn,* 353 n. 32.

21. Weddle, *French Thorn,* 12–15.

22. Quoted by Weddle, *French Thorn,* 42. See also the same author's *Wilderness Manhunt,* 7–14. The latter treats at least eighteen expeditions between 1686 and 1698, nine by sea and nine by land.

23. On July 13, 1995, Texas Historical Commission archaeologists announced the discovery of *La Belle.* Still listing to starboard, as a Spanish diarist noted in 1687, the remarkably preserved oak hull and its contents were encased in a cofferdam and painstakingly excavated. The diary of Juan Enríquez Barroto, who told of sighting the wreck of *La Belle* in 1687, has been translated and annotated by Robert S. Weddle, in Weddle, ed., *La Salle, the Mississippi, and the Gulf: Three Primary Documents* (College Station: Texas A&M University Press, 1987), 129–205.

24. Declaration of Miguel, Parral, Apr. 11, 1689, in Hackett, *Historical Documents,* 2:269–73.

25. Weddle, *Wilderness Manhunt* and *French Thorn,* and Hickerson, *Jumanos,* a book dedicated to "the spirit of Juan Sabeata." Declaration of Muygisofac, Parral, Apr. 11, 1689, in Hackett, *Historical Documents,* 2:277–81.

26. While Weddle, *Wilderness Manhunt,* 132–48, accepts the opinion of Géry's Spanish interrogators that the Frenchman was demented, William C. Foster, *Spanish Expeditions into Texas, 1689–1768* (Austin: University of Texas Press, 1995), 5, 292 n. 8, considers him instead an alert and wily survivor. Foster tracks and compares the period's eleven major expeditions with far greater precision than has anyone before him. For a biographical sketch of Alonso de León, see Chipman and Joseph, *Notable Men and Women,* 22–40.

27. Gerhard, *North Frontier,* 325–34.

28. Michael B. McCloskey, *The Formative Years of the Missionary College of Santa Cruz of Querétaro, 1683–1733* (Washington, D.C.: Academy of American Franciscan History, 1955).

29. "Letter of fray Damián Massanet to don Carlos de Sigüenza, 1690," in Bolton, *Spanish Exploration*, 353–87 (quotation, 361). This and other related documents are provided in Spanish by Lino Gómez Canedo, ed., *Primeras exploraciones y poblamiento de Texas (1686–1694)* (Monterrey: Instituto Tecnológico y de Estudios Superiores, 1968).

30. Itinerary of Alonso de León, 1689, in Bolton, *Spanish Exploration*, 388–404 (quotation, 398).

31. Excavation of the eight iron cannon—three three-pounders, three four-pounders, and two six-pounders—in 1996 by Curtis Tunnell of the Texas Historical Commission confirmed the site of Fort Saint-Louis, identified first by Herbert E. Bolton in 1914. It lies some five miles up Garcitas Creek from Lavaca Bay, an inlet of Matagorda Bay, on the Keeran Ranch in Victoria County, Texas.

32. Rick Hendricks and Meredith D. Dodge, eds., *Two Hearts, One Soul: The Correspondence of the Condesa de Galve, 1688–96* (Albuquerque: University of New Mexico Press, 1993), 85; Weddle, *Wilderness Manhunt*, 214–15, 250–63, and *French Thorn*, 15–16, 69, 119. There is some confusion in the secondary sources about the Talon children, which Weddle, "The Talon Interrogations: A Rare Perspective," clears up in *La Salle, the Mississippi, and the Gulf*, 209–24.

33. L'Archevêque quoted by Weddle, *Wilderness Manhunt*, 173.

34. Massanet to Siguenza, 1690, in Bolton, *Spanish Exploration*, 363–64.

35. Itinerary of León, 1689, in Bolton, *Spanish Exploration*, 398. It seems doubtful that any part of the temporary fort had a second "story"; I would change that word (*techo*) to "roof." Gómez Canedo, *Primeras exploraciones*, 99. Sketched by Juan Bautista Chapa, a crude plan of the fort, corresponding to León's description and showing the location of the eight scattered cannon, is reproduced in Chipman and Joseph, *Notable Men and Women*, 30.

36. Massanet to Siguenza, 1690, in Bolton, *Spanish Exploration*, 369. "Storeship," instead of "sloop," renders the Spanish *urca* more precisely.

37. Massanet to Siguenza, 1690, in Bolton, *Spanish Exploration*, 383, 387.

38. Juan Bautista Chapa in *Historia de Nuevo León con noticias sobre Coahuila, Tamaulipas, Texas y Nuevo México, escrita en el siglo XVII por el Cap. Alonso de León, Juan Bautista Chapa y el Gral. Fernando Sánchez de Zamora*, ed. Israel Cavazos Garza (Monterrey: Gobierno del Estado de Nuevo León, 1961), 222. The implication that fray Damián was wearing a blue habit is interesting. Friars of the missionary colleges wore gray habits, but since Massanet had been sent to the missions of Coahuila from Jalisco, he might still have been wearing the blue of the Franciscan provinces. McCloskey, *Formative Years*, 62; Gómez Canedo, *Primeras exploraciones*, xiv, 4.

39. I discuss the pivotal, three-stage Pueblo-Spanish war in John L. Kessell, "Spaniards and Pueblos: From Crusading Intolerance to Pragmatic Accommodation," *CC1*, 127–38.

40. Declaration of Naranjo, Dec. 19, 1681, in Hackett and Shelby, *Revolt*, 2:247–48.

41. Fray Silvestre Vélez de Escalante to fray Juan Agustín Morfi, Santa Fe, Apr. 2, 1778, in Ralph Emerson Twitchell, *The Spanish Archives of New Mexico*, 2 vols. (Cedar Rapids: The Torch Press, 1914), 2:268–80 (quotations, 273).

42. Kessell, *Kiva, Cross, and Crown*, 122–29, 239; Alden C. Hayes, *The Four Churches of Pecos* (Albuquerque: University of New Mexico, 1974), 22–23, 32–35.

43. Declaration of Juan, Dec. 18, 1691, in Hackett and Shelby, *Revolt,* 2:235.

44. The Otermín attempt at reconquest is covered in great detail in Hackett and Shelby, *Revolt*. See also Vina Walz, "History of the El Paso Area, 1680–1692" (Ph.D. diss., University of New Mexico, 1951); Jane C. Sánchez, "Spanish-Indian Relations during the Otermín Administration, 1677–1683," *NMHR* 58 (April 1983), 133–51; and the Introduction to John L. Kessell and Rick Hendricks, eds., *By Force of Arms: The Journals of don Diego de Vargas, New Mexico, 1691–93* (Albuquerque: University of New Mexico Press, 1992).

45. Opinion of Ayeta, Hacienda of Luis de Carbajal, Dec. 23, 1681, in Hackett and Shelby, *Revolt,* 2:305–318 (quotations, 309, 316).

46. Otermín to Ayeta, San Lorenzo, Apr. 5, 1682, quoted by Walz, "History of the El Paso Area," 87.

47. Walz, "History of the El Paso Area," 127–34; Hickerson, *Jumanos,* 127–45. Domínguez de Mendoza's itinerary, from December 1683 through May 1684, is translated in Bolton, *Spanish Exploration,* 320–43.

48. Documents relating to the 1684 uprisings and the Spanish response appear in Naylor and Polzer, *Presidio and Militia,* 1:506–47. Walz, "History of the El Paso Area," 135–50. The Juan de Archuleta killed at Ojito in 1684 may have been a cousin of the other Juan de Archuleta who returned to upriver New Mexico in 1693. The latter seems to have been a great-grandson of Asensio. Chávez, *Origins of New Mexico Families,* 6–7, 131–32.

49. Navarro García, *Sonora y Sinaloa,* 264–75. For further context, see Cynthia Radding, *Wandering Peoples: Colonialism, Ethnic Spaces, and Ecological Frontiers in Northwestern Mexico, 1700–1850* (Durham, N.C.: Duke University Press, 1997), 267, 280–82.

50. The wide-ranging band peoples known as Mansos, Sumas, Janos, and Jocomes, with whom the Spaniards of El Paso and Casas Grandes warred in the 1680s and 1690s, were likely Uto-Aztecan speakers undergoing the last stages of cultural absorption by Athapascan-speaking Apaches. See Thomas H. Naylor, "Athapaskans They Weren't: The Suma Rebels Executed at Casas Grandes in 1685," in David R. Wilcox and W. Bruce Masse, eds., *The Protohistoric Period in the North American Southwest, AD 1450–1700* (Tempe: Arizona State University, 1981), 275–81. Evidently, the nonagricultural hunting and gathering Mansos and Sumas were distinct groups, and neither was related to any of the various peoples labeled Jumanos by Spaniards. Bill Lockhart, "Protohistoric Confusion: A Cultural Comparison of the Manso, Suma, and Jumano Indians of the Paso del Norte Region," *Journal of the Southwest* 39 (Spring 1997), 113–49.

51. Ernest J. Burrus, ed., "A Tragic Interlude in the Reconquest of New Mexico," *Manuscripta* 29 (1985), 154–65.

52. Walz, "History of the El Paso Area," 158–82.

53. It may be that Reneros de Posada was a favored relative of fray Alonso de Posada, former custos of New Mexico and the most influential Franciscan at the viceregal court in the mid-1680s. "El Paso del Norte Presidio Muster," 1684, in Naylor and Polzer, *Presidio*

and Militia, 1:512–27. "List of the soldiers," Sept. 23, 1681, in Hackett and Shelby, *Revolt*, 2:134–42.

54. Kessell and Hendricks, *By Force of Arms*, 24–27; Walz, "History of the El Paso Area," 221–63.

55. Fray Silvestre Vélez de Escalante, Extracto de noticias, Biblioteca Nacional, Mexico City, Archivo Franciscano 19/397 and 20/428.1. Supposedly, Bartolomé de Ojeda also gave Jironza data regarding the boundaries of individual pueblos so that the Spanish governor, upon reentry, might make reassuring land grants to these communities. Badly executed nineteenth-century renderings of the so-called Cruzate grants have been identified as forgeries, although intriguing questions remain.

CHAPTER 7

The three epigraphs are quoted in Irving Albert Leonard, ed., *The Mercurio Volante of don Carlos de Sigüenza y Góngora: An Account of the First Expedition of don Diego de Vargas into New Mexico in 1692* (Los Angeles: The Quivira Society, 1932), 88; Gómez Canedo, *Primeras Exploraciones*, 60; and Burrus, *Kino and the Cartography*, 15.

1. For background on Diego de Vargas and his family, see John L. Kessell, ed., *Remote beyond Compare: Letters of don Diego de Vargas to His Family from New Spain and New Mexico, 1675–1706* (Albuquerque: University of New Mexico Press, 1989), 3–29 (the proof of legitimacy from which the quotation is taken is cited on 108 n. 54).

2. Quoted in Kessell, *Remote beyond Compare*, 168. Vargas's time at El Paso is treated in greater detail in Kessell and Hendricks, *By Force of Arms*. Walz ("History of the El Paso Area," v-vi) succinctly compared Vargas and his predecessors: "Of the four governors who served in El Paso during this period, Otermín had the supplies and lacked the character; Jironza had character and wanted resources; Reneros had neither; Vargas had both."

The standard narrative of the third or restoration stage of the Pueblo-Spanish war is J. Manuel Espinosa, *Crusaders of the Río Grande: The Story of Don Diego de Vargas and the Reconquest and Refounding of New Mexico* (Chicago: Institute of Jesuit History, 1942). The Vargas Project at the University of New Mexico is making available the primary sources; volumes published to date are: Kessell, *Remote beyond Compare*; Kessell and Hendricks, *By Force of Arms*; Kessell, Hendricks, and Meredith D. Dodge, eds., *To the Royal Crown Restored: The Journals of don Diego de Vargas, New Mexico, 1692–94* (Albuquerque: University of New Mexico Press, 1995); Kessell, Hendricks, and Dodge, eds., *Blood on the Boulders: The Journals of don Diego de Vargas, New Mexico, 1694–97*, 2 books (Albuquerque: University of New Mexico, 1998); and Kessell, Hendricks, Dodge, and Larry D. Miller, eds., *That Disturbances Cease: The Journals of don Diego de Vargas, New Mexico, 1697–1700* (Albuquerque: University of New Mexico Press, 2000).

3. Quoted by Kessell, *Remote beyond Compare*, 170.

4. Vargas's campaign journal, Oct. 24, 1692, in Kessell and Hendricks, *By Force of Arms*, 518–19.

5. Leonard, *Mercurio Volante,* includes a complete facsimile, 91–128. Espinosa, *Crusaders,* 112–13.

6. Vargas in Kessell, Hendricks, and Dodge, *To the Royal Crown Restored,* 182–220 (quotation, 218).

7. Kessell, Hendricks, and Dodge, *To the Royal Crown Restored,* 223–343.

8. Weddle, *Wilderness Manhunt,* 194–98, 249–52, 258, and *French Thorn,* 105. Paul Trujillo, "'Los Franceses' of Seventeenth-Century New Mexico: Jean L'Archeveque, Jacques Grolet and Pedro Meusnier," *Herencia: The Quarterly Journal of the Hispanic Genealogical Research Center of New Mexico* 3 (January 1995), 17–24.

9. Fontcuberta in Hackett, *Historical Documents,* 2:282–85.

10. Gómez Canedo, *Primeras exploraciones,* 60.

11. For the Terán de los Ríos entrada of 1691–92 and the Salinas Varona resupply expedition of 1693, see Foster, *Spanish Expeditions,* 51–93; Weddle, *French Thorn,* 87–98; Elizabeth A. H. John, *Storms Brewed in Other Men's Worlds: The Confrontation of Indians, Spanish, and French in the Southwest, 1540–1795,* 2d ed. (Norman: University of Oklahoma Press, 1996), 190–95; and F. Todd Smith, *The Caddo Indians: Tribes at the Convergence of Empires, 1542–1854* (College Station: Texas A&M University Press, 1996), 31–35.

12. J. Charles Kelley, "Juan Sabeata and Diffusion in Aboriginal Texas," *American Anthropologist* 57 (October 1955), 981–95. Kelley characterizes Sabeata as "an inveterate gossip and a master at frontier intrigue" (981). Hickerson, *Jumanos,* 199–208.

13. Escalante y Mendoza, August 19, 1693, quoted in Gómez Canedo, *Primeras exploraciones,* 315 n. 8, and Massanet to Galve, San Francisco de los Tejas, June 14, 1693, with report, 309–15.

14. There appears to be little agreement regarding which Native peoples Urrutia lived with, Hasinais or their various allies. John (*Storms,* 192–94) suggests that he might have replaced Juan Sabeata, who disappeared from the record in 1692, as leader of an anti-Apache coalition. Weddle, *French Thorn,* 180, 374 n. 3; Foster, *Spanish Expeditions,* 90; Smith, *Caddo Indians,* 178 n. 56.

15. Massanet in Gómez Canedo, *Primeras exploraciones,* 317–21.

16. Weddle, *French Thorn,* 105–10. For a fuller account, including biographical sketches of Pez and Sigüenza, and documents, see Irving A. Leonard, ed., *Spanish Approach to Pensacola, 1689–1693* (Albuquerque: The Quivira Society, 1939), 19–54, 145–207 (Sigüenza's chart is reproduced after p. 323).

17. Escalante y Mendoza, Fiscal's reply, Mexico City, Mar. 18, 1694, in Kessell, Hendricks, and Dodge, *Blood on the Boulders,* 86–87, 88.

18. Galve to Vargas, Directive, Mexico City, Mar. 26, 1694, in Kessell, Hendricks, and Dodge, *Blood on the Boulders,* 93–94.

19. For the 1693 recolonizing expedition, the battle of Santa Fe, and events leading to the Pueblo revolt of 1696, see Espinosa, *Crusaders,* 112–243, and Kessell, Hendricks, and Dodge, *To the Royal Crown Restored* and *Blood on the Boulders.*

20. Vargas to Galve, Summary of everything, Santa Fe, Jan. 20, 1694, in Kessell, Hendricks, and Dodge, *Blood on the Boulders,* 668–69. Details of pueblo construction over the governor's palace between 1680 and 1693 by Santa Fe's Indian occupants, and the work of Vargas and his successors to reclaim the structure architecturally, are sketchy at best. Tigges, *Santa Fe Historic Plaza Study,* vol. 1.

21. Kessell, Hendricks, and Dodge, *Blood on the Boulders,* 320–21.

22. Kessell, *Remote beyond Compare,* 74, 181–83.

23. Casañas to fray Francisco de Vargas, Bernalillo, Apr. 18, 1696, in J. Manuel Espinosa, ed., *The Pueblo Indian Revolt of 1696 and the Franciscan Missions in New Mexico: Letters of the Missionaries and Related Documents* (Norman: University of Oklahoma Press, 1988), 228–30.

24. Fray Francisco de Vargas to the Commissary General, Santa Fe, July 21, 1696, in Espinosa, *Pueblo Indian Revolt of 1696,* 243–46.

25. Espinosa, *Crusaders,* 250–51, 271, and *Pueblo Revolt of 1696,* 250 n. 2.

26. Kessell, *Kiva, Cross, and Crown,* 288–92.

27. Kessell, Hendricks, and Dodge, *Blood on the Boulders,* 723–964. Espinosa, *Crusaders,* 244–306. See also John B. Colligan, *The Juan Páez Hurtado Expedition of 1695: Fraud in Recruiting Colonists for New Mexico* (Albuquerque: University of New Mexico Press, 1995). McCloskey, Formative Years, 73.

28. Vargas to Ignacio López de Zárate, Santa Fe, Sept. 30, 1698, in Kessell, *Remote beyond Compare,* 185–91. Rick Hendricks, "Pedro Rodríguez Cubero: New Mexico's Reluctant Governor, 1697–1703," *NMHR* 68 (January 1993), 13–39. Espinosa, *Crusaders,* 307–62.

29. Vargas to López de Zárate, Santa Fe, Mar. 11, 1699, in Kessell, *Remote beyond Compare,* 195–98. Documents from the years of contention when sitting governor and former governor both resided in Santa Fe are presented in Kessell, Hendricks, Dodge, and Miller, *That Disturbances Cease.*

30. Kessell, *Remote beyond Compare,* 65–93.

31. Ernest J. Burrus, ed., *Kino and Manje, Explorers of Sonora and Arizona: Their Vision of the Future* (Rome: Jesuit Historical Institute, 1971), 47–55 (Manje quotation, 49–50).

32. Burrus, drawing on his published translation of Kino's biography of Saeta, analyzes the work in *Kino and Manje,* 75–92. For coverage of warfare on the Sonora frontier and the Pima revolt of 1695, see Bolton, *Rim of Christendom,* 288–333, and Naylor and Polzer, *Presidio and Militia,* 1:582–718.

33. González quoted in Burrus, *Kino and Manje,* 79–81. Bolton (*Rim of Christendom,* 334–46, 384–90) describes in detail criticisms of Kino by his young superior in the field from 1694 to 1697, Father Francisco Javier de Mora.

34. Bolton, *Rim of Christendom,* 342–51 (quotation, 346). For his 1695–96 effort, Kino relied on a map of New Mexico from an earlier period before the abandonment of a number of pueblos in the 1670s. Curiously, no map of New Mexico has survived from the turbulent years of the Pueblo-Spanish war. Kino's general map and another smaller one he sketched of Pimería Alta showing Father Saeta kneeling to receive the arrows of two poised Pimas are reproduced in Burrus, *Kino and the Cartography,* following p. 40.

35. On Jesuit Baja California, see the splendidly detailed study by Harry W. Crosby, *Antigua California: Mission and Colony on the Peninsular Frontier, 1697–1768* (Albuquerque: University of New Mexico Press, 1994). Salvatierra's 1697 crossing is covered on 10–26.

36. Bolton, *Rim of Christendom,* 445–87 (quotations, 452, 460, 461, 471); Burrus, *Kino and Manje,* 107–37 and appendixes.

37. Eymer quoted by Bolton, *Rim of Christendom,* 464, also 556, 577. Burrus, *Kino and the Cartography,* 14, 27.

38. Burrus, *Kino and the Cartography,* 29, 150. Kino's post-1701 maps, including a 1724 copy of his culminating achievement of 1710, discovered by Father Burrus in Paris in 1962, are reproduced following 44, 46, and 50.

39. Kino quoted by Bolton, *Rim of Christendom,* 269. "Saint Kino: Bishops from three countries discuss possible canonization of humble priest," *Tucson Daily Citizen* (c. July 1, 1990).

40. Quoted by Bolton, *Rim of Christendom,* 369.

41. Kino quoted by Burrus, *Kino and Manje,* 91.

42. Kino quoted by Burrus, *Kino and Manje,* 92.

43. Naylor and Polzer, *Presidio and Militia,* 1:654.

44. Herbert E. Bolton, ed., *Kino's Historical Memoir of Pimería Alta,* 2 vols. (Berkeley: University of California Press, 1948), 1:198. Burrus, *Kino and Manje,* 212 n. 63, 375 n. 78.

45. Hendricks, "Pedro Rodríguez Cubero," 29–31. Montgomery, Smith, and Brew, *Franciscan Awatovi,* 20–24. John P. Wilson, "Awatovi—More Light on a Legend," *Plateau* 44 (Winter 1972): 125–30.

46. Burrus, *Kino and Manje,* 51 n. 18, 52–55, 417 n. 36. Eleanor B. Adams, "Two Colonial New Mexico Libraries, 1704, 1776," *NMHR* 19 (April 1944), 135–67. A copy of the three-volume *Mística Ciudad* (Madrid, 1670) showed up as item 26 of Vargas's small New Mexico library.

47. Manje quoted by Kessell, "Miracles or Mystery," 135. Bolton, *Rim of Christendom,* 414–18. Burrus, *Kino and Manje,* 395–96, 404, 417–20, 437.

48. Bolton, *Kino's Historical Memoir,* 1:198. Burrus, *Kino and Manje,* 442–43.

CHAPTER 8

The lead quotations are from Marc Simmons, *Albuquerque: A Narrative History* (Albuquerque: University of New Mexico, 1982), 86, and Alfred Barnaby Thomas, ed., *After Coronado: Spanish Exploration Northeast of New Mexico, 1696–1727* (Norman: University of Oklahoma Press, 1935), 146.

1. On the Rivera inspection, see Thomas H. Naylor and Charles W. Polzer, eds., *Pedro de Rivera and the Regulations for Northern New Spain, 1724–1729* (Tucson: University of Arizona Press, 1988); Jack Jackson and William C. Foster, eds., *Imaginary Kingdom: Texas as Seen by the Rivera and Rubí Military Expeditions, 1727 and 1767* (Austin: Texas State Historical

Association, 1995); Luis Navarro García, *Don José de Gálvez y la Comandancia General de las Provincias Internas del Norte de Nueva España* (Sevilla: Escuela de Estudios Hispano-Americanos, 1964), 71–78; and Weber, *Spanish Frontier*, 214–26.

2. Harry W. Crosby's *Antigua California* remains the prime source for the Jesuits' entire seventy-year tenure in Baja California. For the period 1697–1701, see 27–60 (quotations, 36, 43).

3. Quoted by Crosby, *Antigua California*, 59–60.

4. Radding, *Wandering Peoples*, 67, 284.

5. Crosby, *Antigua California*, 154. Setting the word in quotation marks, Crosby terms Ugarte's laborers "'volunteer' neophyte warriors from missions on the Río Yaqui" (84). Elsewhere (439 n. 76), he mentions that such neophytes "were 'borrowed' to act as foot soldiers during California explorations. No mention was made of their compensation, if any."

6. Crosby, *Antigua California*, 87–101.

7. Quoted by Bolton, *Rim of Christendom*, 583.

8. Kessell, *Mission of Sorrows*, 28–37; Bolton, *Rim of Christendom*, 510–15; Peter M. Dunne, "Captain Anza and the Case of Father Campos," *Mid-America* 23 (1941), 45–60.

9. Crosby, *Antigua California*, 507 n. 66.

10. Velarde quoted by Bolton, *Rim of Christendom*, 584–85. Misinterpreting the burial entry written by Campos, Kino's "companion of eighteen years," Bolton had a fit: "Kino spent a decade in man-killing explorations and endless demonstrations that California was a peninsula. . . . And now, at the end, in the very obituary . . . California is referred to as 'the Island'" (586). Campos, it appears, was referring not to California, but to the large Isla de la Presentación discovered by Kino at the delta of the Colorado River. See Burrus, *Kino and the Cartography*, 50–51.

11. Kessell, *Mission of Sorrows*, 37 n. 39.

12. Burrus (*Kino and the Cartography*, 52) does not comment on Kino's up-to-date inclusion of Albuquerque.

13. Simmons, *Albuquerque*, 81–94 (quotation, 83). Eleanor B. Adams and Fray Angélico Chávez, eds., *The Missions of New Mexico, 1776: A Description by Fray Francisco Atanasio Domínguez with Other Contemporary Documents* (Albuquerque: University of New Mexico Press, 1956), 145 n. 1.

14. Rick Hendricks, ed., "The Last Years of Francisco Cuervo y Valdés," *La Crónica de Nuevo México* (Historical Society of New Mexico) 36 (July 1993), 2–3. See also Ovidio Casado Fuente, *Don Francisco Cuerbo y Valdés, Gobernador de Nuevo México, Fundador de la Ciudad de Alburquerque* (Oviedo: Instituto de Estudios Asturianos, 1983). During Cuervo's rule in Coahuila, Franciscans, to please the governor, had named one of their Coahuiltecan missions San Francisco Xavier.

15. Gerhard, *North Frontier*, 197; Adams and Chávez, *Missions of New Mexico*, 146 n. 1; Cheryl English Martin, *Governance and Society in Colonial Mexico: Chihuahua in the Eighteenth Century* (Stanford, Calif.: Stanford University Press, 1996), 22.

16. Also like Vargas, Cuervo y Valdés gave his first-born natural son the same name as his second-born legitimate son, Francisco Antonio. Hendricks, "Last Years." Kessell, Hendricks, and Dodge, *To the Royal Crown Restored*, 245. Chávez, *Origins of New Mexico Families*, 183.

17. See Rick Hendricks and John P. Wilson, eds., *The Navajos in 1705: Roque Madrid's Campaign Journal* (Albuquerque: University of New Mexico Press, 1996).

18. Thomas W. Kavanagh, *Comanche Political History: An Ethonohistorical Perspective, 1706–1875* (Lincoln: University of Nebraska Press, 1996), 63. Stanley Noyes, *Los Comanches: The Horse People, 1751–1845* (Albuquerque: University of New Mexico Press, 1993), 16–17.

19. Ulibarrí's campaign journal is translated in Thomas, *After Coronado*, 59–80 (quotations, 69, 72, 74). The flight of the Picuris and some Tewas in 1696 to the Plains Apaches, along with Vargas's pursuit and retrieval of eighty-four of them, is documented in Kessell, Hendricks, and Dodge, *Blood on the Boulders*, 1016–57. Hendricks and Wilson, *Navajos in 1705*, 118–20, 126–28. Some scholars place El Cuartelejo in eastern Colorado and others in Kansas.

20. Robert S. Weddle, *San Juan Bautista: Gateway to Spanish Texas* (Austin: University of Texas Press, 1968), 18–48; Weddle, *French Thorn*, 179–81.

21. Weddle, *French Thorn*, 119–78 (quotation, 171). Chipman, *Spanish Texas*, 101–104. For French enterprise in Lower Louisiana and its effect on the Native peoples, see Daniel H. Usner, Jr., *Indians, Settlers, and Slaves in a Frontier Exchange Economy: The Lower Mississippi Valley before 1763* (Chapel Hill: University of North Carolina Press, 1992).

22. Weddle, *San Juan Bautista*, 75–86 (Ramón quotation, 77).

23. Quoted by Foster, *Spanish Expeditions*, 303 n. 18.

24. Foster, *Spanish Expeditions*, 95–105, points out that the route of the 1709 reconnaissance was not the same as that of Terán de los Ríos in 1691, but rather a new track followed by subsequent colonizing expeditions.

25. Weddle, *San Juan Bautista*, 87–113, and *French Thorn*, 190–97 (quotation, 194). Chipman, *Spanish Texas*, 103–12. John, *Storms*, 196–206. See also "Francisco Hidalgo/Louis Juchereau de St. Denis: Resolute Missionary/Canadian Cavalier," in Chipman and Joseph, *Notable Men and Women*, 41–61. Father Hidalgo's long missionary career is covered admiringly in George P. Hammond, Agapito Rey, Vivian C. Fisher, and W. Michael Mathes, eds., *Apostolic Chronicle of Juan Domingo Arricivita: The Franciscan Mission Frontier in the Eighteenth Century in Arizona, Texas, and the Californias*, 2 vols. (Berkeley, Calif.: Academy of American Franciscan History, 1996), 1:269–93.

26. Smith, *Caddo Indians*, 36–46 (quotation, 36). See also Daniel A. Hickerson, "Historical Processes, Epidemic Disease, and the Formation of the Hasinai Confederacy," *Ethnohistory* 44 (Winter 1997), 31–52.

27. Weddle, *French Thorn*, 197–203. Foster, *Spanish Expeditions*, 109–23.

28. The post-Vargas struggle for power and profit in New Mexico, featuring manipulation of the presidial payroll, is especially evident in Ted J. Warner, "Don Félix Martínez and the Santa Fe Presidio, 1693–1730," *NMHR* 45 (October 1970), 269–310, and Lansing B. Bloom, "The Vargas Encomienda," *NMHR* 14 (October 1939), 366–417. On Valverde, see

Rebecca A. Gudiño Quiroz, *Don Antonio Valverde y Cossío, Gobernador de Nuevo México: una aproximación a su vida pública y privada,* Cuadernos de Trabajo, 24 (Ciudad Juárez: Universidad Autónoma de Ciudad Juárez, 1994).

29. The diary of Valverde's 1719 campaign is translated in Thomas, *After Coronado,* 110–33 (quotations, 116, 120, 124). Chávez, *Origins of New Mexico Families,* 136, 304. William Brandon, *Quivira: Europeans in the Region of the Santa Fe Trail, 1540–1820* (Athens: Ohio University Press, 1990), 165, identifies the noxious plant as poison sumac.

30. Documents concerning the Villasur expedition are in Thomas, *After Coronado,* 133–37, 141–48, 162–87, 222–60 (quotations, 161, 164).

31. Thomas E. Chávez, "The Villasur Expedition and the Segesser Hide Paintings," in *Spain and the Plains: Myths and Realities of Spanish Exploration and Settlement on the Great Plains,* ed. Ralph H. Vigil, Frances W. Kaye, and John R. Wunder (Niwot: University Press of Colorado, 1994), 90–113, and "The Segesser Hide Paintings: History, Discovery, Art," *El Palacio* 92 (Winter 1986), 18–27 (color illustration, 24–25).

32. Gudiño Quiroz, *Don Antonio Valverde y Cossío.* Partial proceedings against Valverde appear in Thomas, *After Coronado,* 219–45. See also Warner, "Don Félix Martínez," 293–300.

33. Naylor and Polzer, *Pedro de Rivera,* 79, 150–52 (quotations, 152).

34. Naylor and Polzer, *Pedro de Rivera,* 281–86.

35. Gudiño Quiroz, *Don Antonio Valverde y Cossío,* 23.

36. On the Anzas and their Basque network in Sonora, see Donald T. Garate, "Who Named Arizona? The Basque Connection," *Journal of Arizona History* 40 (Spring 1999), 53–82.

37. Naylor and Polzer, *Pedro de Rivera,* 80–82, 112–13 (quotation, 82).

38. Fay Jackson Smith, *Captain of the Phantom Presidio: A History of the Presidio of Fronteras, Sonora, New Spain, 1686–1735* (Spokane, Wash.: Arthur H. Clark, 1993), 95–128 (quotation, 127).

39. A translation of Rivera's terse diary and an assessment of the inspector's recommendations regarding Texas appear in Jackson and Foster, *Imaginary Kingdom,* 2–67 (quotation, 28). See also Foster, *Spanish Expeditions,* 163–75, and Naylor and Polzer, *Pedro de Rivera,* 83–87, 113–16, 157–65.

40. Quoted by Jesús F. de la Teja, *San Antonio de Béxar, A Community on New Spain's Northern Frontier* (Albuquerque: University of New Mexico Press, 1995), 18. See also Foster, *Spanish Expeditions,* 127–43, and Chipman, *Spanish Texas,* 116–18.

41. Foster, *Spanish Expeditions,* 120, 145–61; Chipman, *Spanish Texas,* 119–26; Weddle, *San Juan Bautista,* 159–64, and *French Thorn,* 215, 234–36. Chipman (122–25) reproduces Aguayo's proposed designs for the four Texas presidios—Nuestra Señora del Pilar de los Adaes, Nuestra Señora de los Dolores (de los Tejas), San Antonio de Béxar, and Nuestra Señora de Loreto (La Bahía)—none of which in reality appeared so formidable. Marion A. Habig, *Spanish Texas Pilgrimage: The Old Franciscan Missions and Other Spanish Settlements of Texas, 1632–1821* (Chicago: Franciscan Herald Press, 1990), inventories "the 38 Spanish mis-

sions" and sorts out the competitive establishments of friars from the Franciscan colleges of Querétaro and Zacatecas. See also Chipman and Joseph, *Notable Men and Women*, 62–102.

Robert E. Wright, "Local Church Emergence and Mission Decline: The Historiography of the Catholic Church in the Southwest during the Spanish and Mexican Periods," *U.S. Catholic Historian* 9:1–2 (Winter-Spring 1990), 27-48, points out how neglected has been the role of secular, or diocesan, clergymen, particularly in Texas during the late-colonial and Mexican periods. "The repeated accounts of the 'decline of the missions,'" he maintains (27), "almost totally ignore the gradual emergence of resilient local churches on the northern frontier of New Spain and then Mexico."

42. Naylor and Polzer, *Pedro de Rivera*, 157.

43. Naylor and Polzer, *Pedro de Rivera*, 158–62.

44. Navarro García, *José de Gálvez*, 124–26. Jackson and Foster, *Imaginary Kingdom*, 12–13, 61–67.

CHAPTER 9

The lead quotation appears in Thomas, *After Coronado*, 214.

1. Rivera in Thomas, *After Coronado*, 209–17 (quotations, 211). Noyes, *Los Comanches*, xxiv, 317 n. 12. For the natural and human context of the Comanches' rise to power on the Great Plains, see Pekka Hamalainen, "The Western Comanche Trade Center: Rethinking the Plains Indian Trade System," *Western Historical Quarterly* 29 (Winter 1998), 485–513.

2. See Frank Norall, *Bourgmont, Explorer of the Missouri, 1698–1725* (Lincoln: University of Nebraska Press, 1988), 15–89 (quotations, 34, 73, 74); Noyes, *Los Comanches*, 18–22.

3. Weddle, *San Juan Bautista*, 168–71; John, *Storms*, 258–61; and De la Teja, *San Antonio de Béxar*, 8–10.

4. Gilbert R. Cruz, *Let There Be Towns: Spanish Municipal Origins in the American Southwest, 1610–1810* (College Station: Texas A&M University Press, 1988), 68–80; De la Teja, *San Antonio de Béxar*, 31–34; John, *Storms*, 263–64; and Weddle, *San Juan Bautista*, 191–93.

5. Quoted by De la Teja, *San Antonio de Béxar*, 11.

6. Quoted by Chipman, *Spanish Texas*, 139. See also John, *Storms*, 264–71; Jack Jackson, *Los Mesteños: Spanish Ranching in Texas, 1721–1821* (College Station: Texas A&M University Press, 1986), 55–57; and Herbert Eugene Bolton, *Texas in the Middle Eighteenth Century* (1915; repr., Austin: University of Texas Press, 1970), 27–30. When José de Urrutia died in 1740, his son Toribio took command at San Antonio, as did a grandson, Luis Antonio Menchaca, in 1763.

7. Smith, *Captain of the Phantom Presidio*, 129–36, 197–201 (quotations, 199, 200, 201).

8. Naylor and Polzer, *Pedro de Rivera*, 155, 274. For Manuel Bernal de Huidobro, first governor of Sinaloa-Sonora, Anza wrote a telling report in 1735 describing the warfare he conducted from Fronteras. See Charles W. Polzer and Thomas E. Sheridan, eds., "Juan

Bautista de Anza Discusses Apache and Seri Depredations and the Need for a Presidio at Terrenate (1729–1735)," in *The Presidio and Militia on the Northern Frontier of New Spain: A Documentary History,* vol. 2, part 1, *The Californias and Sinaloa-Sonora, 1700–1765* (Tucson: University of Arizona Press, 1997), 303–12, and Thomas E. Sheridan, *Empire of Sand: The Seri Indians and the Struggle for Spanish Sonora, 1645–1803* (Tucson: University of Arizona Press, 1999), 122–38.

9. Kessell, *Kiva, Cross, and Crown,* 325–29. Adams, *Bishop Tamarón's Visitation,* 13–16, 95–106.

10. Kessell, *Mission of Sorrows,* 37–59 (quotations, 53, 54).

11. Dunne, "Captain Anza," 55–60 (quotation, 59). Sheridan, *Empire of Sand,* 123.

12. About the planchas de plata, the settlement called Arizona, and the latter name's Basque origin, see Garate, "Who Named Arizona?"

13. Kessell, *Mission of Sorrows,* 60–69. Polzer and Sheridan, "Juan Bautista de Anza." Daniel S. Matson and Bernard L. Fontana, eds., *Before Rebellion: Letters and Reports of Jacobo Sedelmayr, S.J.* (Tucson: Arizona Historical Society, 1996), xviii-xix, 3–4, 46–47.

14. Crosby, *Antigua California,* 101–17 (quotation, 110). Polzer and Sheridan, "Indian Raid on the Manila Galleon, 1735," *Presidio and Militia,* 2:1, 67–81.

15. Radding, *Wandering Peoples,* 283–85, 299. Crosby, *Antigua California,* 117–26, 153–54, 453 n. 91. For detailed treatments of the massive 1740 revolt, see Evelyn Hu-Dehart, *Missionaries, Miners, and Indians: Spanish Contact with the Yaqui Nation of Northwestern New Spain, 1533–1820* (Tucson: University of Arizona Press, 1981), 59–87, and Luis Navarro García, *La sublevación yaqui de 1740* (Sevilla: Escuela de Estudios Hispano-Americanos, 1966). Hu-Dehart (125 n. 32) challenges the huge death tolls alleged by some scholars. Susan M. Deeds sees the Yaquis' rebellion not as an effort to purge everything Spanish but instead to restore the colonial pact on their terms. "Indigenous Rebellions on the Northern Mexican Mission Frontier: From First-Generation to Later Colonial Responses," in *CG,* 32–51.

16. Polzer and Sheridan, "Royal Cédula of King Philip V on the California Missions, 1744," *Presidio and Militia,* 2:1, 185–93 (quotation, 186). Crosby, *Antigua California,* 126.

17. Kessell, *Kiva, Cross, and Crown,* 387–91 (quotation, 387); Noyes, *Los Comanches,* 22–24; John, *Storms,* 315–16, 319–21; and Brandon, *Quivira,* 202–206, 220–22. See also Donald J. Blakeslee, *Along Ancient Trails: The Mallet Expedition of 1739* (Niwot: University Press of Colorado, 1995), who places the Mallets' venture in the context of historic plains travel.

18. Bolton, *Texas in the Middle Eighteenth Century,* 32–41.

19. Lawrence F. Hill, *José de Escandón and the Founding of Nuevo Santander: A Study in Spanish Colonization* (Columbus: Ohio State University Press, 1926). See also Jones, *Los Paisanos,* 65–78; Cruz, *Let There Be Towns,* 81–104; Gerhard, *North Frontier,* 358–68; Foster, *Spanish Expeditions,* 171; and Chipman and Joseph, *Notable Men and Women,* 124–49.

20. Chipman, *Spanish Texas,* 154–56, and Chipman and Joseph, *Notable Men and Women,* 103–23. See also the damning letter of fray Mariano Francisco de los Dolores y Viana to

Viceroy Conde de Revillagigedo in Diana Hadley, Thomas H. Naylor, and Mardith K. Schuetz-Miller, eds., *The Presidio and Militia on the Northern Frontier of New Spain*, vol. 2, part 2, *The Central Corridor and the Texas Corridor, 1700–1765* (Tucson: University of Arizona Press, 1997), 500–510. Ten days after their mass excommunication, Rábago and all but two of the men of his command had requested and received the sacrament of penance.

21. Kessell, *Mission of Sorrows,* 102–18; Matson and Fontana, *Before Rebellion;* Radding, *Wandering Peoples,* 285–88; Polzer and Sheridan, *Presidio and Militia,* 2:1. War against the Seris in 1749 and 1750, including Ortiz Parrilla's invasion of Tiburón Island, is documented in Sheridan, *Empire of Sand,* 143–231.

22. Chipman, *Spanish Texas,* 156–63 (quotation, 159). Robert S. Weddle, *The San Sabá Mission, Spanish Pivot in Texas* (Austin: University of Texas Press, 1964).

23. Terreros quoted by Weddle, *San Sabá Mission,* 56, 60.

24. Molina quoted by Weddle, *San Sabá Mission,* 75. A recent translation and transcription of Molina's report appears in Hadley, Naylor, and Schuetz-Miller, *Presidio and Militia,* 2:2, 511–26.

25. Molina quoted in Hadley, Naylor, and Schuetz-Miller, *Presidio and Militia,* 2:2, 516, 518.

26. Weddle, *San Sabá Mission,* 72–89. V. Kay Hindes, Mark R. Wolf, Grant D. Hall, and Kathleen Kirk Gilmore, *The Rediscovery of Santa Cruz de San Sabá, A Mission for the Apache in Spanish Texas* (Austin: Texas Historical Foundation and Texas Tech University, 1995). The mission buildings, according to the report, had been mainly of wattle-and-daub construction.

27. Quoted by Chipman, *Spanish Texas,* 163. Weddle, *San Sabá Mission,* 118–28 (quotations, 120, 121).

28. Weber, *Spanish Frontier,* 199–200.

29. Weddle, *San Sabá Mission,* 147–81, is somewhat harder on Rábago than Chipman, *Spanish Texas,* 174–79.

30. Sam D. Ratcliffe, "'*Escenas de Martirio*': Notes on the Destruction of Mission San Sabá," *SWHQ* 94 (April 1991), 506–34. The friars' account of the San Sabá debacle appears in Hammond, Rey, Fisher, and Mathes, *Apostolic Chronicle,* 2:46–74.

CHAPTER 10

The two epigraphs are quoted, respectively, by Eleanor B. Adams, "Fray Silvestre and the Obstinate Hopi," *NMHR* 38 (April 1963), 99–100, and Weber, *Spanish Frontier,* 206.

1. Quoted by Weddle, *San Sabá Mission,* 140.

2. Kessell, *Mission of Sorrows,* 125–26, 148, 155–57, 173–80 (quotations, 177, 180). For a complete itinerary, consult the diary of Rubí's chief engineer as translated by Lawrence Kinnaird, ed., *The Frontiers of New Spain: Nicolás de Lafora's Description, 1766–1768* (Berkeley: Quivira Society, 1958), and for context, Weber, *Spanish Frontier,* 204–24. Background for

founding the Tubac presidio is presented in "Opinions of the Best Location for the Presidio, 1752," and "Junta Regarding Tubac," in Polzer and Sheridan, *Presidio and Militia,* 2:1, 409–42.

3. For the Texas portion of the Rubí inspection, see Jackson and Foster, *Imaginary Kingdom,* 68–228, which includes a translation of the pertinent part of Rubí's previously unpublished diary (quotations, 114, 115, 116, 129). Foster, *Spanish Expeditions,* 176–93. Chipman and Joseph, *Notable Men and Women,* 178–90.

4. Rubí's *Dictamen* of Apr. 10, 1768, in Jackson and Foster, *Imaginary Kingdom,* 171–207 (quotations, 173, 182, 192, 201).

5. Kessell, *Mission of Sorrows,* 181–87 (quotation, 181). Crosby, *Antigua California,* 371–74.

6. Theodore E. Treutlein, ed., *Missionary in Sonora: The Travel Reports of Joseph Och, S.J., 1755–1767* (San Francisco: California Historical Society, 1965), 56.

7. Quoted by John L. Kessell, *Friars, Soldiers, and Reformers: Hispanic Arizona and the Sonora Mission Frontier, 1767–1856* (Tucson: University of Arizona Press, 1976), 14.

8. Kessell, *Friars, Soldiers, and Reformers,* 13–21 (quotation, 20), and "Friars versus Bureaucrats: The Mission as a Threatened Institution on the Arizona-Sonora Frontier, 1767–1842," *Western Historical Quarterly* 5 (April 1974), 151–62. See also Kieran R. McCarty, *A Spanish Frontier in the Enlightened Age: Franciscan Beginnings in Sonora and Arizona, 1767–1770* (Washington, D.C.: Academy of American Franciscan History, 1981).

9. Crosby, *Antigua California,* 374–86 (quotation, 385).

10. Warren L. Cook, *Flood Tide of Empire: Spain and the Pacific Northwest, 1543–1819* (New Haven: Yale University Press, 1973), 50–51; Maynard J. Geiger, *The Life and Times of Fray Junípero Serra, O.F.M.,* 2 vols. (Washington, D.C.: Academy of American Franciscan History, 1959), 1:179–81. For a fuller treatment, see Michael E. Thurman, *The Naval Department of San Blas: New Spain's Bastion for Alta California and Nootka, 1767–1798* (Glendale, Calif.: Arthur H. Clark, 1967).

11. Kessell, *Friars, Soldiers, and Reformers,* 22–25; McCarty, *Spanish Frontier,* 35–36.

12. Radding, *Wandering Peoples,* 276–77; Kessell, *Friars, Soldiers, and Reformers,* 47, 50. For an extensive report of Colonel Elizondo's war on the Seris, see Sheridan, *Empire of Sand,* 274–402.

13. Quoted by Irving Berdine Richman, *California under Spain and Mexico, 1535–1847* (1911; repr., New York: Cooper Square Publishers, 1965), 69–70.

14. Geiger, *Life and Times of Fray Junípero Serra,* 1:200–207 (quotation, 1:205); Crosby, *Antigua California,* 387–93; Weber, *Spanish Frontier,* 242–46.

15. Quoted by Thurman, *Naval Department of San Blas,* 71.

16. Geiger, *Life and Times of Fray Junípero Serra,* 1:208–27 (quotations, 1:220, 224).

17. Geiger, *Life and Times of Fray Junípero Serra,* 228–54 (quotations, 237, 248). Thurman, *Naval Department of San Blas,* 80–81, 95–96.

18. Radding, *Wandering Peoples,* 43–44, 179–80, and "The Colonial Pact and Changing Ethnic Frontiers in Highland Sonora, 1740–1840," in *CG,* 62.

19. Kessell, *Friars, Soldiers, and Reformers,* 42–57 (quotation, 42); McCarty, *Spanish Frontier,* 97–108. For the Querétaran friars' continued struggle with reformers to maintain control of their missions, see Kessell, "Friars versus Bureaucrats."

20. Navarro García, *Don José de Gálvez,* 200–202, 215–18; Jackson and Foster, *Imaginary Kingdom,* 79–84; Weber, *Spanish Frontier,* 215–20.

21. Quoted in Jackson and Foster, *Imaginary Kingdom,* 199.

22. On O'Conor and his tenure as commandant-inspector, see Donald C. Cutter, ed., *The Defense of Northern New Spain: Hugo O'Conor's Report to Teodoro de Croix, July 22, 1777* (Dallas: Southern Methodist University Press, 1994).

23. Max L. Moorhead, *The Apache Frontier: Jacobo Ugarte and Spanish-Indian Relations in Northern New Spain, 1769–1791* (Norman: University of Oklahoma Press, 1968), 115–42.

24. Quoted by Weber, *Spanish Frontier,* 227.

25. Bernardo de Gálvez, *Instructions for Governing the Interior Provinces of New Spain, 1786,* ed. Donald E. Worcester (Berkeley: Quivira Society, 1951), 27–85 (quotations, 34, 40, 79).

26. Kessell, *Friars, Soldiers, and Reformers,* 29–47 (quotation, 29), and "The Making of A Martyr: The Young Francisco Garcés," *NMHR* 45 (July 1970), 181–96 (quotations, 188, 190).

27. Kessell, "Friars, Bureaucrats, and the Seris of Sonora," *NMHR* 59 (January 1975), 73–95 (quotations, 89). See also Hammond, Rey, Fisher, and Mathes, *Apostolic Chronicle,* 2:230–40, and Sheridan, *Empire of Sand,* 405–42.

28. Kessell, *Friars, Soldiers, and Reformers,* 93–100 (quotation, 93); Geiger, *Life and Times of Fray Junípero Serra,* 2:135; Weber, *Spanish Frontier,* 249–53. See also Herbert E. Bolton's *Outpost of Empire: The Story of the Founding of San Francisco* (New York: Alfred A. Knopf, 1931).

29. Adams, "Fray Silvestre," *NMHR* 38 (April 1963), 97–138 (quotations, 109, 122, 132), and "Fray Francisco Atanasio Domínguez and Fray Silvestre Vélez de Escalante," *Utah Historical Quarterly* 44 (Winter 1976), 40–58 (quotation, 48).

30. Joseph P. Sánchez, *Explorers, Traders, and Slavers: Forging the Old Spanish Trail, 1678–1850* (Salt Lake City: University of Utah Press, 1997), treats Juan María Antonio Rivera's two expeditions in 1765 to the country of the Utes and translates his diaries. Twitchell, *Spanish Archives of New Mexico,* 2:255.

31. See Adams and Chávez, *Missions of New Mexico* (quotations, 12, 279).

32. Adams and Chávez, *Missions of New Mexico* (quotations, 283, 284). Kessell, *Friars, Soldiers, and Reformers,* 110–21.

33. Fray Angélico Chávez and Ted J. Warner, eds., *The Domínguez-Escalante Journal: Their Expedition through Colorado, Utah, Arizona, and New Mexico in 1776* (Provo: Brigham Young University Press, 1976), quotations, 72, 99–100, and Herbert E. Bolton, *Pageant in the*

Wilderness: The Story of the Escalante Expedition to the Interior Basin, 1776 (Salt Lake City: Utah State Historical Society, 1950).

34. Kessell, *Friars, Soldiers, and Reformers,* 130–46. Alfred Barnaby Thomas, *Teodoro de Croix and the Northern Frontier of New Spain, 1776–1783* (Norman: University of Oklahoma Press, 1941), quotations, 222, 231, 238. For the full story, see Mark Santiago, *Massacre at the Yuma Crossing: Spanish Relations with the Quechans, 1779–1782* (Tucson: University of Arizona Press, 1998). The four martyred Franciscans are eulogized in Hammond, Rey, Fisher, and Mathes, *Apostolic Chronicle,* 2:246–74.

35. Weber, *Spanish Frontier,* 266–67.

36. William H. Broughton, "Francisco Rendón: Spanish Agent in Philadelphia 1779–1786, Intendant of Spanish Louisiana 1793–1796" (Ph.D. diss., University of New Mexico, 1994).

CHAPTER 11

The lead quotation is from Noel M. Loomis and Abraham P. Nasatir, *Pedro Vial and the Roads to Santa Fe* (Norman: University of Oklahoma Press, 1967), 276.

1. Although several historians have alluded in print to this remarkable case, no one has described it fully. The documents reside in the Spanish Archives of New Mexico (SANM), Series II, nos. 673 and 690 (microfilm reel 10, frames 752–88 and 859–66), New Mexico State Records Center and Archives, Santa Fe. For background, see Charles R. Cutter, *The Legal Culture of Northern New Spain, 1700–1810* (Albuquerque: University of New Mexico Press, 1992).

2. Alfred Barnaby Thomas, ed., *The Plains Indians and New Mexico, 1751–1778* (Albuquerque: University of New Mexico Press, 1940), 49–59, 190–211 (quotations, 191, 198), and ed., *Forgotten Frontiers: A Study of the Spanish Indian Policy of Don Juan Bautista de Anza, Governor of New Mexico, 1777–1787* (Norman: University of Oklahoma Press, 1932), and *Teodoro de Croix,* 35–47. John, *Storms,* 500–22.

3. Quoted in Thomas, *Plains Indians,* 134–35.

4. Kessell, *Kiva, Cross, and Crown,* 397–401 (quotations, 400, 401; map of the campaign, evidently by Miera y Pacheco, following p. 358). Relevant documents are in Thomas, *Forgotten Frontiers,* 119–42. For recent refinements regarding Anza's route, see Ronald E. Kessler, ed., "The Diary of Juan Bautista de Anza," *The San Luis Valley Historian* 26:1 (1994), 4–38, and Phil Carson, *Across the Northern Frontier: Spanish Explorations in Colorado* (Boulder: Johnson Books, 1998), 134–54, who attempted in vain to track where Cuerno Verde's head-dress may have ended up (149, 226 n. 34).

5. Pertinent correspondence between Anza and Croix is translated in Thomas, *Forgotten Frontiers,* 142–71, 221–45 (quotations, 236, 244). John, *Storms,* 593–601. Adams, "Fray Francisco Atanasio Domínguez and Fray Silvestre Vélez de Escalante," 57.

6. Kessell, *Kiva, Cross, and Crown,* 348, 378.

7. Robert H. Jackson, *Indian Population Decline: The Missions of Northwestern New Spain, 1687–1840* (Albuquerque: University of New Mexico Press, 1995), 118. Kessell, *Friars, Soldiers, and Reformers,* 142.

8. Marc Simmons, "New Mexico's Smallpox Epidemic of 1780–81," *NMHR* 41 (October 1966), 319–26. Kessell, *Friars, Soldiers, and Reformers,* 142. Cook, *Flood Tide of Empire,* 80, 95.

9. Documents in Thomas, *Forgotten Frontiers,* 171–221 (quotation, 180). John, *Storms,* 601–605. See also Marc Simmons, "Spanish Attempts to Open a New Mexico-Sonora Road," *Arizona and the West* 17 (Spring 1975), 5–20.

10. A redrawing of the 1779 Miera map with a translation of the headnote are in Adams and Chávez, *Missions of New Mexico,* 2–4.

11. Thomas, *Teodoro de Croix,* 107–108, and *Forgotten Frontiers,* 379 n. 59. The tension between New Mexicans and their reforming governor is well described by Carlos R. Herrera, "The King's Governor: Juan Bautista de Anza and Bourbon New Mexico in the Era of Imperial Reform, 1778–1788" (Ph.D. diss., University of New Mexico, 2000).

12. Rick Hendricks, "Church-State Relations in Anza's New Mexico, 1777–1787," *Catholic Southwest* 9 (1998), 24–42; Herrera, "King's Governor," 147–245. In 1776, with a full roster, there had been twenty-six subsidized Franciscans, with four others serving as parish priests in El Paso and the villas of Santa Fe, Santa Cruz, and Albuquerque.

13. Thomas, *Forgotten Frontier,* 374 (quotation, 364). John, *Storms,* 609–11. Navarro García, *Don José de Gálvez,* 429–43, 506.

14. Kessell, *Kiva, Cross, and Crown,* 401–407 (quotations, 403). John, *Storms,* 668–89. The documents are in Thomas, *Forgotten Frontiers,* 292–364. Trade advantages to the Comanches are considered by Hamalainen, "Western Comanche Trade Center," 503–504.

15. Moorhead, *Apache Frontier,* 143–69; Alfred Barnaby Thomas, "San Carlos, A Comanche Pueblo on the Arkansas, 1787," *The Colorado Magazine* 6 (May 1929), 79–91; John, *Storms,* 732–35.

16. Navarro García, *Don José de Gálvez,* 506. Moorhead, *Apache Frontier,* 193–96.

17. John, *Storms,* 654–68, 718–32, 739–49 (quotation, 727); Loomis and Nasatir, *Pedro Vial,* 262–318 (including translations of the diaries); Kessell, *Kiva, Cross, and Crown,* 353.

18. Loomis and Nasatir, *Pedro Vial,* 327–68 (quotations, 349, 353); John, *Storms,* 448–53, 525, 612–13, 704–705, 742–49; Chipman, *Spanish Texas,* 186–87; and Chipman and Joseph, *Notable Men and Women,* 150–225, for chapters on Athanase de Mézières, Antonio Gil Ybarbo, and Domingo Cabello.

19. Moorhead, *Apache Frontier,* 193–96.

20. Kessell, *Friars, Soldiers, and Reformers,* 127–28, 136, 160–63, 169–77.

21. Navarro García, *Don José de Gálvez,* 486–87; Moorhead, *Apache Frontier,* 278–79.

22. Cook, *Flood Tide of Empire,* 54–84 (quotations, 61, 82); Geiger, *Life and Times of Fray Junípero Serra,* 2:5–11. See also Iris H. W. Engstrand, "Seekers of the 'Northern Mystery': European Exploration of California and the Pacific," in *CE,* 78–110.

23. Francis F. Guest, "Junípero Serra and His Approach to the Indians," in *SCSH*, 89–129. William E. Evans, "The Confirmation Controversy of 1779," in *SCSH*, 131–38. See also the concise demographic summary in Weber, *Spanish Frontier*, 258–65.

24. Geiger, *Life and Times of Fray Junípero Serra*, 2:343–74 (quotation, 369). The custody of San Carlos in Sonora, the only one of Reyes's four proposed custodies actually set in motion, functioned erratically between 1783 and 1791, when it was abolished by royal decree and the old order restored. See Kessell, *Friars, Soldiers, and Reformers*, 151–59, 164–68.

25. Geiger, *Life and Times of Fray Junípero Serra*, 2:58–67 (quotation, 65).

26. A representative sample of essays about the California missions appears in *CC1*:303–497. See also Robert H. Jackson, "The Formation of Frontier Indigenous Communities: Missions in California and Texas," in *NV*, 131–56, and several essays in *CE*. Albert L. Hurtado, *Intimate Frontiers: Sex, Gender, and Culture in Old California* (Albuquerque: University of New Mexico Press, 1999), 1–19, discusses sexuality in multicultural Franciscan California.

27. Loomis and Nasatir, *Pedro Vial*, 369–407 (quotation, 373).

CHAPTER 12

The epigraph is quoted by Abraham P. Nasatir, *Borderlands in Retreat: From Spanish Louisiana to the Far Southwest* (Albuquerque: University of New Mexico Press, 1976), 126.

1. Cook, *Flood Tide of Empire*, 85–179 (quotations, 105, 130, 172, 179).

2. Cook, *Flood Tide of Empire*, 200–49 (quotation, 235).

3. Noel M. Loomis, "Philip Nolan's Entry into Texas in 1800," in John Francis McDermott, ed., *The Spanish in the Mississippi Valley, 1762–1804* (Urbana: University of Illinois Press, 1974), 120–32 (quotations, 124, 132); Jackson, *Los Mesteños*, 451–61 (quotation, 456); Chipman, *Spanish Texas*, 212–15.

4. Loomis and Nasatir, *Pedro Vial*, 408–48 (quotations, 408, 410). Chávez, *Origins of New Mexico Families*, 202.

5. Lansing B. Bloom, *Early Vaccination in New Mexico* (Santa Fe: Santa Fe New Mexican Publishing Corp., 1924). De la Teja, *San Antonio de Béxar*, 21.

6. Ross Frank, "Demographic, Social, and Economic Change in New Mexico," in *NV*, 57–58.

7. Janie Louise Aragón, "The People of Santa Fe in the 1790s," *Aztlán* 7 (Fall 1976), 391–417.

8. Adrian Bustamante and Marc Simmons, eds., *The Exposition on the Province of New Mexico, 1812, by Pedro Baptista Pino* (Albuquerque: University of New Mexico Press, 1995), 7 n. 2. Kessell, *Kiva, Cross, and Crown*, 415–22.

9. "Report of Governor Chacón, 1803," in Marc Simmons, *Coronado's Land: Essays on Daily Life in Colonial New Mexico* (Albuquerque: University of New Mexico Press, 1991), 162–72 (quotation, 165–66).

10. "Spanish Arizona in 1804," in Kieran McCarty, *Desert Documentary: The Spanish Years, 1767–1821* (Tucson: Arizona Historical Society, 1976), 82–92 (quotations, 87–88, 91); Kessell, *Friars, Soldiers, and Reformers*, 177–206 (quotation, 187). See also Henry F. Dobyns, *Spanish Colonial Tucson: A Demographic History* (Tucson: University of Arizona Press, 1976), and Daniel S. Matson and Bernard L. Fontana, eds., *Friar Bringas Reports to the King: Methods of Indoctrination on the Frontier of New Spain, 1796–97* (Tucson: University of Arizona Press, 1977).

11. Salomé Hernández, "No Settlement without Women: Three California Settlement Schemes, 1790–1800," in *SCSH*, 309–38 (quotation, 333). Antonia I. Castañeda, "Engendering the History of Alta California, 1769–1848," in *CE*, 230–59 (quotation, 241).

12. Weber, *Spanish Frontier*, 265.

13. Cook, *Flood Tide of Empire*, 389–96 (quotations, 393). Donald C. Cutter presents the observations of Spanish naval officers who called at Monterey the same year in *California in 1792: A Spanish Naval Visit* (Norman: University of Oklahoma Press, 1990).

14. Robert Archibald, "The Economy of the Alta California Missions, 1803–21," in *SCSH*, 339–51; Maynard Geiger, *Franciscan Missionaries in Hispanic California, 1769–1848: A Biographical Dictionary* (San Marino: The Huntington Library, 1969), 136–42, 235–39; Geiger, *Life and Times of Fray Junípero Serra*, 2:26–27; Weber, *Spanish Frontier*, 262–64; Steven W. Hackel, "Land, Labor, and Production: The Colonial Economy of Spanish and Mexican California," in *CE*, 111–46.

15. Quoted in David J. Weber, ed., *Foreigners in Their Native Land: Historical Roots of the Mexican Americans* (Albuquerque: University of New Mexico Press, 1973), 66.

16. Weber, *Spanish Frontier*, 289–91. See also Stephen E. Ambrose, *Undaunted Courage: Meriwether Lewis, Thomas Jefferson, and the Opening of the American West* (New York: Simon and Schuster, 1996), 51–79.

CHAPTER 13

The initial quotation is from Loomis and Nasatir, *Pedro Vial*, 244.

1. Cook, *Flood Tide of Empire*, 446–90 (quotations, 453). Cook, utilizing documentation from all sides, first pointed out convincingly that Spaniards "made repeated efforts of considerable magnitude to intercept Lewis and Clark, and came surprisingly and dangerously close to achieving their objective" (461 n. 72). Loomis and Nasatir, *Pedro Vial*, 171–204, 412.

2. Kessell, *Kiva, Cross, and Crown*, 434–35.

3. Cook, *Flood Tide of Empire*, 470–83 (quotation, 476). Donald Jackson, ed., *The Journals of Zebulon Montgomery Pike with Letters and Related Documents*, 2 vols. (Norman: University of Oklahoma Press, 1966), 2:57–58.

4. Jackson, *Journals of Zebulon Montgomery Pike*, 1:290–385, 2:147–53 (quotation, 2:147). Cook (*Flood Tide of Empire*, 477–83) argues persuasively that Melgares in 1806 had no knowledge of Pike's exploration, even though the latter convinced himself that the Spaniards were searching specifically for him. Melgares, instead, had meant to turn

back Freeman and Custis on the Red (already met by Viana) or Lewis and Clark on
the Missouri had he intercepted either party.

5. Jackson, *Journals of Zebulon Montgomery Pike,* 1:385–412, 2:59–62 (quotations, 1:391, 396, 405, 407). Editor Jackson, on the basis of Pike's extensive correspondence, believed that the American lieutenant truly thought he and his men were on the headwaters of the Red, not the Rio Grande. See also Arthur Gómez, "Royalist in Transition: Facundo Melgares, the Last Spanish Governor of New Mexico, 1818–1822," *NMHR* 68 (October 1993), 371–87.

As a prisoner in New Spain, Zalmon Coley found himself caught in a maelstrom. Recalled from Santa Fe to Chihuahua, he cheated death in the roll of dice among Nolan's survivors, only to be imprisoned in Acapulco, freed by Mexican insurgents, recaptured by royalists, and executed by firing squad in 1812. Ernest R. Liljegren, "Zalmon Coley: The Second Anglo-American in Santa Fe," *NMHR* 62 (July 1987), 263–86.

6. On the remarkable Walker, see Elizabeth A. H. John, "The Riddle of Map Maker Juan Pedro Walker," in *Essays on the History of North American Discovery and Exploration,* ed. Stanley J. Palmer and Dennis Reinhartz (College Station: Texas A&M University Press, 1988), 102–32.

7. Jackson, *Journals of Zebulon Montgomery Pike,* 1:412–48, 2:364–68 (quotations, 1:412–13, 423, 424, 425; 2:241, 255).

8. Jackson, *Journals of Zebulon Montgomery Pike,* 1:436–48 (quotations, 1:438, 439, 440; 2:80). Chipman, *Spanish Texas,* 224–30. Jack Jackson (*Los Mesteños,* 485–90, 525) discusses certain of Cordero's edicts "addressing the laxities he saw around Béxar" (487).

9. For a biography of Pike, see W. Eugene Hollon, *The Lost Pathfinder: Zebulon Montgomery Pike* (Norman: University of Oklahoma Press, 1949).

10. Cook, *Flood Tide of Empire,* 491–95. Loomis and Nasatir (*Pedro Vial,* 459–534) translated Amangual's 1808 diary.

11. Jesús F. de la Teja, "Rebellion on the Frontier," in Gerald E. Poyo, ed., *Tejano Journey, 1770–1850* (Austin: University of Texas Press, 1996), 15–30, and "Spanish Colonial Texas," in *NV,* 106–30 (Cabello quotation, 114); Félix D. Almaráz, Jr., *Tragic Cavalier: Governor Manuel Salcedo of Texas, 1808–1813* (Austin: University of Texas Press, 1971), 22–129 (quotation, 112); Chipman, *Spanish Texas,* 216–34 (quotation, 230); Jackson, *Los Mesteños,* 525–30; and Gómez, "Royalist in Transition," 378–79.

12. Bustamante and Simmons, *Exposition on the Province of New Mexico* (quotations, 10, 18 n. 8, 41 n. 1, 44); Jim F. Heath and Frederick M. Nunn, "Negroes and Discrimination in Colonial New Mexico: Don Pedro Bautista Pino's Startling Statement of 1812 in Perspective," *Phylon* 31 (1970), 372–78. See also Frank McNitt, *Navajo Wars: Military Campaigns, Slave Raids, and Reprisals* (Albuquerque: University of New Mexico Press, 1972), 41–47; David J. Weber, *The Mexican Frontier, 1821–1846: The American Southwest under Mexico* (Albuquerque: University of New Mexico Press, 1982), 16–18; Kessell, *Friars, Soldiers, and Reformers,* 218; Almaráz, *Tragic Cavalier,* 66–67.

Robert E. Wright, "How Many Are 'A Few'?: Catholic Clergy in Central and Northern New Mexico, 1780–1851," in Thomas J. Steele, Paul Rhetts, and Barbe Awalt, eds., *Seeds of Struggle/Harvest of Faith: The History of the Catholic Church in New Mexico*

(Albuquerque: LPD Press, 1998), 219–61, seeks to put exaggerated claims like Pino's about the spiritual backwardness of New Mexico in historical context.

13. Jackson, *Los Mesteños,* 530–51; Chipman, *Spanish Texas,* 233–37 (quotation, 235); Almaráz, *Tragic Cavalier,* 130–82 (quotation, 167); Teja, "Rebellion on the Frontier." See also Chipman and Joseph, *Notable Men and Women,* 226–49. Jackson, *Journals of Zebulon Montgomery Pike,* 2:17–18 n. 20, has James B. Wilkinson dying in 1813 at Dauphin Island, Alabama.

14. Quoted by Chipman, *Spanish Texas,* 298 n. 82. Weber, *Mexican Frontier,* 9–10, 294 n. 21.

15. Cook, *Flood Tide of Empire,* 495–506 (quotation, 498). C. Alan Hutchinson, *Frontier Settlement in Mexican California: The Híjar-Padrés Colony, and Its Origins, 1769–1835* (New Haven: Yale University Press, 1969), 32–39.

16. Cook, *Flood Tide of Empire,* 514–22 (quotation, 518–19).

17. Cook, *Flood Tide of Empire,* 513; Loomis and Nasatir, *Pedro Vial,* 455–56, 536–40; Gómez, "Royalist in Transition," 379–86.

18. Chipman, *Spanish Texas,* 239–40; Jackson, *Los Mesteños,* 561–71.

19. Kessell, *Friars, Soldier, and Reformers,* 233.

20. Weber, *Mexican Frontier,* 1–14 (quotation, 8); W. H. Timmons, *El Paso: A Borderland History* (El Paso: Texas Western Press, 1990), 70–72; Gómez, "Royalist in Transition," 386–87.

21. David J. Weber, ed., "An Unforgettable Day, Facundo Melgares on Independence," *NMHR* 48 (January 1973), 27–44 (quotations, 37, 40, 42).

22. Thomas James, *Three Years among the Indians and Mexicans* (1846; repr., Philadelphia: J. B. Lippincott Co., 1962), 87–88, 89.

23. A. H. Clark in the foreword to D. W. Meinig, *Southwest: Three Peoples in Geographical Change, 1600–1970* (New York: Oxford University Press, 1971). Meinig (3) takes on the Southwest, referring to it initially as "a distinctive place to the American mind but a somewhat blurred place on American maps." For an idea of how complex defining the region has become, see articles in the *Journal of the Southwest* during the 1990s, especially those by James Byrkit (Autumn 1992) and Michael J. Riley (Autumn 1994).

GLOSSARY

Adelantado. Medieval Castilian office transferred to the New World by which a wealthy individual contracted with the crown to conquer and defend a specified territory in turn for administrative and economic privileges.

Alcalde mayor. In New Spain and South America an administrative officer equivalent to a governor or corregidor; in New Mexico one of six or eight district officers appointed by the governor.

Alcalde ordinario. Local magistrate of a municipality.

Alcaldía mayor. District administered by an alcalde mayor.

Alférez (Afz.). Ensign, lowest-ranking commissioned officer.

Americano. Citizen or resident of the United States.

Antigua California. Baja California, present-day Mexican state and territory.

Atole. A maize (cornmeal) gruel or thin porridge.

Audiencia. Superior civil tribunal and legislative council in the Spanish Indies.

Auto de fe. Public spectacle of sentencing by the Inquisition and resulting punishment of prisoners by the secular authorities, auto da fé (from the Portuguese).

Barranca. Deep gully or canyon.

Bejareño. Citizen or resident of greater San Antonio de Bexar, Texas.

Belduque. Trade knife.

Bidarka. Portable skin boat of Alaskan and Aleut Natives.

Bozal. African-born black imported as a slave.

Caballero. Warrior knight; man on horseback; gentleman.

Cabecera. Head mission village and residence of the missionary.

Cabildo. Municipal council.

Cacique. Hereditary chief among the Native peoples of the Caribbean; title extended to other Indian headmen; in New Mexico, chief sacred leader among the Pueblos.

Californio. Culturally Hispanic citizen or resident of Spanish or Mexican California.

Camino real. Government road or highway; *Camino Real de la Tierra Adentro,* the main trunk road from Mexico City through Zacatecas to Santa Fe.

Casas reales. Town hall, government buildings.

Castas. Mixed-bloods, as opposed to Spaniards and Indians.

Chichimeca. Member of numerous mostly hunter-gatherer peoples of the Gran Chichimeca; Indians considered wild by Europeans.

Churro. Variety of small, lean sheep with long-stapled, greaseless wool.

Cíbolo. Buffalo or bison.

Ciudad. City, highest municipal designation.

Coahuila. Province carved out of Nueva Vizcaya and Nuevo León south of the Rio Grande, capital Monclova; presently a Mexican state bordering on Texas.

Conde. Count, noble title of Castile ranking with *marqués*.

Congrega. A sort of bastard encomienda employed in eighteenth-century Nuevo León to round up Native work gangs.

Congregación. Mission congregation brought together from diverse villages or pueblos.

Convento. Franciscan dwelling, from rooms attached to a mission complex to the *Convento Grande* in Mexico City, headquarters of the Holy Gospel Province.

Cortes. Parliament.

Coureur de bois. French woodsman, hunter, trapper, and trader, often employed by a fur company, *voyageur*.

Coyote. Mixed-blood of mestizo and mulatto ancestry, but often applied imprecisely; sometimes synonymous with *mestizo*.

Criollo. Person of Spanish origin born in the colonies, creole.

Cuartel. Houseblock, as among the Pueblo Indians; barracks; district or quarter as of a city.

Cuera. Protective several-ply leather jacket, often sleeveless and thigh length.

Custody. Franciscan administrative unit, beneath and dependent on a province.

Despoblado. Largely uninhabited region, wasteland.

Doctrina. Native congregation, mission; catechism.

Don, doña. Form of respectful address, once only of the nobility, Spanish or Native, but relaxed subsequently; used properly with given or full name, never with surname alone.

Donado. In sixteenth-century New Spain, an Indian boy entrusted to the Franciscans, raised by them, and in their service as assistant and catechist.

Ducat (ducado). Unit of Spanish currency somewhat lower in value, when considered in money of account, than the peso, but taken in Spain as roughly equivalent.

Empresario. Contractor in colonization, like Stephen F. Austin.

Encomienda. Grant of Indian labor or tribute; *encomendero*, holder of an encomienda.

Entrada. Expedition or exploration, entry.

Esclavo de guerra. Native taken in just war and enslaved.

Esclavo de rescate. Ransomed slave allegedly in bondage among Native peoples.

Espada ancha. Short, broad sword.

Español. Spaniard, culturally or racially.

Española. Hispaniola, or Santo Domingo, the Caribbean island of which Haiti occupies the western third and the Dominican Republic the remainder.

Español mexicano. Spaniard from Mexico City and environs.

Establecimiento de paz. Peace camp, settlement of pacified Indians, for example of Apaches.

Estancia. Stockraising property, general smaller and less diversified than a hacienda; *estanciero,* holder of an estancia.

Fandango. Lively regional Spanish dance and its music.

Fanega. Regionally variable dry measure of between 1.5 and 3.0 bushels or the area planted with that quantity of seed.

Filibustero. Filibuster, freebooter, mercenary.

Fiscal. Royal prosecutor and chief legal adviser to the viceroy; Native mission official.

Fray. Member of a mendicant order, priest or lay brother, friar; properly used only with given or full name, not with surname alone; Jesuits are not friars.

Genízaro. Ransomed or captured Indian acculturated in Hispanic New Mexico or a descendant, member of the underclass.

Gente de razón. Literally, people of reason; persons culturally Hispanic and not identified as Indians.

Gobierno. A governor's jurisdiction.

Gran Chichimeca. The vast, mostly high desert north from Zacatecas and including today's states of Durango and Chihuahua; home of the Chichimeca Indians.

Grande. One of the great noble lords of Spain permitted to call the king cousin.

Guerrilla. Irregular warfare; literally, little war.

Hechicero. Native spiritual leader, shaman, medicine man.

Hidalgo. Member of Spain's lowest-ranking nobility or gentry.

Indio ladino. Hispanicized, Spanish-speaking Indian, *ladino.*

Indios bárbaros. Native nations that resisted Spanish domination; literally, barbarous Indians.

Isleño. Islander, specifically a member or descendant of the Canary Island families that settled in Texas.

Jacal. Hut; type of pole and earth construction.

Juicio plenario. The second stage of a legal proceeding, during which the parties offered judicial proofs of their positions.

Junta. Governing council.

Kachina. A spirit being among the Pueblo Indians of New Mexico and Arizona often represented by a masked human male.

Kiva. Ceremonial chamber among the Pueblo Indians, circular or rectangular, below or above ground.

Lay brother. Member of a religious order not ordained as a priest.

League. In northern New Spain, generally about 2.6 miles.

Lobo. Mixed-blood of Indian and mestizo ancestry, but often used imprecisely.

Macana. Obsidian-edged, wooden sword; any Indian war club.

Maestre de campo. Field-grade officer; often second-in-command, as of the Coronado and Oñate expeditions; commander of the militia, as in seventeenth-century New Mexico.

Manta. As an item of Indian tribute in New Mexico, a piece of cotton cloth less than six-feet square.

Marqués. Marquis, noble title of Castile ranking with *conde*.

Menino. Noble page in Spain's royal household.

Merced de tierra. Land grant.

Mestizo. Mixed-blood of European and Indian ancestry; loosely, any mixed-blood.

Mitote. Among Chichimecas, a wild victory ceremonial.

Montañés. Native of the northern Spanish province of Santander.

Mulatto. Mixed-blood of African and European ancestry.

Naboría. Free Indian wageworker.

New Spain, Nueva España. The name given by Hernán Cortés to his conquest in 1521; a viceroyalty after 1535 with jurisdiction over the area of present-day Mexico, territory north and south, and the Philippines.

Norteño. A person from the north; a member of certain Native nations north of Texas allied with or including Comanches.

Nueva California. Alta California, a part of the present-day U.S. state.

Nueva Galicia. From the 1530s to 1560s, all of northwestern New Spain out of which Nueva Vizcaya and other provinces emerged, capital Zacatecas.

Nueva Vizcaya. Vast province north of Nueva Galicia and south of New Mexico, capital Durango; present-day Mexican states of Durango and Chihuahua.

Nuevo León. Province in northeastern Mexico, capital Monterrey; presently a Mexican state east of Coahuila bordering on Texas.

Nuevo Santander. Province on the Gulf of Mexico formed in the 1740s out of unclaimed land, Coahuila, and Nuevo León, including territory on both sides of the lower Rio Grande; today's Mexican state of Tamaulipas.

Pascua Florida. Easter.

Patronato Real. Administration of the Roman Catholic Church in Spain and its empire conceded by the Papacy to the Spanish monarchy.

Peninsular. Person born in Spain on the Iberian Peninsula.

Peñol. Steep-sided mesa, like that of Acoma in New Mexico.

Pimería Alta. Land of the northern Piman peoples; today's Sonora north of the Altar River and Arizona south of the Gila.

Poblador. Settler, colonist.

Presidio. Garrison of salaried soldiers or the post they occupied.

Protector de indios. Official, culturally Hispanic, assigned as attorney for an Indian group.

Provincial. Superior of a province of one of the religious orders, father or minister provincial.

Provincias Internas. The General Command of the Interior Provinces set up in 1776 and comprising the Californias, Sonora, Nueva Vizcaya, New Mexico, Coahuila, and Texas.

Ranchería. Indian village less compact than a pueblo and the people who belong to it.

Real. Mining camp or town; the eighth part of a peso.

Reconquista. The Roman Catholic reconquest of the Iberian Peninsula from the Muslims, eighth century to 1492; also other reconquests, as of New Mexico in the 1690s.

Regidor. Town councilman.

Religioso. Religious, member of a religious order.

Repartimiento. Labor levy.

Requerimiento. C. 1512, a nine-hundred-word statement read by law to Indians before a conquistador could commence hostilities.

Residencia. Judicial review of an official's term of office at its conclusion.

Rico. Member perceived to be of the rich upper class.

Santafecino. Citizen or resident of Santa Fe.

Sargento mayor. Third in command of Oñate's army; officer in command of New Mexico's militia in the seventeenth century.

Sentencia. The final stage of a legal proceeding, when acquittal or punishment was proclaimed.

Sinaloa. Province on the west coast of New Spain south of Sonora and governed as Sinaloa-Sonora after 1733; current Mexican state.

Situado. Government subsidy, as for the administration and defense of Florida or the Philippines.

Sonora. Province north of Sinaloa; today's Mexican state plus former Pimería Alta.

Sumaria. The fact-finding first stage of a legal proceeding.

Tlatole. Native call to arms; *tlatolero,* Native agitator.

Vaquero. Cattle hand, cowboy.

Vara. Linear measure, approximately thirty-three inches; five thousand varas equaled a league.

Vecino. Citizen or householder, neighbor.

Villa. Chartered municipality ranking below a *ciudad,* or city, and above a *pueblo,* or town.

Visita. Secondary mission village, preaching station; inspection.

Voyageur. Employee of a fur-trading company; French woodsman, hunter, trapper, and trader, *coureur de bois.*

Yuca. Cassava root.

Zemi. Among the Taino Indians of the Caribbean a small, cotton, wood, or stone image representing a spirit.

WORKS CITED

PUBLISHED PRIMARY SOURCES

Adams, Eleanor B., ed. *Bishop Tamarón's Visitation of New Mexico, 1760.* Albuquerque: Historical Society of New Mexico, 1954.

Adams, Eleanor B., and Fray Angélico Chávez, eds. *The Missions of New Mexico, 1776: A Description by Fray Francisco Atanasio Domínguez with Other Contemporary Documents.* Albuquerque: University of New Mexico Press, 1956.

Bolton, Herbert E., ed. *Kino's Historical Memoir of Pimería Alta.* 2 vols. Berkeley: University of California Press, 1948.

———, ed. *Spanish Exploration in the Southwest, 1542–1706.* 1908. Reprint, New York: Barnes and Noble, 1967.

Burrus, Ernest J., ed. *Kino and Manje, Explorers of Sonora and Arizona: Their Vision of the Future.* Rome: Jesuit Historical Institute, 1971.

———, ed. "A Tragic Interlude in the Reconquest of New Mexico." *Manuscripta* 29 (1985), 154–65.

Bustamante, Adrian, and Marc Simmons, eds. *The Exposition on the Province of New Mexico, 1812, by Pedro Baptista Pino.* Albuquerque: University of New Mexico Press, 1995.

Chapa, Juan Bautista. "Historia del Nuevo Reino de León de 1650 á 1690 por Juan Bautista Chapa." In *Historia de Nuevo León con noticias sobre Coahuila, Tamaulipas, Texas y Nuevo México, escrita en el siglo XVII por el Cap. Alonso de León, Juan Bautista Chapa y el Gral. Fernando Sánchez de Zamora.* Edited by Israel Cavazos Garza. Monterrey: Gobierno del Estado de Nuevo León, 1961.

Chávez, Fray Angélico, ed. *The Oroz Codex.* Washington, D.C.: Academy of American Franciscan History, 1972.

Chávez, Fray Angélico, and Ted J. Warner, eds. *The Domínguez-Escalante Journal: Their Expedition through Colorado, Utah, Arizona, and New Mexico in 1776.* Provo: Brigham Young University Press, 1976.

Clayton, Lawrence A., Vernon James Knight, Jr., and Edward C. Moore, eds. *The De Soto Chronicles: The Expedition of Hernando de Soto to North America in 1539–1543.* Tuscaloosa: University of Alabama Press, 1993.

Covey, Cyclone, ed. *Cabeza de Vaca's Adventures in the Unknown Interior of America.* Albuquerque: University of New Mexico Press, 1983.

Craddock, Jerry R., ed. "Juan de Oñate in Quivira." *Journal of the Southwest* 40 (Winter 1998), 481–540.

———, ed. "Philological Notes on the Hammond and Rey Translation of the '[Relación de la] Entrada que hizo en el Nuevo México Francisco Sánchez Chamuscado en junio de [15]81' by Hernán Gallegos, Notary of the Expedition." *Romance Philology* 49 (May 1996), 351–63.

Cutter, Donald C., ed. *The California Coast: A Bilingual Edition of Documents from the Sutro Collection.* Norman: University of Oklahoma Press, 1969.

———, ed. *California in 1792: A Spanish Naval Visit.* Norman: University of Oklahoma Press, 1990.

———, ed. *The Defense of Northern New Spain: Hugo O'Conor's Report to Teodoro de Croix, July 22, 1777.* Dallas: Southern Methodist University Press, 1994.

Espinosa, J. Manuel, ed. *The Pueblo Indian Revolt of 1696 and the Franciscan Missions in New Mexico: Letters of the Missionaries and Related Documents.* Norman: University of Oklahoma Press, 1988.

Favata, Martin A., and José B. Fernández, eds. *The Account: Alvar Núñez Cabeza de Vaca's "Relación."* Houston: Arte Público Press, 1993.

Foster, William C., ed. *The La Salle Expedition to Texas: The Journal of Henri Joutel, 1684–1687.* Translated by Johanna S. Warren. Austin: Texas State Historical Association, 1998.

Gálvez, Bernardo de. *Instructions for Governing the Interior Provinces of New Spain, 1786.* Edited by Donald E. Worcester. Berkeley: Quivira Society, 1951.

García Icazbalceta, Joaquín, ed. *Nueva colección de documentos para la historia de México.* 5 vols. 1886–92. Reprint, Mexico City: Editorial Salvador Chávez Hayhoe, 1941.

Gibson, Charles, ed. *The Spanish Tradition in America.* New York: Harper and Row, 1968.

Gómez Canedo, Lino, ed. *Primeras exploraciones y poblamiento de Texas (1686–1694).* Monterrey: Instituto Tecnológico y de Estudios Superiores, 1968.

Hackett, Charles Wilson, ed. *Historical Documents Relating to New Mexico, Nueva Vizcaya, and Approaches Thereto, to 1773.* 3 vols. Washington, D.C.: Carnegie Institution, 1923–37.

Hackett, Charles Wilson, ed., and Charmion Clair Shelby, trans. *Revolt of the Pueblo Indians of New Mexico and Otermín's Attempted Reconquest, 1680–1682.* 2 vols. Albuquerque: University of New Mexico Press, 1942.

Hadley, Diana, Thomas H. Naylor, and Mardith K. Schuetz-Miller, eds. *The Presidio and Militia on the Northern Frontier of New Spain.* Vol. 2, part 2. *The Central Corridor and the Texas Corridor, 1700–1765.* Tucson: University of Arizona Press, 1997.

Hammond, George P., and Agapito Rey, eds. *Don Juan de Oñate, Colonizer of New Mexico, 1595–1628.* 2 vols. Albuquerque: University of New Mexico Press, 1953).

———, eds. *Narratives of the Coronado Expedition, 1540–1542.* Albuquerque: University of New Mexico Press, 1940.

———, eds. *The Rediscovery of New Mexico, 1580–1594: The Explorations of Chamuscado, Espejo, Castaño de Sosa, Morlete, and Leyva de Bonilla and Humaña.* Albuquerque: University of New Mexico Press, 1966.

Hammond, George P., Agapito Rey, Vivian C. Fisher, and W. Michael Mathes, eds. *Apostolic Chronicle of Juan Domingo Arricivita: The Franciscan Mission Frontier in the*

Eighteenth Century in Arizona, Texas, and the Californias. 2 vols. Berkeley, Calif.: Academy of American Franciscan History, 1996.

Hendricks, Rick, ed. "The Last Years of Francisco Cuervo y Valdés." *La Crónica de Nuevo México* 36 (July 1993), 2–3.

Hendricks, Rick, and Meredith D. Dodge, eds. *Two Hearts, One Soul: The Correspondence of the Condesa de Galve, 1688–96.* Albuquerque: University of New Mexico Press, 1993.

Hendricks, Rick, and John P. Wilson, eds. *The Navajos in 1705: Roque Madrid's Campaign Journal.* Albuquerque: University of New Mexico Press, 1996.

Hodge, Frederick Webb, George P. Hammond, and Agapito Rey, eds. *Fray Alonso de Benavides' Revised Memorial of 1634.* Albuquerque: University of New Mexico Press, 1945.

Jackson, Donald, ed. *The Journals of Zebulon Montgomery Pike with Letters and Related Documents.* 2 vols. Norman: University of Oklahoma Press, 1966.

Jackson, Jack, and William C. Foster, eds. *Imaginary Kingdom: Texas as Seen by the Rivera and Rubí Military Expeditions, 1727 and 1767.* Austin: Texas State Historical Association, 1995.

Kessell, John L., ed. *Remote beyond Compare: Letters of don Diego de Vargas to His Family from New Spain and New Mexico, 1675–1706.* Albuquerque: University of New Mexico Press, 1989.

Kessell, John L., and Rick Hendricks, eds. *By Force of Arms: The Journals of don Diego de Vargas, New Mexico, 1691–93.* Albuquerque: University of New Mexico Press, 1992.

Kessell, John L., Rick Hendricks, and Meredith D. Dodge, eds. *Blood on the Boulders: The Journals of don Diego de Vargas, New Mexico, 1694–97.* 2 books. Albuquerque: University of New Mexico, 1998.

———, eds. *To the Royal Crown Restored: The Journals of don Diego de Vargas, New Mexico, 1692–94.* Albuquerque: University of New Mexico Press, 1995.

Kessell, John L., Rick Hendricks, Meredith D. Dodge, and Larry D. Miller, eds. *That Disturbances Cease: The Journals of don Diego de Vargas, New Mexico, 1697–1700.* Albuquerque: University of New Mexico Press, 2000.

Kessler, Ronald E., ed. "The Diary of Juan Bautista de Anza," *The San Luis Valley Historian* 26:1 (1994), 4–38.

Kinnaird, Lawrence, ed. *The Frontiers of New Spain: Nicolás de Lafora's Description, 1766–1768.* Berkeley: Quivira Society, 1958.

Leonard, Irving A., ed. *The Mercurio Volante of don Carlos de Sigüenza y Góngora: An Account of the First Expedition of don Diego de Vargas into New Mexico in 1692.* Los Angeles: The Quivira Society, 1932.

———, ed. *Spanish Approach to Pensacola, 1689–1693.* Albuquerque: The Quivira Society, 1939.

Lynch, Cyprian J., ed., and Peter P. Forrestal, trans. *Benavides' Memorial of 1630.* Washington, D.C.: Academy of American Franciscan History, 1954.

Matson, Daniel S., and Bernard L. Fontana, eds. *Before Rebellion: Letters and Reports of Jacobo Sedelmayr, S.J.* Tucson: Arizona Historical Society, 1996.

————, eds. *Friar Bringas Reports to the King: Methods of Indoctrination on the Frontier of New Spain, 1796–97.* Tucson: University of Arizona Press, 1977.

McCarty, Kieran, ed. *Desert Documentary: The Spanish Years, 1767–1821.* Tucson: Arizona Historical Society, 1976.

Milanich, Jerald T., and William C. Sturtevant, eds. *Francisco Pareja's 1613 Confessionario: A Documentary Source for Timucuan Ethnography.* Tallahassee: Florida Department of State, 1972.

Morrow, Baker H., ed. *A Harvest of Reluctant Souls: The Memorial of Fray Alonso de Benavides, 1630.* Niwot: University Press of Colorado, 1996.

Naylor, Thomas H., and Charles W. Polzer, eds. *Pedro de Rivera and the Regulations for Northern New Spain, 1724–1729.* Tucson: University of Arizona Press, 1988.

————, eds. *The Presidio and Militia on the Northern Frontier of New Spain: A Documentary History, Volume One, 1570–1700.* Tucson: University of Arizona Press, 1986.

Pérez de Villagrá, Gaspar. *Historia de la Nueva México, 1610.* Edited by Miguel Encinias, Alfred Rodríguez, and Joseph P. Sánchez. Albuquerque: University of New Mexico Press, 1992.

Polzer, Charles W., ed. "The Franciscan Entrada into Sonora, 1645–1652: A Jesuit Chronicle." *Arizona and the West* 14 (Autumn 1972), 253–78.

Polzer, Charles W., and Thomas E. Sheridan, eds. *The Presidio and Militia on the Northern Frontier of New Spain: A Documentary History.* Vol. 2, part 1. *The Californias and Sinaloa-Sonora, 1700–1765.* Tucson: University of Arizona Press, 1997.

Pupo-Walker, Enrique, and Frances M. López-Morillas, eds. *Castaways: The Narrative of Alvar Núñez Cabeza de Vaca.* Berkeley: University of California Press, 1993.

Reff, Daniel T., Maureen Ahern, and Richard K. Danford, eds. *History of the Triumphs of Our Holy Faith Amongst the Most Barbarous and Fierce Peoples of the New World, by Andrés Pérez de Ribas.* Tucson: University of Arizona Press, 1999.

Schroeder, Albert H., and Dan S. Matson, eds. *A Colony on the Move: Gaspar Castaño de Sosa's Journal, 1590–1591.* Santa Fe: School of American Research, 1965.

Sheridan, Thomas E., ed. *Empire of Sand: The Seri Indians and the Struggle for Spanish Sonora, 1645–1803.* Tucson: University of Arizona Press, 1999.

Tello, Antonio. *Crónica miscelánea de la Santa Provincia de Xalisco por fray Antonio Tello, Libro Segundo.* C. 1650. 2 vols. Reprint, Guadalajara: Universidad de Guadalajara, 1968.

Thomas, Alfred Barnaby, ed. *After Coronado: Spanish Exploration Northeast of New Mexico, 1696–1727.* Norman: University of Oklahoma Press, 1935.

————, ed. *Forgotten Frontiers: A Study of the Spanish Indian Policy of Don Juan Bautista de Anza, Governor of New Mexico, 1777–1787.* Norman: University of Oklahoma Press, 1932.

————, ed. *The Plains Indians and New Mexico, 1751–1778.* Albuquerque: University of New Mexico Press, 1940.

————, ed. *Teodoro de Croix and the Northern Frontier of New Spain, 1776–1783.* Norman: University of Oklahoma Press, 1941.

Treutlein, Theodore E., ed. *Missionary in Sonora: The Travel Reports of Joseph Och, S. J., 1755–1767.* San Francisco: California Historical Society, 1965.

Varela, Consuelo, ed. *El viaje de don Ruy López de Villalobos a las islas del Poniente, 1542–1548.* Milan: Instituto Editoriale Cisalpino-La Goliardica, 1983.

Weber, David J., ed. "An Unforgettable Day, Facundo Melgares on Independence." *NMHR* 48 (January 1973), 27–44.

Weddle, Robert S., ed. *La Salle, the Mississippi, and the Gulf: Three Primary Documents.* College Station: Texas A&M University Press, 1987.

SECONDARY SOURCES

Adams, Eleanor B. "Fray Francisco Atanasio Domínguez and Fray Silvestre Vélez de Escalante." *Utah Historical Quarterly* 44 (Winter 1976), 40–58.

————. "Fray Silvestre and the Obstinate Hopi." *NMHR* 38 (April 1963), 97–138.

————. "Two Colonial New Mexico Libraries, 1704, 1776." *NMHR* 19 (April 1944), 135–67.

Adorno, Rolena. "The Negotiation of Fear in Cabeza de Vaca's *Naufragios.*" In *New World Encounters.* Edited by Stephen Greenblatt. Berkeley: University of California Press, 1993.

Ahern, Maureen. "The Cross and the Gourd: The Appropriation of Ritual Signs in the *Relaciones* of Alvar Núñez Cabeza de Vaca and Fray Marcos de Niza." In *Early Images of the Americas.* Edited by Jerry Williams and Robert Lewis. Tucson: University of Arizona Press, 1993.

Aiton, Arthur Scott. *Antonio de Mendoza, First Viceroy of New Spain.* Durham, N.C.: Duke University Press, 1927.

Alessio Robles, Vito. *Francisco de Urdiñola y el norte de la Nueva España.* 1931. Reprint, Mexico City: Editorial Porrúa, 1981.

Almaráz, Félix D., Jr. *Tragic Cavalier: Governor Manuel Salcedo of Texas, 1808–1813.* Austin: University of Texas Press, 1971.

Ambrose, Stephen E. *Undaunted Courage: Meriwether Lewis, Thomas Jefferson, and the Opening of the American West.* New York: Simon and Schuster, 1996.

Aragón, Janie Louise. "The People of Santa Fe in the 1790s." *Aztlán* 7 (Fall 1976), 391–417.

Archibald, Robert. "The Economy of the Alta California Missions, 1803–21." In *SCSH.*

Bakewell, Peter J. *Silver Mining and Society in Colonial Mexico: Zacatecas, 1546–1700.* Cambridge: Cambridge University Press, 1971.

Bishop, Morris. *The Odyssey of Cabeza de Vaca*. New York: The Century Co., 1933.

Blakeslee, Donald J. *Along Ancient Trails: The Mallet Expedition of 1739*. Niwot: University Press of Colorado, 1995.

Bloom, Lansing B. *Early Vaccination in New Mexico*. Santa Fe: Santa Fe New Mexican Publishing Corp., 1924.

———. "The Vargas Encomienda." *NMHR* 14 (October 1939), 366–417.

Bolton, Herbert E. *Coronado: Knight of Pueblos and Plains*. Albuquerque: University of New Mexico Press, 1949.

———. *Outpost of Empire: The Story of the Founding of San Francisco*. New York: Alfred A. Knopf, 1931.

———. *Pageant in the Wilderness: The Story of the Escalante Expedition to the Interior Basin, 1776*. Salt Lake City: Utah State Historical Society, 1950.

———. *Rim of Christendom: A Biography of Eusebio Francisco Kino, Pacific Coast Pioneer*. New York: Macmillan, 1936.

———. *Texas in the Middle Eighteenth Century*. 1915. Reprint, Austin: University of Texas Press, 1970.

Brandon, William. *Quivira: Europeans in the Region of the Santa Fe Trail, 1540–1820*. Athens: Ohio University Press, 1990.

Broughton, William H. "Francisco Rendón: Spanish Agent in Philadelphia 1779–1786, Intendant of Spanish Louisiana 1793–1796." Ph.D. diss., University of New Mexico, 1994.

Burrus, Ernest J. *Kino and the Cartography of Northwestern New Spain*. Tucson: Arizona Pioneers' Historical Society, 1965.

Bushnell, Amy Turner. "Republic of Spaniards, Republic of Indians." In *The New History of Florida*. Edited by Michael Gannon. Gainesville: University Press of Florida, 1996.

———. *Situado and Sabana: Spain's Support System for the Presidio and Mission Provinces of Florida*. New York: American Museum of Natural History, 1994.

Carmack, Robert M. "The Spanish Conquest of Central America: Comparative Cases from Guatemala and Costa Rica." In *CC3*.

Carson, Phil. *Across the Northern Frontier: Spanish Explorations in Colorado*. Boulder: Johnson Books, 1998.

Casado Fuente, Ovidio. *Don Francisco Cuerbo y Valdés, Gobernador de Nuevo México, Fundador de la Ciudad de Alburquerque*. Oviedo: Instituto de Estudios Asturianos, 1983.

Castañeda, Antonia I. "Engendering the History of Alta California, 1769–1848." In *CE*.

Chávez, Fray Angélico. "The Carpenter Pueblo." *New Mexico Magazine* 49 (September-October 1971), 26–33.

———. *Coronado's Friars*. Washington, D.C.: Academy of American Franciscan History, 1968.

———. *Origins of New Mexico Families: A Genealogy of the Spanish Colonial Period*. Rev. ed. Santa Fe: Museum of New Mexico Press, 1992.

———. "Pohé-yemo's Representative and the Pueblo Revolt of 1680." *NMHR* 25 (April 1967), 85–126.

Chávez, Thomas E. "The Segesser Hide Paintings: History, Discovery, Art." *El Palacio* 92 (Winter 1986), 18–27.

———. "The Villasur Expedition and the Segesser Hide Paintings." In *Spain and the Plains: Myths and Realities of Spanish Exploration and Settlement on the Great Plains.* Edited by Ralph H. Vigil, Frances W. Kaye, and John R. Wunder. Niwot: University Press of Colorado, 1994.

Chevalier, Francois. *Land and Society in Colonial Mexico: The Great Hacienda.* Translated by Alvin Eustis. Edited by Lesley Byrd Simpson. Berkeley: University of California Press, 1966.

Chipman, Donald E. *Nuño de Guzmán and the Province of Pánuco in New Spain, 1518–1533.* Glendale, Calif.: Arthur H. Clark, 1967.

———. "In Search of Cabeza de Vaca's Route across Texas: An Historiographical Survey." *SWHQ* 91 (October 1987), 127–48.

———. *Spanish Texas, 1519–1821.* Austin: University of Texas Press, 1992.

Chipman, Donald E., and Harriett Denise Joseph. *Notable Men and Women of Spanish Texas.* Austin: University of Texas Press, 1999.

Colligan, John B. *The Juan Páez Hurtado Expedition of 1695: Fraud in Recruiting Colonists for New Mexico.* Albuquerque: University of New Mexico Press, 1995.

Cook, Warren L. *Flood Tide of Empire: Spain and the Pacific Northwest, 1543–1819.* New Haven: Yale University Press, 1973.

Cramaussel, Chantal. *La Provincia de Santa Bárbara en Nueva Vizcaya, 1563–1631.* Chihuahua: Universidad Autónoma de Ciudad Juárez, 1990.

Crosby, Alfred W., Jr. *The Columbian Exchange: Biological and Cultural Consequences of 1492.* Westport, Conn.: Greenwood Press, 1972.

———. *Ecological Imperialism: The Biological Expansion of Europe, 900–1900.* Cambridge: Cambridge University Press, 1986.

Crosby, Harry W. *Antigua California: Mission and Colony on the Peninsular Frontier, 1697–1768.* Albuquerque: University of New Mexico Press, 1994.

Cruxent, José María. "The Origin of La Isabela: First Spanish Colony in the New World." In *CC1.*

Cruz, Gilbert R. *Let There Be Towns: Spanish Municipal Origins in the American Southwest, 1610–1810.* College Station: Texas A&M University Press, 1988.

Cutter, Charles R. *The Legal Culture of Northern New Spain, 1700–1810.* Albuquerque: University of New Mexico Press, 1992.

Day, A. Grove. *Coronado's Quest: The Discovery of the Southwestern States.* Berkeley: University of California Press, 1940.

De la Teja, Jesús F. "Rebellion on the Frontier." In *Tejano Journey, 1770–1850.* Edited by Gerald E. Poyo. Austin: University of Texas Press, 1996.

———. *San Antonio de Béxar, A Community on New Spain's Northern Frontier*. Albuquerque: University of New Mexico Press, 1995.

———. "Spanish Colonial Texas." In *NV*.

Deagan, Kathleen A. "La Isabela, Europe's First Foothold in the New World." *National Geographic* 181 (January 1992), 40–53.

———. *Puerto Real: The Archaeology of a Sixteenth-Century Spanish Town in Hispaniola*. Gainesville: University Press of Florida, 1995.

———. "Sixteenth-Century Spanish-American Colonization in the Southeastern United States and the Caribbean." In *CC2*.

Deagan, Kathleen A., and José María Cruxent. "From Contact to *Criollos:* The Archaeology of Spanish Colonization in Hispaniola." *Proceedings of the British Academy* 81 (1993), 67–104.

Deeds, Susan M. "Indigenous Rebellions on the Northern Mexican Mission Frontier: From First-Generation to Later Colonial Responses." In *CG*.

Dobyns, Henry F. *Spanish Colonial Tucson: A Demographic History*. Tucson: University of Arizona Press, 1976.

Dozier, Edward P. *The Pueblo Indians of North America*. New York: Holt, Rinehart and Winston, 1970.

Duncan, David Ewing. *Hernando de Soto: A Savage Quest in the Americas*. New York: Crown Publishers, 1995.

Dunne, Peter M. "Captain Anza and the Case of Father Campos." *Mid-America* 23 (1941), 45–60.

———. *Pioneer Black Robes on the West Coast*. Berkeley: University of California Press, 1940.

Dutton, Bertha P. *American Indians of the Southwest*. Albuquerque: University of New Mexico Press, 1983.

Ebright, Malcolm. *Land Grants and Lawsuits in Northern New Mexico*. Albuquerque: University of New Mexico Press, 1994.

Engstrand, Iris H. W. "Seekers of the 'Northern Mystery': European Exploration of California and the Pacific." In *CE*.

Engstrand, Iris H. W., and Donald C. Cutter. *Spanish Settlement in the Far Southwest: Arizona, California and New Mexico, 1530–1821*. Golden, Colo.: Fulcrum Publishing, 1996.

Espinosa, J. Manuel. *Crusaders of the Río Grande: The Story of Don Diego de Vargas and the Reconquest and Refounding of New Mexico*. Chicago: Institute of Jesuit History, 1942.

Esquibel, José Antonio. "Doña Eufemia, La Valerosa: The Great Martesia of Oñate's Colony." *Herencia* 2 (April 1994), 19–28.

Evans, William E. "The Confirmation Controversy of 1779." In *SCSH*.

Flint, Richard. "Armas de la Tierra: The Mexican Indian Component of Coronado Expedition Material Culture." In *CETN*.

———. "The Coronado and de Soto Expeditions: A Contrast in Attitudes or Differences in External Conditions?." *El Viaje*. Coronado Trail Association Newsletter 1 (April 1992), 4–8.

———. "Great Cruelties Have Been Reported: The 1544 Investigation of the Coronado Expedition." Ph.D. diss., University of New Mexico, 1999.

Floyd, Troy S. *The Columbus Dynasty in the Caribbean, 1492–1526*. Albuquerque: University of New Mexico Press, 1973.

Fontana, Bernard L. *Entrada: The Legacy of Spain and Mexico in the United States*. Tucson: Southwest Parks and Monuments Association, 1994.

Forbes, Jack D. *Apache, Navaho, and Spaniard*. 2d ed. Norman: University of Oklahoma Press, 1994.

Foster, George M. *Culture and Conquest: America's Spanish Heritage*. Chicago: Quadrangle Books, 1960.

Foster, William C. *Spanish Expeditions into Texas, 1689–1768*. Austin: University of Texas Press, 1995.

Frank, Ross. "Demographic, Social, and Economic Change in New Mexico." In *NV*.

Garate, Donald T. "Who Named Arizona? The Basque Connection." *Journal of Arizona History* 40 (Spring 1999), 53–82.

Geiger, Maynard. *Franciscan Missionaries in Hispanic California, 1769–1848: A Biographical Dictionary*. San Marino: The Huntington Library, 1969.

———. *The Life and Times of Fray Junípero Serra, O.F.M.* 2 vols. Washington, D.C.: Academy of American Franciscan History, 1959.

Gerhard, Peter. *The North Frontier of New Spain*. Rev. ed. Norman: University of Oklahoma Press, 1993.

———. *Pirates of the Pacific, 1575–1742*. Lincoln: University of Nebraska Press, 1990.

Gómez, Arthur. "Royalist in Transition: Facundo Melgares, the Last Spanish Governor of New Mexico, 1818–1822." *NMHR* 68 (October 1993), 371–87.

Gradie, Charlotte M. "Discovering the Chichimecas." *The Americas* 51 (July 1994), 67–88.

Gudiño Quiroz, Rebecca A. *Don Antonio Valverde y Cossío, Gobernador de Nuevo México: una aproximación a su vida pública y privada*. Ciudad Juárez: Universidad Autónoma de Ciudad Juárez, 1994.

Guest, Francis F. "Junípero Serra and His Approach to the Indians." In *SCSH*.

Gunnerson, Dolores A. *The Jicarilla Apaches: A Study in Survival*. DeKalb: Northern Illinois University Press, 1974.

Gutiérrez, Ramón A. *When Jesus Came, the Corn Mothers Went Away: Marriage, Sexuality, and Power in New Mexico, 1500–1846*. Stanford, Calif.: Stanford University Press, 1991.

Haas, Jonathan. "Warfare among the Pueblos: Myth, History, and Ethnography." *Ethnohistory* 44 (Spring 1997), 235–61.

Habig, Marion A. *Spanish Texas Pilgrimage: The Old Franciscan Missions and Other Spanish Settlements of Texas, 1632–1821*. Chicago: Franciscan Herald Press, 1990.

Hackel, Steven W. "Land, Labor, and Production: The Colonial Economy of Spanish and Mexican California." In *CE*.

Hallenbeck, Cleve. *The Journey of Fray Marcos de Niza*. Edited by David J. Weber. Dallas: Southern Methodist University Press, 1987.

Hamalainen, Pekka. "The Western Comanche Trade Center: Rethinking the Plains Indian Trade System." *Western Historical Quarterly* 29 (Winter 1998), 485–513.

Hann, John H. *Apalachee: The Land between the Rivers*. Gainesville: University Presses of Florida, 1988.

———. *A History of the Timucua Indians and Missions*. Gainesville: University Press of Florida, 1996.

———. "The Missions of Spanish Florida." In *The New History of Florida*. Edited by Michael Gannon. Gainesville: University Press of Florida, 1996.

Hayes, Alden C. *The Four Churches of Pecos*. Albuquerque: University of New Mexico, 1974.

Heath, Jim F., and Frederick M. Nunn. "Negroes and Discrimination in Colonial New Mexico: Don Pedro Bautista Pino's Startling Statement of 1812 in Perspective." *Phylon* 31 (1970), 372–78.

Hendricks, Rick. "Church-State Relations in Anza's New Mexico, 1777–1787." *Catholic Southwest* 9 (1998), 24–42.

———. "Pedro Rodríguez Cubero, New Mexico's Reluctant Governor, 1697–1703." *NMHR* 68 (January 1993), 13–39.

Hendricks, Rick, and Gerald J. Mandell. "Juan Manso, Frontier Entrepreneur." *NMHR* 75 (July 2000), 339–67.

Hernández, Salomé. "No Settlement Without Women: Three California Settlement Schemes, 1790–1800." In *SCSH*.

Herrera, Carlos E. "The King's Governor: Juan Bautista de Anza and Bourbon New Mexico in the Era of Imperial Reform, 1778–1788." Ph.D. diss., University of New Mexico, 2000.

Hickerson, Daniel A. "Historical Processes, Epidemic Disease, and the Formation of the Hasinai Confederacy." *Ethnohistory* 44 (Winter 1997), 31–52.

Hickerson, Nancy P. "How Cabeza de Vaca Lived With, Worked Among, and Finally Left the Indians of Texas." *JAR* 54 (Summer 1998), 199–218.

———. *The Jumanos: Hunters and Traders of the South Plains*. Austin: University of Texas Press, 1994.

———. "The *Servicios* of Vicente de Zaldívar: New Light on the Jumano War of 1601." *Ethnohistory* 43 (Winter 1966), 127–44.

———. "The Visits of the 'Lady in Blue': An Episode in the History of the South Plains, 1629." *JAR* 46 (Spring 1990), 67–90.

Hill, Lawrence F. *José de Escandón and the Founding of Nuevo Santander: A Study in Spanish Colonization*. Columbus: Ohio State University Press, 1926.

Hindes, Kay, Mark R. Wolf, Grant D. Hall, and Kathleen Kirk Gilmore. *The Rediscovery of Santa Cruz de San Sabá, A Mission for the Apache in Spanish Texas*. Austin: Texas Historical Foundation and Texas Tech University, 1995.

Hoffman, Paul E. "Hernando de Soto: A Brief Biography." In *The De Soto Chronicles: The Expedition of Hernando de Soto to North America in 1539–1543*. Edited by Lawrence A. Clayton, Vernon James Knight, Jr., and Edward C. Moore. Tuscaloosa: University of Alabama Press, 1993.

————. *A New Andalucia and a Way to the Orient: The American Southeast During the Sixteenth Century*. Baton Rouge: Louisiana State University Press, 1990.

Hollon, Eugene. *The Lost Pathfinder: Zebulon Montgomery Pike*. Norman: University of Oklahoma Press, 1949.

Hordes, Stanley M. "The Sephardic Legacy in New Mexico: A History of the Crypto-Jews." *Journal of the West* (October 1996), 82–90.

Hu-Dehart, Evelyn. *Missionaries, Miners, and Indians: Spanish Contact with the Yaqui Nation of Northwestern New Spain, 1533–1820*. Tucson: University of Arizona Press, 1981.

Hurtado, Albert L. *Intimate Frontiers: Sex, Gender, and Culture in Old California*. Albuquerque: University of New Mexico Press, 1999.

Hutchinson, Alan. *Frontier Settlement in Mexican California: The Híjar-Padrés Colony, and Its Origins, 1769–1835*. New Haven: Yale University Press, 1969.

Ives, Ronald L. "Adam Aigenler's Field Manual." *Journal of Geography* 52 (October 1953), 291–99.

Ivey, James E. "Convento Kivas in the Missions of New Mexico." *NMHR* 73 (April 1998), 121–52.

————. "Pueblo and Estancia: The Spanish Presence in the Pueblo, A.D. 1620–1680." In *Current Research on the Late Prehistory and Early History of New Mexico*. Edited by Bradley J. Vierra. Albuquerque: New Mexico Archaeological Council, 1992.

Jackson, Jack. *Los Mesteños: Spanish Ranching in Texas, 1721–1821*. College Station: Texas A&M University Press, 1986.

Jackson, Robert H. "The Formation of Frontier Indigenous Communities: Missions in California and Texas." In *NV*.

————. *Indian Population Decline: The Missions of Northwestern New Spain, 1687–1840*. Albuquerque: University of New Mexico Press, 1995.

James, Thomas. *Three Years among the Indians and Mexicans*. 1846. Reprint, Philadelphia: J. B. Lippincott Co., 1962.

John, Elizabeth A. H. "The Riddle of Map Maker Juan Pedro Walker." In *Essays on the History of North American Discovery and Exploration*. Edited by Stanley J. Palmer and Dennis Reinhartz. College Station: Texas A&M University Press, 1988.

———. *Storms Brewed in Other Men's Worlds: The Confrontation of Indians, Spanish, and French in the Southwest, 1540–1795.* 2d. ed. Norman: University of Oklahoma Press, 1996.

Jones, Oakah L., Jr. *Nueva Vizcaya: Heartland of the Spanish Frontier.* Albuquerque: University of New Mexico Press, 1988.

———. *Los Paisanos: Spanish Settlers on the Northern Frontier of New Spain.* Norman: University of Oklahoma Press, 1979, 1996.

———. *Pueblo Warriors and Spanish Conquest.* Norman: University of Oklahoma Press, 1966.

Kavanagh, Thomas W. *Comanche Political History: An Ethnohistorical Perspective, 1706–1875.* Lincoln: University of Nebraska Press, 1996.

Kelley, J. Charles. "Juan Sabeata and Diffusion in Aboriginal Texas." *American Anthropologist* 57 (October 1955), 981–95.

Kelsey, Harry. *Juan Rodríguez Cabrillo.* San Marino: Huntington Library, 1986.

Kessell, John L. "Diego Romero, the Plains Apaches, and the Inquisition." *The American West* 15 (May-June 1978), 12–16.

———. "Esteban Clemente, Precursor of the Pueblo Revolt." *El Palacio* 86 (Winter 1980–81), 16–17.

———. "Friars, Bureaucrats, and the Seris of Sonora," *NMHR* 59 (January 1975), 73–95.

———. *Friars, Soldiers, and Reformers: Hispanic Arizona and the Sonora Mission Frontier, 1767–1856.* Tucson: University of Arizona Press, 1976.

———. "Friars versus Bureaucrats: The Mission as a Threatened Institution on the Arizona-Sonora Frontier, 1767–1842." *Western Historical Quarterly* 5 (April 1974), 151–62.

———. *Kiva, Cross, and Crown: The Pecos Indians and New Mexico, 1540–1840.* Washington, D.C.: National Park Service, 1979.

———. "The Making of A Martyr: The Young Francisco Garcés." *NMHR* 45 (July 1970), 181–96.

———. "Miracles or Mystery: María de Agreda's Ministry to the Jumano Indians of the Southwest in the 1620s." In *Great Mysteries of the West.* Edited by Ferenc Morton Szasz. Golden, Colo.: Fulcrum Publishing, 1993.

———. *Mission of Sorrows: Jesuit Guevavi and the Pimas, 1691–1767.* Tucson: University of Arizona Press, 1970.

———. "Spaniards and Pueblos: From Crusading Intolerance to Pragmatic Accommodation." In *CC1.*

Knaut, Andrew L. *The Pueblo Revolt of 1680: Conquest and Resistance in Seventeenth-Century New Mexico.* Norman: University of Oklahoma Press, 1995.

Ladd, Edmund J. "Zuni on the Day the Men in Metal Arrived." In *CETN.*

LeCompte, Janet. "Coronado and Conquest." *NMHR* 64 (July 1989), 279–304.

Liljegren, Ernest R. "Zalmon Coley: The Second Anglo-American in Santa Fe." *NMHR* 62 (July 1987), 263–86.

Lockhart, Bill. "Protohistoric Confusion: A Cultural Comparison of the Manso, Suma, and Jumano Indians of the Paso del Norte Region." *Journal of the Southwest* 39 (Spring 1997), 113–49.

Lockhart, James. *Spanish Peru, 1532–1560: A Colonial Society*. Madison: University of Wisconsin Press, 1968.

Loomis, Noel M. "Philip Nolan's Entry into Texas in 1800." In *The Spanish in the Mississippi Valley, 1762–1804*. Edited by John Francis McDermott. Urbana: University of Illinois Press, 1974.

Loomis, Noel M., and Abraham P. Nasatir. *Pedro Vial and the Roads to Santa Fe*. Norman: University of Oklahoma Press, 1967.

Lyon, Eugene. *The Enterprise of Florida: Pedro Menéndez de Avilés and the Spanish Conquest of 1565–1568*. Gainesville: University Presses of Florida, 1976.

———. "Track of the Manila Galleons." *National Geographic* 178 (September 1990), 5–37.

MacLachlan, Colin M. *Spain's Empire in the New World: The Role of Ideas in Institutional and Social Change*. Berkeley: University of California Press, 1988.

Marrinan, Rochelle A., John F. Scarry, and Rhonda L. Majors. "Prelude to de Soto: The Expedition of Pánfilo de Narváez." In *CC2*.

Martin, Cheryl English. *Governance and Society in Colonial Mexico: Chihuahua in the Eighteenth Century*. Stanford, Calif.: Stanford University Press, 1996.

Mathers, William M. "*Nuestra Señora de la Concepción*." *National Geographic* 178 (September 1990), 39–53.

Mathes, W. Michael. *Vizcaíno and Spanish Expansion in the Pacific Ocean, 1580–1630*. San Francisco: California Historical Society, 1968.

McCarty, Kieran. "Franciscans North from Mexico, 1527–1580." In *Franciscan Presence in the Americas: Essays on the Activities of the Franciscan Friars in the Americas, 1492–1900*. Edited by Francisco Morales. Washington, D.C.: Academy of American Franciscan History, 1983.

———. *A Spanish Frontier in the Enlightened Age: Franciscan Beginnings in Sonora and Arizona, 1767–1770*. Washington, D.C.: Academy of American Franciscan History, 1981.

McCloskey, Michael B. *The Formative Years of the Missionary College of Santa Cruz of Querétaro, 1683–1733*. Washington, D.C.: Academy of American Franciscan History, 1955.

McNitt, Frank. *Navajo Wars: Military Campaigns, Slave Raids, and Reprisals*. Albuquerque: University of New Mexico Press, 1972.

Mecham, J. Lloyd. *Francisco de Ibarra and Nueva Vizcaya*. New York: Greenwood Press, 1968.

Meinig, D. W. *Southwest: Three Peoples in Geographical Change, 1600–1970*. New York: Oxford University Press, 1971.

Milanich, Jerald T., and Charles Hudson. *Hernando de Soto and the Indians of Florida*. Gainesville: University Press of Florida, 1993.

Montgomery, Ross G., Watson Smith, and John O. Brew. *Franciscan Awatovi*. Cambridge, Mass.: Peabody Museum, 1949.

Moorhead, Max L. *The Apache Frontier: Jacobo Ugarte and Spanish-Indian Relations in Northern New Spain, 1769–1791*. Norman: University of Oklahoma Press, 1968.

Morison, Samuel Eliot. *The European Discovery of America: The Southern Voyages, A.D. 1492–1616*. New York: Oxford University Press, 1974.

Morris, John Miller. *El Llano Estacado: Exploration and Imagination on the High Plains of Texas and New Mexico, 1536–1860*. Austin: Texas State Historical Association, 1997.

Murga Sanz, Vicente. *Juan Ponce de León, fundador y primer gobernador del pueblo Puertorriqueño, descubridor de la Florida y del Estrecho de las Bahamas*. San Juan: Universidad de Puerto Rico, 1959.

Nasatir, Abraham P. *Borderlands in Retreat: From Spanish Louisiana to the Far Southwest*. Albuquerque: University of New Mexico Press, 1976.

National Geographic Society. "The Southwest" (Map). Washington, D.C.: National Geographic Society, 1982.

Navarro García, Luis. *Don José de Gálvez y la Comandancia General de las Provincias Internas del Norte de Nueva España*. Sevilla: Escuela de Estudios Hispano-Americanos, 1964.

———. *Sonora y Sinaloa en el siglo XVII*. Sevilla: Escuela de Estudios Hispano-Americanos, 1967.

———. *La sublevación yaqui de 1740*. Sevilla: Escuela de Estudios Hispano-Americanos, 1966.

Naylor, Thomas H. "Athapaskans They Weren't: The Suma Rebels Executed at Casas Grandes in 1685." In *The Protohistoric Period in the North American Southwest, AD 1450–1700*. Edited by David R. Wilcox and W. Bruce Masse. Anthropological Research Papers, 24. Tempe: Arizona State University, 1981.

Norall, Frank. *Bourgmont, Explorer of the Missouri, 1698–1725*. Lincoln: University of Nebraska Press, 1988.

Noyes, Stanley. *Los Comanches: The Horse People, 1751–1845*. Albuquerque: University of New Mexico Press, 1993.

Ortiz, Alfonso. "Popay's Leadership: A Pueblo Perspective." *El Palacio* 86 (Winter 1980–81), 18–22.

———, ed. *Southwest*. Vols. 9 and 10. *Handbook of North American Indians*. Edited by William C. Sturtevant. Washington, D.C.: Smithsonian Institution Press, 1979, 1983.

Phares, Ross. *Cavalier in the Wilderness: The Story of the Explorer and Trader Louis Juchereau de St. Denis*. Baton Rouge: Louisiana State University Press, 1952.

Powell, Philip Wayne. *Mexico's Miguel Caldera: The Taming of America's First Frontier, 1548–1597*. Tucson: University of Arizona Press, 1977.

———. *Soldiers, Indians, and Silver: The Northward Advance of New Spain, 1550–1600*. Berkeley: University of California Press, 1952.

Radding, Cynthia. "The Colonial Pact and Changing Ethnic Frontiers in Highland Sonora, 1740–1840. In *CG*.

———. *Wandering Peoples: Colonialism, Ethnic Spaces, and Ecological Frontiers in Northwestern Mexico, 1700–1850*. Durham, N.C.: Duke University Press, 1997.

Ramenofsky, Ann F. "The Problem of Introduced Infectious Diseases in New Mexico: A.D. 1540–1680." *JAR* 52 (Summer 1996), 161–84.

Ratcliffe, Sam D. "'*Escenas de Martirio*': Notes on The Destruction of Mission San Sabá." *SWHQ* 94 (April 1991), 506–34.

Reff, Daniel T. "Anthropological Analysis of Exploration Texts: Cultural Discourse and the Ethnological Import of Fray Marcos de Niza's Journey to Cibola." *American Anthropologist* 93 (1991), 636–55.

———. "Contextualizing Missionary Discourse: The Benavides *Memorials* of 1630 and 1634." *JAR* 50 (Spring 1996), 51–67.

———. *Disease, Depopulation, and Culture Change in Northwestern New Spain, 1518–1764*. Salt Lake City: University of Utah Press, 1991.

———. "The Jesuit Mission Frontier in Comparative Perspective: The Reductions of the Río de la Plata and the Missions of Northwestern Mexico, 1588–1700." In *CG*.

———. "The 'Predicament of Culture' and Spanish Missionary Accounts of the Tepehuan and Pueblo Revolts." *Ethnohistory* 42 (Winter 1995), 64–90.

———. "Text and Context: Cures, Miracles, and Fear in the *Relación* of Alvar Núñez Cabeza de Vaca." *Journal of the Southwest* 38 (Summer 1996), 115–38.

Richman, Irving Berdine. *California under Spain and Mexico, 1535–1847. 1911*. Reprint, New York: Cooper Square Publishers, 1965.

Riley, Carroll L. *The Kachina and the Cross: Indians and Spaniards in the Early Southwest*. Salt Lake City: University of Utah Press, 1999.

———. *Rio del Norte: People of the Upper Rio Grande from Earliest Times to the Pueblo Revolt*. Salt Lake City: University of Utah Press, 1995.

Rodack, Madeleine Turrell. "Cíbola, from Fray Marcos to Coronado." In *CETN*.

Rouse, Irving. *The Tainos: Rise and Decline of the People Who Greeted Columbus*. New Haven: Yale University Press, 1992.

Sánchez, Jane C. "Spanish-Indian Relations during the Otermín Administration, 1677–1683." *NMHR* 58 (April 1983), 133–51.

Sánchez, Joseph P. *Explorers, Traders, and Slavers: Forging the Old Spanish Trail, 1678–1850*. Salt Lake City: University of Utah Press, 1997.

Sando, Joe S. *The Pueblo Indians*. San Francisco: Indian Historian Press, 1976.

———. *Pueblo Nations: Eight Centuries of Pueblo Indian History*. Santa Fe: Clear Light Publishers, 1992.

Santiago, Mark. *Massacre at the Yuma Crossing: Spanish Relations with the Quechans, 1779–1782*. Tucson: University of Arizona Press, 1998.

Sauer, Carl Ortwin. *The Early Spanish Main*. Berkeley: University of California Press, 1966.

Scholes, France V. *Church and State in New Mexico, 1610–1650*. Albuquerque: University of New Mexico Press, 1937.

———. "Civil Government and Society in New Mexico in the Seventeenth Century." *NMHR* 10 (April 1935), 71–111.

———. "The First Decade of the Inquisition in New Mexico." *NMHR*, 10 (July 1935), 195–241.

———. "Juan Martínez de Montoya, Settler and Conquistador of New Mexico." *NMHR* 19 (October 1944), 337–42.

———. "Royal Treasury Records Relating to the Province of New Mexico, 1596–1683." *NMHR* 50 (January and April 1975), 5–23, 139–64.

———. "The Supply Service of the New Mexican Missions in the Seventeenth Century." *NMHR* 5 (January, April, and July 1930), 93–115, 186–210, 386–404.

———. *Troublous Times in New Mexico, 1659–1670*. Albuquerque: University of New Mexico Press, 1942.

Scholes, France V., and Lansing B. Bloom. "Friar Personnel and Mission Chronology, 1598–1629." *NMHR* 19 (October 1944), 319–36; 20 (January 1945), 58–82.

Schurz, William Lytle. *The Manila Galleon*. New York: E. P. Dutton, 1939.

Simmons, Marc. *Albuquerque: A Narrative History*. Albuquerque: University of New Mexico, 1982.

———. *Coronado's Land: Essays on Daily Life in Colonial New Mexico*. Albuquerque: University of New Mexico Press, 1991.

———. *The Last Conquistador: Juan de Oñate and the Settling of the Far Southwest*. Norman: University of Oklahoma Press, 1991.

———. "New Mexico's Smallpox Epidemic of 1780–81." *NMHR* 41 (October 1966), 319–26.

———. "Settlement Patterns and Village Plans in Colonial New Mexico." *Journal of the West* 8 (January 1969), 7–21.

———. "Spanish Attempts to Open a New Mexico-Sonora Road." *Arizona and the West* 17 (Spring 1975), 5–20.

Smith, F. Todd. *The Caddo Indians: Tribes at the Convergence of Empires, 1542–1854*. College Station: Texas A&M University Press, 1996.

Smith, Fay Jackson. *Captain of the Phantom Presidio: A History of the Presidio of Fronteras, Sonora, New Spain, 1686–1735*. Spokane: Arthur H. Clark, 1993.

Snow, David H. *New Mexico's First Colonists: The 1597–1600 Enlistments for New Mexico under Juan de Oñate, Adelantado and Gobernador*. Albuquerque: Hispanic Genealogical Research Center of New Mexico, 1998.

———. "A Note on Encomienda Economics in Seventeenth-Century New Mexico." In *Hispanic Arts and Ethnohistory in the Southwest*. Edited by Marta E. Weigle. Santa Fe: Ancient City Press, 1983.

Stevens, John. *A New Spanish and English Dictionary*. London: George Sawbridge, 1706.

Tenenbaum, Barbara A., ed. *Encyclopedia of Latin American History and Culture*. 5 vols. New York: Charles Scribner's Sons, 1996.

Thomas, Alfred Barnaby. "San Carlos, A Comanche Pueblo on the Arkansas, 1787." *The Colorado Magazine* 6 (May 1929), 79–91.

Thomas, Hugh. *Conquest: Montezuma, Cortés, and the Fall of Old Mexico*. New York: Simon and Schuster, 1995.

Thurman, Michael E. *The Naval Department of San Blas: New Spain's Bastion for Alta California and Nootka, 1767–1798*. Glendale: Arthur H. Clark, 1967.

Tigges, Linda, ed. *Santa Fe Historic Plaza Study*. Vols. 1–4. Santa Fe: City Planning Department, 1990–92.

Timmons, W. H. *El Paso: A Borderlands History*. El Paso: Texas Western Press, 1990.

Trimble, Stephen. *The People: Indians of the American Southwest*. Santa Fe: School of American Research, 1995.

Trujillo, Paul. "'Los Franceses' of Seventeenth-Century New Mexico: Jean L'Archeveque, Jacques Grolet and Pedro Meusnier." *Herencia* 3 (January 1995), 17–24.

Twitchell, Ralph Emerson. *The Spanish Archives of New Mexico*. 2 vols. Cedar Rapids: The Torch Press, 1914.

Udall, Stewart L. *Majestic Journey: Coronado's Inland Empire*. Santa Fe: Museum of New Mexico Press, 1995.

Usner, Daniel H., Jr. *Indians, Settlers, and Slaves in a Frontier Exchange Economy: The Lower Mississippi Valley before 1763*. Chapel Hill: University of North Carolina Press, 1992.

Vigil, Ralph H. *Alonso de Zorita, Royal Judge and Christian Humanist, 1512–1585*. Norman: University of Oklahoma Press, 1987.

Wagner, Henry R. *The Spanish Southwest, 1542–1794*. 2 parts. Albuquerque: Quivira Society, 1937.

Wagner, Henry R., and Helen Rand Parish. *The Life and Writings of Bartolomé de las Casas*. Albuquerque: University of New Mexico Press, 1967.

Walz, Vina. "History of the El Paso Area, 1680–1692." Ph.D. diss., University of New Mexico, 1951.

Warner, Ted J. "Don Félix Martínez and the Santa Fe Presidio, 1693–1730." *NMHR* 45 (October 1970), 269–310.

Weber, David J. *The Mexican Frontier, 1821–1846: The American Southwest under Mexico*. Albuquerque: University of New Mexico Press, 1982.

———. *The Spanish Frontier in North America*. New Haven: Yale University Press, 1992.

———. "The Spanish-Mexican Rim." In *The Oxford History of the American West*. Edited by Clyde A. Milner II, Carol A. O'Conor, and Martha A. Sandweiss. New York: Oxford University Press, 1994.

Weber, David J., ed. *Foreigners in Their Native Land: Historical Roots of the Mexican Americans*. Albuquerque: University of New Mexico Press, 1973.

————, ed. *What Caused the Pueblo Revolt of 1680?* Boston: Bedford/St. Martin's, 1999.

Weddle, Robert S. *The French Thorn: Rival Explorers in the Spanish Sea, 1682–1762.* College Station: Texas A&M University Press, 1991.

————. *San Juan Bautista: Gateway to Spanish Texas.* Austin: University of Texas Press, 1968.

————. *The San Sabá Mission, Spanish Pivot in Texas.* Austin: University of Texas Press, 1964.

————. *Spanish Sea: The Gulf of Mexico in North American Discovery, 1500–1685.* College Station: Texas A&M University Press, 1985.

————. *Wilderness Manhunt: The Spanish Search for La Salle.* Austin: University of Texas Press, 1973.

When Cultures Meet: Remembering San Gabriel del Yunge Oweenge, Papers from the October 20, 1984 Conference Held at San Juan Pueblo, New Mexico. Santa Fe: Sunstone Press, 1987.

Wilson, John P. "Awatovi—More Light on a Legend." *Plateau* 44 (Winter 1972), 125–30.

Wood, Peter H. "La Salle: Discovery of a Lost Explorer." *American Historical Review* 89 (April 1984), 294–323.

Wright, Robert E. "How Many Are 'A Few'?: Catholic Clergy in Central and Northern New Mexico, 1780–1851." In *Seeds of Struggle/Harvest of Faith: The History of the Catholic Church in New Mexico.* Edited by Thomas J. Steele, Paul Rhetts, and Barbe Awalt. Albuquerque: LPD Press, 1998.

——. "Local Church Emergence and Mission Decline: The Historiography of the Catholic Church in the Southwest during the Spanish and Mexican Periods." *U.S. Catholic Historian* 9:1–2 (Winter-Spring 1990), 27–48.

Young, Gloria A., and Michael P. Hoffman, eds. *The Expedition of Hernando de Soto West of the Mississippi, 1541–1543.* Fayetteville: University of Arkansas Press, 1993.

INDEX

All references to illustrations are in italic type.

St. Louis Community College
at Meramec
Library